6. Can a local account be used in a trust relationship? Explain.

7. In a complete trust domain model that uses 4 different domains, what is the total number of trust relationships required to use a complete trust domain model?

Exam Questions

The following questions are similar to those you will face on the Microsoft exam. Answers to these questions can be found in section Answers and Explanations, later in the chapter. At the end of each of those answers, you will be informed of where (that is, in what section of the chapter) to find more information..

1. ABC Corporation has locations in Toronto, New York, and San Francisco. It wants to install Windows NT Server 4 to encompass all its locations in a single WAN environment. The head office is located in New York. What is the best domain model for ABC's directory services implementation?

A. Single-domain model

B. Single-master domain model

C. Multiple-master domain model

D. Complete-trust domain model

2. JPS Printing has a single location with 1,000 users spread across the LAN. It has special printers and applications installed on the servers in its environment. It needs to be able to centrally manage the user accounts and the resources. Which domain model would best fit its needs?

A. Single-domain model

B. Single-master domain model

C. Multiple-master domain model

D. Complete-trust domain model

5. What must be created to allow a user account from one domain to access resources in a different domain?

A. Complete Trust Domain Model

B. One Way Trust Relationship

C. Two Way Trust Relationship

D. Master-Domain Model

Answers to Review Questions

1. Single domain, master domain, multiple-master domain, complete-trust domain. See section, Windows NT Server 4 Domain Models, in this chapter for more information. (This question deals with objective Planning 1.)

2. One user, one account, centralized administration, universal resource access, synchronization. See section, Windows NT Server 4 Directory Services, in this chapter for more information. (This question deals with objective Planning 1.)

6. Local accounts cannot be given permissions across trusts. See section, Accounts in Trust Relationships, in this chapter for more information. (This question deals with Planning 1.)

Answers and Explanations: For each of the Review and Exam questions, you will find thorough explanations located at the end of the section. They are easily identifiable because they are in blue type.

Exam Questions: These questions reflect the kinds of multiple-choice questions that appear on the Microsoft exams. Use them to become familiar with the exam question formats and to help you determine what you know and what you need to review or study more.

Suggested Readings and Resources

The following are some recommended readings on the subject of installing and configuring NT Workstation:

1. Microsoft Official Curriculum course 770: *Installing and Configuring Microsoft Windows NT Workstation 4.0*

   • Module 1: Overview of Windows NT Workstation 4.0

   • Module 2: Installing Windows NT Workstation 4.0

2. Microsoft Official Curriculum course 922: *Supporting Microsoft Windows NT 4.0 Core Technologies*

   • Module 2: Installing Windows NT

   • Module 3: Configuring the Windows NT Environment

3. *Microsoft Windows NT Workstation Resource Kit Version 4.0* (Microsoft Press)

   • Chapter 2: Customizing Setup

   • Chapter 4: Planning for a Mixed Environment

4. Microsoft TechNet CD-ROM

   • *MS Windows NT Workstation Technical Notes*

     • MS Windows NT Workstation Deployment Guide – Automating Windows NT Setup

     • An Unattended Windows NT Workstation Deployment

5. Web Sites

   • www.microsoft.com/train_cert

Suggested Readings and Resources: The very last element in each chapter is a list of additional resources you can use if you wish to go above and beyond certification-level material or if you need to spend more time on a particular subject that you are having trouble understanding.

Exam 70-067 Implementing and Supporting Microsoft Windows NT Server 4.0

Planning (Chapter 1)

THIS OBJECTIVE	IS COVERED HERE:
Plan the disk drive configuration for various requirements. Requirements include: · Choosing a file system · Choosing a fault-tolerance method	Choosing a disk configuration, ch. 1, p. 25 Windows NT File Systems, ch. 1, p. 29 Fault Tolerance Methods, ch. 1, p. 33
Choose a protocol for various situations. Protocols include: · TCP/IP · NWLink /SPX Compatible Transport · NetBEUI	Choosing a Windows NT Network Protocol, ch. 1, p. 37 TCP/IP, ch. 1, p. 37 NWLink, ch. 1, p. 40 NetBEUI, ch. 1, p. 41

Installation and Configuration (Chapters 2, 3, and 4)

THIS OBJECTIVE	IS COVERED HERE:
Install Windows NT Server on Intel-based platforms.	Installation Requirements, ch. 2, p. 60 Installation Procedure, ch. 2, p. 65
Install Windows NT Server to perform various server roles. Server roles include: · Primary domain controller · Backup domain controller · Member server	Choosing a Server Type, ch. 2, p. 64
Install Windows NT Server by using various methods. Installation methods include: · CD-ROM · Over-the-network · Network Client Administrator · Express versus custom	Installation Procedure, ch. 2, p. 65 CD-ROM, ch. 2, p. 65 Network Installs, ch. 2, p. 66 Network Installs, ch. 2, p. 66

MONITORING AND OPTIMIZATION (CHAPTER 8)

THIS OBJECTIVE	IS COVERED HERE:
Monitor performance of various functions by using Performance Monitor. Functions include: · Processor · Memory · Disk · Network	Peformance Monitor, ch. 8, p. 425
Identify performance bottlenecks.	Bottleneck—The Limiting Resource, ch. 8, p. 434

TROUBLESHOOTING (CHAPTER 9)

THIS OBJECTIVE	IS COVERED HERE:
Choose the appropriate course of action to take to resolve installation failures.	Troubleshooting Installation, ch. 9, p. 458
Choose the appropriate course of action to take to resolve boot failures.	Troubleshooting Boot Failures, ch. 9, p. 461
Choose the appropriate course of action to take to resolve configuration errors.	Troubleshooting Configuration Errors, ch. 9, p. 480
Choose the appropriate course of action to take to resolve printer problems.	Troubleshooting Printer Problems, ch. 9, p. 490
Choose the appropriate course of action to take to resolve RAS problems.	Troubleshooting RAS, ch. 9, p. 495
Choose the appropriate course of action to take to resolve connectivity problems.	Troubleshooting Connectivity Problems, ch. 9, p. 497
Choose the appropriate course of action to take to resolve resource access problems and permission problems.	Troubleshooting Access and Permission Problems, ch. 9, p. 501
Choose the appropriate course of action to take to resolve fault-tolerance failures. Fault-tolerance methods include: · Tape backup · Mirroring · Stripe set with parity · Disk duplexing	Recovering from Fault-Tolerance Failures, ch. 9, p. 502 Windows NT Backup, ch. 9, p. 503 Recovering from a Failed Mirror Set, ch. 9, p. 511 Recovering from a Failed Element of a Stripe Set with Parity, ch. 9, p. 512 Troubleshooting Partitions and Disks, ch. 9, p. 513

MANAGING RESOURCES (CHAPTERS 5 AND 6)

CONNECTIVITY (CHAPTER 7)

MCSE

Second Edition

Windows NT®
Server 4

Exam: 70-067

New Riders

DENNIS MAIONE

MCSE Training Guide: Windows NT® Server 4, Second Edition

Copyright © 1998 by New Riders Publishing

International Standard Book Number: 1-56205-916-5

Library of Congress Catalog Card Number: 98-85732

Printed in the United States of America

First Printing: September, 1998

00   4

Trademarks

Warning and Disclaimer

EXECUTIVE EDITOR
Mary Foote

ACQUISITIONS EDITOR
Nancy Maragioglio

DEVELOPMENT EDITOR
Ami Frank

MANAGING EDITOR
Sarah Kearns

PROJECT EDITOR
Mike La Bonne

COPY EDITOR
Audra McFarland

INDEXER
Joy Dean Lee

TECHNICAL EDITOR
Alain Guilbault

SOFTWARE DEVELOPMENT SPECIALIST
Jack Belbot

PRODUCTION
Mary Hunt
Gina Rexrode
Nicole Ritch

Contents at a Glance

Table of Contents

PART I: Exam Preparation

1 Planning   11

2 Installation and Configuration Part 1: Installation of NT Server   57

7 Connectivity   369

PART II: Final Review

PART III: **Appendixes**

About the Author

Dennis Maione lives in Winnipeg, Canada, where he is a full-time trainer for PBSC Computer Training Centres, the largest Canadian ATEC. He is an MCSE and has been in the computer training business for three years. He has a computer science degree and more than 15 years of experience programming and administering networks in a variety of environments (who'da thought that a TRS-80 would take me so far?).

Dennis is also the author of *MCSE Training Guide: Windows NT Workstation 4 Second Edition*, and is co-author of *CLP Training Guide: Lotus Notes*. You should buy them; they're both really good!

Dennis is married to a wonderfully supportive wife, Debra, and has three stunningly intelligent children: Emma, Alexander, and Noah. He never sees them any more though because he spends all his free time at his hobbies (this is the product of one of them).

Dennis would like to be a rock star when he grows up and if you hear that Matchbox-20 is looking for a new lead singer, email him at **Dennis_Maione@PBSC.COM**. You can email him at that address if you have comments or questions about the book (or if any other famous bands are looking for lead singers).

Dedication

This book is dedicated to my family:

Debra: *I'm still thankful you said "Yes" and keep saying "Yes" every time you sacrifice something of your life to allow me to pursue my dreams and "hobbies."*

Emma, **Alexander**, *and* **Noah**: *For all the little things that only you can do to encourage me when I am down..."my butterflies."*

My parents *(biological and adoptive): For giving to me when I could never give back and teaching me the way to walk.*

God: *How can I thank you for being Father and supporter to me...so this is what grace is like.*

Acknowledgments

I have to acknowledge all the people who made this project possible:

Nancy: Thanks for the "gentle" prodding to get this all done and thanks for a chance to write again (OK, I'll take the pins out now!)

Ami, **Alain**, and **Luther**: How could I have done it without your expert advice?

Brian, **Tammi**, **Rob**, and **Jason**: You have and continue to encourage me to be the best at what I do...thanks for the chance to do that.

All the people who supported me and my family during long hours of writing, without whose prayers and encouragement we would have fallen apart long ago.

Tell Us What You Think!

As the reader of this book, *you* are our most important critic and commentator. We value your opinion and want to know what we're doing right, what we could do better, what areas you'd like to see us publish in, and any other words of wisdom you're willing to pass our way.

As the Executive Editor for the Certification team at Macmillan Computer Publishing, I welcome your comments. You can fax, email, or write me directly to let me know what you did or didn't like about this book—as well as what we can do to make our books stronger.

Please note that I cannot help you with technical problems related to the topic of this book, and that due to the high volume of mail I receive, I might not be able to reply to every message.

When you write, please be sure to include this book's title and author, as well as your name and phone or fax number. I will carefully review your comments and share them with the author and editors who worked on the book.

Fax: 317-581-4663

Email: certification@mcp.com

Mail: Executive Editor
             Certification
             Macmillan Computer Publishing
             201 West 103rd Street
             Indianapolis, IN 46290 USA

How to Use This Book

New Riders Publishing has made an effort in the second editions of its Training Guide series to make the information as accessible as possible for the purposes of learning the certification material. Here, you have an opportunity to view the many instructional features that have been incorporated into the books to achieve that goal.

CHAPTER OPENER

Each chapter begins with a set of features designed to allow you to maximize study time for that material.

List of Objectives: Each chapter begins with a list of the objectives as stated by Microsoft.

Objective Explanations: Immediately following each objective is an explanation of it, providing context that defines it more meaningfully in relation to the exam. Because Microsoft can sometimes be vague in its objectives list, the objective explanations are designed to clarify any vagueness by relying on the authors' test-taking experience.

OBJECTIVES

Microsoft provides the following objectives for "Connectivity":

Add and configure the network components of Windows NT Workstation.

▶ This objective is necessary because someone certified in the use of Windows NT Workstation technology must understand how it fits into a networked environment and how to configure the components that enable it to do so.

Use various methods to access network resources.

▶ This objective is necessary because someone certified in the use of Windows NT Workstation technology must understand how resources available on a network can be accessed from NT Workstation.

Implement Windows NT Workstation as a client in a NetWare environment.

▶ This objective is necessary because someone certified in the use of Windows NT Workstation technology must understand how NT Workstation can be used as a client in a NetWare environment and how to configure the services and protocols that make this possible.

Use various configurations to install Windows NT Workstation as a TCP/IP client.

▶ This objective is necessary because someone certified in the use of Windows NT Workstation technology must understand how TCP/IP is important in a network environment and how Workstation can be configured to use it.

CHAPTER 4

Connectivity

Chapter Outline: Learning always gets a boost when you can see both the forest and the trees. To give you a visual image of how the topics in a chapter fit together, you will find a chapter outline at the beginning of each chapter. You will also be able to use this for easy reference when looking for a particular topic.

STUDY STRATEGIES

▶ Disk configurations are a part of both the planning and the configuration of NT Server computers. To study for Planning Objective 1, you will need to look at both the following section and the material in Chapter 2, "Installation Part 1." As with many concepts, you should have a good handle on the terminology and know the best applications for different disk configurations. For the objectives of the NT Server exam, you will need to know only general disk configuration concepts—at a high level, not the nitty gritty. Make sure you memorize the concepts relating to partitioning and know the difference between the system and the boot partitions in an NT system (and the fact that the definitions of these are counter-intuitive). You should know that NT supports both FAT and NTFS partitions, as well as some of the advantages and disadvantages of each. You will also need to know about the fault-tolerance methods available in NT—stripe sets with parity and disk mirroring—including their definitions, hardware requirements, and advantages and disadvantages.

Of course, nothing substitutes for working with the concepts explained in this objective. If possible, get an NT system with some free disk space and play around with the Disk Administrator just to see how partitions are created and what they look like.

You might also want to look at some of the supplementary readings and scan TechNet for white papers on disk configuration.

▶ The best way to study for Planning Objective 2 is to read, memorize, and understand the use of each protocol. You should know what the protocols are, what they are used for, and what systems they are compatible with.

As with disk configuration, installing protocols on your NT Server is something that you plan for, not something you do just because it feels good to you at the time. Although it is much easier to add or remove a protocol than it is to reconfigure your hard drives, choosing a protocol is still an essential part of the planning process because specific protocols, like spoken languages, are designed to be used in certain circumstances. There is no point in learning to speak Mandarin Chinese if you are never around anyone who can understand you. Similarly, the NWLink protocol is used to interact with NetWare systems; therefore, if you do not have Novell servers on your network, you might want to rethink your plan to install it on your servers. We will discuss the uses of the major protocols in Chapter 7, "Connectivity." However, it is important that you have a good understanding of their uses here in the planning stage.

Study Strategies: Each topic presents its own learning challenge. To support you through this, New Riders has included strategies for how to best approach studying in order to retain the material in the chapter, particularly as it is addressed on the exam.

INSTRUCTIONAL FEATURES WITHIN THE CHAPTER

These books include a large amount and different kinds of information. The many different elements are designed to help you identify information by its purpose and importance to the exam and also to provide you with varied ways to learn the material. You will be able to determine how much attention to devote to certain elements, depending on what your goals are. By becoming familiar with the different presentations of information, you will know what information will be important to you as a test-taker and which information will be important to you as a practitioner.

Objective Coverage Text: In the text before an exam objective is specifically addressed, you will notice the objective is listed and printed in color to help call your attention to that particular material.

Warning: In using sophisticated information technology, there is always potential for mistakes or even catastrophes that can occur through improper application of the technology. Warnings appear in the margins to alert you to such potential problems.

EXAM TIP

Only One NTVDM Supports Multiple 16-bit Applications
Expect at least one question about running Win16 applications in separate memory spaces. The key concept is that you can load multiple Win16 applications into the same memory space only if it is the initial Win16 NTVDM. It is not possible, for example, to run Word for Windows 6.0 and Excel for Windows 5.0 in one shared memory space and also run PowerPoint 4.0 and Access 2.0 in another shared memory space.

Exam Tip: Exam Tips appear in the margins to provide specific exam-related advice. Such tips may address what material is covered (or not covered) on the exam, how it is covered, mnemonic devices, or particular quirks of that exam.

Note: Notes appear in the margins and contain various kinds of useful information, such as tips on the technology or administrative practices, historical background on terms and technologies, or side commentary on industry issues.

---

8   **Chapter 1** PLANNING

INTRODUCTION

Microsoft grew up around the personal computer industry and established itself as the preeminent maker of software products for personal computers. Microsoft has a vast portfolio of software products, but it is best known for its operating systems.

Microsoft's current operating system products, listed here, are undoubtedly well-known to anyone studying for the MCSE exams:

- ◆ Windows 95
- ◆ Windows NT Workstation
- ◆ Windows NT Server

NOTE

Strange But True Although it sounds backward, it is true: Windows NT boots from the system partition and then loads the system from the boot partition.

Some older operating system products—namely MS-DOS, Windows 3.1, and Windows for Workgroups—are still important to the operability of Windows NT Server, so don't be surprised if you hear them mentioned from time to time in this book.

Windows NT is the most powerful, the most secure, and perhaps the most elegant operating system Microsoft has yet produced. It languished for a while after it first appeared (in part because no one was sure why they needed it or what to do with it), but Microsoft has persisted with improving interoperability and performance. With the release of Windows NT 4 which offers a new Windows 95-like user interface, Windows NT has assumed a prominent place in today's world of network-based computing.

WINDOWS NT SERVER AMONG MICROSOFT OPERATING SYSTEMS

WARNING

Don't Overextend Your Partitions and Wraps It is not necessary to create an extended partition on a disk; primary partitions might be all that you need. However, if you do create one, remember that you can never have more than one extended partition on a physical disk.

As we already mentioned, Microsoft has three operating system products now competing in the marketplace: Windows 95, Windows NT Workstation, and Windows NT Server. Each of these operating systems has its advantages and disadvantages.

Looking at the presentation of the desktop, the three look very much alike—so much so that you might have to click the Start button and read the banner on the left side of the menu to determine which operating system you are looking at. Each offers the familiar Windows 95 user interface featuring the Start button, the Recycling

STEP BY STEP

5.1 Configuring an Extension to Trigger an Application to Always Run in a Separate Memory Space

1. Start the Windows NT Explorer.

2. From the View menu, choose Options.

3. Click the File Types tab.

4. In the Registered File Types list box, select the desired file type.

5. Click the Edit button to display the Edit File Type dialog box. Then select Open from the Actions list and click the Edit button below it.

6. In the Editing Action for Type dialog box, adjust the application name by typing **cmd.exe /c start /separate** in front of the existing contents of the field (see Figure 5.15).

FIGURE 5.15
Configuring a shortcut to run a Win16 application in a separate memory space.

Step by Step: Step by Steps are hands-on tutorial instructions that walk you through a particular task or function relevant to the exam objectives.

Figure: To improve readability, the figures have been placed in the margins so they do not interrupt the main flow of text.

---

14   Chapter 1   PLANNING

You must use NTFS if you want to preserve existing permissions when you migrate files and directories from a NetWare server to a Windows NT Server system.

Windows 95 is Microsoft's everyday workhorse operating system. It provides a 32-bit platform and is designed to operate with a variety of peripherals. See Table 1.1 for the minimum hardware requirements for the installation and operation of Windows 95. Also, if you want to allow Macintosh computers to access files on the partition through Windows NT's Services for Macintosh, you must format the partition for NTFS.

MAKING REGISTRY CHANGES

To make Registry changes, run the REGEDT32.EXE program. The Registry in Windows NT is a complex database of configuration settings for your computer. If you want to configure the Workstation service, open the HKEY_LOCAL_MACHINE hive, as shown in Figure 3.22.

The exact location for configuring your Workstation service is

    HKEY_LOCAL_MACHINE\System\CurrentControlSet\Services\
    LanmanWorkstation\Parameters

To find additional information regarding this Registry item and others, refer to the Windows NT Server resource kit.

This summary table offers an overview of the differences between the FAT and NTFS file systems.

In-Depth Sidebar: These more extensive discussions cover material that perhaps is not as directly relevant to the exam, but which is useful as reference material or in everyday practice. In-Depths may also provide useful background or contextual information necessary for understanding the larger topic under consideration.

REVIEW BREAK

Choosing a File System

But if the system is designed to store data, mirroring might produce disk bottlenecks. You might only know whether these changes are significant by setting up two identical computers, implementing mirroring on one but not on the other, and then running Performance Monitor on both under a simulated load to see the performance differences.

This summary table offers an overview of the differences between the FAT and NTFS file systems.

Review Break: Crucial information is summarized at various points in the book in lists or tables. At the end of a particularly long section, you might come across a Review Break that is there just to wrap up one long objective and reinforce the key points before you shift your focus to the next section.

CASE STUDIES

Case Studies are presented throughout the book to provide you with another, more conceptual opportunity to apply the knowledge you are developing. They also reflect the "real-world" experiences of the authors in ways that prepare you not only for the exam but for actual network administration as well. In each Case Study, you will find similar elements: a description of a Scenario, the Essence of the Case, and an extended Analysis section.

CASE STUDY: REALLY GOOD GUITARS

ESSENCE OF THE CASE

Here are the essential elements in this case:

· need for centralized administration

· the need for WAN connectivity nation-wide

· a requirement for Internet access and e-mail

· the need for Security on network shares and local files

· an implementation of Fault-tolerant systems

SCENARIO

Really Good Guitars is a national company specializing in the design and manufacture of custom acoustic guitars. Having grown up out of an informal network of artisans across Canada, the company has many locations but very few employees (300 at this time) and a Head Office in Churchill, Manitoba. Although they follow the best traditions of hand-making guitars, they are not without technological savvy and all the 25 locations have computers on-site which are used to do accounting, run MS Office applications, and run their custom made guitar design software. The leadership team has recently begun to realize that a networked solution is essential to maintain consistency and to provide security on what are becoming some very innovative designs and to provide their employees with e-mail and Internet access.

RGG desires a centralized administration of its

continues

Essence of the Case: A bulleted list of the key problems or issues that need to be addressed in the Scenario.

Scenario: A few paragraphs describing a situation that professional practitioners in the field might face. A Scenario will deal with an issue relating to the objectives covered in the chapter, and it includes the kinds of details that make a difference.

Analysis: This is a lengthy description of the best way to handle the problems listed in the Essence of the Case. In this section, you might find a table summarizing the solutions, a worded example, or both.

CASE STUDY: PRINT IT DRAFTING INC.

continued

too, which is unacceptable. You are to find a solution to this problem if one exists.

ANALYSIS

The fixes for both of these problems are relatively straightforward. In the first case, it is likely that all the programs on the draftspeople's workstations are being started at normal priority. This means that they have a priority of 8. But the default says that anything running in the foreground is getting a 2-point boost from the base priority, bringing it to 10. As a result, when sent to the background, AutoCAD is not getting as much attention from the processor as it did when it was the foreground application. Because multiple applications need to be run at once without significant degradation of the performance of AutoCAD, you implement the following solution:

1. On the Performance tab of the System Properties dialog box for each workstation, set the Application Performance slider to None to prevent a boost for foreground applications.

2. Recommend that users keep the additional programs running alongside AutoCAD at a minimum (because all programs will now get equal processor time).

The fix to the second problem is to run each 16-bit application in its own NTVDM. This ensures that the crashing of one application will not adversely affect the others, but it still enables interoperability between the applications because they use OLE (and not shared memory) to transfer data. To make the fix as transparent as possible to the users, you suggested that two things be done:

1. Make sure that for each shortcut a user has created to the office applications, the Run in Separate Memory Space option is selected on the Shortcut tab.

2. Change the properties for the extensions associated with the applications (for example, .XLS and .DOC) so that they start using the /separate switch. Then any file that is double-clicked invokes the associated program to run in its own NTVDM.

CHAPTER SUMMARY

KEY TERMS

Before you take the exam, make sure you are comfortable with the definitions and concepts for each of the following key terms:

• FAT

• NTFS

• workgroup

• domain

This chapter discussed the main planning topics you will encounter on the Windows NT Server exam. Distilled down, these topics revolve around two main goals: understanding the planning of disk configuration and understanding the planning of network protocols.

◆ Windows NT Server supports an unlimited number of inbound sessions; Windows NT Workstation supports no more than 10 active sessions at the same time.

◆ Windows NT Server accommodates an unlimited number of remote access connections (although Microsoft only supports up to 256); Windows NT Workstation supports only a single remote access connection.

Key Terms: A list of key terms appears at the end of each chapter. These are terms that you should be sure you know and are comfortable defining and understanding when you go in to take the exam.

Chapter Summary: Before the Apply Your Learning section, you will find a chapter summary that wraps up the chapter and reviews what you should have learned.

EXTENSIVE REVIEW AND SELF-TEST OPTIONS

At the end of each chapter, along with some summary elements, you will find a section called "Apply Your Learning" that gives you several different methods with which to test your understanding of the material and review what you have learned.

Chapter 1 PLANNING   23

APPLY YOUR LEARNING

This section allows you to assess how well you understood the material in the chapter. Review and Exam questions test your knowledge of the tasks and concepts specified in the objectives. The Exercises provide you with opportunities to engage in the sorts of tasks that comprise the skill sets the objectives reflect.

Exercises

1.1   Synchronizing the Domain Controllers

The following steps show you how to manually synchronize a backup domain controller within your domain. (This objective deals with Objective Planning 1.)

Time Estimate: Less than 10 minutes.

1. Click Start, Programs, Administrative Tools, and select the Server Manager icon.

2. Highlight the BDC (Backup Domain Controller) in your computer list.

3. Select the Computer menu, then select Synchronize with Primary Domain Controller.

12.2   Establishing a Trust Relationship between Domains

The following steps show you how to establish a trust relationship between multiple domains. To complete this exercise, you must have two Windows NT Server computers, each installed in their own domain. (This objective deals with objective Planning 1.)

Time Estimate: 10 minutes

1. From the trusted domain select Start, Programs, Administrative Tools, and click User Manager for Domains. The User Manager.

FIGURE 1.2
The login process on a local machine.

2. Select the Policies menu and click Trust Relationships. The Trust Relationships dialog box appears.

4. When the trusting domain information has been entered, click OK and close the Trust Relationships dialog box.

Review Questions

1. List the four domain models that can be used for directory services in Windows NT Server 4.

2. List the goals of a directory services architecture.

3. What is the maximum size of the SAM database in Windows NT Server 4.0?

4. What are the two different types of domains in a trust relationship?

5. In a trust relationship which domain would contain the user accounts?

Exercises: These activities provide an opportunity for you to master specific hands-on tasks. Our goal is to increase your proficiency with the product or technology. You must be able to conduct these tasks in order to pass the exam.

Review Questions: These open-ended, short-answer questions allow you to quickly assess your comprehension of what you just read in the chapter. Instead of asking you to choose from a list of options, these questions require you to state the correct answers in your own words. Although you will not experience these kinds of questions on the exam, these questions will indeed test your level of comprehension of key concepts.

6. Can a local account be used in a trust relationship? Explain.

7. In a complete trust domain model that uses 4 different domains, what is the total number of trust relationships required to use a complete trust domain model?

Exam Questions

The following questions are similar to those you will face on the Microsoft exam. Answers to these questions can be found in section Answers and Explanations, later in the chapter. At the end of each of those answers, you will be informed of where (that is, in what section of the chapter) to find more information..

1. ABC Corporation has locations in Toronto, New York, and San Francisco. It wants to install Windows NT Server 4 to encompass all its locations in a single WAN environment. The head office is located in New York. What is the best domain model for ABC*is* directory services implementation?

A. Single-domain model

B. Single-master domain model

C. Multiple-master domain model

D. Complete-trust domain model

2. JPS Printing has a single location with 1,000 users spread across the LAN. It has special printers and applications installed on the servers in its environment. It needs to be able to centrally manage the user accounts and the resources. Which domain model would best fit its needs?

A. Single-domain model

B. Single-master domain model

C. Multiple-master domain model

D. Complete-trust domain model

5. What must be created to allow a user account from one domain to access resources in a different domain?

A. Complete Trust Domain Model

B. One Way Trust Relationship

C. Two Way Trust Relationship

D. Master-Domain Model

Answers to Review Questions

1. Single domain, master domain, multiple-master domain, complete-trust domain. See section, Windows NT Server 4 Domain Models, in this chapter for more information. (This question deals with objective Planning 1.)

2. One user, one account, centralized administration, universal resource access, synchronization. See section, Windows NT Server 4 Directory Services, in this chapter for more information. (This question deals with objective Planning 1.)

6. Local accounts cannot be given permissions across trusts. See section, Accounts in Trust Relationships, in this chapter for more information. (This question deals with Planning 1.)

Exam Questions: These questions reflect the kinds of multiple-choice questions that appear on the Microsoft exams. Use them to become familiar with the exam question formats and to help you determine what you know and what you need to review or study more.

Answers and Explanations: For each of the Review and Exam questions, you will find thorough explanations located at the end of the section. They are easily identifiable because they are in blue type.

Suggested Readings and Resources

The following are some recommended readings on the subject of installing and configuring NT Workstation:

1. Microsoft Official Curriculum course 770: *Installing and Configuring Microsoft Windows NT Workstation 4.0*

    • Module 1: Overview of Windows NT Workstation 4.0

    • Module 2: Installing Windows NT Workstation 4.0

2. Microsoft Official Curriculum course 922: *Supporting Microsoft Windows NT 4.0 Core Technologies*

    • Module 2: Installing Windows NT

    • Module 3: Configuring the Windows NT Environment

3. *Microsoft Windows NT Workstation Resource Kit Version 4.0* (Microsoft Press)

    • Chapter 2: Customizing Setup

    • Chapter 4: Planning for a Mixed Environment

4. Microsoft TechNet CD-ROM

    • *MS Windows NT Workstation Technical Notes*

       • MS Windows NT Workstation Deployment Guide – Automating Windows NT Setup

       • An Unattended Windows NT Workstation Deployment

5. Web Sites

    • www.microsoft.com/train_cert

    • www.prometric.com/testingcandidates/ assessment/chosetest.html (take online

Suggested Readings and Resources: The very last element in every chapter is a list of additional resources you can use if you want to go above and beyond certification-level material or if you need to spend more time on a particular subject that you are having trouble understanding.

Introduction

MCSE Training Guide: Windows NT Server 4, 2nd Edition is designed for advanced end users, service technicians, and network administrators with the goal of certification as a Microsoft Certified Systems Engineer (MCSE). The "NT Server 4" exam (#70-067) measures your ability to implement, administer, and troubleshoot information systems that include Windows NT Server 4 alone and with NetWare.

WHO SHOULD READ THIS BOOK

This book is designed to help you meet the goal of certification by preparing you for the "Networking Essentials" exam.

This book is your one-stop shop. Everything you need to know to pass the exam is in here, and Microsoft has approved it as study material. You do not *need* to take a class in addition to buying this book to pass the exam. However, depending on your personal study habits or learning style, you may benefit from taking a class in addition to the book.

This book also can help advanced users and administrators who are not studying for the exam but are looking for a single-volume reference on networking.

HOW THIS BOOK HELPS YOU

This book leads you on a self-guided tour of all the areas covered by the "NT Server 4" exam and teaches you the specific skills you need to achieve your MCSE

certification. You'll also find helpful hints, tips, real-world examples, exercises, and references to additional study materials. Specifically, this book is designed around four general concepts to help you learn.

◆ **Organization.** This book is organized first by major exam topics and then by individual exam objectives. Every objective you need to know for the "NT Server 4" exam is covered in this book. We attempted to make the information accessible in several different ways:

- The full list of exam topics and objectives is included in this introduction.

- Each chapter begins with a list of the objectives covered in that particular chapter, as well as the author's personal explanation of that objective.

- Each chapter opener includes a Study Strategy, provided by the author, to guide you in the best ways to prepare for that particular section of the exam, whether it be memorization, hands-on practice, or conceptual understanding.

- Each chapter also begins with an outline that provides an overview of the material in the chapter and the page numbers where particular topics can be found.

Individual objectives appear in color like this, immediately preceding the text that covers that particular objective.

- To help you quickly locate where the objectives are addressed in the chapter, you will notice the objective listed and printed in color to help direct your attention to that particular material.

- The information on where the objectives are covered is also conveniently condensed on the tear card at the front of this book.

◆ **Instructional Features.** This book has been designed to provide you with multiple ways to access and reinforce the exam material. The book's instructional features include the following:

- *Objective Explanations.* As mentioned earlier, each chapter begins with a list of the objectives covered in the chapter. In addition, immediately following each objective is an explanation of it, in context that defines it more meaningfully.

- *Study Strategies.* The beginning of the chapter also includes strategies for how to approach studying and retaining the material in the chapter, particularly as it is addressed on the exam.

- *Exam Tips.* Exam tips appear in the margin to provide specific exam-related advice. Such tips may address what material is covered (or not covered) on the exam, how it is covered, mnemonic devices, or particular quirks of that exam.

- *Reviews and Summaries.* Crucial information is summarized at various points in the book in lists or tables. Each chapter ends with a summary as well.

- *Key Terms.* A list of key terms appears at the end of each chapter.

- *Notes and Tips.* These appear in the margin and contain various kinds of useful information, such as tips on the technology or administrative practices, historical background on terms and technologies, or side commentary on industry issues.

- *Warnings.* When you use sophisticated information technology, there is always potential for mistake or even catastrophe that can occur through improper application of the technology. Warnings appear in the margin to alert you to such potential problems.

- *In-Depth Sidebars.* These more extensive discussions cover material that is, perhaps, not directly relevant to the exam, but which is useful as reference material or in everyday practice. In-depth sidebars might also provide useful background or contextual information necessary for understanding the larger topic under consideration.

- *Step by Steps.* These are hands-on tutorial instructions that walk you through particular tasks or functions relevant to the exam objectives.

- *Exercises.* Found at the end of the chapters in the "Apply Your Knowledge" section, Exercises may include additional tutorial material as well as other types of problems and questions.

- *Case Studies.* Case studies are presented throughout the book. They provide you with another, more conceptual opportunity to apply the knowledge you are gaining. They include a description of a scenario, the essence of the case, and an extended analysis section. They also reflect the "real-world" experiences of the authors in ways that prepare you not only for the exam but for actual network administration as well.

◆ **Extensive Practice Test Options.** The book provides numerous opportunities for you to assess your knowledge and practice for the exam. The practice options include:

- *Review Questions*. These open-ended questions appear in the "Apply Your Learning" section at the end of each chapter. They allow you to quickly assess your comprehension of what you just read in the chapter. Answers to the questions are provided later in the chapter.

- *Exam Questions*. These questions also appear in the "Apply your Knowledge" section. They reflect the kind of multiple-choice questions that appear on the Microsoft exams. Use them to practice for the exam and to help you determine what you know and what you need to review or study further. Answers and explanations for them are provided.

- *Practice Exam*. A Practice Exam is included in the "Final Review" section. The Final Review section and the Practice Exam are discussed below.

- *TestPrep*. The Top Score software included on the CD-ROM provides further practice questions.

> **NOTE**
> **Top Score** For a complete description of New Riders' Top Score test engine, see Appendix D, "Using the Top Score Software."

◆ **Final Review**. This part of the book provides you with three valuable tools for preparing for the exam.

- *Fast Facts*. This condensed version of the information contained in the book will prove extremely useful for last-minute review.

- *Study and Exam Preparation Tips*. Read this section early on to help you develop study strategies. It also provides you with valuable exam-day tips and information on new exam

question formats, such as adaptive tests and simulation-based questions.

- *Practice Exam*. A full practice exam is included. Questions are written in the styles used on the actual exam. Use it to assess your readiness for the real thing.

The book includes other features, such as a section titled "Suggested Readings and Resources" at the end of each chapter that directs you toward further information that could aid you in your exam preparation or your actual work. There are several valuable appendixes as well, including a glossary (Appendix A), an overview of the Microsoft certification program (Appendix B), and a description of what is on the CD-ROM (Appendix C). These and all the other book features mentioned above provide you with thorough preparation for the exam.

For more information about the exam or the certification process, contact Microsoft:

Microsoft Education: (800) 636-7544

Internet:
ftp://ftp.microsoft.com/Services/MSEdCert

World Wide Web:
http://www.microsoft.com/train_cert

CompuServe Forum: GO MSEDCERT

WHAT THE NT SERVER 4 EXAM (#70-067) COVERS

The "NT Server 4" exam (#70-067) covers the four main topic areas represented by the conceptual groupings of the test objectives. Each chapter represents one or more of these main topic areas. The exam objectives are listed by topic area in the following sections.

Planning

Plan the disk drive configuration for various requirements. Requirements include:

- Choosing a file system
- Choosing a fault-tolerance method

Choose a protocol for various situations. Protocols include:

- TCP/IP
- NWLink IPX/SPX Compatible Transport
- NetBEUI

Installation and Configuration

Install Windows NT Server on Intel-based platforms.

Install Windows NT Server to perform various server roles. Server roles include:

- Primary domain controller
- Backup domain controller
- Member server

Install Windows NT Server by using various methods. Installation methods include:

- CD-ROM
- Over-the-network
- Network Client Administrator
- Express versus custom

Configure protocols and protocol bindings. Protocols include:

- TCP/IP
- NWLink IPX/SPX Compatible Transport
- NetBEUI

Configure network adapters. Considerations include:

- Changing IRQ, IO base, and memory addresses
- Configuring multiple adapters

Configure Windows NT Server core services. Services include:

- Directory Replicator
- License Manager
- Other services

Configure peripherals and devices. Peripherals and devices include:

- Communication devices
- SCSI devices
- Tape device drivers
- UPS devices and UPS service
- Mouse drivers, display drivers, and keyboard drivers

Configure hard disks to meet various requirements. Requirements include:

- Allocating disk space capacity
- Providing redundancy
- Improving performance
- Providing security
- Formatting

Configure printers. Tasks include:

- Adding and configuring a printer
- Implementing a printer pool
- Setting print priorities

Configure a Windows NT Server computer for various types of client computers. Client computer types include:

- Windows NT Workstation
- Microsoft Windows 95
- Microsoft MS-DOS-based

Managing Resources

Manage user and group accounts. Considerations include:

- Managing Windows NT groups
- Managing Windows NT user rights
- Administering account policies
- Auditing changes to the user account database

Create and manage policies and profiles for various situations. Policies and profiles include:

- Local user profiles
- Roaming user profiles
- System policies

Administer remote servers from various types of client computers. Client computer types include:

- Windows 95
- Windows NT Workstation

Manage disk resources. Tasks include:

- Copying and moving files between file systems
- Creating and sharing resources
- Implementing permissions and security
- Establishing file auditing

Connectivity

Configure Windows NT Server for interoperability with NetWare servers by using various tools. Tools include:

- Gateway Services for NetWare
- Migration Tool for NetWare

Install and configure Remote Access Service (RAS). Configuration options include:

- Configuring RAS communications
- Configuring RAS protocols
- Configuring RAS security
- Configuring Dial-Up Networking clients

Monitoring and Optimization

Monitor performance of various functions by using Performance Monitor. Functions include:

- Processor
- Memory
- Disk
- Network

Identify performance bottlenecks.

Troubleshooting

Choose the appropriate course of action to take to resolve installation failures.

Choose the appropriate course of action to take to resolve boot failures.

Choose the appropriate course of action to take to resolve configuration errors.

Choose the appropriate course of action to take to resolve printer problems.

Choose the appropriate course of action to take to resolve RAS problems.

Choose the appropriate course of action to take to resolve connectivity problems.

Choose the appropriate course of action to take to resolve resource access problems and permission problems.

Choose the appropriate course of action to take to resolve fault-tolerance failures. Fault-tolerance methods include:

- ◆ Tape backup
- ◆ Mirroring
- ◆ Stripe set with parity
- ◆ Disk duplexing

It is somewhat easier to obtain access to the necessary computer hardware and software in a corporate business environment. It can be difficult, however, to allocate enough time within the busy workday to complete a self-study program. Most of your study time will occur after normal working hours, away from the everyday interruptions and pressures of your regular job.

ADVICE ON TAKING THE EXAM

More extensive tips are found in the Final Review section in the chapter titled "Study and Exam Preparation Tips." But keep the following suggestions in mind as you study:

- ◆ **Read all the material.** Microsoft has been known to include material on its exams that's not expressly specified in the objectives. This book has included additional information not reflected in the objectives in an effort to give you the best possible preparation for the examination and for the real-world network experiences to come.

- ◆ **Do the Step by Steps and complete the Exercises in each chapter.** They will help you gain experience using the Microsoft product. All Microsoft exams are task- and experienced-based and require you to have used the Microsoft product in a real networking environment.

- ◆ **Use the questions to assess your knowledge.** Don't just read the chapter content; use the questions to find out what you know and what you don't. Then study some more, review, and assess your knowledge again.

- ◆ **Review the exam objectives.** Develop your own questions and examples for each topic listed. If you can make and answer several questions for each topic, you should not find it difficult to pass the exam.

> **NOTE**
>
> **No Guarantees**   Although this book is designed to prepare you to take and pass the NT Server 4 certification exam, there are no guarantees. Read this book and work through the questions and exercises, and when you feel confident, take the Practice Exam and additional exams using the Top Score test engine. This should tell you whether or not you are ready for the real thing.
>
> When taking the actual certification exam, make sure you answer all the questions before your time limit expires. Do not spend too much time on any one question. If you are unsure about an answer, answer the question as best you can and mark it for later review; you can go back to it when you have finished the rest of the questions.

Remember, the primary object is not to pass the exam—it is to understand the material. If you understand the material, passing the exam should be simple. Knowledge is a pyramid: To build upward, you need a solid foundation. This book and the Microsoft Certified Professional programs are designed to ensure that you have that solid foundation.

Good luck!

NEW RIDERS PUBLISHING

The staff of New Riders Publishing is committed to bringing you the very best in computer reference material. Each New Riders book is the result of months of work by authors and staff who research and refine the information contained within its covers.

As part of this commitment to you, the NRP reader, New Riders invites your input. Please let us know if you enjoy this book, if you have trouble with the information or examples presented, or if you have a suggestion for the next edition.

Please note, however, that New Riders staff cannot serve as a technical resource during your preparation for the Microsoft certification exams or for questions about software- or hardware-related problems. Please refer instead to the documentation that accompanies the Microsoft products or to the applications' Help systems.

If you have a question or comment about any New Riders book, you can contact New Riders Publishing in several ways. We will respond to as many readers as we can. Your name, address, or phone number will never become part of a mailing list or be used for any purpose other than to help us continue to bring you the best books possible. You can write to us at the following address:

New Riders Publishing
Attn: Publisher
201 W. 103rd Street
Indianapolis, IN 46290

If you prefer, you can fax New Riders Publishing at (317) 817-7448.

You also can send email to New Riders at the following Internet address:

```
certification@mcp.com
```

NRP is an imprint of Macmillan Computer Publishing. To obtain a catalog or information, or to purchase any Macmillan Computer Publishing book, call (800) 428-5331.

Thank you for selecting *MCSE Training Guide: NT Server 4, Second Edition!*

Exam Preparation

Microsoft provides the following objectives for "Planning":

▶ **Plan the disk drive configuration for various requirements. Requirements include choosing a file system and choosing a fault-tolerance method.**

This objective is necessary because someone certified in the use of Windows NT Server technology must understand the basic advantages and disadvantages of the two file systems when choosing a file system for a given situation. In addition, one must understand the capabilities of various fault-tolerance methods and again be able to apply that understanding when choosing a method for use in a particular situation.

▶ **Choose a protocol for various situations. Protocols include TCP/IP, NWLink, IPX/SPX Compatible Transport, and NetBEUI.**

This objective is necessary because someone certified in the Microsoft NT Server technology should understand the network protocols available in NT and be able to decide when it is appropriate to use a particular protocol or protocols. Each protocol has a specifically recommended use, and you should be well versed in their applications.

CHAPTER 1

Planning

▶ Disk configurations are a part of both the planning and the configuration of NT Server computers. To study for the first Planning objective, you will need to look at both the following section and the material in Chapter 2, "Installation and Configuration Part 1: Installation of NT Server." As with many concepts, you should have a good handle on the terminology and know the best applications for different disk configurations. For the objectives of the NT Server exam, you will need to know only general disk configuration concepts—at a high level, not the nitty gritty. Make sure you memorize the concepts relating to partitioning and know the difference between the system and the boot partitions in an NT system (and the fact that the definitions of these are counter-intuitive). You should know that NT supports both FAT and NTFS partitions, as well as some of the advantages and disadvantages of each. You will also need to know about the fault-tolerance methods available in NT—*stripe sets with parity* and *disk mirroring*—including their definitions, hardware requirements, and advantages and disadvantages.

Of course, nothing substitutes for working with the concepts explained in this objective. If possible, get an NT system with some free disk space and play around with the Disk Administrator just to see how partitions are created and what they look like.

You might also want to look at some of the supplementary readings and scan TechNet for white papers on disk configuration.

▶ The best way to study for the second Planning objective is to read, memorize, and understand the use of each protocol. You should know what the protocols are, what they are used for, and what systems they are compatible with.

As with disk configuration, installing protocols on your NT Server is something that you plan for, not something you do just because it feels good to you at the time. Although it is much easier to add or remove a protocol than it is to reconfigure your hard drives, choosing a protocol is still an essential part of the planning process because specific protocols, like spoken languages, are designed to be used in certain circumstances. There is no point in learning to speak Mandarin Chinese if you are never around anyone who can understand you. Similarly, the NWLink protocol is used to interact with NetWare systems; therefore, if you do not have Novell servers on your network, you might want to rethink your plan to install it on your servers. We will discuss the uses of the major protocols in Chapter 7, "Connectivity." However, it is important that you have a good understanding of their uses here in the planning stage.

This chapter will help you prepare for the "Planning" section of Microsoft's Exam 70-067 by giving you information necessary to make intelligent choices regarding the file system or systems you will use on your Windows NT Server machine and the fault-tolerance methods you will employ.

This chapter will also introduce you to the major supported protocols in the NT Server environment and the benefits and drawbacks of each.

INTRODUCTION

Microsoft grew up around the personal computer industry and established itself as the preeminent maker of software products for personal computers. Microsoft has a vast portfolio of software products, but it is best known for its operating systems.

Microsoft's current operating system products, listed here, are undoubtedly well-known to anyone studying for the MCSE exams:

◆ Windows 95 (soon this will include Windows 98)

◆ Windows NT Workstation

◆ Windows NT Server

Some older operating system products—namely MS-DOS, Windows 3.1, and Windows for Workgroups—are still important to the operability of Windows NT Server, so don't be surprised if you hear them mentioned from time to time in this book.

Windows NT is the most powerful, the most secure, and perhaps the most elegant operating system Microsoft has yet produced. It languished for a while after it first appeared (in part because no one was sure why they needed it or what to do with it), but Microsoft has persisted with improving interoperability and performance. With the release of Windows NT 4 which offers a new Windows 95-like user interface, Windows NT has assumed a prominent place in today's world of network-based computing.

This chapter introduces you to Windows NT Server and Windows NT Workstation, which are the two flavors (you might say) of Windows NT. To help you better understand the application of Windows NT technology, we compare Windows NT to Windows 95 and also compare the workgroup and the domain (the two basic network architecture types of Windows NT networking). We conclude by examining some planning issues you need to address before you set up your Windows NT network: specifically, choosing a disk configuration and choosing a network protocol.

NOTE **Using Windows NT to Apply to Both Workstation and Server** Although Windows NT Server 4.0 and Windows NT Workstation 4.0 are considerably different in their application, power, and capabilities, they are very similar in many ways. Therefore, this chapter might make reference to them as a collective operating system using the term Windows NT. In absence of the words Server or Workstation, you can assume that it is referring to features or capabilities that are common to both operating systems.

WINDOWS NT SERVER AMONG MICROSOFT OPERATING SYSTEMS

As you already know, Microsoft has three operating system products now competing in the marketplace: Windows 95, Windows NT Workstation, and Windows NT Server. Each of these operating systems has its advantages and disadvantages. Looking at the presentation of the desktop, the three look very much alike—so much so that you might have to click the Start button and read the banner on the left side of the menu to determine which operating system you are looking at. Each offers the familiar Windows 95 user interface featuring the Start button, the Recycling Bin, My Computer, and the ever-useful Explorer, but each is its own product designed for specific situations. The following sections describe these operating systems and outline their similarities and differences.

Table 1.1 outlines the installation requirements for the three operating systems. We will refer to these requirements often as we look at each system in detail.

TABLE 1.1

MINIMUM REQUIREMENTS FOR OPERATING SYSTEM INSTALLATION

Component	Windows 95	NT Workstation	NT Server
Processor	386DX/20	486DX/33	486DX/33
RAM	4MB	12MB	16MB
Free disk space	40MB	120MB	130MB

Windows 95

Windows 95 is Microsoft's everyday workhorse operating system. It provides a 32-bit platform and is designed to operate with a variety of peripherals. See Table 1.1 for the minimum hardware requirements for the installation and operation of Windows 95.

Like Windows NT, Windows 95 supports preemptive multitasking; unlike Windows NT, however, Windows 95 doesn't support multiple processors. Windows 95 supports Plug and Play, not to mention a vast number of hardware devices and device drivers (more than Windows NT).

Although Windows 95 runs only on Intel platforms, it supports 16-bit and 32-bit Windows and MS-DOS applications, including applications that access the hardware directly.

Windows 95 supports two file systems: FAT and FAT32. The FAT file system is a standard among most operating systems and is also supported by Windows NT (although NT's NTFS file system is much superior in most ways). FAT32 is a new file system that is much more efficient than the original FAT system. It is available with the OEM Release 2 of Windows 95 and with Windows 98; however, Windows NT 4.0 does not support FAT32.

You can network a Windows 95 computer in a *workgroup* (described later in this chapter in the section "Workgroups"), and you can use a Windows 95 computer as a client in a domain-based Windows NT network. However, Windows 95 alone cannot provide a network with centralized authentication and security.

Windows NT Workstation

The original Windows NT operating systems, Windows NT 3.1 and Windows NT 3.1 Advanced Server have evolved into a pair of operating system products that we now know as Windows NT Workstation and Windows NT Server. These two products are, on the surface, very similar; however, they are tuned very differently and include some very different tools that make them useful for radically different purposes. NT Server, discussed in the next section, is designed to operate as a network server and domain controller. NT Workstation, like Windows 95, is designed to serve as a network client and desktop operating system.

When Windows 95 first appeared, it seemed that Microsoft planned for Windows 95 to inherit the market of Windows 3.1 (general-use desktop computing for business and consumer) and for Windows NT to focus on the specialty market of professionals (such as programmers who require extra processing power). Now, however, it seems that Windows NT Workstation (with its stability, portability, and advanced security) is poised to assume a large share of the corporate desktop market. Windows NT Workstation can serve as a standalone operating system, act as a client in a domain-based NT network, or participate in a workgroup.

The most striking difference between Windows NT Workstation and Windows 95 is security. Windows NT Workstation is an extremely secure operating system, and there are security implications for almost every facet of Windows NT administration and configuration. Windows NT provides security for files, directories, printers, and nearly everything else. In fact, a user must be authenticated through a mandatory login to use Windows NT at all.

Windows NT Workstation also requires somewhat more powerful hardware than does Windows 95. Refer back to Table 1.1 for the minimum hardware requirements for the installation and operation of Windows NT Workstation.

Windows NT is designed to provide system stability; each application can run in its own memory address space. Windows NT supports preemptive multiprocessing as well as true symmetric multiprocessing (more than one processor).

On the other hand, Windows NT doesn't support as many devices as Windows 95 and seems a bit more myopic when it comes to detecting and installing new hardware. But although Windows NT doesn't support the vast array of devices Windows 95 supports, it supports more processor platforms. Because Windows NT is written mostly in C, it can be compiled separately for different processors. In addition to its Intel platform, versions of Windows NT are available for RISC, MIPS, DEC Alpha, and PowerPC-based systems; however, Microsoft is phasing out ongoing development for the MIPS and PowerPC platforms so those will not be supported in future releases (although Microsoft says it will continue to release bug fixes for these platforms).

Microsoft designed Windows NT for limited backward-compatibility with MS-DOS 5.0, Windows 3.1x, and OS/2 1.x and for lateral-compatibility with POSIX-based applications. No other operating system supports such a broad spectrum of applications. For security and stability reasons, however, Windows NT doesn't allow applications to directly access the hardware; MS-DOS applications and other legacy applications that attempt to access the hardware directly will run into trouble with Windows NT.

Windows NT Server

Due to the success of Windows 3.1, Microsoft branched into the network operating system market. Originally, two products were released: Windows NT 3.1 and Windows NT Advanced Server 3.1 (the NT stands for New Technology). When these two operating systems debuted, the marketplace experienced quite a bit of confusion over what the distinction was between the two products. Windows NT Advanced Server had some clear advantages, however. For example, unlike Windows NT 3.1, it supported Macintosh clients and provided its users software-based RAID fault tolerance. Still, if you only needed a file or print server, Windows NT 3.1 performed just as well as Windows NT Advanced Server 3.1. This lack of differentiation resulted in a potentially unprofitable situation for Microsoft.

When it introduced Windows NT Workstation 3.5 and Windows NT Server 3.5, Microsoft tweaked the two operating systems to make them different from one another in terms of performance, capacity, and features. With version 4, NT Server and NT Workstation continue to distinguish themselves as they adapt to their respective markets. The next few sections outline the most notable differences between Windows NT Workstation and Server.

Features

The following features are available on Windows NT Server but not on Windows NT Workstation:

- Services for Macintosh
- RAID fault tolerance
- Domain logon validation
- Export server in directory replication
- Windows NT Directory Services (NTDS)
- Multiprotocol routing and advanced network services, such as DNS, DHCP, and WINS

Capacity

Capacity refers to the number of clients supported, speed of performance, and performance efficiency. In many areas, similar or identical functions are present in the two versions of NT, but one is clearly superior in capacity. This does not necessarily mean, though, that the operating system with the higher capacity (usually NT Server) is a better choice in all circumstances; actually, using NT Server when NT Workstation will do might be overkill.

Windows NT Workstation and Server differ in capacity in the following areas:

◆ *Concurrent client sessions.* Windows NT Server supports an unlimited number of inbound sessions; Windows NT Workstation supports no more than 10 active sessions at the same time.

◆ *Remote access sessions.* Windows NT Server accommodates an unlimited number of remote access connections (although Microsoft only supports up to 256); Windows NT Workstation supports only a single remote access connection.

◆ *Multiprocessors.* Although both Windows NT Workstation and Server can support up to 32 processors in an OEM (original equipment manufacturer) configuration, Windows NT Workstation can support only two processors out-of-the-box, whereas Windows NT Server can support four.

◆ *Internet Service.* Both NT Workstation and NT Server come with Internet-type server applications, but the NT Server application (Internet Information Server) is capable of more concurrent connections and, because it runs on an operating system platform tuned for server performance, it is better suited to environments in which it will serve many requests per day than is the NT Workstation application (Peer Web Services), which is designed primarily for light-duty applications.

◆ *BackOffice Support.* Both NT Workstation and NT Server provide support for the administration of the Microsoft Back-Office family of software products (SQL Server, Systems Management Server, SNA Server, Exchange Server) but require the core components to be run on an NT Server.

Performance

Since the time of Windows NT 3.1 and Windows NT Advanced Server, Microsoft has implemented performance tuning into its operating systems to ensure that they can function well in the environments for which they were designed. This continues with Windows NT Workstation 4.0 and Windows NT Server 4.0. Some of the differences include the following:

◆ Windows NT Workstation preloads a Virtual DOS Machine (VDM), which is the 32-bit MS-DOS emulator that supports legacy applications. Because older applications are more likely to run on a workstation than on a server, the preloading of the VDM speeds up the load time of the first DOS or Win16 application started, at the expense of the RAM used by the VDM (which most likely would need to be loaded anyway). Windows NT Server devotes that RAM to caching and other server operations because it is less likely that an MS-DOS-based or Win16-based application will be run on a server. (This does not mean that servers cannot run such applications, but only that the first applications executed are slower to load.)

◆ Caching is handled differently on workstations and servers, which enables better network throughput on Windows NT Server and better local disk access time on Windows NT Workstation.

◆ Windows NT Server includes a configurable server service with which you can tune the server as an application server or as a file/print server. Windows NT Workstation does not provide this feature because it is limited to 10 inbound sessions.

◆ The server files system driver used in both Windows NT Workstation and Server (SRV.SYS) is more subject to paging under Windows NT Workstation than it is under Windows NT Server. When Windows NT Workstation runs out of physical RAM, it pages the server code out to disk, which means its network sharing performance takes a hit but local application performance gets a boost. Windows NT Server does not page much of the server code out; because it is designed as a server, it would not make much sense to impair that side of its functionality.

Minimum Hardware Requirements

The minimum requirements for NT Server and NT Workstation are roughly the same, but NT Server needs a little more RAM and a little more disk space. See Table 1.1 for the minimum hardware requirements for the installation and operation of Windows NT Server.

WORKGROUPS AND DOMAINS

Every networked Windows NT-based computer participates in a workgroup or a domain. Essentially, a *workgroup* is a collection of computers that maintain their own individual lists of user accounts and that maintain the security of their resources individually. On the other hand, a *domain* is a collection of computers defined by a list of user accounts on a computer called a domain controller. In a domain environment, when a user logs in, he or she is validated not by the local computer, but by a domain controller. As a result, the list of accounts and passwords need only be maintained in one place (instead of on every computer, as is the case in a workgroup).

Users must log on to Windows NT to use a Windows NT-based computer; such a logon process is *mandatory*. The access token identifies the user and all processes spawned by the user. No action can take place on a Windows NT system without a valid access token attached to it.

When a user successfully logs on to Windows NT, the system generates an *access token*, which contains the user's security identifier and group identifiers as well as the user rights granted through the User Rights policy in User Manager or User Manager for Domains. (For more information on User Manager for Domains, see Chapter 5, "Managing Resources Part 1: Managing Users and User Environments.")

Workgroups

The computers in a workgroup are defined by network connectivity: They must share a common protocol in order to communicate with other computers in the workgroup, and a common workgroup name must be defined in the Network properties sheet for each machine. In a workgroup, each computer is like a sovereign state with its own set of security policies and accounts. The security information necessary to verify a user's credentials and generate an access token resides on the local machine. Thus, every Windows NT computer in a workgroup must contain an account for each person who might ever need to access resources on that computer (see Figure 1.1). This involves a great deal of administration in workgroups that consist of more than a few members. If a user changes her password on her own workstation, that password must be changed for the corresponding account on every other workstation in the workgroup; otherwise, she cannot access resources beyond her own computer.

A workgroup is, however, simpler than a domain and easier to install. A workgroup does not require an NT Server machine acting as a domain controller, and the decentralized administration of a workgroup can be an advantage in small networks because it does not depend on the health of a few key server and controller machines.

Unless a Windows NT Server computer is configured as a stand-alone server, it cannot participate in a workgroup (see Chapter 2, "Installation and Configuration Part 1: Installation of NT Server"). Windows NT Workstation computers, Windows 95 computers, and older networked Microsoft systems such as Windows for Workgroups, can participate in workgroups.

When you log on to a Windows NT machine in a workgroup, you are logging on to that specific machine. The local security database verifies your credentials. When you log on to a Windows NT computer directly, the local machine performs the following steps (as depicted in Figure 1.2):

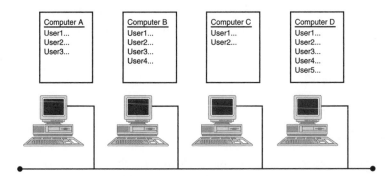

FIGURE 1.1
In a workgroup, each computer is responsible for its own security, and each computer maintains its own accounts database.

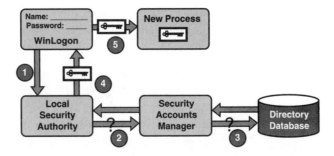

FIGURE 1.2
The login process on a local machine.

1. WinLogon asks for your username and password, which it then sends to the Local Security Authority (LSA).

2. The LSA sends the username and password to the Security Accounts Manager (SAM).

3. The SAM checks the directory database for the presence of the username/password combination you entered and then notifies the LSA whether they are approved.

4. If they are approved, the LSA creates an access token with your assigned rights and passes it to the WinLogon process.

5. The WinLogon process completes the logon by starting a new process (usually Explorer.exe) for you. Your access token is attached to the new process.

Domains

In a domain environment, all nodes must authenticate logon requests with a domain controller that contains the central accounts database for the entire domain (see Figure 1.3). The first and central domain controller is called the primary domain controller (PDC). It contains the main copy of the account database. Other domain controllers can be configured to make login more efficient, especially at remote sites. These secondary domain controllers are called backup domain controllers (BDCs); they contain a copy of the account database, which is synchronized with the PDC's copy on a regular basis.

In a domain environment, a password needs to be changed only once—in the central account database—to be usable on any member computer of the domain. Likewise, a user needs only a single account to access resources anywhere in the domain. Only Windows NT Server machines can serve as domain controllers in a Windows NT network.

The logon process is somewhat more complicated for a domain because logon information must pass from the local machine (on which the user is working) to the domain controller and back again. This network logon process requires the NetLogon service to establish a secure channel to a domain controller so that its accounts database can be queried.

The following steps outline the domain logon procedure (illustrated in Figure 1.4):

1. WinLogon sends the username and password to the Local Security Authority (LSA).

2. The LSA passes the request to the local NetLogon service.

3. The local NetLogon service sends the logon information to the NetLogon service on the domain controller.

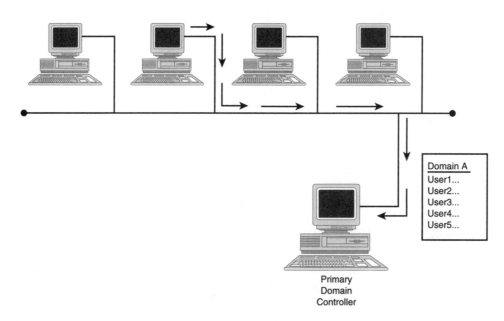

Primary
Domain
Controller

FIGURE 1.3

In a domain, security and account information resides on one or more domain controllers, and logon requests pass across the network to the domain controller for authentication.

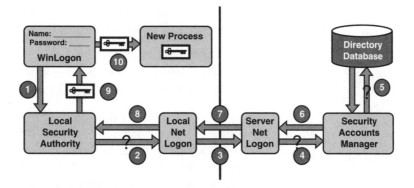

FIGURE 1.4
The login process in a domain environment.

4. The NetLogon service on the domain controller passes the information to the domain controller's Security Accounts Manager (SAM).

5. The SAM asks the domain directory database for approval of the username and password.

6. The SAM passes the result of the approval request to the domain controller's NetLogon service.

7. The domain controller's NetLogon service passes the result of the approval request to the client's NetLogon service.

8. The client's NetLogon service passes the result of the approval request to the LSA.

9. If the logon is approved, the LSA creates an access token and passes it to the WinLogon process.

10. WinLogon completes the logon by creating a new process for the user and attaching the access token to the new process.

CHOOSING A DISK CONFIGURATION

Plan the disk drive configuration for various requirements. Requirements include choosing a file system and choosing a fault-tolerance method.

One of the first tasks in planning a network is deciding on a disk configuration for each of the computers that will make up the network. Each computer will have its own disk configuration, but this book (and the Windows NT Server exam) targets the disk configuration options available in Windows NT Server systems.

The following sections highlight these specific planning issues related to disk configuration under Windows NT:

◆ *Partitions.* Partitions define limits to logical units of disk space, which are treated by your operating system as separate hard drives (often referred to as *logical drives*).

◆ *Primary and extended partitions.* A primary partition is a partition that your computer sees as bootable because it contains the files required to begin the boot process (in NT, the system partition must be a primary partition). An extended partition is a partition that can be further subdivided into logical drives. You might want to place a different kind of data on each extended partition (such as the boot files for NT, or applications, or data).

◆ *The System and the boot partitions.* You must consider the location of the boot and system partitions when you plan an installation. The system partition must be on an active partition and must contain files specifying where to go to get the NT program files. The boot partition is the one that contains the NT program files (often located in a folder called WINNT); it is used to start and run NT on your computer.

◆ *Windows NT file systems.* The file systems you use will influence what kind of security you can implement, what kind of clients you can support, and what kind of disk tools you can use. Although it's possible to change file systems without having to format your partitions, you will want to make the major decisions before you actually install NT on your computer.

◆ *Windows NT fault-tolerance methods. Fault tolerance* enables an operating system to continue functioning even when a catastrophic failure occurs (like a hard disk crash). Implementing fault tolerance after your system crashes might prevent further loss in server availability, but it will not help you recover lost data or server time that you lose during the recovery. Be sure to consider fault-tolerance methods during the planning stages of your NT implementation.

The topic of hard disks in Windows NT arises again in Chapter 4, "Installation and Configuration Part 3: Configuring NT Server Disks and Peripherals" which looks at disk configuration issues, and in Chapter 6, "Managing Resources Part 2: Managing Disk Resources," which looks at managing disk resources. The following sections concentrate on planning issues and provide the background you need to understand the later material.

Partitions

A partition is a logical organization of a physical disk. NT Server can subdivide a disk drive into several partitions, each of which is then formatted separately. NT Server assigns a different drive letter to each of the partitions, and users interact separately with the individual partitions as if each is a separate physical disk drive.

Partitioning is the act of defining a partition and associating that partition with an area (or areas) of free space on a hard disk. You must partition an area of free space before you can format it with a file system. After you format the partition with a supported file system, you can use the partition to store files and directories.

As you plan your Windows NT configuration, you must make some decisions about the arrangement of partitions on your disk drive. You must choose whether each partition will be a primary partition or an extended partition. You also need to designate a system partition and a boot partition for your Windows NT installation. The following sections discuss these concepts.

Primary and Extended Partitions

Windows NT supports two types of partitions:

◆ *Primary partitions*. A primary partition cannot be subdivided and is capable of supporting a bootable operating system. One hard disk can contain up to four primary partitions. Thus, you can assign up to four drive letters to a disk if you use only primary partitions. Note, however, that MS-DOS 5.0 and earlier MS-DOS systems cannot recognize more than one primary partition per disk.

◆ *Extended partitions*. An extended partition can be subdivided into smaller logical drives (see Figure 1.5). This enables you to assign more than four drive letters to one disk. However, an extended partition does not support a bootable operating system. The system partition, therefore, cannot reside on an extended partition (see the next section for details). One hard disk can contain only one extended partition.

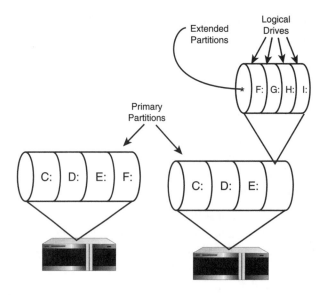

FIGURE 1.5
A physical disk can consist of up to four primary partitions or up to three primary partitions
and one extended partition. An extended partition can be subdivided into logical drives.

Don't Overextend Your Partitions!
It is not necessary to create an
extended partition on a disk; primary partitions might be all that you
need. However, if you do create
one, remember you can never have
more than one extended partition
on a physical disk.

(margin label: WARNING)

If you choose to use an extended partition of a hard disk, you are
limited to three (rather than four) primary partitions for that disk.

On an Intel-based computer, one primary partition must be marked
as *active*. The active partition is then used to boot the computer (as
explained in the next section). Because any primary partition of sufficient size can support a bootable operating system, one advantage
of using multiple primary partitions is that you can isolate different
operating systems on different partitions.

If you install Windows NT on a computer that has another operating system in place, the active partition does not change. If you
install Windows NT on a new computer, the partition created by
Setup becomes the active partition.

Boot and System Partitions

The *system partition* is the partition that contains the files necessary
to boot the operating system. (See Chapter 2 for a description of
which files these are.) The system partition does not have to be the
partition on which Windows NT is installed.

The partition that holds the Windows NT operating system files is
called the *boot* partition. If your system boots from drive C and you
install Windows NT on drive D, drive C is your system partition
and drive D is your boot partition (see Figure 1.6). If you boot from
drive C and Windows NT is installed on drive C, drive C is both
the system partition and the boot partition.

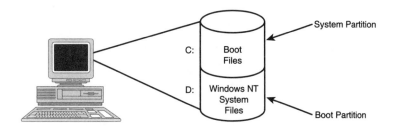

FIGURE 1.6
The partition that boots the computer is the system partition; the partition that holds the Windows NT directory is the boot partition. Note that these names are counter-intuitive.

Recall from the preceding section that the active partition is the partition used to boot the system. The system partition must, therefore, be the active partition.

Active partitions are only a relevant concept for Intel-based computers; RISC-based computers use a hardware configuration utility to designate the system partition.

> **NOTE**
>
> **Strange But True**   Although it sounds backward, it is true: Windows NT boots from the system partition and then loads the system from the boot partition.

Windows NT File Systems

After a partition is created, it must be formatted with a supported file system. A *file system* provides a means for organizing and managing the data on a disk. Windows NT supports three file systems: FAT (File Allocation Table), NTFS (New Technology File System), and CDFS (Compact Disc File System). CDFS is a read-only file system for CD-ROMs, so you can immediately rule it out for hard disk partitions.

Each partition must use either the FAT file system or the NTFS file system. You need to understand the advantages and limitations of each file system before you can decide which is best for your system. The following sections introduce you to the FAT and NTFS file systems. Chapter 2 explains more about these file systems.

FAT

The venerable File Allocation Table (FAT) file system was originally invented for MS-DOS. FAT is now supported by Windows NT, Windows 95, DOS, and OS/2, making it the most universally accepted and supported file system (see Figure 1.7). For this reason alone, you should seriously consider using FAT for your partitions if your computer supports more than one operating system booting locally (a *multiple boot* configuration).

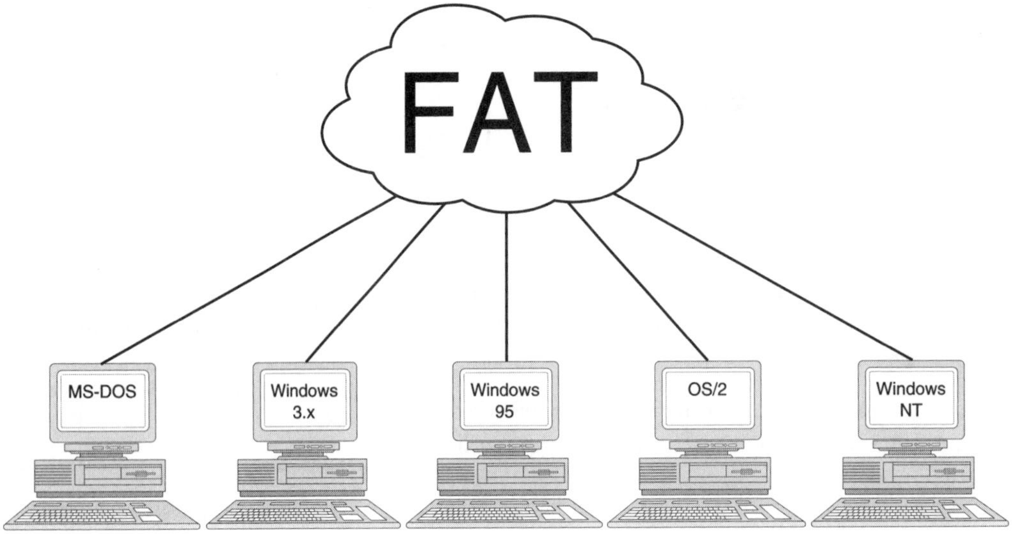

FIGURE 1.7
The FAT file system is supported by more operating systems than NTFS is, but FAT doesn't provide the advantages NTFS does.

> **FAT and Long Filenames** Earlier versions of FAT forced users to use short filenames (consisting of no more than eight characters plus a three-character extension). But Windows NT overcomes the 8.3 limitation on FAT partitions. Users can create filenames with up to 255 characters and can include spaces in the filename. (Short filenames are still maintained, however, for compatibility with legacy applications and dual-boot systems.)

FAT has a lower overhead than its high-tech counterpart NTFS (less than 1MB, compared to an average of 5–10MB for NTFS), and FAT is typically the more efficient file system for small partitions (under 400MB).

Some of the disadvantages of FAT include the following:

◆ FAT is generally slower than NTFS. It takes longer to find and access files. For partitions greater than 400MB, FAT performance degrades quickly.

◆ The maximum file, directory, or partition size under FAT is only 4GB. Also, because Windows NT does not support any FAT compression software (including Microsoft's own DriveSpace and DoubleSpace), you cannot conserve space by compressing files on a FAT partition.

◆ FAT does not offer the security features offered by NTFS (see the following section).

◆ If the power fails during a disk transaction, the FAT file system may be left with cross-linked files or orphan clusters.

You should use the FAT file system if you will be dual-booting your computer with another operating system and you want to access the partition from the other operating system. You might dual boot if your security needs require Windows NT but your software needs require Windows 95. Some people install Windows NT on computers that are currently running Windows 95 in order to make the transition from one to the other more smooth. In addition, if applications are not supported under NT (some DOS and even some Windows 95 software isn't), you will need to dual boot to get the software to run.

NTFS

The New Technology File System (NTFS) is designed to fully exploit the features and capabilities of Windows NT. For partitions larger than 400MB, the NTFS file system far outshines the FAT file system. The biggest drawback with using NTFS is that only the Windows NT operating system can locally access NTFS partitions. If you plan to configure your computer to boot some other operating system (such as MS-DOS or Windows 95) in addition to NT, you should be aware that the other operating system cannot access an NTFS partition.

NTFS is generally faster than FAT, and NTFS supports bigger partitions; the theoretical maximum for an NTFS partition is 16 exabytes (an exabyte is one billion gigabytes, or 2^{64} bytes). NTFS supports *sector sparing*, also known as *hot fixing*, on SCSI hard drives. This means that if a sector fails on an NTFS partition of a SCSI hard drive, NTFS tries to write the data to a good sector (if the data is still in memory) and map out the bad sector so that it is not reused.

NTFS also keeps a transaction log while it works. Therefore, if the power fails and leaves NTFS in a possibly corrupt state, the CHKDSK command that executes when the system is rebooted attempts to either redo the transaction (in the case of a delete, for example) or undo the transaction (in the case of a file write, where the data is no longer in memory).

Two other principal advantages of NTFS include the following:

◆ *File-level security.* NTFS enables you to assign specific permissions to individual files and directories.

◆ *File compression.* NTFS partitions support file-level compression by built-in compression algorithms. Traditional FAT compression utilities, including Microsoft's own DriveSpace and DoubleSpace, do not provide the functionality of NTFS compression and are not supported under Windows NT.

NOTE

Format the C: Drive Correctly! If your Windows NT computer is a RISC-based system, your C drive must be formatted with FAT and have at least 2MB of free space.

You must use NTFS if you want to preserve existing permissions when you migrate files and directories from a NetWare server to a Windows NT Server system. Also, if you want to allow Macintosh computers to access files on the partition through Windows NT's Services for Macintosh, you must format the partition for NTFS.

Because NTFS has a higher overhead, somewhere between 4.5 and 10MB for the file system itself, you cannot use the NTFS file system for floppy disks.

This summary table offers an overview of the differences between the FAT and NTFS file systems.

REVIEW BREAK

FAT VERSUS NTFS

Feature	FAT	NTFS
Filename length	255	255
8.3 filename compatibility	Yes	Yes
File size	4GB	16EB
Partition size	4GB	16EB
Directory structure	Linked list	B-tree
Local security	No	Yes
Transaction tracking	No	Yes
Hot fixing	No	Yes
Overhead (avg. 4.5–10)	1 MB	>2MB
Required on system partition for RISC-based computers	Yes	No
Accessible from MS-DOS/Windows 95	Yes	No
Accessible from OS/2	Yes	No
Case-sensitive	No	POSIX only
Case preserving	Yes	Yes
Compression	No	Yes
Efficiency	200MB	400MB
Windows NT formattable	Yes	Yes
Fragmentation level	High	Low
Floppy disk formattable	Yes	No

Windows NT provides a utility called Convert.exe that converts a FAT partition to NTFS. There is no utility for directly converting an NTFS partition to FAT. To change an NTFS partition to FAT, back up all files on the partition, reformat the partition, and then restore the files to the reformatted partition (see Chapter 3).

Fault-Tolerance Methods

Fundamentally, *fault tolerance* is the system's capability to compensate in the event of hardware disaster. The standard for fault tolerance is known as Redundant Array of Inexpensive Disks (RAID). RAID consists of several levels (or categories) of protection that offer a mixture of performance, reliability, and cost.

Deciding on a RAID fault-tolerance method might be one of the steps in planning your Windows NT system because planning relates not only to the installation of your NT Server, but also to the ongoing operation of it. A good plan for recovering your system can begin before you ever install NT on a computer. Deciding to implement a RAID method can save you a lot of trouble in your ongoing operations if a catastrophic failure ever occurs.

Windows NT Server offers the following two RAID fault-tolerance methods:

◆ *Disk mirroring (RAID Level 1).* Windows NT writes the same data to two physical disks. If one disk fails, the data is still available on the other disk.

◆ *Disk striping with parity (Raid Level 5).* Windows NT writes data across a series of disks (anywhere from 3 to 32). The data is not duplicated on the disks (as it is with disk mirroring), but Windows NT records parity information that it can use to regenerate missing data if a disk should fail.

The following sections introduce you to disk mirroring and disk striping with parity. Chapter 5 explains more about these important fault-tolerance methods.

It is important to note that the fault-tolerance methods available through Windows NT are software-based RAID solutions. Several hardware vendors offer hardware-based RAID solutions. Hardware-based RAID solutions are beyond the scope of this book and the Windows NT Server exam.

EXAM TIP

RAID Terminology For the exam, it is important that you understand the terminology used to refer to RAID implementations and how the RAID levels (1 and 5) are implemented in NT. For example, you may be told in a planning scenario that you are going to implement RAID Level 1. If you are not familiar with the concept of disk mirroring or you don't know that RAID Level 1 is implemented in NT as disk mirroring, you will be lost as to the implication of the RAID method. In addition, be careful of the terminology Microsoft uses in the exams. Don't assume that it means one thing when it says another. You will frequently see questions that refer to "disk striping." Note that this is not the same as "disk striping with parity." Disk striping with parity is fault tolerant; disk striping is not. Implementing disk striping will allow you to create a single logical drive out of a number of smaller partitions, but it is by no means a fault-tolerant system (some would say it is just the opposite: a fault waiting to happen).

Disk Mirroring (RAID Level 1)

Disk mirroring calls for all data to be written to two physical disks (see Figure 1.8). A mirror is a redundant copy of a disk partition. You can use any partition, including the boot and system partitions, to establish a mirror.

You can measure the disk utilization of a fault-tolerance method by checking the percent of the total disk space devoted to storing the original information. Fifty percent of the data in a disk-mirroring system is redundant data. Thus the percentage utilization is also 50 percent, making disk mirroring less efficient than disk striping with parity. The startup costs for implementing disk mirroring are typically lower, however, because disk mirroring requires only two physical disks (rather than 3–32).

Disk mirroring slows down write operations slightly (because Windows NT has to write to two disks simultaneously). Read operations are actually slightly faster, though, because NT can read from both disks simultaneously.

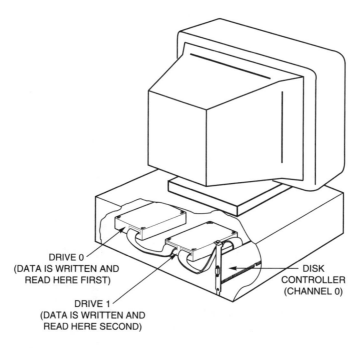

DRIVE 0
(DATA IS WRITTEN AND
READ HERE FIRST)

DRIVE 1
(DATA IS WRITTEN AND
READ HERE SECOND)

DISK
CONTROLLER
(CHANNEL 0)

FIGURE 1.8
How disk mirroring works.

MORE ABOUT DISK MIRRORING

The performance change in your NT Server caused by disk mirroring may or may not be significant to you or your user community. In a system dedicated to the storage of data or the retrieval of data, however, you might see noticeable increases or decreases in system performance as a result of using this fault tolerant method. In a system in which the primary operation a user performs is queries on a database, the increase in read performance might be significant in terms of throughput. But if the system is designed to store data, mirroring might produce disk bottlenecks. You might only know whether these changes are significant by setting up two identical computers, implementing mirroring on one but not on the other, and then running Performance Monitor on both under a simulated load to see the performance differences. For more information on monitoring, see Chapter 8, "Monitoring and Optimization."

In a typical disk mirroring scenario, a single disk controller writes to both members of the mirror set. If a mirrored disk fails, the user can keep working. If the disk controller fails, however, Windows NT cannot access either disk.

Disk duplexing is a special kind of disk mirroring that provides a solution for this potential pitfall. In a disk duplexing system, each of the mirrored disks has its own disk controller. The system can therefore endure either a disk failure or a controller failure. Disk duplexing also has some performance advantages because the two disk controllers can act independently (see Figure 1.9).

Disk Striping with Parity (RAID Level 5)

A stripe set with parity writes information in stripes (or rows) across 3 to 32 disks. For each stripe, there is a parity stripe block on one of the disks. If one of the disks fails, Windows NT can use the parity stripe block to regenerate the missing information. The parity stripe block is the only data that is additional to what the system would need to record the original data without fault tolerance. Disk striping with parity is therefore more efficient than disk mirroring.

The percentage of disk space available for storing data is:

% Utilization = (no. of disks–1) / no. of disks × 100%

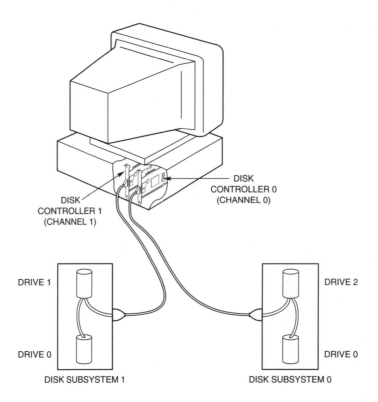

DISK
CONTROLLER 0
(CHANNEL 0)

DISK
CONTROLLER 1
(CHANNEL 1)

DRIVE 1

DRIVE 2

DRIVE 0

DRIVE 0

DISK SUBSYSTEM 1

DISK SUBSYSTEM 0

FIGURE 1.9
Disk duplexing is demonstrated here.

For example, if you have five disks, 80 percent of your disk space is available for storing data (as compared to 50 percent for a disk mirroring system). The more disks you add, the more efficient your fault-tolerance becomes. But at the same time, your setup costs also increase as you add disks.

Windows NT must perform the parity calculations as it writes data to a stripe set with parity. As a result, write operations take three times as much memory if you are using a stripe set with parity. If all disks are working properly, read operations are faster under a stripe set with parity than they are under a mirror set. If a disk fails, however, Windows NT must create the missing data from the parity information, and read operations will slow down considerably.

Any partition except the boot partition and the system partition can be part of a stripe set with parity.

CHOOSING A WINDOWS NT NETWORK PROTOCOL

Choose a protocol for various situations. Protocols include TCP/IP, NWLink IPX/SPX Compatible Transport, and NetBEUI.

A network *protocol* is a collection of rules and procedures governing communication among the computers on a network. In a sense, a protocol is a language your computer uses when speaking to other computers. If two computers don't use the same protocols, they cannot communicate. Windows NT includes several protocols designed for different situations and different networking environments. Later chapters discuss these protocols in more detail. This chapter examines some planning issues relating the three principal Windows NT networking protocols, as follows:

◆ *TCP/IP.* A widely-used routable protocol that is the basis for communication on the Internet.

◆ *NWLink IPX/SPX Compatible Transport.* Microsoft's rendition of Novell's proprietary IPX/SPX protocol suite. NWLink is a routable protocol designed to enable Windows NT computers to interoperate with Novell NetWare networks.

◆ *NetBEUI.* A very fast but non-routable protocol used on Microsoft networks. Because NetBEUI is non-routable, it is suitable only for local area networks (LANs).

You should learn the advantages and disadvantages of each of these protocols and understand when to use each.

TCP/IP

Transmission Control Protocol/Internet Protocol (TCP/IP) Windows NT. TCP/IP is the only protocol supported on the Internet (which is why it is the global standard protocol).

Windows NT's version of the TCP/IP protocol, Microsoft TCP/IP, is a 32-bit suite of protocols. It requires more configuration than other protocols, but Microsoft also provides some excellent configuration tools. The end result is a cross-platform, industry-standard, routable network implementation that you can expect to grow in popularity (just think, you may see the day when every toaster, garage door opener, and Coke machine has a TCP/IP address!).

Here's a list of important things to remember about TCP/IP:

◆ *TCP/IP is routable.* Because TCP/IP packets can be forwarded through routers, you can use TCP/IP on wide area networks (WANs). (The NetBEUI protocol, by contrast, can be used only on local area networks.)

◆ *TCP/IP is the language of the Internet.* If your Windows NT computer will be connected to the Internet, you need to use TCP/IP.

◆ *TCP/IP is a widely accepted standard.* You can interconnect with more networks worldwide if you are using TCP/IP. You can also implement communication in a heterogeneous environment, allowing UNIX, NetWare, OS/2, Banyan Vines, and NT systems to all talk to one another through this common protocol.

TCP/IP comes with a number of useful utilities, such as PING, Tracert, and IPConfig, that facilitate network configuration and administration. For a look at PING and IPConfig, see Exercise 1.2 and the end of this chapter. Chapter 3 explains more about those TCP/IP utilities.

You implement TCP/IP on your network with the help of three important services: Dynamic Host Configuration Protocol (DHCP), Domain Name System (DNS), and Windows Internet Name Service (WINS). To plan your TCP/IP network, you need a basic understanding of these services, especially if you plan to connect your local LAN with a wide area network or the Internet.

The Internet Protocol (the IP in TCP/IP) sends packets using a network adapter's *IP address*, which is a unique 32-bit binary number that no other computer on the network can possess. The 32-bit IP address usually is expressed as four octets (or 8-bit numbers), which then are represented in decimal form. An 8-bit number can have a value of anywhere from 0 to 255, so an IP address consists of four numbers between 0 and 255 separated by decimal points (for example, 111.12.3.141).

Every computer on a TCP/IP network must have an IP address. You can configure a permanent IP address for each computer, or you can configure each computer to receive a dynamically assigned IP address from a Dynamic Host Configuration Protocol (DHCP) server. (See

Chapter 2 for more information on configuring TCP/IP.) A DHCP server is assigned a range of IP addresses, referred to as the *DHCP scope*. The DHCP server then "leases" (assigns for a limited duration) these IP addresses to DHCP clients in the subnet. A computer running Windows NT Server can act as a DHCP server, a DHCP client, or a DHCP relay agent. A DHCP relay agent forwards DHCP broadcast messages across an IP router to a DHCP server on a different subnet.

The decimal octet form of an IP address is easier to remember than its binary equivalent, but even such a number as 111.12.3.141 is not really very easy to remember. Therefore, the Domain Name System (DNS) was created. It is a feature of TCP/IP networks that enables you to map an IP address to an alphanumeric name that is theoretically even easier for humans to remember than is the decimal octet. (Internet domain names, such as newriders.mcp.com, are now easily recognizable in this age of email and Web browsers.) NT Server's DNS service can map IP addresses to domain names on a TCP/IP network. In addition, it can also interact with non-NT DNS servers on other operating systems, such as UNIX. In this way, the DNS servers that are already configured on the Internet can be used to resolve addresses that have not been statically assigned in your DNS Server.

Windows NT's WINS service is similar to DNS except that, instead of mapping IP addresses to domain names, WINS maps IP addresses to NetBIOS names. NetBIOS names are used to identify resources on Microsoft networks. If a WINS server is configured on your Microsoft network, every computer that starts up will register itself with that WINS machine. In this way, a dynamic list of all the computers and their TCP/IP addresses can be maintained on your network. NetBIOS names follow the familiar Universal Naming Convention (UNC) format you use to locate resources from the Windows NT command prompt:

   *computername**sharename**path*

Whereas DNS requires a static listing of all IP addresses assigned to a machine/domain the WINS service can automatically associate NetBIOS names with IP addresses. However, only Microsoft computers will register themselves with WINS. So, if you have UNIX hosts or other TCP/IP machines on your network, you will have to use DNS to associate their names with TCP/IP addresses.

NWLink

The primary purpose of Microsoft's NWLink IPX/SPX Compatible Transport protocol is to provide connectivity with the many thousands of Novell NetWare networks. NWLink is, however, a fully functional and fully routable protocol, and you can use NWLink to network Windows NT machines with or without the involvement of NetWare resources. Chapter 2 describes how to configure NWLink on your Windows NT Server system, and Chapter 6 discusses some issues related to NetWare connectivity.

NWLink provides compatibility with IPX/SPX-based networks, but NWLink alone does not necessarily enable a Windows NT computer to interact with NetWare networks. Windows NT includes several services that provide connectivity with NetWare services after NWLink is in place. Refer to Chapter 4 for more on connecting to NetWare resources using NWLink.

In general, you should remember the following important points about NWLink:

◆ The NWLink protocol provides compatibility with Novell NetWare IPX/SPX networks.

◆ A Windows NT Workstation computer running Client Services for NetWare (CSNW) and the NWLink protocol or a Windows NT Server computer running Gateway Services for NetWare (GSNW) and the NWLink protocol can connect file and print services on a NetWare server.

◆ A Windows NT computer using the NWLink protocol can connect to client/server applications on a NetWare server (without requiring additional NetWare-connectivity services).

◆ Any Microsoft network client that uses Server Message Block (Windows NT, Windows 95, or Windows for Workgroups) can access NetWare resources through a NetWare gateway on a Windows NT Server computer running Gateway Services for NetWare. The NetWare resources will appear to the Microsoft network client as Windows NT resources.

NetBEUI

Because NetBEUI is a non-routable protocol, it is generally used for what Microsoft calls "department-sized LANs." In addition, NetBEUI is still used to connect to other Microsoft networks running only NetBEUI. The recent emphasis on internetworking means that, in all but the smallest and most isolated networks, NetBEUI is usually not the ideal choice for a primary network protocol.

NetBEUI was designed for Microsoft networks, and one of the advantages of NetBEUI is that it enables Windows NT machines to interact with older Microsoft network machines that use NetBEUI (for instance, Windows for Workgroups 3.1 or Microsoft LAN Manager).

NetBEUI is also extremely easy to implement. It is self-tuning and self-configuring. (If you try to configure NetBEUI through the Protocols tab of Windows NT's Network application, you receive a message that says Cannot configure the software component.) In addition, because NetBEUI was designed for an earlier generation of lower-performance computers, it also comes with a smaller memory overhead.

The speed and simplicity of NetBEUI comes with a downside, however: NetBEUI relies heavily on network broadcasts, which can degrade performance on large and busy subnets.

> **NOTE** **Overcoming NetBEUI's Routing Limitations** You cannot use NetBEUI with a router, but you can use a bridge to connect LAN segments operating with the NetBEUI protocol. A *bridge* is a hardware device that connects two LANs to form what appears to be a single LAN.

Planning for Network Clients

The Windows NT CD-ROM includes client software for a number of operating systems that are not as naturally networkable as Windows NT or Windows 95. Some of those client software packages include the following:

◆ Microsoft Network 3.0 for MS-DOS

◆ LAN Manager 2.2c for MS-DOS client

◆ LAN Manager 2.2c for OS/2 client

Microsoft Network Client 3.0 for MS-DOS enables MS-DOS machines to participate in Windows NT networks. An MS-DOS client using Microsoft Client 3.0 for MS-DOS configured with the full redirector can perform the following tasks on a Windows NT network:

◆ Log on to a domain

◆ Run logon scripts

◆ Access IPC mechanisms, such as RPCs, named pipes, and WinSock

◆ Use RAS (version 1.1)

Note, however, that a Microsoft Client 3.0 for MS-DOS client cannot browse the network unless a Windows NT computer or a Windows for Workgroups computer is in the same workgroup.

The LAN Manager 2.2c for MS-DOS client includes some features not found in the OS/2 version, including support for the Remoteboot service (described later in this chapter) and the capability to connect to a NetWare server.

Table 1.2 describes which network protocols and which TCP/IP services each of the client systems supports.

TABLE 1.2

NETWORK PROTOCOL AND TCP/IP SERVICE SUPPORT FOR VARIOUS WINDOWS NT CLIENT SYSTEMS

Client OS	NetBEUI	IPX	IPX/SPX	TCP/IP	DLC	DHCP Client	WINS Client	DNS Client
Network Client for MS-DOS	X	X		X	X	X	X	
LAN MAN 2.2c for MS-DOS	X		X	X	X	X	X	
LAN MAN 2.2c for OS/2	X			X				
Windows 95	X		X	X	X	X	X	X
Windows NT Workstation	X		X	X	X	X	X	X
Windows NT Server	X		X	X	X	X	X	X

CASE STUDY: REALLY GOOD GUITARS

ESSENCE OF THE CASE

This case requires that you establish the following essential elements:

- centralized administration
- WAN connectivity nationwide
- Internet access and email
- security on network shares and local files
- fault-tolerance methods

SCENARIO

Really Good Guitars is a national company specializing in the design and manufacturing of custom acoustic guitars. Having grown up out of an informal network of artisans across Canada, the company has many locations but very few employees (300 at this time) and a head office in Churchill, Manitoba. Although they follow the best traditions of hand-making guitars, they are not without technological savvy; all 25 locations have computers onsite that are used for accounting, running MS Office applications, and running the company's custom guitar design software. The leadership team recently realized that a network solution is essential for maintaining consistency, providing security on what are becoming some very innovative designs, and providing their employees with email and Internet access.

RGG desires a centralized administration of its network security with only a limited base of support at its branch locations. As well, because their designs are the lifeblood of their operation, they require support for both network-based and local security on all machines, as well as fault tolerance to protect their work in the case of catastrophic disk failure.

ANALYSIS

In any planning scenario, you must consider issues of compatibility with existing systems, security, connectivity, and expandability. The essence can be boiled down to considerations of network architecture, usability of existing hardware, local security and recoverability, and WAN connectivity. After you identify the major considerations, you can make recommendations regarding the implementation of a network solution.

continues

CASE STUDY: REALLY GOOD GUITARS

continued

In terms of network architecture, a Windows NT domain model is definitely the way to go. The client requires centralized administration of security and administrative tasks, this cannot be accomplished either with a workgroup structure or with independent local LANs. In addition, the domain model allows for ease of expandability without reconfiguration; a factor which needs to be taken into consideration when looking to implement an architecture.

Network architecture and the physical layout of the network inform us as to the WAN connectivity needs. They want email, Internet access, and the ability to communicate from location to location using routers. The obvious choice, therefore, is to use TCP/IP as a protocol. Because there are no existing networks to interact with (either Microsoft or NetWare), there is no need to install either NWLink or NetBEUI on any of the machines, thereby making TCP/IP the only protocol.

In order to maintain reasonable access to a domain controller for login authentication (instead of having to communicate across the country to the primary domain controller in Churchill every time a user logs in), a reasonable solution would be to set up a backup domain controller at every site. This BDC then would be the obvious choice as a DHCP server to minimize the administration involved in maintaining TCP/IP addresses.

Finally, the need for security on files, both over the network and locally on each machine, as well as the need for fault-tolerant disk setups require the presence of NTFS partitions on both the file servers and the client machines, which means that NT Workstation is required for the clients. The clients can then be configured with NTFS security to allow access only to those individuals who need it. In addition, a scheme involving disk mirroring and disk striping with parity can be implemented to provide fault tolerance in addition to the obvious backups that would be made of the data.

The following data summarizes the solution.

OVERVIEW OF THE REQUIREMENTS AND SOLUTIONS IN THIS CASE STUDY

Requirement	Solution Provided By
Centralized administration	Implementation of NT domain with PDC and BDCs
Nationwide WAN connectivity	Implementation of TCP/IP as the only networking protocol
Internet and email support	Implementation of TCP/IP as the only networking protocol
Security on network shares and local files	Installation of NT Server and Workstation with NTFS partitions
Fault tolerance on server data	Implementation of disk-mirroring and stripe sets with parity on Server volumes

CHAPTER SUMMARY

This chapter discussed the main planning topics you will encounter on the Windows NT Server exam. Distilled down, these topics revolve around two main goals: understanding the planning of disk configuration and understanding the planning of network protocols. In addition, the chapter also highlighted two points that are not specifically covered in the objectives but that you might be tested on: planning for domain implementation and planning for NT Server installation (primarily, deciding whether to use NT Server and whether existing hardware is sufficient to meet the needs of an NT Server installation).

Disk configuration is important because it allows you to plan for organization (partitions), security and functionality (file systems), and disaster recovery (fault-tolerance). To correctly answer exam questions regarding scenarios, you must be able to correctly put together information from all of these areas to come up with solutions to problems.

Protocol planning is equally important because your choice of protocol will determine both the scalability of your NT implementation (network growth may be curtailed if you do not choose to implement TCP/IP) and the interoperability with other Network types (NWLink is essential for interoperating with Novell networks, and NetBEUI is essential for maintaining network connectivity with older Microsoft networks). If proper protocols are not established in the planning stage, a lot of redesign may be needed as the network grows.

Finally, this chapter covered the miscellaneous but not insignificant topics of network security architecture (domain vs. workgroup) and operating system planning (Windows 95 vs. Windows NT Workstation vs. Windows NT Server) in order to give you a picture of the role that NT Server plays in a network configuration (almost always in a domain model).

KEY TERMS

Before taking the exam, make sure you are comfortable with the definitions and concepts for each of the following key terms. Appendix A is a glossary you can use for quick reference.

- FAT
- FAT32
- NTFS
- workgroup
- domain
- primary domain controller (PDC)
- backup domain controller (BDC)
- WinLogon
- Local Security Authority (LSA)
- Security Accounts Manager (SAM)
- NetLogon
- partition
- primary partition
- extended partition
- system partition
- boot partition
- fault tolerance
- disk mirroring
- disk duplexing
- disk striping with parity
- protocol
- TCP/IP
- NWLink
- NetBEUI
- DNS
- WINS
- DHCP

APPLY YOUR LEARNING

This section allows you to assess how well you understood the material in the chapter. Review and exam questions test your knowledge of the tasks and concepts specified in the objectives. The exercises provide you with opportunities to engage in the sorts of tasks that comprise the skill sets the objectives reflect.

For more review- and exam-type questions, see the TestPrep test engine on the CD-ROM that comes with this book.

Exercises

Each chapter of this book contains some exercises that give you first-hand knowledge of the chapter's topics. This chapter does not offer the same opportunities for first-hand exploration that later chapters provide, but the following exercises provide a glimpse of two very important concepts: NTFS file permissions and IP addresses. If you are an experienced NT administrator, you have probably undertaken these exercises many times, and you may want to move on to Chapter 2. If you are just starting to explore Windows NT and its features, try the following exercises.

1.1: Exploring NTFS

This exercise helps you explore NTFS file permissions, one of the principal features that distinguish FAT from NTFS.

Estimated Time: 10 minutes

1. Log on as an administrator to a Windows NT Server system.

2. Right-click on the Start button and select Explore to start Explorer.

3. Scroll to an NTFS partition on your system.

4. Find a file on the NTFS partition, right-click on the file icon, and choose Properties. The File Properties dialog box appears.

5. Click on the Security tab. You will see separate buttons for file Permissions, Auditing, and Ownership (see Figure 1.10). (You will learn more about how to manage and configure file security in later chapters.)

6. Click on the Permissions button. The File Permissions dialog box appears (see Figure 1.11). From within the File Permissions dialog box, you can specify which type of access to the file each user or group will receive. Clicking on the Add button enables you to add new users and groups to the access list.

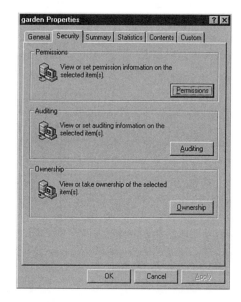

FIGURE 1.10
The Security tab of the File Properties dialog box.

APPLY YOUR LEARNING

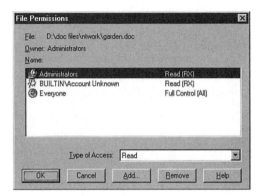

FIGURE 1.11
The File Permissions dialog box.

7. Close the File Permissions dialog box and the File Properties dialog box. You return to Explorer. Make sure the file you selected in step 4 is still selected.

8. Pull down the Explorer's Edit menu and choose Copy.

9. Scroll through the left pane of the Explorer window to a directory on a FAT partition. Select the directory.

10. Pull down the Edit menu and select Paste. A copy of the file you selected in step 4 appears in the FAT directory.

11. Right-click on the new file icon and choose Properties.

12. Examine the File Properties dialog box for the new file. Notice that the Security tab is missing. Because the FAT file system does not enable you to set user and group access to files, you cannot craft a specific security environment for the file as you can through the Security tab and the File

Permissions dialog box of the NTFS file. File-level security is one of the biggest advantages of using NTFS partitions.

1.2: PING and IPCONFIG

In this exercise, you will learn how to use the important TCP/IP utilities IPCONFIG and PING to verify your TCP/IP configuration.

Estimated Time: 10 minutes

1. Make sure TCP/IP is installed on your network.

2. Choose Start, Programs, Command Prompt.

3. At the command prompt, type **IPCONFIG**. The IPCONFIG command is supposed to return the IP address, subnet mask, and default gateway for all network adapters to which TCP/IP is bound. (Chapter 2 explains more about TCP/IP configuration and adapter bindings.)

4. Press Enter. If TCP/IP is working properly on your system, the IPCONFIG utility outputs the IP address, subnet mask, and default gateway for your network adapter(s). If your computer needs to obtain an IP address from a DHCP that is not working at this time (for instance, if you have a dial-up adapter that you use to access the Internet with an Internet service provider and you are not presently connected), the IP address and subnet mask appear as 0.0.0.0. If you have a duplicated IP address, the address appears, but the subnet mask appears as 0.0.0.0. Write down your IP address.

5. Type **ping 127.0.0.1**. The PING utility (Packet INternet Groper) tests your TCP/IP connection. You can specify the IP address of another

APPLY YOUR LEARNING

computer with the `ping` command to make sure your connection with the other computer is working. The format for the `ping` command is as follows:

```
ping <IP address>
```

The address you just typed (127.0.0.1) is a special address called the loopback address. The loopback address verifies that TCP/IP is working correctly on your system.

6. Ping the IP address of your own computer. This confirms that your IP address is configured correctly and lets you know if any duplicate IP addresses exist on your network. This also checks the network adapter of the machine.

7. Ping the address of another computer on your subnet. If a system has a default gateway (see step 4), it is a common practice to ping the default gateway to ensure that your connection to the gateway is working.

8. If you know the IP address of a computer beyond the gateway, ping the IP address of the remote computer to ensure that you can connect to remote resources.

Review Questions

1. A Windows NT Server machine must be installed as what in order to participate in a workgroup? Which partition holds the files necessary to boot your computer?

2. At what partition size does the NTFS file system become more efficient that FAT?

3. What is the principle disadvantage of the NetBEUI protocol?

4. What two software-based fault-tolerance methods does NT Server support, and what are their respective disk utilization percentages?

5. What NT Server service is available for minimizing TCP/IP address allocation administration

6. What is the NWLink protocol primarily used for in an NT network environment?

7. For which four clients are the installation files provided on the NT Server CD-ROM?

8. What does Microsoft recommend as the minimum hardware requirements for the installation of Windows NT Server on an Intel-based computer?

9. What is the core of a Windows NT domain?

Exam Questions

The following questions will test your knowledge of the information in this chapter. For additional questions, please see the exclusive Top Score test engine included with the CD-ROM and Appendix D, "Using Top Score Software."

1. You are the network administrator in an environment with the following characteristics:

   Two physically disconnected LANs, each consisting of a workgroup containing Windows 3.11 clients and Windows 95 clients running NetBEUI protocol.

APPLY YOUR LEARNING

Required Result:

To provide centralized account and security administration

Optional Desired Results:

To provide each user with access to resources in each LAN

To provide Internet access to all users

Proposed Solution:

Install the 32-bit TCP/IP protocol for Windows 3.11 clients and the MS TCP/IP protocol on the Windows 95 clients, and then install a router in each of the physical LANs with dedicated Internet connectivity.

Analysis:

Which of the following statements best describes the proposed solution?

A. The proposed solution produces the required result and both of the optional desired results.

B. The proposed solution produces the required result but only one of the optional desired results.

C. The proposed solution produces the required result but does not produce any of the optional desired results.

D. The proposed solution does not produce the required result.

2. You need to select an operating system that enables you to run your MS-DOS–based legacy applications. You have been told by your MIS department that these applications are written for speed and hence sometimes directly access hardware devices. Which of the following operating system(s) should you choose to run these applications? Choose all that apply.

A. Windows NT Workstation

B. Windows NT Server

C. Windows 95

D. Windows for Workgroups

3. For a multithreaded database application that your company is developing, you need an operating system that supports multiple CPUs. Which of the following operating systems support multiple processors? Choose all that apply.

A. Windows 95

B. Windows NT Workstation

C. Windows NT Server

D. Windows for Workgroups

4. Your Windows NT Server has a 2GB hard drive and a 1GB hard drive that are currently configured in the following way: one 1GB FAT partition that serves as the system/boot partition, 1GB of free space on the first disk, and 1GB of free space on the second disk.

Required Result:

To implement file-level security on your system/boot partition without reinstalling the operating system.

Optional Desired Results:

To use the free 2GB as a mirror set that will hold data network users place in shares.

To preserve the users' long filenames in those shares.

APPLY YOUR LEARNING

Proposed Solution:

Use CONVERT.EXE to convert the system/boot partition to NTFS, create two 1GB extended partitions with the free space, create a mirror set, and format the mirror as FAT.

Analysis:

Which of the following statements best describes the proposed solution?

A. The proposed solution produces the required result and both of the optional desired results.

B. The proposed solution produces the required result but only one of the optional desired results.

C. The proposed solution produces the required result but does not produce any of the optional desired results.

D. The proposed solution does not produce the required result.

5. What are the system requirements for running Windows NT Workstation?

A. 486DX/33 CPU
   8MB of RAM
   120MB free disk space

B. 486DX/33 CPU
   12MB of RAM
   85MB free disk space

C. 486DX/33 CPU or RISC-based processor
   12MB of RAM
   120MB free disk space

D. RISC-based processor
   12MB of RAM
   120MB free disk space

6. You need for Macintosh users to be able to connect to and store files on a computer. Which of the following operating systems can serve this purpose? Choose all that apply.

A. Windows NT Workstation

B. Windows 95 with the computer to MAC and Back third-party add-on

C. Windows for Workgroups

D. Windows NT Server

7. You get a call from a user stating that he is trying to share a directory with all the users in his office. But not all users can connect to his NT Workstation. His office consists of 15 users, running a mix of NT Workstation and Windows for Workgroups. What could be the problem?

A. The users running Windows for Workgroups need to upgrade to NT Workstation before they can attach his computer.

B. If he intends to share resources, he really should upgrade to NT Server.

C. He has used up all his licensed sessions. NT Workstation only allows 10 simultaneous sessions.

D. He needs to restart his computer; the problem should go away.

8. You are evaluating operating systems for a mission-critical application your MIS department is in the process of developing. You must choose an operating system that gives you basic data protection features, such as disk mirroring, RAID support, and the capability to secure the data against unauthorized individuals. Which of the following operating systems must you choose? Choose all correct answers.

APPLY YOUR LEARNING

A. Windows NT Server

B. Windows NT Workstation

C. Windows 95

D. MS-DOS

9. At a weekly management meeting, the director of the sales department relays concerns from her salespeople that when they try to dial in to the network, they usually get busy signals. Currently, 10 salespeople are out in the field, but this number is expected to double in the next six months. Currently, all the sales people are accessing the network via RAS (Remote Access Service) running on a dedicated Windows NT Workstation computer. What can you suggest to enable more simultaneous connections?

A. Nothing more can be done.

B. Upgrade the dial-in computer to Windows NT Server, which can support up to 256 RAS users. NT Workstation supports only one RAS user at a time.

C. You must set up a bank of 10 computers all running NT Workstation so that you can provide an adequate number of connections. When the new salespeople are hired, you must purchase an additional 5 to 10 computers.

10. What are the minimum hardware requirements for running Windows NT Server 4?

A. 386 DX/33 or higher CPU
16MB of RAM
130MB of disk space

B. 386 DX2/66 or higher CPU
12MB of RAM, 130MB of disk space

C. Pentium or higher CPU
16MB of RAM
130MB of disk space

D. 486 DX/33 or higher CPU
16MB of RAM
130MB of disk space

11. Users of the HR workgroup come to you and complain that every time someone joins or leaves their department, they have to create new user accounts and deactivate existing ones on each one of their 10 workstations. They are running Windows NT Workstation on all their computers. One user asks why this has to be done. Which of the following best describes why this is so?

A. In a workgroup model, account information is stored on each machine participating in the workgroup. To access a resource on another machine in the workgroup, you must have an account on that computer. To use a single user ID and password for all computers, you must install NT Server in a domain model.

B. This is a known problem in NT Workstation and is easily remedied by downloading a bug fix from Microsoft.

C. The user needs to designate one of the NT Workstations as the master controller for the workgroup and then transfer all the user account information to that machine. After this is done, users are authenticated by that dedicated workstation and, therefore, need only one user ID and password.

12. To organize your users and groups in a domain, which type of operating system must you install as the domain controller?

APPLY YOUR LEARNING

A. NT Workstation running in dedicated mode

B. Windows 95

C. Windows for Workgroups

D. Windows NT Server

13. You are planning to install Windows NT in a dual-boot configuration on a computer currently running Windows 95. The network users are accustomed to using long filenames. The other computers on the network are a mixture of Windows NT and Windows 95 computers, and you have opted for the dual-boot configuration so that users can access file resources from either operating system. Which file system should you use?

A. NTFS

B. FAT

C. HPFS

D. Either A or B

14. You plan to collect several large directories on a single partition. The directories require a total of 5GB in an uncompressed state. You should then do which of the following?

A. Format the partition for the FAT file system.

B. Format the partition for FAT and use DriveSpace file compression.

C. Format the partition for NTFS.

D. Either B or C.

15. You have a Windows NT Server system with three physical disks. One disk has a single partition that serves as the boot and system partitions.

The second disk has two partitions of approximately equal size, one formatted for FAT and one for NTFS. The third disk is currently free space. What fault-tolerance method(s) can be used given the current configuration?

A. Disk mirroring

B. Disk striping with parity

C. All of the above

D. None of the above

16. Users on your Windows NT network occasionally have to exchange messages with users on a Novell NetWare 4.0 network via the Internet. To enable such communication, you must use which of the following protocols?

A. TCP/IP

B. NWLink

C. Both A and B

D. None of the above

ANSWERS AND EXPLANATIONS

The answers to the review and exam questions are provided here, along with explanations as to why those answers are correct (when feasible).

Answers to Review Questions

1. In order to participate in a workgroup, an NT Server must be installed as a standalone server. NT Server allows for the installation of two types of non-domain controller servers: member and

APPLY YOUR LEARNING

standalone. Technically, a member server is an NT Server that participates in a domain, and a standalone server is one that does not. For more information, see the section "Workgroups."

2. At 400MB, it becomes most efficient to use NTFS partitions. Because of the high overhead of the NTFS file system (typically 5–10MB), you should not install NTFS on a partition smaller than 400MB. In addition, because of the linked-list structure of FAT partitions, their performance tends to downgrade as the number of files on the partition increases; frequently, a larger partition means more files and, therefore, worse performance. For more information, see the section "Windows NT File Systems."

3. The principle disadvantage of using NetBEUI is the fact that it is not routable. NetBEUI is provided as a convenience to give connectivity to early Microsoft network configurations. However, because the protocol is not routable, it cannot be used effectively in an environment larger than a single physical departmental LAN. This means that large scale networks (LANs with many users or WANs) cannot be implemented using NetBEUI. For more information, see the section "NetBEUI."

4. The two software-based fault-tolerance methods that NT Server supports are disk mirroring and disk striping with parity. They provide 50% disk utilization and (#ofdisks–1)/#ofDisks*100% disk utilization, respectively. Disk mirroring creates a redundant partition that becomes a dynamic backup of an existing partition. Because it is a redundant partition, half of the total disk space is used to provide fault tolerance (for example, two 500MB partitions provide only 500MB of useable storage). Disk striping with parity

basically requires that 3–32 partitions in the stripe set be reserved for fault-tolerant parity information. As a result, the percentage of useable space increases along with the number of disks. For example, in an environment with three 500MB partitions, 500MB would be reserved to provide fault tolerance and, therefore, 66% of the space would be available for data storage. In an environment with ten 500MB partitions, 500MB would still be required to provide fault tolerance; however, now 90% of the total space would be available for data storage. For more information, see the section "Fault-Tolerance Methods."

5. The service available for minimizing TCP/IP address allocation and configuration administration is the Dynamic Host Configuration Protocol (DHCP) service. When installed on an NT Server, DHCP will lease TCP/IP addresses, completely configured, to all clients capable of requesting those addresses; these clients include NT Servers, NT Workstations, Windows 95 workstations, and Windows 3.11 workstations with the 32-bit TCP/IP protocol installed. For more information, see the section "TCP/IP."

6. The primary use for NWLink is to provide connectivity to Novell networks. The NWLink protocol is Microsoft's emulation of the IPX/SPX protocol native to the Novell NetWare network environment. Although NWLink can be used as the primary protocol in an all-Microsoft network, it is most frequently used to provide access to NetWare resources. For more information, see the section "NWLink."

7. The clients provided on the NT Server CD-ROM are Windows 95, MS-DOS client 3.0, LAN Manager 2.2c for MS-DOS client, and LAN Manager 2.2c for OS/2 client. The

Windows NT Server CD-ROM provides full installation files for each of these clients for the convenience of network administrators. For more information, see the section "Planning for Network Clients."

8. Microsoft recommends the following minimum hardware requirements for installation of NT Server on an Intel machine: 486DX/33 processor, 16MB of RAM, and 130MB of free disk space. For more information, see the section "Minimum Hardware Requirements."

9. The core of a Windows NT domain is an NT Server configured as a primary domain controller (PDC). Centralized account management is provided by the primary domain controller in your domain. Aided by backup domain controllers (if present), it also validates user login. Without a primary domain controller, a true Windows NT Domain cannot exist. For more information, see the section "Domains."

Answers to Exam Questions

1. **D.** This solution does not produce the required result. The scenario identifies the primary result as the ability to provide centralized account and security administration in the network environment; that result can be accomplished only by installing a Windows NT Server as a primary domain controller (PDC) on the network. The solution will provide TCP/IP-based connectivity between the physical LANs and will provide users with Internet access, but it will not produce the primary goal. For more information, see the section "Domains."

2. **C. and D.** Windows 95 and Windows for Workgroups (3.11) will enable MS-DOS applications to directly access hardware; NT Workstation and Server will not. For more information, see the sections "Windows 95" and "Windows NT Workstation."

3. **B. and C.** Only Windows NT Workstation and Server provide support for true symmetric multiprocessing. For more information, see the section "Windows NT Workstation."

4. **A.** This solution produces all of the results, both required and optional. File-level security is provided only through the use of an NTFS partition. To avoid reformatting the system/boot partition, you can run the CONVERT.EXE program to convert the FAT partition to NTFS without the loss of any data. Then, using the free space on each of the disks, you can create a mirror set, format it as FAT, and create shares on the mirror set. Because all partition types on NT support long filenames, you will be able to provide your users with that functionality. For more information, see the sections "NTFS" and "Choosing a File System."

5. **C.** Like NT Server, NT Workstation requires either a 486 Intel or RISC-based processor. It requires 12MB of RAM and at least 120MB of free hard disk space. For more information, see the section "Windows NT Workstation."

6. **D.** Windows NT Server is the only one that allows you to install the service necessary to support Macintosh users. For more information, see the section "Windows NT Server."

7. **C.** Unlike Windows NT Server, which can support an unlimited number of concurrent user connections, Windows NT Workstation can sup-

port only 10 simultaneous network connections. For more information, see the section "Windows NT Server."

8. **A.** Although Windows NT Workstation will allow you to provide security against unauthorized individuals, only NT Server provides software-based fault tolerance in the form of disk mirroring and disk striping with parity (RAID levels 1 and 5). For more information, see the section "Windows NT Server."

9. **B.** Windows NT Server can support up to 256 simultaneous RAS connections; Workstation can support only 1. Replacing the Workstation-based RAS server with a Server-based RAS server provides the sales department with the connectivity they desire. For more information, see the section "Windows NT Server."

10. **D.** NT Server requires a 486DX/33 or higher CPU, 16MB of RAM, and at least 130MB of free disk space. For more information, see the section "Windows NT Server."

11. **A.** In a workgroup, each computer maintains its own accounts database. This means that each machine must be manually synchronized when a new user needs access to the workgroup resources or when an existing user no longer needs access. In addition, whenever a user changes his or her password on one machine, the password must be changed on all machines. For more information, see the section "Workgroups."

12. **D.** Only Windows NT Server can be installed as a domain controller. For more information, see the section "Domains."

13. **B.** In order to give access to all data on the computer to either boot configuration, you must format your hard drives with a file system that's readable by both; FAT is the only file system that fulfills that requirement. For more information, see the section "FAT."

14. **C.** Because FAT does not support partitions greater than 4GB, you must format the partition with NTFS. For more information, see the section "NTFS."

15. **A.** Disk mirroring can be accomplished using two hard drives and will support the system and boot partitions. In order to implement disk striping with parity, you must have free space on at least three physical disks, which you do not have in this configuration. For more information, see the sections "Disk Mirroring" and "Disk Striping with Parity."

16. **A.** Of the options listed, only TCP/IP is capable of being used via the Internet. NWLink is routable, but it is not an Internet supported protocol. For more information, see the section "TCP/IP."

APPLY YOUR LEARNING

Suggested Readings and Resources

We recommend the following resources for further study in the area of planning:

1. Microsoft Official Curriculum course 922: *Supporting Microsoft Windows NT 4.0 Core Technologies*

   - Module 1: The Windows NT 4.0 Environment

   - Module 5: Managing File Systems

   - Module 6: Managing Partitions

   - Module 7: Managing Fault Tolerance

   - Module 10: Configuring Windows NT Protocols

   - Module 15: Implementing Network Clients

2. *MS Windows NT Server 4.0 Networking Guide* (Microsoft Press)

   - Chapter 1: Windows NT 4 Networking Architecture

   - Chapter 6: TCP/IP Implementation Details

   - Chapter 13: Using NetBEUI with Windows NT

3. Microsoft TechNet CD-ROM

   - *Concepts and Planning: MS Windows NT Server 4.0*

   - Chapter 1: Managing NT Server Domains

   - Chapter 7: Protecting Data

   - Chapter 11: Managing Client Administration

4. Web Sites

   - www.microsoft.com/ntserver (check out the online seminars)

   - www.microsoft.com/train_cert

   - www.prometric.com/testingcandidates/assessment/chosetest.html (take online assessment tests)

Microsoft provides the following objectives for the "Installation" portion of "Installation and Configuration":

▶ **Install Windows NT Server on Intel-based platforms.**

This objective is necessary because someone certified in the use of Windows NT Server technology must understand the process and all the options regarding the installation of the product. Because the Intel platform is by far the platform most commonly used for NT Server, the exam focuses on installation for Intel. You will need to understand all the facets of installation, including the phases, the methods, and the GUI setup options.

▶ **Install Windows NT Server to perform various server roles. Server roles include those of primary domain controller, backup domain controller, and member server.**

This objective is necessary because someone certified in the use of Windows NT Server technology must understand the roles an NT server can play on a network and how those roles relate to the installation process. You will need to understand the implications of installing a server as a primary domain controller (PDC), a backup domain controller (BDC), and a member server in a domain. This includes meeting the requirements of both the computer and the network (for example, having a PDC available and online during installation of a BDC).

▶ **Install Windows NT Server by using various methods. Installation methods include CD-ROM, over-the-network, Network Client Administrator, Express versus Custom.**

This objective is necessary because someone certified in the use of Windows NT Server technology must understand the valid methods for installing NT Server. This extends beyond the different methods to address how those methods are alike and how they differ, and what you will need in advance to make them work properly.

C H A P T E R 2

Installation and Configuration Part 1: Installation of NT Server

OUTLINE

▶ Because server roles are relatively straightforward, you should understood them simply by reading through the materials that follow. However, for a complete understanding of the installation of each, you might need to actually perform an installation of each type. This will require at least two machines: one that can be installed as a primary domain controller and one that can be installed as both a member server and a backup domain controller through the use of a dual-boot configuration.

▶ You cannot escape questions on installation on the NT Server exam. As a result, you need to be very familiar with the concepts and the practical application of installation. The best way to study is to understand the theory presented here and then to go out and implement it. Get a machine that meets the minimum hardware requirements and install NT Server. If you have a couple of machines to work with, that's even better. You can try an installation from the CD-ROM using the setup disks, and you can install a PDC and then do an over-the-network installation of a BDC. You can try installing NT Server using the /B option and see how that differs from the regular WINNT installation. Also, play around with the different options in the GUI interface to see what the results are.

In short, understanding installation really requires practice. Although you may be able to get away with memorizing the concepts in this book to pass the exam, you really might never understand installation until you do it.

This chapter will help you prepare for the "Installation" part of the "Installation and Configuration" section of Microsoft's Exam 70-67. Installing and configuring an NT Server correctly is the first step to ensuring that your networking environment is stable and easy to administer. The test covers all aspects of installation; be prepared for all sorts of questions regarding the various forms of installation.

INTRODUCTION

Because the section "Installation and Configuration" is so large, it has been divided into three chapters. This first chapter, "Installation of NT Server" deals with the topics relating to the actual installation of NT server software.

A knowledge of installation is the first step toward understanding the operation of any NT server. The protocols, the services, and the roles of the server and the domain are all things to be considered when installing the server software.

Moving from the planning stage to the installation stage, you take the plan and implement it, complete with naming conventions, disk configuration, and initial server configuration.

This chapter provides an overview of the installation requirements and procedure.

REQUIREMENTS FOR INSTALLATION

To install Windows NT server efficiently, it is best to do some planning in advance so you can be prepared for the questions the setup program will ask. Take the time to determine which installation method will work best for you. The following section discusses Windows NT Server installation.

Hardware Requirements

Install Windows NT Server on Intel-based platforms.

Before you install Windows NT Server, you need to make sure that your hardware can support it. Windows NT Server doesn't support anywhere near the number of devices that Windows 95 supports, so don't assume that Windows NT Server can support the hardware you currently use for MS-DOS or Windows 95.

You receive lots of advice in this chapter. First and foremost, be sure to consult the Hardware Compatibility List (HCL) before you try to install Windows NT Server and certainly before you purchase any new hardware on which to run Windows NT Server. The HCL includes the vendor and model names for all systems and devices tested and approved for use with Windows NT Server.

You should know the following things about the HCL:

◆ The HCL that ships with the product is now obsolete. However, the HCL is frequently updated, and the most recent version can be found on TechNet (Microsoft's monthly product support CD-ROM), as well as on The Microsoft Network, CompuServe, the Internet (`www.microsoft.com/hwtest/hcl`), and other online services.

◆ Even if a product is listed on the HCL, it might not be fully 100 percent compatible. Check the fine print; usually, you can find a footnote or endnote including caveats regarding supporting a device under Windows NT Server.

◆ A product might be listed on the HCL even if it hasn't been tested yet. Before giving up hope, ask the vendor if any drivers are available for Windows NT 4. Recognize, however, that if the device isn't on the HCL, Microsoft probably will just refer you back to the vendor for technical support issues.

◆ If a product isn't on the HCL and the vendor doesn't have a Windows NT 4 driver, ask the vendor if any compatible drivers are available. For instance, a modem might be Hayes-compatible, or a network card might be NE2000-compatible. Should a problem arise down the road, however, you probably won't be able to rely on Microsoft or the vendor for technical support.

The specific hardware requirements differ depending on the platform on which you intend to install Windows NT.

Intel and RISC-based Requirements

Intel-based computers form the largest segment of the Windows NT installation base, owing to the worldwide predominance of Intel-based computers. If you plan to install Windows NT Server on an Intel-based computer, make sure that your hardware meets the following minimum requirements:

◆ *Processor.* Intel-based computers require a 32-bit Intel or Intel-compatible CPU (80486 DX-33 or higher); Pentium CPUs give optimal performance.

◆ *Memory.* The specifications for Windows NT Server indicate that it will install with as few as 16MB of RAM, but you can expect increases in performance as you add RAM.

◆ *Hard disk.* Windows NT Server installation requires at least 125MB of free hard disk space for Intel-based machines and 160MB for RISC-based machines.

On any platform, cluster size also is important. Microsoft recommends that a Windows NT Server with 32KB clusters have at least 200MB free space.

You also need a VGA (or higher) video card. And if you install Windows NT on an Intel-based computer and intend to use the three setup diskettes in conjunction with your CD-ROM installation, you might need a 3 ½-inch disk drive.

Other devices, while not mandatory, certainly are quite valuable. For example, it's difficult to get by these days without a mouse or similar pointing device, a CD-ROM drive (optional on Intel only, required for RISC), and a network adapter card. If you're using a PowerPC with an NE-2000 compatible network card, make sure that the computer's firmware is version 1.24 or later.

Multiboot Requirements

You can install Windows NT Server alongside another operating system on the same machine; this provides you with the capability to boot either of the installed operating systems at system startup. If you need or want to do so, you should read whichever of the following sections apply to the operating systems you want to use.

Windows NT Server

An unlimited number of Windows NT variants and roles can coexist on the same computer. Be careful to install each operating system in a separate directory, though. A Windows NT-based operating system will automatically create and update a boot loader menu if it finds other operating systems on the system.

NOTE

Overcoming the 540MB Limit Any supported hard disk suffices, but Windows NT might have a problem addressing IDE drives roomier than 540MB. If your IDE controller is compatible with the Western Digital WD1003 standard, Windows NT can handle your EIDE drive; if it isn't compatible with the standard, a BIOS upgrade should solve the problem. A utility for MS-DOS called Disk Manager (published by OnTrack Systems) also might do the trick; it alters the BIOS on the hard disk so that MS-DOS (and Windows NT) can correctly handle the drive.

EXAM TIP

You Don't Need to Know Non-NT Operating Systems for the Exam Although Microsoft wants you to know about multibooting Windows NT Server with other operating systems, you are not required to know how any of the other systems function except where that extends to support by NT. For example, you are not expected to know OS/2 just because NT can multiboot with it; however, you do need to know about the OS/2 subsystem that is a part of NT.

Windows 95

Windows 95 and Windows NT can coexist on the same machine, but not in the same directory root because each OS has files that differ in content but are the same in name and location. Therefore, you must reinstall Win95 applications under Windows NT Server before you can use them with both operating systems. Again, Windows NT will detect Windows 95 if it's present and will create or update the boot loader menu.

There is currently no upgrade path from Windows 95 to Windows NT.

MS-DOS

If your MS-DOS installation includes Windows 3.x or Windows for Workgroups, you can install Windows NT in the existing Windows root directory. The benefit of this arrangement is a synchronized desktop environment. Also, such an arrangement frees you from having to reinstall your Windows applications before you can use them under Windows NT.

OS/2

You can install Windows NT on a system that currently runs OS/2, but doing so disables OS/2's Boot Manager in favor of the Windows NT Boot Loader. If you want to use the OS/2 Boot Manager, you must re-enable it through Disk Administrator by marking the Boot Manager active after Windows NT successfully installs. When Boot Manager is active, you can boot to Windows NT by choosing MS-DOS from the Boot Manager menu. Choosing MS-DOS invokes the Windows NT Boot Loader, from which you can boot either Windows NT or MS-DOS.

Early versions of OS/2 (version 1.x) don't have Boot Manager. Instead, you must use the BOOT command: Type **BOOT /DOS** from inside OS/2 and reboot to bring up the Windows NT Boot Loader, or type **BOOT /OS2** from MS-DOS and reboot to bring up OS/2.

CHOOSING A SERVER TYPE

Install Windows NT Server to perform various server roles. Server roles include those of primary domain controller, backup domain controller, and member server.

When installing Windows NT Server, you must make an important choice: You have to decide what role your NT Server machine will play on your network. You can choose from three server roles:

◆ *Primary domain controller (PDC).* The PDC contains the master copy of the directory database (which contains information on user accounts) for the domain. There must be one—and only one—primary domain controller per domain, and the primary domain controller must be the first machine installed.

◆ *Backup domain controller (BDC).* The backup domain controller helps the primary domain controller. The primary domain controller copies the directory database to the backup domain controller(s). The BDC can authenticate users just as the PDC can. If the PDC fails, a BDC can be promoted to a PDC by an administrator; however, if a BDC is promoted, any changes that were made to the directory database since the last time it was copied from the old PDC are lost. A domain can have more than one BDC.

◆ *Member or Standalone Server.* A *standalone server* is a Windows NT Server machine that doesn't participate in a domain environment. It is an NT server configured to operate in a workgroup. A standalone server can provide all Windows NT Server functions (file service, print service, Internet service, and so on) but provides only local authentication.

Member servers, on the other hand, are Windows NT Servers that are not configured as domain controllers yet still participate as part of a domain. Member servers are useful for keeping a file or print server free from the overhead of authenticating users, which provides faster access to data and applications and, in turn, reduces the load on the domain controllers by reducing the file, print, and application services they must provide to the domain.

Choosing the server type during the planning process is important because after you install a machine, you cannot change its role without reinstalling NT. A domain controller must always remain a domain controller, and a non-domain controller must always remain as such. You can, however, configure an NT Server as a standalone server and then reconfigure it later to participate in a domain as a member server, and vice versa.

INSTALLATION PROCEDURE

Install Windows NT Server by using various methods. Installation methods include CD-ROM, over-the-network, Network Client Administrator, express vs. custom.

You can get Windows NT Server installation files from one of two sources:

◆ The Windows NT installation CD-ROM

◆ A network sharepoint containing the installation files for the appropriate hardware platform on which the program is to be installed

Most installation procedures consist of two distinct phases: a file copying phase that takes place under a minimal text-mode version of Windows NT and a configuration phase that runs under the full GUI Windows NT Setup Wizard.

The details of the Windows NT installation process depend on the details of your system; different prompts and dialog boxes may ask you for additional information depending on the devices on your system and the components you want to install.

CD-ROM

Windows NT Server can be installed from the CD-ROM containing the program files. This installation can be initiated in one of three ways. First, you can boot to the first of three installation floppy disks. These disks allow you to install Windows NT on a computer that does not support CD-ROM boot and does not support drivers for the CD-ROM drive in the machines. To begin the CD-ROM installation process, boot from Setup Disk 1. Setup asks for all three of the setup disks before it asks for the CD-ROM. (You'll learn how to regenerate these disks should the need arise later in this chapter.)

Second, you can begin the installation from a local CD-ROM from within your existing operating system. Setup copies the installation files from the CD-ROM to your hard drive and asks you to restart your computer.

Third, you can begin the installation by booting your computer to the CD-ROM. You can use this method on machines configured to boot to the CD-ROM when detected. In this case, the Autoplay screen appears, and you can choose the Windows NT Setup icon to begin the file copying process.

If you are initiating the installation from the Setup disks, you must boot from the Setup disks; don't type the standard run a:\setup. Because Setup is a Windows NT program, in order for it to run, Windows NT must be running; the programs winnt.exe and winnt32.exe are the setup programs for NT Server and will be discussed later in this chapter. When you boot from the initial setup disk, a minimal version of Windows NT loads and initializes.

Network Installs

If you have to roll out many Windows NT Servers in a short period of time, or if you simply want a fast installation of NT, a CD-ROM-based installation may be impractical. Perhaps not all of your servers have CD-ROM drives, or perhaps you don't have as many copies of the CD-ROM as you do servers. A network install is really a CD-ROM install; an initial preinstallation phase is added, in which the contents of the CD-ROM are copied across the network from the server to the client computer. After all the installation files have been copied, the client computer reboots (optionally) from the setup disks and proceeds with the installation as if it were a CD-ROM install (in this case, the "CD-ROM" is the hard drive). You can use Windows NT's Client Administrator application to create a network installation startup disk that will enable you to boot the client machine and connect to the shared directory with the installation files. The Client Administrator startup disk is described later in this chapter.

To start an installation across the network, you must first redirect an MS-DOS drive letter to the network sharepoint containing the installation files. From a NetWare client, you use the MAP command; from a Windows 95 client, you utilize the Network Neighborhood and connect to a drive; from an MS-DOS client, you use the NET USE command; from a Windows for Workgroups client, you choose Disk, Connect Network Drive in File Manager. In short, establish network connections however you ordinarily do it.

NOTE

Installation from a Disk-Based Network Share Is Always Faster Than Sharing the CD-ROM   To improve performance, copy the contents of the CD-ROM to the hard drive and share the hard disk's copy rather than the CD's. Hard disks are much faster than CD-ROM drives.

After you map a drive to the installation share, change to the drive and run a program called WINNT.EXE. (If you install from a previous version of NT, the system prompts you to run WINNT32.EXE instead of WINNT.EXE.) Except for the fact that WINNT and WINNT32 run on different platforms, they are virtually identical in their use and their results. Therefore, in the discussion that follows, I will make reference to both programs using the name WINNT.EXE. WINNT.EXE is an MS-DOS program that generates the three necessary Setup disks and copies the Windows NT installation files from the server to the local hard drive. After all the files are copied, WINNT.EXE prompts you to insert Setup Disk 1 so it can reboot the computer and begin the installation process.

> **NOTE**
>
> **Help Available for NET Command** If you have questions about net commands, type **net help** at the prompt. If you require assistance on the specific command, type `net help` followed by the command, such as **net help view** or **net help logoff**.

WINNT.EXE Switches

The following switches enable you to customize how WINNT.EXE begins the setup process.

/B No Boot Floppies

The /B switch instructs WINNT.EXE not to create the three setup disks. Instead, WINNT.EXE creates images of these disks on your system partition, requiring an extra 4 or 5MB of disk space. The boot sector of the hard disk is modified to point to the temporary directory that contains the images (WIN_NT.~BT).

The /B switch can significantly speed up the installation process. If the computer crashes during Setup, however, you may not be able to reboot to your old operating system. Keeping an MS-DOS or Windows 95 bootable disk around should solve that problem. After you boot to your former operating system, type **Sys C:** (to transfer the system files to the C: drive), and then reboot your system to the hard drive.

> **EXAM TIP**
>
> **Setup Disks Created in Reverse Order** One interesting quirk about WINNT.EXE: When it asks you to insert each of the three blank formatted disks necessary to create the setup disks, it does so in reverse order. It asks for Disk 3 first, then Disk 2, and finally Disk 1. Microsoft did this for your convenience, believe it or not: One less disk swap occurs in this scenario. Try it and see. Still, it confuses many first-time installers who try to reboot their machine from Disk 3, believing it to be Disk 1.

/S Source File Location

When WINNT.EXE executes, it immediately asks the user for the location of the Windows NT source files, even if the user is in the same directory from which WINNT.EXE was run. To avoid answering this question, supply the information up-front using the syntax
`WINNT.EXE /S:<path>`.

/U **Unattended Installation**

The Unattended Installation option automates the installation or upgrade process so you don't have to sit at the keyboard and respond to Setup prompts. You must tell WINNT.EXE in advance where to find the installation files, so you must use the /u switch and the /s switch. Normally, the unattended installation operates unattended only through the copy phase, the text mode portion of Setup, and the initial reboot; after that, Setup requires the user to enter the computer name, network settings, and so on. You can, however, enter a colon and a filename after the /u switch, as follows:

```
winnt /u:c:\answer.txt
```

The file called answer.txt is an answer file, which contains responses to the final Setup prompts. By using the /u switch with an answer file, you can automate the entire installation.

You can use the Setup Manager utility to create an answer file, or you can use any text editor to edit the answer file template called unattend.txt (found on the Windows NT installation CD-ROM). You can save the answer file with any legal name.

You can also use an answer file in conjunction with the (Uniqueness Database File) /UDF switch.

/UDF **Uniqueness Database File**

A Uniqueness Database File (UDF) lets you tailor an unattended installation to the unique attributes of specific machines. The UDF contains different sections, each of which is identified with a string called a *uniqueness ID*. Each section contains machine-specific information for a single computer or a group of computers. You can then use a single answer file for all the network installations but reference machine-specific information by providing the uniqueness ID with the /UDF switch.

/T:drive_letter **Temporary Drive**

This switch tells WINNT or WINNT32 to put the installation files on the specified drive.

/OX **Only Make Boot Diskettes (Local Install)**

The /OX switch creates the three setup disks required to begin the installation of NT from a CD-ROM where this initial phase is necessary.

/F Don't Verify Files

Although you can shave a bit of time off the installation process by skipping the verification of the files copied to the boot disks, the savings are negligible. It doesn't take that much time to verify the files, and it certainly takes much longer to restart the installation if the disks are corrupt. Still, such corruption during file copying is rare, so if you aren't averse to the occasional odds-favorable risk, go for it.

/C Don't Check for Free Space

This switch tells WINNT.EXE not to check for the required free space on the setup boot disks. You should not use this switch for two reasons:

- ◆ The disks are pretty packed; if you have other files on the disks, you probably won't be able to fit all of the required Setup files anyway.

- ◆ The amount of time you can save by using this switch is approximately equal to the amount of time it takes to type the switch.

THE INSTALLATION PHASES

Microsoft divides the Windows NT installation process into four phases:

- ◆ Phase 0: Pre-installation
- ◆ Phase 1: Gathering information about your computer
- ◆ Phase 2: Installing Windows NT Networking
- ◆ Phase 3: Finishing Setup

The following sections take you through these installation phases.

Phase 0: Pre-installation

During pre-installation, Setup copies the necessary installation files to your hard drive and assembles the information it needs for the install by detecting hardware and by asking the user for configuration information. Before you begin studying the installation process, you should look at what's on the three Windows NT Setup disks.

Setup Disk One

When your computer boots from this disk, the Master Boot Record loads and passes control to NTLDR, the Windows NT Boot Loader. NTLDR, in turn, loads the kernel (NTKRNLMP.EXE). Next, one of three Hardware Abstraction Layers (HAL) is loaded: HAL486C.DLL, HALMCA.DLL, or HALAPIC.DLL, depending on which platform is detected.

Setup Disk Two

This disk contains SETUPREG.HIV, a minimal Registry used by Setup. This Registry contains single-entry instructions that tell Windows NT to load the main installation driver, SETUPDD.SYS. After loading SETUPDD.SYS, Windows NT loads generic drivers for video (VIDEOPRT.SYS), keyboard (I8042PRT.SYS and KBDUS.DLL), floppy drive (FLOPPY.SYS), and the FAT file system (FASTFAT.SYS). This disk also includes the setup font (VGAOEM.FON), locale-specific data (C_1252.NLS, \C_437.NLS, and L_INTL.NLS), and the first of many SCSI port drivers, the rest of which are on the third Setup disk.

Setup Disk Three

Disk three contains additional SCSI port drivers, of which only one or two are typically loaded (depending on which, if any, SCSI adapters are installed). Windows NT loads additional file system drivers, such as NTFS.SYS, from this disk. This disk also includes drivers for specific types of hard disks, specifically ATDISK.SYS for ESDI or IDE and ABIOSDSK.SYS for Micro Channel.

After the SCSI drivers have been loaded, Windows NT should recognize supported SCSI CD-ROM drives. Windows NT also detects IDE CD-ROM drives, but it may not detect proprietary Mitsumi or Panasonic drives; you must manually inform Windows NT of their presence.

The Phase 0 Process

In Phase 0, Setup loads a minimal version of Windows NT into memory and asks if you want to perform an installation or an upgrade.

Between Setup disks two and three, the Welcome screen appears, informing you of your options: You can install Windows NT, repair an existing installation, or learn more about the setup process. Take a moment to read the online help if you want. When you're ready to begin, press Enter to begin the installation.

During this phase of the installation, Setup asks you to verify certain information about your hardware and your hardware-related software components. The following sections describe the questions Setup asks.

Mass Storage Devices

Setup asks if you want it to attempt to detect the mass storage devices attached to your computer. A note informs you that Setup can automatically detect floppy controllers and standard ESDI/IDE hard disks. (Some other mass storage devices, such as SCSI adapters and certain CD-ROM drives, can cause the computer to malfunction or become unresponsive.)

Type **S** to skip mass storage device detection and manually select SCSI adapters, CD-ROM drives, and special disk controllers. Or, press Enter to let Setup detect mass storage devices on your computer. If you allow autodetection, Setup asks for Setup Disk 3 and attempts to detect the mass storage devices. Setup then asks you to verify the list. Press Enter if you have no additional devices, or type **S** to specify an additional device.

Hardware and Components

Setup looks for certain hardware and software components, such as a keyboard, a mouse, a video screen, and the accompanying drivers. Setup then presents a list of components and asks if you want to make any changes. Press Enter to accept the list. Or, to change an item, select the item using the arrow keys and press Enter to see alternatives.

Partitions

After you identify your SCSI adapters and CD-ROM drivers, Windows NT Setup needs to know which partition it should install Windows NT on. Setup displays a screen showing the existing partitions on your hard drive and the space available for creating new partitions. Do one of the following:

◆ Press Enter to install Windows NT on the highlighted partition or on unpartitioned space.

◆ Type **C** to create a new partition in unpartitioned space.

◆ Type **D** to delete a partition.

NTFS

Setup then presents the following options:

◆ Format the partition using the FAT file system.

◆ Format the partition using the NTFS file system.

◆ Convert the partition to NTFS.

◆ Leave the current file system intact.

NOTE

Conversion Takes Place *After* Rebooting   The conversion to NTFS isn't performed during installation; rather, it occurs after Windows NT is completely installed and the computer reboots for the first time. The end result is the same: Before the user can log on to Windows NT, the partition has been converted.

Because it was specifically designed for Windows NT, New Technology File System (NTFS) offers some advantages, including better performance and increased security. However, NTFS isn't compatible with non-NT operating systems. The other optional file system for NT hard drives is FAT. If you choose FAT, you lose all data that's currently on the partition.

The default choice is to leave the current file system intact. If your system is now running MS-DOS, Windows 3.x, or Windows 95, the current file system is the FAT file system. If you ever plan to access the partition after locally booting to MS-DOS or Windows, you must select the FAT file system.

See Chapter 6, "Managing Resources Part 2: Managing Disk Resources," for more on the file systems that Windows NT supports.

NT Root Directory

Next, Setup asks what name you want to give the Windows NT root directory. By default, Setup suggests \WINNT of the system partition as the installation directory.

If Setup detects an installation of Windows NT already in the selected directory, you are given the options of replacing the existing installation or choosing another location.

Hard Disk Corruption

Setup examines your hard disk(s) for corruption by automatically performing a basic examination. You can then choose whether you want Setup to perform an exhaustive secondary examination, which may take several minutes. Press Enter to do so, or press Esc to skip the secondary examination.

Reboot

A progress bar appears while Setup copies files to your hard disk. This may take several minutes.

Finally, the last text-mode screen announces that this portion of Setup is complete and asks that you remove the disk from your floppy drive and restart your computer. Press Enter to restart your computer.

Phase 1: Gathering Information

After your computer restarts, Setup asks you to approve the licensing agreement and begins copying files from the disks, CD-ROM, or network to the Windows NT root directory. The Windows NT Setup Wizard then appears, announcing the three remaining parts of the setup process:

1. Gathering information about your computer.
2. Installing Windows NT Networking
3. Finishing Setup

Name and Company Name

For legal and registration reasons, Setup asks for your name and organization, which it uses as the defaults for additional software installed under Windows NT. You must enter a value in the Name field, but you can leave the Company Name blank if you want.

Setup also asks for your Product ID number, which you'll find on a sticker attached to the CD-ROM sleeve. You must enter this number before you can continue with the installation.

WARNING

Dual Boot Not Recommended on NT Servers   Because of the specialized jobs of NT servers, it is not recommended that you configure an NT server to dual boot or multiboot. In a test lab, a dual-booted NT Server is fine. In a production environment, though, you want to lose the NT Server while you are booting to another operating system because even the presence of that operating system is a risk, as it can be a back-door into your data that bypasses NT security. Therefore, you will generally not choose a FAT partition on an NT Server just for the sake of a dual-boot opportunity.

WARNING

Don't Install Windows NT in the Same Directory As Windows 95! Windows NT can peacefully coexist with Windows 3.x in the same directory tree, but do not—under any circumstances—install Windows NT in the same directory as Windows 95; currently the two operating systems cannot coexist in the same directory structure.

Licensing Mode

When installing Windows NT Server, you must specify a licensing mode. These are your options:

◆ *Per server license.* Clients are licensed to a particular server, and the number of concurrent connections to the server cannot exceed the maximum specified in the license. When the maximum number of concurrent connections is reached, Windows NT returns an error to any user who attempts to connect and prohibits access. An administrator can still connect after the maximum is reached, however.

◆ *Per seat license.* Clients are free to use any server they want, and an unlimited number of clients can connect to a server.

If you can't decide which mode to select, choose per server mode. You have a one-time chance to convert the per server license to a per seat license by using the Control Panel Licensing application.

Computer Name

Every networked Windows NT-based computer must have a unique computer name, even if the computers are split among multiple domains. The computer name is a typical NetBIOS name: that is, it can consist of up to 15 characters. Because workgroup and domain names also use NetBIOS names, the computer name must be unique among all of these names as well. NetBIOS names aren't case-sensitive; they always appear in uppercase letters.

Server Type

When installing Windows NT Server, you must specify whether the computer is to be a primary domain controller, a backup domain controller, or a standalone server. These server type options were discussed in the section titled "Choosing a Server Type," earlier in this chapter.

Administrator Password

Setup asks you to enter a password for the Administrator account. The length of the password must be 14 characters or less (see Chapter 5 for more on Windows NT accounts). You need the

Administrator account to create and manage other accounts within Windows NT.

Don't forget to write down the Administrator account password and store it in a safe place.

Emergency Disk

The Setup Wizard asks if you want to create an emergency repair disk. Chapter 9, "Troubleshooting," discusses the Emergency Repair Disk (ERD) in detail. It's essentially a clone of the information stored in the \REPAIR directory in case that directory or even the hard disk becomes corrupt or inaccessible. Creating an ERD for every computer in your company is a good idea. Label each ERD with the serial number of the computer to which it is paired.

The wizard then presents you with a list of components to choose from, of which the most common ones are already selected by default. You can accept the defaults, or you can add or remove components as required.

If you only want to view the list of components, you can choose the Choose Components option to view the list, and then click on Next, leaving the list unchanged to accept the defaults.

Phase 2: Installing Windows NT Networking

Next, the Setup Wizard announces that it is ready to begin installing Windows NT Networking. The following sections describe the Networking phase of the setup.

Network Participation

The next screen asks if your computer will participate in a network and if so, whether it will be wired to the network or whether it will access the network through a modem. Click Yes if your computer will be part of a network. If you intend to connect via both a modem and an ISDN adapter or network adapter, check both boxes.

If you click the No button (indicating that your computer will not participate in a network), the wizard proceeds to Phase 3, "Finishing Setup."

Internet/Intranet Service

When you're installing Windows NT Server, Setup asks if you want to install Internet Information Server 2.0 (IIS); the default is to install IIS. It should be noted that, as of the printing of this book, the current version of IIS is 4.0, and it can be obtained by downloading the Windows NT 4.0 Option Pack from www.microsoft.com.

Network Adapter Card

The next screen asks if you want Setup to search for your network adapter card. Click on Start Search if you know that NT will detect your card or if you have never let NT try to detect this kind of card before. Setup stops after it finds the first card, and the Start Search button changes into a Find Next button. If you have another network adapter card, choose Find Next.

If NT does not detect your card, you can choose Select from List to select your adapter card from a list. Or, you can click the Have Disk button in the Select Network Adapter dialog box if you want to install the software for the adapter card. To install the driver manually, you need to obtain a Windows NT 4 driver from your vendor and supply the path to the driver in the dialog box.

If Setup successfully autodetects your network adapter card, it displays its findings so that you can confirm the network adapter card and its settings. If it cannot detect the card, Setup expects you to manually select a network adapter card from a list of drivers supplied with Windows NT.

After selecting or confirming your network adapter card, you may see a dialog box with card configuration options. These options might include the interrupt request (IRQ), base I/O address, transceiver type, and other card-specific parameters. Confirm these options before proceeding because Windows NT doesn't always pick all of these up correctly, especially if you added your card manually (skipping detection). It is worth noting that some network cards cannot be configured from within, and their settings must be changed using utilities that come with the cards.

If you don't have a network card, you can still install the networking services on top of the Remote Access Service (RAS). You'll be prompted to install RAS during Setup only if you do not select a network card at all. See Chapter 7, "Connectivity," for more information about RAS.

Network Protocols

The next screen enables you to specify networking protocols for your network. You can check TCP/IP, NWLink, IPX/SPX Compatible Transport, or NetBEUI. Click Select from List to access a new window with some additional options, including AppleTalk, DLC, Point to Point Tunneling Protocol, and Streams Environment. This new window also provides a Have Disk option, which you can use if you want to install your own protocol software.

By default, only TCP/IP is installed on an Intel-based computer. You should carefully consider your current network configuration and your needs before you accept the default protocols, however. If your network currently runs mostly NetWare, you might want to use NWLink instead of TCP/IP. If your network uses both NetWare and UNIX, you might want both NWLink and TCP/IP. If your network is a small self-contained workgroup, you might want to use NetBEUI only. See Chapter 1, "Planning," for more information about network transport protocols.

Network Services

When the basic network options are established, Setup asks what optional network services you want to install.

The other chapters of this book discuss many of the network service options. If you don't install a particular service during Setup, you can always add it later by using the Services tab of the Control Panel's Network application.

Network Components

Setup asks if you want to change any of your previous choices, and then it proceeds to install your networking components. Depending on the components and options you selected, various dialog boxes may appear as the components are installed. The Setup Wizard might try to find your modem, for example, or you might be asked whether you want to use Dynamic Host Configuration Protocol (DHCP). You also might be prompted for the IP address and default gateway.

After installing the network components, Setup announces that it's ready to start the network so you can complete the network installation. Setup asks for the name of the workgroup or domain to which your computer will belong. Select Workgroup or Domain, and then type the name.

If Setup successfully starts the network, it immediately begins to copy additional files, which takes a few minutes. If Setup is unsuccessful at starting the network, it asks if you want to change your network adapter card's configuration parameters. It's a good idea not to proceed any further until the network starts correctly—particularly if you're doing a network installation—because if your computer doesn't have a CD-ROM drive, you may find yourself unable to load additional drivers after Windows NT restarts. If you cannot get the network to start after multiple attempts, go ahead and proceed with the installation, but you won't be able to join a domain until the network services are successfully started.

If you have installed networking components, you must join either a domain or a workgroup; you cannot join both.

Joining a workgroup requires nothing more than providing the name of that workgroup. The workgroup doesn't have to exist prior to this point; you can create it just by joining it. In a workgroup, everyone is an administrator. Every Windows NT-based computer has its own account database, and sharing resources between computers requires an immense amount of administration or a significant lack of security.

If you're installing a Windows NT server as a member server in a domain, that domain must already exist; that is, a primary domain controller (PDC) must be defined and available on the network. If Setup cannot find a Windows NT Server acting as a primary domain controller for that domain on the network, you can't join the domain. This is necessary because, in order to join a domain, a computer account must be either created or verified to exist on the PDC for that domain. If this computer account has not already been created by an administrator using Server Manager on the PDC, you will be prompted for an account and password that has the user right "create computer accounts in the domain."

> **WARNING**
>
> **You Cannot Install a BDC If the Network Will Not Start**   If you are trying to install a BDC and the network will not start, you must resolve your networking problem before you can continue. You do not have the choice of proceeding without installing the network because BDC status requires NT to contact the PDC during the installation to receive the accounts database. If you cannot get the network to start, all you can do is cancel the installation, resolve your problems, and then begin the installation again.

Phase 3: Finishing Setup

After the network components are installed, setup is almost complete. The Setup Wizard announces that you are ready for Phase 3: Finishing Setup. The following sections describe the Phase 3 installation steps.

Time Zone

You can set your computer's current date and time and select the appropriate time zone from a Setup dialog box. Specify the date and time on the Date & Time tab. Specify a time zone on the Time Zone tab. If you choose a time zone that switches from standard time to daylight savings time and back, it is possible to have Windows NT automatically make this change for you. To do so, select the Automatically Adjust Clock for Daylight Savings Changes check box.

Exchange Configuration

If you chose to install Microsoft Exchange as an optional component in Phase 1, Setup now requests some information for configuring Exchange.

Display Settings

Setup detects the video display adapter. If the adapter uses a chipset that Windows NT can detect, the name of the chipset appears onscreen.

You must confirm the video driver that NT chooses. If you want to change it, you must wait until setup is complete. Then you can come back to the video configuration and modify the video drivers. If the video drivers have been detected properly, you can change video resolution, number of colors, and video refresh rate at this time.

If you make changes, Setup doesn't let you proceed until you test the settings you have selected. Because Windows NT cannot detect your monitor settings, you could pick a resolution or refresh rate that your card supports but that your monitor does not. When you click on the Test button, the screen briefly goes blank, and then a test pattern appears. If everything looks okay, confirm the settings for the card when the Windows NT Setup interface returns. Otherwise, choose a new setting and click Test again. If your test is unsuccessful, Windows NT probably doesn't work right under that setting.

A few monitors go blank and stay blank during testing, even though the chosen settings are supported. If that happens during your installation and you're sure that both the adapter card and monitor support your configuration, you can lie and tell Setup that the test was

WARNING

Watch Out for Specific Time Zones!   Note that certain geographical locations (such as Arizona in the U.S. and Saskatchewan in Canada) have their own time zones because they do not follow daylight savings time rules like other regions in their physical area. If this is the case for your time zone, be sure to choose the correct time zone for your location.

successful. If Windows NT restarts in an unusable video state when you reboot, reboot again and choose Boot Loader, Windows NT Server 4.0 [VGA mode].

Pentium Patch

The last bit of detection Setup performs is for the presence of the Intel Pentium floating-point division error. If you get an error, Setup asks you if you want to disable the floating-point hardware and enable floating-point emulation software.

Disabling the hardware makes your floating-point calculations much more accurate, but at the expense of performance (because the software isn't as fast as the native floating-point hardware). The nice thing about this software solution, however, is that Windows NT continues to detect the hardware error every time it boots. If and when the processor is upgraded to an error-free Pentium or higher processor, the emulation software will be automatically disabled, and the floating-point hardware will be re-enabled.

Emergency Repair Directory and Disk

When installation is almost complete, Setup copies files to your Windows NT root directory. The screen then clears except for a progress gauge called Saving Configuration. Setup is now backing up the configuration Registry files to the \REPAIR directory it created in the Windows NT root directory. This procedure may take a few minutes, but when it is complete, the \REPAIR directory will contain the information necessary to repair most damaged Windows NT installations.

If you previously told Setup you wanted to create an Emergency Repair Disk (refer to the section "Emergency Disk," earlier in this chapter), Setup now creates an Emergency Repair Disk. Insert a disk into the floppy drive. (The disk you supply does not have to be blank or formatted.) Setup automatically formats the disk to ensure that it has no media errors. When it finishes creating the Emergency Repair Disk, Setup informs you that installation is complete and prompts you to reboot.

UNINSTALLING WINDOWS NT

If you no longer want Windows NT Server on your computer, you can remove it using a variety of methods, depending on how much of the information resident on your computer you want to preserve. For example, removing NT from a machine that is dual-booting with Windows 95 is a different process than removing NT from a machine on which it is the only operating system.

If you are dual-booting Windows NT and another operating system (such as MS-DOS or Windows 95), create a startup disk for the other operating system before you uninstall Windows NT. If MS-DOS, Windows 3.x, or Windows 95 doesn't boot properly after you remove NT, boot to the startup disk and type SYS C: to reinstall your system files onto the hard drive.

> **WARNING**
>
> **Use the Add/Remove Programs Applet**   To create a startup disk in Windows 95, go to the Add/Remove Programs applet in Control Panel and select the Startup Disk tab.

STEP BY STEP

2.1: Removing Windows NT Server from Your Computer

1. Remove all the NTFS partitions from within Windows NT and reformat them with FAT (this ensures that these disk areas will be accessible by non-NT operating systems).

   If the system and/or boot partitions are on NTFS partitions, boot to DOS with a floppy disk and use FDISK or DELPART to remove the NTFS partitions; the FDISK that comes with DOS 6.x and Windows 95 is capable of removing NTFS partitions. If you use this method, NT is

   continues

continued

removed from your machine and you can install another operating system—or at the very least, SYS (the system partition) to make it bootable again.

2. Boot to another operating system, such as Windows 95 or MS-DOS.

3. Delete the Windows NT installation directory tree (usually WINNT).

4. Delete pagefile.sys.

5. Turn off the Hidden, System, and Read-Only attributes for NTBOOTDD.SYS, BOOT.INI, NTLDR, and NTDETECT.COM, and then delete those files. You might not have all of these on your computer, but they would all be located in the root directory of your drive C.

6. Make the hard drive bootable by placing another operating system on it (or SYS it with DOS or Windows 95 to allow the operating system that does exist to boot).

CLIENT ADMINISTRATOR INSTALLATION AIDS

The Network Client Administrator application, in the Administrative Tools group, lets you configure your Windows NT Server system to assist you with the process of installing client machines on the network. Figure 2.1 shows the Network Client Administrator dialog box.

The first two options are designed to help with installing network clients:

◆ *Make Network Installation Startup Disk* shares the client installation files on the network and creates an installation startup

FIGURE 2.1
The Network Client Administrator dialog box gives you options for creating installation disks for a variety of clients and for updating the cur-

disk you can use to connect to the server from the client machine and then download the installation files.

◆ *Make Installation Disk Set* creates a set of floppies you can use to install network client software on a client computer.

The following sections discuss these two installation options.

Network Installation Startup Disk

The Make Network Installation Startup Disk option in the Network Client Administrator enables you to set up a share containing installation files and then create a network startup floppy disk that will enable you to connect to the installation files from the client machine. Client Administrator adds the necessary files to an MS-DOS system disk so that you can boot from the disk and connect to the network share.

You can use this option to create a network startup disk for any of the following operating systems:

◆ Windows NT Server versions 3.5, 3.51, 4.0

◆ Windows NT Workstation versions 3.5, 3.51, 4.0

◆ Windows 95

◆ Windows for Workgroups version 3.11

◆ Microsoft Network Client for MS-DOS version 3.0

The installation files for Windows 95 and Microsoft Network Client for MS-DOS are included on the Windows NT Server CD-ROM, and you'll have the option of copying them to the share you create through Client Administrator. If you plan to install a Windows NT Server, Windows NT Workstation, or Windows for Workgroups system, either manually copy the installation files from the appropriate CD-ROM to the shared directory on the installation server or use the Copy Files to a New Directory, and Then Share option when using the Network Client Administrator.

EXAM TIP

Intel Computers Only   The Windows NT Server and Workstation startup disks work only for Intel computers.

Although Windows 95 installation files are included on the Windows NT Server CD-ROM, you still have to purchase a license for each Windows 95 client you install. The same applies to Windows NT Server, Windows NT Workstation, and Windows for Workgroups installation files that you copy from the appropriate CD-ROM to the installation drive. As with any Windows installation, you are limited to one install per license. You are, however, at liberty to install Microsoft Client for MS-DOS as many times as you want.

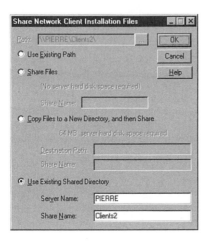

FIGURE 2.2
The Share Network Client Installation Files dialog box.

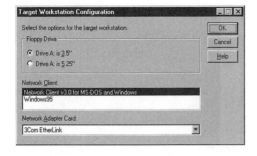

FIGURE 2.3
The Target Workstation Configuration dialog box.

STEP BY STEP

2.2 Creating a Network Installation Startup Disk

1. Select the Make Network Installation Startup Disk radio button in the Network Client Administrator dialog box. The Share Network Client Installation Files dialog box appears (see Figure 2.2).

2. You can either copy the files to your hard disk and share them, or you can share them directly from the Windows NT Server CD-ROM.

   Click the Share Files radio button to share the files directly from the CD-ROM (which doesn't require any hard disk space). Choose the Copy Files to a New Directory, and then Share radio button to copy the files to your hard disk (you'll need 64MB of hard disk space). The Use Existing Shared Directory radio button tells Client Administrator to set up the installation disk to use an existing share; if you choose it, you can specify a server name and a share name.

   When you have configured the location of the installation files, click OK.

3. The Target Workstation Configuration dialog box appears (see Figure 2.3). Specify the size of the floppy disk, the type of network client software, and a network adapter card for the client machine. Then click OK.

4. The Network Startup Disk Configuration dialog box appears. Specify a computer name, user name, domain,

network protocol, and any TCP/IP settings for the client machine. The Destination Path is the path to the floppy drive.

5. Insert a formatted high-density MS-DOS system disk in the destination drive and click on OK.

6. You now can use the network installation startup disk to boot the client machine and connect to the installation files.

Make Installation Disk Set

The Make Installation Disk Set radio button in the Network Client Administrator dialog box enables you to create a set of floppy installation disks you can use to install the following network client packages:

◆ Microsoft Network Client 3.0 for MS-DOS and Windows

◆ Microsoft LAN Manager 2.2c for MS-DOS

◆ Microsoft LAN Manager 2.2c for OS/2

◆ Microsoft Remote Access Service Client version 1.1 for MS-DOS

◆ Microsoft TCP/IP for Windows for Workgroups

STEP BY STEP

2.3 Making an Installation Disk Set

1. In the Network Client Administrator dialog box, select the Make Installation Disk Set radio button and click on Continue. The Share Network Client Installation Files dialog box appears (refer to Figure 2.2 and discussion in the preceding section).

2. After that, you'll see the Make Installation Disk Set dialog box (shown in Figure 2.4). Choose the network software you want to install on the client, choose a destination drive, and click on OK.

FIGURE 2.4
The Make Installation Disk Set dialog box.

CHAPTER SUMMARY

KEY TERMS

Before taking the exam, make sure you are familiar with the definitions of and concepts behind each of the following key terms. Appendix A provides a glossary of terms for quick reference purposes.

- Hardware Compatibility List
- multi-boot
- primary domain controller (PDC)
- backup domain controller (BDC)
- member server
- standalone server
- WINNT.EXE
- WINNT32.EXE
- Emergency Repair Disk
- licensing mode
- network protocols
- Network Services
- workgroup
- domain
- installation disk set

Summarized briefly, this chapter covered the following main points.

- ◆ *Installing Windows NT Server on Intel-based platforms.* This includes ensuring that the CD-ROM drive, 3 ½" floppy drive, VGA card, and network card are present in the machine and are on the Windows NT HCL. This also includes planning for multiple booting machines (if that is a consideration) and recognizing that NT Server can, but is not limited to, multibooting with NT Workstation, Windows 95, MS-DOS, and OS/2.

- ◆ *Installing Windows NT Server to perform various server roles.* These roles include both domain controllers (primary and backup) and member servers (standalone servers if the NT machine is not to participate in a domain). This chapter focused not only on the fact that these roles were available, but that a movement from domain controller to non-domain controller (or vice versa) is not possible without a reinstallation of NT Server.

- ◆ *Installing Windows NT Server by using various methods.* These methods included installation with a set of setup disks and a CD-ROM and network installation (the most popular types of installations on an Intel platform). We also discussed the various switches available with the WINNT or WINNT32 installation programs.

Installation and configuration of NT Server form a major component of the exam. Correct understanding of and ability to implement installation and configuration are essential both to passing the exam and to working with NT in the real world. Once the concepts in Chapter 1 ("Planning") are understood and you have installed and configured your NT server, you are ready for the management of NT resources. Before you look at that chapter, however, apply your knowledge with some exercises and questions that will reinforce this chapter's concepts.

APPLY YOUR LEARNING

Exercises

2.1 Creating an NT Setup Diskette Set

In Exercise 2.1, you learn how to create the three-disk set required for installing Windows NT and required for repairing your server using the Emergency Repair Disk (discussed in Chapter 9, "Troubleshooting"). This will introduce you to one of the fundamental installation and repair tools that you will always need to keep on hand.

Estimated Time: 10 minutes

1. From any computer running Windows NT 4.0, format three floppy disks using this method.

    a. Open My Computer

    b. Insert the first disk into the drive (ensure it is not write protected).

    c. Right-click the floppy disk icon and choose Format from the pull-down menu.

    d. When the Format dialog box appears, click the Start button at the bottom.

    e. Repeat c and d for each disk.

2. Insert the Windows NT Server 4.0 CD-ROM into the CD-ROM drive of the above-mentioned Windows NT 4.0 machine.

3. From the Start menu, choose Run. In the dialog box that appears, type the following:

    ```
    <CD-DRIVE>:\I386\WINNT32 /OX
    ```

    where *<CD-DRIVE>* is the letter of your CD-ROM drive.

    Figure 2.5 shows the dialog box that appears upon successful initiation of WINNT32.

FIGURE 2.5
This dialog box asks you to confirm the location of the files necessary to create the NT setup disks.

4. Click the Continue button in the Windows NT 4.0 Upgrade/Installation dialog box. Figure 2.6 shows the message box that appears.

FIGURE 2.6
This dialog box prompts you to continue the creation of the setup disks by inserting a blank disk and clicking OK.

5. Label a formatted disk (created in step 1) "Windows NT Server Setup Disk #3" and insert it into the floppy drive. Click the OK button to continue.

6. When you're prompted to do so, label a formatted disk "Windows NT Server Setup Disk #2" and insert it into the floppy drive. Click the OK button to continue.

7. When you're prompted to do so, label a formatted disk "Windows NT Server Setup Boot Disk" and insert it into the floppy drive. Click the OK button to continue.

8. When the process is complete, remove the final disk and put the set away pending disk use.

2.2   Installing a Primary Domain Controller on an Intel Platform

Exercise 2.2 shows you how to install Windows NT Server in the role of a primary domain controller on your network. Be aware that because hardware configuration varies from system to system, you will need to know how NT references network adapter drivers and video drivers on your particular system. In order to complete this exercise you will need the following:

◆ A computer capable of supporting Windows NT Server (with a CD-ROM drive)

◆ The three setup disks you created in Exercise 2.1

◆ A formatted disk to use as an Emergency Repair Disk

◆ The Windows NT Server 4.0 CD-ROM

Estimated Time: 45 minutes

1. Power off your machine, insert Disk 1 of the three-disk set, and power the machine back on.

2. When prompted, insert Disk #2 and press Enter to continue.

3. When the "Welcome to Setup" screen appears, press Enter to continue.

4. When the screen appears asking whether you want Setup to detect mass storage devices, press Enter to continue.

5. When prompted, insert Disk #3 and press Enter to continue. At this point, drivers for mass storage devices will be loaded, and yours will be detected.

6. When Setup returns with a list of mass storage devices in your system, press Enter to continue.

7. When prompted, insert the NT Server CD-ROM into your CD-ROM drive. Press Enter to continue.

8. When the license agreement page appears, press the Page Down key to move to the end of the document, and then press the F8 key to accept the agreement.

9. When the detected hardware components list appears, press Enter to continue.

10. When the list of partitions appears, use the up and down arrow keys to select the one on which you want to install NT. Then press Enter to continue.

11. When prompted for the file system, choose the default option of Leave the Current File System Intact. Press Enter.

12. A prompt appears, indicating that the default path for the NT program files is WINNT. Press Enter to accept that location.

13. Press Enter to initiate a thorough scan of your hard drives in preparation for NT installation.

    Once the Setup program has scanned the disks, it will begin to copy files from the CD-ROM to a temporary place on your hard drive in preparation for the installation of NT.

14. When prompted, remove the disk from your floppy drive and press Enter to reboot to the GUI portion of setup (you do not need to remove your Windows NT CD-ROM).

15. When the Windows NT Server Setup dialog box appears with selection 1 highlighted, press Enter to allow NT to gather information about your computer.

APPLY YOUR LEARNING

16. When prompted, enter your name, press Tab, enter your organization (optional), and press Enter.

17. When prompted, enter the key pasted on the back of your NT Server CD-ROM and press Enter to continue.

18. When the Licensing Modes screen appears, enter **10** in the Per Server field and press Enter.

19. When the Computer Name screen appears, enter the name **TRAIN_SERVER** and press Enter.

20. When the Server Type screen appears, press Enter to accept the role of primary domain controller.

21. In the Administrator Account screen, enter the word **password** in both the Password and Confirm Password fields and press Enter.

22. In the Emergency Repair Disk screen, press Enter to accept the creation of an ERD.

23. On the Select Components screen, click the check box beside Accessories to clear the box, and then click it again to select all the accessories. Then press Enter to continue.

24. When the Windows NT Setup screen appears with selection 2 highlighted, press Enter to install networking.

25. When prompted, click the Next button to indicate that you are wired to the network.

26. When you're asked if you want to install IIS, clear the check box and press Enter.

27. To set up a network adapter, click the Start Search button. If an adapter appears, click the Next button; if not, either click the Select from List button and choose your network adapter

from the list or click the Have Disk button and specify the driver's location on the floppy disk. Click the Next button to go to the Protocols screen.

28. When prompted for protocols, make sure that only TCP/IP is selected and press Enter to continue.

29. When prompted for Network Services, press Enter to accept the defaults.

30. When you're prompted to do so, press Enter to complete the networking installation. If configuration dialog boxes appear, configure your network adapter appropriately for its correct operation.

31. When the TCP/IP setup dialog box appears, press Enter to accept the default of no address acquisition from a DHCP server (you will configure TCP/IP yourself).

32. When the Microsoft TCP/IP Properties dialog box opens, configure it with the following settings:

IP address: 10.10.10.1

Subnet mask: 255.255.255.0

Default gateway: (leave this blank)

Press Enter to continue.

33. When the bindings page appears, press Enter to accept the defaults.

34. When prompted to start the network, press Enter.

35. When prompted for computer and domain names, click in the Domain field and type **TRAINING**. Then press Enter.

APPLY YOUR LEARNING

36. When the Windows NT Setup screen appears with selection 3 highlighted, press Enter to finish setup.

37. When the Date/Time properties dialog box appears, click the drop-down arrow next to the default time zone (GMT) and select your time zone from the list.

38. Click the Date/Time tab and make sure that the date and time indicated are correct. Then press Enter to continue.

39. When the Detected Display dialog box appears, press Enter to accept the video adapter that NT finds.

40. In the Display Properties dialog box, select the desired number of colors and the desired resolution, and then click the Test button to test the choices for correct operation. When prompted, press the Enter key to initiate the display test.

    At this point, the screen will display a test pattern. If the pattern does not appear, indicate that you did not see the bitmap properly and change your settings so that they work. If the pattern appears to be fine, click the Yes button. Finally, click OK to accept the message displayed in the message box that follows; you will return to the setup screen.

41. Press the Enter key to continue. Setup will copy the files required by your selections and then save your configuration to the hard drive.

42. When prompted, insert a floppy disk labeled "Emergency Repair Disk" into the floppy drive and press Enter to create the ERD.

43. Finally, remove the ERD and press Enter to restart your computer. The installation is complete.

Review Questions

1. What must you do to change a member server into a backup domain controller?

2. What programs are available to install Windows NT Server over a network, and in what context is each used?

3. To install Windows NT Server on an Intel-based machine without a network connection, what do you need?

4. What are the minimum hardware requirements (processor, RAM, and free disk space) for the installation of Windows NT Server on an Intel-based computer?

5. To uninstall Windows NT server, what steps must you take?

6. What are the four roles an NT server can be configured for?

7. In order to install a backup domain controller, what must you first have done?

Exam Questions

1. You're considering purchasing a file server for the Accounting department to run Windows NT Server 4. What's the first thing you should do?

    A. Verify that all the hardware to be contained in the server is on Microsoft's Hardware Compatibility List (HCL).

    B. Purchase the parts and put the server together yourself so you know you're obtaining a quality computer.

    C. Buy the server hardware only from a reputable dealer licensed to sell Microsoft Windows NT Server.

D. Contact Microsoft and ask them to direct you to a Microsoft-certified hardware vendor in your area.

2. You're installing Windows NT Server 4 on a machine that has an existing installation of OS/2. After the final reboot of the installation program, you notice that the OS/2 boot manager menu isn't appearing. What could be the problem?

A. When you installed NT you actually upgraded from OS/2 to NT, thus overwriting the OS/2 installation.

B. Nothing; you can't boot OS/2 when Windows NT 4 is installed.

C. Windows NT has disabled the boot manager, and you need to re-enable it via Disk Administrator by marking the Boot Manager active.

D. Nothing, but you need to install DOS, create a FAT partition, and then reinstall OS/2.

3. When you installed Windows NT Server 4, during the installation process, you selected Server as the type of installation. You now want to make the server a backup domain controller. What must you do to convert the server?

A. Nothing. The next time you restart the server, simply select NT Server - Domain Controller from the boot menu.

B. Under Control Panel, System, change the server type to Domain Controller.

C. Under Control Panel, Network, change the server type to Domain Controller.

D. You cannot change the server from a member server to a domain controller unless you reinstall NT Server.

4. Which of the following must a domain have? (Select all that apply.)

A. A BDC and a PDC

B. Only a BDC

C. A PDC

D. A PDC and at least one BDC

5. What is the main difference between an NT Server acting as a domain controller and an NT Server not installed as a domain controller?

A. A domain controller maintains a copy of the directory database; a non-domain controller does not.

B. A non-domain controller maintains a copy of the directory database; a domain controller does not.

C. A non-domain controller validates user logons; a domain controller does not.

D. NT Server 4 cannot be installed as a domain controller.

6. You want to install NT Server on four new servers simultaneously. Which installation method would provide you with the fastest installation?

A. Floppy disk

B. CD-ROM

C. Over-the-network

D. Direct cable connection through the COM ports

APPLY YOUR LEARNING

7. What must you do to perform an NT installation using the over-the-network method?

   A. Copy the entire CD-ROM contents to a Web server, and then access the server installation files using a Web browser installed on the new server.

   B. Install from the CD-ROM to an existing NT Server, and then transfer the program files to the new server by using the NetTransfer program included on the CD-ROM.

   C. First either copy a hardware-specific installation directory from the CD-ROM to a share point on an existing server or share the directory directly from the CD-ROM. Then connect to the share point using a network-aware client and run the WINNT or WINNT32 program.

   D. Purchase a CD-ROM drive that has an Ethernet card in it and share the CD-ROM over the network. Then run the client software on the computer on which you are going to install NT and run the WINNT program.

8. To save time, you want to install Windows NT without first making the three boot floppies. Which command-line switch should you use with the WINNT program to bypass that step?

   A. /OX

   B. /NF

   C. /O

   D. /B

9. You're upgrading from Windows NT 3.5 to 4. How should you proceed with the installation?

   A. Restart the computer in DOS and run the WINNT program from the CD-ROM.

   B. In the Program Manager, choose the File, Run command and run the WINNT program.

   C. In the Program Manager, choose the File, Run command and run the WINNT32 program.

   D. You cannot directly upgrade to NT 4 because of the new user interface. You must install a fresh copy.

10. While installing NT Server, you were prompted for a computer name. Which statement best describes the purpose of the computer name?

    A. The computer name is the NetBIOS name. It identifies the computer on the network. It's okay to have two computers with the same computer name as long as they are separated by a router.

    B. The computer name is the NetBIOS name. It identifies the computer on the network. Under no circumstances should two computers have the same name.

    C. The computer name identifies the computer to the domain controller. The computer name must be at least two characters and must include the domain name as part of the computer name.

    D. Computer names are case-sensitive and must be entered when the user logs on to the computer for the first time.

APPLY YOUR LEARNING

11. What is the default network protocol installed with Windows NT on an Intel-based platform?

    A. NetBEUI

    B. AppleTalk

    C. IPX/SPX

    D. TCP/IP

12. A user calls you and asks how he can make his NT Server a member of a workgroup and domain. He needs to share files with users in his department and access the file server at the same time. How does he make his server a member of both the workgroup and the domain at the same time?

    A. He cannot. An NT Server computer cannot be a member of a domain and a workgroup at the same time.

    B. Under Control Panel, Network enter the workgroup name and the domain name, and then restart the server.

    C. He can be a member of both only if the workgroup and domain names are the same.

    D. He needs to reinstall Windows NT Server and specify the domain and workgroup during the installation.

13. A user calls you and states that during the course of installing NT Server as a member server, he tried to enter the domain name when prompted but could not continue. The computer said something along the lines of You do not have sufficient authority to join the domain. Without reinstalling his software, what do you need to do so that he can join the domain?

    A. Nothing. A Windows NT Server cannot be a member of a domain, only a workgroup.

    B. Grant his domain userid the authority to create computer accounts in the domain and tell him to try it again.

    C. Give him the domain administrator's userid and password and tell him to try it again.

    D. Create a computer account for the user in Server Manager and ask him to try entering the domain name again.

14. You're trying to install Windows NT on a RISC-based computer. Which of the following requirements must you meet?

    A. A Microsoft-certified hardware reseller must supply the RISC-based computer, and the vender must install NT on the computer.

    B. You must install NT from a CD-ROM and have at least a 2MB FAT partition.

    C. You must install NT using the over-the-network installation method because NT doesn't support CD-ROM devices on RISC-based computers.

    D. You must request the special RISC-based CD-ROM when ordering Windows NT.

15. Which statement best describes the differences between a per server license and a per seat license?

    A. In per server license mode, a certain number of connections are assigned to the server; in per seat mode, a license is assigned to each client connecting to the server.

    B. In per seat mode, a certain number of connections are assigned to the server; in per seat

APPLY YOUR LEARNING

mode, a license is assigned to each client connecting to the server.

C. You can convert from a per seat license to a per server license for a one-time charge from Microsoft.

D. You can convert from a per server license to a per seat license for a one-time charge from Microsoft.

Answers to Review Questions

1. There is no configuration option for changing a member server into a BDC. You must reinstall NT Server in that role. For more information, see the section "Choosing a Server Type."

2. Two programs are available for installing NT Server over the network: WINNT and WINNT32. They are virtually identical except for one distinguishing feature: WINNT32 can only be used to install NT Server from a machine already running NT. WINNT is used for all other NT Server Network installations. For more information, see the section "Installation Procedure."

3. At minimum, you need the Windows NT Server CD-ROM and a CD-ROM drive in your computer, and if the operating system you are installing from does not recognize the CD-ROM drive, you need the three setup disks. For more information, see the section "Intel Requirements."

4. To install Windows NT Server you need the following minimum hardware requirements: a 486DX-33 processor, 16MB of RAM, and

125MB of free hard disk space. For more information, see the section "Intel Requirements."

5. To uninstall NT server, you must do the following:

a) Remove all the NTFS partitions.

b) Remove the Windows NT boot directory (usually WINNT).

c) Delete pagefile.sys.

d) Delete NTBOOTDD.SYS, BOOT.INI, NTLDR, and NTDETECT.COM.

e) Make the hard drive bootable by placing another operating system on it.

For more information, see the section "Uninstalling Windows NT."

6. NT Server can be configured for the following four roles: primary domain controller, backup domain controller, member server in a domain, and standalone server in a workgroup. For more information, see the section "Choosing a Server Type."

7. In order to install a backup domain controller, you must first have installed and started a primary domain controller for the domain in which the BDC is to be a member. If you do not do that first, the installation of the BDC will fail. For more information, see the section "The Installation Phases."

Answers to Exam Questions

1. **A.** In order to ensure that all hardware in the server is compatible with NT 4.0, you should check it against the most current version of the

HCL. For more information, see the section "Hardware Requirements."

2. **C.** By marking the OS/2 partition as active, you can again boot to it. For more information, see the section "Multiboot Requirements."

3. **D.** You cannot change a server's function from a non-domain controller to a domain controller without reinstalling NT. For more information, see the section "Choosing a Server Type."

4. **C.** A domain is defined by the configuration of its PDC. A domain cannot exist if a PDC has not been installed. For more information, see the section "Choosing a Server Type."

5. **A.** In a domain, every domain controller maintains a copy of the directory database, which enables it to validate the logins of domain users. For more information, see the section "Choosing a Server Type."

6. **C.** By copying the contents of a hardware-specific installation directory onto a file server and then sharing that directory, you can ensure that your simultaneous installations will be smooth and fast. For more information, see the section "Installation Procedure."

7. **C.** In order to install NT over the network, you must connect to a share containing a copy of the hardware-specific installation files (in this case, I386), and then you must run the WINNT or WINNT32 program from that share. For more information, see the section "Installation Procedure."

8. **D.** The /OX switch ensures that you will never be prompted to create the setup floppy disks during the installation process. For more information, see the section "Installation Procedure."

9. **C.** To install Windows NT (whether a new installation or an upgrade) from another NT version, you must use the WINNT32 program. For more information, see the section "Installation Procedure."

10. **B.** NetBIOS names are used by many programs to identify computers on the network. You can never have a computer, domain, or workgroup name that is the same, whether the computers are on a single LAN or a routed WAN. For more information, see the section "The Installation Phases."

11. **D.** When you install Windows NT Server, the TCP/IP protocol is the default. For more information, see the section "The Installation Phases."

12. **A.** A computer cannot be a member of both a domain and a workgroup at the same time; it must be one or the other. For more information, see the section "the Installation Phases."

13. **D.** In order for a Windows NT computer to participate in a domain, a computer account must be created for a machine. It is not desirable to give the user the ability to create computer accounts (there is probably a reason why he does not already have this permission), so it is best for you to create this account and then have him enter the domain name and try again. For more information, see the section "The Installation Phases."

14. **B.** On a RISC machine, you must install NT from a CD-ROM, and the system partition must be FAT. This system partition can be as small as 2MB. For more information, see the section "Hardware Requirements."

15. **A, D.** In per server license mode, you indicate how many concurrent connections can be made to a specific machine. If that limit is reached,

APPLY YOUR LEARNING

additional users will be prevented from connecting to the sever. In per seat license mode, each user is licensed to make as many concurrent connections to as many servers as necessary. No limits are imposed by any servers. You can upgrade from per server to per seat for a one-time charge. For more information, see the section "The Installation Phases."

APPLY YOUR LEARNING

Suggested Readings and Resources

The following are some recommended readings in the area of installation:

1. Microsoft Official Curriculum course 922: *Supporting Microsoft Windows NT 4.0 Core Technologies*

   • Module 2: Installing Windows NT

2. *MS Windows NT Server 4.0 Networking Guide* (Microsoft Press)

   • Chapter 2: Network Security and Domain Planning

3. *MS Windows NT Server 4.0 Resource Guide* (Microsoft Press)

   • Chapter 1: Deploying Windows NT Server

4. Web sites

   • www.microsoft.com/ntserver

   • www.microsoft.com/train_cert

   • www.prometric.com/testingcandidates/ assessment/chosetest.html (take online assessment tests)

Microsoft provides the following objectives for the "Network Configuration" portion of "Installation and Configuration":

Configure protocols and protocol bindings. Protocols include: TCP/IP, NWLink IPX/SPX Compatible Transport, and NetBEUI.

▶ This objective is necessary because someone certified in the use of Windows NT Server technology must understand the different protocols that NT supports and the use for each. This extends to the options available when installing each, as well as the circumstances in which it would make sense to install each.

Configure network adapters. Considerations include: Changing IRQ, IO base, and memory addresses and configuring multiple adapters

▶ This objective is necessary because someone certified in the use of Windows NT Server technology must have the ability to understand the installation and configuration of the software component relating to network cards. This will include installing a variety of adapters and knowing how to configure them for proper operation.

Configure Windows NT Server computer for various types of client computers. Client computer types include: Windows NT Workstation; Microsoft Windows 95; Microsoft MS-DOS-based.

▶ This objective is necessary because someone certified in the use of Windows NT Server technology must understand the different clients that are supported by NT Server, the clients that are available on the NT Server CD-ROM, and the protocols required on an NT server to allow these clients to connect. In addition, knowing about the services that NT Server provides and knowing which are available to which clients is also essential.

C H A P T E R 3

Installation and Configuration Part 2: Configuration of NT Server Network Components

Configure Windows NT Server core services. Services include: Directory Replicator, License Manager, and other services.

▶ This objective is necessary because someone certified in the use of Windows NT Server technology must understand the core services that can be provided by an NT Server. This includes services that are configured by default (Replicator and License Manager) as well as services that you install manually (such as DHCP, WINS, and DNS). In addition to understanding that these service are present, you ought to know what they do, how to install them, how to configure them, and what NT Server components must be present for them to function properly.

This chapter will help you prepare for the "Installation and Configuration" section of Microsoft's Exam 70-67. Installing and configuring an NT Server correctly is the first step toward ensuring that your networking environment is stable and easily administered. Testing occurs on all aspects of installation and configuration; be prepared for all sorts of questions regarding the various forms of installation as well as the configuration options available.

▶ Although the installation of protocols is very straightforward, the questions on the exam might be a bit tricky. You will need to know about not only the protocols, but also the environments in which they are used and the connectivity situations in which they are essential. For example, for NetWare connectivity, you will need NWLink. To connect to the Internet, you will need TCP/IP. Of course, you will also need to understand the configuration of each of the protocols, particularly TCP/IP. Therefore, the best strategy is to install the protocols on an NT Server machine and investigate the settings. Remember that TCP/IP can be configured two ways: manually and using DHCP. In addition, you need to know that the TCP/IP configurations that are essential are the IP address and the subnet mask; everything else is optional, including the default gateway.

▶ The NT Server exam does not focus very much on the "Configure Network Adapters" objective. Because the adapter configurations vary greatly, you cannot possibly know the configurations of specific adapters. However, you cannot just ignore this objective because you might get a general question or two about adapter configuration. Knowing the material in this section should sufficiently carry you through the exam questions.

▶ As with the adapter configuration objective, Microsoft does not focus a great deal on configuration for the purposes of supporting clients on its Server exam. You will need to know what clients are available on the NT Server CD-ROM, as well as the protocols and services supported by each. Table 3.1 gives you the required information.

▶ The services discussed in the "Core Services" objective section are those that Microsoft considers to be core to the day-to-day operation of an NT Server. As a result, you will be tested on most of them on a Server exam. Pay particular attention to the functions of the server, workstation, browser, and replication services. You will need to understand what those services do, especially for scenario questions.

Because the server and workstation services have very few, if any, configuration options, all you really need to know is what they do. Likewise, you will need to understand how the browser works, but because you really can't see it operating, a theoretical knowledge of its operation will be sufficient. However, where the browser is concerned, you will need to know how elections work, what the results of a low-level machine winning an election are, and how the browser service is used on the network.

Regarding the Replicator, make sure you know the difference between an import and an export computer and what kinds of machines can serve each function. Also, know how the process of replication works and what gets replicated.

The License Manager is not going to come up very often on an exam. Although it is mentioned in the objective, it is not essential to the function of NT and, therefore, is rarely mentioned on the test. You will need to know what it does, but the information in this chapter is sufficient for the exam.

Of course, you will also need to know where services are installed and where they are managed because you might be asked questions about enabling a service to start when NT starts and how to do that.

INTRODUCTION

This is the second of three chapters covering the "Installation and Configuration" section of the exam. This chapter, "Configuration of NT Server Network Components," deals with the topics surrounding NT and the network environment in which it is installed.

Because NT Server is almost always installed in a networked environment, a knowledge of the configuration of the networking tools and components of NT Server is essential to configuring an NT Server properly and to passing the NT Server exam. As a result, in this chapter you will learn about the basic components of NT Server networking and their configuration. Those components include protocols, adapters, clients, and core services.

CONFIGURING PROTOCOLS AND PROTOCOL BINDINGS

Configure protocols and protocol bindings. Protocols include: TCP/IP, NWLink IPX/SPX Compatible Transport, and NetBEUI.

The Control Panel's Network application is a central location for entering and altering network configuration information. The following list describes the five tabs of the Network application:

◆ *Identification.* The Identification tab specifies the computer name for the computer and the domain to which it belongs (see Figure 3.1). Click the Change button to change the values. If your Windows NT computer is a domain controller, you cannot move to a different domain, but you can change the domain's name using the Change button. If your Windows NT computer is a member server, the Change button offers several alternatives (see Figure 3.2). You can join a workgroup or domain, or you can set up an account for the computer in the domain's security database.

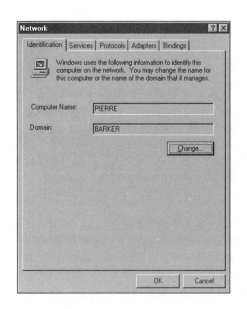

FIGURE 3.1
The Network application's Identification tab.

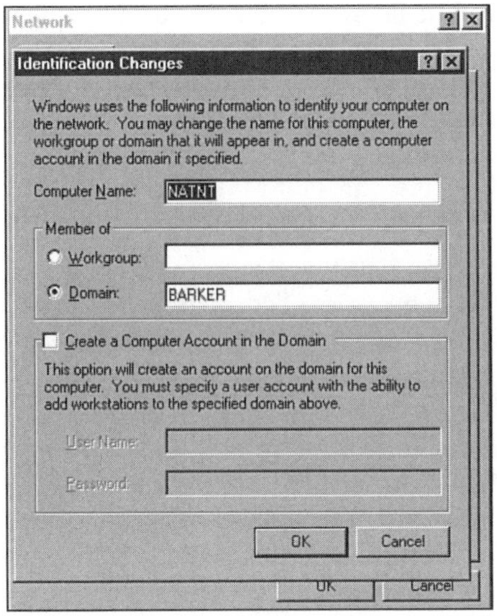

FIGURE 3.2
The Identification Changes dialog box for a non-domain controller, which was invoked from the Network application's Identification tab.

◆ *Services.* The Services tab lets you add, remove, or configure network services (see Figure 3.3). Network services were described earlier in this chapter. Click Add to view a list of available network services, or click the Properties button to view configuration information for the service.

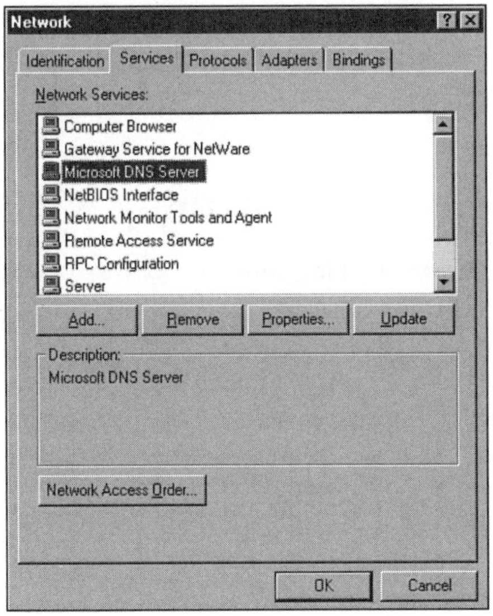

WARNING

Changing the Name of a Domain Controller Can Be Tricky! You must take care when changing the domain name of a Domain controller. In many instances, although the domain name is modified, references to the old domain continue to persist in configurations and databases. If the old domain name still appears in a browse list, for example, people browsing your network may be confused as to which computers and domains are available and which are not (because some domains displayed in Network Neighborhood will not respond). Similarly, if the old domain name remains in the WINS registration database and if you try to name another computer, workgroup, or domain with the name formerly used by the current domain, you might be told that the name is unusable because it is already registered with WINS. Therefore, you should not undertake to change the name of a production domain without giving a lot of thought to the consequences of your action.

FIGURE 3.3
The Network application's Services tab.

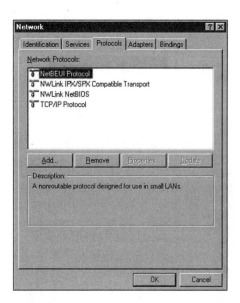

FIGURE 3.4
The Network application's Protocols tab.

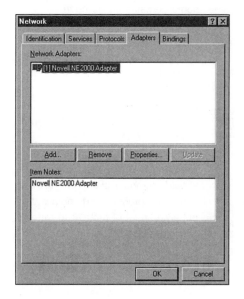

FIGURE 3.5
The Network application's Adapters tab.

◆ *Protocols.* The Protocols tab lets you add, remove, and configure network protocols (see Figure 3.4). Some of the protocol configuration options are discussed later in this chapter.

◆ *Adapters.* The Adapters tab lets you add, remove, and configure network adapter cards for the system (see Figure 3.5). Click Add to view a list of available network adapter card drivers. The Properties button lets you configure the IRQ and port address for some types of adapters (others must be configured using software supplied by the card's manufacturer).

◆ *Bindings.* A binding is a potential pathway from a particular network service to a network protocol to a network adapter. The Bindings tab tabulates the bindings for the system. As you can see in Figure 3.6, the Workstation service is bound to the NetBEUI Protocol, WINS Client (TCP/IP), and NWLink NetBIOS. Click the plus sign beside a protocol to reveal the adapters that are bound to the protocol for the particular service. Much of the binding configuration takes place automatically. If you install Remote Access Service and enable TCP/IP, for example, the Remote Access WAN Wrapper appears beneath the WINS Client (TCP/IP) protocol. It is important to note that the order of bindings is important. The protocol bound closest to the adapter will be the "default" protocol; therefore, you should make sure that—for efficiency sake—the protocol that is to be used most frequently is bound nearest to the card.

Installing and Configuring NWLink

All Windows NT networking components are installed and configured in the Control Panel's Network application. If you want to install the NWLink protocol, choose the Protocols tab and click the Add button. The message Building Network Protocol Option List appears briefly, and then you are prompted to select a networking component.

Select NWLink IPX/SPX Compatible Transport. You need to steer Setup toward the original source files at this point. (You might need to point Setup to the Microsoft Windows NT Server CD-ROM.) If

Remote Access Services is installed on your system, Setup asks if you want to configure RAS to support NWLink. After the NWLink files are installed, an icon labeled NWLink IPX/SPX Compatible Transport appears in the Network Protocols list on the Protocols tab. You must shut down and restart your computer to put the changes into effect. Figure 3.7 shows the NWLink IPX/SPX Properties dialog box.

To reach the NWLink IPX/SPX Properties dialog box, select NWLink IPX/SPX Compatible Transport in the Network application's Protocols tab, and then click the Properties button. Windows NT automatically detects your network adapter during startup. If you know which frame type is in use on your network, you can use this dialog box to manually set Windows NT to match it. By default, Windows NT is configured to autodetect the frame type, which it does by sending out a Routing Information Protocol (RIP) request on all frame types when NWLink is initialized. One of the following scenarios will then occur:

◆ *No response from any of the frame types.* NWLink uses the default frame type, which is 802.2, when Windows NT is first installed.

◆ *A response from one of the frame types.* NWLink uses this frame type, which also becomes the default protocol the next time autodetection occurs.

◆ *Multiple responses are received.* NWLink steps through this list (in order) until it finds a frame type that was one of the multiple responses:

> Ethernet 802.2
>
> Ethernet 802.3
>
> Ethernet II
>
> SNAP

You can configure both Windows NT Workstation and Windows NT Server for multiple frame types, but only for NT Server can you use Control Panel's Network application to set the configuration. If you want Windows NT Workstation to use multiple frame types, you must edit the Registry directly with REGEDIT. To do so, first find the following key:

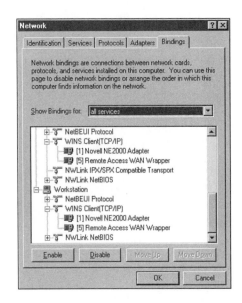

FIGURE 3.6
The Network application's Bindings tab.

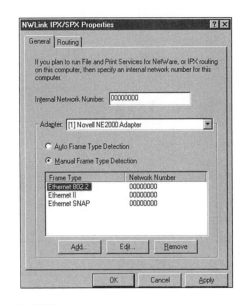

FIGURE 3.7
The NWLink IPX/SPX Properties dialog box.

```
HKEY_LOCAL_MACHINE\SYSTEM\CurrentControlSet\Services\
NWlnkIpx\~NetConfig\<NIC_Driver>
```

Then change the PktType value (which is of type REG_MULTI_SZ) to any combination of the following numbers:

0 Ethernet II

1 Ethernet 802.3

2 Ethernet 802.2

3 Ethernet SNAP

4 ARCnet

Make sure you're using the correct frame type for your network; an incorrect frame type can cause an immense slow down in network performance. If, because Auto Frame Type Detection is selected, you cannot determine what frame type your Windows NT-based computer is using, use the IPXROUTE CONFIG command from the command prompt. As a result, you will get an instant report of the frame type(s) in use.

If you're not sure which frame type(s) your other servers and clients are using, here is a list of the frame types and which particular servers use them:

◆ *802.2.* Windows NT Workstation 3.5x, Windows NT Server 3.5x, NetWare 4.x, NetWare 3.12, Windows for Workgroups 3.11 from the Windows NT Server CD, Microsoft Network Client 3.0

◆ *802.3.* Windows NT 3.1, Windows NT Advanced Server 3.1, NetWare 3.11 and below, Windows for Workgroups 3.x retail.

The operating systems listed here use the specified frame types as their defaults; however, your mileage (as they say) may vary. To verify the frame type on a NetWare server, check its AUTOEXEC.NCF file.

The Network Number field at the bottom of the NWLink IPX/SPX Properties dialog box reveals one additional configuration parameter: the Internal Network Number.

The Internal Network Number is similar to a subnet address on a TCP/IP network: It determines which servers are considered local and which are considered remote. The default setting here is 0, which forces Windows NT to send out a RIP request and wait for the closest NetWare server to respond with the proper internal network number.

Working with TCP/IP

Of all the protocols that ship with Windows NT, TCP/IP requires the most configuration by the administrator. Nevertheless, TCP/IP is an integral part of the Internet, and it's becoming an increasingly popular protocol for private networks as well. The section defines some important TCP/IP concepts, describes how to configure TCP/IP on a Windows NT machine, and looks at some of the important commands and tools that will assist you in implementing TCP/IP on your network. This discussion is by no means complete or exhaustive; NRP's *MCSE Training Guide: TCP/IP* provides a thorough discussion of TCP/IP addressing and configuration. This book discusses the basics—the parameters that are necessary to install any TCP/IP network client. Another good source for information is Drew Heywood's *Networking with Microsoft TCP/IP, 2nd Edition*, also from New Riders.

IP Address

In any type of network, communication between computers is possible only when you have a bulletproof way of uniquely identifying any computer on the network. At the lowest level, packets are sent from one network card to another, and the serial numbers burned into the card itself serve to identify the sender and receiver.

However, because most networks cannot see that far down, they apply another level (or perhaps more than one level) of addressing to ensure compatibility across different platforms. The Internet Protocol (the IP in TCP/IP) sends packets using a computer's IP address (a unique 32-bit binary number that no other computer on the network can possess). But it's about time to stop speaking in terms of computers and begin speaking in terms of network interface cards (NICs): Each NIC requires its own IP address.

Because a 32-bit binary address isn't any easier to remember than the hexadecimal NIC address burned into the card (try

WARNING

TCP/IP Coverage on Server and Enterprise Exams TCP/IP is one of those broad topics that is difficult to position in either the MCSE Server or Enterprise exam. Microsoft's exam objectives include TCP/IP protocols and bindings with the Server exam but reserve TCP/IP-related topics such as DHCP, WINS, and DNS for the Enterprise exam. Nevertheless, it is difficult to even describe how to configure TCP/IP without at least touching on DHCP, WINS, and DNS. Microsoft's Windows NT Core Technologies course includes material on DHCP, WINS, and DNS, and these services are an important component of even smaller Microsoft networks.

100000110110101100000001011001000 on for size!), the 32-bit address usually is expressed as four octets, or eight-bit numbers, which then are presented in decimal form. An eight-bit number can have a value of anywhere from 0 to 255, so an IP address consists of four numbers between 0 and 255, separated by decimal points. The 32-bit binary address in the beginning of this paragraph can also be written like this: 131.107.2.200.

Subnet Mask

Each IP address consists of a netid and a hostid. The *netid* is the leftmost portion of the address (the first one, two, or three octets), and it assigns an address to every NIC on the same physical network shares. If other physical networks are interconnected via routers (these physical networks are called subnetworks or simply, subnets), each of the networks must have its own unique netid. The *hostid* is the rightmost portion of the IP address (the last one, two, or three octets), and a unique hostid must be assigned to every network adapter that shares a common netid.

The netid/hostid split isn't always fifty-fifty; a parameter called the *subnet mask* determines how many bits are devoted to each field. The subnet mask also is a 32-bit number, and each bit set to 1 denotes a bit assigned to the netid; each bit set to 0 denotes a bit assigned to the hostid.

Some platforms' implementations of TCP/IP do not require the administrator to configure a subnet mask. That doesn't mean that the subnet mask isn't required, just that the operating system is using *default subnet masks*. Default subnet masks are defined by these three Internet classes of IP addresses:

◆ *Class A.* The first octet belongs to the netid, and the others belong to the hostid. Class A netids can range from 0 to 127 (although both 0 and 127 are excluded; see the section "The Rules," later in this chapter), which means that there can be only 126 Class A networks in the entire Internet. But because three octets are available for the hostid, each of these 126 networks can host more than 16 million NICs. Odds are, you probably won't be using one of these.

◆ *Class B.* The first two octets define the netid, and the next two octets define the hostid. The first octet of the netid can range from 128 to 191. Combined with the unrestricted second octet, this allows for more than 16,000 Class B networks, each with the capacity for more than 65,000 NICs. These are more common than Class A networks, but they are still a bit of overkill for most networks.

◆ *Class C.* The first three octets define the netid, and the last octet is the hostid. The first octet of the netid can range from 192 to 223; therefore, combined with the second and third octets, you can have more than two million Class C networks on the Internet. Each of these is restricted to only 254 hosts, however (the extremes in either field are always excluded). As you can see, this is the most common type of IP address the InterNIC assigns.

You can see that the problem of relying on the default subnets is that if you have more than 254 NICs to support on a single network, you need to either segment your network or move to a Class B address (and probably waste many of the 65,000 hostids that cannot be assigned elsewhere). That's why the subnet mask comes in handy.

Here are the subnet masks for the various classes of networks:

Class A: 255.0.0.0
Class B: 255.255.0.0
Class C: 255.255.255.0

Defaults are an all-or-nothing deal, but by borrowing some bits from the hostid and tacking them on to the netid, you can take a Class B address and share it among multiple physical networks. If you need to do so, you really should check out the *TCP/IP Training Guide* because unless you are already a TCP/IP administrator, you need more depth than this book offers.

Default Gateway

A default gateway is a *router*, a device that sends packets on to a remote network. A router can be a device created for that purpose, such as those that Cisco and 3Com make, or it can be a Windows NT-based computer that has at least two network cards (for spanning two networks). When a packet is sent to a remote netid, IP forwards the packet to the default gateway, hoping that it knows where to send the packet. Although strictly speaking, default gateways are optional parameters, without one, communications are limited to the local subnet.

Putting It Together

An important point to remember is that every computer on the internetwork must have a unique IP address. When your internetwork is the Internet, that's pretty hard to ensure. Here are a few things to keep in mind:

◆ If you're on the public Internet, apply for a range of addresses from the Internet Network Information Center (InterNIC). The InterNIC is the closest thing the Internet has to a governing body, and it's the organization responsible for tracking and assigning the usage of IP addresses. You can reach the InterNIC via email at hostmaster@internic.net and via the U.S. Postal Service at 505 Huntmar Park Drive, Herndon, VA, 22070.

◆ If you aren't on the public Internet, consider applying to the InterNIC anyway. You'll probably be on the Internet sooner or later.

◆ If you're absolutely sure that you don't need Internet connectivity, either because you are planning to use a proxy server or because your corporate needs do not include such access, you can use any IP addresses you want, as long as they're unique within your private internetwork and they follow the rules.

The Rules

This section doesn't pretend to be a complete discussion of IP addressing requirements, but it does lay out a couple cardinal rules that every TCP/IP administrator must know.

◆ *Rule #1.* Don't go to extremes. Hostids cannot be set to all zeroes or all ones because such ids denote broadcast messages rather than specifically targeted messages. An easy rule of thumb is to stay away from 0 and 255 when assigning octets.

◆ *Rule #2.* Don't use 127 as a netid. When 127 is used as the first octet of a netid, TCP/IP recognizes the address as a special diagnostic address called the *loopback address* (so called because any message to this address is returned to its sender). 127 addresses are used to test the configuration of TCP/IP-based computers.

◆ *Rule #3.* All netids on a subnet must match. If one NIC doesn't have the same netid as the rest of the NICs on its subnet, the host can't communicate with the other hosts on the subnet. Likewise, if a host on a remote subnet is configured using the netid of the local subnet, communication between the two subnets becomes impossible; the packets are never routed because they appear to the local host as the local netid.

◆ *Rule #4.* All hostids in a subnet must be unique. If, on a subnet, two hosts share a hostid, the results are unpredictable— and certainly unwanted. If a Windows NT-based computer attempts to join the network with a duplicate hostid, Windows NT doesn't let it join the network; instead it sends a message to both the usurper and the usurped explaining the problem. If a non-Windows NT-based host joins the network with a duplicate hostid, the results can range from interception of the other host's packets to locking up of the computer that's trying to use an already allocated TCP/IP address (and perhaps the locking up of the computer currently using the TCP/IP address as well if it isn't a Windows NT-based computer). In short, keep careful tabs on your IP addresses, or use the DHCP protocol described later in this chapter.

Installing TCP/IP

The installation and initial configuration of TCP/IP is straightforward (see Step by Step 3.1). However, it can be tedious if you are configuring the protocol manually. If you do, you will have to enter the TCP/IP address, the subnet mask, the default gateway (if used), and the WINS and DNS servers if these are available. On the other hand, if you are installing TCP/IP on a DHCP client, all you have to do is install the protocol, and DHCP takes care of the rest.

STEP BY STEP

3.1 Installing TCP/IP

1. Open the Control Panel and start the Network application.

2. Choose the Protocols tab and click the Add button.

3. Select the TCP/IP protocol and click OK.

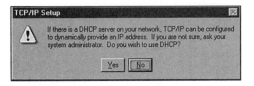

FIGURE 3.8
The DHCP prompt in TCP/IP.

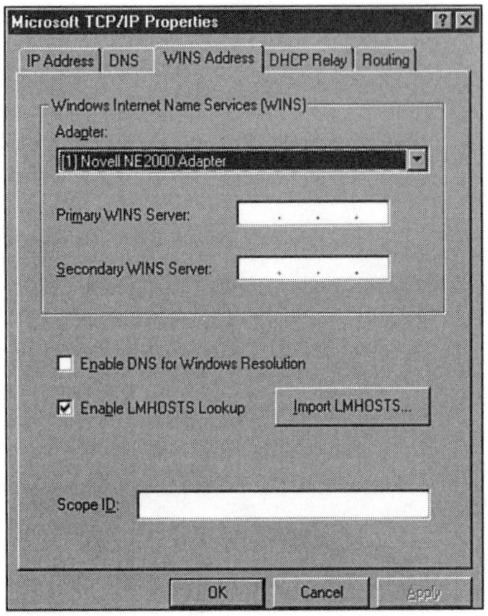

FIGURE 3.9
The Microsoft TCP/IP Properties dialog box.

Configuring TCP/IP with DHCP

When you install TCP/IP, Setup asks if you want to use DHCP to dynamically provide IP addresses. (DHCP stands for Dynamic Host Configuration Protocol.) So that you don't have to keep tabs on where your IP addresses have been assigned at any given moment, a Windows NT Server running DHCP can do it for you. A DHCP server leases addresses to clients when they join the network.

If a DHCP server services your subnet, consider choosing Yes in response to the dialog box shown in Figure 3.8. If you do, the DHCP client is assigned an IP address automatically when it restarts.

Selecting the DHCP option here enables DHCP for all network interface cards in the computer. To selectively assign DHCP to individual NICs in a multihomed computer (a computer with more than one NIC), don't select DHCP at this time. Choose No now, and you can configure each NIC separately in the Microsoft TCP/IP Properties dialog box.

If Remote Access Services (RAS) is installed on your system, Setup asks if you want to configure RAS to support the TCP/IP protocol. After the installation finishes, choose Close in the Network application's main window, and the Microsoft TCP/IP Properties dialog box appears (see Figure 3.9).

In the Adapter drop-down list on the IP Address tab of the Microsoft TCP/IP Properties dialog box, you can select any of the network adapters you have installed on your computer. After you select a network adapter, you have one more chance to enable automatic DHCP configuration. If you enable the Obtain an IP Address from a DHCP Server radio button, the IP Address and Subnet Mask fields for this network adapter become grayed out because henceforth that information will come from a DHCP server. Although you can still specify a default gateway by clicking the Advanced button, this information can come from a DHCP server as well. However, any information you enter on this tab overrides DHCP-assigned information.

The Advanced button opens the Advanced IP Addressing dialog box (see Figure 3.10). The Advanced IP Addressing dialog box lets you enter multiple IP addresses for a single network adapter, which enables administrators to create logical networks within a single physical network—virtual subnets, you might say. Each IP address also requires its own subnet mask entry. By default, Server accepts up to five IP addresses, and additional ones can be added with a Registry edit. You also can enter multiple default gateways for each network adapter. The arrow buttons allow you to adjust the order in which the gateways are tried. If the gateway at the top of the list fails, the second one is used; if it too fails, the third one is used; and so on down the list.

Select the Enable Security check box and click Configure to open the TCP/IP Security dialog box, which lets you selectively enable TCP ports, UDP ports, and IP protocols.

Configuring TCP/IP Manually

If you really want to configure TCP/IP manually, you must enter an IP address and subnet mask for each NIC. Although Windows NT doesn't consider the default gateway mandatory, you probably should enter your router's IP address here (that is, if you want to communicate with remote subnets). To enable IP routing, select the Routing tab in the Microsoft TCP/IP Properties dialog box, and then enable the Enable IP Routing check box.

WINS

WINS stands for Windows Internet Name Service. The WINS Address tab in the Microsoft TCP/IP Properties dialog box lets you specify IP addresses for primary and secondary WINS servers (see Figure 3.11).

WINS is a service that maps NetBIOS names to IP addresses. For the convenience of humans, TCP/IP interfaces allow the use of decimal values to represent the 32-bit binary addresses that TCP/IP uses to communicate. However, these addresses are not very easy to remember or work with.

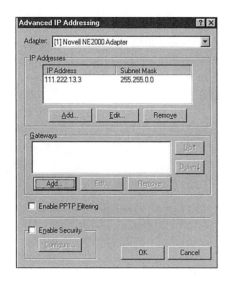

FIGURE 3.10
The Advanced IP Addressing dialog box.

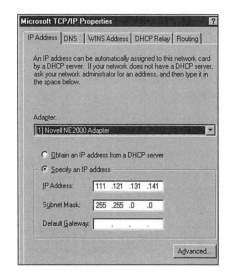

FIGURE 3.11
The WINS Address tab of the Microsoft TCP/IP Properties dialog box.

To make things more user-friendly and to maintain the UNC convention across the board, Windows NT includes a NetBIOS layer that resides just above TCP/IP. This component, called NetBT, allows communication using standard Microsoft NetBIOS computer names, such as \\NTServer.

This is great news for users, but it doesn't change the fact that TCP/IP requires IP addresses in order to communicate. To resolve the NetBIOS names to IP addresses, Windows NT must broadcast the name of the server and wait for it to respond with its IP address. This takes time, causes network broadcast traffic, and generally doesn't work across subnets (because most routers do not forward broadcast messages).

Here's where WINS comes in. WINS maintains a database of active names on the network. When a WINS client needs to contact another server, the WINS server resolves the NetBIOS name and responds with the server's IP address.

If you have a WINS server on your network, you can enter its IP address in the Primary WINS Server field. If you have more than one WINS server, you can enter another server's IP address in the Secondary WINS Server field. Again, however, you also can let DHCP assign this information.

At the bottom of the WINS Address tab are these three Windows Networking parameters:

- ◆ *Enable DNS for Windows Resolution.* Selecting this check box instructs Windows NT to look up NetBIOS names against a Domain Name Server, which is usually a service running on Windows NT Server or a daemon running on UNIX. DNS is a static database usually reserved for TCP/IP hostnames, such as ftp.microsoft.com, but NT 4.0 provides WINS/DNS integration so that you can use DNS for NetBIOS resolution as well.

- ◆ *Enable LMHOSTS Lookup.* This check box incorporates a text database mapping of NetBIOS names to IP addresses into the name resolution process. This name resolution technique predates WINS, and although it's harder to keep up-to-date, it causes less network traffic than WINS because name resolution occurs on the client itself before it attempts to use network name resolution resources.

- ◆ *Scope ID.* This option enables administrators to create logical IP networks that are invisible to one another. Hosts must belong to the same NetBIOS scope in order to communicate.

DNS

DNS is a service that maps computer host names to TCP/IP addresses. Like WINS, configuring a DNS Server entry for a client machine
(see Step by Step 3.2) means that you will be able to use names to
locate TCP/IP hosts instead of the TCP/IP addresses. Unlike WINS,
however, DNS can help you locate TCP/IP hosts that are not
Microsoft based and/or that are not part of your network but instead
are Internet based. DNS resolution allows you to access any TCP/IP
computer that's recognized by your DNS Server or any DNS Servers
it has access to.

STEP BY STEP

3.2 Configuring a DNS Client

1. Open the Microsoft TCP/IP Properties dialog box and
   select the DNS tab.

2. In the Hostname field, enter the name of this machine.

3. (Optional) In the Domain field, enter the DNS domain
   that this computer belongs to (such as widgets.com).

4. Click the Add button under the DNS Service Search
   Order box, and then enter the addresses of the DNS
   Servers on your network.

   You can change the search order of the DNS servers using
   the Up and Down buttons to the right of the box.

5. Click the Add button under the DNS Suffix Search order
   to define a search order for DNS domain names.

TCP/IP Diagnostics

A host of TCP/IP utilities are included with Windows NT. Some of
the more useful ones are IPCONFIG, PING, and TRACERT.

IPCONFIG

IPCONFIG displays the TCP/IP configuration parameters of the
local host. The /ALL switch can be used to display every field, including DHCP and WINS information.

PING

PING is a diagnostic utility used to test the connection between two hosts on an internetwork. It uses the Internet Control Message Protocol (ICMP) echo and reply functions to send messages to and from a remote host. If the connection is successful, PING returns four responses similar to the following:

```
Pinging ftp.microsoft.com [198.105.232.1] with 32 bytes of
➡data:
Reply from 198.105.232.1: bytes=32 time=227ms TTL=51
Reply from 198.105.232.1: bytes=32 time=221ms TTL=51
Request timed out.
Reply from 198.105.232.1: bytes=32 time=205ms TTL=51
```

Note that the third attempt timed out. This can happen on the Internet during busy periods, which is why PING makes four attempts at a connection. Four timeouts would indicate that a connection is unlikely for the time being.

TRACERT

The TRACERT utility traces the hops that a packet takes on its way from the local host to a remote host, as well as the amount of time it takes to reach each destination (allowing three tries from each source to each destination). To see how TRACERT works, study TRACERT's analysis of the route from a Portland, Oregon MSN connection to Microsoft's FTP Server:

```
Tracing route to ftp.microsoft.com [198.105.232.1]
over a maximum of 30 hops:
1    161 ms    154 ms    156 ms   Max3.Seattle.WA.MS.UU.NET
➡Æ[204.177.253.3]
2    198 ms    190 ms    160 ms   Cisco2.San-
➡Francisco.CA.MS.UU.Net Æ[137.39.2.63]
3    185 ms    184 ms    214 ms   San-Jose3.CA.ALTER.NET
➡Æ[137.39.100.17]
4    195 ms    192 ms    213 ms   mae-
➡west.SanFrancisco.mci.net Æ[198.32.136.12]
5    264 ms    191 ms    346 ms   borderx2-hssi2-
➡Æ0.SanFrancisco.mci.net [204.70.158.117]
6     *        212 ms    218 ms   core2-fddi-
➡1.SanFrancisco.mci.net Æ[204.70.158.65]
7    220 ms    229 ms    202 ms   core1-hssi-
➡2.Sacramento.mci.net Æ[204.70.1.146]
8    253 ms    435 ms    269 ms   core-hssi-3.Seattle.mci.net
➡Æ[204.70.1.150]
9    236 ms    263 ms    205 ms   border1-fddi-
➡0.Seattle.mci.net Æ[204.70.2.146]
10     *        204 ms      *      nwnet.Seattle.mci.net
➡Æ[204.70.52.6]
11   242 ms    242 ms    234 ms   seabr1-gw.nwnet.net
➡Æ[192.147.179.5]
12   197 ms    209 ms    199 ms   microsoft-t3-gw.nwnet.net
```

```
➥Æ [198.104.192.9]
13    *        259 ms    232 ms   131.107.249.3
14    220 ms   245 ms    228 ms   ftp.microsoft.com
➥[198.105.232.1]
Trace complete.
```

Armed with these three utilities, you can troubleshoot connectivity problems between two hosts. Say, for instance, you're trying to reach Microsoft's FTP server, but the connection fails. You might work through the following procedure.

First, use IPCONFIG to confirm that you do indeed have TCP/IP correctly initialized on your computer. Also, check the default gateway and name resolution information because incorrect configuration of these items affects your ability to connect to remote hosts.

If everything looks okay, ping 127.0.0.1 (a loopback diagnostic address), and it will confirm that TCP/IP is correctly initialized and bound on your computer. If this step isn't successful, shut down and restart your computer, and then try again. If this step still isn't successful, check the network bindings listed on the Bindings tab of the Control Panel's Network application.

Next, ping your own IP address to confirm that your computer is configured with the correct address and to ensure that no other hosts on the network have your IP address. If this step is unsuccessful, use IPCONFIG to check for a typo in your IP address. If the address looks fine but you still cannot ping yourself, check the Event Viewer for a message indicating that another host has your IP address. A message always appears when you do this, but it's easy to dismiss the message without reading it.

If you are able to successfully ping yourself, try pinging your default gateway. If the router is down, you can't communicate with any remote hosts. However, if that step is successful, move on to the next step: Ping the remote host. If this step is successful, you should be able to form a connection. If this step is unsuccessful, a router probably is down somewhere between your default gateway and the remote host. You can confirm that by using the TRACERT utility to see where the communication breakdown is occurring.

CONFIGURING NETWORK ADAPTERS

Configure network adapters. Considerations include: Changing IRQ, I/O base, and memory addresses and configuring multiple adapters.

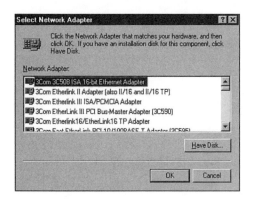

FIGURE 3.12
The Select Network Adapter dialog box.

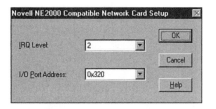

FIGURE 3.13
The Network Card Setup dialog box.

The Adapters tab of the Control Panel's Network application lets you add and configure network adapters for your system (refer to Figure 3.5).

To add a new network adapter, click the Add button. In the Select Network Adapter dialog box that appears, you can select an adapter from a list (see Figure 3.12). Click Have Disk to install an adapter that isn't on the list.

To configure the IRQ and I/O port address (base-memory I/O address expressed in decimals), access the Network application's Adapters tab and either double-click on an adapter or select an adapter and click the Properties button. The Network Card Setup dialog box appears (see Figure 3.13).

CONFIGURING WINDOWS NT SERVER FOR CLIENT COMPUTERS

Configure a Windows NT Server computer for various types of client computers. Client computer types include Windows NT Workstation, Microsoft Windows 95, and Microsoft MS-DOS-based.

A wide variety of clients may log in to or connect over the network to an NT Server computer. This list of clients includes NT Workstation, Windows 95, and DOS.

Very little configuration is needed to allow NT Server to be the server for those clients listed. Most of the necessary configurations areg listed elsewhere in this book. However, the following sections also outline the necessary configurations just to make sure you have a good idea of what needs to be done.

Configuring NT Server for NT Workstation Clients

The NT Workstation client is unique in the realm of NT Server clients. Because it is so similar to NT Server, some of the configuration that is required for, say, Windows 95, is unnecessary. An example of this is printer drivers. Because the print architecture of Windows NT Workstation is basically the same as that of NT Server, the print drivers are the same. In fact, NT Workstation simply downloads any updated drivers the server has when it prints.

What NT Workstation does require in order to participate in a domain controlled by an NT Server is a computer account. A computer account is what identifies a particular NT Workstation as being part of a domain, and it is this account that allows a user to use the computer to log in to the domain. Without a computer account in the domain, a user would not have the option of logging in to a domain controller; instead he would only be able to log in to the local workstation.

A computer account can be created in three ways: during an NT Workstation installation, from the NT Workstation's network properties, or from the Server Manager on an NT Server. In all both cases, the computer account becomes part of the domain accounts list and allows a secure communications channel to be established between the client and its domain controller. In order to create a computer account from the workstation, you have to be an administrator of the domain. In order to create a computer account from Server Manager, you must be an administrator or a member of the Account Operators group.

Because creating a group from Server Manager is expressly an NT Server task, it is covered here and is demonstrated in Step by Step 3.3.

WHY IT'S IMPORTANT TO JOIN A DOMAIN

You will notice that after a computer account has been created, the icon for the new computer is gray. That is because the account is not really "initialized" until the client itself chooses to join the domain; all that you have done is grant it permission to join. Microsoft recommends that you treat this as a security risk until the computer joins the domain. It is possible that another user who is not supposed to have access to your domain from his or her computer could rename that computer to the computer name you have just created an account for and then join your domain. Therefore, you should keep the creation of new computer accounts relatively quiet until the computer has been configured to join the domain.

FIGURE 3.14
The Add Computer to Domain dialog box allows you to create a new computer account for an NT Workstation, Server, or BDC.

STEP BY STEP

3.3 Creating a Computer Account Through Server Manager

1. Log in to the server using an account that is part of the Administrators, Domain Admins, or Account Operators group.

2. From the Start menu, choose Programs, Administrative Tools (Common), Server Manager.

3. From the Computer menu, choose Add to Domain. The Add Computer to Domain dialog box appears (see Figure 3.14).

4. Under Computer Type, choose Windows NT Workstation or Server.

5. In the Computer Name box, type the NetBIOS name of the client computer.

6. Click the Add button to create the computer account.

Other than the obvious network communication configuration (network card, cabling, common protocols, and so on) and the computer account, no other setup is required to allow an NT Workstation to be the client of an NT Server .

Configuring NT Server for Windows 95 Clients

Unlike Windows NT Workstation clients, Windows 95 clients do not support computer accounts and, therefore, do not require such configuration. In order for a Windows 95 client to participate in an NT domain, the client must be configured to allow login into the domain of the user's choice. That configuration is handled from the Windows 95 client, not from the NT Server. The two NT Server configurations that are required are for printer drivers and profiles.

Because Windows 95 printer drivers are different from those used by Windows NT, simply having the NT drivers installed on the server is not sufficient to allow a Windows 95 client to print to a printer shared from the NT Server. In addition to installing the local printer on the server and sharing it, to allow the Windows 95 client to connect to it, you also must specifically configure the printer to allow printing from a Windows 95 client. This involves installing additional printer drivers at the time the printer is installed.

When you share a local printer on an NT Server computer, you are given the option of loading printer drivers for use by other clients; Windows 95 is listed among those clients (see Figure 3.15). By choosing to install the Windows 95 printer driver, you give those clients the ability to print to your shared printer. You will be prompted for the Windows 95 CD-ROM to complete the installation of these drivers. For more information on sharing printers, see Chapter 4.

The other thing you must configure especially for Windows 95 clients are profiles and policies for users who log on using those client stations. Although profiles and policies are discussed in depth in Chapter 5, some discussion is valuable here.

A *profile* is a set of configuration settings for a specific user. *Policies* are system configurations that define restrictions and settings for all users, groups of users, or specific users. Profiles and policies are frequently stored on domain controllers and are accessed by clients when at logon. Profiles for Windows NT-based clients are created from a Windows NT machine and are made available on a domain controller. Policies for Windows NT-based clients are created using the NT policy editor. However, neither NT policies nor profiles are compatible with Windows 95 because some of the settings modify the Registry of the client, and the Registries of Windows 95 and Windows NT are very different. As a result, if Windows 95-based users who log on to your domain need to access profiles and policies, you will have to execute Step by Step 3.4 to give them that permission.

FIGURE 3.15
The Sharing tab on the Printer Properties dialog box allows you to configure all sharing properties, including the driver to install for client use.

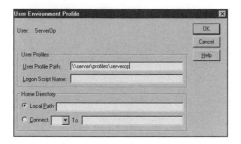

FIGURE 3.16
The User Enviroment Profile dialog box allows you to specify the path to a user's profile, either Windows NT or Windows 95.

STEP BY STEP

3.4 Creating Windows 95-Compatible Policies or Profiles

1. Create Windows 95 system policies and profiles using the Windows 95 configuration tools found on a Windows 95 computer (this must be done from a Windows 95 machine). For more detailed information, consult the *Windows 95 Resource Kit* from Microsoft Press or the Microsoft Official Curriculum course Supporting Windows 95.

2. Copy the Windows 95 system policy into the NetLogon share of the Windows NT domain controllers using the filename Config.pol (as opposed to NTConfig.pol for the NT policies).

3. Copy the Windows 95 user profile into the users folder, created in the Policies share on the domain controller.

4. Configure the domain user accounts logging in from Windows 95 machines to use these profiles. To do so, in User Manager for Domains, access the user properties (see Figure 3.16) and click the Profile button.

Configuring NT Server for MS-DOS Clients

Because the DOS client is quite a bit simpler in its architecture than the Windows NT or even the Windows 95 client is, less configuration is required. Most of the configuration is actually performed on the DOS machine itself because DOS does not have an inherent ability to communicate over a network. As a result, in order to get a DOS client to talk to an NT Server, the NT DOS Networking client must first be installed on the DOS machine (for more information see Chapter 2, "Installation and Configuration Part 1: Installation of NT Server"). No other configuration of the NT Server is required to allow these DOS clients to access it or to log on.

Because much of the general configuration of an NT Server is done to ease the administration of client access, a concluding discussion of network protocols and NT Services that are supported by the various clients is in order. Table 3.1 gives a list of many of the clients supported by NT Server and the services and protocols of they can be the clients. For more information about these protocols and services, see "Configuring Protocols and Protocol Bindings" and "Windows NT Core Services," both earlier in this chapter.

TABLE 3.1

NETWORK PROTOCOL AND TCP/IP SERVICE SUPPORT FOR VARIOUS WINDOWS NT CLIENT SYSTEMS

Client OS	NetBEUI	IPX	IPX/SPX	TCP/IP	DLC	DHCP Client	WINS Client	DNS Client
Network Client for MS-DOS	X	X		X X	X	X		
LAN MAN 2.2c for MS-DOS	X		X	X X	X	X		
LAN MAN 2.2c for OS/2	X			X				
Windows 95	X		X	X X	X	X	X	
Windows NT Workstation	X		X	X X	X	X	X	
Windows NT Server	X		X	X X	X	X	X	

WINDOWS NT CORE SERVICES

Configure Windows NT Server core services. Services include: Directory Replicator, License Manager, and other services.

A *service* is a built-in application that provides support for other applications or other components of the operating system. Windows NT includes dozens of services, each of which performs a highly specialized function. Many of Windows NT's Services support NT's networking capabilities.

Examples of Windows NT Services include:

◆ Windows Internet Name Service (WINS), which maps IP addresses to NetBIOS names.

◆ UPS service, which interacts with an Uninterruptible Power Supply system to prevent your system from abruptly shutting down.

◆ Server service, which accepts I/O requests from the network and routes the requested resources back to the client.

◆ Workstation service, which accepts I/O requests from the local system and redirects the requests to the appropriate computer on the network.

Services are background processes that perform specific functions in Windows NT. Typically, services don't interact with the user interface in any way (including appearing in the Task List), so users shouldn't be aware of their existence. Think of a Windows NT Service as the equivalent of UNIX daemon or, if you are more comfortable with NetWare, the equivalent of a NetWare Loadable Module (NLM).

This section gives you a closer look at some important Windows NT services and how to configure them.

The Services Application

The Control Panel's Services application manages the services on your system. The Services application writes directly to the following key, where configuration data for Windows NT Services is maintained:

```
HKEY_LOCAL_MACHINE\SYSTEM\CurrentControlSet\Control\Services
```

Double-click on the Services icon in Control Panel to open the Services dialog box (shown in Figure 3.17).

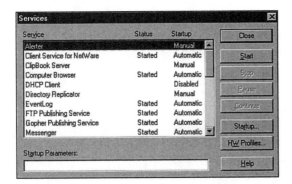

FIGURE 3.17
The Control Panel's Services application.

The Services dialog box lists the services on your system, as well as the service's status (whether or not it is started) and startup type. The startup type describes whether the service will start automatically or manually or whether it is disabled. Automatic services start at the very end of the boot process, after the "Welcome: Press Ctrl+Alt+Del to Log On" window appears. (Because services are Win32 programs, they require a fully functional operating system before they can be opened.) Manual services start when you select the service in the Services dialog box and click the Start button.

Note that the Services dialog box also includes buttons that stop a service, pause a service, and continue a service that has been paused. When you pause a service, the service continues to handle the processes it's currently serving but does not take on any new clients. For example, the Server service must be running on a server in order for the server to accept connections from a client. Stopping the Server service causes all connections to be immediately dropped, but pausing the service preserves existing connections while rejecting new connection attempts.

To enable a service for a given hardware profile, click HW Profiles in the Services dialog box, select a profile, and click OK.

Double-click on a service to open a configuration dialog box called the Service dialog box (as opposed to the Services dialog box) in which you can configure a startup type and define a logon account for the service.

The *logon account* defines a security context for the service. Because services are Win32 programs, they must run under the auspices of a user account. The problem is, services continue to execute even when nobody is logged on to the computer, so the administrator must configure the service to use a specific user account. Services are often configured to use one of the following accounts:

◆ *System account.* An internal account, called SYSTEM, can be used either by the operating system or by the service. This method isn't recommended, however, because you can't fine-tune rights and permissions without possibly affecting the performance and stability of the operating system and other services that may use this account.

◆ *This account.* You can designate any user account from your account database here. You should create a separate account for each service for which you want to configure rights and permissions; for example, you might create a SQLAdmin account for the SQL server service or an SMSAdmin account for the SMS service.

Network Services

The Services tab of the Control Panel's Network application lets you add, configure, and remove services that support network functions (refer to Figure 3.3). The Add button opens the Select Network Service dialog box, which provides a list of available Windows NT network services. Select a service and click OK to add the service to your configuration. Or, click the Have Disk button if you are attempting to install a new service from a disk.

Some of the services in the Network Services list are configurable through the Network application, and some are not. Select a service and click the Properties button to open a configuration dialog box for the service (if there is one). Figure 3.18 shows the configuration dialog box for the Server service.

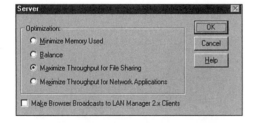

FIGURE 3.18
The Server dialog box.

Many of the network components you'll read about elsewhere in this book (DHCP, WINS, DNS, RAS, and Gateway Services for NetWare) are actually services that, though often configured elsewhere, can still be added, started, stopped, and managed through the Network Services tab of the Control Panel's Services application. For the most part, anything you do on the network occurs through some form of network service.

The following sections examine these important topics relating to Windows NT services:

- Directory replication
- Client license management
- The browser process

Directory Replication

Directory replication is a facility that lets you configure Windows NT Servers to automatically transmit updated versions of important files and directories to other computers on the network.

The purpose of directory replication is to simplify the task of distributing updates for logon scripts, system policy files, Help files, phone lists, and other important files. The network administrator updates the file(s) on a single server (called the export server), and the export server automatically distributes the file(s) to other network servers or even to network workstations. The computer receiving the update is called the *import computer*. A Windows NT Server, a Windows NT Workstation, or a LAN Manager OS/2 server can act as an import computer.

Directory replication is performed by the Directory Replicator service. You can start and stop the Directory Replicator service from the Control Panel's Services application. The parameters for the Directory Replicator service are found in this Registry key:

```
HKEY_LOCAL_MACHINE\SYSTEM\CurrentControlSet\Services\
Replicator\Parameters
```

NOTE

The Directory Replicator Registry Key Most of the parameters in the Registry key HKEY_LOCAL_MACHINE\SYSTEM\CurrentControlSet\Services\Replicator\Parameters can be configured within Server Manager (described later in this chapter). However, there are two important exceptions:

Interval. This REG_WORD value defines how often an export server checks for updates. The range is from 1 to 60 minutes, and the default is 5 minutes.

GuardTime. This REG_WORD value defines how long a directory must be stable before its files can be replicated. The range is 0 to one-half of the Interval value. The default is 2 minutes. See the section "Configuring the Export Computer," later in this chapter, for a discussion of the Wait Until Stabilized check box.

The export directory on the export server holds the files and directories are replicated across the network. The default export directory is

```
\<winnt_root>\System32\Repl\Export
```

For each group of files that you wish to replicate, create a subdirectory in the export directory. When the Directory Replicator service starts, NT shares the export directory with the share name Repl$.

Each import computer has a directory called the import directory, and the default directory is \<winnt_root>\System32\Repl\Import. The Directory Replicator service copies files from the export server's export directory to the import directories of the import computers. In addition to copying files, the Directory Replicator service automatically creates any necessary subdirectories in the import directory so that after each replication, the directory structure of the import directory matches the directory structure of the export directory.

The following steps describe the process:

1. The export server periodically checks the export directory for changes, and if changes have occurred, it sends update notices to the import computer.

2. The import computer receives the update notices and calls the export computer.

3. The import computer reads the export directory on the export server, copies any new or changed files from the export directory to its own import directory, and deletes files that exist in its import directory but not in the export directory.

The following sections describe how to set up the export and import computers for directory replications.

Configuring the Export Computer

In an export-import relationship, the first machine normally configured is the export computer. This machine, which must be an NT Server, will contain the directory structure to be duplicated on the import computer (see Step by Step 3.5).

STEP BY STEP

3.5 Setting Up an Export Server for Directory Replication

1. Create a new account for the Directory Replicator service. (See Chapter 5 for more on creating accounts using User Manager for Domains.) The Directory Replicator account must be a member of the Backup Operator group or the Replicator group for the domain. When you set up the new account, be sure to enable the Password Never Expires option and to disable the User Must Change Password at Next Logon option. Also, make sure the account has logon privileges for all hours.

2. In the Control Panel, double-click the Services icon and start the Directory Replicator service; you *must* have done step 1 to perform this step.

3. Start the Server Manager application in the Administrative Tools program group. Server Manager, shown in Figure 3.19, is a tool for managing network servers and workstations from a single location.

NOTE

Import, Export, or Both A Windows NT Server can serve as an export server, an import computer, or both. The left side of the Directory Replication dialog box defines export properties. The right side of the Directory Export dialog box defines import properties.

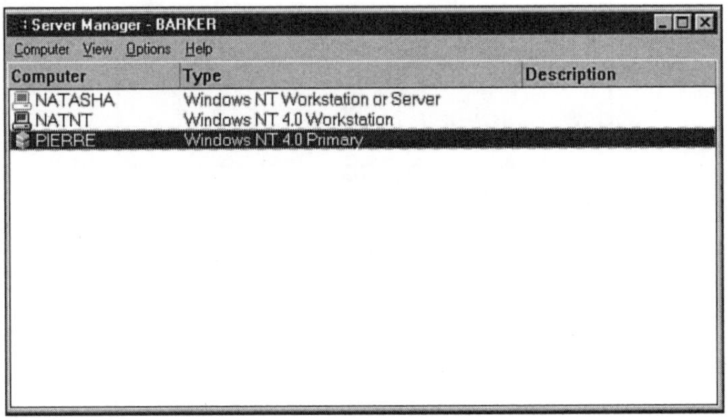

FIGURE 3.19
The Server Manager main screen.

continues

continued

4. In the Server Manager, double-click the export server to open the Server Properties dialog box (see Figure 3.20).

5. Click Replication to open the Directory Replication dialog box (see Figure 3.21).

6. In the Directory Replication dialog box, select the Export Directories radio button. The default path to the export directory then appears in the From Path box. Click the Add button to open the Select Domain dialog box (see Figure 3.22).

FIGURE 3.20
The Server Properties dialog box.

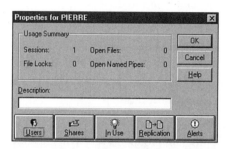

FIGURE 3.21
The Directory Replication dialog box.

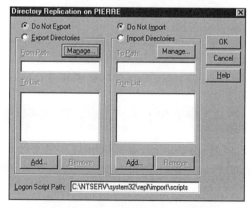

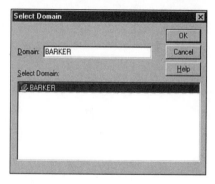

FIGURE 3.22
The Select Domain dialog box.

7. Click a domain to select it. Double-click a domain to display the computers within that domain (see Fig. 3.23). If you select a whole domain, all import servers in the domain receive the replicated data. If you choose a specific computer, only that computer receives the replicated data. You can choose any combination of domains and specific computers.

8. In the Directory Replication dialog box, click the Manage button to open the Manage Exported Directories dialog box (see Figure 3.24). Subdirectories within the export directory are listed in the Sub-Directory list. You can add or remove subdirectories from the list by clicking on the Add or Remove buttons.

   Notice the check boxes at the bottom of the screen. Enabling the Wait Until Stabilized check box tells the Directory Replicator service to wait at least two minutes after any change to the selected subdirectory tree before exporting. Enabling the Entire Subtree check box tells the Directory Replicator service to export all subdirectories beneath the selected subdirectory. The Add Lock button lets you lock the subdirectory so it can't be exported. More than one user can lock a subdirectory. (Consequently, a subdirectory can have more than one lock.) To remove a lock, click the Remove Lock button.

9. Click OK in the Manage Exported Directories dialog box, the Directory Replication dialog box, and the Server Properties dialog box.

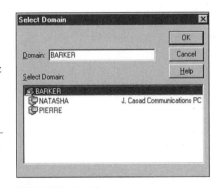

FIGURE 3.23
The Select Domain dialog box displaying specific computers within the domain.

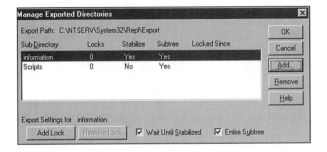

FIGURE 3.24
The Manage Exported Directories dialog box.

CONFIGURING EXPORT DIRECTORIES

Be careful about how you configure the export directories. Normally, it is a good practice to create directories with subdirectories that contain their own subdirectories in order to best organize your data. However, in replication, this is a bad idea. When a directory is considered for replication, a check is made at the root directory (any directory present directly in the export directory) to see if a change has been made to any file in its subdirectory structure. If a change has been made, the entire tree is replicated. This may result in a lot of excess replication if you have a complex and deep tree in which only a few files ever change. Because of that, consider creating a very shallow structure with most of the directories located in the export directory. That way, you can minimize the amount of traffic generated by replication.

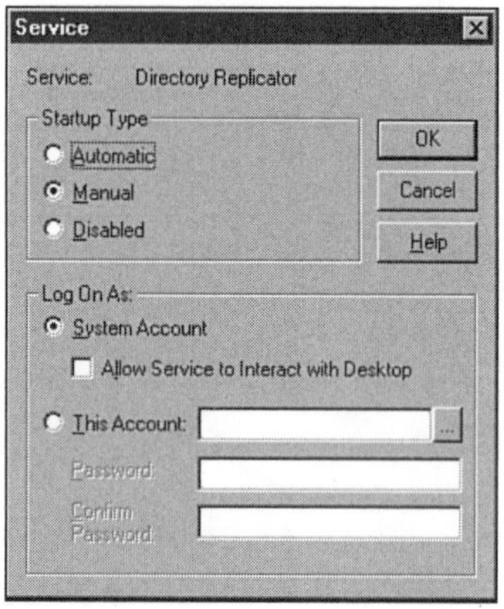

FIGURE 3.25
The Service dialog box.

Remember to Create a Replication User Account If the import computer and the export server aren't part of the same domain or a trusting domain, you must create a replication user account on the import computer and give that account permission to access the Repl$ share on the export server. Then enter that account and password in the Service dialog box in step 2.

Configuring the Import Computer

The import computer finds the changes that are present on the export computer and makes its directory structure identical to that on the export computer. The import computer can be any NT machine (server or workstation). Step by Step 3.6 walks you through setting up an import computer for directory replication.

STEP BY STEP

3.6: Setting Up an Import Computer for Directory Replication

1. Double-click the Services icon in the Control Panel. Then select the Directory Replicator service and click the Startup button to open the Service dialog box (see Figure 3.25).

2. In the Startup Type frame, select the Automatic radio button. In the Log On As frame, select the This Account radio button and enter a username and password for the replicator account you created on the export server.

3. Start Server Manager, select the computer you're now configuring, and click the Replication button in the Properties dialog box. The Directory Replication dialog box appears. This time, you're concerned with the import side (the right side) of the dialog box, but the configuration steps are similar to those for configuring the export side.

4. The default import directory appears in the To Path box. Click the Add button to add a domain or a specific export server (see step 7 in the preceding section). Click the Manage button to open the Manage Imported Directories dialog box, from which you can manage the import directories (see Figure 3.26).

5. In the Manage Imported Directories dialog box, click Add or Remove to add or remove a subdirectory from the list. Click Add Lock to add a lock to the subdirectory (see preceding section).

Troubleshooting Directory Replication

The Status column in the Manage Exported Directories and the Manager Imported Directories dialog boxes gives the status of the directory replication for a subdirectory. The following list outlines each of the possible values and their meanings:

Value	Meaning
OK	The export server is sending regular updates, and the import directory matches the export directory.
No Master	The import computer isn't receiving updates, which means that either the export server or the Directory Replicator service on the export server may not be running.
No Sync	The import directory has received updates, but the data in the updates isn't what it should be; this could signify an export server malfunction, a communication problem, open files on either the import or the export computer, or a problem with the import computer's access permissions.

continues

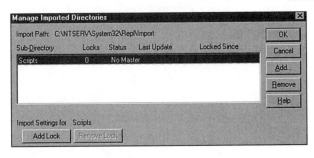

FIGURE 3.26
The Manage Imported Directories dialog box.

continued

Value	Meaning
[Blank]	Replication has never occurred. This can result from improper configuration on either the import or the export computer.

When the Directory Replication service generates an error, check Event Viewer to find out as much as you can about the cause.

For the following common replication errors, Microsoft recommends the given solutions:

◆ *Access denied.* The Directory Replicator service might not be configured to log on to a specific account. Check Event Viewer. Also check the Startup dialog box in the Control Panel's Services application to see if an account is specified, and use User Manager for Domains to check the permissions for the logon account.

◆ *Exporting to specific computers.* Designate specific export servers for each import server, and designate specific import computers for each export server. If you just choose a domain in the dialog box opened by clicking the Add button in the Directory Replication dialog box, every domain computer receives replicated data, and every import computer receives updates from every export server in the domain.

◆ *Replication over a WAN link.* When transmitting replication data across a WAN link, specify the computer name, not just the domain name when you click the Add button in the Directory Replication dialog box.

◆ *Logon scripts for member servers and workstations.* NT Workstations and non-controller NT Servers must use the default logon script directory:

```
C:\<winnt_root>\System32\Repl\Import\Scripts
```

Windows NT Client Licenses

Microsoft requires that every client accessing a resource on a computer running Windows NT Server have a Client Access License (CAL). The Client Access License is separate from the license for the client's operating system. Your Windows 95 or Windows NT Workstation doesn't include implied permission to access resources on a Windows NT Server; to access NT Server resources you must have a CAL.

Microsoft provides two options for purchasing Client Access Licenses:

◆ *Per server mode.* Client Access Licenses are assigned to each server. A Windows NT Server might be licensed for, say, 10 simultaneous client connections. No more than 10 clients will be able to access the server at one time; additional clients will not be able to connect.

◆ *Per seat mode.* A Client Access License is assigned to each client machine. You purchase a CAL for every client computer on the network. If the total number of simultaneous connections on all Windows NT Servers exceeds the number of per seat licenses, a client can still connect.

Microsoft allows you to make a one-time switch from per server to per seat licensing mode. If you aren't sure which option to choose, you can choose per server mode and change later to per seat mode if you determine that per seat mode is more cost effective.

If your network has only one server, Microsoft recommends that you choose per server licensing mode. If you have more than one server on your network, Microsoft suggests that you use the following formulas to determine which mode is best for you:

A = number of servers

B = number of simultaneous connections to each server

C = total number of seats (clients) accessing computers

If A*B<C, use per server licensing (number of CALs = A*B).

IF A*B>C, use per seat licensing (number of CALs = C).

Interpreted, this means that if the total number of simultaneous connections to your servers is greater than the number of users in your

FIGURE 3.27
The Choose Licensing Mode dialog box.

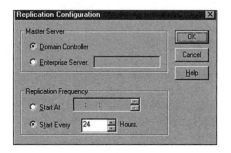

FIGURE 3.28
The Replication Configuration dialog box.

organization, you should use per seat licensing. Otherwise, you should use per server.

Windows NT Server provides two tools for managing client licenses:

- ◆ The Licensing application
- ◆ License Manager

The following sections describe these Windows NT license-managing tools.

The Licensing Application

The Control Panel Licensing application opens the Choose Licensing Mode dialog box (see Figure 3.27). From the Choose Licensing Mode dialog box, you can add or remove client licenses or switch from Per Server to Per Seat licensing mode.

The Replication button opens the Replication Configuration dialog box (shown in Figure 3.28). You configure license replication using the options in this dialog box.

License replication is a convenient feature that lets individual servers send their licensing information to a master server. The master server creates and updates a database of licensing information for the entire network. This provides a single central location for licensing information.

License Manager

License Manager, a tool in the Administrative Tools program group, displays licensing information for the network (see Figure 3.29).

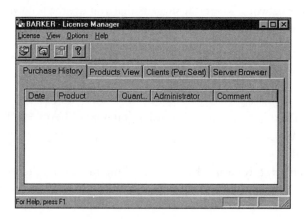

FIGURE 3.29
The License Manager window.

You can maintain a history of client licenses, examine your network's per server and per seat licenses by product, and browse for client license information on particular network clients.In addition, you can monitor server usage by per seat clients and even revoke a client's permission to access a server.

You also can use License Manager to add or edit license groups. A license group is a group of users mapped to a group of per seat licenses. License groups provide a means of tracking per seat license usage in situations where an organization has more users than computers (or in some cases, more computers than users). For example, a retail outlet may have 10 employees sharing three per-seat-licensed computers.

Computer Browser Service

One of the most important network services is the Computer Browser service. The Computer Browser service oversees a hierarchy of computers that serve as browsers for the network. A *browser* is a computer that maintains a central list of network servers. (In this case, a server is any computer that makes resources available to the network.) That list then becomes available to clients who are "browsing" the network looking for remote computers, printers, and other resources. The list that appears when you open the Network Neighborhood application, for instance, comes from a network browser list.

The advantage of using the browser process is that it allows a small number of network computers to maintain browse lists for the whole network, thereby minimizing network traffic and eliminating duplication of efforts. (The alternative would be for all computers to constantly poll the network in order to maintain their own lists.) In order for the browser process can function efficiently, however, it must be highly organized so that clients know where to find a list and so that contingencies can take effect when a browser fails.

In a Windows NT domain, each computer assumes one of five browser roles:

◆ *Master browser.* Each workgroup or domain subnet must have a master browser. At startup, all computers running the Server service (regardless of whether they have resources available for the network) register themselves with the master browser. The master browser compiles a list of available servers on the workgroup or subnet and forwards the list to the domain master browser. The master browser then receives a complete browse list for the entire domain from the domain master browser.

◆ *Domain master browser.* The domain master browser requests subnet browse lists from the master browsers and merges the those lists into a master browse list for the entire domain. It also forwards the domain browse list back to the master browsers and to a WINS server (if one is available). The primary domain controller (PDC) serves as the domain master browser for a Windows NT domain.

◆ *Backup browsers.* The backup browser gets a copy of the browse list from the master browser (on the subnet) and distributes that list to subnet clients who request it. If the master browser fails, a backup browser can serve as the master browser for the subnet. The number of backup browsers is determined based on the number of computers registered on the network.

◆ *Potential browser.* A potential browser is a computer that isn't presently serving as a browser but that could become a browser at the request of the master browser or as a result of a browser election (described later in this section).

◆ *Non-browser.* A non-browser is a computer that cannot serve as a browser.

The first time a client computer attempts to access the network, it obtains a list of backup browsers for the subnet or workgroup from the master browser. It then asks a backup browser for a copy of the browse list.

If a master browser fails, a new master browser is chosen automatically in what is known as a *browser election.* A browser election occur when a client or backup browser cannot access the master browser or when a domain controller is started on the LAN. A browser election isn't exactly an election; it's really more of a contest. The browsers and potential browsers rank themselves according to a number of criteria, and the machine with the highest ranking becomes the new master browser. Some of the criteria used in a browser election include the following:

◆ *Operating system.* Windows NT Server gets a higher score than Windows NT Workstation, which gets a higher score than Windows 95.

◆ *Version.* Windows NT Server 4 gets a higher score than Windows NT Server 3.51, and so forth.

◆ *Present browser role.* A backup browser scores higher than a potential browser.

You can configure a Windows NT computer to always, never, or sometimes participate in browser elections. To do so, you use the MaintainServerList parameter in the following Registry key:

```
HKEY_Local_Machine\System\CurrentControlSet\Services\
Browser\Parameters
```

The possible values are described here:

Value	Description
Yes	The computer always participates in browser elections. (This is the default for Windows NT Server domain controllers.)
No	The computer never participates in browser elections.
Auto	The computer is classified as a potential browser. (This is the default for Windows NT Workstations and Windows NT Servers that aren't acting as domain controllers.)

CHAPTER SUMMARY

KEY TERMS

Before taking the exam, make sure you are familiar with the definitions and concepts behind each of the following key terms. Appendix A provides a glossary of terms for quick reference purposes.

- protocol
- service
- adapter
- binding
- IPX/SPX
- NWLink
- frame type
- TCP/IP
- IP address
- subnet mask
- default gateway
- DHCP
- WINS
- DNS
- IPCONFIG
- PING
- TRACERT
- directory replication
- import computer
- export computer

This chapter dealt with four main topics: configuring protocols, configuring adapters, configuring for clients, and core services. Each of these topics has a role in the proper functioning of an NT Server in a network environment.

In the protocols section, you learned about the protocols you will be likely to encounter in NT configuration and on the exam. In an NT environment, the three major protocols are TCP/IP, NWLink IPX/SPX Compatible Transport, and NetBEUI. TCP/IP was identified as the most common (and default) protocol installed on NT Server; it is routable and is the protocol used to communicate over the Internet. Because the configuration of TCP/IP is quite complex, you should automatically configure with DHCP if possible. You were shown that the NWLink protocol is the protocol of choice when connecting NT Networks with NetWare (Novell) networks. Being a routable protocol, NWLink could be used for general network communication. However, it is not as popular as TCP/IP and, therefore, is not used as frequently when NetWare servers are not involved. Finally, you learned that the NetBEUI protocol was designed for small local networks. As a result, NetBEUI is usually configured on NT Servers only when the network implementation is small or when connectivity with an existing NetBEUI network is desired. NetBEUI is not routable and not practical for most network applications.

Regarding the configuration of network adapters, you were given a brief look at network adapters, their installation, and configuration. This included information about adding new adapters to your NT system and then configuring them with appropriate IRQ, IO base, and memory addresses whenever possible.

In the section on configuring a Windows NT Server computer for various types of client computers, you learned about which clients are supported by Windows NT Server, the protocols each client can understand, and the services each one can take advantage of.

Regarding configuration of Windows NT Server core services, you examined the services in general and then the operation of some specific services. Services are programs NT executes that perform certain optional system functions. These services, which are added in the Network properties, include the Directory Replicator service (for copying files from one server to another on schedule), the License Manager (for managing the number and kind of licenses available in your NT environment), and the Browser service (for managing browse lists and producing them in environments such as the Network Neighborhood).

- Client Access License
- per server licensing mode
- per client licensing mode
- License Manager
- browser
- domain master browser
- master browser
- backup browser
- potential browser
- non-browser

APPLY YOUR LEARNING

Exercises

3.1 The Server and Workstation Services

In this exercise, you learn about starting and stopping services using the Services application in the Control Panel, and you study the functions of the Server and Workstation services.

Estimated Time: 15 minutes

1. Start two Windows NT PCs on your network that each provide shared resources. This exercise will refer to those computers as Computer A and Computer B.

2. Using Network Neighborhood, browse Computer B from Computer A. Then browse Computer A from Computer B. Make sure the shared resources are available.

3. On Computer B, start the Control Panel's Services application and shut down the Server service. Windows NT will ask if it's okay to shut down the Computer Browser service, too. Click OK. Then click Close to close the Services application.

4. Now try to browse Computer B from Computer A. You'll get the following message:

   ```
   <\\computer_name> is not accessible. The
   network path was not found.
   ```

5. Restart the Server service in the Control Panel's Services application. Then try to browse Computer B from Computer A again. The shared resources are now available.

6. In the Control Panel's Services application, shut down the Workstation service. Notice that you can still browse Computer B from Computer A.

7. With the Computer B Workstation service stopped, try to browse Computer A from Computer B. You'll get the following message:

   ```
   Unable to browse the network. The network is
   not present or not started.
   ```

8. Restart the Computer B Workstation service. Once again, you can browse Computer A from Computer B.

3.2 Directory Replication

In this exercise, you learn how to set up directory replication on your network.

Estimated Time: 20 minutes

1. Set up the Windows NT Server export computer for directory replication. Use the following steps:

   a. From the Start menu, choose Programs, Administrative Tools (Common), Server Manager.

   b. In the Server Manager dialog box, double-click the name of the export computer.

   c. In the Server Properties dialog box, click the Replication button.

   d. In the Directory Replication dialog box, choose the Export Directories radio button, and then type the name of the import computer in the To list.

2. Set up the Windows NT Server import computer for directory replication. Use the following steps:

   a. From the Start menu, choose Programs, Administrative Tools (Common), Server Manager.

b. From the Server Manager dialog box, double-click the name of the import computer.

c. In the Server Properties dialog box, click the Replication button.

d. In the Directory Replication dialog box, choose the Import Directories radio button, and then type the name of the export computer in the From list.

3. Create a folder called Test in the export directory of the export computer (if you kept the default, this will probably be
`C:\WINNT\System32\Repl\Export`). Then copy some files into it.

4. Wait a few minutes. The Test folder will appear on the import computer and will contain the files you placed in it.

3.3 Network Bindings

Even if a protocol is properly installed, you might not be able use it with a particular network adapter. In order for you to use a protocol with a network adapter, a *binding* must exist between the protocol and the adapter. This exercise studies the effect of removing a network binding.

Estimated Time: 10 minutes

1. Log on to a Windows NT Server system that uses the TCP/IP protocol, and then go to the command prompt.

2. Ping the loopback address: 127.0.0.1 (see Exercise 1.2 in Chapter 1). The loopback address verifies that TCP/IP is properly configured for your system. You should get four replies.

3. Next, ping the IP address of the computer you are now using. The IP address is actually

associated with your network adapter. Again, you should get four replies.

4. Start Control Panel's Network application and select the Bindings tab.

5. In the Show Bindings For: box, select all adapters.

6. Expand the tree for your network adapter and select the TCP/IP protocol.

7. Click the Disable button to disable the TCP/IP binding for your network adapter card. Click OK.

8. When Windows NT asks if you want to restart your system, click Yes.

9. Restart your system, log on, and go to the command prompt.

10. Ping the loopback address again. You should still get four replies.

11. Ping the IP address of your own computer. You'll get a message that says `Destination host unreachable` four times. Your network adapter is unreachable because you have disabled the binding that associates your adapter with the TCP/IP protocol.

12. Now ping another computer on your network. You should get the `Destination host unreachable` message for other PCs, too, because disabling the binding has disrupted the pathway through which your computer communicates with the network.

13. Return to the Bindings tab of the Network application. In the box labeled Show Bindings For:, select all adapters. Expand the tree for your network adapter and enable the TCP/IP protocol. Then shut down and restart your system.

APPLY YOUR LEARNING

Review Questions

1. Which Control Panel application allows you to change the IRQ setting of a network adapter if it is configurable from within NT?

2. Which protocol needs to be installed on a Windows NT Server in order for that server to connect to a NetWare Server, and what native NetWare protocol does that protocol emulate?

3. What service is available for the automatic assignment and configuration of TCP/IP on a Microsoft network?

4. Which Windows NT Server service allows you to synchronize the files on two machines? What are the two roles that computers can play in this synchronization?

5. What service is responsible for providing information necessary for the population of Network Neighborhood? What happens on a network if no computer to be responsible for providing this information?

6. If you have four servers and 100 users on your network, and any user might need to access one or more of the servers at any one time, what is the best server license mode to use?

Exam Questions

1. Of the following, which are required TCP/IP properties in a routed environment?

   A. TCP/IP address

   B. subnet mask

   C. default gateway

   D. DNS Server entry

2. Company XYZ wants to deploy a network consisting of 10 servers and 200 clients. All of these machines are NT Servers, NT Workstations, or Windows 95 computers. They require connectivity between all the computers and have installed a network to ensure such. They want to be able to use TCP/IP and to allow users to connect to other computers using their computer names. They also would like to be able to use Internet Explorer to connect to sites on the Internet by name. None of the NT Servers have any services configured except those that are installed by default.

Primary Objective:

To minimize the amount of administration required to maintain TCP/IP configurations on all the computers on the network.

Secondary Objectives:

To allow users to use computer names to connect to other computers on their network.

To allow users to use WWW addresses (such as www.widgets.com) to access Internet sites.

Proposed Solution:

Configure all the computers as DHCP clients and configure an NT Server as a DHCP server with all the TCP/IP configurations set up in its scope.

Analysis:

Which of the following best describes the effectiveness of the proposed solution?

   A. The proposed solution fulfills the primary objective and all of the secondary objectives.

   B. The proposed solution fulfills the primary objective and one of the secondary objectives.

C. The proposed solution fulfills the primary objective but none of the secondary objectives.

D. The proposed solution does not fulfill the primary objective.

3. What does WINS do?

A. It maps host names to TCP/IP.

B. It maps NetBIOS names to TCP/IP addresses.

C. It resolves TCP/IP addresses to MAC addresses.

D. It automatically configures TCP/IP addresses.

4. Of the following, which cannot be a DHCP client?

A. Windows NT Workstation

B. Windows NT Server

C. Network Client for MS-DOS

D. LAN MAN 2.2c client for OS/2

5. Which of the following correctly describes the process of directory replication?

A. At a time defined by the Interval setting in the Registry, an export computer checks for changes in its export directory. If changes have occurred, it contacts its list of import computers. When contacted, the import computers pull information from the changed directories to make their corresponding import directories identical to the export directories.

B. At a time defined by the Interval setting in the Registry, an export computer checks for

changes in its export directory. If changes have occurred, it contacts its list of import computers and pushes information to them. When the process is finished, the import directories that information was pushed to are identical to the export directories that information was pushed from.

C. At a time defined by the Interval setting in the Registry, an export computer checks for changes in its export directory. If changes have occurred, it contacts its list of import computers. When contacted, the import computers pull information from the changed directories to merge new items into the corresponding import directories.

D. At a time defined by the Interval setting in the Registry, an import computer contacts the export computer to check for changes in its export directory. If changes have occurred, the import computers pull information from the changed directories to make their corresponding import directories identical to the export directories.

6. A computer that is configured to participate in browser elections but has not been selected to be a browser is referred to as a(n):

A. incumbent browser

B. backup browser

C. potential browser

D. non-browser

7. Which of the following is the rule of thumb regarding which license type an organization should use?

APPLY YOUR LEARNING

A. If the total number of simultaneous logons is greater than the total number of users, an organization should use per server licensing.

B. If the total number of simultaneous connections to all its servers is greater than the number of users in the organization, an organization should use per server licensing.

C. If the total number of network share points is greater than the total number of users, an organization should use per seat licensing.

D. If the total number of simultaneous connections to all its servers is greater than the number of users in the organization, an organization should use per seat licensing.

8. Which of the following tools can be used to display the current TCP/IP configuration of your network adapter(s)?

A. PING

B. IPCONFIG

C. ARP

D. WINS

9. You have installed a service on your NT Server, but it does not start automatically when your server reboots. How can you configure it to start automatically?

A. In the Network dialog box, choose the Services tab, double-click the service you want to start, click the Startup Configuration button, and choose Automatic.

B. Double-click the Services icon in the Control Panel, select the service you want to start, click the Startup Configuration button, and choose Automatic.

C. From the Start menu, choose Programs, Administrative Tools, and the manager of the service you want to start. From the manager dialog box, select the menu choice Server, Automatic Start.

D. Double-click the Control Panel icon corresponding to the service you want to start. From the manager dialog box, select the menu choice Server, Automatic Start.

10. What is the difference between pausing the Server service and stopping it?

A. When you pause the Server service, current users maintain their connections, but new users cannot connect to the server.

B. When you stop the Server service, current users maintain their connections, but new users cannot connect to the server.

C. When you pause the Server service, current users are dropped from the server, but new users can connect to the server.

D. When you stop the Server service, current users are dropped from the server, but new users can connect to the server.

11. Which of the following occurrences will cause a browser election to be called?

A. A Windows 95 machine starts on the LAN

B. A domain controller starts on the LAN

C. A computer cannot find a master browser on the LAN

D. A Windows NT Server machine starts on the LAN

12. Which of the following parameters can be set to ensure that a Windows NT machine will never become a browser?

    A. MaintainBrowserList

    B. BecomeBrowser

    C. IncumbantElector

    D. MaintainServerList

13. Which of the following can function as an import computer for replication?

    A. Windows NT Server

    B. Windows NT PDC

    C. Windows NT Workstation

    D. Windows 95 workstation

14. Which of the following can function as an export computer for replication?

    A. Windows 95 workstation

    B. Windows NT PDC

    C. Windows NT Workstation

    D. Windows NT Server

15. Which of the following tools aids you in tracking license purchases in your domain?

    A. License Manager

    B. Purchase Manager

    C. Client Licenser

    D. None of the above; no such tool exists.

Answers to Review Questions

1. You can change the IRQ setting of a network adapter from within the Network application. For more information, see the section "Configururing Network Adapters."

2. In order to connect to a NetWare server, you must have the NWLink protocol installed on your NT machine. This protocol is Microsoft's emulation of the NetWare protocol IPX/SPX. For more information, see the section "Installing and Configuring NWLink."

3. The service that assigns and configures TCP/IP addresses is called Dynamic Host Configuration Protocol (DHCP). For more information, see the section "Windows NT Core Protocols."

4. The server service designed to synchronize files on two machines is called the Replicator. Two roles must be configured: export computer and import computer. For more information, see the section "Directory Replication."

5. The service responsible for the information required to populate the Network Neighborhood is the Browser service. If no browser can be found on a network, a browser election is called to choose a new one from among the computers available to become browsers. For more information, see the section "Computer Browser Service."

6. The rule of thumb for client licensing is this: If the number of simultaneous connections to all your servers exceeds the total number of users, you should use per seat licensing. Because "any user can be expected to be accessing one or more of these servers at any one time," you can assume that it's very likely the total number of connections will exceed the number of users; therefore,

you should use per seat licensing. For more information, see the section "Windows NT Client Licenses."

Answers to Exam Questions

1. **A, B, C.** For TCP/IP to function at all, you must have at least an address and a subnet mask. However, in order to function in a routed environment, a default gateway must also be configured to allow your machine to communicate with hosts in other subnets. For more information, see the section "Working with TCP/IP."

2. **C.** Although configuring DHCP will ensure that all clients have TCP/IP addresses and that the TCP/IP protocol is completely configured, no allowances have been made for name resolution. To form a complete solution, an NT Server should have been configured with the WINS service to provide name resolution among the Microsoft computers, and DNS should have been configured to provide name resolution outside of the company (to Internet hosts). For more information, see the section "Windows Core Services."

3. **B.** The WINS service is responsible for dynamically collecting and mapping NetBIOS names to TCP/IP addresses. For more information, see the section "Windows Core Services."

4. **D.** Of the operating systems listed, each can be a client of a DHCP server (i.e., can receive TCP/IP configuration) except LAN MAN 2.2c client for OS/2. For more information, see the section "Configuring Windows NT Server for Client Computers."

5. **A.** A basic replication event involves the export computer telling one or more import computers that they should come and get data. At that point, the import computer(s) pull data from the export computer. For more information, see the section "Directory Replication."

6. **C.** All computers that can possibly become browsers—but are not necessarily browsers yet—are initially configured as *potential browsers*. When an election is held, one computer becomes the master browser; others may become backup browsers depending on the number of clients on the network; and others remain as potential browsers until they're needed. Some computers are configured as non-browsers, which means they can never become browsers and are never potential browsers. For more information, see the section "Computer Browser Service."

7. **D.** The rule of thumb for choosing a license type is this: If the total number of simultaneous connections will ever exceed the number of users, you should be licensing on a per seat basis because some of your users are using more than one connection at one time. For more information, see the section "Windows NT Client Licenses."

8. **B.** The IPCONFIG command line utility will tell you what your current TCP/IP configuration is. If you use the /all switch with this utility, you will get a complete listing of all the configuration settings for TCP/IP on your computer. For more information, see the section "Working with TCP/IP."

9. **B.** Service startup configuration can be changed from within the Services program, which is accessible from the Control Panel. In that program, you can select the service you desire to change, click the Startup Configuration button, and choose automatic. For more information, see the section "The Services Application."

APPLY YOUR LEARNING

10. **A.** Pausing the Server service does not stop the service. Therefore, the users who are currently connected via that service maintain their connections. However, pausing the service does not allow new users to connect. Stopping the service disconnects all users who are connected to the computer via the network. For more information, see the section "The Services Application."

11. **B, C.** Several things can force a browser election on a network. Two of these are the starting of a domain controller and the lack of response from a browser when a client requests the browse list. For more information, see the section "Computer Browser Service."

12. **D.** To ensure that a Windows NT computer never becomes a browser, you set the MaintainServerList parameter in the `HKEY_Local_Machine\System\CurrentControlSet\ Services\Browser\Parameters` Registry key. For more information, see the section "Computer Browser Service."

13. **A, B, C.** Of the operating systems listed, all can function as an import computer in directory replication except for the Windows 95 workstation. For more information, see the section "Directory Replication."

14. **B, D.** Any NT Server can function as an export machine in directory replication. Therefore, a PDC in particular (which must be an NT Server) must be listed as a correct answer. For more information, see the section "Directory Replication."

15. **A.** The License Manager can be used to track the purchase of client licenses in a domain. For more information, see the section "Windows NT Client Licenses."

APPLY YOUR LEARNING

Suggested Readings and Resources

The following are some recommended readings related to the configuration of NT Server network components:

1. Microsoft Official Curriculum course 922: *Supporting Microsoft Windows NT 4.0 Core Technologies*

    • Module 2: Installing Windows NT

    • Module 3: Configuring the Windows NT Environment

    • Module 10: Configuring Windows NT Protocols

    • Module 11: Windows NT Network Services

    • Module 15: Implementing Network Clients

    • Module 16: Implementing Directory Replication

2. *Microsoft Windows NT Networking Guide* (Microsoft Press; also available with the NT Server Resource Kit)

    • Chapter 1: Windows NT 4 Networking Architecture

    • Chapter 6: TCP/IP Implementation Details

    • Chapter 13: Using NetBEUI with Windows NT

3. Microsoft TechNet CD-ROM

    • *Concepts and Planning: MS Windows NT Server 4.0*

        • Chapter 1: Managing NT Server Domains

        • Chapter 11: Managing Client Administration

    • *Workstation Resource Guide*

        • Chapter 30: Microsoft TCP/IP and Related Services for Windows NT

        • Chapter 31: Microsoft TCP/IP Architecture

4. Web sites

    • www.microsoft.com/ntserver

    • www.microsoft.com/train_cert

    • www.prometric.com/ testingcandidates/ assessment/ chosetest.html (take online assessment tests)

Microsoft provides the following objectives for the disk and peripheral portion of the "Installation and Configuration" objective:

Configure peripherals and devices. Peripherals and devices include: communication devices, SCSI devices, tape device drivers, UPS devices and UPS service, mouse drivers, display drivers, and keyboard drivers.

▶ This objective is necessary because someone certified in the use of Windows NT Server technology must understand the different peripherals that can be attached to an NT Server and the installation and configuration of each. This section covers the Control Panel configuration of each peripheral.

Configure hard disks to meet various requirements. Requirements include: allocating disk space capacity, providing redundancy, improving performance, providing security, and formatting.

▶ This objective is necessary because someone certified in the use of Windows NT Server technology must understand the different disk configuration options. This includes file types, fault tolerance, performance tuning, and security. As well, you should understand when each of these options is appropriate for use.

Configure printers. Tasks include: adding and configuring a printer, implementing a printer pool, and setting print priorities.

▶ This objective is necessary because someone certified in the use of Windows NT Server technology must understand the NT printing process and the installation, configuration, and sharing of one or more printers. A complete understanding of the appropriate use of different print configurations is important.

CHAPTER 4

Installation and Configuration Part 3: Configuring Windows NT Server Disks and Peripherals

OUTLINE

STUDY STRATEGIES

A variety of strategies relate to studying the material in this chapter. In order to make it most helpful, each objective will be discussed separately.

▶ The first note to make on studying is that the sections on the NT Registry are mostly for information. You will be asked questions about the Registry only as it relates to other topics, not as a topic of its own. As a result, you do not have to study that material in depth. However, you should know what the Registry is, what the editors are, and how they work.

The Microsoft NT Server exams rarely delve into the minutiae of installing and configuring peripherals such as those covered in the peripherals section. However, it is still a good idea to be familiar with the elements of the Control Panel, what devices or software they configure, and what options are available for each device. Although you can get much of the information here, you will also want to go to a Windows NT Server computer and explore a bit on your own. Actually, installing some of the hardware components and configuring them will do wonders for your understanding and retention of details for the exam.

One element to watch for in particular is the configuration of a UPS, especially the /noserialmice setting that is inserted into the BOOT.INI file to prevent detection of serial mice by NT at startup (because the detection process has a tendency to shut down some UPSs).

▶ You can expect a number of questions related to disks and disk configurations on the NT Server exam—especially in scenario format, where the disk configuration is one of many factors you need to take into account. Because the configuration of disks can mean the difference between having enough space for all your data or not, between having the security you need or not, and between having the recoverability you need or not, it is a major focus of the exam.

The author's suggestion is that you first understand the underlying functions and configuration of partitions, how they are created, how they are lettered, and how ARC paths work. After that, look at formatting and the implication of the file systems NT supports. Finally, study the fault-tolerance methods.

Once you have a good grasp of the theory presented here and in the supplementary readings, play with the configurations in a live situation. If possible, get a computer with multiple physical drives so that you can practice working with stripe sets with parity and mirrored sets. As well, format FAT and convert to NTFS just to see how conversion works. In short, get inside your disk configuration by experimenting with it, and you will be well prepared for the exam.

▶ Finally, as a study strategy for printing, you really need to know what the process looks like on a theoretical level first. Study the processes and the terminology used to describe the component parts. The exams like to test your knowledge of the difference between a printer and a print device, especially because not all operating systems use the terms the same way. As well, understand how printer drivers are distributed (that they are downloaded by an NT client at print time and installed when the network connection is first made everywhere else). Finally, you should understand things like permissions on printers, methods for clearing the spooler, and what a printer pool is and how it works.

Of course, you should also install a couple of printers on an NT system and share them, just to get a feel for those processes.

INTRODUCTION

This chapter begins with an overview of the Windows NT Registry and the Registry Editors available with NT Server, then moves to disk configuration and then to printer configuration. Because these topics are so important to the day-to-day operation of your NT Server computer, they frequently show up in both multiple-choice and scenario questions on the exam.

WINDOWS NT AND THE REGISTRY

The Registry is Windows NT's storehouse for configuration information. In order to understand Windows NT, you certainly must have an understanding of what the Registry is and how it works. And yet, direct references to the Registry are conspicuously absent from Microsoft's exam objectives for the Windows NT Server exam. It could be that Microsoft finds it impossible to write an exam question on the hundreds of Registry keys, subkeys, and values that is anything other than pure memorization. Whatever the reason, it is important to know that *any* configuration you do in Windows NT somehow finds its way into the Registry and, because this is a chapter on Windows NT configuration, it wouldn't be complete without a discussion of the Registry itself.

The Registry is a configuration database that was designed to replace the plethora of INI files used to configure both the operating system and applications under other versions of Windows. Unfortunately, Windows 95, which is on its way to becoming Registry-based, is not quite there yet. The Registry has several advantages over the older system:

◆ *Centralization.* Instead of a PROGMAN.INI, a CPANEL.INI, and a host of other such files for your applications, Windows NT stores all its configuration data in the Registry. As a result, any Windows NT component and Windows NT-based application can easily find information about any other aspect of the computer. In addition, the Registry supports remote administration: An administrator sitting at her own workstation can alter another computer's configuration by remotely editing its Registry.

◆ *Structure.* The Registry can contain subsections within sections, something that was impossible with INI files. The end result is a much more orderly, logical record.

◆ *Flexibility.* INI files contained ASCII text. The Registry can contain text, but it also can hold binary and hexadecimal values. It can even hold executable code or entire text files. The Registry also contains preferences and restrictions for individual users, something that INI files never have done. This provides a configuration database that stores not only computer-specific information but also user-specific information.

◆ *Security.* You can protect the Registry just like any object in Windows NT. An Access Control List can be defined for any Registry key, and a special set of permissions exists specifically for dealing with the Registry.

When you view it from this perspective, you might wonder how users survived without the Registry. However, the Registry has its drawbacks:

◆ *It's cryptic.* Unlike INI files, the assumption with many parts of the Registry seems to be that humans just don't go here. It isn't always easy to determine why certain entries are present or how to effectively configure them.

◆ *It's sprawling.* Imagine all the INI files on an average Windows 3.x-based computer merged into a single file, with some additional hardware information as well. The Registry begins its life big, and it only gets bigger.

◆ *Editing can be dangerous.* If you make a mistake when editing an INI file, or if you aren't sure about the potential effect of a change, you can always exit the text editor without saving the file. Even a fatal change to an INI file can be fixed by booting to MS-DOS and using a text editor to alter the problematic file. Not so with the Registry: Direct changes to the Registry are often dynamic and potentially irreversible.

Windows NT provides the following three tools for editing and managing Registry information:

◆ Registry Editors

◆ Control Panel

◆ System Policy Editor

Later in this chapter, you'll learn more about the Registry Editors and some of the Control Panel applications.

How Windows NT Uses the Registry

You now know what the Registry is, at least conceptually. But when and how is it used? The when is easy: constantly. The how is a bit harder to answer, but only because the scope of the Registry is so broad.

Windows NT accesses the Registry in the following situations:

◆ *When changes are made to the Control Panel.* All changes to values in the Control Panel are written to the Registry. Even when the Control Panel serves merely to confirm values already in place, the information is read from the Registry.

◆ *During setup.* The main Windows NT Setup program or a setup program for a Win32 application always examines the Registry for existing configuration information before entering new configuration information.

◆ *With the use of Administrative Tools.* User Manager, Event Viewer, and other Administrative Tools all read and write their information to various parts of the Registry.

◆ *During the boot process.* When Windows NT boots, hardware information is fed into the Registry. In addition, the kernel reports its version and build number to the Registry and extracts the name and order of the device drivers that must be loaded. These device drivers communicate with the Registry as well, reporting the resources they're using for the current session.

◆ *When changes are made to security.* Whenever changes are made to the accounts database, the new information is stored in the Registry.

How Users Use the Registry

Although users can read entries in the Registry, they should not change any of them, and frankly, the Registry should be transparent to them. User settings can be modified indirectly through the

Control Panel. Only experienced administrators should work directly with the Registry.

How Administrators Use the Registry

Just because administrators can directly modify the Registry doesn't mean they should do so. Even administrators should continue to use the Control Panel, Windows NT Setup, and other front–end devices whenever possible. Only edit the Registry directly when there is no other option for accomplishing the configuration task at hand.

The Registry is so delicate that Microsoft always includes this disclaimer with any instructions about making changes: "Edit the Registry only with the specific steps spelled out and only after creating a current emergency repair disk (ERD)." For more on the Windows NT emergency repair disk, see Chapter 9, "Troubleshooting."

Using the Registry Editors

Windows NT comes with two Registry Editors: REGEDT32.EXE and REGEDIT.EXE. REGEDT32 is the traditional Registry Editor that comes with NT. The other, REGEDIT, functions the same as the Windows 95 Registry Editor and displays Registry keys in an "Explorer"-like fashion.

Although the two tools are similar in that they both allow you to view Registry settings and make modifications to them, they are also different in their functionality. You cannot perform all the tasks you may want with either one, so being able to use both will greatly enhance your capabilities at Registry modification. Advantages of REGEDIT.EXE (shown in Figure 4.1) include the simplicity of the interface (you see all the keys in an Explorer-like interface) and its enhanced key-value-finding capabilities.

Advantages of REGEDT32.EXE (shown in Figure 4.2) are its capability to create and edit a larger variety of key values and to change security settings for Registry keys.

FIGURE 4.1
A typical REGEDIT window.

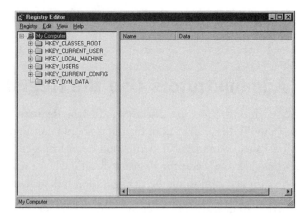

Both editors allow you to create new keys and modify the contents of any key value to which you have enough access. You will note that although both are installed with Windows NT Server, neither is given an icon in any program group. This fact is a sure sign that they are to be used infrequently—and then only by someone knowledgeable to know what keys to look for and modify and exactly what the implications of those modifications will be.

You can find both programs in the System32 subdirectory of your Windows NT root directory. Before exploring the Registry in the next sections, you should know about a couple of recommendations and one major warning:

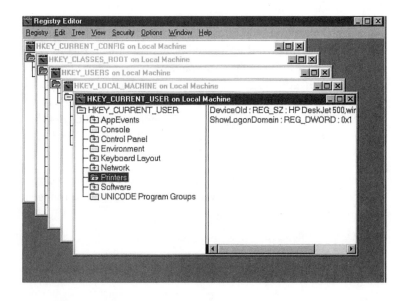

FIGURE 4.2
A typical REGEDT32 window.

◆ Whenever possible, you should use REGEDT32 because it allows you to work in Read Only mode to prevent inadvertent modifications to the Registry, and it allows you to modify security settings.

◆ Upon entering REGEDT32, configure it for Read Only mode (choose Options, Read Only Mode) and leave it that way until the moment you want to make a Registry modification. When the desired modification is complete, set it back to Read Only mode. This procedure helps prevent accidental modification of Registry settings.

◆ Upon entering REGEDT32, configure it to confirm deletions (choose Options, Confirm on Delete) to ensure that any deletions you make are really intentional, and not accidental. As in Read Only mode, a check mark precedes the option on the menu when it has been selected. If the option isn't selected, pressing the Delete key irretrievably erases the selected Registry key and all its subkeys. By default, Confirm on Delete is selected, and it's automatically enabled when you work in Read Only mode. In fact, in Read Only mode, you cannot turn off Confirm on Delete.

◆ If you're using a production computer to explore the Registry, back up Registry files before you go any further.

Comparing the Registry Editors

The REGEDIT.EXE and REGEDT32.EXE programs essentially perform the same function: They allow you to navigate and modify the Windows NT Registry. However, they have different looks, and each has unique features in addition to the common ones.

Both editors allow you to navigate through the Registry and observe the contents. Both editors also allow you to make modifications to the contents of Registry keys (where the configuration settings in the Registry are actually kept).

For the purposes of adding keys and modifying their values, REGEDT32.EXE is a superior tool. This is because it allows you to make more specific the kind of value it presents in the key itself. Whereas REGEDIT allows you to define only three kinds of Registry values, REGEDT32 allows you to define five.

WARNING

Microsoft Technical Assistants Will Not Fix Your Registry Before you change anything using either Registry Editor, you should understand that Microsoft washes its hands of its technical support responsibility if you edit the Registry directly. In other words, you're on your own. If your computer does not boot after you alter the Registry, you can call Microsoft's Product Support Service Engineers, and they probably will do their best to help you. But their best may not be good enough. You may have to reinstall the operating system or, at the very least, undertake the emergency repair process described in Chapter 9. Because the Registry Editor can write binary, ASCII, hex, or executable code directly into the Registry, a simple mistyped character can have disastrous consequences.

For the purpose of adding security to Registry keys, REGEDT32 is the only one that allows you to do this. With REGEDT32, you can modify key-level security to define the modification privileges (defined in the accounts database) that individuals or groups have on specific keys.

However, REGEDIT is clearly superior to REGEDT32 in the area of key value searching. It is often necessary to locate a key based on the content of that key; for example, suppose you are searching for where a specific application stores its dictionary and you want to search for any keys containing the string "custom.dic." REGEDT32 will allow you to search only key names themselves. It will not allow you to search into the content of those keys, which is necessary to do the previously-mentioned search. REGEDIT does allow you to search down to the value of keys.

Navigating the Registry

Look back at the Registry Editor main window shown in Figure 4.2 and examine it for a minute. Refer to it as you read the next section, which introduces some important MCSE terminology.

Notice that the Registry Editor contains five child windows. If you conceptualize the Registry as a giant tree with branches and sub-branches and leaves, these five windows are the roots of the tree. In Windows NT-parlance, these roots are called *subtrees* (and occasionally, *predefined key handles*). The five subtrees are:

- ◆ *HKEY_LOCAL_MACHINE.* Stores all the computer-specific configuration data.

- ◆ *HKEY_USERS.* Stores all the user-specific configuration data.

- ◆ *HKEY_CURRENT_USER.* Stores all configuration data for the user who's currently logged on.

- ◆ *HKEY_CLASSES_ROOT.* Stores all OLE and file association information.

- ◆ *HKEY_CURRENT_CONFIG.* Stores information about the hardware profile specified at startup.

Before delving into a discussion of these subtrees, take a closer look at the foreground window in the Registry Editor. You might find it

---

EXAM TIP

Referring to REGEDT32 on Exam
Because the NT Server exam will almost always make reference to REGEDT32, the following discussion will also reference that application. Note, however, that most of what is discussed in these sections applies equally, regardless of the application you are using to navigate and modify the Registry. Exceptions will be noted where appropriate.

somewhat similar in appearance to Explorer. This is intentional: Conceptually, it helps if you picture the Registry as a series of directories, subdirectories, and files. Unfortunately, the Registry doesn't really work that way.

Several files collectively comprise the Registry, but they don't break down as evenly as they do in the interface. In fact, they hardly break down below the top level at all. Some of the data in the Registry actually never gets written to disk: It's dynamically collected every time the system boots and is stored in memory until the system is shut down.

Each of the folders you see in the left pane of the subtree window represents a *key*. A key is a category, a fitting abstraction, because keys don't really exist anywhere outside Registry Editor. As you also can see from the diagram, keys can contain *subkeys* (or subcategories); there is no limit to how far a branch can reach.

Eventually, however, branches sprout leaves. In the Registry, keys produce values. A value has three components: a name by which it is referenced in the Registry, a data type (text, binary, and so on), and the data itself.

The types of data that can be stored in the Registry have been defined, but look at how these data types are referenced in the Registry Editor:

- ◆ *REG_BINARY.* Indicates that binary data follows. The binary data, however, actually is stored as a string of hexadecimal pairs, which represent byte values (2 hex digits give a range of 0 to 255 for each byte).

- ◆ *REG_DWORD.* Indicates that the data is stored in a word, a term applied to a four-byte number. Words can range in value from 0 to 4,294,967,295 (a 4GB range, which is enough to accommodate the full address range of a 32-bit operating system).

- ◆ *REG_SZ.* Denotes a string value. A string is simply text.

- ◆ *REG_MULTI_SZ.* Denotes a multiple string, which actually appears as a list in the Registry, with the list items separated by null characters.

- ◆ *REG_EXPAND_SZ.* Indicates an expandable string, which really is a variable. For instance, %SystemRoot% is an expandable string that Windows NT would interpret as the actual root directory for the operating system.

It is helpful to note that only three data types are referenced from REGEDIT: REG_BINARY, REG_DWORD, and REG_SZ. The data type REG_SZ allows you to view and modify all three of the string types accessible from REGEDT32; it just does not describe them as such and does not provide as nice an interface for viewing and modifying them.

HKEY_LOCAL_MACHINE

HKEY_LOCAL_MACHINE contains all configuration information relevant to the local machine (see Figure 4.3). Every piece of information that applies to the local computer, regardless of who (if anyone) is logged on, gets stored somewhere in this subtree.

This subtree has five subkeys: HARDWARE, SAM, SECURITY, SOFTWARE, and SYSTEM, which are discussed in the following sections.

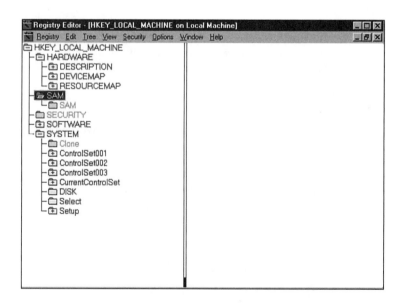

FIGURE 4.3
The Registry tree HKEY_LOCAL_MACHINE.

HARDWARE

The Hardware key is the only volatile key in
HKEY_LOCAL_MACHINE; its data is never saved to or read from
a file. Instead, Windows NT automatically detects the current hardware every time the operating system is booted and stores that information under the Hardware key's three subkeys: Description,
DeviceMap, and ResourceMap (see Figure 4.4).

Description

The Description subkey contains the hardware database that's detected by Windows NT during system boot. On Intel-based computers,
the Windows NT hardware recognizer (NTDETECT.COM)
autodetects this information. On RISC-based computers, the computer's firmware passes this information to the Registry. Entries for
the CPU (CentralProcessor), math coprocessor
(FloatingPointProcessor), and <multifunction_adapter>, which is
usually called *Multifunction Adapter* (except in EISA computers,
where it is called EisaAdapter) are listed at the top of the following
tree:

HKEY_LOCAL_MACHINE\HARDWARE\DESCRIPTION\
System

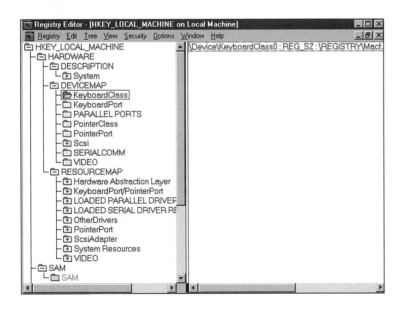

FIGURE 4.4

The Hardware key of the
HKEY_LOCAL_MACHINE subtree.

The <multifunction_adapter> entry enumerates the rest of the devices on the system, including the hard disk controller and serial and parallel ports.

Each device key has an Identifier value, which contains the "name" of each detected device—information that can prove helpful when troubleshooting hardware information.

DeviceMap

The subkeys of this subkey enumerate the Windows NT device drivers currently in use and point to the configuration information for each driver, which is contained elsewhere in the following Registry key:

    HKEY_LOCAL_MACHINE\SYSTEM\CurrentControlSet\Services

ResourceMap

The ResourceMap key tracks IRQ and DMA settings and other resource allocation for and by each driver. If two devices are competing for a specific resource, the information in ResourceMap can tell you which devices are conflicting. Of course, the information isn't readable; you need to use another front-end, like Windows NT Diagnostics (WINMSD.EXE), to view it in a readable form. (See Chapter 9 for more information on WINMSD.)

SAM

SAM, Security Accounts Manager, is the Registry key that contains the entire user and group account database. As such, it sure is tempting to poke around in it a bit. Unfortunately for would-be techno-predators, but fortunately for administrators, this key is off limits even to administrators. The only way to modify the data in SAM is to use the User Manager utility (or User Manager for Domains on a Windows NT Server domain controller). SAM is actually a subkey of the SECURITY key:

    HKEY_LOCAL_MACHINE\SECURITY\SAM

SECURITY

Besides mirroring the SAM key, SECURITY also contains all the policy information discussed in Chapter 4, as well as local group membership information. As with SAM, this key is off limits to all users (including administrators). To modify this information, an administrator must use an application such as User Manager to make a call to the Windows NT Security API.

SOFTWARE

SOFTWARE is a particularly busy key: It defines and maintains configuration data for all Win32 software on the computer, including Windows NT (see Figure 4.5). At least five, and often more, subkeys are available here: Classes, Microsoft, Program Groups, Secure, and Windows 3.1 Migration Status, and perhaps additional subkeys for other software vendors besides Microsoft.

Classes

File association and OLE information are stored in this subkey (see Figure 4.6), which evolved from the old Windows 3.x configuration Registry. In fact, to maintain compatibility with the old Windows 3.x Registry addressing scheme, this information is mirrored in the HKEY_CLASSES_ROOT subtree. The applications themselves handle OLE configuration, and file association using File Manager hasn't changed since Windows 3.1.

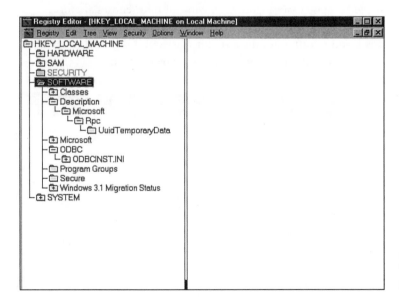

FIGURE 4.5
The Software key of the HKEY_LOCAL_MACHINE subtree.

FIGURE 4.6
The Software\Classes subkey of the
HKEY_LOCAL_MACHINE subtree.

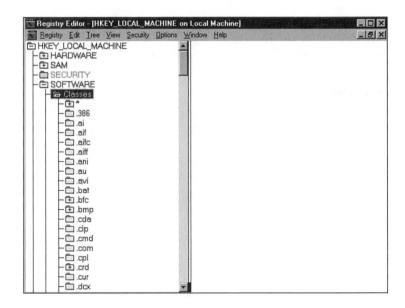

FIGURE 4.6
The Software\Classes subkey of the
HKEY_LOCAL_MACHINE subtree.

Microsoft

One of the more populated keys in the Registry, this key contains
subkeys for all Microsoft software installed on the Windows NT-
based computer (see Figure 4.7). Most of these entries are for
Windows NT and its related components (Browser, Clipbook Server,
Mail, and so on), but others are for Microsoft Office, Cinemania 96,
or whatever Microsoft applications may be installed.

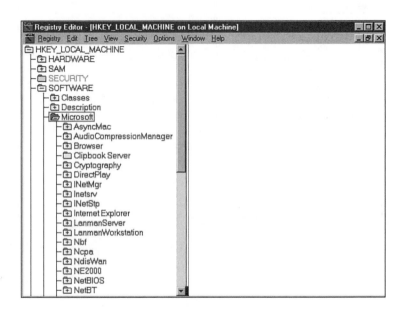

FIGURE 4.7
The Software\Microsoft subkey of the
HKEY_LOCAL_MACHINE subtree.

This key sets the rule for other vendors' keys. Typically, you can expect to find one key at this level for each software vendor and sub-keys for each installed title published by that vendor.

Of particular interest is the following key:

HKEY_LOCAL_MACHINE\SOFTWARE\Microsoft\Windows NT\CurrentVersion

You can find various items of useful information under this key, such as the name and company of the user who installed the operating system (which you can change from here), the current build number, the current Service Pack, and other items specific to Windows NT.

Program Groups

In Windows NT, the program groups in the Programs menu can be either personal (in which case they appear only on the desktop of the user that created them) or common (in which case they appear on the desktop of anyone who logs on at the computer). The HKEY_LOCAL_MACHINE\SOFTWARE\Program Groups Registry subkey contains a list of the common program groups for this computer (the personal program groups are stored under HKEY_USERS because that is user-specific information).

Secure

This key actually goes completely unused by Windows NT, although other applications (such as Microsoft Exchange Server) use it to maintain configuration data that's restricted to administrator access.

Windows 3.1 Migration Status

If you installed Windows NT Server in a directory that previously contained an old copy of Windows 3.x or Windows for Workgroups 3.x, certain computer-specific configuration items from Windows 3.x were migrated to Windows NT when the system rebooted for the first time. These items include the REG.DAT file and certain WIN.INI settings. The presence of this key indicates that the migration is complete. To force the migration to occur again, you can simply delete this key.

SYSTEM

The critical HKEY_LOCAL_MACHINE\SYSTEM subkey maintains information about the device drivers and services installed on a

Windows NT-based computer (see Figure 4.8). The SYSTEM key contains numerous subkeys, most of which are called ControlSets because they contain configuration settings used to control the devices and services on the computer. Each ControlSet contains four subkeys: Control, Enum, Hardware Profiles, and Services. The Control key maintains information necessary to control the computer, such as the current time zone, the list of drivers to load during system boot, and the name of the computer that's displayed on the network. The Services key configures background processes that control hardware devices, file systems, network services, and so on.

Typically, you see a ControlSet001 and ControlSet002. You also might see a ControlSet003 and even a ControlSet004. Potentially, the four possible ControlSets are:

◆ *Current.* The ControlSet used to successfully boot the computer for the current session.

◆ *Default.* The ControlSet to be used to boot the system the next time the computer reboots.

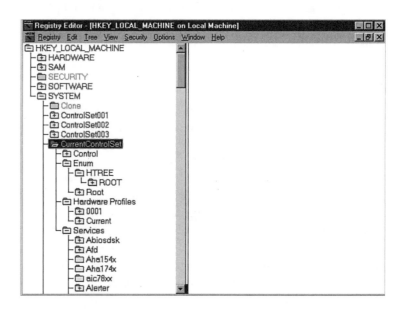

FIGURE 4.8
The System/CurrentControlSet subkey of the HKEY_LOCAL_MACHINE subtree.

◆ *Failed.* The ControlSet that attempted but failed to boot the system for this current session.

◆ *LastKnownGood.* The ControlSet that was used to successfully boot the computer for the current session and has been backed up in case the Default ControlSet fails the next time the system is rebooted.

Each of the ControlSet00x entries maps to at least one of these four types of ControlSets. You can view the mappings by examining the HKEY_LOCAL_MACHINE\SYSTEM\Select key. The values for this key are entries for each of the preceding ControlSets. The data for each value is the *x* in a ControlSet00x entry.

Typically, only two ControlSet00x entries appear. One of these maps to both Current and Default and, because the Current ControlSet was successful, it's used as the Default ControlSet for the next reboot. The other ControlSet00x entry maps to LastKnownGood.

If you do see a third ControlSet00x entry, it probably indicates a configuration change that has been made during the current session. Because the Current ControlSet (the one used to boot the system) no longer is the Default ControlSet (the one used to boot the system next time), a separate ControlSet00x entry must exist for Current and Default.

A fourth ControlSet00x entry should exist only if your computer failed to restart and had to resort to the LastKnownGood configuration. In that case, the ControlSet that was Default and would have been Current becomes Failed, and LastKnownGood becomes Current.

The Clone subkey of the SYSTEM key is a temporary holding area that Windows NT uses for creating the LastKnownGood ControlSet, and the CurrentControlSet subkey is a mirror of whichever ControlSet00x entry contains the Current ControlSet. The final subkey is the Setup key, which the Windows NT Setup program uses. Administrators and users have no need to go there.

HKEY_CLASSES_ROOT

As mentioned earlier, the HKEY_CLASSES_ROOT subtree is a mirror of HKEY_LOCAL_MACHINE\SOFTWARE\Classes. It's mirrored here to provide compatibility with the Windows 3.x registration database, which also is accessed using the HKEY_CLASSES_ROOT handle.

HKEY_CURRENT_USER

The HKEY_CURRENT_USER subtree contains the user profile for the user who is currently logged on (refer to Figure 4.2). Profiles contain all user preferences and restrictions, including Control Panel settings, personal program groups, printer connections, network drive connections, bookmarks in WinHelp, and even the most recently accessed documents in Microsoft Word. User profiles are discussed in detail later in this chapter.

HKEY_CURRENT_USER maps to HKEY_USERS\<*SID_of_current_user*>, in which *SID* is the lengthy security identifier associated with the user. Occasionally, keys in this subtree duplicate keys found in HKEY_LOCAL_MACHINE but contain different values. HKEY_CURRENT_USER almost always overrides HKEY_LOCAL_MACHINE.

HKEY_USERS

HKEY_USERS can potentially contain the user profiles for all users defined in the accounts database, although in practice it usually contains only the default user profile (HKEY_USERS\.DEFAULT) and the profile for the currently logged on user (HKEY_USERS\<*SID_of_current_user*>, which is also mapped to HKEY_CURRENT_USER). Figure 4.9 shows the HKEY_USERS subtree.

People frequently ask why Microsoft chose not to load all the user profiles in this subtree. The answer is that it isn't necessary and probably would not be advantageous. Remember that the Registry resides in memory. The more data in the Registry, the more memory the Registry uses. Because the only user profile required in memory at

any given time is the profile in use by the current user, loading other
user profiles as well is unnecessary. If you do need to alter another
user's profile, however, you can do so.

HKEY_CURRENT_CONFIG

The HKEY_CURRENT_CONFIG subtree contains information
about the current hardware profile for the system. You'll learn more
about hardware profiles later in this chapter.

Editing the Registry

To edit any value in the Registry, simply double-click on the value in
Registry Editor. A dialog box appears with the current value selected.
You may enter the data for a new value at this point. Choosing OK
effectively enters the value in the Registry. Don't look for a "Save
Settings?" message when you close Registry Editor; your changes are
saved as soon as you make them.

For configuration purposes, you might need to add a value to the
Registry (see Step by Step 4.1).

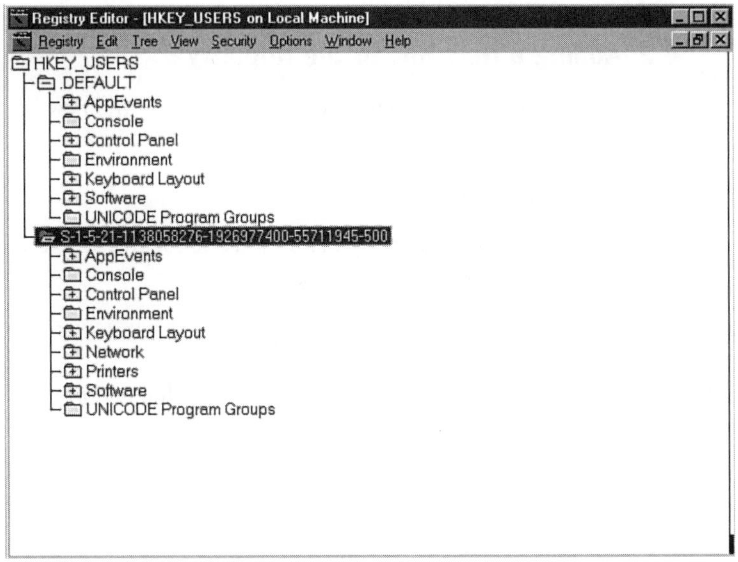

NOTE

**Write Must Be Enabled to Change
Registry** You must leave Read Only
mode to add a Registry value or key.
To do so, choose the Options menu
and deselect Read Only Mode.

FIGURE 4.9
The HKEY_USERS subtree.

FIGURE 4.10
Adding a value to an existing key.

STEP BY STEP

4.1 Adding a Value to an Existing Key

1. Select the key for which you want to add a value.

2. Choose Edit, Add Value to open the Add Value dialog box (see Figure 4.10).

3. In the Value Name text box, enter the name of the new value.

4. Select the appropriate data type from the Data Type combo box and choose OK.

5. In the String Editor dialog box, enter the data for the new value.

Sometimes you don't just need to add a value to a key that exists. You may need to actually create a key to add a new value to (see Step by Step 4.2).

STEP BY STEP

4.2 Adding a New Key to the Registry

1. Select the key under which you want to insert the new key.

2. Choose Edit, Add Key.

3. In the Add Key dialog box, enter a name for the new key in the Key Name box and choose OK.

To delete a key or a value, simply select the key or value and press

Delete. Again, be cautious: You cannot undo deletions any more than you can undo additions or changes. Every action you take in Registry Editor is irreversible (except through manual intervention). Therefore, to prevent accidental deletions, you should enable Confirm on Delete from the Options menu. If it's already activated, a check mark appears immediately to its left.

Searching the Registry

In order to thoroughly search the Registry, you use must a variety of techniques and both of the Registry Editors. Here are your options:

◆ *View, Find Key (in REGEDT32).* Searches only the Registry keys for the desired search string. You can't search for specific values using Find Key. Also, the Find Key command works only in the selected subtree, and within that subtree, it works only from the current key forward. You can't search more than one subtree using a single Find Key command.

◆ *Edit, Find* (in REGEDIT). Searches only the Registry for the desired search string in any keys, values, or data. Unlike the View, Find Key command in REGEDT32, this command enables you to search the entire Registry in a single Find session.

◆ *Registry, Save Subtree As.* Saves up to an entire subtree in a text file that you can view in any ASCII text editor or word processor. Before choosing this command, choose the key you want to use as the top level of your subtree. Registry Editor populates the text file with that key and its children. In the file, you can perform a search using a word processor or text editor.

◆ *Registry, Print Subtree.* Converts the selected key and its descendants into text. Instead of saving the key to a text file, however, this command directs its output to a printer.

NOTE **Know the Registry**   True masters of Windows NT are well-schooled on the Windows NT Registry, and the best way to understand the Registry is to print a copy of each subtree using the Print Subtree command. Armed with a hard copy of your Registry, begin to peruse the Windows NT Resource Guide, which thoroughly documents the major (and most of the minor) Registry entries. Wherever the Resource Guide misses, the REGENTRY.HLP file, which accompanies the Resource Guide on CD-ROM, more than picks up the slack. REGENTRY.HLP is an excellent hypertext guide to the Registry. You can download REGENTRY.HLP free from Microsoft's FTP server: ftp.microsoft.com.

R E V I E W   B R E A K

To summarize, the following are the key points relating to the Registry and Registry editing tools:

◆ The Registry is a unified database of Windows NT configuration information.

◆ The Registry consists of five subtrees: HKEY_LOCAL_MACHINE, HKEY_USERS, HKEY_CURRENT_USER, HKEY_CLASSES_ROOT, and HKEY_CURRENT_CONFIG.

◆ Two tools are available for viewing and modifying Registry information: REGEDT32 and REGEDIT.

WINDOWS NT CONTROL PANEL

The Windows NT Control Panel is a collection of small applications (applets) that each provide an interface to the Registry for the purpose of editing some specific Windows NT component (see Figure 4.11). The Control Panel is usually the first place to look if you need to make a change to your Windows NT configuration.

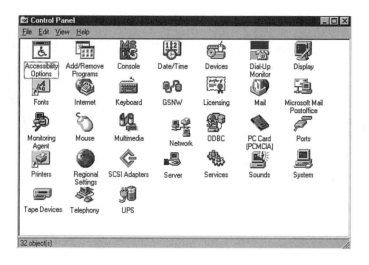

FIGURE 4.11
The Control Panel window.

To open the Control Panel, choose Start, Settings, Control Panel. Each Control Panel application has a specific purpose, and you'll hear them described throughout this book. This section introduces you to the Control Panel's System application. In later sections, you'll learn about the Network application, the Licensing application, and the various Control Panel applications that let you install and configure peripherals and other devices.

A typical Control Panel application, the System application is a smorgasbord of system wide configuration parameters. Because the System application is a fairly important configuration tool, and because it doesn't fall very neatly into any of the later sections in this chapter, I'll describe it for you here as an example of a Control Panel application.

When you double-click on the System icon in Control Panel, the System Properties dialog box appears. Five of the six tabs in the System Properties dialog box are discussed in the following sections. User profiles are discussed in detail in Chapter 5, "Managing Resources Part 1: Managing Users and User Environments."

Startup/Shutdown

The Startup/Shutdown tab (see Figure 4.12) enables you to set the default boot menu option for the system startup. It also enables you to define some recovery options the system can fall back on if it encounters a Stop error.

When a Windows NT-based computer is booted, the information in BOOT.INI is used to build the Boot Loader menu that appears before Windows NT loads. Boot Loader menu options typically include Windows NT Server 4, Windows NT Server 4 [VGA mode], and any other operating system that's set up to dual boot with Windows NT. Although BOOT.INI is a text file, you take a risk when you edit it directly; a mistyped character can have disastrous results. The Startup/Shutdown tab provides a safe way to configure the default operating system and the length of time the Boot Loader waits for the user to make a selection before proceeding to load the default operating system (specified in the Startup box).

The Recovery section of the Startup/Shutdown tab determines what happens in the event of a system crash. You can use any one or all of these four options at any given time:

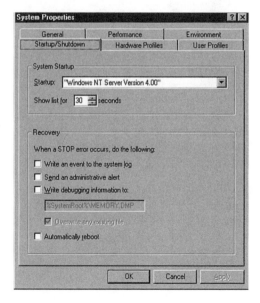

FIGURE 4.12
The Startup/Shutdown tab in the System Properties dialog box.

◆ *Write an Event to the System Log.* This option records an event that can be viewed using Event Viewer.

◆ *Send an Administrative Alert.* If the Alerter and Messenger services are running, alerts are sent to designated users and workstations if the system crashes.

◆ *Write Debugging Information To.* This option launches a program called SAVEDUMP.EXE whenever a system crash occurs. SAVEDUMP.EXE writes the entire contents of the computer's memory to the pagefile and flags it so that when the system reboots, the pagefile will be copied to the file specified in this option. Note that you can overwrite an existing file that may have been generated by an old crash dump, and then you can send the dump file to a debugger or a PSS Engineer for analysis. In order for this option to work, your computer's boot partition must have a pagefile at least as large as your computer's memory.

◆ *Automatically Reboot.* This option may be useful if a power surge or an errant application causes a crash (although the latter is extremely unlikely). If the problem is hardware-related, however, the same problem may occur after you restart the system.

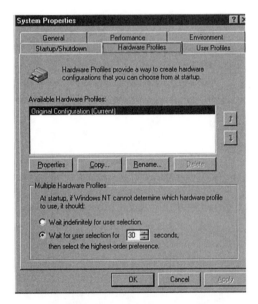

FIGURE 4.13
The Hardware Profiles tab in the System Properties dialog box.

Hardware Profiles

The Hardware Profiles tab enables you to create new hardware profiles and change the order of precedence among hardware profiles (see Figure 4.13). You can click on the Properties button to define a docking state for a portable computer or to enable or disable network hardware.

To create a new hardware profile, select an existing profile and click on the Copy button. In the subsequent Copy Profile dialog box, enter a name for the new hardware profile. The new hardware profile will then appear in the Available Hardware Profiles list.

The up and down arrows to the right of the Available Hardware Profiles list let you change the preference order of the hardware profiles. The radio buttons at the bottom of the Hardware Profiles tab let you specify whether Windows NT should wait indefinitely for you to choose a hardware profile, or whether the choice should default to the highest-preference profile after a specified amount of time.

If you define more than one hardware profile, Windows NT will display a menu of hardware profiles at startup and ask which profile you want to use. The profile you specify becomes the active hardware profile. Any changes you make to your hardware configuration affect the active hardware profile.

Environment

The Environment tab enables you to define system and user environment variables (see Figure 4.14). The system environment variables are written to the following Registry key:

> HKEY_LOCAL_MACHINESYSTEM\
> CurrentControlSetControl\Session Manager\Environment

You have to be an administrator to alter the System environment variables using Control Panel. The User Variables section is the only area of this tab that nonadministrators can access and configure (see Step by Step 4.3).

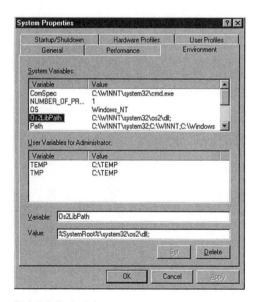

FIGURE 4.14
The Environment tab in the System Properties dialog box.

STEP BY STEP

4.3 Setting or Changing a User Environment Variable

1. Select the environment variable you want to change. (The variable and value appear in the Variable and Value text boxes.)

2. Position the cursor at (or tab down to) the Variable text box or the Value text box.

3. Change the variable or value (or both).

4. Click the Set button.

If none of the existing environment variables contain the information you want to store, you must create a new one as described in Step by Step 4.4.

STEP BY STEP

4.4 Creating a New Environment Variable and Setting Its Value

1. Click in the System Variables list box if you want to add a system variable. Click in the User Variables for Administrator list box if you want to add a user variable.

2. Click in the Variable text box and enter the name of the new variable.

3. Click in the Value text box and enter the value for the new variable.

4. Click the Set button.

If an existing environment variable is no longer useful, you can delete it (see Step by Step 4.5).

STEP BY STEP

4.5 Deleting an Environment Variable

1. Select the variable in the System Variables list or the User Variables for Administrator list.

2. Click the Delete button.

Performance

In the Application Performance section on the Performance tab, you can set the response time for the foreground application (see Figure 4.15). Drag the Boost control to the right to increase the response time, or drag to the left to decrease it.

In the Virtual Memory section, you can click on the Change button to open the Virtual Memory dialog box, which maintains settings for paging file sizes and the Registry size (see Figure. 4.16).

General

The General tab of the System Properties dialog box displays some basic information about your computer, such as the operating system and version number, the processor type and the amount of RAM, and the registration names from Windows NT Setup.

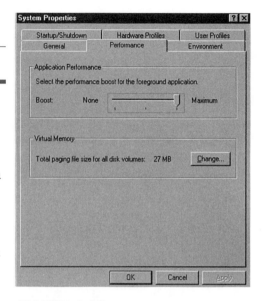

FIGURE 4.15
The Performance tab in the System Properties dialog box.

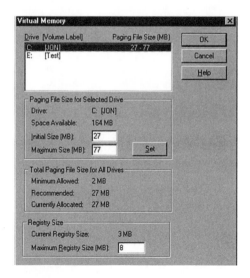

FIGURE 4.16
The Virtual Memory dialog box.

To summarize, the following are important points to remember about the Control Panel:

◆ The Control Panel consists of small applications (applets) that allow you to manipulate certain aspects of the Registry from within a controlled environment.

◆ The Startup/Shutdown tab in the System Properties dialog box allows you to control which operating system boots by default and how long you have to choose an operating system during system startup.

◆ The Hardware Profiles tab in the System Properties dialog box allows you to define different hardware configurations for the current machine that you can choose from during the boot process.

◆ The Environment Profiles tab in the System Properties dialog box allows you to configure system variables.

◆ The Performance tab in the System Properties dialog box allows you to boost foreground applications and configure virtual memory settings.

◆ The General tab in the System Properties dialog box provides you with basic information about your NT version, registration, and hardware.

CONFIGURING PERIPHERALS AND DEVICES

Configure peripherals and devices. Peripherals and devices include: communications devices, SCSI devices, tape device drivers, UPSs and UPS service, mouse drivers, display drivers, and keyboard drivers.

Control Panel includes several applications that help you install and configure peripherals and devices. You should be familiar with how to use those applications to install drivers and configure peripherals and hardware. Upcoming sections examine the following applications:

- Devices
- Multimedia
- Ports
- UPS
- SCSI Adapters
- Tape Devices
- PC Card
- Modems
- Keyboard
- Mouse
- Display

You should be familiar with how to use these applications for installing and configuring peripherals and devices.

Devices

The Devices application (SRVMGR.CPL) writes to HKEY_LOCAL_MACHINE\SYSTEM\CurrentControlSet\Services. You can start, stop, or disable device drivers in this Control Panel applet (see Figure 4.17).

The main Devices display area is divided into three columns: Device, Status, and Startup. The Device column identifies the name of the device driver as it appears in the Registry; the Status column reads Started if the driver is active, and appears blank otherwise; the Startup column denotes when each driver is configured to initialize.

To set the Startup value, select the device driver you want to modify and choose the Startup button. In the Device dialog box, shown in Figure 4.18, choose one of the following startup types and click OK.

EXAM TIP

Don't Memorize Specific Registry Keys   Although the following discussion mentions specific Registry keys that are changed through Control Panel applications, the actual keys are never the subject of NT Server exam questions. For the exam, it is sufficient for you to know that these icons exist and what they do.

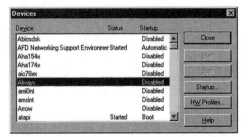

FIGURE 4.17
The Devices application.

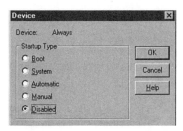

FIGURE 4.18
The Device dialog box.

◆ *Boot.* These devices start first, as soon as the kernel is loaded and initialized (see Chapter 9, "Troubleshooting," for more details about the boot process). These devices have a Start value of 0 in the Registry. Atdisk, the hard disk driver, is an example of a boot device.

◆ *System.* These devices start after the boot devices and after the HKEY_LOCAL_MACHINE subtree has begun to be built. These devices have a start value of 1 in the Registry. The video driver is a system device.

◆ *Automatic.* These devices start late in the boot process, when the Registry is almost entirely built but just before the WinLogon screen appears. These devices have a start value of 2 in the Registry. Serial (the serial port driver) is an automatic device.

◆ *Manual.* These devices are never started without administrator intervention. They may be manually started through the Control Panel Devices menu. These devices have a start value of 3 in the Registry.

◆ *Disabled.* These devices cannot be started at all unless their startup type is changed to something other than Disabled. These devices have a start value of 4 in the Registry. File system drivers are disabled by default. (However, file system recognizers are started with the system devices, and if any file system is "recognized," the startup type of the file system driver is changed to System.)

To start a device that isn't active, select the device and choose the Start button. If the Start button is grayed out, the device is already started or is disabled.

To stop a device that's active, select the device and choose the Stop button. A grayed-out stop button indicates that the device already is inactive.

To enable or disable a device for a given hardware profile, select the device, click on HW Profiles, select Enable or Disable to change to the desired status, and click on OK. (You'll learn more about hardware profiles later in this chapter.)

Multimedia

The Multimedia application (MMSYS.CPL) writes to
HKEY_LOCAL_MACHINE\SYSTEM\CurrentControlSet\Services.
Multimedia device drivers are added and configured from this
Control Panel applet. The Multimedia application also provides set-
tings for CD music, audio, video, and MIDI.

Ports

The Ports application (PORTS.CPL) writes directly to the following
key:

> HKEY_LOCAL_MACHINE\SYSTEM\
> CurrentControlSet\Services\Serial

This Control Panel interface lists only those serial ports that are
available but are not in use as serial ports. In other words, if a mouse
is connected to your COM1 port, COM1 doesn't show up in the
Control Panel Ports dialog box. All serial ports, regardless of whether
they appear in Control Panel Ports, are logged in the Registry under
the following key:

> HKEY_LOCAL_MACHINE\HARDWARE\Description\System\
> *<multifunction_adapter>*\0\˜SerialController\
> *<COM_port_number>*

Clicking the Settings button in the Ports application displays values
for the port's baud rate, data bits, parity, stop bits, and flow control.

If you need an additional port for use under Windows NT, choose
the Add button. In the Advanced Settings for New Port dialog box
(see Figure 4.19), you can assign a different COM port number, base
I/O port address, or IRQ, or you can enable a First In-First Out
(FIFO) buffer for that port.

To remove a port, simply select it in the Ports application and click
on the Delete button.

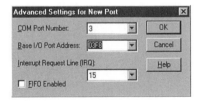

FIGURE 4.19
You can add a new port and configure its settings.

UPS

The UPS application (UPS.CPL) writes to the following Registry key:

HKEY_LOCAL_MACHINE\SYSTEM\CurrentControlSet\
Services\UPS

If your computer is equipped with an Uninterruptible Power Supply (UPS), Windows NT can be configured to communicate with it. The specific voltages requested in the UPS Configuration area depend on the UPS manufacturer and model. You may need to consult with your vendor to get these values. Armed with the correct information, Windows NT can recognize the following:

◆ *Power Failure Signal.* The point when an event is logged and the Server service is paused. No new connections to this server can be made, but existing connections will still function.

◆ *Low Battery Signal at Least 2 Minutes Before Shutdown.* As the name implies, Windows NT recognizes when the UPS battery is about to be exhausted.

◆ *Remote UPS Shutdown.* Signals Windows NT that the UPS is shutting down.

The Execute Command File option enables an administrator to specify a batch or executable file that will be run immediately preceding a shutdown. The program has 30 seconds before the system shuts down. The program cannot open a dialog box because that would require an attendant user.

If no Low Battery Signal option is configured, the administrator can enter the Expected Battery Life and the Battery Recharge Time Per Minute of Run Time in the lower-left corner of the dialog box.

After the initial PowerOut alert is raised (the Power Failure Signal has been received), Windows NT waits until the Time Between Power Failure and Initial Warning Message time has elapsed, and then it sends an alert to all interactive and connected users.

Windows NT repeats the alert every time the Delay Between Warning Messages time elapses.

If the UPS is about to run out of steam, the system shuts down safely. If power is restored, users are notified, an event is logged, and the Server service resumes.

SCSI Adapters

This application is one of the great misnomers in Windows NT. As it suggests, this application opens the SCSI Adapters dialog box, which is used to install SCSI adapter drivers. However, this dialog box also is used to install and remove IDE CD-ROM drivers as well as drivers for CD-ROM drives that use proprietary interfaces, such as Mitsumi or Panasonic drives. See Step by Step 4.6 for instructions on adding an adapter or driver.

When a SCSI adapter or CD-ROM device driver is no longer used on your system, you will need to remove it (see Step by Step 4.7).

STEP BY STEP

4.6 Adding a SCSI Adapter or CD-ROM Device Driver

1. Double-click in the SCSI Adapters application in the Control Panel.

2. In the SCSI Adapters dialog box, choose the Drivers tab and click on the Add button.

3. Select the driver from the list of available drivers in the Install Driver dialog box. If your driver isn't listed but you have a disk from the manufacturer with a Windows NT driver, click on the Have Disk button.

4. Choose OK. You must point Windows NT toward the original installation files (or the disk that contains the driver) and restart the computer in order for the new driver to initialize.

STEP BY STEP

4.7 Removing a SCSI Adapter or CD-ROM Device Driver

1. Select the Drivers tab in the SCSI Adapters dialog box.

2. Select the driver you want to remove.

3. Click the Remove button.

Tape Devices

Almost identical to the SCSI Adapter Setup dialog box in both appearance and function, this dialog box allows the installation and removal of tape drives (see Step by Step 4.8) for use with a Windows NT Backup program.

When a tape device is no longer present on your NT Server, you can remove it using the procedure outlined in Step by Step 4.9.

STEP BY STEP

4.8 Adding a Tape Drive Device Driver

1. Double-click the Tape Devices icon in Control Panel.

2. Select the Drivers tab.

3. Click the Add button.

4. Select the driver from the list of available drivers. If your driver isn't listed but you have a disk from the manufacturer with a Windows NT Driver, click the Have Disk button.

5. Choose OK. You must point Windows NT toward the original installation files (or the disk that contains the driver) and restart the computer in order for the new driver to initialize.

STEP BY STEP

4.9 Removing a Tape Drive Device Driver

1. Select the driver from the list of installed drivers in the Tape Devices dialog box of the Drivers tab.

2. Choose the Remove button.

PC Card (PCMCIA)

The PC Card application helps you install and configure PCMCIA device drivers. Select a PC card and click on Properties. Select the Drivers tab and then choose Add, Remove, or Configure as necessary.

A red X next to a device in the PC card list indicates that NT doesn't support the device.

Modems

The Modems application enables you to add or remove a modem. You can ask NT to detect your modem, or you can select a modem from a list.

STEP BY STEP

4.10 Adding a Modem

1. Double-click the Modems icon in the Control Panel.

2. In the Modems Properties dialog box (see Figure 4.20), click Add.

3. In the Install New Modem dialog box, click Next if you want NT to try to detect your modem. If NT detects your modem successfully, you're done.

   If you want to select your modem from the list or if you're providing software for a modem not listed, enable the Don't Detect... check box (see Figure 4.21), and then click Next. Then proceed to step 4.

FIGURE 4.20

The Modems Properties dialog box.

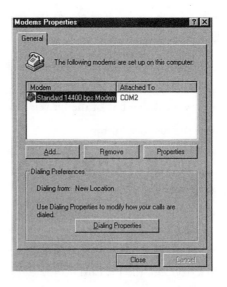

FIGURE 4.21

The Install New Modem dialog box.

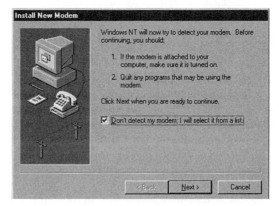

4. Select a manufacturer and a model, and click Next. Or click the Have Disk button if you're installing software for a modem not shown on the list.

5. Select a port for the modem, or select All ports. Click Next.

In the Modems Properties dialog box, select a modem in the Modems list and click on Properties to change the parameters for that modem. A new dialog box opens, with two tabs: General and Connection. The General tab enables you to set the port number and the maximum speed. The Connection tab enables you to define some connection preferences, such as the data bits, stop bits, and parity. Click on Advanced for additional settings.

The Dialing Properties button in the Modems Properties dialog box calls up the My Location tab, which is also in the Telephony application. The My Locations tab enables you to set the dialing characteristics for the modem. If you have a portable computer, you can define additional locations (see Step by Step 4.11) and configure a complete set of dialing properties for each location. If you sometimes travel to a certain hotel in Paris, for instance, you can define a location called Paris and specify the dialing properties you want to use for the Paris hotel. The next time you're in Paris, you have to change only the location setting in the I Am Dialing From box at the top of the My Location tab. The other settings automatically change to the settings you defined for Paris.

Keyboard

The Keyboard application opens the Keyboard Properties dialog box, which enables the user to set the keyboard repeat rate, the repeat delay, the cursor blink rate, and the keyboard layout properties. The keyboard driver appears on the General tab in the Keyboard Type text box (see Figure 4.22).

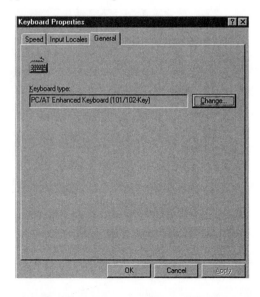

FIGURE 4.22
The Keyboard Properties dialog box.

STEP BY STEP

4.11 Adding a New Location

1. Click the New button at the top of the My Locations tab. (NT announces that a new location has been created.)

2. The new location has the name "New Location" (followed by a number if you already have a location called New Location). Click on the name and change it if you want to give your location a different name. (NT might not let you erase the old name completely until you add your new name. Add the new name and then backspace over the old text if necessary.)

3. Change any necessary dialing properties. The new properties will apply to your new location.

To select a new driver, click the Change button. The Select Device dialog box appears (see Figure 4.23).

Click the Show All Devices radio button to view a list of available drivers in the Models list. Then choose the keyboard model that matches your hardware. If your keyboard comes with its own installation disk for a model that isn't in the list, click the Have Disk button.

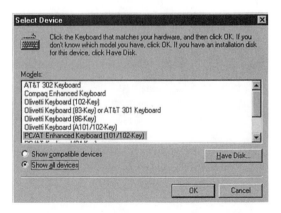

FIGURE 4.23
The Select Device dialog box.

Mouse

The options in this application control the mouse speed, sensitivity, and left- or right-handedness. The one new setting added to this dialog box since its Win 3.x predecessor is the Snap to Default option in the Motion tab, which instantly positions the pointer over the default button in the active dialog box. From the Pointers tab, you can select a pointer type. The General tab lets you install a new mouse driver. The procedure for selecting a mouse driver is similar to the procedure for selecting a keyboard driver (described in the preceding section).

Display

The Display application configures the values in the following key, including the video driver, screen resolution, color depth, and refresh rate:

HKEY_LOCAL_MACHINE\SYSTEM\CurrentControlSet\
Services\<*video_driver*>\ Device0\

The Display Properties dialog box, shown in Figure 4.24, offers the following five tabs:

◆ *Background.* Defines the wallpaper for the desktop.

◆ *Screen Saver.* Defines the screen saver for the desktop.

◆ *Appearance.* Defines window properties.

◆ *Plus!.* The Visual Enhancements tab from the Microsoft Plus! package for Windows 95 lets you configure the desktop to use large icons or to stretch the wallpaper to fit the screen.

◆ *Settings.* Defines desktop colors, refresh frequency, and other screen-related settings.

The Settings tab also contains a Test button. You should always test new display settings before you make changes permanent. Although Windows NT can detect the capabilities of your video card, it can't do the same with your monitor. Testing these settings before you apply them enables you to confirm that both the video card and monitor can support the new settings. Step by Step 4.12 demonstrates how to change the video adapter.

Unlike Windows 95, Windows NT doesn't let you change video resolution on-the-fly. The computer must be restarted for the changes to take effect.

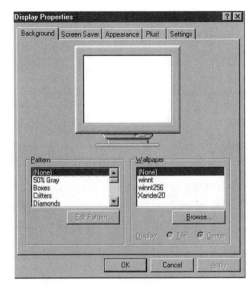

FIGURE 4.24
The Display Properties dialog box.

NOTE

Using [VGA mode] When Booting NT
All hardware, including monitors, break eventually. When a monitor dies, you often can dig up an older model to use temporarily. Often, however, such a resurrected monitor isn't as advanced as the one that just died, and when you restart Windows NT, video card settings such as the resolution and refresh rate aren't supported. Typically, this means that you no longer can view anything onscreen.

If this happens, reboot the computer using the [VGA mode] option on the Boot Loader menu. Windows NT boots using the standard VGA driver at 640×480 resolution. When the system is fully loaded, log on and go to the Settings tab of the Control Panel's Display application, and then choose optimal settings for your temporary monitor.

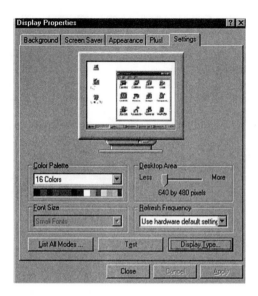

FIGURE 4.25
The Settings tab in the Display Properties dialog box.

FIGURE 4.26
The Display Type dialog box.

FIGURE 4.27
The Change Display dialog box.

STEP BY STEP

4.12 Changing the Video Display Adapter

1. Start the Control Panel's Display application and click on the Settings tab (see Figure 4.25).

2. Click the Display Type button, and the Display Type dialog box appears (see Figure 4.26).

3. Click the Change button in the Adapter Type frame. The Change Display dialog box appears (see Figure 4.27). Select an adapter from the list and click OK. Or, if you have a manufacturer's installation disk, click on Have Disk and click OK.

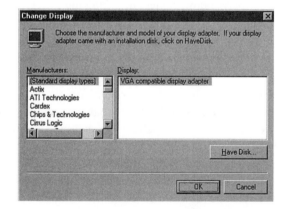

The following table provides a recap of this section's contents.

CONFIGURING PERIPHERALS AND DEVICES

Control Panel Applet	*Enables You To...*
Devices	Determine which devices are started and configure startup parameters. Also allows you to add a device to a hardware profile.
Multimedia	Add and configure audio and video devices.
Ports	Add and configure communication ports on your server. Remember that only those ports that are not currently being used are displayed in this dialog box.
UPS	Configure an Uninterruptible Power Supply for your server. If your UPS is being shut off at system boot, try adding the /NoSerialMice switch to the boot line in the BOOT.INI file.
SCSI Adapters	Add and configure SCSI devices and IDE drives.
Tape Devices	Add and configure digital tape devices for use in backups.
PC Card	Add and configure PC Cards (PCMCIA). This applet will function only if you have a PCMCIA controller installed on your computer.
Modems	Add and configure modems. A wizard will guide you through the installation process.
Keyboard	Configure your keyboard.
Mouse	Install and configure a mouse for your NT Server.
Display	Configure your display. This includes screen savers, color schemes, and background colors, as well as print drivers and colors and resolution.

CONFIGURING HARD DISKS

Configure hard disks to meet various requirements. Requirements include: allocating disk space capacity, providing redundancy, improving performance, providing security, and formatting.

Chapter 1 discussed some important concepts related to disk configuration, such as file systems, primary partitions, extended partitions, and fault tolerance. This section describes how to apply those concepts to an actual disk configuration using Windows NT's Disk Administrator disk utility. To access Disk Administrator, you must use an administrator account.

The Disk Administrator

The Disk Administrator was designed to allow you to maintain your disk configurations. From it, you can create and format partitions. In addition, you can create special data storage structures such as stripe sets and volume sets, as well as fault-tolerant structures such as mirror sets and stripe sets with parity.

To access the Disk Administrator, choose Start, Programs, Administrative Tools (common), Disk Administrator.

When you open the Disk Administrator for the first time, a message box appears, telling you the following:

```
No signature found on Disk 0.access this disk from other
➡operating systems, such as DOS.
If you choose not to write a signature, the disk will be
➡inaccessible to the Windows NT Disk Administrator program.
Do you want to write a signature on Disk 0 so that the
➡Disk Administrator can access the drive?
```

Choose Yes to write a 32-bit signature that uniquely identifies the disk written to the primary partition. This enables the system to recognize the disk as the original even if it is has been used with a different controller or its identification has changed.

Customizing the Display

The status bar at the bottom of the Disk Administrator's main window displays basic disk information (see Figure 4.28). Along with the status bar, a color-coded legend displays the different representations for partition colors and patterns. When you're working with multiple disks, you might want to hide one or both of these options to create a larger area for viewing information. To do so, choose Options, and then select Status Bar, Legend, or both.

NOTE

Commit Changes to Continue   If you attempt to make any modifications on a disk(s), a message appears, warning you that certain changes (such as deleting a partition) are irreversible and require user approval. The changes don't become permanent until you exit the program or choose Partition, Commit Changes Now.

Until you commit changes, your commands aren't actually carried out, and you can change your mind if necessary. If you exit Disk Administrator without first choosing the Commit Changes Now command, Disk Administrator asks you whether it should save your changes (which is the same as committing them). That's the last chance you get to back out gracefully.

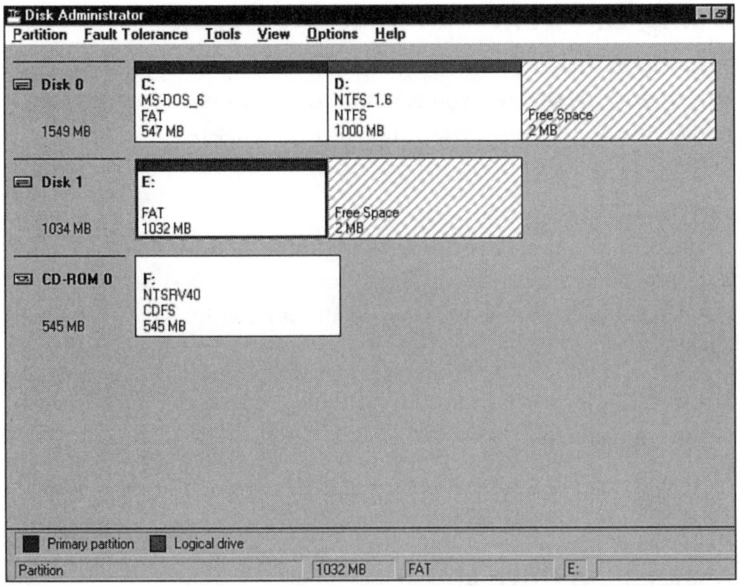

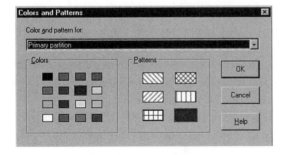

FIGURE 4.28
The Disk Administrator main window.

You also can set different colors and patterns to distinguish among different disks and disk characteristics for the primary partition, logical drive, mirror set, and volume set. To change the default settings, choose Options, Colors and Patterns. The Colors and Patterns dialog box appears (see Figure 4.29).

Initially, each disk represented in the main display window is sized proportionately. By choosing Options, Region Display, you open the Region Display Options dialog box, which contains several options for customizing the appearance of each region (see Figure 4.30).

FIGURE 4.29
Disk Administrator's Colors and Patterns dialog box.

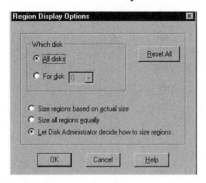

FIGURE 4.30
Disk Administrator's Region Display Options
dialog box.

Using the Disk Administrator Tools

A variety of tools are available in the Disk Administrator's Tools menu. With these tools, you can format a partition, assign a drive letter, view a disk's properties, and create and delete partitions.

Formatting

In order to function, a partition or logical drive must be divided into logical sections that enable a disk to locate data in a systematic fashion. This process is called *formatting* and is described in Step by Step 4.13.

You also can format partitions from the command prompt using the following command:

```
FORMAT <drive_letter>: /FS:FAT¦NTFS
```

Assigning a Drive Letter

Windows NT assigns drive letters to partitions using the following pattern:

1. Beginning from the letter C:, assign consecutive letters to the first primary partition on each physical disk.

2. Assign consecutive letters to each logical drive, completing all on one physical disk before moving on to the next.

3. Assign consecutive letters to the additional primary partitions, completing all on one physical disk before moving on to the next.

If you want to override the normal drive-naming algorithm, choose Tools, Assign Drive Letter. You may change the drive designation to any other unused letter, or you may simply remove the drive letter altogether. The latter option may seem of dubious value, but it allows an administrator to "hide" a partition and its files by not providing the computer a "handle" (drive letter) by which to access it. If the administrator needs to recover the data, the partition can be reassigned a drive letter. This procedure is secure because only administrators can work with Disk Administrator (see Step by Step 4.14).

STEP BY STEP

4.13 Formatting a Partition Using the Disk Administrator

1. Select the newly created partition you want to format.

2. Choose Partition, Commit Changes Now. Click on Yes to save the changes.

3. Choose Tools, Format.

4. In the Format dialog box, enter the volume label to identify the partition.

5. Select the type of file system to use, and then click OK.

   If you enable the Quick Format check box, the Disk Administrator doesn't scan for bad sectors during the format process. This option isn't available when you format mirror sets or stripe sets with parity.

6. Choose Yes from the Confirmation dialog box to begin the process.

   A dialog box appears indicating the current progress of the format. The format progress window lets you cancel the process, but if you do cancel it, you can't be sure that the volume will be returned to its original state.

STEP BY STEP

4.14 Changing a Drive Letter Using the Disk Administrator

1. Select the partition or logical drive that you want to assign a drive letter.

2. Choose Tools, Assign Drive Letter. A message box appears, indicating the remaining drive letters for assignment.

3. In the Assign Drive Letter dialog box, select the letter to use and choose OK.

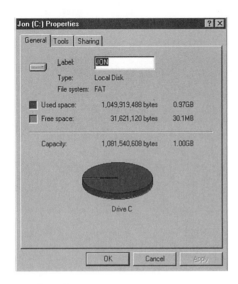

FIGURE 4.31
The Volume Properties dialog box.

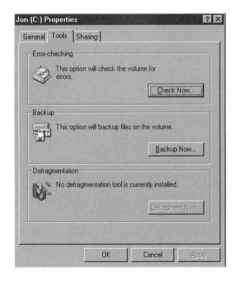

FIGURE 4.32
The Tools tab of the Volume Properties dialog box.

Certain programs make references to a specific drive letter, so be careful when changing drive letter assignments, especially to the active primary partition.

Properties

If you click a volume and choose Tools, Properties, the Properties dialog box for the volume appears (see Figure 4.31). (This is the same dialog box that will appear if you right-click on the disk in Explorer and choose Properties.) The General tab presents a graphical representation of the free and used space on the volume.

The Sharing tab of the Disk Properties dialog box lets you create and configure a network share for the volume. The Tools tab lets you back up or defragment the volume or check the volume for errors (see Figure 4.32).

In contrast to earlier versions of NT, in which the only way to scan a volume for errors was to use CHKDSK (which you had to execute from a VDM), NT 4 provides a graphical method of checking hard disks for errors.

To check for disk problems from Disk Administrator, select the partition you want to check, choose Tools, Properties, and select the Tools tab from the Properties dialog box. Click on the Check Now button to open the Check Disk dialog box, which offers the following options:

◆ Automatically Fix File System Errors

◆ Scan for and Attempt Recovery of Bad Sectors

Choose either or both options and click on the Start button to begin checking the partition.

Saving and Restoring Configuration Information

The Configuration command on Disk Administrator's Partition menu enables you to save or restore a disk configuration by using a floppy disk. You can save the disk configuration to a blank floppy, a floppy with a previous disk configuration, or an emergency repair disk.

You can use the Configuration Save option if you want to change your disk configuration but think you may someday want to return to the configuration you have now. Also, Microsoft recommends that you save a copy of your disk configuration before upgrading Windows NT.

The Configuration Restore option restores a saved disk configuration from a floppy.

The Configuration command includes a third option, Search, which searches your hard drive for other Windows NT installations. If you find any, you can then choose to update your disk configuration to match the configuration of one of the other Windows NT installations on the list.

Both the Restore and Search options come with a warning that you are about to overwrite your disk configuration. The Restore and Search operations don't create or delete partitions, but they do affect drive letters, volume sets, stripe sets, parity stripes, and mirrors.

Partitioning

Partitioning is the method of making hard disks usable. Windows NT includes options for creating six kinds of partitions and collections of partitions (sets) with the Disk Administrator:

- Primary partition
- Extended partition
- Volume set
- Stripe set
- Mirror set
- Stripe set with parity

Of the preceding partition types, three are not fault tolerant (primary, volume set, and stripe set), two are fault tolerant (and will be discussed in the next major section), and extended partitions are in a class of their own. Let us first discuss primary and extended partitions and volume and stripe sets.

Primary Partitions

A primary partition is a bootable partition. Every physical disk can have up to four partitions: All four of them can be primaries or, if you want to create an extended partition, three can be primaries and the other can be an extended partition. Although you do not need a primary partition on each physical drive, in order to be able to boot your computer, there must be at least one primary partition on your disk set.

A primary partition can be created only in free space that has not been allocated for anything else; it cannot be created inside of an extended partition. Step by Step 4.15 walks you through the process of creating a primary partition. After you create a primary partition, it is automatically assigned a drive letter and then can be formatted.

If you want to boot from a primary partition, you need to mark it active (see Step by Step 4.16). This indicates to your computer's ROM that the particular primary partition so marked is the one to boot from. Only one partition on any computer can be marked active.

Notice that an asterisk appears in the color bar of the active partition (see Figure 4.33).

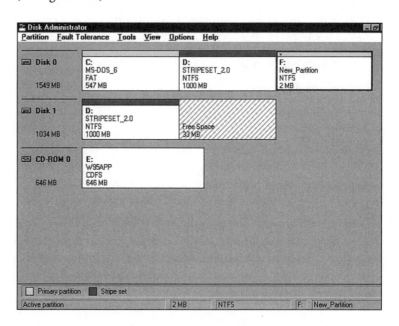

FIGURE 4.33
The Disk Administrator main window displays active stripe sets (indicated with colored bars).

STEP BY STEP

4.15 Creating a Primary Partition Using the Disk Administrator

1. Start Disk Administrator

2. Select an area of free space on a disk.

3. Choose Partition, Create. A message box appears, indicating the possible minimum and maximum sizes for a new primary partition.

4. In the Create Primary Partition dialog box, enter the size of the partition you want to create and click OK.

STEP BY STEP

4.16 Marking a Partition Active

1. Start Disk Administrator

2. Select a primary partition on one of your hard drives

3. From the Partition menu, choose Mark Active.

4. A Disk Administrator message appears, indicating the new active partition will be booted from the next time your computer is started. Click OK to accept.

Extended Partitions

An extended partition is a partition type that allows you to overcome the restriction of having only four primary partitions. An extended partition can be subdivided into as many parts as you like. Each of these parts is referred to as a *logical drive*. Through the use of logical drives, you can create dozens of drives on your computer. Step by Step 4.17 demonstrates how to create an extended partition using Disk Administrator.

Because extended partitions can be subdivided, they are not given drive letters when they're created. What you end up with is a portion of free disk space that is distinct from the rest of the disk and can be subdivided. As a result, you could have an extended partition that contains both logical drives (which have been lettered) and formatted and free space.

Extended partitions have two limitations:

◆ You cannot create a primary partition inside an extended partition.

◆ You cannot boot from a logical drive inside an extended partition (in other words, a logical drive cannot be your NT system partition, but it can be your NT boot partition).

In order to make an extended partition usable, you must either divide it into one or more logical drives or make it part of a larger set. To create a logical drive within an extended partition, select the extended partition and choose Partition, Create. If this command is unavailable, you probably have selected another partition instead of the extended one.

Volume Sets

A volume set offers one of two non-fault-tolerant methods for joining more than one area of free space into a single logical unit. Volume sets can be created out of anywhere from 2–32 separate areas of free space (see Step by Step 4.18). They can (but do not have to) span multiple hard drives, and these hard drives can be comprised of different technology types (SCSI and IDE, for example).

A volume set is filled one area at a time, and if formatted NTFS, it can have additional pieces added to it by extending the set. The loss of one area of the volume set will destroy the data in the whole set.

STEP BY STEP

4.17 Creating an Extended Partition Using the Disk Administrator

1. Select an area of free space on a disk.

2. Choose Partition, Create Extended. A message box appears, indicating the possible minimum and maximum sizes for a new extended partition.

3. In the Create Extended dialog box, enter the size of the extended partition you want to create and click OK.

STEP BY STEP

4.18 Creating a Volume Set Using the Disk Administrator

1. Select the areas of free space you want to include with a volume set.

2. Choose Partition, Create Volume Set. A message box appears, indicating the possible minimum and maximum sizes for a new extended partition.

3. In the Create Volume Set dialog box, enter the size of the volume set you want to create and click OK.

After you create a volume set, you must format it before you can use it. NTFS and FAT are both supported. To format the new volume, you must save the changes by choosing Partition, Commit Changes Now or by responding to the prompts when exiting the Disk Administrator. You also must restart the system before formatting.

Before you can reclaim any of the disk space that a volume set uses, you must delete the volume set entirely.

Sets Are Not Accessible Locally Outside of NT If NT is configured to support multiple operating systems (such as DOS), when a volume set or stripe set is created, the other systems cannot see the set when booted to locally. Therefore, these sets cannot be accessed by the other operating systems, regardless of how they are formatted. This applies only to locally booting an operating system, though; it does not apply to network clients.

Configuring volume sets and ordinary partitions are different in the following ways:

◆ The system and boot partitions cannot be part of a volume set. Windows NT must be running before these volume sets can be addressed; if Windows NT itself is on a volume set, there is no way to address the volume set.

◆ You can extend an NTFS volume set (but not a FAT volume set) by selecting the volume set in Disk Administrator and simultaneously selecting at least one area of free space (hold down the Ctrl key to select more than one area at a time). Choose Partition, Extend Volume Set to get a chance to enter a new size for the volume set.

◆ You can never shrink a volume set; after creating or extending it, it's set in stone. You can delete the entire volume set, but not any individual area within it.

If you choose to implement a volume set, be aware of the following drawbacks and dangers:

◆ Only Windows NT supports volume sets; if you're booting between Windows NT and Windows 95, MS-DOS, or another operating system, your volume set will be inaccessible if Windows NT isn't active.

◆ If the disk on which any of the volume segments exists fails, your volume set will break, and you are likely to lose all your data. Be sure to back up your data to ensure the possibility of restoring it. If it becomes necessary to do so, shut down the system, replace the bad drive, reformat the volume set, and then restore your data from backup.

To extend a volume set (see Step by Step 4.19), you must first verify that it is formatted NTFS. If necessary, use CONVERT.EXE to convert from FAT to NTFS.

STEP BY STEP

4.19 Extending a Volume Set Using the Disk Administrator

1. Select an NTFS volume, and then select the area(s) of free space you want to add. (Hold down the Ctrl key while you select the areas of free space.)

2. Choose Partition, Extend Volume Set. A dialog box appears, indicating the possible minimum and maximum sizes for the creation of an extended partition.

3. In the Create Extended Volume Set dialog box, enter the size of the volume you want to create and click OK.

Stripe Sets

Stripe sets are similar to volume sets in that they also combine anywhere from 2–32 areas of free space into a single logical drive. However, stripe sets differ from volume sets in that the free space areas must all be equally sized areas from separate physical disks.

Data is read from and written to the stripe set in 64KB blocks, disk by disk, row by row. If multiple controllers service your stripe set, or if your single controller can perform concurrent I/O requests, you can improve performance dramatically because you can then use multiple drives simultaneously.

Windows NT Server has a more robust method of improving performance while maintaining fault tolerance, called stripe sets with parity. Use a stripe set with parity if you really want the performance boost from striping. This fault tolerance technology is called Redundant Array of Inexpensive Disks (RAID). Step by Step 4.20 teaches you how to create a stripe set.

The same rules apply for both stripe sets and volume sets: no limit on drive types, no limit for the file system, and no system and boot partitions. However, you cannot extend a stripe set the way you can a volume set, and you cannot shrink one.

A stripe set can support IDE, EIDE, and SCSI drive types.

> **WARNING**
>
> **Failure of a Single Member of the Stripe Set Destroys the Whole Set** Not only do the same dangers apply to stripe sets that apply to volume sets, but the potential disaster is even more dire. If any single member of a stripe set fails, the entire volume becomes inaccessible to the point that—because your data is contiguous only for 64KB at a time—not even a disk editor can help you. If you didn't back up, your data is gone for good.

When creating a stripe set, you must make sure that the space on each disk is the same size (see Figure 4.34). If it's not, the Disk Administrator approximates the sizes for each to make them equal.

As with a volume set, you must format the stripe set before you can use it. To format the new volume, save the changes by choosing Partition, Commit Changes Now or by responding to the prompts when exiting the Disk Administrator. You also must restart the system before formatting.

Deleting Partitions

From Disk Administrator, you can delete any partition except for the system and boot partitions (but you can't delete those because Windows NT is using them). Simply select the partition you want to delete, and then choose Partition, Delete. Confirm your action to officially remove the partition from the interface. Again, until you commit changes, nothing officially happens. If you make a mistake, just exit Disk Administrator without saving or committing changes.

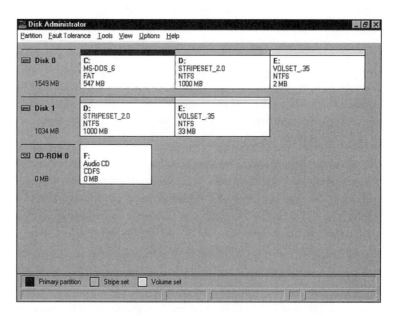

FIGURE 4.34

The Disk Administrator main window displays stripe set information.

STEP BY STEP

4.20 Creating a Stripe Set Using the Disk Administrator

1. Select at least two areas of free space on different hard drives.

2. Choose Partition, Create Stripe Set. A dialog box appears, indicating the possible minimum and maximum sizes for the creation of an extended partition.

3. In the Create Stripe Set dialog box, enter the size of the stripe set you want to create and click OK.

Fault-Tolerant Partitions

Fundamentally, fault tolerance is the system's capability to recover in the event of hardware disaster.

The standard for fault tolerance is known as Redundant Array of Inexpensive Disks (RAID). Chapter 1 introduced disk mirroring and disk striping with parity, the two RAID fault-tolerance methods available with Windows NT. The following sections describe how to configure these fault-tolerance methods through Disk Administrator.

Disk Mirroring

Disk mirroring is a RAID level 1 fault-tolerance method. A *mirror* is a redundant copy of another disk partition that uses the same or a different hard disk controller. You can use any partition, including the boot or system partition, to establish a mirror. Step by Step 4.21 teaches you to create a mirror with Disk Administrator.

In the past, disk mirroring was one of the more expensive solutions of protecting against disk failure. However, because a mirror requires only two hard disks for implementation, if you take into account global reductions in cost for hard disks, this method now is an effective alternative to other forms of fault tolerance.

STEP BY STEP

4.21 Creating a Mirror Using the Disk Administrator

1. Select at least two areas of free space on different hard drives.

2. Choose Fault Tolerance, Establish Mirror.

The Disk Administrator then creates spaces of equal size on the disks and assigns a drive letter to them.

Stripe Sets with Parity

A stripe set with parity is considered a RAID level 5 fault-tolerance method. It differs from other approaches because it writes information across all disks in the array, but it accomplishes fault tolerance by keeping the data and parity on separate disks. Step by Step 4.22 demonstrates how to create a stripe set with parity.

Parity information exists as a stripe block in each row that spans the array, so at least three drives must be used (instead of just two). If a single drive fails, enough information is distributed across the drives for it to be completely reconstructed. When creating a stripe set with parity, you may use all partitions except for the boot and system partitions.

The Disk Administrator calculates the stripe set with parity's total size (based on the number of disks selected) and creates a space that is equal on each disk. It then combines the drives into one logical volume. If you have selected free areas that are disproportionate, the Disk Administrator rounds to the closest value.

As with other new volumes, you must format the stripe set before you can use it. To format the new volume, save the changes by choosing Partition, Commit Changes Now or by answering the prompts when exiting the Disk Administrator. You also must restart the system before formatting.

STEP BY STEP

4.22 Creating a Stripe Set with Parity

1. Select between 3 and 32 areas of free disk space on separate drives.

2. Choose Fault Tolerance, Create Stripe Set with Parity. A dialog box appears, indicating the possible minimum and maximum sizes for a new extended partition.

3. In the Create Stripe Set with Parity dialog box, enter the size of the stripe set to create and click OK.

Securing the System Partition on RISC Machines

The system partition on a RISC computer must be a FAT partition. Because Windows NT cannot provide the same security for a FAT partition that it provides for an NTFS partition, the RISC version of Windows NT includes a special Secure System Partition command that provides an extra layer of security for RISC-based system partitions. This command specifies that only members of the local Administrators group have access to the system partition.

REVIEW BREAK

The following is a summary of the important points in the preceding section. Make sure you understand all of these concepts before proceeding.

◆ The system partition is where your computer boots, and it must be on an active partition.

◆ The boot partition is where the WINNT folder is located, and it contains the NT program files. It can be on any primary partition or logical drive (but not on a set).

◆ NT supports two forms of software-based fault tolerance: disk mirroring (RAID 1) and stripe sets with parity (RAID 5).

◆ Disk mirroring uses two hard drives and provides 50% disk space utilization.

◆ Stripe sets with parity use between 3 and 32 hard drives and provides a $(n–1)/n*100\%$ utilization (where n = number of disks in the set).

◆ Disk duplexing provides better tolerance than mirroring because it performs mirroring with separate controllers on each disk.

◆ NT supports three file systems: NTFS, FAT, and CDFS. It no longer supports HPFS (the OS/2 file system), nor does it support FAT32 (a file system used by Windows 95).

CONFIGURING PRINTING

Configure printers. Tasks include: adding and configuring a printer, implementing a printer pool, and setting print priorities.

The printing process is an important part of an operating system, and network administrators spend a significant amount of time chasing down printing problems. For the NT Server exams, you should become familiar with the following printer-related topics:

◆ Understanding Windows NT printing architecture

◆ Installing printers

◆ Configuring printers

◆ Sharing printers

◆ Setting up a printer pool

◆ Printing from MS-DOS applications

In this section, you will examine each of the preceding topics and how printing works under Windows NT, both locally and remotely.

Windows NT Printing Architecture

Most of us visualize a printer as a device that receives data from the computer and converts it into a rendered hard copy. In Windows NT, however, the term printer refers to the software that controls a specific printing device or devices.

Windows NT uses the term printing device to refer to the hardware that produces the actual output.

It's interesting to note that under Windows NT, a single printer can control more than one printing device. When a single printer (software) controls more than one printing device (hardware), the resulting configuration is called a *printer pool*. Printer pools are discussed in more detail later in this chapter.

You should become familiar with the components of the Windows NT printing process for the MCSE exam. The process goes roughly as follows:

1. When an application on an NT client sends a print job, Windows NT checks to see if the version of the printer driver on the client is up-to-date with the version on the print server. If it isn't, Windows NT downloads a new version of the printer driver from the print server to the client.

2. The printer driver sends the data to the client spooler. The client spooler spools the data to a file and makes a remote procedure call to the server spooler, thus transmitting the data to the server spooler on the print server machine.

3. The server spooler sends the data to the Local Print Provider.

4. The Local Print Provider passes the data to a print processor, where it's rendered into a format legible to the printing device. Then, if necessary, the Local Print Provider sends the data to a separator page processor, where a separator page is added to the beginning of the document. The Local Print Provider lastly passes the rendered data to the print monitor.

5. The print monitor points the rendered data to the appropriate printer port and, therefore, to the appropriate printing device.

The following sections discuss the components of the NT printing process.

Printer Drivers

In the first step of the printing process, Windows NT checks to see whether the printer driver on the print client is current. If it isn't, Windows NT downloads a new copy of the printer driver from the print server.

NOTE

Print Queue Defined Other operating systems—NetWare, for example—use the term "print queue" for what Windows NT calls a "printer." Windows NT also uses the term "print queue," but in NT, a print queue is simply the list (queue) of documents waiting to print.

Automatic Update of Printer Drivers This automatic update of the printer driver on the client is a fundamental element of Windows NT printing and, as such, is frequently a tested item. When you set up a Windows NT printer, the Setup wizard asks for the operating systems and hardware platforms of all client machines that are going to access the printer. The wizard then places the appropriate printer drivers on the server so they will be available for downloading.

Because the printer driver is responsible for generating the data stream that forms a print job, the success of the print job relies on the printer driver's health. The Windows NT printer driver is implemented as a combination of two dynamic link libraries (or DLLs) and a printer-specific minidriver or configuration file.

Typically, Microsoft supplies the two dynamic link libraries with Windows NT, and the original manufacturer of the printer supplies the minidriver or configuration file. The following list describes these three files:

◆ *The Printer Graphics Driver DLL.* This dynamic link library consists of the rendering or managing portion of the driver; it's always called by the Graphics Device Interface.

◆ *The Printer Interface Driver.* This dynamic link library consists of the user interface or configuration management portion of the printer driver; it's used by an administrator to configure a printer.

◆ *The Characterization File.* This component contains all the printer-specific information, such as memory, page protection, soft fonts, graphics resolution, paper orientation and size, and so on; it's used by the other two dynamic link libraries whenever they need to gather printer-specific information.

These three components of a printer driver (printer graphics driver, printer interface driver, and configuration file) are all located in the following directory, according to their Windows NT platforms (w32x86, w32mips, w32alpha, and w32ppc) and version numbers (0 = version 3.1, 1 = version 3.5x, 2 = version 4.x):

winnt_root\system32\spool\drivers.directory

The printer driver is specific to both the operating system and the hardware platform. You can't use a Windows 95 printer driver with Windows NT, and you can't use an Intel Windows NT printer driver on an Alpha Windows NT machine. Figure 4.35 shows a sample list of drivers from which to choose.

Spooler

The Spooler is a Windows NT service that operates in the background to manage the printing process. The spooler consists of a series of DLLs that work together to accept, process, and distribute print jobs.

You need to understand that the spooler really runs the show. Specifically, the Spooler service is responsible for the following functions:

◆ Keeping track of what jobs are destined for which printers

◆ Keeping track of which ports are connected to which printers

◆ Routing print jobs to the correct port

◆ Managing printer pools

◆ Prioritizing print jobs

The NT Spooler service must be running on both the client and the print server machines for the printing process to function properly. Logically, however, you can think of the print spooler as a single process occurring on the client and on print server machines.

By default, the spool file folder is the winnt_root\system32\ spool\PRINTERS directory. You can change the spool folder by using the Advanced tab of the print server Properties dialog box. (The print server Properties dialog box gets more attention later in this chapter.) You also can use Registry Editor to set the spool directory, like so:

◆ *For all printers:*

> HKEY_LOCAL_MACHINE\SYSTEM\
> CurrentControlSet\Control\Print\Printers
> DefaultSpoolDirectory:REG_SZ:<*New Spool Path*>

◆ *On a per-printer basis:*

> HKEY_LOCAL_MACHINE\SYSTEM\
> CurrentControlSet\Control\Print\Printers\
> <*printer*>SpoolDirectory:REG_SZ:<*New Spool Path*>

If a print job gets stuck in the spooler to the point that an administrator or print operator cannot delete or purge it, you can stop the

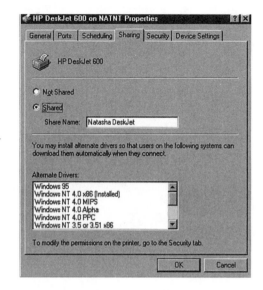

FIGURE 4.35
Choosing a printer driver from the Sharing tab of the printer's Properties dialog box.

Spooler service and restart it by using the Control Panel's Service application.

You also can start or stop the Spooler service by using the following commands at the command prompt:

```
net start spooler
net stop spooler
```

Router

The print router receives the print job from the spooler and routes it to the appropriate print processor.

The Print Processor

The process of translating print data into a form that a printing device can read is called *rendering*. The rendering process begins with the printer driver. The print processor is responsible for completing the rendering process. The tasks performed by the print processor differ depending on the type of print data.

The primary Windows NT print processor is called WINPRINT.DLL and is located in winnt_root\system32\spool\ prtprocs\platform. WINPRINT.DLL recognizes the following data types:

◆ *Raw data*. Fully rendered data that is ready for the printer. A postscript command, for instance, reaches the print processor as raw data.

◆ *Windows NT Enhanced Metafile (EMF)*. A standard file format that many different printing devices support. Instead of the raw printer data being generated by the printer driver, the Graphical Device Interface generates NT EMF information before spooling. After the NT EMF is created, control returns to the user. The NT EMF is then interpreted in the background on a 32-bit printing subsystem spooler thread and sent to the printer, which supports the PSCRIPT1 data type. The PSCRIPT1 data type is for print data sent from Macintosh clients to non-PostScript printing devices.

Print Monitors

A print monitor controls access to a specific device, monitors the status of the device, and communicates this information back to the spooler, which relays the information via the user interface. The print monitor essentially controls the data stream to one or more printer ports. Its responsibilities include writing a print job to the output destination and taking care of port access (opening, closing, configuring, reading from, writing to, and acquiring or releasing ports).

To install a new print monitor, click on Add Port in the Ports tab of the printer's Properties dialog box. Then click on the New Monitor button in the Printer Ports dialog box that appears (see Figure 4.36).

In addition, the print monitor performs the following duties:

◆ Detects unsolicited errors (such as Toner Low).

◆ Handles true end-of-job notification. The print monitor waits until the last page has been printed to notify the spooler that the print job has finished and can be discarded.

◆ Monitors printer status to detect printing errors. If necessary, the print monitor notifies the spooler so that the job can continue or be restarted.

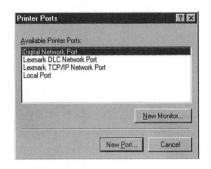

FIGURE 4.36
The Printer Ports dialog box.

Windows NT provides some standard print monitors. These include print monitors for the following:

◆ Local output to LPTx, COMx, remote printer shares, and named pipes (\WINNT_ROOT\SYSTEM32\ LOCALMON.DLL).

◆ Output to Hewlett-Packard network interface printing devices (\WINNT_ROOT\SYSTEM32\HPMON.DLL), which can support up to 225 (configured for 64) Hewlett-Packard network interface printing devices. This print monitor requires the DLC protocol.

◆ Output to Digital network port printers (DECPSMON.DLL), supporting both TCP/IP and DECnet protocols. The DECnet protocol doesn't ship with Windows NT.

◆ Output to LPR (Line Printer) ports (LPRMON.DLL), allowing Windows NT to print directly to UNIX LPD print servers or network interface printing devices over the TCP/IP protocol.

◆ Output to PJL Language printing device (PJLMON.DLL).

◆ Output to Apple Macintosh PostScript printers (SFMMON.DLL), for Windows NT servers with services for the Apple Macintosh installed.

Printers Folder

The Printers folder is the Windows NT printing system's primary user interface. The Printers folder replaces Print Manager, the printing interface that was used in previous versions of NT. You can reach the Printers folder through Control Panel or through the Settings item in the Start menu.

From the Printers folder, you install, configure, administer, and remove printers. You also supervise print queues; pause, purge and restart print jobs; share printers; and set printer defaults. The following sections discuss two of the principal activities managed through the Printers folder: adding printers and configuring printers.

You can install printers on your Windows NT Workstation in two ways: by installing a printer on your own workstation or by connecting to a remote printer. Installing your own printer is much more involved than connecting to a remote printer, and it requires Administrative or Power User-level rights. You add a new printer or connect to a remote printer using the Add Printer icon in the Printers folder. You also can connect to a remote printer via Network Neighborhood.

From the Printers folder, double-click on the Add Printer icon to open the Add Printer Wizard (see Figure 4.37).

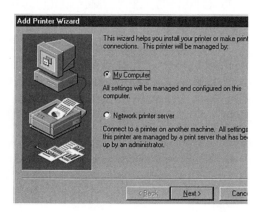

FIGURE 4.37
The Add Printer Wizard screen.

The first screen of the Add Printer Wizard asks whether the new printer will be attached to your computer (the My Computer option) or connected to another machine and accessed via the network (the Network printer server option). The My Computer option requires Administrator or Power User rights, whereas the Network printer server option does not. You don't have to be an Administrator or a Power User to connect to a shared printer on another machine; you simply must have been granted access to it by the administrator on the other machine.

Adding a Printer on Your Own Machine

If you select the My Computer option from the Add Printer Wizard screen and then click Next, the wizard asks you what port you want to use (see Figure 4.38). You must select a port for the new printer. The wizard won't let you proceed until you have either checked one of the ports or added a new port.

The next screen asks you to specify the manufacturer and model of the new printer (see Figure 4.39). Select a manufacturer, and a list of drivers for printers by that manufacturer appears. Or, if you want to install an unlisted printer driver from a disk, click the Have Disk button.

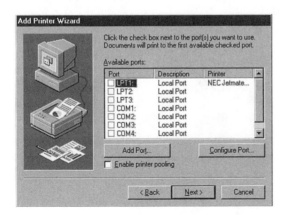

FIGURE 4.38

The Add Port button enables you to add a new digital network port, local port, or PJL language monitor to your printing system.

FIGURE 4.39

The manufacturer and model options screen of the Add Printer Wizard.

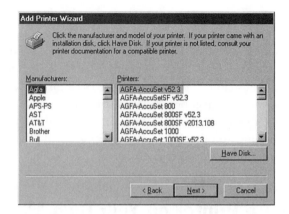

The next screen asks for a printer name and asks whether you want the printer to become the default printer for Windows-based programs. As with all objects in Windows NT, a printer requires a name. The printer name can be as long as 32 characters and doesn't have to reflect the name of the driver in use. You should avoid using the full 32 characters, however, because you might sometimes need to type the printer name to connect to it from a remote computer.

The next screen asks whether you want to share the printer (see Figure 4.40). If you want to share the printer with other computers on the network, you must also specify a share name (the default share name is the printer name you specified in the preceding screen). The wizard also asks you to specify the operating systems of all computers that will be sharing the printer. Your only choices are Windows 95 and a number of NT versions and platforms.

> **N O T E**
>
> **Strange but True** Although it sounds backward, it is true: Windows NT boots from the system partition and then loads the system from the boot partition.

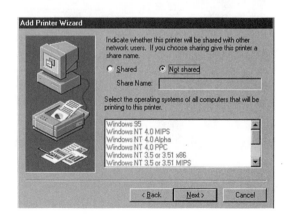

FIGURE 4.40

The Add Printer Wizard asks whether you want to share the printer.

The Add Printer Wizard then attempts to install the printer driver. You may be asked to supply the Windows NT installation disk. (Also, if you designate Windows 95 as the operating system of a computer sharing the printer, you may be prompted to supply the Windows 95 installation CD-ROM.) The wizard then asks if you want to print a test page. Printing a test page enables you to test the accuracy of your configuration.

When the installation is complete, the Add Printer Wizard displays the Properties dialog box for the new printer. You can read more about the Properties dialog box later in this chapter.

Adding a Network Print Server

If you choose the Network Printer Server option in the first screen of the Add Printer Wizard, the wizard opens the Connect to Printer dialog box (see Figure 4.41), where you specify the shared printer to which you want to connect. Click on the workstation to which the printer is attached, and then select the printer.

The wizard then asks whether you want the printer to serve as a default printer. Then it completes the installation. If the installation is successful, an icon for that printer appears in the Printers folder.

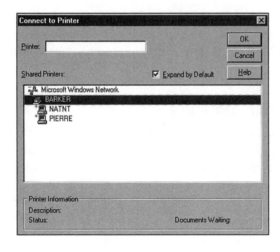

NOTE

Establish a Network Connection Before Connecting to a Network Printer The Add Printer Wizard doesn't know enough to open a network connection for you; if you don't open a connection using the workstation you select in the Connect to Printer dialog box, the printers attached to that workstation don't appear in the list. If this happens, double-click the Network Neighborhood icon, double-click the icon for the workstation, and then enter your username and password to establish a connection. As long as you're in Network Neighborhood, you might as well establish the printer connection through Network Neighborhood.

FIGURE 4.41
Use the Connect to Printer dialog box to specify the network printer you want to connect to.

Configuring Printers

Almost all the configuration settings for a printer in Windows NT 4 are accessible through the following three commands in the Printers folder window:

- ◆ File, Document Defaults
- ◆ File, Server Properties
- ◆ File, Properties

Selecting the File, Document Defaults command opens the Default Document Properties dialog box, which holds page setup and document settings for a given printer.

The Server Properties dialog box appears when you select the File, Server Properties command. This dialog box holds information specific to the computer's print server activities. Therefore, the Server Properties dialog box is independent of any particular printer (which is why the Server Properties command appears in the File menu regardless of whether a printer is selected).

You find most of the configuration settings for a given printer in the Properties dialog box, which appears when you select the File, Properties command. In NT 4, the printer Properties dialog box serves as a central location for printer configuration information.

You also use the File, Sharing command for some configuration settings—specifically, to set up the printer as a shared printer on the network. The File, Sharing command is actually just a different path to the Sharing tab of the Properties dialog box.

Document Defaults

Choose File, Document Defaults to open the Default Document Properties dialog box shown in Figure 4.42. The Default Document Properties dialog box contains document settings for the documents that are to print on the selected printer. A good example of a document setting you can control by using the Default Document Properties dialog box is the Orientation setting.

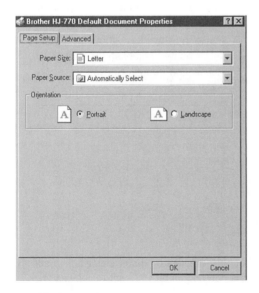

FIGURE 4.42
The Page Setup tab of the Default Document Properties dialog box allows you to indicate default page settings for this printer, such as paper size and orientation.

The Page Setup tab defines the Paper Size, Paper Source, and Orientation options for the document you want to print. You change the size, source, and orientation settings in the Advanced tab, which also contains settings for graphics resolution, color adjustment, and print quality (see Figure 4.43).

Server Properties

Choose File, Server Properties to open the Print Server Properties dialog box (see Figure 4.44). The following sections discuss the three tabs in the Print Server Properties dialog box.

Forms

The Forms tab of the Print Server Properties dialog box defines the print forms available on the computer. Think of a print form as a description of a piece of paper that might be in a printer tray. A print form tells NT the size of the paper and where to put the printer margins. Step by Step 4.23 walks you through creating a new form from the Forms tab.

FIGURE 4.43
The Advanced tab of the Default Document Properties dialog box allows you to set more advanced print options such as graphic resolution and print quality.

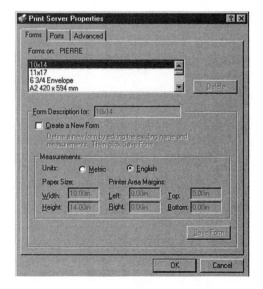

NOTE

Assigning a Form to a Tray The Device Settings tab of the printer Properties dialog box lets you assign a print form to an actual tray. Thus, you can tell NT the size of the paper in each printer tray, and the size of the printer margins. This facility is useful when you have multiple printer trays with different sizes of paper in each, or when one of your printer trays contains a particular type of paper, such as corporate letterhead paper, which requires a different top or bottom margin from the standard tray.

FIGURE 4.44
The Forms tab of the Print Server Properties dialog box allows you to define the print forms available on the computer.

STEP BY STEP

4.23 Creating a New Form from the Forms Tab

1. Open the Print Server Properties dialog box and click on an existing form in the Forms On list.

2. Select the Create a New Form check box.

3. Change the name of the form, and then change the form measurements to the new settings.

4. Click the Save Form button.

Ports

The Ports tab of the Print Server Properties dialog box maintains a list of available ports. You can add, delete, or configure a port. The Ports tab here is similar to the Add Printer Wizard's Ports tab (discussed earlier in this chapter) and the printer Properties Ports tab (discussed later in this chapter). The difference is that you don't have to select a port because you aren't associating a port with a particular printer; rather, you are merely viewing the ports that are available for all printers.

Advanced

The Advanced tab of the Print Server Properties dialog box provides the location of the spooler and an assortment of logging and notification options (see Figure 4.45).

Properties

You'll find most of the printer configuration settings in the printer Properties dialog box (see Figure 4.46). To open the printer Properties dialog box, select a printer in the Printers folder and choose File, Properties, or right-click on the printer and choose Properties. The following sections discuss the six tabs of the printer Properties dialog box.

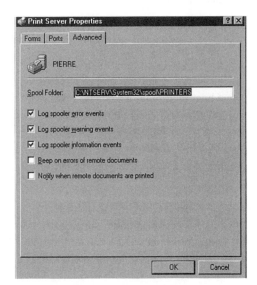

FIGURE 4.45
The Advanced tab of the Print Server Properties dialog box allows you to specify the location of the spooler and miscellaneous logging properties.

The General Tab

The General tab lets you install a new driver for the printer. You can select an existing driver from the Driver drop-down list, or you can click the New Driver button and follow the instructions for adding a new driver to the system.

The Print Test Page button provides a convenient method for testing to see whether a printer connection is working. The Separator Page and Print Processor buttons are a bit more complicated, however.

Separator Page

By default, Windows NT doesn't separate print jobs with even a blank sheet of paper. To print a separator page between print jobs, you must configure a separator file, three of which are included with Windows NT. You can create your own or use one of these three:

- ◆ *SYSPRINT.SEP.* Prints a separator page for PostScript printers; stored in the \<winnt_root>\SYSTEM32 directory.

- ◆ *PSCRIPT.SEP.* Switches Hewlett-Packard printers to PostScript mode for printers incapable of autoswitching; located in the \<winnt_root>\SYSTEM32 directory.

- ◆ *PCL.SEP.* Switches Hewlett-Packard printers to PCL mode for printers not capable of autoswitching (and prints a separator page before each document); located in the \<winnt_root>\SYSTEM32 directory.

You also may choose to design your own separator page. If so, use a text editor and consult the escape codes listed in Table 4.1. The escape codes are special symbols that prompt Windows NT to replace them with specific pieces of data. For instance, /N is the escape code that instructs Windows NT to print the username of the user who printed the job, and /D represents the date the job was printed.

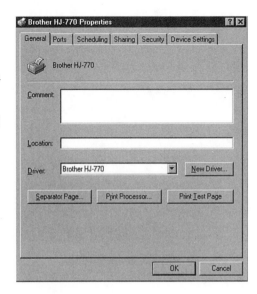

FIGURE 4.46

The printer Properties dialog box allows you to adjust the default printer administration settings.

TABLE 4.1	

WINDOWS NT PRINTING ESCAPE CODES

Code	Instruction for Windows NT
\<number>	Skip specified number of lines (0–9)
\B\M	Print text in double-width block mode
\B\S	Print text in single-width block mode
\D	Print current date using Control Panel International format
\E	Eject the page
\F<filename>	Print the specified file
\H<code>	Send printer-specific hexadecimal ASCII code
\I	Print job number
\L<text>\L	Print the specified text
\N	Print username of job owner
\T	Print time the job was printed using Control Panel International format
\U	Turn off block mode (see \B\M and \B\S)
\W<width>	Set width of the page (< =256)

To specify a separator file, click on the Separator Page button in the printer Properties General tab, and then either enter the name of the file or click on Browse and locate the separator file.

Print Processor

Don't mess with the print processor; it's the component of the printing subsystem that actually performs the rendering. Typically, WINPRINT.DLL performs the print processor functions. If it becomes necessary to replace it, Windows NT does it for you.

WINPRINT.DLL supports the following five data types:

◆ *Raw.* Fully rendered data ready for printing.

◆ *RAW (FF appended).*

◆ *RAW (FF auto).*

◆ *NT EMF (Enhanced Metafile Format).* A device-independent file format. An EMF file can be spooled directly to the print server and rendered at the server into the correct print format.

◆ *TEXT Raw.* Unformatted ASCII text ready for printing as is.

The Ports Tab

The printer Properties Ports tab lets you select a port for the printer and add or delete a port from the tab (see Figure 4.47). The Configure Port button allows you to specify the Transmission Retry time (the amount of time that must elapse before NT notifies you that the printing device isn't responding). The Transmission Retry setting applies not only to the selected printer but to all printers that use the same driver.

The Scheduling Tab

The printer Properties Scheduling tab lets you designate when the printer is to be available and set the printer priority (see Figure 4.48). It also displays some miscellaneous settings that define how the printer processes print jobs. The next few sections discuss the important settings on the Scheduling tab.

Available

The Available setting lets you limit the availability of a printer to a specific period of time. Note that just because a printer is restricted to a certain period of time doesn't mean the print device must be similarly restricted. For example, to keep long monthly reports from monopolizing a device during business hours, you could create two printers for the same printing device. One could be used for short print jobs and be available during the day, and the other could be used for long reports and print only at night.

Priority

The default priority for a printer is 1, but it can be set as high as 99. Changing this setting from its default of 1 is useful when you have more than one printer printing to the same printing device, in which case the printer with higher priority (99 being the highest) prints before printers of lower priority (1 being the lowest). Note that the Printer Priority setting is not related to the print job priority.

FIGURE 4.47
The printer Properties Ports tab allows you to configure the port or ports this printer is to use when printing.

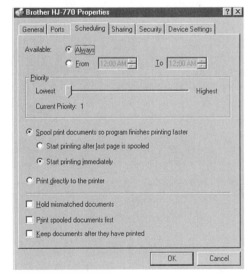

FIGURE 4.48
The printer Properties Scheduling tab allows you to specify when the printer will print documents sent to it (among other things).

Spool Print Documents or Print Directly to Printer

If you spool print documents, the computer and the printer don't have to wait for each other. It's almost always more efficient to spool print documents, so you rarely have reason to change this default. One advantage, however, of printing directly to the printer is that doing so might allow you to troubleshoot a problem with the spooler. If you can print to the printer but you can't print via the spooler, you may have a problem with your spooler.

Under the Spool Print Documents... option are two other options:

◆ Start Printing After the Last Page Is Spooled

◆ Start Printing Immediately

The first choice is (in part) a holdover from earlier versions of NT; NT used to wait until a job was completely spooled before beginning to print it. This could take a long time for reports that were hundreds of pages long, so more recent versions offered a Job Prints While Spooling option to let the printer start printing before the spooler finishes. In NT 4, Start Printing Immediately is the default option, but you still have the option of not printing until after the last page spools.

Hold Mismatched Documents

In other Windows-based operating environments, improperly configured print jobs—a print job, for example, requesting a paper tray that isn't present—can be sent to a printer, which usually causes the printer to hang with an error message. In NT, however, if you select the Hold Mismatched Documents option, Windows NT examines the configuration of both the print job and the printer to make sure they are in agreement before it sends the job.

Print Spooled Documents First

Ordinarily, Windows NT prints documents on a first-come, first-served basis: The document at the top of the queue prints before the documents below it. If the document at the top of the queue takes a long time to spool and the Job Prints While Spooling option isn't selected, you might want to enable the Print Spooled Documents First setting. Windows NT always prints the first available completely spooled print job. But if this setting is used in conjunction with

Job Prints While Spooling, all the completely spooled documents ahead of the spooling document print first. The spooling document is then processed next, even if completed documents are waiting behind it in the queue.

Keep Documents After They Have Printed

Normally, Windows NT cleans up after itself as it finishes printing each job. If you enable the Keep Documents After They Have Printed option, however, Windows NT keeps the print document after it prints. One reason you might check this box is if you want to have a record of completed print jobs that all users can access. Although you can choose to have completed print jobs recorded in the Event Log, nonadministrative users cannot view the Event Log.

The Sharing Tab

The Sharing tab lets you share the printer with other computers on the network (see Figure 4.49). If you didn't install the printer as a shared printer but decide later that you want to share it, you can change the printer to a shared printer as described in Step by Step 4.24.

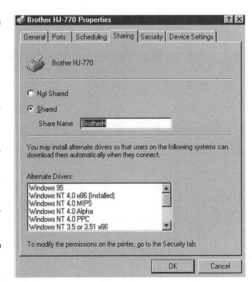

FIGURE 4.49
The printer Properties Sharing tab allows you to indicate what name will be displayed for this printer over the network and the drivers that will be installed for client use.

STEP BY STEP

4.24 Sharing a Printer

1. Select the Sharing tab in the printer Properties dialog box.

2. Specify a share name (or accept the default, which is the first eight characters of the printer name).

3. Specify what operating systems the other workstations will be using (so NT can automatically download the necessary print drivers to the connecting computers).

4. Click OK.

You can access the Sharing tab directly either by clicking on a printer and choosing File, Sharing in the Printers folder or by right-clicking on a printer and choosing Sharing.

FIGURE 4.50
The printer Properties Security tab is the jumping-off place for security, auditing, and ownership configuration.

FIGURE 4.51
In the Printer Permissions dialog box, you indicate who can use the printer and what permissions they have to administrate it.

The Security Tab

The Security tab lets you configure permissions, auditing, and ownership settings for the printer (see Figure 4.50).

Windows NT printers are Windows NT resources, and Windows NT resources are Windows NT objects. Windows NT objects are protected by the Windows NT security model: They have owners and Access Control Lists that owners can use to protect the printers.

To set or change permissions for a printer, a user must be the owner, an Administrator, a Power User, or a user who has Full Control permissions on the printer's ACL. To set permissions for a printer, select the Security tab in the printer Properties dialog box and click on the Permissions button. You see the Printer Permissions dialog box, which displays common user groups and the permission levels granted to each group for the use of the selected printer (see Figure 4.51).

Windows NT offers four possible permission levels:

◆ *No Access.* Completely restricts access to the printer.

◆ *Print.* Allows a user or group to submit a print job and to control the settings and print status for that job.

◆ *Manage Documents.* Allows a user or group to submit a print job and to control the settings and print status for all print jobs.

◆ *Full Control.* Allows a user to submit a print job and to control the settings and print status for all documents as well as for the printer itself. In addition, the user or group may share, stop sharing, change permissions for, and even delete the printer.

These permissions affect both local and remote users. By default, permissions on newly created printers comply with the scheme outlined in Table 4.2.

To change the permission level for a group, select the group in the Name list, and then enter a new permission level in the Type of Access combo box or open the combo box and select a permission level. To add a group or user to the permissions list, click on the Add button. The Add Users and Groups dialog box opens (see Figure 4.52).

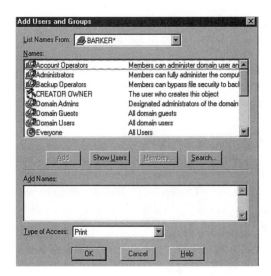

FIGURE 4.52
The Add Users and Groups dialog box allows you to choose from a list who has permission to use a printer.

TABLE 4.2

DEFAULT PERMISSIONS ON A NEW PRINTER (BY GROUP)

Group	Permission
Administrators	Full Control
Creator/Owner	Manage Documents
Everyone	Print
Power Users	Full Control
Print Operators	Full Control
Server Operators	Full Control

To add a group to the permissions list, select a group in the Names list of the Add Users and Groups dialog box and click Add. The name of the group then appears in the Add Names box. Click OK to add the name to the permissions list.

To add an individual user to the permissions list, click the Show Users button in the Add Users and Groups dialog box. This adds users to the Names list. Select the user and click Add. The name of the user then appears in the Add Names box. Click OK to add the name to the permissions list.

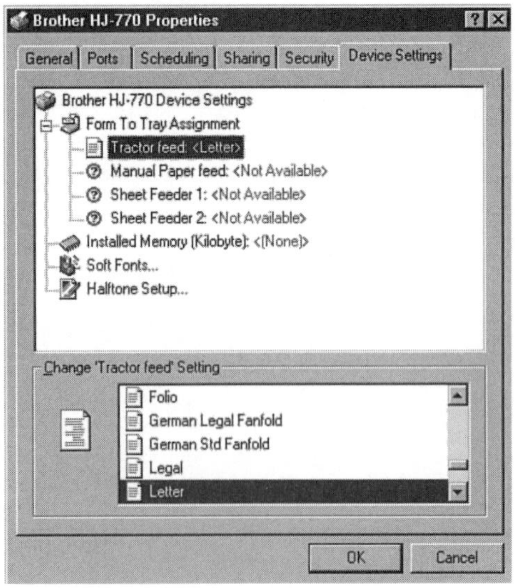

FIGURE 4.53
The printer Properties Device Settings tab allows you to associate a specific form with a paper tray and to indicate the amount of memory and fonts installed in the printer.

NOTE

Place Pooled Printers Near One Another When printing to a printer pool, the user has no control over which device prints the job. Therefore, printer pools are incredibly annoying if the print devices aren't located in the same place.

After you add the group or user to the permissions list, you can change the permission level for that group or user (as described earlier in this section).

The printer Properties Security tab also enables you to set up auditing for the printer and to take ownership of the printer.

The Device Settings Tab

The printer Properties Device Settings tab maintains settings for the printing device (see Figure 4.53). These settings differ depending on your printing device. The Form To Tray Assignment setting allows you to associate a print form with an actual paper tray on the printing device.

Sharing Printers

When you install a new printer, you can designate it to be shared over the network. The section "Adding a Printer on Your Own Machine" earlier in this chapter describes how to do this.

You can share a printer that already has been installed by using the Sharing tab in the printer Properties dialog box. See the section "The Sharing Tab," earlier in this chapter.

Use the Security tab in the printer Properties dialog box to set or change permissions for printers.

Setting Up a Printer Pool

A printer pool presents interesting possibilities for some office environments. A *printer pool* is essentially a single printer that prints to more than one print device; it prints jobs sent to it to the first available print device (and, therefore, provides the throughput of multiple print devices with the simplicity of a single printer definition).

If a printer controls a printer pool, Windows NT ensures that no single device is ever sent more than one document at a time if other devices currently are available. This characteristic ensures the most efficient utilization of your print devices. Step by Step 4.25 walks you through the creation of a printer pool.

Printer pools are an extremely efficient way of streamlining the printing process, although they don't necessarily work for every environment. Before your network can use a printer pool, it must meet the following criteria:

◆ You must have at least two print devices capable of using the same printer driver because the entire pool is treated as a single logical device and is managed by a single printer driver.

◆ The print devices should be in close proximity. Users aren't notified which actual device prints their jobs and should be able to check all the print devices rapidly and easily.

STEP BY STEP

4.25 Creating a Printer Pool

1. Install a printer from the Printers folder in the Control Panel or open the properties for an existing one.

2. On the Ports tab of the printer Properties dialog box, select the Enable Printer Pooling check box.

3. Also on the Ports tab, select the ports connected to the print devices that are to be part of the pool.

4. Click OK to save the changes.

Printing from MS-DOS Applications

MS-DOS applications provide their own printer drivers and automatically render printer data to the RAW data type or to straight ASCII text. The print data is then intercepted by the client spooler and routed through the Windows NT printing system.

The MS-DOS application typically isn't equipped to process UNC names. So if it is printing to a remote printer, you should map a physical port to the remote printer by using this command:

```
net use LPTx: \\pserver\printer_name
```

Because the application itself renders the printer data, an MS-DOS application that prints graphics and formatted text must have its own printer driver for the printing device. An MS-DOS application can print ASCII text output without a vendor-supplied printer driver.

CASE STUDY: SMITH, PENNER, AND SMENT

ESSENCE OF THE CASE

Here are the essential elements of this case:

- The need for high security to protect documents

- The need for central administration by a single person

- Global access to resources across the company

- The need for fault tolerance and ease of data recovery in the event of system failure

- The need for high print performance and volume

SCENARIO

Smith, Penner, and Sment, Attorneys at Law, have decided to implement a corporate networking strategy to support their firm's business. Although their main office is in Chicago, IL, they also maintain two smaller sites in rural Illinois. In total, they employ 150 people, 125 at their main office.

Currently, all documents produced by the firm are dictated by the lawyers to assistants, who collate the information and send it to a central typing pool to have the documents typed (this typing is currently being done on manual typewriters). Documents produced in the two satellite locations are typed onsite, faxed to the main office to be retyped, and then are returned to the satellite locations by courier when the final drafts are complete.

The partners have a desire to incorporate the latest technology into their organization to make the process more efficient and to eliminate redundant work. However, they are concerned about the security of their information, both from unauthorized access and from system failure. They want documents to be available to anyone who needs them, and they want to be able to print even the longest documents quickly whenever necessary, especially at the main office.

They think they need a computer professional on staff to maintain the new systems, but they want to hire only one person at this time.

CASE STUDY: SMITH, PENNER, AND SMENT

ANALYSIS

The questions and concerns of the partners at Smith, Penner, and Sment are common in companies that are moving to replace paper systems with technological ones. Who has access to our information? What happens if the system fails? Will we be more efficient or less efficient? These questions must be addressed when a proposal is presented.

A number of factors need to be addressed in the analysis. Because the main branch wants to keep some control over the new system and because a single administrator is to be hired, a domain model is the most reasonable type of network. This model also ensures central security and keeps security issues out of the hands of end-users.

With this model, however, comes the question of performance for remote users. Because the domain is to be administered from a central location, the question of user login and the performance considerations that go along with making users log on from remote sites over a wide area network need to be addressed. It's possible that login will take longer than desired if validation by the PDC is required. To alleviate this, a BDC can be installed at each of the branch locations. The BDC solution also offers two other advantages: It allows for speed of validation when the remote users log on, and the BDC machines can be used as print and file servers at the remote locations. Despite having a server at the remote sites, all but the most complex of administration tasks on these BDCs can still be done centrally from the Chicago office using the domain management

tools available on the PDC. A BDC will also be installed at the Chicago office to ensure failover capabilities should the PDC go down unexpectedly or for scheduled maintenance.

The need for global access to resources is, of course, satisfied by the implementation of a network and the use of home directories and publicly shared space on the file servers. Using TCP/IP as the only protocol will ensure not only that the network communication is routable, but also that this company is prepared for access to the Internet should the company direction ever lead there. However, you must stress that the potential for global access to documents and printers does not necessarily mean that everyone will have access to everything; on the contrary, security will be implemented to ensure that people have access only to what they need. This will guarantee restricted access not only from outside the organization, but also from within. This is implemented through domain accounts and the utilization of the security inherent in the domain model.

Although recoverability is not covered in this module, you stress the need for a good backup strategy and indicate that it should be implemented as soon as the network is in place. Likewise, the implementation of a fault-tolerance system will enable quicker recovery if catastrophic failure occurs. Mirror sets and stripe sets with parity can be configured for all hard drives that store essential data. (Of course, the implementation of hardware-based RAID is always a consideration, but it's beyond the scope of this discussion.) Moreover, the simple installation of UPS systems on all the

continues

CASE STUDY: SMITH, PENNER, AND SMENT

continued

computers will reduce the chance of failure during power outages and brownouts.

Finally, the need for a good printing solution is necessary. Because this firm relies on quick turnaround of documents, you will need to propose a robust printing solution. (As an aside, the need for quick turnaround will increase as they begin to rely on the system you put in place: Where quick turnaround may have meant a few days in the past, with the new networked system in place, they may begin to redefine that phrase to mean a few hours.) You will need to plan for that and propose a robust system that will be effective into the reasonably long-term future.

In order to provide proper print resources to a number of people with high volume and high speed on their minds, you may want to propose that one or more high-speed printers be

installed at the main office. If more than one printer is required, a printer pool would be advantageous because it gives the additional throughput that may be necessary during crisis times in projects. These printers will be controlled by a member server that is configured as a print server. (As an alternative, you could use the BDC as a print server if the idea of having three NT servers at the head office is thought to be excessive.) To justify the member server, however, you stress that it could also be the location for all the document storage, in addition to being the print server for the location. You will also want to have printers installed at the branch locations to ensure that drafts of documents and additional copies can be printed when they are needed. These remote printers can be configured to be controlled by the BDCs at the remote branches.

The following table summarizes the solution.

A SUMMARY OF THE REQUIREMENTS AND SOLUTIONS IN THIS CASE STUDY

Requirement	Solution Provided By
Centralized administration	Implementation of NT domain with PDC and BDCs
Global access to resources	Installation of TCP/IP
	Access to home and public folders
Fault tolerance and recoverability	Implementation of backup strategy
	Installation of multiple hard drives on file server
	Configuration of stripe sets with parity and mirror sets
	UPS systems for each location
High printer performance	Member server as print server
	Printer pool at head office
	Printers at branch offices

CHAPTER SUMMARY

In summary, this chapter covered three major sections: configuring peripherals in general, configuring disk drives, and configuring printers.

The chapter began with a discussion of the Windows NT Registry and the tools available to manipulate it. Although the Registry is not the topic of an exam objective, a knowledge of how to use and manipulate the Registry is expected of an NT Server expert and is expected on the NT Server exam.

Having studied the Registry in detail, you then moved to the configuration of peripherals. That section gave you a guided tour of the Control Panel and the programs available from it. A knowledge of the configuration options discussed in that section is essential. However, as you learned at the beginning of the section, the material regarding the Registry keys that are modified when you make changes in the Control Panel was for your information only; you do not need to memorize that material.

Understanding the Disk Administrator is very important because it helps you understand disk configuration. You learned about creating partitions and the different sorts of partitions available, and then you learned about fault tolerance, a major topic on the exam (especially in scenario questions).

Finally, the chapter discussed printing. Beginning with an overview of the printing process, the section moved on to cover installing and configuring printers. This included the configuration of both local printers and network printers. In addition, you looked at sharing printers for the purpose of allowing clients to connect to them as network printers. The chapter finished by briefly discussing printer pools and printing from DOS.

KEY TERMS

Before taking the exam, make sure you are familiar with the definitions of and concepts behind each of the following key terms. Appendix A provides a glossary of terms that you can use for quick reference purposes.

- Registry
- REGEDT32.EXE
- REGEDIT.EXE
- Registry tree
- Registry key
- HKEY_LOCAL_MACHINE
- Control Panel
- UPS
- SCSI adapter
- Disk Administrator
- partition
- primary partition
- extended partition
- logical drive
- volume set
- stripe set
- active partition
- fault tolerance
- disk mirroring
- disk striping with parity
- printer
- print device
- spooler
- printer driver
- printer pool

APPLY YOUR LEARNING

Exercises

The following exercises will help to reinforce the concepts you learned in this chapter. Although they're not all-inclusive, they do give you an overview of some of the tools and procedures you studied.

4.1   Creating a Volume Set from Free Space

This exercise will help you explore the Disk Administrator by creating a volume set using two partitions in free space on your hard drive. If you do not have the free space available that is indicated, use whatever free space is available and adjust the exercise accordingly. This exercise also assumes that you have one contiguous area of free space on your hard drive and, as a result, does a bit of fudging to allow you to create the volume set. Some of these steps would not be necessary if you already had a number of segmented areas of free space.

Estimated Time: 10 minutes

1. Log on as an administrator to a Windows NT Server system.

2. Start the Disk Administrator by choosing Start, Programs, Administrative Tools (Common), Disk Administrator.

3. Select the free space. Then open the Partition menu and choose Create (see Figure 4.54).

4. When the Create Logical Drive dialog box appears, type **50** and press Enter.

5. Select the free space. Then open the Partition menu and choose Create. When the Create Logical Drive dialog box appears, type **10** and press Enter.

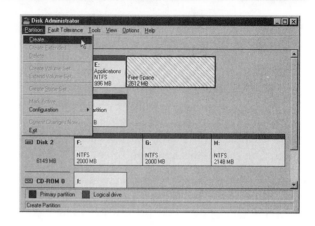

FIGURE 4.54
Use the Disk Administrator to create a new partition.

6. Select the free space. Then open the Partition menu and choose Create. When the Create Logical Drive dialog box appears, type **50** and press Enter.

7. Select the free space. Then open the Partition menu and choose Create. When the Create Logical Drive dialog box appears, type **10** and press Enter.

8. Select the logical drive you created in step 4. Then open the Partition menu and choose Delete.

9. Select the logical drive you created in step 6. Then open the Partition menu and choose Delete.

   At this point, you have created three separate areas of free space, as shown in Figure 4.55.

10. Select the first area of free space, press and hold down the Ctrl key, and select the second area (both should now be selected). Then open the Partition menu and choose Create Volume Set (see Figure 4.56).

APPLY YOUR LEARNING

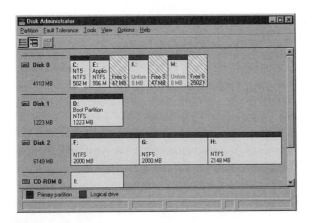

FIGURE 4.55
Having completed this much of the procedure, your drive should look like this one.

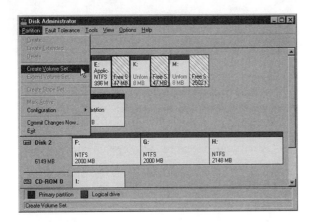

FIGURE 4.56
Use the Disk Administrator to create a volume set.

11. When the Create Volume Set dialog box appears, press Enter to accept a volume set consisting of all the free space selected.

12. From the Partition menu, choose Commit Changes Now to make the changes permanent so you can format the new partition.

If you are prompted to restart your computer, do so (be sure to read and approve any questions and message boxes that appear).

4.2 Formatting and Converting a Partition

This exercise continues your exploration of the Disk Administrator. Here you take the volume set you created in Exercise 4.1, format it as FAT, add a file to it, and then convert it to NTFS.

Estimated Time: 10 minutes

1. Log on as an administrator to a Windows NT Server system.

2. Start the Disk Administrator by choosing Start, Programs, Administrative Tools (Common), Disk Administrator.

3. Select the volume set you created in Exercise 4.1. Then open the Tools menu and choose Format.

4. When the Format dialog box appears (see Figure 4.57), click the Start button to format. When you're asked to approve the format, click OK.

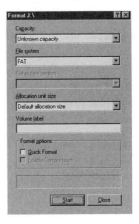

FIGURE 4.57
The Format dialog box enables you to set the properties for formatting.

APPLY YOUR LEARNING

5. Exit the Disk Administrator and open a window for the new partition in either Explorer or My Computer. Right-click on the partition and select New, Text Document. When the new document appears, type the name **FAT Test.txt** and press Enter (see Figure 4.58).

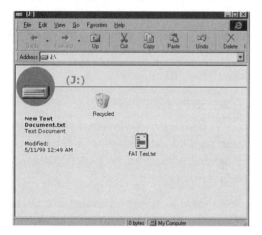

FIGURE 4.58
Create a new text document on the volume set that you just created.

> ⓃⓄⓉⒺ **This Is Only a Test** The document you are creating is only a test. When you convert this partition from FAT to NTFS in the next sequence of steps, you need to be able to confirm that the conversion is, in fact, not destructive to files. This is how you test that.

6. Choose Start, Run and type the following command in the Run dialog box:

```
convert j: /fs:ntfs
```

where *j* is the letter Windows NT assigned to your volume set.

7. You should see the message shown in Figure 4.59. Type **Y**, and then restart your system to allow the conversion to take place.

FIGURE 4.59
If the system cannot gain exclusive access to a drive, you must restart Windows NT for conversion to occur.

8. After your system restarts, open a window displaying the contents of your volume set and verify that the FAT Test.txt file is still present in that partition.

9. Restart the Disk Administrator to verify that the volume set is now formatted NTFS.

APPLY YOUR LEARNING

4.3   Extending a Volume Set

In this exercise, you will continue exploration of Disk Administrator by extending the volume set you have been working with. This process will extend the memory available for the volume set.

Estimated Time: 10 minutes

1. Start the Disk Administrator by choosing Start, Programs, Administrative Tools (Common), Disk Administrator.

2. Select the volume set you converted to NTFS in Exercise 4.2, press and hold the Ctrl key, and then click the free space available on your hard drive. Both the volume and the free space are now selected.

3. From the Partition menu, choose Extend Volume Set. When the Extend Volume Set dialog box appears, type **150** and press Enter to extend the volume set from 100MB to 150MB. The volume set will now appear as three separate sections with the same drive letter (see Figure 4.60).

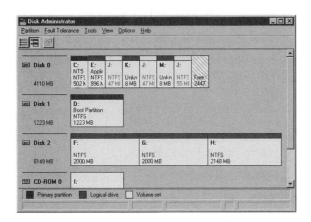

FIGURE 4.60
The volume set shows up as three yellow sections in the Disk Administrator.

4. Close the Disk Administrator and display the contents of the volume set in a window to verify that the FAT Test.txt document still exists.

4.4   Deleting a Partition

In this exercise, you conclude your exploration of the Disk Administrator by deleting the volume set you have been working with. This releases the involved partitions, making them into free space once again.

Estimated Time: 10 minutes

1. Log on as an administrator to a Windows NT Server system.

2. Start the Disk Administrator by choosing Start, Programs, Administrative Tools (Common), Disk Administrator.

3. Select the volume set you have been working with, open the Partition menu, and choose Delete.

4. A warning appears, indicating that all data will be lost from the partition that's being deleted. Click Yes to delete the volume set.

   The space allocated to the volume set reverts to free space.

4.5   Installing a Local Printer

This exercise will help you explore printers as you walk through the installation of a local printer on your Windows NT Server.

Estimated Time: 10 minutes

1. Log on as an administrator to a Windows NT Server system.

2. Choose Start, Settings, Printers to open the Printers dialog box (see Figure 4.61).

APPLY YOUR LEARNING

FIGURE 4.61
The process of printer installation begins in the Printers dialog box.

3. In the Printers dialog box, double-click the Add Printer icon. This invokes the Add Printer Wizard (see Figure 4.62).

FIGURE 4.62
The Add Printer Wizard walks you through the printer installation process.

4. In the first Add Printer Wizard dialog box, select the My Computer radio button and click Next.

5. When prompted for the port to use, select the check box beside LPT1. Then click Next.

6. When prompted for the printer manufacturer and model, choose HP and HP LaserJet 4 (see Figure 4.63).

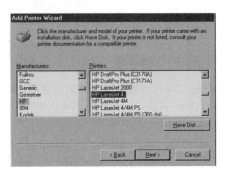

FIGURE 4.63
When prompted, choose the manufacturer and model of the printer you want to install.

7. When asked for the local name of the printer, type **Local Printer** in the dialog box and click Next.

8. When asked whether this printer is to be shared, select the Not Shared option and click Next.

9. When you're asked whether you want to print a test page, select No and click Finish.

   If the source of the Windows NT installation files is not readily available, you will be prompted for the location of the printer driver. Insert the CD-ROM at this time, or type a path where NT can find the proper printer driver.

4.6 Sharing a Local Printer

This exercise walks you through the steps for sharing the printer you just installed on your Windows NT system.

Estimated Time: 10 minutes

APPLY YOUR LEARNING

1. Log on as an administrator to a Windows NT Server system.

2. Choose Start, Settings, Printers to open the Printers dialog box.

3. Right-click on the printer you want to share and choose Sharing from the context menu that appears. The printer Properties dialog box appears (see Figure 4.64).

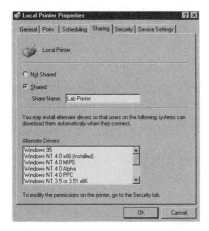

FIGURE 4.64
Printer sharing can be configured from the Sharing tab of the printer Properties dialog box.

4. In the printer Properties dialog box, type **Lab Printer** in the Share Name field and click OK.

5. You will be warned that the share name you chose may not be accessible by DOS clients. Click Yes to complete the sharing.

   A hand now appears to be holding the printer icon, which indicates that it is shared.

Review Questions

1. In Windows NT terminology, what is a printer controlling two or more print devices called?

2. What two disk maintenance methods are available to collect multiple areas of free space into a single logical drive without providing fault tolerance?

3. The Windows NT Server implementations of RAID 1 and RAID 5 are referred to as what?

4. Which Control Panel application would be used to install and configure Panasonic CD-ROM devices?

5. In print configuration, what term is used to refer to the software component? The hardware component?

6. Name the two programs used to view and modify the Registry.

7. What is the minimum permission that's required for a user to be able to delete any and all documents from the print queue?

8. What are the five subtrees of the NT Registry?

9. What are the four options you can choose from as actions to take when a system crash (Stop error) occurs?

10. What Control Panel applet is used to configure certain devices for use in particular hardware profiles?

APPLY YOUR LEARNING

Exam Questions

1. Your Windows NT Server has two 4GB hard drives, partitioned as described here:

   Drive 1: 1GB primary partition; 1GB extended partition (two logical partitions defined); 2GB free space

   Drive 2: 1GB primary partition; 1GB primary partition; 2GB extended partition (two logical partitions defined).

   Given that the drive lettering has been left up to Windows NT, if you create another primary partition in the free space of Drive 1, what drive letter will be assigned to it?

   A. G

   B. H

   C. I

   D. D

2. Which statement best describes the purpose of the Registry?

   A. The Registry is a configuration database that replaces the INI files used by previous versions of Windows.

   B. The Registry is a configuration database that Windows NT uses to keep domain account information (that is, registered information).

   C. Windows 3.x applications use the Registry instead of INI files to store configuration information.

   D. The Registry stores all the domain information for ease of removal in the event that a Windows NT Server domain controller must be moved from one domain to another.

3. Which utilities are available in NT to directly edit the Registry? Choose all that apply.

   A. REGEDIT.EXE

   B. EDITREG.EXE

   C. REGEDT32.EXE

   D. CHGREG.EXE

4. What five subtrees make up the Registry?

   A. HKEY_LOCAL_MACHINE
      HKEY_ALL_USERS
      HKEY_CURRENT_USER
      HKEY_ROOT
      HKEY_CURRENT_CONFIG

   B. HKEY_LOCAL_MACHINE
      HKEY_COMMON
      HKEY_CURRENT_USER
      HKEY_CLASSES_ROOT
      HKEY_CURRENT_CONFIG

   C. HKEY_MACHINE
      HKEY_CLASSES_ROOT
      HKEY_CURRENT_USER
      HKEY_USERS
      HKEY_CURRENT_CONFIG

   D. HKEY_LOCAL_MACHINE
      HKEY_USERS
      HKEY_CURRENT_USER
      HKEY_CLASSES_ROOT
      HKEY_CURRENT_CONFIG

5. Which Registry subtree contains information about the current configuration of the computer?

   A. HKEY_CURRENT_USER

   B. HKEY_CURRENT_MACHINE

   C. HKEY_LOCAL_MACHINE

   D. HKEY_CLASSES_ROOT

6. The least risky method of modifying the Registry is to use the _____ utility?

    A. Registry Editor (REGEDT32.EXE)

    B. Control Panel

    C. REGEDIT.EXE

    D. None of the above. (The Registry is a system database that should never be modified by any user.)

7. A user calls you and tells you that he was trying to verify his hardware settings for his COM ports by looking at Control Panel, Ports, but he doesn't see any listing for his serial mouse, which is on COM1. Why is this?

    A. The user doesn't actually have a serial mouse. He has a bus mouse and that's why it's not listed on a port.

    B. The user is mistaken; he probably doesn't have a mouse attached to his system.

    C. The user has a mouse, but he needs to look under Control Panel, Mouse to see his device settings.

    D. Control Panel, Ports shows only available ports, not ports in use.

8. Your mission-critical NT Server just crashed as the result of a power failure. You purchase a UPS (Uninterruptible Power Supply) and attach it to the NT Server computer. How can you configure the operating system so that it shuts down gracefully before the UPS runs out of power?

    A. You cannot. You must manually shut down the server before the UPS runs out of power.

    B. Choose the Control Panel, System option, select UPS, and then configure the estimated runtime of the UPS. Be sure to select a number of minutes less than the actual runtime of the UPS.

    C. Open the Control Panel's UPS applet and configure the COM Port, Run Time, and signaling methods of the UPS.

    D. Because NT is Plug and Play compatible, you don't need to configure the UPS. The next time you restart the Server, the device will automatically be configured.

9. A user calls you and states that after creating a new partition on his hard drive, he cannot select Format from the Tools menu in Disk Administrator. What does he need to do to be able to format the drive?

    A. He must reboot the computer in DOS, and then use the `format` command to format the hard disk.

    B. He has to commit the changes in Disk Administrator before the partition can be formatted.

    C. He has to use the low-level format program in the computer's BIOS to prepare the disk.

    D. He must first partition the disk using FDISK and format it with DOS. Then he can convert it to NTFS to make it ready for use.

10. You installed a new hard disk in your NT Server computer, and you partitioned it and formatted it as a FAT partition. You want to add this disk space to an existing volume to extend the disk space. However, when you attempt to extend the volume, you cannot. Why?

    A. The volume that you created must already include four primary partitions and cannot be extended any further.

APPLY YOUR LEARNING

B. You must commit the changes before you can proceed.

C. You can extend only a volume that has been formatted NTFS.

D. You can extend only volumes that have been formatted or converted to FAT.

11. **Scenario:** Herbert has an NT Server that consists of four physical disks with 500MB of free space on each. The first is the NT system and boot partition, and the other three have applications loaded on them.

   Required Result:

   Create a multidisk set that provides the largest possible usable data area.

   Optional Desired Results:

   Provide fault tolerance in case of disk failure.

   Provide the ability to format with NTFS.

   Provide the ability to add to the set in the future without reformatting it.

   Proposed Solution:

   Create a stripe set using the free space on the three disks that do not contain the system and boot partitions.

   Analysis:

   Which of the following statements best describes the proposed solution?

   A. The proposed solution produces the required result and all of the optional desired results.

   B. The proposed solution produces the required result but only one of the optional desired results.

C. The proposed solution produces the required result but does not produce any of the optional desired results.

D. The proposed solution does not produce the required result.

12. **Scenario:** Herbert has an NT Server that consists of four physical disks with 500MB of free space on each. The first is the NT system and boot partition, and the other three have applications loaded on them.

   Required Result:

   Create a multidisk set that provides the largest possible fault-tolerant area.

   Optional Desired Results:

   Provide the ability to format with NTFS.

   Provide the ability to add to the set in the future without reformatting it.

   Proposed Solution:

   Create a volume set using the free space on the three disks that do not contain the system and boot partitions.

   Analysis:

   Which of the following statements best describes the proposed solution?

   A. The proposed solution produces the required result and all of the optional desired results.

   B. The proposed solution produces the required result but only one of the optional desired results.

   C. The proposed solution produces the required result but does not produce any of the optional desired results.

D. The proposed solution does not produce the required result.

13. Which of the following is a type of disk system that makes an exact copy of all data from one disk partition and places it on another disk partition?

    A. RAID

    B. Disk saving

    C. Disk mirroring

    D. Hot fixing

14. Which of the following are not fault-tolerant (select all correct answers)?

    A. Volume sets

    B. Disk striping with parity

    C. Disk striping without parity

    D. Disk mirroring

15. In a Windows NT environment, what is the term that refers to the object that actually performs the printing process?

    A. Printer

    B. Print device

    C. Print queue

    D. Print server

16. A user states that she's trying to load a printer driver for her laser printer, but she cannot find one specifically written for Windows NT. She wants to know whether the one she has for Windows 95 will work. Which statement best describes the relationship between printer drivers for different NT platforms?

A. The Windows NT printer drivers are platform-specific. You cannot use a Windows 95 driver on an NT computer. You also must be sure to use the printer driver for the platform on which you're running NT.

B. The NT printer drivers are interchangeable and can be used on any NT platform.

C. The NT printer drivers and Windows 95 drivers are interchangeable because both operating systems are 32-bit. However, you cannot substitute 16-bit drivers for NT drivers.

D. Printer drivers are interchangeable as long as they are for the same printer.

17. A print job isn't printing properly but you cannot remove it from the printer. What can you do to fix the problem?

    A. Nothing.

    B. Wait a couple hours until the Spooler service detects the problem and corrects it.

    C. Take the print server down and restart it.

    D. Stop the Spooler service on the print server and then restart it.

18. Which statement best describes the procedure for updating the printer driver on all your Windows NT computers?

    A. Create a disk with the new printer driver on it, and then go to each computer and load the new version of the printer driver.

    B. You must purchase and configure the SMS product from Microsoft if you want to automatically configure NT computers to update printer drivers.

C. Load the new driver on the computer acting as the print server. The NT computers will automatically copy down the new printer driver the next time they print.

D. Put the printer driver in a shared directory and have your NT users install the new driver manually.

19. How do you install a new printer driver? Select all correct answers.

    A. Choose Start, Settings, Printers. Run the Add Printer Wizard.

    B. Start Print Manager and add the printer from the Printer menu.

    C. Open Control Panel, click on the Printers icon, and then double-click on the Add Printer icon.

    D. Run the Windows NT Setup program and install the printer driver under the Configuration menu.

20. If you have a printer that has multiple paper trays, how can you make it easier for users to select the proper paper tray for the type of paper they want to print on?

    A. Tell the users the type of paper that's in each of the paper trays so that they can select the proper tray when printing.

    B. Assign particular types of paper to the paper trays via the printer Properties dialog box. The users can select the type of paper on which to print without knowing which tray the paper is in.

    C. The users must select manual feed and then notify the printer operator when they're printing on nonstandard paper types.

    D. The users must select manual feed and then feed the correct type of paper when they print their documents.

21. **Scenario:** Emma is a network administrator for an NT domain. She is configuring a print device in the Sales Office that is connected to an NT member server acting as a print server.

    Required Result:

    Provide a way for users to direct large jobs to print between 6:00 p.m. and 6:00 a.m. and to direct small jobs to print immediately.

    Optional Desired Results:

    Configure managers' small print jobs to take priority over all other users' jobs.

    Prevent people in the Accounting Department from using the print device.

    Proposed Solution:

    Install three printers on the print server, all of which print to the port the print device is connected to. Configure the first printer so that only the Managers group has Print access and the Administrators group has Full Control. Give this printer a priority of 99.

    Configure the second printer so that the Everyone group has Print access and the Administrators group has Full Control. Give this printer a priority of 1.

    Configure the last printer so that the Everyone group has Print access and the Administrators group has Full Control. Leave the print priority at default and make it available only between 6:00 p.m. and 6:00 a.m.

    Tell the Managers to print regular documents to the first printer and large documents to the third.

Tell all other salespeople to print regular documents to the second printer and large documents to the third.

Analysis:

Which of the following statements best describes the proposed solution?

A. The proposed solution produces the required result and all of the optional desired results.

B. The proposed solution produces the required result but only one of the optional desired results.

C. The proposed solution produces the required result but does not produce either of the optional desired results.

D. The proposed solution does not produce the required result.

22. **Scenario:** Noah is a network administrator for an NT domain. He is configuring a print device in the Sales Office that is connected to an NT member server acting as a print server.

Required Result:

Provide a way for users to direct large jobs to print between 6:00 p.m. and 6:00 a.m. and to direct small jobs to print immediately.

Optional Desired Results:

Configure managers' small print jobs to take priority over all other users' jobs.

Prevent people in the Accounting department from using the print device.

Proposed Solution:

Install three printers on the print server, all of which print to the port the print device is

connected to. Configure the first so that only the Managers group has Print access and the Administrators group has Full Control. Give this printer a priority of 99.

Configure the second printer so that the Sales group has Print access and the Administrators group has Full Control. Give this printer a priority of 1.

Configure the last printer so that the Sales group has Print access and the Administrators group has Full Control. Leave the print priority at default and make it available only between 6:00 p.m. and 6:00 a.m.

Tell the Managers to print regular documents to the first printer and large documents to the third. Tell all other salespeople to print regular documents to the second printer and large documents to the third.

Analysis:

Which of the following statements best describes the proposed solution?

A. The proposed solution produces the required result and all of the optional desired results.

B. The proposed solution produces the required result but only one of the optional desired results.

C. The proposed solution produces the required result but does not produce either of the optional desired results.

D. The proposed solution does not produce the required result.

23. You have two groups of users who need to print to the same printer. However, one group's print

APPLY YOUR LEARNING

jobs must have priority over the other group's print jobs. How best can you accomplish this arrangement?

A. You must install two separate printing devices and assign each group to print to one of the printing devices.

B. Make the users that need the higher printing priority Printer Operators so they can adjust the order of print jobs in the printer.

C. Set up a printing pool with multiple printers.

D. Install two printers that are connected to the same printing device. Assign different priorities and groups to each printer.

24. Some of the users on your network habitually select the incorrect printer driver when printing to your laser printer. How can you make sure that improperly formatted documents don't print on the printer and possibly cause it to hang?

A. Tell the users to always check the printer driver they've selected before printing their documents.

B. Install a printer that supports both PostScript and PCL printing definition languages.

C. Select the Hold Mismatched Documents option in the printer Properties dialog box. This tells the NT print server to hold any documents that don't match the printer language.

D. You shouldn't have to worry about it. The newer printer drivers can automatically translate page formatting language to match the printer.

25. **Scenario:** Alexander is in charge of supporting the administrators in a large corporate office.

There are three HP LaserJet 4 printers in the office. The problem is that two of the devices are heavily used, but the other is hardly used at all. Alexander has been asked to resolve the problem in the most effective way.

Required Result:

Ensure that all three printers are used equally.

Optional Desired Results:

Make the user intervention in the use-balancing process as small as possible.

Ensure that Alexander's manual intervention in balancing is kept to a minimum.

Proposed Solution:

Locate all three print devices in a central place in the office and connect them to three ports on the same print server.

Configure a printer pool to allow a single printer to print to whichever print device is available at the time.

Analysis:

Which of the following statements best describes the proposed solution?

A. The proposed solution produces the required result and all of the optional desired results.

B. The proposed solution produces the required result but only one of the optional desired results.

C. The proposed solution produces the required result but does not produce either of the optional desired results.

D. The proposed solution does not produce the required result.

26. To print from a DOS application to a network printer under Windows NT, what two things must be done?

    A. The LPT device must be redirected to the network printer share using the NET USE command.

    B. The LPT device must be redirected to the network print queue using the CAPTURE command.

    C. The correct printer driver must be selected in Windows NT, and it must be set as the default printer.

    D. The correct printer driver and LPT port must be selected in the DOS application.

Answers to Review Questions

1. A printer configured to control two or more print devices is referred to as a *printer pool*. For more information, see the section "Setting Up a Printer Pool."

2. The two non-fault-tolerant methods for joining multiple areas of free space into a single logical drive are volume sets and stripe sets. For more information, see the section "Partitioning."

3. In Windows NT Server, RAID 1 is implemented using mirror sets, and RAID 5 is implemented using stripe sets with parity. For more information, see the section "Fault Tolerance."

4. The Control Panel application that would be used to install and configure Panasonic CD-ROM devices is SCSI Adapters. For more information, see the section "Devices."

5. In print configuration, the software component is referred to as a *printer*, and the hardware component is referred to as a *print device*. For more information, see the section "Windows NT Printing Architecture."

6. The two programs that are used to modify the Registry in NT are REGEDT32.EXE and REGEDIT.EXE. For more information, see the section "Using the Registry Editors."

7. In order to delete any and all documents from an NT print queue, you need at least Manage Documents permission on the printer. For more information, see the section "Configuring Printers."

8. The five subtrees of the NT Registry are: HKEY_LOCAL_MACHINE, HKEY_USERS, HKEY_CURRENT_USER, HKEY_CLASSES_ROOT, and HKEY_CURRENT_CONFIG. For more information, see the section "Navigating the Registry."

9. The four actions you can configure the system to take in the event of a system crash (Stop error) are: Write an event to the system log, send an administrative alert, write debugging information to, and automatically reboot. For more information, see the section "Startup/Shutdown."

10. The Devices applet is used to configure a device for use in a specific hardware profile. For more information, see the section "Devices."

Answers to Exam Questions

1. **C.** Drive lettering begins with the first primary partition on each physical disk, then moves back

to the first disk and letters each logical drive, and then moves to each additional disk and letters each of their logical drives. Finally, the additional primary drives on each physical disk are lettered. This would mean that the first primary on Drive 1 is C:, the primary on Drive 2 is D:, the logicals on Drive 1 are E: and F:, the logicals on Drive 2 are G: and H:, and the second primary on Drive 1 is I:. For more information, see the section "Partitioning."

2. **A.** The Registry contains the complete configuration for most aspects of a Windows NT server and domain (in the case of a domain controller). It replaces the .INI files for most programs, and it contains configuration for a myriad of other things. For more information, see the section "How Windows NT Uses the Registry."

3. **A, C.** Both REGEDIT and REGEDT32 are NT utilities for editing the Registry. For more information, see the section "Using the Registry Editors."

4. **D.** The five Registry subtrees are HKEY_LOCAL_MACHINE, HKEY_USERS, HKEY_CURRENT_USER, HKEY_CLASSES_ROOT, and HKEY_CURRENT_CONFIG. For more information, see the section "Navigating the Registry."

5. **C.** The subtree that contains information about the current configuration of the computer is HKEY_LOCAL_MACHINE. For more information, see the section "Navigating the Registry."

6. **B.** The Control Panel icons allow controlled access to the Registry. These icons have been created to allow access to the Registry only in ways that are predictable. For more information, see the section "How Users Use the Registry."

7. **D.** Expecting that you want to assign a new device to a COM port through the COM port utility in the Control Panel, the utility shows you only those COM ports that are not being used. For more information, see the section "Ports."

8. **C.** If the UPS is configured properly from the UPS application in the Control Panel, it should warn you when a power failure has occurred and then it should shut down the system gracefully when power is running low. For more information, see the section "Devices."

9. **B.** After creating a new partition, you must commit the changes in order to format that partition. This can be done through the Format menu or by exiting out of Disk Administrator. For more information, see the section "Committing Changes."

10. **C.** Only volumes that are formatted NTFS can be extended. If the partition is formatted FAT, you can use the CONVERT.EXE program to convert it to NTFS, and then you can extend the volume. For more information, see the section "Partitioning."

11. **B.** Both a volume set and a stripe set will provide an equal amount of usable space in this case, so this solution does produce the required result. A stripe set does not provide fault tolerance nor is it expandable without reformatting. However, a stripe set can be formatted NTFS, so this solution also produces one of the optional desired results. A stripe set with parity would have provided fault tolerance, but because of the overhead involved in providing fault tolerance, it would not have given the largest usable data area. For more information, see the section "Partitioning."

APPLY YOUR LEARNING

12. **D.** Because a volume set is not fault tolerant, it does not produce the required result (despite the fact that it does produce both of the optional desired results). For more information, see the section "Partitioning."

13. **C.** As the name implies, a mirror set creates an exact duplicate of a partition onto free space of the same size. For more information, see the section "Fault Tolerant Partitions."

14. **A, C.** Although volume sets and disk striping provide functionality over and above regular partitions, they are not fault tolerant, and because they are spread out over many physical disks, they actually have a higher chance of being destroyed by a disk failure. For more information, see the section "Partitioning."

15. **B.** In NT, a *printer* is a software device that controls printing, and the *print device* is the hardware component. For more information, see the section "Windows NT Printing Architecture."

16. **A.** A printer driver for another operating system or another NT hardware platform will not work, even if the driver is for the same print device. For more information, see the section "Windows NT Printing Architecture."

17. **D.** Stopping the Spooler service clears the print buffer, thus allowing you to remove jobs that are not printing properly. For more information, see the section "Windows NT Printing Architecture."

18. **C.** Every time an NT machine prints to a print server, it downloads the latest version of the printer driver. If a new driver exists, that driver will be loaded locally. For more information, see the section "Windows NT Printing Architecture."

19. **A, C.** Both answers amount to the same thing, they just get to the printer configuration in different ways. For more information, see the section "Configuring Printers."

20. **B.** You can configure the properties of various paper sizes and types to include the tray in which they are found. A new type could be created for specialty paper, like letterhead, which is found in a different tray from the regular white paper. For more information, see the section "Configuring Printers."

21. **B.** The configuration allows for large jobs to be printed at night and small jobs to be printed anytime. It also allows for managers' jobs to be printed before everyone else's. However, because the Everyone group was given Print permission, it does not restrict the Accounting group from printing to the printer. For more information, see the section "Configuring Printers."

22. **A.** As with the previous scenario, the proposed solution allows for printing at different times and with different priorities. However, in this case because the Sales group is given access but Accounting is not mentioned, the Accountants will not be able to access the printer. For more information, see the section "Configuring Printers."

23. **D.** You can install more than one printer that is configured to print to the same print device. These printers can then be configured with different print priorities. The printer with the highest printing priority will always take precedence over waiting jobs that come from the lower priority printer. For more information, see the section "Configuring Printers."

APPLY YOUR LEARNING

24. **C.** Holding mismatched documents is one way to prevent documents formatted for one printer from printing on another print device. For more information, see the section "Configuring Printers."

25. **A, B, C.** A printing pool can be successfully implemented only if the printers all use the same printer driver, are controlled by the same print server, and are in close proximity to one another. The first two are criteria of the operating system;

the last is a criterion of your users. For more information, see the section "Setting Up a Printer Pool."

26. **A, D.** In order to print to a network printer from DOS, the operating system must be able to access the printer through a network share, and you must inform your DOS applications of the printer port and printer type. For more information, see the section "Printing from MS-DOS Applications."

Suggested Readings and Resources

The following are some recommended readings in the area of configuring peripherals:

1. Microsoft Official Curriculum course 803: *Administering Windows NT*
   - Chapter 7: Setting Up a Network Printer
   - Chapter 8: Administering Network Printers

2. Microsoft Official Curriculum course 922: *Supporting Microsoft Windows NT 4.0 Core Technologies*
   - Module 6: Managing Partitions
   - Module 7: Managing Fault Tolerance

3. *Windows NT Server Networking Guide* (Microsoft Press; also available in the NT Server Resource Kit)
   - Chapter 1: Windows NT 4 - Networking Architecture
   - Chapter 6: TCP/IP Implementation Details
   - Chapter 13: Using NetBEUI with Windows NT

4. Microsoft TechNet CD-ROM
   - *Workstation Resource Guide*
   - Chapter 7: Printing
   - Chapter 17: Disk and File System Basics
   - Chapter 18: Choosing a File System
   - Chapter 22: Disk, File System, and Backup Utilities
   - Chapter 23: Overview of the Windows NT Registry
   - Chapter 24: Registry Editors and Registry Administration
   - Chapter 25: Configuration Management and the Registry

5. Web sites
   - www.microsoft.com/ntserver
   - www.microsoft.com/train_cert
   - www.prometric.com/testingcandidates/ assessment/chosetest.html (take online assessment tests)

Microsoft provides the following objectives for "Managing Resources":

Manage user and group accounts. Considerations include managing Windows NT groups, managing Windows NT user rights, managing Windows NT account policies, and auditing changes to the user account database.

▶ This objective is necessary because someone certified in the use of Windows NT Server technology must understand the account types available and how to create and manage them, as well as the implications of the various management decisions.

Create and manage policies and profiles for various situations. Policies and profiles include local user profiles, roaming user profiles, and system policies.

▶ This objective is necessary because someone certified in the use of Windows NT Server technology must understand the configuration of the user's environment. This includes a complete understanding of the various profile types, as well as system policies.

Administer remote servers from various types of client computers. Client computer types include Windows 95 and Windows NT Workstation.

▶ This objective is necessary because someone certified in the use of Windows NT Server technology must understand how to configure a client machine to administer a server by using the administrative tools that are available on the NT Server CD-ROM.

CHAPTER 5

Managing Resources Part 1: Managing Users and User Environments

The Windows NT Server exam does not put much emphasis on the concepts discussed in this chapter; rather, most of the focus regarding managing resources deals with the topic of the next chapter: disk resources. This does not mean that you do not need to look closely at this chapter. It simply means that you should look at it more for its overall concepts and typical scenarios than for its in-depth detailed information.

▶ You need to be familiar with the User Manager for Domains because all the points in the "Managing User and Group Accounts" objective deal with that tool. You should be able to create a user and configure that user, and you should be familiar with the various configuration options for a user. In addition, make sure you know how to create both local and global groups and that you understand how users, global groups, and local groups interact. You will also need to know about the accounts and groups that are created by NT. Through experimentation and research, you can become familiar with the tasks these accounts and groups are capable of. Finally, you must know how account policies are set and what you can do with them because these ideas are often included in test material.

▶ Next, be sure you understand all the profile options and how they are implemented. Test them by creating some profiles and then logging in to your server to see what the results are. In addition, be sure you know what a system policy does and how to create and configure system policies. Both of these points, policies and profiles, are best learned by doing, not by reading. When you are familiar with the concepts in this book, spend some time experimenting with them.

▶ Finally, understand what remote administration looks like. If you have another system available, install NT Workstation and/or Windows 95 on it and see what the tools look like from that perspective. You should understand how the tools are made available and what exactly you get on each operating system. You can get away with just memorizing the concepts if you do not have another computer to experiment with, but seeing the concepts in action is important.

This chapter will help you prepare for the user management portion of the "Managing Resources" section of Microsoft's Exam 70-67. This will include information on NT accounts, policies and profiles, and administration of NT servers from client computers.

INTRODUCTION

This chapter examines some important topics related to managing resources on a Windows NT network. Managing resources is, of course, a very broad topic, but Microsoft has narrowed it somewhat in its objectives for the Windows NT Server exam. This chapter considers user and group accounts and the important tool User Manager for Domains, which you will use to manage accounts on an NT domain. This chapter also discusses user profiles, hardware profiles, and system policies—three important features that help administrators define the user environment. You will learn about the remote administration tools available through Windows NT Server for administering NT resources from client machines.

MANAGING USER AND GROUP ACCOUNTS

Manage user and group accounts. Considerations include managing Windows NT groups, managing Windows NT user rights, managing Windows NT account policies, and auditing changes to the user account database.

Windows NT users get their rights and permissions in either of two ways: They are explicitly assigned a right or permission through their individual accounts, or they are assigned them by virtue of membership in a group that has been given a right or permission.

An administrator creates an account (or maybe more than one) for each person who will use the system. When you boot Windows NT, your first interaction with the operating system is with the WinLogon process (see Chapter 1, "Planning"). Figure 5.1 illustrates the basic WinLogon process.

When a user logs on locally to a Windows NT machine, the following process is initiated:

1. The WinLogon process presents the Logon dialog box, and then passes the information that's entered in it to the Local Security Authority.

2. The Local Security Authority passes the information to the local Security Accounts Manager.

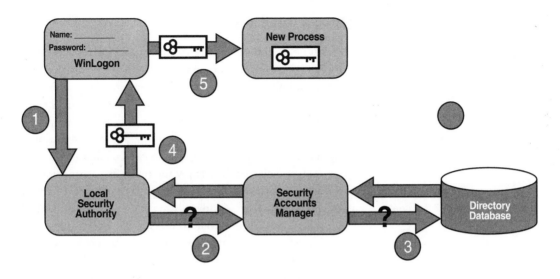

3. The Security Accounts Manager queries the directory database to verify the validity of the username and password entered by the user.

4. When the Security Accounts Manager receives verification, it passes the information back to the Local Security Authority, which generates an access token based on the information for that account that was obtained from the directory and passes the token back to the WinLogon process.

5. The WinLogon then spawns the first process for the user (usually Explorer), which has the access token attached to it.

The access token that's generated is attached to all subsequent processes generated by the user. It indicates the system rights and access permissions to system resources.

The intermediate step in which WinLogon passes its request through the Local Security Authority to the Security Accounts Manager is necessary because in a domain logon, a domain controller must validate the logon. In this case, the Local Security Authority, recognizing that validation is not done locally, passes the logon information to another process called the NetLogon process. This process creates a secure channel to the NetLogon process for the domain controller and passes the user account name and password to the domain controller. It is then that the Security Accounts Manager on the domain controller queries the domain directory database and validates the user's credentials.

FIGURE 5.1
Locally logging on to a Windows NT computer.

Users and Groups

Windows NT administrators can create two types of accounts: accounts for users and accounts for groups. *User accounts* belong to one person only; rights and permissions assigned to a user account affect only the person who uses that account to log on. A *group account* is an account that allows for the collection of users who hold common rights and permissions by virtue of their association with the group. The number of people who can belong to a group is unlimited, and all members enjoy the rights and permissions (or rue the lack thereof) assigned to the group. In practice, a group is a vehicle for assigning rights and permissions to an individual user. If you determine that a certain group of users in your environment requires a specific set of rights and permissions, you can create a group that has those rights and permissions and add users to the new group. It is important to note that there is no order of precedence among user and group accounts. No one group takes priority over any other group, and group accounts do not take priority over user accounts (or vice versa).

For management purposes, it is easier to use group accounts when assigning rights and permissions. First, it's cleaner: Users can be members of as many groups as necessary, and group names can be more descriptive than user names. When looking at the permissions list for a file, for example, you probably would understand why Vice Presidents have access to sensitive financial information before you would understand why JackS, JanetP, and BillG are allowed in. Second, it's simpler: If you need to give a user the right to back up files and directories, you can add that user to a built-in group, called Backup Operators, which was designed specifically for that purpose.

Windows NT has two types of groups: local groups and global groups.

On a Windows NT standalone or member server of a domain, a *local group* is an entity that exists for assigning rights and permissions to resources on the local machine. (Remember that such resources consist of drive space and printers on that specific computer.) That local group exists only on that computer.

This changes slightly at the domain level. A local group created on a domain controller appears on all domain controllers within that domain. This is because—like all accounts—local groups are stored in the accounts directory database, and in a domain situation, the same database is present on all the domain controllers. A local group created on one backup domain controller (BDC) also appears on the primary domain controller (PDC) and all other BDCs within that domain. You then can assign this local group rights and permissions.

A *global group* is a collection of user accounts within the domain. Global groups have *no* power by themselves. Instead, global groups must be assigned to local groups to gain any access to the local resources. You use a global group as a container for users that you can then add to local groups.

When a Windows NT server becomes part of a domain, the built-in domain global groups (described later in this chapter) join the corresponding local groups in the workstation's local security database. The global group Domain Admins, for example, becomes a member of the local group Administrators. Each user account in the domain database is a member of an appropriate global group. The Administrator account, for example, is a member of the Domain Admins global group. By nesting global groups in the local groups of individual machines, Windows NT provides users with seamless access to resources across the domain.

In terms of the actual implementation of user accounts, local groups, and global groups, Microsoft recommends the following pattern (see Figure 5.2):

1. Create user accounts.

2. Create global groups for the domain and populate the groups with user accounts.

> **NOTE**
>
> **Global Groups Can't Contain Other Groups** Global groups can contain only users; they cannot contain other groups. Local groups can contain both users and global groups, but they cannot contain other local groups.

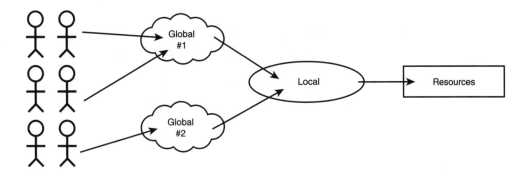

FIGURE 5.2
Users are placed into global groups, which are placed into local groups, which are assigned permissions to resources.

3. Create local groups and assign them rights and permissions to resources and programs in the domain.

4. Place global groups into the local groups you have created, thereby giving the users who are members of the global groups access to the system and its resources.

Built-In Groups on Domain Controllers

Windows NT domain controllers oversee eight built-in local groups and three built-in global groups. These groups create a wide range of access levels for network resources.

The Windows NT domain local groups include the following:

- ◆ Administrators
- ◆ Users
- ◆ Guests
- ◆ Backup Operators
- ◆ Replicator
- ◆ Print Operators
- ◆ Server Operators
- ◆ Account Operators

Administrators

The local group Administrators is the most powerful group in Windows NT. Because Administrators has complete control over the entire Windows NT environment, you should use caution when adding users to this group. If you will be the administrator for a Windows NT machine, consider creating an ordinary user account as well for safety reasons. If an administrator walks away from a computer while she is still logged on, anyone can walk up to that computer and make unauthorized changes. Even if you are extremely conscientious, mistakes happen. An application that malfunctions and deletes files can wreak more havoc if it runs under an administrative account than if it runs under a user account. Use administrator-level accounts only when necessary.

In the following situations, it is necessary to use administrator-level accounts:

- ◆ To create other administrator-level accounts
- ◆ To modify or delete users, regardless of who created them

◆ To manage the membership of built-in groups

◆ To unlock workstations, regardless of who locked them

◆ To format a hard disk

◆ To upgrade the operating system

◆ To back up or restore files and directories

◆ To change the security policies

◆ To connect to administrative shares

Users

By default, new accounts become members of the Users group automatically (in a domain, all users become members of the Domain Users global group, which is added to the local Users group). The Users group provides users with everything they need to run applications safely and to manage their own local environments (local to the user, that is, not to the computer). Users can perform the following tasks:

◆ Run applications

◆ Manage their own files and directories (but not share them)

◆ Use printers (but not manage them)

◆ Connect to other computers' directories and printers

◆ Save their settings in personal profiles

Because users cannot affect files to which they have not been granted access, and they cannot format hard disks, delete accounts, and so on, it is safest to use the Users account unless you need to perform a task that only an administrator or power user has the right to perform.

Guests

Windows NT also provides a relatively powerless group called Guests. Because Windows NT requires accounts for everyone who accesses the system, you can use the Guest account (described later in this chapter) and the Guests group to provide limited access to users who don't possess an account on your computer. Because the default Guest account does not require a password, it can pose a security risk. The actual extent of the access provided to the Guests group depends on how you implement it. If you are concerned about security, leave the Guest account disabled, which it is by default.

Backup Operators

Backup Operators have a singular purpose: to back up files and directories and to restore them later. Although any user can back up and restore files to which he has been granted permissions, backup operators can override the security on resources (but only when using the NTBackup program).

Replicator

The Replicator group is a special group used by the Directory Replication Service. See Chapter 3, "Installation and Configuration Part 2: Configuration of NT Server Network Components," for more information on this group.

Print Operators

Members of the Print Operators group wield the power to create, manage, and delete print shares on domain controllers.

Server Operators

The members of the Server Operators group have the power to administer primary and backup domain controllers. They can log on to and shut down servers, lock and unlock servers, change the system time, back up and restore files, and manage network shares.

Account Operators

The members of the Account Operators group have the ability to create, delete, and modify users. They can also create, delete, or modify the membership of global and local groups with the exceptions of the Server Operators group and the Administrators group.

Built-In Global Groups

Windows NT domain controllers also oversee the following three global groups:

◆ *Domain Admins.* This is a global group of administrator accounts. The Domain Admins group is a member of the Administrators local group for the domain, and it is, by default, a member of the local group for every computer in the domain running Windows NT Server or NT Workstation. A domain administrator, therefore, can perform administrative functions on local computers.

◆ *Domain Users.* This is a global group of user-level accounts. During setup, the domain's Administrator account is part of the Domain Users global group. All new domain accounts are automatically added to the Domain Users group.

◆ *Domain Guests.* This is a global group for users with guest-level accounts. The domain's Guest account is automatically a member of the Domain Guests group.

Built-In Groups on Member Servers

Windows NT Server member servers (servers that are not domain controllers) have the following built-in local groups:

◆ Administrators

◆ Backup Operators

◆ Power Users

◆ Guests

◆ Replicator

◆ Users

The descriptions for these groups are the same as the descriptions for their domain controller counterparts, except in the case of the Power User group, which is not a built-in group on Windows NT domain controllers. Power users live somewhere between the kingdom of administrators and the masses of users. Power users have considerably more power than ordinary users, but nowhere near the amount of control an administrator has.

A principle similar to that for administrator-level rights applies here: Do not use or give out Power user accounts unless doing so is necessary for performing a task. Power user accounts are ideal for the following types of tasks:

◆ Sharing (and revoking) directories on the network

◆ Creating, managing, and sharing printers

◆ Creating accounts (but not administrator-level accounts)

◆ Modifying and deleting accounts (but only those accounts that the power user has created)

◆ Setting the date and time on the computer

◆ Creating common program groups (groups accessible by any user logging in to a machine locally)

Power users cannot touch any of the security policies on a Windows NT system, and their powers are limited in scope. It is best, therefore, to use a Power User account instead of an Administrator account if you can accomplish what you need to as a power user.

Windows NT member servers and workstations don't control any global groups because global groups can be created and administered only on domain controllers. Nevertheless, global groups play an important part in assigning local rights and permissions to server and workstations resources. The following section describes how global groups interact with local accounts.

Member Server Accounts

Windows NT Server machines acting as member servers maintain local account databases and manage a set of local accounts and groups independent of any domain affiliations. You can understand the need for these local accounts when you consider the emphasis on security in Windows NT. A user must provide credentials in order to access a Windows NT system, even if that system is not and has never been attached to a domain. The local account information controls the account's access to the machine's resources.

Domain users can access resources on server and workstation machines logged in to the domain because (by default) each domain user is a member of the global group Domain Users, and the global group Domain Users is a member of the machine's local group Users. In the same way, domain administrators are part of the global group Domain Admins, which is part of the machine's local Administrators group.

System Groups

Windows NT maintains the following four system groups, which are not user-modifiable:

◆ Everyone

◆ Creator Owner

◆ Network

◆ Interactive

Everyone

The Everyone group includes anyone who accesses your network. These could be people in your domain, people in a workgroup on your LAN, or even people who are clients of other network operating systems (such as NetWare users). The Everyone group is given full control of all new network shares by default.

Creator Owner

The Creator Owner group is used to track who has ownership of a particular resource. Ownership falls to either the creator or the last person to take ownership of a resource. Unlike most of the other groups, this group exists for each individual resource, and its membership is usually different for each resource.

Network

The Network group contains a list of all the people who are currently accessing a shared resource on a local computer over the network.

Interactive

This group consists of the person who is currently logged in to an NT machine locally. This is the person who actually sat down at the machine and logged on to it.

Built-In User Accounts

Groups are the center of power in Windows NT, but groups need members in order to have any effect at all. At least two accounts are created when you install Windows NT Workstation. Those two user accounts and their group memberships are discussed next.

Administrator

The Administrator account, the first account created during an installation, is a member of the Administrators group. This is an important concept because the Administrator account by itself is powerless; you could remove it from the Administrators group and place it in the Guests group, and you would have a really wimpy

NOTE

Hard-Coded Capabilities So far, only the hard-coded characteristics of the Windows NT built-in groups have been discussed; in other words, there are some things you can change and some things you can't. For example, all the things you just learned about groups are things that cannot be changed; users cannot share directories, and power users cannot be prevented from sharing directories (to which they have access, of course). You cannot modify these characteristics (also called *hard-coded capabilities*), but you can change user rights.

An administrator can grant or revoke a user right at any time. Only administrators have the hard-coded capability to manage this policy. At this point, then, it is important to clearly distinguish between user rights and resource permissions. *User rights* define what a user can and cannot do on a system. *Resource permissions* establish the scope where these rights can be used. In other words, user rights control what you can do, and resource permissions control where you can do those things.

Administrator account. Power in Windows NT comes not from the user accounts, but from the group membership.

The Administrator account is permanent. You cannot disable or delete it, although it might not be a bad idea to rename it.

Guest

The Guest account is another permanent account. It is a member of the Guests group, but its affiliation can be changed. Like the Administrator account, the Guest account itself has no inherent power or lack thereof; it is the group membership for the account that establishes its scope.

Unlike the Administrator account, however, you can disable the Guest account, and it is disabled by default in a Windows NT environment. You might want to disable the account if you are in a secure environment. Otherwise, users who don't have an account on your system can log on as guests. At the very least, you should consider adding a password to the Guest account.

User Manager for Domains

Windows NT Server includes a tool called User Manager for Domains that you can use to administer user and group accounts. User Manager for Domains is similar to the User Manager tool available with Windows NT Workstation. However, User Manager is primarily used to oversee local workstation accounts, whereas User Manager for Domains includes additional features that enable it to manage accounts at the domain level and even to interact with other domains.

To access User Manager for Domains, open the Start menu, choose Programs, choose Administrative Tools (Common), and then select User Manager for Domains. The User Manager for Domains main screen appears (see Figure 5.3).

User Manager for Domains enables you to administer any domain over which you have administrative rights. The Select Domain option in the User menu (see Figure 5.4) enables you to choose a different domain. You can choose to administer any domain to which you have administrative rights.

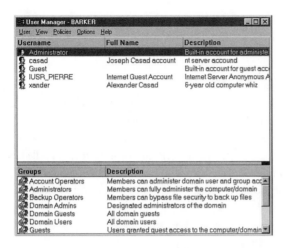

FIGURE 5.3
User Manager for Domains allows you to add new accounts, configure group memberships, set user rights, and perform general account maintenance tasks.

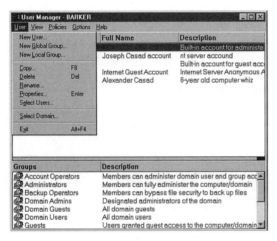

FIGURE 5.4
You are not restricted to administering accounts from the domain that you are in. You can also select other domains to administer as long as you have the correct rights to do so.

Some of the tasks you can perform with User Manager for Domains include the following:

◆ Creating new user and group accounts

◆ Viewing and configuring the properties of user and group accounts

◆ Adding new members to groups and removing members from groups

◆ Viewing and configuring account policy restrictions

◆ Adding user rights to users and groups

◆ Auditing account-related events

◆ Establishing, viewing, and configuring trust relationships

You will find most commands related to administration and configuration on the User and Options menus.

Creating a User

Before a new user can log on to your computer or in to your domain, you must create the user account, as described in Step by Step 5.1. Only two pieces of information are required to create an account: a username and a password. The username is a short "handle" by which the system identifies the user. The password enables the user to prove that the user account actually belongs to the person attempting to use it.

STEP BY STEP

5.1 Creating a New User

1. From the User menu, choose New User. The New User dialog box appears (see Figure 5.5).

2. Enter a username.

3. Enter and confirm a user password.

4. Click the Add button.

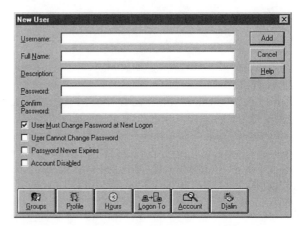

FIGURE 5.5
In the New User dialog box, you can create and modify user account information.

The name in the Username field must be unique to the accounts directory database in which it is being created. That means that no other user or group in this particular domain or on a local machine (depending on which accounts directory database you are interacting with) can have the same name. The username can be as long as twenty characters and is not case-sensitive.

The password entered in the Password field is case-sensitive; in fact, the most common logon-related problem reported by Windows NT users is solved just by pressing the Caps Lock key. The Password field can be left blank (although that's not recommended for obvious reasons), or it can be as long as fourteen characters. When you enter a password, it appears onscreen as a series of asterisks, so you don't need to worry about someone looking over your shoulder. In addition, when you return to the user properties after an account has been created, the password field always shows 14 asterisks, whether the password has 14 characters or none. Because the password does not appear as you type it, you must confirm the password just to make certain that you did not mistype any characters behind those asterisks.

The other fields in this dialog box are optional but useful. The Full Name is a free text field that can be used for the user's full name, including spaces and initials. Having both a username and a full name enables a user to log on quickly (using the username), but still be listed and available by her full name.

The Description field is also free text. You might use it to specify the department to which a user belongs, or maybe a location or project team.

Enabling the User Must Change Password at Next Logon check box option is useful when you're creating an account. Because a new account has a preset password specified by the administrator, this option forces the user to change the password immediately the next time he logs on after you set this option. When the user attempts to log on, he sees the message You are required to change your password at first logon. After the user dismisses the message, a Change Password dialog box appears.

Enabling the User Cannot Change Password check box prevents users from making any changes to their passwords at any time. You might want to use this for the Guest account and any other account that several people might share.

Forcing a user to change his or her password and telling the system that the account password cannot be changed are mutually exclusive rules. Therefore, if you check both of these boxes, NT will issue an error and prevent the user account from being created until one or the other is cleared.

Enabling the Password Never Expires check box overrides any blanket password expiration date defined in the Account policy. Again, the Guest account is a likely candidate for this option.

Enabling the Account Disabled check box turns off the account but does not remove it from the database. In general, you should disable user accounts instead of removing them. If a person leaves the organization and then later returns, you can reactivate his account. If the user never returns, you can rename the account and reactivate it for the new user who replaces the former user. All rights and permissions for the original user are then transferred to the new user. Other serious implications regarding deleting and disabling accounts are covered later in this chapter; see the section "Deleting Versus Disabling" for more information.

You can click any of the six buttons at the bottom of the New User dialog box to opens its corresponding dialog box described here:

◆ *Groups*. Enables you to add and remove group memberships for the account. The easiest way to grant rights to a user account is to add that account to a group that possesses those rights.

◆ *Profile*. Enables you to add a user profile path, a logon script name, and a home directory path to the user's environment profile. You'll learn more about the Profile button in the next section.

◆ *Hours*. Enables you to define specific times when the users can access the account. (The default is always.)

◆ *Logon To*. Enables you to specify up to eight workstations from which the user can log on. (The default is all workstations.)

◆ *Account*. Enables you to provide an expiration date for the account. (The default is never.) You also can designate the account as global (for regular users in this domain) or domain local.

◆ *Dialin*. Enables you to specify whether the user can access the account via a dial-up connection. You also can configure the callback properties from here.

WARNING

Don't Confuse Domain Local Accounts with Local Groups or Local Computer Accounts Don't confuse a domain local account with a local group membership or a local account on a workstation. A domain local account is designed to give access to users from other domains with which a formal relationship between the domains (trust) has not been established. If an account called EmmaM with a password of "Password" exists in another domain, you can allow that user to access resources in your domain by creating a domain local account called EmmaM with a password of "Password." This would allow EmmaM to access resources to which your EmmaM account has been given permission, even though EmmaM is from another domain and should not technically be given access to your resources.

User Environment Profiles

The Profile button invokes the User Environment Profile dialog box, which consists of two frames: User Profiles and Home Directory (see Figure 5.6).

The User Profiles section of this dialog box enables you to specify the user profile path and the logon script name. The user profile path is needed when a roaming or mandatory profile for the user will reside on another computer. If the user will log on to both Windows NT 3.x and Windows NT 4 computers, include the user profile filename in the user profile path. If the user will use only a computer running Windows NT 4, the user profile path should point to the user profile directory and should not include the filename. If the directory does not exist, Windows NT creates it when the roaming profile is created (see the discussion of roaming profiles later in this chapter), but note that the local machine must have access to the roaming profile directory by way of a network share.

In the Logon Script Name text box, you can specify a logon script for the user. *Logon scripts* are .CMD or .BAT files that contain a series of valid Windows NT commands. A logon script might re-establish a series of network drive connections or display a welcome message. Notice that the dialog box asks only for the name, not the full path. Windows NT already has a directory for logon scripts, but it is buried pretty deep:

Typically, logon scripts are not used on Windows NT machines. User profiles can accomplish most things that logon scripts can.

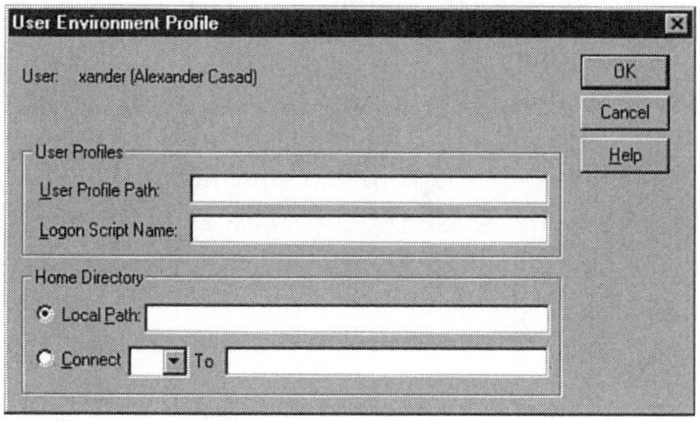

FIGURE 5.6
The User Environment Profile dialog box.

The Home Directory section of the User Environment Profile dialog box is used when a user opens or saves a file in an application or when a user opens a command prompt window. The default home directory is \USERS\DEFAULT; if a workstation will support more than one user, consider establishing a separate home directory for each user. Note that users are not restricted to or from these home directories (unless you establish that security separately); this is just where they start by default when working with documents.

You do not have to create the home directory; User Manager will do it for you as long as you ask it to create only a single directory at a time. You might have User Manager create a home directory called c:\ken, for example, but it could not create c:\ken\home if the \ken directory did not already exist. That is just a limitation of User Manager.

Click on the Local Path radio button to specify a local path for the home directory. To specify a home directory on the network, click on the Connect radio button, select a drive letter from the drop-down list, and enter the network path in the To text box.

When you use User Manager for Domains to create a user's home directory on an NTFS partition, the default permissions for that directory grant that user Full Control and restrict access to all other users.

> **NOTE**
>
> **Home Directory Creation** If you would like the home directory name to be the same as the user's username, you can use a special environment variable in this dialog box: %USERNAME%. The actual username replaces %USERNAME% after the account is created. This is not really any faster than just typing in the actual username, but it can save time when you're copying accounts (described later in this chapter).

Creating a Group

You can create new global and local groups by way of the New Global Group and New Local Group options on the User menu in User Manager for Domains. Figure 5.7 shows the New Global Group dialog box. Note that, by default, the Administrator account is automatically a member of the new group. Only user accounts can be members of a global group. To add a member to the new global group, select a user in the Not Members list and click on the Add button to add the user to the Members list. To remove a user account from the group, select the account in the Members list and click the Remove button.

Figure 5.8 shows the New Local Group dialog box. To add additional members to the new local group, click on the Add button. Both individual users and global groups can join a local group.

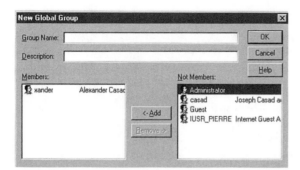

FIGURE 5.7
The New Global Group dialog box.

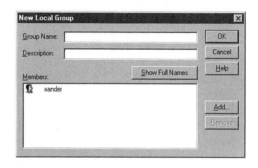

If you select one or more users in the User Manager for Domains main screen, those users automatically appear in the membership list for the new local group. This shortcut can save you a step, but you also need to be careful to make sure no users are selected in the main screen that you don't want to be part of the new group.

FIGURE 5.8
The New Local Group dialog box.

You cannot directly add rights to a group. Instead, you have to add the group to the list of groups that have a particular right. To add groups to a right, you select the User Rights option from the Policies menu (described later in this chapter).

User and Group Properties

Selecting the Properties command from the User menu of the User Manager screen opens a Properties dialog box for the selected object. The User Properties dialog box resembles the New User dialog box (refer to Figure 5.5) except that all the information is already filled in. Use the User Properties dialog box to edit user properties after you create an account.

The group Properties dialog boxes for global and local groups also resemble their respective creation dialog boxes (see the preceding section).

Administering Account Policy

Figure 5.9 shows the Policies menu in User Manager for Domains.

Choose the Account option to open the Account Policy dialog box (see Figure 5.10).

The Account Policy dialog box contains a lot of information, but all the options revolve around a single concept: passwords.

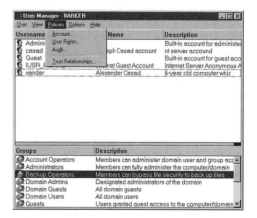

FIGURE 5.9
The User Manager for Domains Policies menu.

FIGURE 5.10
The Account Policy dialog box.

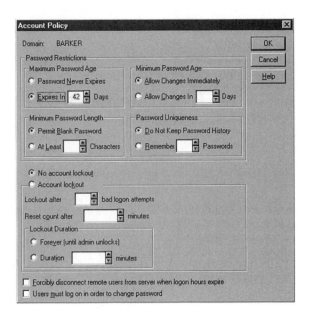

Maximum Password Age

In a secure environment, the longer a password is in use, the greater the chance that an unauthorized user will discover it and break in repeatedly. Setting a maximum password age forces users to choose a new password periodically. You have a choice here. If you don't care about password ages, leave the setting at its default of Password Never Expires; if you do want a maximum password age, choose the Expires In radio button and enter the number of days to use as the limit. (The default is 42, but the value can range from 1–999.)

When a maximum password age is in effect, users get a warning 14 days before the password is set to expire. When the user receives the first warning message, she can either change the password or choose to wait. If she waits, the password expiration message appears each time the user logs on, until the maximum password age is reached. At that point, the user cannot access the system until the password is changed. See the section "User Must Log On in Order to Change Password" (later in this chapter) for more information.

Minimum Password Age

Users can get very attached to their passwords, and some resent having to change them. A classic user trick is to change the password when forced to and then immediately change it back, thereby retaining the old password. Setting a minimum password age circumvents this problem.

The default setting, Allow Changes Immediately, enables users to perform the favorite-password sleight-of-hand just mentioned. However, the Allow Changes In setting forces users to wait anywhere from 1–999 days (at the administrator's discretion) before making changes.

Minimum Password Length

Users also get tired of typing in long passwords. Given the opportunity, many users will use short 3- or 4-character (or fewer) passwords. Setting a minimum password length forces users to choose a longer password. Although you can require up to 14 characters, using 6 to 8 usually suffices.

Password Uniqueness

Even if you force users to set a longer password and wait a week or two before changing it, some tenacious users still swap between two passwords continuously. The Password Uniqueness setting tells Windows NT to remember each password (up to 24) that a user sets. As long as a password is in a user's password history cache, the user cannot reuse it. A Remember setting of 24 combined with a Minimum Password Age of seven days forces users to wait almost six months before reusing a password.

Even all these password options combined won't prevent a user from changing his or her password from "password" to "passworda," "passwordb," "passwordc," and so on. NT can do only so much, though; the rest is up to you as an administrator.

Account Lockout

The bottom half of the Account Policy dialog box deals with unauthorized logon attempts and allows you to set account lockout policies (see Step by Step 5.2).

Windows NT will lock out an account after a certain number of bad logon attempts (in which the user provides the incorrect password/username combination) within a certain period of time. You can enable this feature by choosing the Account Lockout radio button. If you do, you must supply a couple of parameters: How many bad attempts should trigger the lockout, how long should the system wait following a bad logon attempt before resetting the counter, and how long should the account stay locked out? If you choose Forever for the last option, the administrator must manually unlock the account in User Manager; otherwise, you can elect to set a duration after which the account will be unlocked.

STEP BY STEP

5.2 Setting Account Lockout Policy

1. In User Manager, choose Policies, Account.

2. Choose the Account Lockout radio button.

3. In the Lockout After Bad Logon Attempts field, enter the number of bad logons required to trigger the lockout.

4. In the Reset Count After field, enter the timeout period for resetting the bad logon count.

5. Choose a lockout duration: Forever (Until Admin Unlocks) or a specific Duration (in minutes).

If a user violates the lockout rules, you are forced to unlock his or her account manually (see Step by Step 5.3). This must be done from User Manager for Domains.

STEP BY STEP

5.3 Unlocking a User Account

1. Select the username in User Manager for Domains.

2. Choose User, Properties.

3. Clear the Account Locked Out check box.

NOTE

You Can't Manually Lock an Account
No one can lock an account through the User Manager. The only way an account can become locked is by violation of the login rules configured here.

By default, the Account Lockout feature is turned off. Windows NT has tight security as it is, and the potential is there for this feature to be misused. It is entirely possible, for example, that a user could deliberately lock out a coworker's or supervisor's account by purposefully entering bad passwords with that person's username. For this reason, the built-in Administrator account can never be locked out. Many administrators don't care for this "out." The Administrator account is arguably the one you need to protect the most. Yet, if the Administrator account were to become locked out, it is possible that no one else could get on the system to unlock it. This is another reason you should rename the Administrator account after installation.

Someone trying to break into the system will have to discover both the username and password.

If a user attempts to log on with a locked account, the following message appears:

```
Unable to log you on because your account has been locked
out, please contact your administrator.
```

Forcibly Disconnect Remote Users from the Server After Logon Hours Expire

You can use the Hours button in the New User and User Properties dialog boxes to specify when the user is allowed to access the system. Enable this check box to have the user forcibly disconnected after the specified logon hours expire. If you do not enable forcible disconnection, the user can choose when to log off. If after the logon hours expire, the user tries to log on again, he or she will be prevented from doing so until the start of the login hours range. However, if a user does not manually log off, he or she will be able to continue to work indefinitely.

User Must Log On in Order to Change Password

This check box item relates to the password expiration settings discussed earlier. When a user's password nears expiration, the user is prompted at each logon to change it. If the user declines and the password age is exceeded, the user cannot log on until the password is changed. If this selection is cleared (the default), the user is presented with the Change Password dialog box and is not allowed to proceed until she changes the obsolete password. If this selection is checked, users are allowed to change the password only after logging on. Because an expired password cannot be used to log on, the administrator must change the user's password from within User Manager before the user can log on again. This is a useful option in a secure environment, and the embarrassment of calling the administrator should prompt users to pay more attention to the warnings that precede a lockout.

Assigning Rights to Groups by Assigning Groups to Rights

In User Manager for Domains, you can choose the User Rights option from the Policies menu to open the User Rights Policy dialog box (see Figure 5.11). There you can assign groups to a particular right.

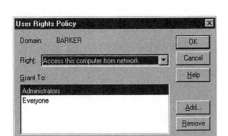

FIGURE 5.11
The User Rights Policy dialog box.

Here you face the most confusing part of User Manager's interface: You cannot view the rights assigned to a particular user. Instead, you must choose a right from the drop-down list so that you can view the users assigned to it. You probably wonder why Microsoft designed the interface this way. The answer is, "Probably to discourage people from messing with it."

Whereas a *permission* is targeted at a specific object (such as a directory or file), a *right* refers to a general right to perform a particular action on the system. This list provides some examples of Windows NT rights:

◆ Log On Locally

◆ Shut Down the System

◆ Restore Files and Directories

◆ Take Ownership of Files or Other Objects

The built-in groups described earlier in this chapter are automatically assigned appropriate user rights. In the User Rights Policy dialog box (refer to Figure 5.11), choose Restore Files and Directories from the Right drop-down list. You will see that administrators, backup operators, and server operators all have the right to restore files and directories.

The Add button in the User Rights Policy dialog box enables you to add a user or group to the list of accounts that are granted a particular right (see Figure 5.12). Step by Step 5.4 walks you through the process of adding a user or group.

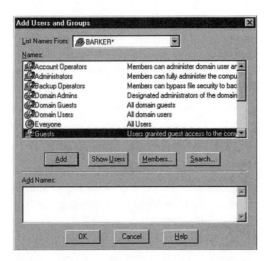

FIGURE 5.12
The Add Users and Groups dialog box.

STEP BY STEP

5.4 Giving a User or Group a Particular Right

1. Choose the right from the Right drop-down list and click on the Add button. The Add Users and Groups dialog box appears (see Figure 5.12).

2. Select the name of a user or group from the Names list and click on the Add button. (By default, only group names appear in the Names list. Click on the Show Users button to include individual users in the list.)

3. The name(s) you selected appear in the Add Names list in the lower frame. Click on the OK button to add the selected user or group to the list of accounts assigned to the right.

Of course, you might not want a user to continue to have certain rights forever. Luckily, you can take away a user right as easily as you can give it, as explained in Step by Step 5.5.

STEP BY STEP

5.5 Removing a Right from a User or Group

1. Choose the right from the Right drop-down list.

2. Select the user or group from the Grant To list.

3. Click on the Remove button.

You should not need to change the user rights policy very often. The built-in groups already are assigned appropriate user rights for most situations. Before you modify the rights policy, make sure that you could not simply add or remove a user from an existing group to accomplish the same end.

Note the Show Advanced User Rights check box at the bottom of the User Rights Policy dialog box (refer to Figure 5.11). Advanced user rights are not shown by default because you rarely need to

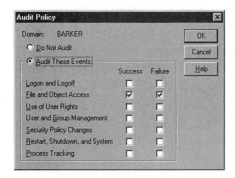

FIGURE 5.13
The Audit Policy dialog box.

> **TIP**
>
> **EXAM**
>
> **Trusts Are Important, but They're Not a Testable Topic** A trust relationship is a relationship between different domains that enables the sharing of resources. In a trust relationship, the trusting domain—having resources to share—allows users from the trusted domain to access those resources. Trust relationships are commonly used in wide area network (WAN) situations, and you will get a heavy dose of them if you ever decide to prepare for the Windows NT Server Enterprise exam. However, this is not a testable topic on the NT Server exam.

change them. These rights include creating a pagefile, logging on as a service, and other rights that programs need but people don't.

Auditing Account-Related Events

Selecting the Auditing command from the Policy menu in the User Manager for Domains invokes the Audit Policy dialog box, which enables you to track certain account-related events (see Figure 5.13). You can track either the success or the failure of the events shown in Figure 5.13. Event information is stored in a security log. You can view the security log by using Event Viewer (see Chapter 9, "Troubleshooting"). After you have configured the audit policy here, you are free to enable auditing on specific resources.

Trust Relationships

The Trust Relationships command on the Policy menu of User Manager for Domains enables you to set up and modify trust relationships for the domain.

Account Administration Tasks

An administrator's job does not end after she creates the accounts; in fact, it has just begun. Changes and modifications inevitably are necessary in day-to-day operations. You can review the properties of any user account by double-clicking on the username in User Manager for Domains or by selecting the username and choosing User, Properties. The User Properties dialog box appears (see Figure 5.14).

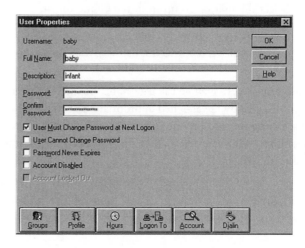

FIGURE 5.14
The User Properties dialog box.

Although you can change most things about a user in the User Properties dialog box, you should be aware of a few unique commands located on the User menu of the User Manager for Domains main window (see Figure 5.15).

Renaming Users

The User Properties dialog box shows that although you can change a user's full name at any time, the username is fixed. To change the username (remember, the username is the logon name), you must choose User, Rename from the User Manager for Domains main window (refer to Figure 5.15).

When you rename an account, it retains all of its other properties, including user rights and resource permissions. Internally, Windows NT is no more fooled by the new moniker than your family would be if you legally changed your own name. This is because Windows NT tracks users with an internally defined Security Identifier (SID), which is like a Social Security Number. Once it's created, an account's SID never changes, even if the account is renamed.

Copying Users

If you need to create multiple users at one time, consider creating a template account and copying it. When you copy an account by choosing User, Copy in User Manager for Domains, you must enter a new username, full name, and password, but the other properties are retained, including the description, group memberships, and profile information. The only exception is the Account Disabled check box, which is cleared automatically.

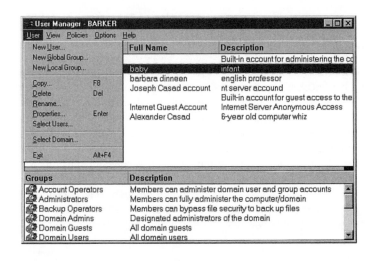

FIGURE 5.15
The User menu of the User Manager for Domains.

Using the home directory tip that was mentioned earlier, if you copied an account called Ken with a home directory of c:\%USERNAME% and named the new account RyanC, a new directory would be created called \RyanC, in addition to the already existing \Ken directory.

Deleting Versus Disabling

Earlier, Security Identifiers (SIDs) were compared to Social Security Numbers. SIDs, however, go one step further than Social Security Numbers do. When people die, their Social Security Numbers are recycled. SIDs are not recycled. When an account is deleted, that account's SID is never reused. If it were, it would be possible for a new account to inherit all the permissions and rights that were assigned to the account that had previously owned the SID.

THE IMPLICATIONS OF THE UNIVERSALLY UNIQUE NATURE OF SIDS

A SID is a universally unique identifier given to many objects in NT. Domains have SIDs, groups have SIDs, and users have SIDs. The notion of "universally unique" means that a duplicate SID cannot exist in anyone else's NT implementation. This uniqueness allows for the continued identification of an account, even if it is renamed.

When permissions to access a resource are given to a user or group account, it is the SID of that account that is registered as having access. This means that if an account is renamed, the account will retain the same access as it did prior to the name change because the SID has not been altered.

Two scenarios allow you to see the value of SID constancy and help you to get a good handle on proper account maintenance procedures.

Scenario 1: FritzW is an employee of your company. Having completed his M.C.S.E., he decides that being an independent contractor is his most lucrative option, and he strikes out on his own. When you are informed by Human Resources that your company no longer employs Fritz, you might be tempted to delete his account; many system administrators would. However, let us say that in a month, FritzW (not having the proper tools to be a successful self-employed person) decides that he would like to return to your company. He returns and is hired back into his former position. Having deleted his user account, you now create another one called FritzW. Unfortunately, this new account has a different SID than the old one did, and his old account's permissions do not apply to the new one. You will have to go through the system resources and add Fritz's new account to all the resource lists.

What you should have done is this. When Fritz left, you should have gone into User Manager for Domains and disabled his account. That would prevent Fritz from accessing company resources. However, when Fritz returned, you could have simply enabled his account again, giving him the same access to the same resources as before.

Scenario 2: BillG is the Marketing Manager for your company. Seeing green grass in an ad for a fencing company, Bill quits and takes a position at another company. To ensure that Bill can no longer access his resources in your domain, you delete his account. Two weeks later, you hire MaxW to fill the position of Marketing Manager. You now have to add Max to all the groups and resource lists to give him access to resources that he needs.

What you should have done is this: Acknowledging that the position of Marketing Manager is permanent and assuming that a replacement would be hired for Bill, you should have disabled Bill's account to ensure that a security breach did not occur. However, once Max was hired, you could have renamed the BillG account to MaxW, and Max would have had access to all the resources that Bill had access to.

The moral of the story: Don't delete accounts if you can avoid it at all.

STEP BY STEP

5.6 Disabling a User Account

1. In User Manager for Domains, select the username of the account you want to disable.

2. Choose User, Properties.

3. In the User Properties dialog box, enable the Account Disabled check box.

An account for an active user that has been disabled will probably need to be re-enabled at some point. Until it is, the user in question will not be able to log on.

FIGURE 5.16
If you attempt to delete a user, you receive this warning.

STEP BY STEP

5.7: Enabling a Disabled Account

1. In User Manager, select the username of the account you want to enable.

2. Choose User, Properties.

3. In the User Properties dialog box, deselect the Account Disabled check box.

If, after careful consideration, you decide that a disabled account will never be needed again, you can delete it as described in Step by Step 5.8. Be sure, however, that you do consider this action carefully before you perform in it.

STEP BY STEP

5.8: Deleting an Account

1. In User Manager, select the username of the account you want to delete.

2. Choose User, Delete.

3. A warning message appears (see Figure 5.16). Click on OK to proceed with the deletion.

REVIEW BREAK

Before you move on to learning about managing policies and profiles, stop and take stock of what you have already learned. You should have learned the following:

◆ Users and groups can be created and maintained using User Manager (or User Manager for Domains).

◆ Although some groups are created for you by NT to allow you to administrate your system more easily, you must create other groups yourself.

◆ Local groups are used to give permissions to access local resources. Global groups are used to group together domain users, and global groups are usually made members of local groups.

◆ The Administrator account is a built-in account that is the
most powerful user in your domain. It is important to protect
this account by changing its name and by changing its password frequently.

◆ The Guest account is a built-in account that should be disabled except in environments with very loose security.

◆ Account policies can be set in User Manager for Domains to
configure password lengths, account lockout parameters, and
so on.

◆ A variety of maintenance Activities can be performed from
within User Manager for Domains, including deleting
accounts, renaming accounts, and unlocking accounts.

Now you will look at user profiles and system policies, two mechanisms you can use to automatically configure a user's environment.

MANAGING POLICIES AND PROFILES

Create and manage policies and profiles for various situations.
Policies and profiles include local user profiles, roaming user profiles,
and system policies.

Policies and profiles are two powerful methods for defining the user
environment. This section focuses on the following subtopics:

◆ User profiles

◆ Hardware profiles

◆ System policies

User Profiles

A *user profile* is stored on a local machine. Because a local profile
resides on the local machine, it does not follow the user if the user
logs on to the network from a different machine. A *roaming profile* is
a profile that can follow the user to other computers on the network
because it is stored at a central location that the other computers can
access at logon.

Local Profiles

Unless you specify a roaming profile (see the following section), Windows NT obtains user-specific settings from a local user profile on the workstation the user is currently using. You will find a local user profile subdirectory for each workstation user in the *<winnt_root>*\profiles directory.

When a user logs on for the first time, the Windows NT logon process checks the user account database to see whether a roaming profile path has been specified for the account (see the following section). If the account database doesn't contain a profile path for the user, Windows NT creates a local user profile subdirectory for the user in the *<winnt_root>*\profiles directory and obtains initial user profile information from the local default user profile, which is stored in the *<winnt_root>*\profiles\Default User subdirectory.

Windows NT saves all changes made to the user profile in the new local user profile. The next time a user logs on at the workstation, Windows NT accesses the local user profile and configures all user-specific settings to match the information in the profile.

Roaming Profiles

A *roaming profile* is a centrally located user profile that other workstations on the network can access at logon. You specify a path to a roaming profile subdirectory in User Manager.

When a user logs on to the domain, the Windows NT logon process checks to see whether the account database contains a roaming profile path for the account. If the account database contains a path to a roaming profile, Windows NT checks to see whether the user has changed the profile type to Local in the User Profile tab of the Control Panel's System application (as described later in this chapter). If the profile type is set to Local, Windows NT uses a version of the profile stored locally instead of downloading a new version from the path specified in the account database. If the user has not changed the type to Local in the Control Panel's System application, Windows NT compares the local version of the profile with the roaming profile specified in the account database. If the local version is more recent, Windows NT asks whether the user would like to use the local version instead of the roaming version. Otherwise, Windows NT downloads the roaming version.

If the user is a guest or if the profile is a mandatory profile, when the user logs off, Windows NT doesn't save the current user profile to the user profile subdirectory. If the user is not a guest and if the profile isn't mandatory, Windows NT saves the current profile information. If the profile type has been set to Local in the User Profile tab of the Control Panel's System application, Windows NT saves the current user profile to the local copy of the profile. If the profile type is set to Roaming, Windows NT saves the current profile information to both the local copy and the version specified in the account database. Step by Step 5.9 demonstrates configuration of a roaming profile.

STEP BY STEP

5.9 Configuring a Roaming Profile for an Account

1. In User Manager for Domains, select the account and choose User, Properties. The User Properties dialog box appears (refer to Figure 5.14). (If you are creating a new account, choose User, New User. The New User dialog box that appears is similar to the User Properties dialog box.)

2. Click on the Profile button, and the User Environment Properties dialog box appears (refer to Figure 5.6).

3. In the User Profiles frame of the User Environment Profile dialog box, specify the user profile path and a logon script name.

Open the Control Panel's System application and choose the User Profiles tab. There you can control whether the computer will use a locally stored version of the profile or download a roaming profile at logon. If you are logged on as an administrator, the user profile list displays all user profiles currently stored on the computer (see Figure 5.17). If you are logged on as a user, the list displays only the profile you are currently using.

The Change Type button enables you to specify whether to use the local version of the profile or whether to download a roaming profile at logon. If you choose the roaming profile option, select the check box labeled Use Cached Profile on Slow Connections if you want Windows NT to use the local profile when the network is running slowly.

NOTE

Different Uses for the Profile Path
The user profile path is for cases in which the account will use a roaming or mandatory profile. If the user will log on to both Windows NT 3.x and Windows NT 4 computers, include the user profile filename in the user profile path. If the user will use only a computer running Windows NT 4, the user profile path should point to the user profile directory and should not include the filename. If the directory does not exist, Windows NT creates it when the roaming profile is created. Note, however, that the local machine must have access to the roaming profile directory by way of a network share. The user profile path should include the full UNC path to the profile, including a computer name, a share name, and the directory path. (See the section on the UNC naming convention later in this chapter.)

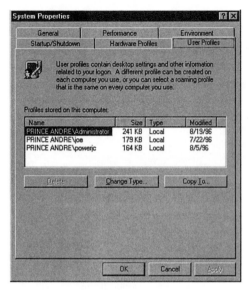

FIGURE 5.17
The User Profiles tab of the System Properties dialog box.

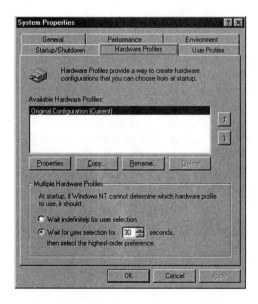

FIGURE 5.18
The Hardware Profiles tab.

Click on the Copy To button box in the User Profiles tab to open the Copy To dialog box, which enables you to copy the user profile to another directory or to another computer on the network. If a different user will use the profile at its new location, you must give that user permission to use the profile. To add a user to the permissions list for the profile, click on the Change button in the Copy To dialog box.

Mandatory Profiles

A *mandatory profile* is a preconfigured roaming profile that the user cannot change. To create a mandatory profile, create a roaming profile subdirectory and specify the path to that directory in User Manager for Domains. Then copy a user profile to the roaming profile subdirectory (using the Copy To button in the User Profile tab of the Control Panel's System application) and rename the NTUSER.DAT file to NTUSER.MAN. The .MAN extension makes the file a read-only file.

Hardware Profiles

A *hardware profile* is a collection of information about devices, services, and other hardware-related settings. Hardware profiles are primarily designed for portable computers. The hardware configuration of a portable computer might change each time the portable is attached to or removed from a docking station. A hardware profile enables the user to define a set of hardware conditions under which the computer will operate at a given time. A different hardware profile can define a different set of conditions.

If you have more than one hardware profile, you are asked to specify a hardware profile at startup. The Registry key HKEY_CURRENT_CONFIG contains information about the hardware profile selected at startup.

The Hardware Profiles tab of the Control Panel's System application enables you to create new hardware profiles and change the order of precedence among profiles (see Figure 5.18). Click on the Properties button to define a docking state for a portable computer or to enable or disable network hardware. Step by Step 5.10 leads you through the creation of a new hardware profile.

STEP BY STEP

5.10 Create a New Hardware Profile

1. Select an existing profile.

2. Click on the Copy button.

3. In the Copy Profile dialog box that appears, enter a name for the new hardware profile. The new hardware profile appears in the Available Hardware Profiles list on the Hardware Profiles tab.

If you have defined more than one hardware profile, Windows NT displays a menu of hardware profiles at startup and asks which profile you want to use. The profile you specify becomes the active hardware profile. Any changes you make to your hardware configuration affect the active hardware profile. For example, you can enable or disable a device for a given hardware profile using the Control Panel's Devices application. Likewise, you can enable or disable a service using the Control Panel's Services Application.

The up and down arrows to the right of the Available Hardware Profiles list enable you to change the preference order of the hardware profiles (refer to Figure 5.18). The radio buttons at the bottom of the Hardware Profiles tab enable you to specify whether Windows NT should wait indefinitely for you to choose a hardware profile or whether the choice defaults to the highest-preference profile after a specified period of time.

Managing System Policy with System Policy Editor

System Policy Editor, a powerful configuration tool included with Windows NT Server, enables a network administrator to maintain machine and user configurations for the entire network from a single location. System Policy Editor can operate in Registry mode or Policy File mode. The following sections discuss these two modes and the two distinct functions associated with each.

Know System Policies for the Exam   The exam objectives for the "Managing Resources" section of the NT Server exam specifically mention *system policies*. This implies that, at least for the purposes of the "Managing Resources" section, the Policy mode functions of System Policy Editor are the more significant. The Windows NT Registry, however, is an extremely important part of Windows NT, and System Policy Editor's Registry mode is an able and important interface to the Registry.

Registry Mode

In Registry mode, System Policy Editor enables whoever is using it to display and change Registry settings of either the local computer or another computer on the network. In form and function, System Policy Editor's Registry mode stakes out a niche somewhere between Control Panel and Registry Editor. It does not provide the complete Registry access that Registry Editor affords, but it is much easier to use, and it provides powerful access to settings you cannot access via Control Panel. System Policy Editor has a hierarchical structure similar to the Registry, and though its interface isn't quite as graphical as that of Control Panel, it is remarkably simple and convenient when you consider its power.

You can use System Policy Editor for the following tasks:

◆ Setting the maximum number of authentication retries

◆ Prohibiting NT from creating 8.3 aliases for long filenames

◆ Defining a logon banner to appear prior to logon

◆ Enabling or disabling a computer's capability to create hidden drive shares

◆ Hiding the Network Neighborhood icon

◆ Removing the Run command from the Start menu

◆ Requiring a specific desktop wallpaper

◆ Disabling Registry editing tools

The best way to get a feel for the kinds of things you can control using System Policy Editor is to browse through the Properties dialog boxes yourself (as described later in this section). As you study for the MCSE exam, spend some time familiarizing yourself with the System Policy Editor settings.

You access System Policy Editor via the Administrative Tools program group. Open the Start menu, choose Programs, select Administrative Tools, and click on the System Policy Editor icon.

System Policy Editor's Registry mode displays a portfolio of Registry settings that enable the administrator to customize the configuration for a specific machine or a specific local user. Step by Step 5.11 walks you through using the System Policy Editor to change Registry settings.

STEP BY STEP

5.11 Changing Registry Settings Using System Policy Editor

1. In the System Policy Editor, choose File, Open Registry. Figure 5.19 shows the System Policy Editor main screen in Registry mode.

2. Click on the Local Computer icon to configure Registry settings for the computer you are currently using. The Local Computer Properties dialog box appears, showing the hierarchy of the local computer (see Figure 5.20).

3. Click on a plus sign to see settings within each of the categories (as shown in Figure 5.21), and then check or uncheck the leaf-level settings to enable or disable the options. If an option requires additional input (such as display text for a logon banner), additional boxes and prompts appear in the space at the bottom of the dialog box.

continues

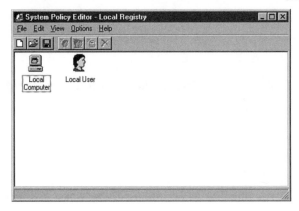

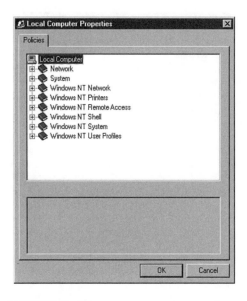

FIGURE 5.19
System Policy Editor in Registry mode.

FIGURE 5.20
The Local Computer Properties dialog box in System Policy Editor's Registry mode.

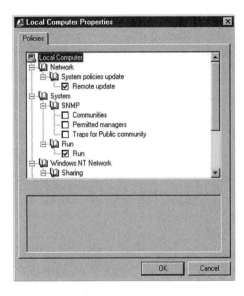

FIGURE 5.21
The Local Computer Properties dialog box with branches expanded.

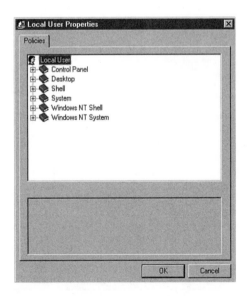

FIGURE 5.22
The Local User Properties dialog box in System Policy Editor's Registry mode.

4. Click on OK to return to the System Policy Editor main window.

5. Click on the Local User icon to configure Registry settings for the user currently logged on to the computer. The Local User settings differ from the Local Computer settings, but the procedure is the same. Figure 5.22 shows the Local User Properties dialog box.

6. Click on a plus sign to see settings within each of the categories (as shown in Figure 5.23), and then check or uncheck the leaf-level settings to enable or disable the options. If an option requires additional input, additional boxes and prompts appear at the bottom of the dialog box.

If you have proper permissions, you can edit the policy file on a remote computer as described in Step by Step 5.12. This allows you to configure policies in remote locations that you cannot physically get to.

STEP BY STEP

5.12 Editing the Policy File on a Remote Computer

1. In the System Policy Editor, choose File, Connect to open the Connect dialog box (see Figure 5.24).

2. Enter the name of the computer you want to reach and click on OK.

3. Another dialog box appears, asking which user account on the remote computer you want to administer. Select an account and click on OK.

4. The System Policy Editor reappears, looking as it did in Figure 5.19, except the name of the remote computer appears in the title bar. Click on the Local Computer icon or the Local User icon, and then change the settings as described in the preceding steps.

A typical System Policy Editor task is to customize the logon process, which you can do by adding a login banner using system policies. Step by Step 5.13 shows you how.

STEP BY STEP

5.13 Adding a Login Banner Using System Policies

1. Start the System Policy Editor.

2. Choose File, Open Registry.

3. Double-click on the Local Computer icon.

4. Click on the plus sign next to Windows NT system.

5. Click on the plus sign next to Logon.

6. Select the Logon Banner check box. Then enter a caption and some text in the text boxes at the bottom of the dialog box (see Figure 5.25). When you finish, click OK.

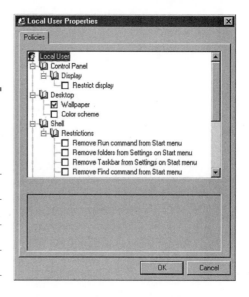

FIGURE 5.23
The Local User Properties dialog box with branches expanded.

FIGURE 5.24
The Connect dialog box.

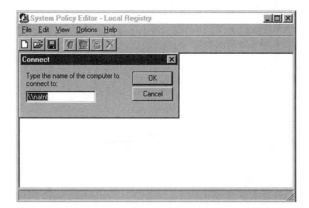

The logon banner caption and text appear under the LegalNoticeCaption and LegalNoticeText values of the following Registry subkey:

\HKEY_LOCAL_MACHINE\Software\Microsoft\Windows NT\ CurrentVersion\Winlogon

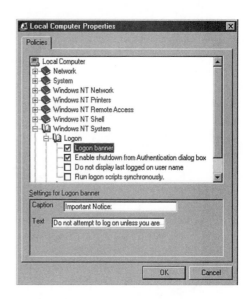

FIGURE 5.25
Enabling a logon banner.

Figure 5.26 also shows another popular System Policy Editor setting. If you select the Do Not Display Last Logged On User Name check box, Windows NT does not display the most recent user in the User Name text box of the Logon dialog box.

Policy File Mode

System Policy Editor's Policy File mode looks similar to Registry mode, but it is significantly different. System Policy is a kind of meta-Registry. The System Policy file can contain settings that override local Registry settings. You can, therefore, use System Policy Editor to impose a configuration on a user or machine that the user cannot change.

For Windows NT machines, the System Policy file is called NTCONFIG.POL. To enable system policy, create the NTCONFIG.POL file (using System Policy Editor) and place it in the *<winnt_root>*\System32\Repl\Import\Scripts folder of the domain controller's boot partition. This directory is shared as \\PDC_*servername*\Netlogon$. (If you're storing system policy information for Windows 95 machines, store it in the file CONFIG.POL instead of NTCONFIG.POL.)

When a Windows NT computer attempts to log on, Windows NT looks for the NTCONFIG.POL file and checks it for system policy information that affects the user or computer. Windows NT merges the system policy information with local Registry settings, overwriting the Registry information if necessary.

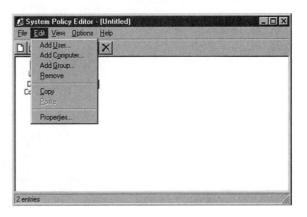

FIGURE 5.26
The System Policy Editor's Edit menu.

System policy information can come in several different forms. You can define a system policy for a specific computer, user, or group, or you can define default system policies. Default computer policies apply to all computers that do not have specific policy settings. Default user policies apply to all users that do not have specific policy settings or that aren't part of a group with specific policy settings.

Computer system policies modify the HKEY_LOCAL_MACHINE Registry subtree. User and group policies modify the HKEY_CURRENT_USER Registry subtree.

The types of settings you can define through System Policy Editor's Policy File mode are similar to the settings you can define through Registry mode, but system policy settings override Registry settings. Also, because you can apply system policy settings to groups, you can simultaneously set policies for several users or even for an entire domain.

A complete set of all system policy information for a given configuration is stored in one big system policy file. You can create different system policy files to test different system policy configurations. The active file (for NT machines), however, must be saved as NTCONFIG.POL. (As was mentioned previously, Windows 95 system policies must be saved in the file CONFIG.POL.)

Windows NT Server includes some system policy templates, which contain preconfigured system policy settings and categories. Those template files include the following:

- ◆ *c:\<winnt_root>\inf\common.adm.* This template contains settings common to both Windows NT and Windows 95 (and not present in the following two files).

- ◆ *c:\<winnt_root>\inf\winnt.adm.* This template contains Windows NT settings.

- ◆ *c:\<winnt_root>\inf\windows.* This template contains Windows 95 settings.

EXAM TIP

Effects of Policies Should Be Remembered!   It is very common to ask questions about the effect of policies on the user who is logging in. Remember the following: When a user logs in, the NTCONFIG.POL is checked. If there is an entry for that specific user, any Registry settings indicated will be merged with—and will overwrite if necessary—the user's Registry. If there is no specific user entry, any settings for groups of which the user is a member will be applied to the user. Following that, computer settings will be applied.

To use a system policy template, choose Options, Policy Template from the System Policy Editor, and then choose a template from the list.

The System Policy templates are written in a proprietary scripting language. (See the Windows NT Resource Kit for more information on the policy template scripting language.) Step by Step 5.14 goes through the steps for defining a system policy.

STEP BY STEP

5.14 Defining a System Policy

1. In the System Policy Editor, choose File, New Policy. The Default Computer and Default User icons appear.

2. Double-click on the appropriate icon to set the default computer or default user policy. (The policy settings appear in a tree structure with check boxes at the leaf level.)

3. Use the Edit menu (shown in Figure 5.27) to add specific users, computers, or groups to the policy file. When you add a computer, user, or group, an icon for whatever you choose appears with the Default Computer and Default User icons in the System Policy Editor main window.

4. Double-click on the computer, user, or group icon to set or change system policy settings. (Select an icon and choose Edit, Remove to remove that item from the policy file.)

5. When you finish making changes to the Policy file, choose File, Save As. Save the file as the following:

   \<*winnt_root*>\System32\Repl\Import\Scripts\ NTconfig

System Policy Editor automatically appends the POL extension.

Or, if you are only experimenting with the Policy file and don't want to use it yet, save it under a different name. After you save the policy file, you can open it by choosing File, Open Policy from the System Policy Editor main screen.

MANAGING WINDOWS NT SERVER FROM CLIENT MACHINES

Administer remote servers from various types of client computers. Client computer types include Windows 95 and Windows NT Workstation.

The Network Client Administrator tool, located in the Administrative Tools program group, makes a set of Windows NT administration tools available to Windows NT clients. The administration tools enable you to perform network administration functions from a client machine.

There are two packages of client-based network administration tools: one for Windows 95 clients and one for Windows NT Workstation clients. The Windows 95 client-based network administration tools include the following:

- ◆ Event Viewer
- ◆ File Security tab
- ◆ Print Security tab
- ◆ Server Manager
- ◆ User Manager for Domains

◆ User Manager Extensions for Services for NetWare

◆ File and Print Services for NetWare

In order to use the Windows 95 client-based network administration package, you must have a 486DX/33 or better Windows 95 computer with 8MB of RAM (highly recommended) and a minimum of 3MB of free disk space in the system partition. The Client for Microsoft Networks must be installed on the Windows 95 computer.

The Windows NT Workstation client-based network administration tools include the following:

◆ DHCP Manager

◆ Remote Access Administrator

◆ Remoteboot Manager

◆ Services for Macintosh

◆ Server Manager

◆ System Policy Editor

◆ User Manager for Domains

◆ WINS Manager

In order to use the client-based network administration package, the Windows NT Workstation must be a 486DX/33 or better with 12MB of RAM and a minimum of 2.5MB of free disk space in the system partition. The Workstation and Server services must be installed on the Windows NT Workstation.

To install the client administration tools on a Windows NT machine (Workstation or NT Server nondomain controller), you must first make them available from the NT server CD-ROM and then install them on the destination machine.

STEP BY STEP

5.15 Making the Client Files Available on a Network Server

1. From a domain controller, choose Start, Programs, Administrative Tools, Network Client Administrator. The Network Client Administrator dialog box appears (see Figure 5.27).

2. Choose the Copy Client-Based Network Administration Tools radio button, and then click the Continue button. The Share Client-Based Administration Tools dialog box appears (see Figure 5.28).

3. Choose the appropriate method of file sharing from the dialog box.

   - *Share Files.* If you're sharing installation files that are already available (on the CD-ROM, for example), choose this radio button, type the path of the file location (if you're sharing from the CD-ROM it is CD-ROM:\clients\srvtools), and type the name of the share.

   - *Copy Files to a New Directory and Share.* If you want to copy the installation files to a hard drive and then share them, choose this radio button, and then type the destination path and the share name.

   - *Use Existing Shared Directory.* If you have already shared the files, choose this radio button and indicate the server name and share name.

   When the share is successfully set up, a message appears, telling you so (see Figure 5.29).

FIGURE 5.27
The Network Client Administrator dialog box.

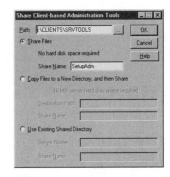

FIGURE 5.28
The Share Client-Based Administration Tools dialog box.

FIGURE 5.29
This message indicates a successful share of the administration tools.

Now that the files are available on the network, you must connect to them from your client and install them, as shown in Step by Step 5.16.

STEP BY STEP

5.16 Installing the Client-Based Administration Tools on a Windows NT Workstation or Member Server

1. Map a drive letter to the share on the server that you prepared in the previous procedure. You must map a drive because the installation will not work if you simply provide a UNC path to the share on the distribution server.

2. Open a command prompt window or select the Start, Run command. At the command line, type **MappedLetter:\Winnt\setup**. This invokes a batch file that installs the platform-specific tools on your workstation or server computer.

3. Create Program Manager icons for as many of the tools as you require. These tools have been installed in the NTROOT\system32 directory.

CASE STUDY: HAROLD'S CROISSANTS AND FILL DIRT

ESSENCE OF THE CASE

The essence of this case revolves around the restriction of rights and accesses to a certain group of users. You need to be able to implement a strategy that will disable the appropriate functionality on all machines that this group of people uses, without causing that restriction to be enforced on the rest of the user community. In addition, you need to ensure not only that the users do not have these rights, but that they cannot get them.

SCENARIO

Harold's Croissants and Fill Dirt is a baked goods and landscaping supply company. The have a large nationwide NT network that they use for a myriad of communications and data-handling applications. In the summer, they frequently hire students to do landscaping jobs. These students need access to their NT system but only occasionally and with limited access. Because many of the students they hire are from Computer Science and Engineering departments at local

CASE STUDY: HAROLD'S CROISSANTS AND FILL DIRT

universities, Harold is concerned about inquisitive hackers accessing his system and wants to implement strict control over the kinds of things that these students can do. He wants to configure default display settings, restrict access to local drives, and disable the ability to map to the network; basically, he wants to ensure that the only access they are allowed is the access that he gives them.

You are a consultant brought in to implement Harold's requests.

ANALYSIS

This is a perfect example of a use for system policies and user groups. Because all the students require the same access to resources and the same restrictions, the following procedure is a sound one:

1. Using User Manager for Domains, create the user accounts for the students (perhaps, for administrative ease, label them as temporary employees).

2. Using User Manager for Domains, create a global group called DomainTemps and populate that group with the user accounts you created in step 1.

3. On each appropriate machine, create a local group called Temps, assign that group to the resources the students need access to, and add the DomainTemps group to that local group.

4. In Policy Editor, create a new policy file and create a policy for the DomainTemps global group. This policy should include all the restrictions that Harold wants. Leave the default user and computer entries as they are to ensure that unwarranted restrictions are not imposed on the rest of the employees in the company. Save this policy file as NTCONFIG.POL in the \\<winnt_root>\System32\Repl\Import\ Scripts folder on the PDC.

5. Confirm that replication is enabled between all of the domain controllers to ensure that the policy is available everywhere a student might be validated.

These procedures ensure that the students get access to only those resources that they need and are restricted from having rights they do not need.

CHAPTER SUMMARY

KEY TERMS

Before taking the exam, make sure you are familiar with the definitions and concepts behind each of the following key terms. Appendix A is a glossary of terms you can use for quick reference purposes.

- NetLogon
- WinLogon
- user account
- group account
- local groups
- global groups
- system groups
- User Manager for Domains
- account lockout
- account policy
- user profiles
- local profile
- roaming profile
- mandatory profile
- system policy
- NTCONFIG.POL
- Client Administration Tools

This chapter covered topics relating to three major objectives for the NT Server exam: managing user and group accounts, managing policies and profiles, and managing Windows NT Server from client machines.

Specifically, you looked at how to create user and group accounts, use User Manager for Domains, and work with account profiles. You also studied topics related to policies and profiles, which identified profiles as configuration settings for specific users and identified policies as configuration scope for a domain. You also learned about using the Policy Editor as a tool for configuring system policies.

Finally, you studied the configuration of client tools installation and worked through the actual installation of domain administration resources on Windows 95 and Windows NT machines.

These topics summarize the exam objectives for the Resource Management section of the NT Server exam.

APPLY YOUR LEARNING	

Exercises

5.1   Creating a User Account

This exercise shows you how to configure Windows NT to audit changes to the user account database, create a user account, and then view the audit log.

Estimated Time: 20 minutes

1. Log on to the domain as an administrator.

2. Choose Start, Programs, Administrative Tools, and then click on User Manager for Domains.

3. In the User Manager for Domains main window, choose Policies, Audit.

4. In the Audit Policy dialog box that appears, select the Success and Failure check boxes for User and Group Management (refer to Figure 5.13).

5. Click on OK.

6. In the User Manager for Domains main window, choose User, New User. The New User dialog box appears.

7. In the Username text box, type **Exer1**.

8. In the Full Name text box, type **Exercise 1**.

9. For a description, type **MCSE Training Guide test account**.

10. For the password, type **exer1**. Type the password again in the Confirm box.

11. Click on the Add button, and then click the Close button. The new user account should appear in the user list in the top panel of the User Manager for Domains main window.

12. Double-click on the account icon in the user list (or select the account and choose User, Properties) to open the User Properties dialog box.

13. Browse through each of the buttons at the bottom of the User Properties dialog box. When you click the Groups button, notice that the new account is a member of the Domain Users group. You can add the account to other groups by selecting a group in the right panel and clicking on the Add button. Click Cancel (or OK if you made changes) to return to the User Manager for Domains main window.

14. Choose Start, Programs, Administrative Tools, and then select Event Viewer.

15. In the Event Viewer main window, choose Log, Security. Look for three security log entries related to creating the new account at or near the top of the list. The Category column for each of the three entries will be marked Account Manager.

16. Double-click on each of the entries for a detailed look at the audit information.

17. Close Event Viewer.

18. In the User Manager for Domains main window, choose Policies, Audit.

19. Deselect the User and Group Management check boxes (unless you want to keep auditing User and Group Management events).

20. If you plan to continue with Exercise 5.2, close User Manager for Domains. If you don't plan to continue with Exercise 5.2, double-click on the icon for the Exer1 account and select the Account Disabled check box in the User Properties dialog

APPLY YOUR LEARNING

box. The next time you need to set up a user account, you can rename the Exer1 account by choosing User, Rename in the User Manager for Domains main window.

> **NOTE**
>
> **Disable Instead of Deleting** As this chapter describes, it is generally a better policy to disable a user account than to delete it. Because the Exer1 account created in this exercise was never used, advantages for disabling it are less significant. You also could delete the account by choosing User, Delete in the User Manager for Domains main window.

5.2   Working with System Policies

This exercise shows you how to use the System Policy Editor to configure a user's desktop environment.

Estimated Time: 20 minutes

1. Log on as an administrator.

2. Choose Start, Programs, Administrative Tools, and then click on System Policy Editor.

3. Choose File, Open Policy.

4. Browse to the *<winnt_root>*\system32\repl\import\scripts folder and look for an NTCONFIG.POL file. If the file exists, select it and click OK. If the NTCONFIG.POL file does not exist, click on Cancel, and then choose File, New Policy.

5. In the System Policy Editor, choose Edit, Add User.

6. In the Add User dialog box, enter **Exer1**. Click on OK.

7. Find the name Exer1 in the main window and double-click its icon.

8. Expand the Shell policy category; then expand the Restrictions subcategory.

9. Select the Remove Run command from the Start menu check box and click on OK.

10. Choose File, Save.

11. If you started with a New Policy in step 4, Windows NT prompts you to enter a filename. Type **ntconfig** in the File Name text box (NT appends the .POL extension) and save the file to the *<winnt_root>*\system32\Repl\Import\Scripts directory.

12. Log on to the domain from a workstation by using the Exer1 account (or whatever account name you established the policy for in step 6). Use the password you created in step 10 of Exercise 5.1.

13. When the Start button appears, click it and examine the Start menu. The Run command is missing from the Start menu.

14. Log off the workstation. Disable or delete the Exer1 account as described in step 20 of Exercise 5.1.

APPLY YOUR LEARNING

Review Questions

1. What is the difference between a permission and a right?

2. What tool is used to specify that a certain profile is to be assigned to a particular user? What must be done to the profile to make it read-only?

3. What are the client-based network administration tools, which clients can they be run on, and what are the essential steps for installing them on a client?

4. Why is it recommended that you not delete accounts unless it's absolutely necessary?

5. What precautions can you take to secure the Administrator account?

6. What is the difference between a user profile and a system policy?

Exam Questions

1. You are the administrator of a Windows NT workgroup. You need to devise a group strategy for the following scenario:

   You have a group of several marketing employees who need access to the contact management database. A second group of people need to access the accounts receivable program, and a third group of people need to be able to modify the inventory database and run general programs.

   Keep in mind that you are trying to minimize your account administration time. Management has just informed you that the number of people in your area is expected to double over the next

quarter. How would you set up group management for each group?

Select the best answer from the following:

A. Create a user account for each user and assign access permissions based on the requirements laid out in the question.

B. Create a global group for each unique group, assign the necessary permissions to each group, and then place the users in the appropriate groups.

C. Create a local group for each unique group, assign the needed permissions to each group, and then place the users in the appropriate groups.

D. Designate one of the NT machines as the central administrator and configure permissions on that machine.

2. Which of the following correctly describes the relationship between deleting and disabling user accounts?

A. Deleting a user account removes the SID from the directory database; disabling the user account does not remove the SID, rather it makes it unusable.

B. Disabling a user account removes the SID from the directory database; deleting the account does not remove the SID, rather it makes it unusable.

C. After deleting an account, to re-establish the user's permissions and access rights, you just have to re-create the userid using the same name it had before, thus restoring the system SID.

APPLY YOUR LEARNING

D. Deleting and disabling are two terms describing the same action.

3. Which one of the following best describes the differences between local groups and global groups?

A. A global group resides in an NT Server user accounts database, and a local group is local to the computer where the resources reside.

B. A local group resides in an NT Workstation or Server computer and is used to grant access permissions to resources on that computer. A global group is created in an NT domain and is used to group domain users with common access needs.

C. Global groups contain local groups that have access to resources on NT Workstation and Windows 95 computers.

D. Local groups are created on NT domain controllers and are used to grant domain users access to resources in the domain. Global groups are used to give users access to resources in other domains.

4. If you suspect that a user is attempting to gain access to directories that contain sensitive information, which feature can you enable in Windows NT Server to create a log of attempted accesses?

A. You can use the System Option in Control Panel to enable the auditing feature of Windows NT.

B. You can use the Windows NT Accounting System.

C. You can use Directory Logging.

D. You can use the User Manager program to enable the Windows NT Audit Policy and then enable auditing on the specific directories.

5. A recently hired system administrator in a remote location calls and complains that the system time on one of the NT Servers is incorrect and when he tries to fix the time, he gets a message that he doesn't have sufficient permissions. What is the best way to allow him to change the time on the system without giving him any more rights?

A. Give him the administrator password and have him log on as administrator and change the system time.

B. Make his userid a member of the Administrator group to give him the permissions he needs to change the time.

C. Grant his userid the Change System Time right in User Manager for Domains.

D. Tell him to restart his computer in MS-DOS and change the time and date in DOS.

6. You want to appoint a user the responsibility of backing up all the Windows NT Workstation and server computers in your domain. What is the best way to give the user the permissions necessary to perform this function?

A. Make the user a member of the Administrator group, which gives her access to all resources on the NT computers.

B. Give the user the administrator password and tell her to log on as administrator to perform the backups.

APPLY YOUR LEARNING

C. Grant the user's account Full Control permissions to all the directories and files that she needs to back up and restore.

D. Create a global group called DomainBackups and place the user in that group. Then add that group to the local Backup Operators group on each machine she is to perform backups on.

7. You have created a number of accounts on your PDC that are to be used by temporary employees. You want to prevent those users from changing their passwords. Which step(s) should you take to perform this?

A. Create mandatory profiles on the domain controller.

B. Configure directory, share, and file permissions.

C. Assign appropriate user rights on a user-by-user basis.

D. Enable the User Cannot Change Password option in User Manager.

8. You are the primary user of your NT Workstation computer, but you occasionally share your computer with a couple of other users in your department. What is the best way to let them use your computer?

A. Create a user account for each user.

B. Create one account and give each user the password for the new account.

C. Let the users use your account but ask them not to change anything on your computer.

D. Tell them the password to the Administrator account on your computer.

9. You share your computer with another user. You need to install Microsoft Word so that it is available to both of you. What type of program group should you create so that the program is available to both you and the other user?

A. Personal

B. Local

C. Global

D. Common

10. Your company hires temporary employees around the holidays each year. These temps typically work the last two weeks in November and the entire month of December. How would you design an account policy to maximize the security of your network? Select all correct answers.

A. Set the account policy to lock out users after three bad logon attempts.

B. Set the account policy so that users' passwords never expire.

C. Set the account policy so that users are logged out of the workstation when their time restrictions are exceeded.

D. Modify the temporary users' accounts so that their accounts are disabled after January first.

11. A user calls you and tells you that she accidentally deleted a group that contains several users on her computer. She is worried that this may have affected the users' rights to certain resources on

APPLY YOUR LEARNING

her computer. She knows the name of the group and the users that were members of the group. How can she restore the group and the permissions back to the way they were?

A. Choose the Undelete option in User Manager to recover the deleted group.

B. Create a new group with the same name and SID as the deleted group.

C. Create a new group with the same name, assign the users to the group, and then reassign the permissions to the group.

D. Re-create the users and group, and reassign the permissions to the group.

12. What are the names of the four system groups in NT Server?

A. Network, Special, Administrators, and Interactive

B. Administrators, Backup Operators, Network, and Local

C. Global, Power Users, Macintosh Users, and Network

D. Network, Creator Owner, Interactive, and Everyone

13. When you connect to a shared directory on another Windows NT computer, which group do you automatically become a member of?

A. Network

B. Administrators

C. Creator Owner

D. Interactive

14. You want a user to be able to create user and group accounts, but you don't want her to be able to assign user rights. Of which groups should you make the user a member?

A. Account Operators

B. Server Operators

C. Administrators

D. Power Users

15. What is the difference between a user account that is locked out and an account that is disabled?

A. A disabled userid keeps its SID, whereas a locked out user account does not.

B. The system administrator can lock out a user account, but the system administrator cannot disable a user account.

C. The system administrator can disable a user account, but the system administrator cannot lock out a user account.

D. A locked out userid keeps its SID, whereas a disabled user account does not.

16. You need to create several user accounts that all have the same properties. What is the best method for doing so?

A. Create a user who has the correct properties, and then use the Replicate option to create as many other users as necessary.

B. Create a user who has the correct properties, and then use the Copy function in User Manager to create as many others as necessary.

APPLY YOUR LEARNING

C. Use the REPLUSER.EXE program to copy a user template that has the correct properties.

D. Run the RDISK.EXE program to make duplicate user accounts for as many users as necessary.

17. You are using a template to create several user accounts with similar properties. However, you want to assign home directories to each user based on his or her userid. Which path should you specify for the home directory in the User Environment Profile dialog box?

A. C:\USERS\DEFAULT

B. C:\USERS\%HOMEDRIVE%

C. C:\USERS\%DOMAINUSERS%

D. C:\USERS\%USERNAME%

18. A user calls you complaining that he cannot log on. He changed his password yesterday, and now he cannot remember it. What can you do to get this user logged on?

A. Create a new user account with no password and tell him to log on.

B. Change the user's password, and then set his account policy so that his password never expires and cannot be changed.

C. Run User Manager and change his password. Then set his account policy so that he must change his password at the next logon. Give the user the password and tell him that he must change it during the logon process.

D. Tell the user to attempt to log on guessing his password at each attempt; hopefully he will remember it sooner or later.

19. A user is going to be on leave for the next two months. How would you keep anyone from using her account yet avoid having to re-create it when she returns?

A. Use Server Manager to disable the user's account from logging on to the workstation.

B. Remove the user's right to log on locally.

C. Disable the user's account in User Manager.

D. Delete the user account.

20. Your boss's secretary complains that she cannot log on to her domain user account. You make a site visit, and she informs you that even though she is entering the correct password, the system tells her that either she is using the incorrect account or her password is incorrect. You question her further and find out that yesterday when she logged on she was required to change her password. Which one of the following may be the cause of her problems?

A. She is entering her userid in lowercase characters and does not realize that the userid is case-sensitive.

B. She is entering her password in lowercase characters and does not realize that the password is case-sensitive.

C. Another system administrator manually locked her account.

D. Her system is caught in a feedback loop resulting from having both the User Cannot Change Password and the User Must Change Password at Next Login boxes checked in User Manager.

APPLY YOUR LEARNING

21. You have a user who uses a laptop computer in a docking station while she's at work and also uses the laptop at home without the docking station. The laptop is configured with Windows NT Workstation. Which of the following describes the best way to configure the laptop for each of the different environments?

    A. Open the Control Panel, click the System icon, and choose the Hardware Profiles tab to create separate hardware profiles for each location. The user can then choose the appropriate configuration when the laptop boots.

    B. There is no way to configure NT with multiple hardware configurations because the operating system does not support Plug and Play.

    C. You don't have to configure the laptop manually. The Plug and Play features of NT automatically detect the difference.

    D. Tell the user to reconfigure the settings for when she is away from the office (before she leaves the office). The next time she reboots, she will have the correct configuration.

22. Which of the following describes the easiest way to make a group of users' desktop environments look the same?

    A. Use Registry Editor, and then place a copy of the configured Registry in each user's home directory.

    B. Use User Profile Editor, and then place a copy of the configured profile in each user's home directory. Give the profile a .MAN extension, and it becomes a mandatory profile that the users cannot change.

    C. Use System Policy Editor and create a POL file that all users will use. Place this POL file in the *<**winnt root**>*\System32\Repl\Import\ Scripts directory, and then assign the policy file for whichever users you want to be able to use it.

    D. You cannot configure a standard desktop automatically, but you can configure each machine manually so that the next time your users log on, they have the configured settings.

23. Which statement is true regarding system policy files between Windows 95 and Windows NT?

    A. The policies are not the same and can't be interchanged.

    B. The policies are the same and can be interchanged.

    C. Windows 95 doesn't have system policies.

    D. Windows 95 policies are local to the machine, whereas Windows NT policies can be stored only on a server.

24. A user calls to complain that every time she changes her desktop, it reverts to its prior state the next time she logs on. How can you explain what is happening?

    A. Tell the user to choose the Save Settings on Exit option from the Start menu properties.

    B. Tell the user that she doesn't have sufficient rights to save her desktop settings and that she should contact Microsoft to obtain a license to change her desktop.

    C. Tell the user that her userid probably is set up to use a mandatory profile that she cannot modify.

D. Tell her she needs to make the changes and save them by using the System Policy Editor. The next time she logs on, the settings should be the same.

25. A user wants to know why his desktop settings change as he moves from workstation to workstation. Which statement best explains this situation?

    A. The user is set up to use a local profile. Because this profile is stored on his machine, it is not available when he moves to a different computer.

    B. The computer policy of the other machine is configured to override his server-based policy.

    C. The user must be logging on with the Ignore Profile setting enabled in the Logon dialog box. Tell him to disable this option.

    D. The user must be set up to use a local policy. Because this policy is stored on his machine, it is not available when he moves to a different computer.

26. The name of the Teachers group needs to be changed to Professors. Which statement best describes the process for changing the name of the group?

    A. The name of the group cannot be changed.

    B. Select the Rename option from the User menu in User Manager, and then enter the new group name.

    C. Create a new group called Professors, and then move the users from the Teachers group to the Professors group.

    D. Create a new group called Professors, and then delete the users from the Teachers group and add them to the Professors group.

Answers to Review Questions

1. A permission is an access level assigned to a specific resource, such as a file or a printer. A right is the ability to perform some system action, such as locally logging on to a domain controller or shutting down a domain controller. For more information, see the section "Managing User and Group Accounts."

2. On a domain controller, the tool used is User Manager for Domains. After bringing up the properties for the specific user, you can click the Profile button to bring up the Profile dialog box where you can specify the profile that the account is to use. In order to make that profile read-only, when you create it, put a .MAN extension on it (to make it mandatory). For more information, see the section "Managing Policies and Profiles."

3. Client-based administration tools are a subset of the tools for domain administration, but they are installed onto a nondomain controller in order to administer your domain from a workstation. These tools can be installed on any Windows 95 or Windows NT machine. The essential steps for installing them are: 1) share the installation files and 2) connect to the share from the client and install the tools. For more information, see the section "Managing Windows NT Server from Client Machines."

4. Because an account gets a unique SID when it's created and that SID is used to grant permissions

APPLY YOUR LEARNING

to access resources, if you delete an account and then realize you did not want to, you cannot simply re-create the user name and expect all the permissions to be restored. You will have to grant the permissions again from scratch. In addition, when one person leaves a company, frequently a person is hired to take his or her place. Therefore, you should rename the old account instead of creating a new one to ensure that the permissions granted to the previous user are automatically transferred to the new user.

One precaution you can take is to disable an inactive account to prevent its unauthorized use. For more information, see the section "Account Administration Tasks."

5. The Administrator account is very powerful. However, certain features of that account make it vulnerable as well. Because it is a very important account in your network, the account cannot be locked out; if it could be locked out, a hacker could cripple your system by purposely entering too many incorrect passwords. You should take the following precautions to protect the Administrator account:

   • *Rename it.* This forces a potential hacker to guess both the account name and the password.

   • *Create another account with few privileges and call it Administrator.* This prevents hackers from accessing the true Administrator account. If a hacker does gain access to the account called Administrator, she will have wasted her time.

   • *Change the password frequently.* This ensures that if someone does get the password, its

lifetime will be limited. Be sure to make the password complex, including odd combinations of numbers and upper- and lowercase characters.

For more information, see the section "Users and Groups."

6. The basic difference between a user profile and a system policy is that a system policy defines the environment in which a user can work, and a user profile defines what configuration a user wants to use within the context of that environment. To use a metaphor, if you are told that you can decorate a room with paint but can choose whatever color you want, the decorating option, paint, is the policy; your specific color choice is the profile. For more information, see the section "Managing Policies and Profiles."

Answers to Exam Questions

1. **C.** Because each machine in the workgroup maintains its own local directory database, groups must be set up locally on each machine; and because this is not a domain, global groups do not exist. For more information, see the section "Managing User and Group Accounts."

2. **A.** Deleting an account permanently removes it from the directory database; disabling an account makes it unusable until it is re-enabled. Because the SID for an account is unique, even if an account is created with the same name as a deleted account, the permissions for that account will not be restored. Avoid deleting accounts whenever possible. For more information, see the section "Managing User and Group Accounts."

APPLY YOUR LEARNING

3. **B.** Global groups are used to group domain resources into manageable units; local groups are used to assign permissions to access local computer resources to users or the members of global groups. For more information, see the section "Users and Groups."

4. **D.** Enabling auditing requires two steps. First, you must enable auditing in User Manager for Domains (or User Manager if you are working with NT Workstation or a standalone NT server). Second, on an NTFS volume, you must enable auditing for the resources you want to track access to. For more information, see the section "Working with NTFS File Permissions and Security."

5. **C.** If you are concerned about giving a user too many rights, you should not make him a member of the Administrators group. In this case, you can simply give him the right to change the system time, and he will not be able to perform any additional administrative functions. For more information, see the section "Managing User and Group Accounts."

6. **D.** Remember that users are added to global groups, global groups are added to local groups, and local groups are given permissions. Because you want to provide the user with the ability to back up any machine in the domain, the best way to give access is to first create a global group containing that user (and any others who need the same ability). Then you place that global group (which is accessible by any machine that is a member of the domain) into the Backup Operators group on each local machine. Because that local group already has the proper permissions to perform backups, nothing else is

necessary. For more information, see the section "Managing User and Group Accounts."

7. **D.** The only step that is necessary is to open User Manager for Domains and enable the User Cannot Change Password option for each user. For more information, see the section "User Manager for Domains."

8. **A.** To secure your machine, you begin by giving each of the additional users his or her own user account. After doing this, you have the ability to enable local security on NTFS partitions and give or remove user rights. For more information, see the section "Managing User and Group Accounts."

9. **D.** Common groups created by an administrator are available to all users via a shortcut. On the other hand, personal groups created by individual users are available only to the users who created them. For more information, see the section "Managing User and Group Accounts."

10. **A, C, D.** All the options listed are reasonable security precautions except passwords that never expire (which reduces security instead of increasing it). For more information, see the section "User Manager for Domains."

11. **C.** Because the SID for the group is unique, there is no way to associate the permissions for the previous group with a new one. The only way to restore the group and its permissions is to re-create the group, assign the users to it, and then assign permissions to the group as before. For more information, see the section "Managing User and Group Accounts."

12. **D.** The Network group contains all the users currently accessing a shared resource on a server. The

APPLY YOUR LEARNING

Creator Owner group is a group maintained on a resource-by-resource basis, and it defines the person who created the resource or who last took ownership of it. The Interactive group contains the name of the person who is currently logged in locally to an NT machine. The Everyone group includes anyone who might access the NT machine, whether in a domain, a workgroup, or a client of another network operating system. For more information, see the section "Users and Groups."

13. **A.** You automatically become a member of the Network group. For more information, see the section "Users and Groups."

14. **A.** The Account Operators group allows for the creation of users and groups but not for the assignment of user rights. For more information, see "Built-In User Accounts."

15. **C.** An administrator can disable an account to render it unusable. The only way to lock out an account is to violate the login rules—by entering an incorrect password too many times in too short a time. For more information, see the section "User Manager for Domains."

16. **B.** By creating a user template account, you can assign properties to it and then copy that account as many times as necessary. For more information, see the section "User Manager for Domains."

17. **D.** The environment variable %USERNAME% contains the name of the user who is currently logged on. By using this variable in conjunction with the user's home directory path (in this case C:\Users), you can ensure that a different home directory is specified for each user. For more

information, see the section "User Manager for Domains."

18. **C.** An administrator can go into User Manager (for Domains) and reset any user's password. Once you have set the user's password to some known value, select the User Must Change Password at Next Logon check box. This means that you only know the user's password until the next time he logs in. For more information, see the section "User Manager for Domains."

19. **C.** By disabling the user's account, you prevent it from being used, while maintaining its permissions for any resources it has access to. When the account is re-enabled, the user's access will be restored. For more information, see the section "User Manager for Domains."

20. **B.** The only valid possibility is that she is entering her password correctly but that the capitalization is incorrect. User account passwords are case-sensitive; user account names are not. An administrator cannot lock an account; he can only disable one. And a feedback loop is not possible. For more information, see the section "Managing User and Group Accounts."

21. **A.** Hardware profiles enable you to configure multiple hardware configurations, one of which can be chosen at system boot. One valid hardware configuration is "Off the Network," which does not try to start any networking services. For more information, see the section "Hardware Profiles."

22. **C.** System policies are much more flexible than profiles and are easier to implement. There need be only one policy file per server, and it can be configured with the environment of any user or

APPLY YOUR LEARNING

group of users. For more information, see the section "Managing System Policy with System Policy Editor."

23. **A.** Because policies modify the Registry of the client machine, Windows 95 and Windows NT are not compatible with each other. This means that you must create separate policy files for your Windows 95 clients and your Windows NT clients. For more information, see the section "Managing System Policy with System Policy Editor."

24. **C.** A mandatory profile loads for a user every time the user logs on and is, by its nature, read-only. This means that the user can make modifications to her desktop configuration, but those settings will be discarded when she logs off and the settings for the mandatory profile will be loaded again at her next logon. For more information, see the section "User Profiles."

25. **A.** The profile that the user is set up to use is local to the machine he normally uses. As a result, it is not available on any other machine. When he logs in to another machine, he gets the default profile for that machine. For more information, see the section "User Profiles."

26. **A.** The name of a group cannot be changed. The only way to simulate a name change is to create a new group, give it the same members as the former one, delete the old group, and then assign the new group to every resource to which the old group had access. For more information, see the section "Users and Groups."

Suggested Readings and Resources

The following are some recommended readings in the area of Managing Users and User Environments:

1. Microsoft Official Curriculum course 803: *Administering Microsoft Windows NT 4.0*

   • Module 2: Setting Up User Accounts

   • Module 3: Setting Up Group Accounts

   • Module 4: Administering Group Accounts

2. Microsoft Official Curriculum course 922: *Supporting Microsoft Windows NT 4.0 Core Technologies*

   • Module 4: Managing System Policies

   • Module 15: Implementing Network Clients

3. Microsoft TechNet CD-ROM

   • *Concepts and Planning: MS Windows NT Server 4.0*

• Chapter 1: Managing NT Server Domains

• Chapter 2: Working with User and Group Accounts

• Chapter 3: Managing User Work Environments

• Chapter 11: Managing Client Administration

4. Web Sites

   • www.microsoft.com/ntserver (check out the online seminars)

   • www.microsoft.com/train_cert

   • www.prometric.com/testingcandidates/ assessment/chosetest.html (take the online assessment tests)

Manage disk resources. Tasks include copying and moving files between file systems, creating and sharing resources, implementing permissions and security, and establishing file auditing.

▶ This objective is necessary because someone certified in the use of Windows NT Server technology must understand how disk resources are managed. This includes knowing how resource permissions are applied on both FAT and NTFS partitions, how security is implemented, how resources are shared and audited, and how permissions are maintained when copying and moving files.

CHAPTER 6

Managing Resources Part 2: Managing Disk Resources

▶ This objective is quite popular for exam questions on the NT Server exam, probably because the concepts are easily testable and fit well into the multiple-choice format. Questions often involve tables of permissions and ask you to sort out access based on group membership, or they might require you to determine what permissions look like after a file copy procedure. Make sure you have a good understanding of the effects of moving or copying so that a portion of any move or copy scenario will not throw you for a loop. Remember that attributes are inherited in all cases but one (the exception being when you move from one location to another on the same partition).

Here are some examples of typical questions:

Question: A file is in the path c:\data and is compressed. If it is copied to the path c:\archive (a directory that is not compressed), what will its attributes be?
Answer: The file will not be compressed because it will inherit the attributes of the destination directory.

Question: A file is in the path c:\data and is compressed. If it is moved to the path d:\archive (a directory that is not compressed), what will its attributes be?
Answer: The file will not be compressed; it maintains its original attributes as a result of the copy and delete function that performs the move between partitions.

Question: A file is in the path c:\data and is compressed. If it is moved to the path c:\archive (a directory that is not compressed), what will its attributes be?
Answer: The file will remain compressed; it retains its original attributes through the move.

Make sure you are familiar with the two programs (compact and convert) mentioned in this chapter and how to use them. Also understand how NTFS and share-level permissions interact to form a complete security model.

The concepts covered in this chapter are very easy to experiment with, so take advantage of it. Take the concepts and play with them until you have a good grasp of the way things work. This will benefit you not only on the exam, but also as you begin to implement access and security strategies on NT Servers.

INTRODUCTION

Manage disk resources. Tasks include copying and moving files between file systems, creating and sharing resources, implementing permissions and security, and establishing file auditing.

This chapter covers the final objectives of Managing Resources by discussing the resources found on your hard drives. A big part of an NT administrator's job is managing file resources for the network. This might include such tasks as assigning permissions, creating directory shares, troubleshooting filename problems, and copying or moving files and directories.

The following sections take a close look at working with file resources and working with file permissions and security.

WORKING WITH WINDOWS NT FILE RESOURCES

File resources are an important aspect of Windows NT administration, and consequently, the file resources topic is an important stop in the objectives list for the Windows NT Server exam. One significant part of managing file resources is managing NTFS security, which you will get a closer look at later in this chapter. But first, the following sections examine these other important topics you need to understand for the Windows NT Server exam:

- ◆ The Universal Naming Convention (UNC)
- ◆ Copying and moving files
- ◆ Long filenames
- ◆ Converting a FAT partition to NTFS
- ◆ NTFS compression
- ◆ Sharing files
- ◆ Synchronizing files

THE UNIVERSAL NAMING CONVENTION (UNC)

Actually, this is the Microsoft Naming Convention, but when you are Microsoft, you can get away with a little hubris. UNC provides a common method for referring to servers on a network and the shares published on these servers. A UNC path begins with a double-backslash immediately followed by a server name, like this:

\\NTServer

To view the shared directories on a computer named NTServer, you would type the following command at the Windows NT command prompt:

```
net view \\NTServer
```

When you want to refer to a specific shared resource, you refer to the system name first, followed by the share name. For example, to map a new drive letter (such as G) to the documents shared on NTServer, you could type the following command at the Windows NT command prompt:

```
net use G: \\NTServer\Documents
```

You can extend the path even further. (From this point forward, it looks like an MS-DOS path.) To refer to the file README.TXT located in the PUBLIC subdirectory of the Documents share on NTServer, you could use the following syntax:

```
\\NTServer\Documents\PUBLIC\README.TXT
```

To make the connection persistent (in other words, if you want Windows NT to reconnect you to this drive every time you log on), you use the /PERSISTENT switch:

```
net use F: \\NTServer\Documents /PERSISTENT:YES
```

To disconnect a network drive, use the /DELETE switch:

```
net use F: /DELETE
```

You can use UNC throughout Windows NT. To view the contents of the documents shared on NTServer, for example, you could type the following:

```
dir \\NTServer\Documents
```

To copy README.TXT from its original location on NTServer to a new location on another server, you could type this command:

```
copy \\NTServer\Documents\PUBLIC\README.TXT
\\ServerTwo\Archive\
```

You don't have to go to the SCS to use UNC, however; you can use UNC as a timesaver from within the Windows NT GUI. A shortcut can use a UNC as a target address, for example. From Network Neighborhood, you can create a shortcut to a file or directory on a network device just as you would to a file or directory on your local machine.

In Explorer, if you know the name of the server to which you need to connect, you don't need to waste time browsing. Choose Tools, Go To and type the UNC path in the Go To Folder dialog box (see Figure 6.1). Then click on OK.

In addition, you can also use the UNC of a server or one of its shares from the Start, Run dialog box by typing either of these commands:

\\servername	to display a dialog box showing all the shares available
\\servername\sharename	to display a dialog box showing the contents of the share requested.

Microsoft operating systems use UNC to connect to network resources regardless of the type of server in use. You can use UNC to connect from a Windows NT Workstation to a NetWare server, for example, just as easily as you can connect to a Windows NT Server.

COPYING AND MOVING FILES

When you copy a file within or between partitions with the Copy command, a new instance of that file is created, and the new file

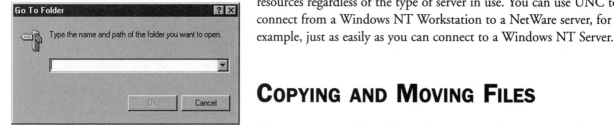

FIGURE 6.1
The Go To Folder dialog box.

inherits the compression and security attributes of its new parent directory. (You will learn more about compression and security later in this chapter.)

You can produce the same effect by moving a file between partitions using the Move command because a move between partitions is really a copy followed by a delete. When a file is moved within a partition, the file retains its original attributes. The attributes do not change because the file itself is never altered. Only the source and target directories change.

LONG FILENAMES

Although all the Windows NT-supported file systems support long filenames, you should be aware of certain issues. These issues differ between FAT partitions and NTFS partitions, so each will be dealt with separately.

FAT Long Filenames

Although, as you learned earlier in this book, the filename length limitations of the FAT file system have been overcome, one limitation that remains is that only 512 directory entries are permitted in the root directory of any partition. Because each long filename requires a directory entry for every thirteen characters (or portion thereof) in its name and an additional entry for its 8.3 alias, you are in danger of quickly reaching the entry limit if you use excessively long filenames in a root directory.

Also, if you are dual booting between Windows NT and Windows 95, you should be aware that although the long filenames are compatible with both operating systems, Windows 95 has a path limitation of 260 characters, including the drive letter. Therefore, if you use a deep hierarchy of subdirectories with long filenames, you may find that Windows 95 cannot access a file buried deep within that directory tree.

The two operating systems also differ in the way they create 8.3 aliases. Both Windows NT and Windows 95 begin by taking the first six legal characters in the LFN (in other words, stripping spaces

and punctuation and converting to uppercase) and tacking on a tilde
(˜) and a number. If the first six legal characters result in a unique
identifier for that file, the number following the tilde is 1. If a file in
that directory already has the same first six legal characters, the
numeric suffix will be 2. For an extension, Windows NT uses the
first three legal characters following the last period in the LFN. To
get an idea of what this looks like, examine this sample directory listing that includes both the long filenames and the 8.3 aliases:

```
Team Meeting Report #3.Doc          TEAMME˜1.DOC
Team Meeting Report #4.Doc          TEAMME˜2.DOC
Team Meeting Report #5.Doc          TEAMME˜3.DOC
Team Meeting Report #6.Doc          TEAMME˜4.DOC
Nov. 1995 Status Report.Doc         NOV199˜1.DOC
```

Both Windows 95 and Windows NT generate aliases in this fashion
until the fifth iteration of the same first six legal characters. At that
point, Windows 95 continues to do so. However, Windows NT does
something altogether different: It takes only the first two legal characters, performs a hash on the filename to produce four hexadecimal
characters, and then appends a ˜1. For every new filename produced, the ˜1 is appended. To illustrate this, Table 6.1 shows aliases
that Windows 95 would generate and Windows NT might generate
if additional reports were saved in the directory used in the preceding list.

TABLE 6.1

COMPARISON OF ALIAS CREATION IN WINDOWS 95 AND
WINDOWS NT

Long Filename	Windows 95 Alias	Windows NT Alias
Team Meeting Report #7.Doc	TEAMME˜5.DOC	TEA4F2˜1.DOC
Team Meeting Report #8.Doc	TEAMME˜6.DOC	TE12B4˜1.DOC
Team Meeting Report #9.Doc	TEAMME˜7.DOC	TE833E˜1.DOC

Windows NT does this for performance reasons. It takes a long time
to search a directory list for a unique filename if it has to go six or
more characters in to find a unique match. Windows 95 eschews this
technique, probably assuming that the performance gains are not
worth the calls from consumers who can't make heads or tails of the
filenames from their 16-bit applications.

Switching back and forth between Windows 95 and Windows NT on LFN-enabled FAT partitions is not a problem. Each time you save the file, the LFN remains intact; however, you may find that the alias is renamed, depending on the operating system and the filenames currently in use in the directory.

If you choose to disable long filename support altogether on a FAT partition, be careful when copying files from a partition that does support LFNs because both the COPY and XCOPY commands always default to using the LFN for their operations. When these commands attempt to write an LFN to an LFN-disabled FAT partition, this error message appears:

```
The file name, directory name, or volume label syntax is
incorrect.
```

If you are copying from an LFN-enabled FAT partition or from an NTFS partition, you can use the /n switch with both COPY and XCOPY to prevent this. The /n switch directs the command to use the alias instead of the LFN.

NTFS Long Filenames

NTFS generates an alias for each LFN the same way that FAT does. This auto-generation takes time, however. If you won't be using 16-bit MS-DOS or Windows 3.x-based applications, you might consider disabling the automatic alias generation by adding a value called NtfsDisable8dot3NameCreation with a type of REG_DWORD and a value of 1 to HKEY_LOCAL_MACHINE\System\ CurrentControlSet\Control\FileSystem. To re-enable alias generation, set the value to 0 or delete the value altogether.

> **WARNING**
>
> **Beware of Third-Party MS-DOS–Based Disk Utilities** When run under Windows NT, such utilities are harmless because they cannot access the hard disk directly. When run under MS-DOS on a dual-boot system, however, they can wreak havoc on your LFN-enabled FAT partitions. You can use Windows 95–specific disk utilities safely, again, when you're running Windows 95 on a multiboot system.

CONVERTING A FAT PARTITION TO NTFS

You can convert a FAT partition to NTFS at any time. You cannot, however, convert an NTFS partition to a FAT partition. Therefore, if you aren't certain which type of file system to use for a partition, you might want to start with FAT and then convert after you are sure there will be no ill effects.

To convert from FAT to NTFS, issue this command at the command prompt (there is no GUI utility for this):

```
CONVERT <drive_letter>: /FS:NTFS
```

The reason for specifying the file system when there has never been more than one choice is probably to accommodate future expansion.

When you perform a conversion, you do not have to back up your data (although you always should, just in case something goes awry); the conversion is done on-the-fly. You usually don't even need to shut down and restart the computer, unless another process currently is using the partition you are converting. In that case, Windows NT performs the conversion after the system reboots, using a special boot-time utility called AUTOCONV. You can see the conversion as it takes place: when the screen turns blue immediately following the CHKDSK output.

NTFS COMPRESSION

Individual files and directories can be marked for compression on NTFS partitions only. (An entire drive can be compressed, too, but all you are really doing is compressing the root directory and the files within it; everything is handled at the file level.)

Compression occurs on-the-fly. All this is transparent to applications and the rest of the operating system.

NTFS compression does not free up as much disk space as most MS-DOS-compatible compression products do. This is not because Microsoft could not write a tight compression algorithm; in fact, they did just that with DriveSpace in Windows 95. The reason for the loose compression in Windows NT is actually to ensure that performance is not adversely affected.

NOTE

NTFS Is Better! Stacker, DoubleSpace, DriveSpace, and other disk compression products are great products, but you never really know how much disk space you have left. Everything is based on an estimated compression ratio, and because the entire drive is compressed (these products allow no granularity), that compression ratio is applied to all files—DOCs and ZIPs alike. Sometimes you run out of disk space even though a directory listing says you should have several megabytes remaining.

With NTFS, each file is compressed individually, so you always know the exact amount of disk space you have left. You can also choose which files to compress, so you don't have to waste time compressing the entire drive if you only want to keep your Word documents down to size.

Typically, disk compression products sacrifice performance for extra compression. In Windows NT, you can get a compression ratio almost as good as that of the MS-DOS 6.22 DriveSpace compression engine, without sacrificing any noticeable performance. When a user marks files for compression, NTFS analyzes the files to see how much disk space will be saved and the amount of time it will take to compress and decompress the files. If NTFS determines that it is not a fair trade, it does not compress the files, no matter how many times the user issues the command to do so. NTFS compression is not at all configurable; all parameters are handled exclusively by the file system.

You can compress any file or directory on an NTFS partition, even if it is the system or boot partition. NTLDR, a Hidden, System, Read-Only file in the root of your system partition, is the only file that you cannot compress. NTLDR is the first file loaded when Windows NT boots, and NTLDR controls the rest of the boot process, including the loading of a mini-NTFS driver needed for bootup. Until NTLDR loads the NTFS minidriver, compressed files are inaccessible. NTLDR must, therefore, always remain uncompressed.

Not all files compress equally. Document files tend to compress the most. Text-based documents and bitmapped graphics, in particular, can shrink to less than one-eighth of their original sizes. Program files compress about 40 or 50 percent, and already-compressed files such as JPG and AVI graphics and videos tend not to compress at all.

Compressing and Uncompressing Files, Directories, and Drives

One of a few ways to compress a file or directory on an NTFS partition is to select the directories and files, and choose File, Compress (see Step by Step 6.1).

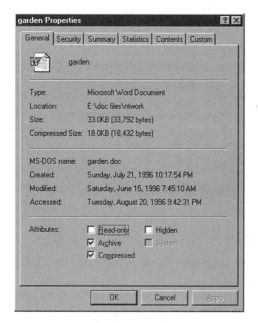

FIGURE 6.2
The file Properties dialog box for a file on an NTFS partition.

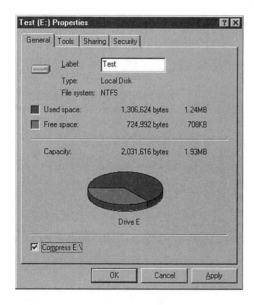

FIGURE 6.3
The General tab of the drive Properties dialog box.

STEP BY STEP

6.1 Compressing NTFS Files

1. Select the files you want to compress. Use the Ctrl key to select multiple files.

2. Choose File, Properties. The Properties dialog box appears.

3. In the Attributes frame, select the Compressed check box (see Figure 6.2).

If you select a directory instead of, or along with, a file, you are asked whether you want to compress all the files and subdirectories within that directory.

To uncompress files or directories, select them and remove the check from the Compressed check box in the Properties dialog box.

When files and directories are compressed, a new Compression attribute is set for those objects. Note that the Compression attribute does not display for non-NTFS partitions.

If you are curious about the amount of disk space NTFS actually is saving you, access the General tab of a file's Properties dialog box (refer to Figure 6.2) and compare the size to the compressed size.

The procedure for compressing a drive is similar to the procedure for compressing a file or directory. Select the drive in My Computer or Explorer, and then choose File, Properties. On the General tab of the drive's Properties dialog box (see Figure 6.3), select the Compress check box.

COMPACT.EXE

In addition to using the properties dialog boxes in the GUI interface, you can also use a command-line utility called COMPACT.EXE to compress files. COMPACT.EXE enables a user to compress files and directories from the command prompt. Table 6.2 lists switches you can use with the COMPACT command.

TABLE 6.2	

SWITCHES USED WITH THE COMPACT COMMAND

Use This Command...	To Do This...
COMPACT <filelist> /C	Compress
COMPACT <filelist> /U	Uncompress
COMPACT <filelist> /S	Compress an entire directory tree
COMPACT <filelist> /A	Compress hidden and system files
COMPACT <filelist> /I	Ignore errors and continue compressing
COMPACT <filelist> /F	Force compression even if the objects are already compressed
COMPACT <filelist> /Q	Turn on quiet mode; that is, display only summary information

Keep the COMPACT /F command in the back of your mind as a troubleshooting tool because when files are marked for compression, their Compressed attribute is determined and set before the actual file is compressed. Although that's not usually a big deal, if the system were to crash during a compression operation, all the selected files would be marked as compressed even though the operation had not been completed. You could try compressing the files again with the /C switch, but the files would all be skipped because their Compressed attributes would already be set. Using the /F switch forces all files in the list to be recompressed, which should solve the problem.

You also can use the COMPACT command without any switches, in which case it just reports on the compression status, size, and ratio for each file in the file list.

Special Notes About Compressed Directories

Directories are not truly compressed; the Compressed attribute for a directory just sets a flag to tell Windows NT to compress all current files and all future files created in the directory. With that in mind, it may be easier to understand that when you copy or move compressed files, the files do not always stay compressed.

When a new file is created in an NTFS directory, it inherits the attributes set for that directory. When a file is created in a compressed directory, for example, that file will be compressed. When a file is created in an uncompressed directory, the file will not be compressed. So when a compressed file is copied to an uncompressed directory, the new copy of the file will not be compressed. Likewise, if an uncompressed file is copied to a compressed directory, the copy of the file will be compressed even though the original is not.

That much probably makes sense. However, Windows NT includes a MOVE command that, when used within a single partition, swaps directory pointers so that a single file appears to move from one directory to another. Note the word "appears." The file does not actually go anywhere; it is the source and target directories that actually record a change. When files are *moved*, attributes do not change. In other words, a compressed file moved into an uncompressed directory stays compressed, and an uncompressed file moved into a compressed directory stays uncompressed.

If you don't think that is complicated enough, Windows NT enables you to use the MOVE command even when the source and target directories are on two different partitions. In this scenario, it is not possible for a directory on one partition to point to a file on another partition. Instead, Windows NT copies the file to the target partition and deletes the original file. Because the target partition now contains a brand-new file, that file inherits the attributes of its new parent directory.

When you copy a file within or between partitions or you move a file between partitions, therefore, the compression attribute of the new copy is inherited from its new parent directory. When you move a file within a single partition, the attributes on the file remain unchanged.

SHARING DIRECTORIES

Sharing refers to publishing resources on a network for public access. When you share a resource, you make it available to users on other network machines. The Windows NT objects most commonly shared are directories and printers. You learned how to share printers in Chapter 4. This section (and the following subsections) look at how to share directories.

Because shares are computer-specific, and because users cannot modify anything that affects the entire computer, shares are off-limits. This restriction is not a default; granting this capability to users is impossible, as is revoking this capability from administrators and power users.

Even if you are an administrator, you must have at least List permissions to a directory in order to share it. Any user who has locked you out of a share probably does not want you to publish it on the network.

There are three methods for creating shared directories:

◆ Using Explorer or My Computer

◆ Using the command prompt

◆ Using Server Manager

The following sections look at these methods for sharing directories and take a look at two special kinds of shares: hidden shares and administrative shares. You also will get a look at how you can view shared resources and monitor access to them by using the Server Manager and the Control Panel's Server application.

Sharing with Explorer and My Computer

You can share directories in Windows NT in a number of ways. The easiest, and usually the most efficient, is to use Explorer or My Computer.

Right-click on the directory you want to share and choose Sharing from the shortcut menu to open the Sharing tab of the Properties dialog box (see Figure 6.4). You also can reach the Sharing tab by choosing File, Properties and clicking the Sharing tab. Additionally, My Computer enables you to choose Sharing directly from the File menu after you select a directory.

The share name defaults to the name of the directory. You can change it, however; doing so does not affect the actual directory

NOTE

Sharing Is Different on NT Than on Other Operating Systems   If you are familiar with NetWare but not with Windows NT, note that by default no NT resources are available to network users. To be made available, resources must be explicity shared. If you are familiar with Windows for Workgroups or Windows 95 but not with Windows NT, you also should understand that Windows NT users cannot share directories on their computers; only administrators and power users have this privilege.

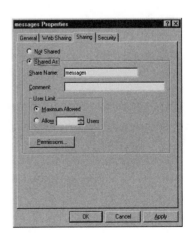

FIGURE 6.4
The Sharing tab of the directory's Properties dialog box.

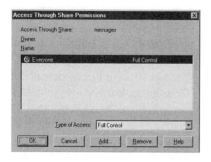

FIGURE 6.5
The Access Through Share Permissions dialog box.

name at all, it just defines the way the directory appears to network users.

Filling in the Comment box is optional. Any comment you enter here becomes a free-text tag line that appears next to the share name to users browsing in Explorer or Network Neighborhood. (Choose View, Details if you want to see the comments.)

Click on the Permissions button to open the Access Through Share Permissions dialog box, from which you can build an Access Control List (ACL) for the share to prevent unauthorized network access (see Figure 6.5) The ACL is a list of people and/or groups for a specific resource, and it indicates what kind of access the people or groups have to that resource. In order to have access to a resource, you must either be explicitly listed in the resource's ACL or have implicit access as a member of a group that is listed.

The share-level permissions are completely independent from the local NTFS permissions. In fact, share-level permissions can even be applied to FAT partitions. Because they apply to the entire share, however, you cannot assign granular file-level permissions unless the partition on which the share resides is NTFS.

The share-level permissions themselves are not that granular. Here are your choices:

◆ *No Access.* Prevents access to the share. Users with No Access to a share can still connect to the share, but nothing appears in File Manager except the message You do not have permission to access this directory.

◆ *Read.* Allows you to display folder and file names, display file content and attributes, run programs, and open folders inside the shared folder.

◆ *Change.* Allows you to create folders and files, change file content, change file attributes, delete files and folders, and do everything the Read permission allows.

◆ *Full Control.* Allows you to change file permissions and do everything the Change permission allows.

As with local NTFS permissions, user and group permissions accumulate, with the exception of No Access, which instantly overrides all other permissions. That means that if a user has a permission of

Read and is in a group that has Change permission, he will have Change permission. However, if a user has a permission of Full Control but is in a group with No Access, she actually has No Access.

If you don't require security, you don't have to touch the share-level permissions. The default permissions grant Full Control to the Everyone group. This means that, by default, everyone who has network connectivity to the machine with the share will be able to exercise Full Control over its contents.

Choose the OK button to implement sharing of the directory. To modify the share configuration, right-click on the directory again and choose Sharing from the shortcut menu.

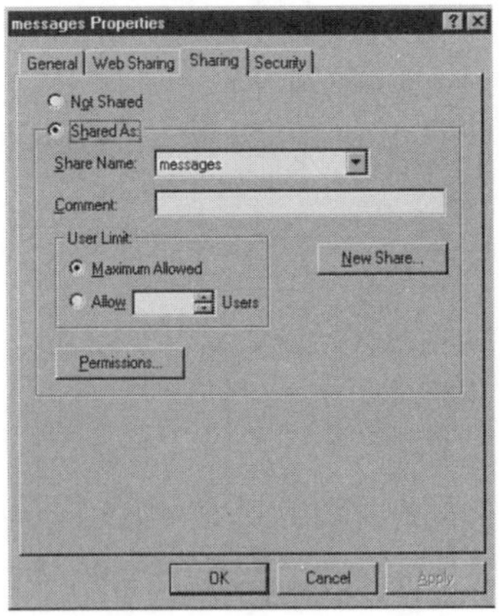

The Sharing tab looks identical to the New Share dialog box, with the exception of the New Share button (see Figure 6.6). Click on the New Share button to share the directory again, with a different name and ACL. This does not remove the original share, it just shares the directory again. In this way, you can share a single directory an unlimited number of times.

FIGURE 6.6
The Sharing tab after sharing has been enabled. Note the New Share button.

Sharing from the Command Prompt

To share from the Windows NT command prompt, use the NET SHARE command, using this syntax:

```
NET SHARE <share_name>=<drive_letter>:<path>
```

For example, to share the C:\PUBLIC directory as Documents, you would use the following command:

```
NET SHARE Documents=C:\PUBLIC
```

To add a comment for browsers, use the /REMARK switch:

```
NET SHARE Documents:=C:\PUBLIC /REMARK:"Public Documents"
```

To set the user limit to the maximum allowed, use the /UNLIMITED switch (although this is the default) as shown here:

```
NET SHARE Documents:=C:\PUBLIC /REMARK:"Public Documents"
/UNLIMITED
```

To set a specific user limit, use the /USERS switch:

```
NET SHARE Documents:=C:\PUBLIC /REMARK:"Public Documents"
/USERS:5
```

To stop a share using the NET SHARE command, use the /DELETE switch:

```
NET SHARE Documents /DELETE
```

Hidden Shares

Regardless of how you created it, you can hide a share by ending the share name with a dollar sign ($) like this:

```
NET SHARE Documents$=C:\Public
```

Users can still connect to these shares, but they must explicitly supply the entire path to do so. And of course, the shares can still be protected using share-level permissions.

Administrative Shares

Every Windows NT–based computer has administrative shares with hard-coded ACLs that grant Full Control to Administrators and No Access to everyone else. Those shares include the following:

◆ *C$ shares the root of the computer's drive C.* If other partitions exist on the drive, those partitions also will have similar shares (but not for CD-ROM or floppy drives). Consequently, administrators can easily connect to other computers on the network.

◆ *ADMIN$ shares the root of the Windows NT installation, regardless of where it may have been installed.* It gives administrators easy access to the operating system directory on any Windows NT–based computer.

You can stop these shares if you want to, but they come back the next time you restart your system. You cannot permanently disable them except through a system policy that disables these shares when the system starts (for more information on system policies, see Chapter 5).

Monitoring and Managing Shares

To see a list of all the shares on the system, open the Server application in the Control Panel. Although you cannot stop sharing a resource from the Server application, you can see a complete list of shared resources, as well as a list of connected users and other server-related items.

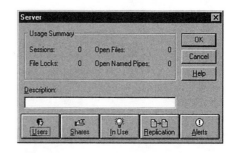

FIGURE 6.7
The Control Panel's Server application.

The Server application (SRVMGR.CPL) is a subset of Windows NT Server's Server Manager application. It is a front end for administering connections to your computer. In the Server dialog box, you can view the Usage Summary for your server (see Figure 6.7).

The Usage Summary tracks the following statistics:

◆ *Sessions.* The number of computers connected to this server.

◆ *Open Files.* The total number of files currently open for access by remote users.

◆ *File Locks.* The total number of file locks placed against this computer by remote users.

◆ *Open Named Pipes.* The total number of named pipes between this computer and connected workstations. (Named pipes are an interprocess communication (IPC) mechanism.)

The Server dialog box also acts as the launch pad for five other server-configuration dialog boxes:

◆ *Users Sessions.* (Click the Users button.) Shows detailed information about current user sessions on your Windows NT-based server.

◆ *Shared Resources.* (Click the Shares button.) Displays detailed information about current shares on your server.

◆ *Open Resources.* (Click the In Use button.) Displays the resources of your computer currently being used by remote users.

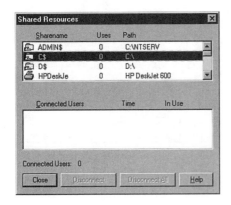

FIGURE 6.8
The Shared Resources dialog box.

◆ *Directory Replication.* (Click on the Replication button.) You can configure the Directory Replicator service in this window.

◆ *Alerts.* (Click on the Alerts button.) Enables an administrator to enter a list of users or workstations to whom messages will be sent in the event of a significant server event.

To view the shared resources on your system, click on the Shares button in the Server application's Server dialog box. The Shared Resources dialog box that appears shows a list of all shares presently configured for your system and the path to each share (see Figure 6.8).

Server Manager, in the Administrative Tools group, offers a similar view of shared resources on the local system and on other network computers as well (see Figure 6.9). Click on a computer icon in the Server Manager main screen to open a dialog box that is similar to that used for the Control Panel's Server application.

In the Server Manager, not only can you view the share information for a remote PC, you can actually create a new shared directory. Select a computer in the Server Manager and choose Computer, Shared Directories. The Shared Directories dialog box appears (see Figure 6.10).

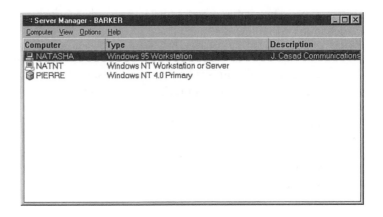

FIGURE 6.9
The Server Manager main screen.

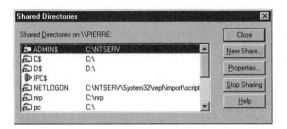

FIGURE 6.10
The Shared Directories dialog box.

The Shared Directories dialog box shows the shared directories for the computer you selected. Click on the New Share button to add a new share. The New Share dialog box that appears asks you to specify a share name, a path, and an optional comment that will appear in descriptions on the share (see Figure 6.11). You can also limit the number of simultaneous users who can access the share. And you can click the Permissions button to specify share-level permissions (as described earlier in this chapter).

Back in the Shared Directories dialog box, the Stop Sharing button enables you to terminate a share. The Properties button opens the Share Properties dialog box, which is similar to the New Share dialog box. See Chapter 3 for a discussion of Server Manager's powerful Directory Replication feature.

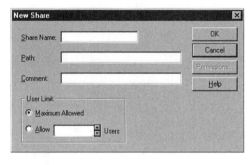

FIGURE 6.11
The New Share dialog box.

SYNCHRONIZING FILES

Windows NT 4, like Windows 95, includes a utility called My Briefcase. My Briefcase helps you synchronize and update files.

My Briefcase is designed to act as a virtual briefcase; you fill it with documents and take it with you when you leave for the office or the airport. Of course, you can copy the documents to a disk without the aid of a high-tech virtual briefcase, but as anyone in business knows, keeping multiple copies of important files poses grave dangers. You might forget which version of the file is current and make changes to the less-current version. Or you might forget about an update to one of the versions and use an older version as the final document.

My Briefcase solves these problems. Assume, for example, that you copy a document to My Briefcase and take it with you on a business trip. When you return, My Briefcase compares the traveling copy with the original, and tells you whether either or both of the files have changed. Then you can choose one of the following options:

◆ *Replace.* Replaces the old version with the changed version. (Or you can tell My Briefcase to replace the changed version with the unchanged version, thereby canceling the changes.)

◆ *Skip.* Skips the update because both versions have changed. (My Briefcase cannot automatically merge the changes when both files have changed, unless the application supports the Briefcase merge feature.)

◆ *Merge.* If the application supports the Briefcase merge feature, My Briefcase merges the changes and updates the files so that both copies get the merged version.

◆ *Delete.* If either the original or the Briefcase copy has been deleted, Briefcase synchronizes the files by deleting the remaining copy.

To open My Briefcase, double-click on the My Briefcase icon located on the desktop. Step by Step 6.2 walks you through some steps involved with using My Briefcase.

STEP BY STEP

6.2 Using My Briefcase

1. Open My Briefcase (see Figure 6.12).

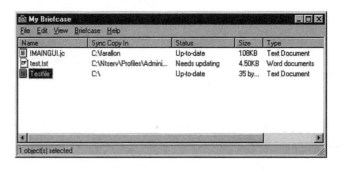

FIGURE 6.12
The My Briefcase main screen.

2. Copy a file or a group of files to My Briefcase using Explorer or My Computer. My Briefcase is designed for drag and drop, so drag a file from Explorer to the My Briefcase window or to the My Briefcase icon. You also can use the Clipboard to copy and paste a file to My Briefcase.

3. Put a disk in your disk drive and drag the My Briefcase icon from the desktop to the disk drive using Explorer or My Computer.

4. Insert the disk into a different computer. (You can use the same computer if you are just doing this as a test.)

5. Open My Briefcase (on the disk), and then open the copy of the file in My Briefcase and make a change to the file. Close the file.

6. In My Briefcase, choose Briefcase, Update All.

7. The Update My Briefcase dialog box appears, asking whether you want to update the unmodified version (see Figure 6.13). Click on the Update button to synchronize the files, or right-click on a file icon to choose a different action from a shortcut menu (see Figure 6.14).

My Briefcase is best known as an aid for users with portable computers, but you also can use My Briefcase to synchronize files on a network.

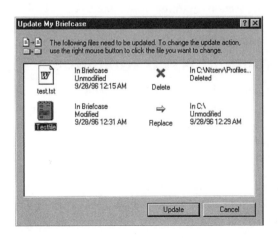

FIGURE 6.13
The Update My Briefcase dialog box.

My Briefcase is part of the user profile for a particular user. This
means that each user can have his or her own briefcase, and that a
user's personal briefcase appears onscreen when he or she logs on.
My Briefcase files are stored in the following directory:

C:\<winnt_root>\Profiles\<username>\Desktop\My Briefcase

WORKING WITH NTFS FILE PERMISSIONS AND SECURITY

The NTFS file system supports a complex arrangement of directory
and file security for which there is no equivalent in the FAT file system.

The following sections examine important aspects of NTFS security.

Ownership of NTFS Resources

Every NTFS file and directory has one account designated as its
owner. The owner of a resource is the only account that has the right
to access a resource, modify its properties, and secure it from outside
access. This feature is available on NTFS partitions and is not available on FAT.

By default, the owner of a resource is the user who created the
resource. Only one user can own a resource at any given time, except
that a user who is a member of the Administrators group cannot be

the sole owner of any resource. Any resource created by an administrator, for example, is co-owned by the entire Administrators group. This is part of a checks-and-balances security model in Windows NT that ensures that an administrator cannot hoard power and resources—yet another reason administrators should not use administrator-level accounts for day-to-day operations. Step by Step 6.3 shows you how to determine who owns a particular resource.

STEP BY STEP

6.3 Identifying the Owner of an NTFS File or Directory

1. Select the file or directory in My Computer or Windows NT Explorer.

2. Choose File, Properties. The Properties dialog box appears.

3. Click on the Security tab (see Figure 6.15).

4. Click on the Ownership button, and the Owner dialog box appears (see Figure 6.16).

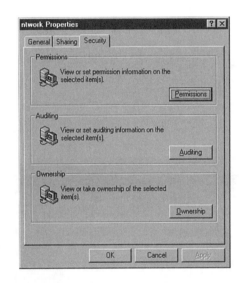

FIGURE 6.15
The Security tab of the file's Properties dialog box.

You can also take ownership away from the current owner by choosing the Take Ownership button in the Owner dialog box. Normally, only administrators can do this: They can take ownership of any resource because they have been granted the "Take Ownership of Files and Directories" user right. You can use User Manager for Domains to revoke the right of administrators to take ownership of files and directories that they did not create or to add another user or group to the list of accounts with the "Take Ownership" right. It is best, however, not to change this right at all; administrators must have this right if the system is to achieve a C2 security rating.

If you are not an administrator, you may still be able to take ownership if the current owner has granted you permission to take ownership. The important concept to grasp for now, however, is that ownership is taken, never given. Ownership involves responsibility, and that responsibility can never be forced on anyone, even by an administrator. Implications to this rule will be discussed shortly.

FIGURE 6.16
The Owner dialog box.

Auditing NTFS Resources

One of the most important aspects of Windows NT security is that system administrators can *audit* access to objects such as directories and files. In other words, you can configure NT to track all attempts (successful or not) to access NTFS resources for various purposes. The record of all access attempts then appear in the Security log of the Event Viewer (see Chapter 9, "Troubleshooting"). By default, file access is not audited; however, Step by Step 6.4 shows you how to enable auditing.

STEP BY STEP

6.4 Configuring Auditing for a File

1. Right-click on an NTFS file in Explorer or My Computer and choose Properties.

2. Click on the Security tab of the File Properties dialog box (refer to Figure 6.15).

3. Click on the Auditing button. The File Auditing dialog box appears (see Figure 6.17). You can audit either successful or failed attempts at any of the actions listed, and you can specify which specific groups or users you want to audit.

4. Click on the Add button to add a group or user to the audit list. Click on the Remove button to delete a group or user from the audit list.

The Directory Auditing dialog box is similar (see Figure 6.18). The procedure for reaching the Directory Auditing dialog box is similar to the procedure for reaching the File Auditing dialog box. Right-click on a directory, choose Properties, choose the Security tab in the Directory Properties dialog box, and then click on the Auditing button. The Directory Auditing dialog box enables you to choose whether the new auditing arrangement you are configuring will replace the auditing on subdirectories or existing files.

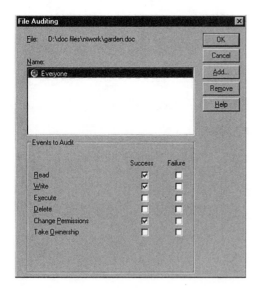

FIGURE 6.17
The File Auditing dialog box.

If you *copy* a file to a directory configured for auditing, the file inherits the directory's auditing configuration. If you *move* a file (dragging a file in Explorer to another directory in the same partition is a move), the file retains its original auditing configuration.

Securing NTFS Resources

The set of permissions on a file or directory is just another attribute (or stream) attached to the file, called an Access Control List (ACL). Each ACL contains a series of Access Control Entries (ACEs), and each Access Control Entry references a specific user or group SID and the type of access granted to or denied that SID. The end of this section explains how Windows NT checks a user's credentials against the Access Control List. First, however, this section reviews how permissions are assigned to the ACL to begin with.

Discretionary Access

Who gets to assign permissions to a resource? The owner of the resource. Who is the owner of the resource? The user who created it. In other words, unlike in other operating systems, security is not the sole domain of the administrator. If you create a file, you—not the administrator—get to secure it. You can, in fact, easily lock administrators out of *your* resources. And that makes sense in many environments.

Picture a typical company network, for example. Along with memos, reports, and routine documents, you might find documents containing salary information, personnel files, and other sensitive data that the administrator and MIS department should not have access to just because they run the network. The users who create these files and work with them are the best ones to judge who should and should not have access. This type of access control, called *discretionary access*, is a hallmark of C2-level security.

Because locking administrators out of files and directories is dangerous, there is a "spare key." An administrator cannot be blocked from taking ownership of a resource, and after the administrator owns the resource, he or she can modify the permissions on the resource so that he or she can access it. Remember, though, that ownership can

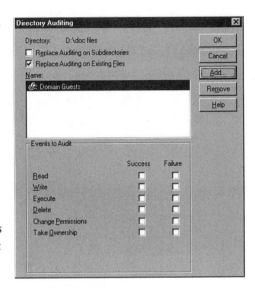

FIGURE 6.18
The Directory Auditing dialog box.

be taken but never given, and that goes for giving back, too. When the administrator owns the resource, he can never return ownership to the original user without that user explicitly taking ownership. And that is how it should be for legitimate situations in which a user might be absent from work when a critical file needs to be accessed. The administrator could get into a sticky situation by accessing files without a legitimate reason.

Permissions Versus User Rights

You might remember that resource permissions are not the same as user rights. User rights are tasks stored with your account information in the Registry, which you can perform on the system as a whole. NTFS permissions are stored with the resource itself, in the ACL property discussed earlier.

It is important to understand the difference between rights and permissions, because that understanding brings light to why the resource permissions assigned to a user cannot be viewed the way trustee assignments in other operating systems (such as Novell NetWare) are viewed. Displaying all the permissions assigned to a user would require searching all the NTFS files and directories on all the NTFS partitions on the workstation and on shared directories of any other workstation or server on the network. It also requires searching for incidences of the user's SID or group SIDs on the ACL of each of those files.

Directory-Level Permissions

Permissions can be placed on both directories and files. When they are, you need to resolve the permissions to figure out the effective permissions for a user.

The owner of a directory can grant a user any of the following permissions:

- ◆ *No Access.* Restricts the user from accessing the directory by any means. The directory appears in the directory tree, but instead of a file list, the user sees the message You do not have permissions to access this directory.

◆ *List.* Restricts the user from accessing the directory, although the user may view the contents list for the directory.

◆ *Read.* Enables the user to read data files and execute program files from the directory but prevents him from making changes of any sort.

◆ *Add.* Prevents the user from reading or even viewing the contents of the directory, but allows him to write files to the directory. If the user writes a file to the directory, he receives the message `You do not have permissions to access this directory`, but he still can save or copy files to it.

◆ *Add & Read.* Gives the user freedom to view and read from the directory and save new files to the directory but does not allow him to modify existing files in any way.

◆ *Change.* Enables the user to view and read from the directory, save new files to the directory, modify and even delete existing files, change attributes on the directory, and even delete the entire directory. (This, by the way, is the most extensive permissions you would ever want to assign anyone.)

◆ *Full Control.* Allows the user to view, read, save, modify, or delete the directory and its contents. In addition, the user can change permissions on the directory and its contents, even if he or she does not own the resource. The user also has permission to take ownership at any time.

Each of these levels of permissions is actually a combination of six basic actions that can be performed against a resource:

Read (R)
Write (W)
Execute (X)
Delete
Change Permissions (P)
Take Ownership (O)

Table 6.3 breaks down these permissions by permission level.

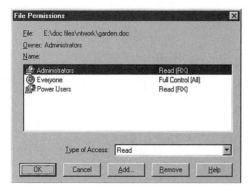

FIGURE 6.19
The File Permissions dialog box.

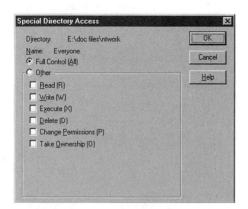

FIGURE 6.20
The Special Directory Access dialog box.

TABLE 6.3

SPECIFIC PERMISSIONS GRANTED BY GENERAL ACCESS LEVELS

Level	Directory Permissions	File Permissions
No Access	None	None
List	RX	Unspecified
Read	RX	RX
Add	WX	Unspecified
Add & Read	RXWD	RX
Change	RXWD	RXWD
Full Control	RXWDPO	RXWDPO

The two custom levels of permissions are Special Directory Access and Special File Access, both of which enable the owner (or any user granted the "P" permission) to custom build an Access Control Entry by using any combination of the six basic actions. Step by Step 6.5 shows you how to create a customized (special) permission for resource access.

STEP BY STEP

6.5 Customizing an Access Control Entry for a Group or User

1. Click on the Permissions button on the Security tab of the File Properties or Directory Properties dialog box.

2. In the File Permissions dialog box that appears, select the group or user for whom you want to establish customized permissions (see Figure 6.19).

3. Choose Special Directory Access from the Type of Access drop-down list.

4. Choose the appropriate permissions in the Special Directory Access dialog box that appears (see Figure 6.20).

When an NTFS partition is created, the default permissions are set so that the Everyone group has Full Control. You may want to change this at the root directory level, but see the section "Special Considerations for the Boot and System Partitions" at the end of this chapter before you do so.

When a new directory or file is created on an NTFS partition, the resource inherits the permissions of its parent directory (the same way it inherits the compression attribute; see the section "NTFS File Compression," earlier in this chapter.)

File-Level Permissions

Although permissions for files are not as varied as they are for directories, NTFS can store permissions for files also. The owner of a file can grant a user the following permissions:

- ◆ *No Access.* The user cannot access this file at all, even though the filename and basic attributes still appear in File Manager.

- ◆ *Read.* The user can read this file if it is a data file or execute it if it is a program file, but she cannot modify it in any way.

- ◆ *Change.* The user can read, execute, modify, or delete this file.

- ◆ *Full Control.* The user can read, execute, write to, or delete this file and can change permissions on it, as well as take ownership away from the current owner.

Refer to Table 6.3 for the breakdown of file permissions based on general access levels.

As with directory permissions, a Special Access level allows anyone who has the capability to change permissions to custom build an Access Control Entry for a user or group.

Setting Permissions

To set permissions on a file or directory, first select the resource in Explorer or My Computer, and then choose File, Properties. Click on the Permissions button on the Security tab of the File Properties dialog box to open the File Permissions dialog box (refer to Figure 6.19).

To remove a user or group from the ACL, select the user and click the Remove button. To add a user or group to the ACL, click the Add button. Clicking the Add button opens the Add Users and Groups dialog box, which includes a list of all the groups in your account database (see Figure 6.21).

If you want to grant access to a specific user, click on the Members button. Otherwise, only the group names are displayed. Choose the users and groups you want to add to the ACL—individually or collectively—and click on the Add button to enter their names in the Add Names list box at the bottom of the dialog box. Don't try to set their access levels here unless all of these accounts are going to be granted the same access level (this type of access setting is all or nothing). When you click on the OK button, you get another chance to modify the permission level for each individual account on the ACL.

Setting permissions for a directory brings up a slightly different dialog box (see Figure 6.22).

In the Directory Permissions dialog box, you can enable either Replace Permissions on Subdirectories or Replace Permissions on Existing Files (the default). If you enable the Replace Permissions on Existing Files check box, the permissions that apply to the directory also apply to the files within the directory, but not to subdirectories or files within subdirectories.

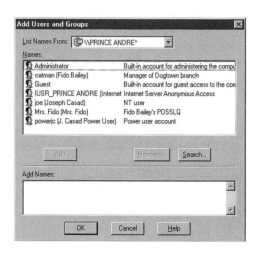

FIGURE 6.21
The Add Users and Groups dialog box.

Enabling only the Replace Permissions on Subdirectories check box modifies the permissions on all directories in the directory tree but not on any files within those directories, even in the top-level directory.

Selecting both check boxes applies these permissions to the entire directory tree and its contents. Enabling neither check box changes the permissions on the top-level directory only.

Local Groups

When you're working with user rights, assigning rights to user and built-in groups usually suffices. When assigning resource permissions, however, adding individual users may be too time-consuming,

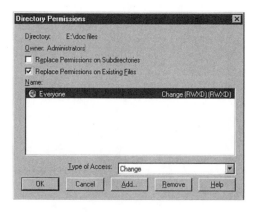

FIGURE 6.22
The Directory Permissions dialog box.

and adding built-in groups may be too inclusive. Imagine having a directory that contains meeting minutes for a project on which you are working. You would like to grant permissions to the people on the project team, but the team is more than thirty people strong. Assigning permissions to everybody would take a long time, and assigning permissions to the Users group would give access to too many people.

In such a case, you would use *local groups*, a separate level of user management in Windows NT. Local groups can be created by any user for any purpose (Headquarters, Marketing, Vice Presidents, Portland, Engineering), and once they're created, they can be reused repeatedly. By creating a local group called MyProject and including all the project team members, you need to grant only a single set of permissions for each meeting report.

Local Groups Versus Built-In Groups

A *local group* is a group used to assign rights or permissions to a local system and local resources. Local groups are similar to built-in groups in that both can contain many users to address a single purpose. In fact, technically, the built-in groups in Windows NT Workstation are local groups.

Local and built-in groups also have similar structures. Both can contain local users, domain users, and global groups, as well as users and global groups from trusted domains. The only type of account that cannot be placed inside a local group is another local group.

The difference between local and built-in groups lies in their intended purposes. The built-in groups are predefined and preassigned to specific rights and capabilities for system management. They are not intended for use in managing access to resources. Local groups are impractical for managing the system but are ideal for assigning permissions to files and directories.

The only other difference between the two types of groups is that built-in groups are permanent members of a computer's account database, whereas local groups can be created and deleted at will.

Defining Local Groups

As with any type of account, you create local groups in User Manager for Domains, as demonstrated in Step by Step 6.6.

STEP BY STEP

6.6 Creating a Local Group in User Manager for Domains

1. Select the user accounts you want to include in the local group (remember to hold down the Ctrl key to select multiple accounts).

2. Choose User, New Local Group to open the New Local Group dialog box (see Figure 6.23).

3. Enter a name (required) and a description (optional) for the group. The users you selected before issuing the New Local Group command should already be listed in the Members list.

4. If you want to add other users, choose the Add button. The Add Users and Groups dialog box appears (refer to Figure 6.21).

   Notice that only users and global groups are displayed, not local groups. Again, local groups cannot be nested, so User Manager does not even tempt you.

5. Choose the users (individual or collective) that you want to add, and click on the Add button to enter their names in the Add Names list at the bottom of the dialog box.

6. Click OK when you are ready to return to the New Local Group dialog box.

7. If you accidentally choose a user who does not belong in the group, click on the Remove button to delete the account from the group. Otherwise, click OK to add the local group to the account database.

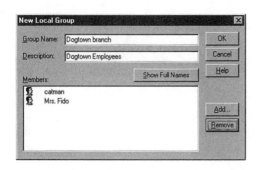

FIGURE 6.23
The New Local Group dialog box.

Managing Local Groups

After you create your local groups, you can manage them much as you manage your user accounts. You should, however, be aware of the following idiosyncrasies concerning local groups:

◆ You cannot rename a local group after it has been created. Groups are referenced throughout the system by their Security Identifiers (SIDs), just as users are. Most likely, Microsoft's programmers just never got around to adding this feature to the code. You can copy a local group and give the new group a new name (in fact, you would have to), but that really is not the same as renaming because none of the permissions granted to the original group would apply to the new copy. There just is not a solution for this one.

◆ You cannot disable a local group after it has been created. If a group were disabled, some implications would be unclear. For example, whether members of that group should be able to log on and whether the group's permissions and rights should apply while it is disabled would be thorny issues. If you must temporarily disable the effects of a group on the system, remove all the users from the group. Do not delete the group and re-create it later, or your new group will have a new SID and a brand new set of default rights and permissions. All the old properties will be irrevocably lost.

◆ If you do want to delete a local group, select the group in User Manager and choose Delete from the User menu. Be aware that you are deleting only the group itself, not the users within the group. The effect stops here.

◆ You can add or remove members from the group by selecting the group in User Manager and choosing User, Properties.

How User and Group Permissions Interact

At this point, you have probably realized that users are likely to be in many different groups. Abigail's user account, for example, may be a member of the Users group, but also the Marketing group, the Department Managers group, the Philadelphia group, and the

Project X group. Each of these user and group accounts is likely to be granted permissions to resources at one time or another, and it is quite likely that more than one of the accounts might occasionally appear on the same Access Control List. In such scenarios, how should the permissions granted to both a user's user account and his group accounts be resolved?

Quite simply, user and group permissions are cumulative: Neither takes precedence over the other. If the Marketing group has Read access to a file, and the Department Managers group has Change access to the same file, Abigail (a member of both groups) has both—or in other words, she has Change access, because Change already includes the R and X permissions that Read incorporates.

The one exception to this rule relates to the No Access permission. No Access overrides all other permissions granted to a user or the user's groups, regardless of where the No Access was assigned. If Abigail was individually granted Read access to a file but the Marketing group was granted No Access, for example, Abigail would not be able to access the file. You cannot—and this cannot be emphasized enough—override a No Access permission.

This might seem worrisome at first. Consider a situation in which Beth is thinking about leaving the company and is updating her résumé. She doesn't want anyone else to have access to this file, so she assigns the following permissions to the file:

Beth: Full Control

Everyone: No Access

You have probably guessed the result: Beth can't access her résumé because she is a member of the Everyone group, and the No Access she assigned to Everyone overrides the Full Control she assigned to her own account. Can Beth somehow retain sole access to her résumé, or does she need to create a group called Everyone But Me and assign it No Access?

Yes, there is an easy way. It involves making the ACL read as follows:

Beth: Full Control

You don't have to specify No Access for a user or group to exclude them from an ACL. The rule in Windows NT is that if you are not on the list, you don't get in. So why does Windows NT include the

No Access command at all if it isn't even necessary to exclude access? Because No Access is intended as a "negator" to remove permissions from a user or group that may already have been implicitly added to the ACL through membership in another group. Beth may not care if her coworkers in the Marketing department know she's thinking about leaving the company, for example, but she would rather her supervisor remain ignorant. She can set the following permissions on the ACL for her résumé file:

Beth: Full Control

Marketing: Read

Abigail: No Access

Because Abigail is a member of the Marketing group, she would have received Read access to Beth's résumé if she had not been excluded by a direct No Access.

How Directory and File Permissions Interact

When you have permissions on both directories and files, as is the case on an NTFS partition, things get just a bit more complicated. Fortunately, you can resolve this situation easily, but a few odd circumstances might surround the situation.

Simply put, file permissions override directory permissions. Even if Abigail had Full Control over the directory that contained Beth's résumé, she could not read Beth's résumé if her account had been granted No Access to that file. Likewise, it is possible to grant a user Read access to a directory and yet still grant Full Control over a single file within that directory.

This can lead to some odd scenarios. Suppose, for example, that Sam doesn't want anyone to view the contents of his private directory. So he assigns the directory this ACL permission:

Sam: Full Control

If Beth tries to view this directory, she gets the message You do not have permission to access this directory. Yet Sam may still want to occasionally grant Beth access to one or two of his files. One day, he grants Beth Read access to a document in his private directory. Beth can read that file, but how can she access it? She can't view the directory contents in Explorer, and she can't view the directory contents by executing the File, Open command in an application either. In order to access the file, Beth must type the full path to the file, from the application in which she wants to view it.

File Delete Child

Consider another odd scenario. Sam decides to grant Everyone Full Control to his private directory, and just apply Read permissions to Everyone for the individual files within the directory. Sam knows that although users might be able to copy and save files in his directory, they can't change the files that are already present because those files have only Read permissions. Sam also knows that no one else can change permissions on the existing files because those files have only Read permissions. However, Sam also thinks that no one can delete his existing files because they only have Read permissions. On this last count, he is wrong.

In addition to the six basic permissions (RXWDPO) granted with Full Control, there is a seventh implicit permission called File Delete Child (FDC). FDC is included for POSIX compatibility, and it grants a user who has Full Control over a directory the capability to delete a top-level file within that directory, even if that user does not have delete permissions to the file itself! Only top-level files can be deleted, not subdirectories or files within subdirectories.

There is a workaround, but you must grant Special Directory Access before you can use it. If you grant Special Directory Access and choose all six permissions instead of just granting Full Control to a directory, the user to whom you grant this level of access won't have the FDC permission. It looks like you are just assigning the equivalent of Full Control, but you are really assigning Full Control minus File Delete Child. By the way, don't waste time searching for File Delete Child in the Explorer interface; it is not there. It's an implicit permission granted only when Full Control is granted over a directory.

An even better workaround is to never grant anyone Full Control over anything, unless you grant it to yourself as the owner. After all, you probably don't want anyone else to have the power to change permissions on your files and lock you out. And you certainly don't want someone to have the capability to take ownership of your files at the same time so that you can't even change permissions back to what they were. A good rule of thumb is to never grant anyone any permissions higher than Change. That is high enough because a user with Change access can delete the resource itself.

Special Considerations for the Boot and System Partitions

When you install Windows NT on an NTFS partition, it is tempting to prevent necessary files from being deleted or overwritten in an attempt to exclude users from accessing the Windows NT installation directory tree. If you examine the Access Control List for that directory, however, you won't see the customary Everyone: Full Control that you normally find on NTFS resources.

The critical entry on the ACL is the SYSTEM: Full Control ACE. Do not, under any circumstances, remove this ACE from the list or modify it. If you do, Windows NT crashes, and you cannot restart the operating system.

If this does happen, don't panic. You can use the Emergency Repair Disk to strip the permissions from the Windows NT installation directory tree. See Chapter 9 for more information on this procedure.

How NT Controls Access to an NTFS Resource

How does Windows NT make the decision whether to grant access to an NTFS resource?

As you may recall, when a user logs on to a Windows NT–based computer, the security accounts manager generates an access token for the user's current session. The access token contains, among other things, the user's user SID and group SIDs.

When a user requests access to an NTFS resource, the Security Reference Monitor (a component of the security subsystem) examines the SIDs contained in the user's access token. The Security

Reference Monitor then parses the Access Control List looking for references to any of the SIDs contained in the user's access token. The search continues until one of the following conditions is met:

◆ The Security Reference Monitor encounters a Deny (the internal representation of No Access) for any SID in the user's access token. At this point, the search stops and access is denied.

◆ The Security Reference Monitor encounters an Allow for any SID in the user's access token. If the Allow specifies the type of access the user seeks, the search stops and access is granted. If the Allow specifies some but not all the permissions requested, the search continues until all permissions are accumulated, at which point access is granted. If the Allow specifies none of the permissions the user requests, the search continues.

◆ The Security Reference Monitor reaches the end of the Access Control List without accumulating all the requested permissions. Access is denied. No partial access is granted.

What is interesting about this process is that it works only if Denies are placed at the top of the ACL. If any Allow precedes a Deny on the ACL, a user can gain access even if No Access has been granted to one of the SIDs in the user's access token because the search stops after the requested permissions have been accumulated and before the No Access is encountered.

Luckily, Windows NT does place all Denies before all Allows, at least in all its built-in applications and interfaces. It is possible, however, for a programmer to write a program so that Denies can be placed anywhere within an ACL (in order to provide maximum compatibility and flexibility in porting existing custom applications to Windows NT). You should not have anything to worry about with any professionally sold Windows NT application, but you definitely want to make certain that any programmer hired for custom development knows how structure affects Access Control Lists.

Handles

After the Security Reference Monitor has approved your access to the file resource, the system creates a *handle* to that resource. (Remember that no user-mode process in Windows NT can access a resource directly.) The handle is entered in the object table of the process that requested the access. The object table contains the list of handles to all resources that process is using, as well as the permissions granted through each handle. When transactions are performed against an open resource, the security subsystem checks the permissions in the object table instead of parsing the entire ACL again, a process that both provides a slight performance boost and guarantees that a user's permissions over a file will not refresh until the file is closed and reopened (which generates a new handle).

Consider a situation in which you might grant a user Change permissions to a file. The user opens the file that contains the requested and granted Change permissions, and while the file is in use, you decide to change the user's permissions to Read. Although the ACL changes immediately, the security subsystem is not checking the ACL anymore because the user has an open handle to the file. The user must close and reopen the file before the new permissions can take effect.

Access Tokens Don't Refresh

As is the case with handles, access tokens are generated only when a user logs on. Any changes to a user's rights and group memberships, for example, do not take effect until the user logs off and back on again. Therefore, you cannot prevent a user who is logged on as a member of the Marketing group from accessing a resource just by removing him from the group. His access token still reflects Marketing membership until the next time he logs on.

CASE STUDY: KING AND VAUGHAN ROADSHOWS

ESSENCE OF THE CASE

Here are the essential elements of this case:

- Access over the network to shared information

- Security on data to ensure that only the owner can access it

- The need for a central location that everyone can read from and write to

SCENARIO

King and Vaughan Roadshows, a booking agency specializing in blues bands, recently installed an NT Network in their Chicago headquarters. Their network consists of a single LAN with 30 Windows 95 users connected to a PDC. When the network was initially installed, each user stored her files on her local hard drive. However, a couple of hard-disk failures caused the company to reassess the prudence of such a configuration. They currently do regular backups on their PDC and want to use the existing backup routine to ensure that personal data is backed up as well. There is some concern, however, about the security of the information if it is held in a central spot. The users want assurance that they will be able to access their information from any computer on the LAN but that no one else will be able to access their data. They also want a central place where anyone can place data so that this data can be accessed by anyone else.

ANALYSIS

There is tension in this case between ease of access and security. The more access you allow to a certain resource, the less secure that resource is. If you consider each element in isolation, it might be easy to come up with solutions, but they will not provide what is required or solve the problems in an efficient manner. For example, it would be tempting to simply create a changed folder for each user on the PDC. Unfortunately, this is a labor-intensive solution because a large number of shares would have to be created. In addition,

CASE STUDY: KING AND VAUGHAN ROADSHOWS

such a solution misses security in one circumstance: local access from the server. On the other hand, NTFS security will provide file- and directory-level security but will not allow sharing. As a result, it will only be effective when users access data locally on the PDC.

The final result must, therefore, be a combination of share-level permissions and local NTFS permissions. If a single data folder is shared—leaving the default Everyone group with Full Control—you can successfully provide access to the data. To control that access, you can implement local security on the folders

assigned to each user. Because the combination of share-level and NTFS security results in the most restrictive being the effective security, the only person who gets access to a particular folder is the one who has been granted access through NTFS security.

To finish the solution, one folder within the data folder can be called Public, and it can retain the default NTFS permission of Everyone: Full Control to allow everyone to both read from and write to it.

The following table summarizes the solution to this study.

A SUMMARY OF THE REQUIREMENTS AND SOLUTIONS IN THIS CASE STUDY

Requirement	Solution Provided By
Access to information over the network	Share a folder on the PDC and place each user's home folder in it.
Security on the data	Ensure the partition with the data on it is formatted NTFS (or converted from FAT). Ensure that permissions are applied to each home folder to allow only the owner to access it; everyone else is denied access.
Central place for all to read and write	Share a folder called Public; give the Everyone group Full Control at the share level and give the Everyone group Full Control locally.

CHAPTER SUMMARY

KEY TERMS

Before taking the exam, make sure you are familiar with the definitions and concepts behind each of the following key terms. Appendix A is a glossary of terms for quick reference purposes.

- UNC
- persistent connection
- filename alias
- CONVERT.EXE
- NTFS compression
- COMPACT.EXE
- sharing
- share permissions
- hidden share
- administrative share
- Take Ownership
- NTFS permissions
- access token

In this chapter you looked specifically at managing access to disk resources. This included learning about the file systems supported under NT and the characteristics of those file systems. You saw the implications of moving and copying files and how long filenames are processed by NT in a FAT environment. In addition, you saw how to convert a FAT partition to NTFS in the case where additional file system efficiency or security is required on your NT system. Finally, you looked at share-level permissions and local NTFS permissions and learned how the two interact to provide a complete resource access security model.

APPLY YOUR LEARNING

Exercises

6.1 Copying and Moving Files

This exercise shows you how to test the differences between copying and moving files on an NTFS partition.

Estimated Time: 10 minutes

1. Start Windows NT Explorer.

2. Right-click any directory on an NTFS partition.

3. Choose File, New, Folder.

4. Create a new subdirectory called **Compressed**.

5. Right-click on the subdirectory named Compressed and choose Properties. On the General tab of the Directory Properties dialog box, select the Compress attribute's check box.

6. Right-click on a file in another directory on the NTFS partition and select Properties.

7. Select the file and choose Edit, Copy. Then choose Edit, Paste. A file called "Copy of *<filename>*" will be created.

8. Select this new file and choose File, Rename.

9. Change the filename to **Copy**. Then create another copy of the original file and change the name of the new file to **Move**.

10. Examine the Compress attribute for the Copy and Move files. Make certain the files are not compressed. (Right-click on each file and choose Properties to view the Compress attribute.)

11. Select the file called Copy and choose Edit, Copy.

12. Double-click on the Compressed directory and choose Edit, Paste. A file called Copy appears in the Compressed subdirectory.

13. Drag the file called Move to the Compressed directory. (Dragging the file within the same partition is a move.)

14. Check the Compress attributes of the Copy and Move files in the Compressed directory. The Copy file is now compressed. (It inherited the Compress attribute from the parent directory.) The Move file retains its uncompressed state.

6.2 Converting a FAT Partition to NTFS

This exercise walks you through the process of converting a drive to NTFS. This assumes that you have a FAT partition available. If you do not, create one from free space if you can and format it as FAT.

Estimated Time: 10 minutes

1. Open My Computer and right-click the drive you want to convert. From the shortcut menu, choose Properties. On the General tab of the Properties dialog box, you should see that the current file system is formatted as FAT.

2. Close the Properties dialog box.

3. Open the Start menu and choose Run.

4. In the Run dialog box, type `convert x hr: / fs:ntfs` (where *x* is the letter of the drive you want to convert).

5. If you're prompted to reboot your system, do so. (If that happens, the conversion will not occur until the reboot begins.)

6. Open My Computer and right-click the drive you just converted. From the shortcut menu, choose Properties. On the General tab of the Properties dialog box, you should see that the current file system is formatted as NTFS.

APPLY YOUR LEARNING

Review Questions

1. What effects do the following actions have on file attributes?

   - Copying a file from one partition to another

   - Copying a file from one folder to another on the same partition

   - Moving a file from one partition to another

   - Moving a file from one folder to another on the same partition

2. What characteristic of NTFS permissions make them inherently more secure than share-level permissions?

3. If both share-level and NTFS permissions are applied to the same folder, what is the resulting effective permission?

4. What program can be used to change a partition from FAT to NTFS without data loss? And what is the syntax for the command if you were to apply it to the C: drive?

5. What NT feature allows an NT administrator to access any drive defined on a server over the network even if no shares have been created by any user?

Exam Questions

1. You need to copy files from an NT-based computer to a Windows 95 computer. However, because you don't have a direct network connection, your only option is to copy the files to a disk. The NT-based computer does not have any FAT partitions. Can you copy the file?

   A. Yes, if you format the disk as NTFS and convert it to the FAT file system by using the CONVERT.EXE utility.

   B. No. This cannot be done because Windows 95 doesn't read NTFS-formatted floppies.

   C. Yes. Copy the files to a FAT-formatted disk, and the Windows 95 computer can read the files.

   D. Yes, but first you must restart the NT-based computer in MS-DOS and copy the files over from DOS to the disk.

2. A user calls you in a panic. He says that he cannot create any files on his C: drive. You probe further and find out that the user is trying to create a file on the root of his C: drive. You also discover that his C: drive is formatted as FAT. He executes DIR and tells you that the system is reporting only 235 files in the root directory. What could be causing this problem, and what should the user do to fix it?

   A. This particular problem has no fix. The problem is with Windows NT, and the only thing he can do is to install a new hard drive and save the files on the new drive.

   B. No problem here. Just tell the user to save the files to disk and then use File Manager to copy them over to the C: drive.

   C. The user's hard drive must be full, and the only solution is to purchase a new hard drive.

   D. The user must be using long filenames, and he probably has used all the directory entries in the root of the drive. The solution is to move some of those files to subdirectories.

APPLY YOUR LEARNING

3. A user calls you and tells you that she is getting a syntax error while trying to copy a file from her FAT partition to a disk. She has booted the computer under MS-DOS and is using the DOS COPY command. The file that she is trying to copy has the file name C:\DOCS\THISISAFILE.TXT. Therefore, the command that the user is entering is COPY C:\DOCS\THISISAFILE.TXT A:. Which of the following command line switches should she be using with the COPY command?

   A. /N

   B. /B

   C. /L

   D. -P

4. You want to further secure your system by storing all your files on an NTFS partition. How can you do this without losing all the data currently stored on your FAT partition?

   A. You cannot.

   B. Using Disk Administrator, format the FAT partition as NTFS.

   C. Back up the current FAT partition and delete it in Disk Administrator. Then re-create the partition and restore the files from the backup.

   D. Use the CONVERT.EXE utility to convert the partition to NTFS without losing the data already on the drive.

5. Recently, you have noticed that your server is running low on disk space. You do not have the budget to go out and purchase a new drive.

What can you do as a temporary fix to give your users more disk space?

   A. Nothing.

   B. Reformat the drives and restore the data from a backup to minimize disk fragmentation and reduce the number of wasted clusters on the drive.

   C. Convert your partitions to NTFS and then implement disk compression.

   D. Convert your partitions to FAT and then install the DriveSpace utility to compress the drive.

6. You can use which of the following pairs of utilities to compress the files on your NTFS partition?

   A. COMPRESS.EXE and File Manager

   B. COMPACT.EXE and Windows NT Explorer

   C. COMPRESS.EXE and Windows NT Explorer

   D. DriveSpace and Windows NT Explorer

7. You copy a file from a folder that has its compression attribute checked to a new folder on the same drive. What attributes will the destination file have?

   A. The destination file will be compressed.

   B. The destination file will not be compressed.

   C. You cannot copy a compressed file without first uncompressing it.

   D. The destination file will inherit the compression attributes of its new parent directory.

APPLY YOUR LEARNING

8. You have been promoted to manager of a new project in another part of the country. Your replacement has asked you to turn over the current project files to him. Which of the following best describes the process for turning over ownership of files and directories?

   A. Email the files to him as attachments and have him save the files in a directory of his choice.

   B. Have the system administrator make the new user the owner of the files and directories.

   C. Give the new user the Take Ownership permission and then have him take ownership of the files and directories.

   D. It is not possible to change the ownership of files and directories.

9. Which of the following statements best describes what happens when ownership of files and directories is changed?

   A. The user taking ownership of the files or directories becomes the current owner of the files and directories.

   B. The groups to which the user who's taking ownership belongs become the current owners of the files and directories.

   C. The user taking ownership of the files and directories becomes the current owner of the files and directories, as do any groups to which the user belongs.

   D. The user taking ownership of the files and directories becomes the current owner of the files and directories, except when the user is a

member of the Administrators group. In that case, the Administrators group becomes the owner of the files and directories.

10. Which of the following describes the default file and directory permissions on an NTFS partition?

    A. Everyone has Read access.

    B. Everyone has No Access.

    C. Everyone has Full Control.

    D. Administrators have Full Control.

11. A user belongs to both the Sales group and the Marketing group. The user has individual Read permission to a directory named DIR1. The Sales group has the Change permission to DIR1, and the Marketing group is not listed in the ACL of DIR1. What are the user's effective rights to DIR1?

    A. The user has Read and Change permissions to DIR1.

    B. The user has no access to DIR1 because the Marketing group is not listed in the ACL of the directory.

    C. The user has only Read access because the user gets only what is assigned to him directly.

    D. The user has Full Control because Read and Change added together equal Full Control.

12. A user belongs to both the Sales group and the Marketing group. The user has individual Read permission to a directory named DIR1. The Sales group has Change permission to DIR1, and the Marketing group has No Access to DIR1. What are the user's effective rights to DIR1?

APPLY YOUR LEARNING

A. The user has Read and Change permissions to DIR1.

B. The user has no permissions to DIR1 because the Marketing group has no permissions to the directory.

C. The user has only Read permission because the user gets only what is assigned to him directly.

D. The user has no access because the Marketing group has No Access.

13. Which one of the following statements best describes what happens to file permissions when files are copied and moved on NTFS partitions?

A. When you copy a file on an NTFS partition, the file inherits the permissions of the destination directory. When you move a file on an NTFS partition, the file retains the permissions it had originally.

B. When you copy a file on an NTFS partition, the file retains the permissions it had originally. When you move a file on an NTFS partition, the file inherits the permissions of the parent directory.

C. When you move or copy a file on an NTFS partition, it always retains its original permissions.

D. When you move or copy a file on an NTFS partition, it always inherits the permissions of the parent directory.

14. A user calls you and states that when he ran a disk diagnostic utility on his FAT partition, it reported errors relating to lost chains and

clusters. Which of the following is the most likely problem?

A. The user is running a disk utility that does not recognize the existence of long filenames and is, therefore, incorrectly reporting errors.

B. The user is running a disk utility that does not recognize the existence of NT; its use should be discontinued immediately.

C. The user should restart the computer in DOS mode and then run the utility.

D. The user should contact the manufacturer of the utility and request a version that is compatible with NT.

Answers to Review Questions

1. The rule of thumb is that attributes are inherited from the destination except when a file is moved from one place to another on the same partition. Therefore, the answers are: inherit from the destination; inherit from the destination; inherit from the destination; keep the same attributes. For more information, see the section "Copying and Moving Files."

2. NTFS permissions are inherently more secure than share-level permissions because they apply both over the network and locally to files and folders (whereas share-level permissions apply only to network access). For more information, see the section "Working with NTFS File Permissions and Security."

3. The combination of NTFS permissions and share permissions results in an effective permission,

APPLY YOUR LEARNING

which is the most restrictive of the two. For more information, see the section "How Directory and File Permissions Interact."

4. The program used to change a FAT partition to NTFS is called CONVERT.EXE, and the syntax for converting the C: drive would be CONVERT C: /fs:ntfs. For more information, see the section "Converting a FAT Partition to NTFS."

5. The feature that allows administrators to access drives on an NT Server despite the lack of user-defined shares is called administrative shares. These shares are hidden, are only accessible by administrators, and use a share name made up of the drive letter followed by a dollar sign (such as C$ for the C: drive). For more information, see the section "Administrative Shares."

Answers to Exam Questions

1. **C.** Floppy disks must always be formatted as FAT. The fact that the source of the files is an NTFS partition is irrelevant because NT will take care of reading the NTFS files and copying them onto the FAT disk. The FAT-formatted disk is readable by Windows 95, and therefore, the files you copy onto it are also readable. For more information, see the section "Converting a FAT Partition to NTFS."

2. **D.** On a FAT partition, long filenames generate not only one primary entry in the FAT table but also a secondary entry for every 13 characters in the filename. Because the root of a FAT partition has a hard-coded maximum of 512 entries, a user could easily hit this barrier with the combination

of long filenames and 235 entries. The user should create some subfolders on the root and copy some of his files into them. For more information, see the section "Long Filenames."

3. **A.** The /N switch uses the short filename alias instead of the long filename that DOS does not like. For more information, see the section "Long Filenames."

4. **D.** CONVERT.EXE enables you to convert a FAT partition to NTFS without losing data. For more information, see the section "Converting a FAT Partition to NTFS."

5. **C.** The NTFS compression attribute allows most files to be compressed without a noticeable loss of performance. For more information, see the section "NTFS Compression."

6. **B.** Two methods are available for compressing files. The first is to set the compression attribute from the GUI interface in Windows Explorer. The second is to use the command line utility COMPACT.EXE. For more information, see the section "NTFS Compression."

7. **D.** In all copy situations, the file being copied inherits the attributes of the destination folder. For more information, see the section "Copying and Moving Files."

8. **C.** You cannot give another user ownership of a file. However, if you are the owner of the file or an administrator, you can give another user the ability to take ownership of a file. If you do this for all the appropriate files, the new manager will be able to take ownership of those files. For more information, see the section "Working with NTFS File Permissions and Security."

APPLY YOUR LEARNING

9. **D.** In all cases except when an administrator takes ownership of a file, the person taking ownership becomes the new owner. When an administrator takes ownership of a file, the entire Administrators group becomes the owner. For more information, see the section "Working with NTFS File Permissions and Security."

10. **C.** Contrary to what may make security sense, the default access to a new NTFS partition is Full Control for the Everyone group. For more information, see the section "Sharing Directories."

11. **A.** Permissions to a resource are cumulative and are not affected by membership in a group that is absent from the ACL. Therefore, the user has the combined permission of Read and Change (which is effectively Change because it includes Read). For more information, see the section "Working with NTFS File Permissions and Security."

12. **D.** Permissions to a resource are cumulative except when a user or a group that a user is member of has No Access explicitly listed in the ACL. In that case, the user has No Access to the directory. For more information, see "Working with NTFS File Permissions and Security."

13. **A.** Copying files always results in inheritance of the attributes of the destination folder. When a file is moved from one folder to another on the same partition, the file retains its original attributes. For more information, see the section "Copying and Moving Files."

14. **A.** Some third-party disk utilities report errors when they encounter the long filenames produced by NT. When that happens, the user should be instructed to try a utility that's known to function properly under NT to determine if the errors are correct or if they are the result of a confused application. For more information, see the section "Long Filenames."

Suggested Readings and Resources

The following are some recommended readings for further research:

1. Microsoft Official Curriculum course 803: *Administering Microsoft Windows NT 4.0*
   - Module 5: Securing Network Resources with Shared Folder Permissions
   - Module 6: Securing Network Resources with NTFS Permissions
   - Module 9: Auditing Resources and Events

2. Microsoft Official Curriculum course 922: *Supporting Microsoft Windows NT 4.0 Core Technologies*
   - Module 5: Managing File Systems

3. *MS Windows NT Server 4.0 Resource Guide* (Microsoft Press; Also available in Windows NT Server 4.0 Resource Kit)
   - Chapter 3: Disk Management Basics
   - Chapter 7: Disk, File System, and Backup Utilities

4. Microsoft TechNet CD-ROM
   - *Concepts and Planning: MS Windows NT Server 4.0*
   - Chapter 4: Managing Shared Resources and Resource Security

5. Web sites
   - www.microsoft.com/ntserver
   - www.microsoft.com/train_cert
   - www.prometric.com/testingcandidates/ assessment/chosetest.html (take online assessment tests)

Microsoft provides the following objectives for "Connectivity":

Configure Windows NT Server for interoperability with NetWare servers by using various tools. Tools include Gateway Services for NetWare and Migration Tool for NetWare.

▶ This objective is necessary because someone certified in the use of Windows NT Server technology must understand the tools available for interoperating with Novell NetWare and must know how to configure them.

Install and configure Remote Access Service (RAS). Configuration options include configuring RAS communications, configuring RAS protocols, configuring RAS security, and configuring Dial-Up Networking clients

▶ This objective is necessary because someone certified in the use of Windows NT Server technology must understand how to configure an NT Server for RAS dialin. This includes the initial configuration and security considerations.

CHAPTER 7

Connectivity

STUDY STRATEGIES

▶ Microsoft places a lot of emphasis on connectivity topics in their NT Server exam—so much so, in fact, that your knowledge of the topics in this chapter can make or break your ability to pass. If you know the material you probably will pass; if you do not know this material, you probably will not pass.

▶ Microsoft expects your knowledge of NetWare interoperability to be thorough. If you can explain all the steps involved in getting a Microsoft NT client connected to NetWare resources (both directly and through a gateway), you've almost got it. However, you also need to know all the services that are provided for the purposes of connectivity and understand the services, when they are used, and for what. In order to get the best picture of how these services work (especially GSNW), you really need a NetWare server to practice with. That will enable you to get some hands-on exposure to the configuration of the NetWare server and the services on NT. This will help reinforce the concepts of account and group creation, as well as those regarding the configuration of GSNW.

▶ As for RAS, again, doing is the best way to study. You will be asked configuration questions couched in terms that require you to know both the server configuration and the client configuration. Practice with a NULL modem cable if you do not have real modem access between two computers. Then you'll have a chance to see how RAS works. Be careful to observe the configuration of authentication because you may be asked questions about the compatibility of authentication methods.

INTRODUCTION

Microsoft believes Windows NT is the best network operating system available, but Microsoft is aware of a strong NetWare presence. One of the driving forces behind the rapid acceptance of Windows NT is the ease with which it integrates into a NetWare environment.

Microsoft has gone to considerable trouble to make Windows NT compatible with Novell NetWare. Windows NT's NetWare-compatibility features include the NWLink network protocol, which is a clone of Novell's IPX/SPX, and a number of special services designed to help Windows NT and NetWare networks link up smoothly. This chapter describes the services you'll need to interoperate with NetWare. NetWare connectivity is extremely important to Microsoft, and you can bet they'll make it important to you when you sit down with the Windows NT Server exam.

Windows NT Remote Access Service (RAS) also offers some important connectivity features. This chapter will describe Windows NT RAS, show you how to install and configure RAS, and show you how to configure Dial-Up Networking.

INTEROPERATING WITH NETWARE

Configure Windows NT Server for interoperability with NetWare servers by using various tools. Tools include Gateway Services for NetWare and Migration Tool for NetWare.

Chapter 3 described how to install and configure NWLink, Microsoft's version of the once-secret IPX/SPX protocol suite. It is important to remember that NWLink by itself does not necessarily provide connectivity with NetWare resources. Microsoft provides a set of services that help Windows NT and NetWare systems interoperate. This section outlines the services and components you'll need to use to interoperate with NetWare for various purposes. You'll learn about these NetWare-related Windows NT services and tools:

◆ Gateway Services for NetWare (GSNW)

◆ Client Services for NetWare (CSNW)

◆ File and Print Services for NetWare (FPNW)

◆ Directory Service Manager for NetWare (DSMN)

◆ Migration Tool for NetWare

You then get a quick look at the components required for NT-based and NetWare-based client/server applications. This section finishes with a quick summary of NetWare connectivity issues.

Gateway Services for NetWare (GSNW)

Gateway Services for NetWare (GSNW) is available only with Windows NT Server. GSNW performs the following functions:

◆ Enables Windows NT Server systems to access NetWare file and print resources directly. (GSNW includes the functionality of Windows NT Workstation's Client Services for NetWare service, CSNW, described later in this chapter.)

◆ Enables a Windows NT Server to act as a gateway to NetWare resources. Non-NetWare clients on a Windows NT network then can access NetWare resources through the gateway as if they were accessing Windows NT resources (see Figure 7.1).

A GSNW gateway can provide Windows NT networks with convenient access to NetWare resources, but it isn't designed to serve as a high-volume solution for a busy network. Because all Windows NT clients must reach the NetWare server through a single connection, performance diminishes considerably with increased traffic. GSNW is ideal for occasional NetWare access, not for large-scale routing.

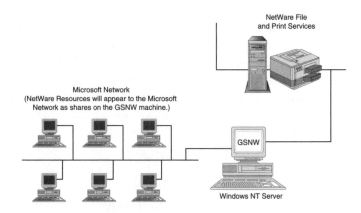

FIGURE 7.1
GSNW enables a Windows NT Server to act as a gateway to NetWare resources.

Network clients with operating systems that use Server Message Block (SMB) (for example, Windows NT, Windows 95, and Windows for Workgroups) can access a share through a GSNW gateway. GSNW supports both NDS-based and bindery-based NetWare systems.

GSNW is a network service. You install it using the Services tab of the Control Panel Network application (see Figure 7.2).

Before installing GSNW, you must remove any NetWare redirectors presently on your system (such as Novell's NetWare services for Windows NT) and reboot. The procedure for installing GSNW is described in Step by Step 7.1.

NOTE

NDS Is NetWare 4.x, Bindery Is NetWare 3.x NetWare Directory Service (NDS) is a distributed database of network resources primarily associated with NetWare 4.x systems. Bindery-based NetWare networks are primarily associated with NetWare 3.x.

STEP BY STEP

7.1 Installing GSNW

1. Choose Start, Settings, Control Panel. Double-click on the Control Panel's Network application icon.

2. In the Network dialog box, select the Services tab. Click the Add button to open the Select Network Services dialog box.

3. Select Gateway (and Client) Services for NetWare in the Network Service list. Then click OK. If NWLink has not already been installed on your server, it will also be installed at this time.

4. Windows NT prompts you for the location of the files (typically, the installation CD-ROM).

5. Windows NT asks if you want to restart your system. You must restart the system to enable the new service.

6. Upon restarting, you will be prompted to fill in specification for Novell login. At this time, you're not going to configure this because you are going to enable the gateway to log in to the NetWare server. Click the Cancel button, and then click Yes when asked to confirm your intentions.

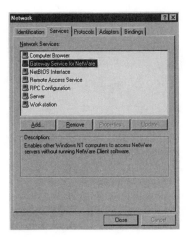

FIGURE 7.2
The Services tab of the Network dialog box.

The basic premise behind the operation of GSNW is that an account created on a NetWare server is configured to access resources, and that access is then transferred to the gateway installed on an NT Server. What this means is that you not only have to prepare the NT Server by installing GSNW and configuring shares, you also have to configure the NetWare server to allow the gateway account to access resources (see Step by Step 7.2).

> **NOTE**
>
> **Both Share Access and NetWare Access Must Be Sufficient**   It is important that the accounts created on the NetWare server have enough access to the NetWare resources required by the Microsoft users. When you give access to the NetWare resources through the gateway, the most access you can grant to the Microsoft users is the maximum access that the NetWare account has been given. Although you can grant any Microsoft users less access than the gateway's account has, you can never grant more. For ease of administration, it is therefore recommended that you grant the gateway account Full Control of the NetWare resources and then control the access from the NT Server.

STEP BY STEP

7.2 Preparing a NetWare Server to Be Accessed by an NT Server

1. Create an account on the NetWare server and give it access to the resources the Microsoft users will need.

2. Create a group on the NetWare server called NTGATEWAY.

3. Put the account created in step 1 into the group created in step 2.

Having prepared the NT Server and the NetWare server, you can now enable the gateway to actually access NetWare resources (see Step by Step 7.3).

STEP BY STEP

7.3 Enabling GSNW to Act as a Gateway to NetWare Resources

1. Double-click the GSNW icon in the Control Panel. The Gateway Service for NetWare dialog box appears (see Figure 7.3). The Preferred Server, Default Tree and Context, Print Options, and Login Script Options frames are discussed in the following section. These options actually configure the server as a NetWare client.

2. To configure Windows NT to act as a gateway, click the Gateway button. The Configure Gateway dialog box appears (see Figure 7.4).

FIGURE 7.3
The Gateway Service for NetWare dialog box.

3. Select the Enable Gateway check box. In the Gateway Account text box, enter the name of the account you created on the NetWare server. Below the account name, enter the password for the account, and then retype the password in the Confirm Password text box.

4. Click the Add button to configure a share to the NetWare server (see Figure 7.5).

5. In the New Share dialog box, enter the name of the share as it is to appear on the NT Server, the UNC path of the share on the NetWare server, a text comment (if desired), the drive letter that is to be mapped from the Gateway server to the NetWare server, and the maximum number of concurrent connections to be allowed. Click the OK button to complete the share setup. At this point, the share will appear in the lower section of the Configure Gateway dialog box (see Figure 7.6).

6. Click the Permissions button to set the NT permissions for the resource. As with any NT share, the default permission is to give the Everyone group Full Control. Don't forget, however, that you cannot grant your NT users any more access than the Gateway has been granted to the NetWare resource.

7. Repeat step 6 for each share you want to which you want to grant access through your gateway.

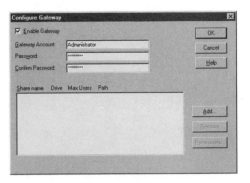

FIGURE 7.4
The Configure Gateway dialog box.

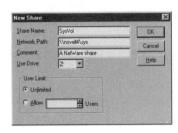

FIGURE 7.5
The New Share dialog box enables you to configure a share to a NetWare server.

GSNW essentially enables you to create a Windows NT share for a resource on a NetWare server. Microsoft network machines that use Server Message Block (SMB) (for example, Windows NT, Windows 95, and Windows for Workgroups), can then access the share even if they don't have NetWare client software. NetWare directories and volumes presently shared through a gateway appear in the Share Name list at the bottom of the Configure Gateway dialog box.

The Remove button in the Configure Gateway dialog box enables you to remove a gateway share. The Permissions button lets you set permissions for a share. (For more information on permissions, see Chapter 6.)

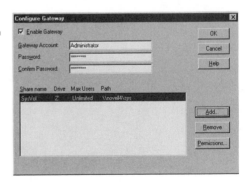

FIGURE 7.6
All the defined shares appear in the Share Name section of the Configure Gateway dialog box.

Client Services for NetWare (CSNW) and the GSNW Client

Client Services for NetWare (CSNW) enables a Windows NT Workstation to access file and print services on a NetWare server (see Figure 7.7). CSNW is incorporated into Windows NT Server's GSNW (described in the preceding section). GSNW and CSNW support both NDS-based and bindery-based NetWare servers.

Both GSNW and CSNW support Novell's NetWare Core Protocol (NCP) and Large Internet Protocol (LIP).

CSNW, like GSNW, is a network service. You install it using the Services tab of the Control Panel's Network application (refer to Figure 7.2). If you're running Windows NT Server, CSNW functions are installed automatically when you install GSNW.

To enable your Windows NT Server computer to act as a NetWare client, install GSNW (as described in the preceding section) and restart your system.

The first time you log on after you install CSNW or GSNW, Windows NT prompts you to enter a preferred server or tree/context (in place of a server for NetWare 4.x) and attempts to validate your credentials for the NetWare network.

The Select Preferred Server for NetWare dialog box shows the name of the user attempting to log on and a drop-down list of available NetWare servers. As the username parameter implies, this is a per-user configuration parameter. The selected server is stored in HKEY_CURRENT_USER, not HKEY_LOCAL_MACHINE.

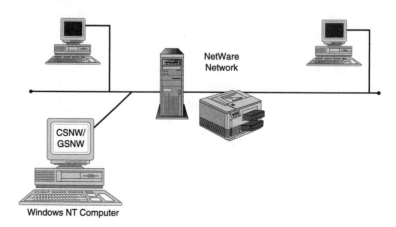

FIGURE 7.7
CSNW, which is incorporated in GSNW, enables a Windows NT computer to access file and print services as a client on a NetWare network.

Choose <None> in the Select Preferred Server for NetWare dialog box if you don't want to have a preferred server authenticate your logon request. Choosing the Cancel button just defers the decision until the next time you log on.

After you select a preferred server, Windows NT always tries to have that server authenticate the user. If the server is unavailable, the user is prompted for a new preferred server. A user can change his or her preferred server at any time via the new CSNW icon in Control Panel (which was added during installation of CSNW).

SYNCHRONIZING NT ACCOUNT AND NOVELL ACCOUNT PASSWORDS

When Windows NT attempts to authenticate a user against the preferred server, the Windows NT-based computer passes the current username and password to the NetWare server. If both the server and the Windows NT-based computer contain the same username/password combination for that user, the user is authenticated immediately. If the preferred server cannot find a match, the user is prompted for a new username and password for the NetWare server.

At first, this is an easy problem to prevent; simply create identical accounts and passwords on each computer. CSNW does not synchronize NetWare passwords with Windows NT passwords, however. So as time goes on and Windows NT users change their passwords, the only way users can keep their passwords in sync is to use the Novell SETPASS command to change their NetWare passwords each time they change their Windows NT passwords. This requires some user education on the part of the administrator and good practice on the part of the users.

Double-click the GSNW icon in Control Panel to open the Gateway Service for NetWare dialog box (refer to Figure 7.3). From this dialog box, you select a preferred server and a default tree and context for the NetWare network. You also can set the following printing options from the Gateway Services for NetWare dialog box:

◆ Add Form Feed completely ejects the last page from the printer when a job has completed.

◆ Notify When Printed causes a pop-up dialog box to appear on the user's screen when the job has been printed successfully.

◆ Print Banner prints a separator page before each job. The page includes the username of the person who sent the job to the printer as well as the date and time the job was submitted.

If you find it necessary or desirable to run a script at logon, you can also choose to run a NetWare logon script by selecting the appropriate check box.

Connecting to NetWare Servers

CSNW (and the client portion of GSNW) is a redirector implemented as a file system driver as is the traditional Windows NT redirector (RDR). As such, it is seamlessly integrated into the Windows NT environment. To connect to a NetWare server's directories, you use Explorer or Network Neighborhood.

To connect to a NetWare server's printers, use the Add Printer Wizard in the Printers folder. In the first wizard screen, select Network Printer Server. A screen similar to Network Neighborhood then appears, in which you can locate the printer on the appropriate server. Alternatively, you can use the traditional Windows NT NET USE command to connect to NetWare servers.

When you install GSNW, it becomes the default network provider. To change the default back to Microsoft Windows Network, click the Network Access Order button on the Services tab of the Control Panel's Network application (this button appears only when you have multiple network providers installed). Clicking the Network Access Order button invokes the Network Access Order dialog box (see Figure 7.8).

The default provider is listed at the top of the Network Access Order dialog box. You can expand any network provider's servers simply by double-clicking on the provider's entry in Network Neighborhood.

When you double-click on a NetWare server, you will notice the final difference between the two types of networks. On a Windows NT Server, directories must be explicitly shared in order for users to access them. On NetWare servers, however, all directories are public. When you expand a volume on a NetWare server, all the directories and subdirectories in that volume are accessible. If you continue to double-click down the hierarchy of directories, the tree expands further.

FIGURE 7.8
The Network Access Order dialog box.

NetWare users are authenticated as soon as the server itself is selected. If the server's directories are accessible, the user has been authenticated. If the user's Windows NT password and NetWare password don't match, an Enter Network Credentials dialog box appears, giving the user a chance to enter the correct NetWare password.

Command Prompt

You can browse the NetWare Network from the command prompt using the NET VIEW command almost as easily as you can browse the Microsoft Windows Network. You just need one extra switch:

```
NET VIEW /NETWORK:NW
```

This command returns a list of available NetWare servers.

To connect to a NetWare server's resource, you can use the NET USE command with no additional parameters:

```
NET USE F: \\NWServer\Sys\Public
```

The preceding example would map drive F to the SYS\PUBLIC directory on NWServer. By design, the syntax is identical, whether you're connecting to a Windows NT Server or a NetWare server (which underscores the word "Universal" in the "Universal Naming Convention" [/UNC/] syntax).

You can use the NET USE command as the equivalent of the NetWare CAPTURE command, too:

```
NET USE LPT1: \\NWServer\Queue
```

Compatibility Issues

Although NetWare commands now can be accessed from the command prompt, some executables cannot function unless a drive is mapped. For example, although you can access SYSCON by typing \\NWSERVER\SYS\PUBLIC\SYSCON at the command prompt, the program terminates with an error message unless you map a drive so that supporting files can also be found.

NOTE

You Won't See Workgroups or Domains   NetWare servers don't appear under the umbrella of a workgroup or domain. That's intentional. After all, workgroups and domains are Microsoft network concepts.

You can run most NetWare utilities (including SYSCON, PCON-SOLE, and SETPASS) from a Windows NT Server running GSNW or from a Workstation running CSNW. However, you might encounter some specific application compatibility problems, in which case you should consult the documentation for GSNW or CSNW.

File and Print Services for NetWare (FPNW)

File and Print Services for NetWare (FPNW) is an add-on utility that enables NetWare clients to access Windows NT file, print, and application services (see Figure 7.9). It does not come with NT Server; rather, it must be purchased as a separate utility.

FPNW doesn't require any additional software (such as Server Message Block support) on the NetWare client. In effect, FPNW enables the Windows NT Server to act like a NetWare 3.12 Server. The NetWare client can access the FPNW machine as it would a NetWare server.

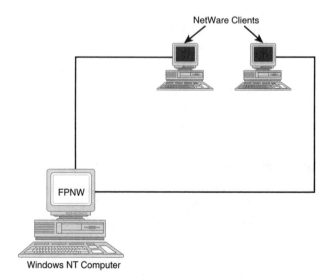

FIGURE 7.9
The add-on utility FPNW lets NetWare clients access resources on a Windows NT system.

Directory Service Manager for NetWare (DSMN)

Directory Service Manager for NetWare (DSMN) is an add-on utility that integrates NetWare and Windows NT user and group account information (see Figure 7.10). Like FPNW, it is not part of the standard NT Server software and must be purchased as a separate utility.

DSMN copies NetWare user and group information to the Windows NT computer. You can use DSMN to manage NetWare accounts from Windows NT. DSMN also can merge server-based NetWare accounts into a single account database, which the Windows NT computer can then propagate back to the NetWare servers. This enables a single network logon for server-based NetWare accounts.

DSMN allows all network accounts (including NetWare accounts) to be managed from User Manager for Domains (see Chapter 5).

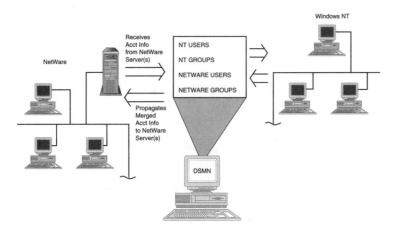

FIGURE 7.10
DSMN integrates NetWare and Windows NT user and group accounts.

Migration Tool for NetWare

Microsoft is so eager for NetWare users to migrate to Windows NT that it developed a tool to automate the migration process. The Migration Tool for NetWare transfers file and directory information and user and group account information from a NetWare server to a Windows NT domain controller. The Migration Tool for NetWare also preserves logon scripts and directory and file effective rights. If you want, you can even specify which accounts, files, or directories you want to migrate. Migration Tool for NetWare cannot preserve the original NetWare password, but it enables users to set a new password from within the tool.

The Migration Tool for NetWare can migrate NetWare resources to the domain controller on which it is running, or it can execute from a separate NT Server or Workstation and migrate the NetWare resources to a domain controller elsewhere on the network (see Figure 7.11). In order to run the Migration Tool for NetWare remotely, you must copy the following files to the workstation from a server's systemroot\system32 folder: NWCONV.EXE, NWCONV.HLP, LOGVIEW.EXE, and LOGVIEW.HLP. In addition, NWLink and Gateway Services for NetWare must be running both on the computer running Migration Tool for NetWare and on the domain controller receiving the migration.

To run the Migration Tool for NetWare, choose Start, Run and type **nwconv** in the Run dialog box.

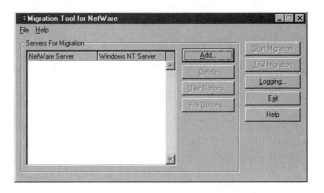

FIGURE 7.11
The Migration Tool for NetWare dialog box.

The Migration Tool for NetWare offers a number of options for transferring file and account information. Always migrate files and directories to an NTFS partition if possible because NTFS file and directory permissions provide an equivalent to the trustee rights specified for these resources in the NetWare environment.

Server and Client/Server Applications

A NetWare client that is equipped with Named Pipes, Windows Sockets, or IPX for NetBIOS can access a server-based application (such as Microsoft SQL Server) that is running on a Windows NT computer as long as the Windows NT computer has the NWLink protocol installed.

A Windows NT computer using NWLink can access a client/server application on a NetWare server without any of the connectivity services described in this chapter.

Exam Tips

The following list outlines facts you learned in this section and will need to memorize for the exam.

- The NWLink protocol provides compatibility between NT and Novell NetWare IPX/SPX networks.

- A Windows NT Workstation computer running CSNW and the NWLink protocol or a Windows NT Server computer running GSNW and the NWLink protocol can connect to file and print services on a NetWare server.

- A Windows NT computer using the NWLink protocol can connect to client/server applications on a NetWare server (without additional NetWare-connectivity services).

- Any Microsoft network client that uses Server Message Block (for example, Windows NT, Windows 95, Windows for Workgroups, or MS-DOS client 3.0) can access NetWare resources through a NetWare gateway on a Windows NT Server computer that is running GSNW. The NetWare resources will appear to the Microsoft network client as Windows NT resources.

- A Windows NT Server system running the add-on utility DSMN can effectively integrate NetWare Server and Windows NT domain account information by copying NetWare account information to Windows NT and propagating the merged information back to the Windows NT Server system. This allows a single network login (across all servers) for NetWare accounts and management of all accounts from User Manager for Domains.

- A Windows NT computer running NWLink, GSNW, and the Migration Tool for NetWare can transfer user and group accounts, directories, files, and login scripts from NetWare servers to a Windows NT domain controller.

- A NetWare client running IPX can access a Windows NT Server system that is running the add-on utility FPNW.

- A NetWare client that supports Named Pipes, Windows Sockets, or IPX with NetBIOS can access an NWLink-enabled Windows NT computer running a server-based application such as Microsoft SQL Server.

CONFIGURING REMOTE ACCESS SERVICE (RAS)

Install and configure Remote Access Service (RAS). Configuration options include configuring RAS communications, configuring RAS protocols, configuring RAS security, and configuring Dial-Up Networking clients.

A second connectivity issue that the NT Server exam focuses on is remote access to a network through an NT Server configured with the Remote Access Service (RAS).

Windows NT's Remote Access Service (RAS) extends the power of Windows NT networking to anywhere you can find a phone line. Using RAS, a Windows NT computer can connect to a remote network via a dial-up connection and fully participate in the network as a network client. RAS also enables your Windows NT computer to receive dial-up connections from remote computers.

As a RAS *server*, an NT Server supports the PPP line protocol, as well as NetBEUI, TCP/IP, and IPX network protocols. Because so many Internet users access their service providers using a phone line, RAS often serves as an Internet interface. NT Server is configured to allow 256 simultaneous RAS clients to connect to it (whereas NT Workstation allows for only one incoming connection).

As a RAS *client*, an NT Server can connect to a server using SLIP or PPP line protocols, as well as NetBEUI, TCP/IP, and IPX network protocols.

The Dial-Up Networking application (located in the Accessories program group) lets you create phonebook entries, which are pre-configured dial-up connections to specific sites. The Telephony application in the Control Panel enables you to preconfigure dialing properties for different dialing locations.

RAS can connect to a remote computer using any of the following media:

◆ *Public Switched Telephone Network (PSTN)*. (This is also known as the phone company.) RAS can connect using a modem through an ordinary phone line or through a dedicated line that uses a technology such as ADSL.

◆ *X.25*. Computers access this packet-switched network via a Packet Assembler Disassembler (PAD) device. X.25 supports dial-up or direct connections.

◆ *Null modem cable*. This cable connects two computers directly, enabling the computers to communicate using their modems (instead of network adapter cards).

◆ *ISDN*. This digital line provides faster communication and more bandwidth than a normal phone line does. A computer must have an ISDN Terminal Adapter to access an ISDN line.

◆ *Cable modem*. This fledgling technology uses the fiber optic cable of a cable-TV service provider to provide fast and dedicated Internet access.

Windows NT 4 also includes a new feature called Multilink protocol. Using Multilink protocol, a Windows NT computer can form a RAS connection using more than one physical pathway. One Multilink connection, for example, can use two modems at once, or one modem line and one ISDN line, or two ISDN channels to form a single logical link. By using multiple pathways for one connection, Multilink protocol can greatly increase bandwidth. Of course, both the client and the server must have access to more than one physical pathway; for example, both could have two modems connected to two phone lines.

RAS Security

Like almost everything else in Windows NT, RAS is designed for security. Here are some of RAS's security features:

◆ *Auditing.* RAS can leave an audit trail, enabling you to see who logged on when, and what authentication they provided.

◆ *Callback security.* You can enable RAS server to use callback (hang up all incoming calls and call the caller back), and you can limit callback numbers to prearranged sites that you know are safe. This causes problems, however, if you have Multilink protocol enabled because you can configure only one callback number, which makes the Multilink protocol configuration useless.

◆ *Encryption.* RAS can encrypt logon information using PAP, CHAP, or MS-CHAP, or it can encrypt all data crossing the connection.

◆ *Security hosts.* In case Windows NT isn't safe enough, you can add an extra dose of security by using a *third-party intermediary security host*—a computer that stands between the RAS client and the RAS server and requires an extra round of authentication.

◆ *PPTP filtering.* You can tell Windows NT to filter out all packets except ultra-safe PPTP packets (described later in this chapter in the section, "PPTP").

RAS Line Protocols

RAS supports the following line protocols:

◆ SLIP (only as a client)

◆ PPP

The following sections describe those protocols.

SLIP

Serial Line Internet Protocol (SLIP) is a standard protocol for serial line connections over TCP/IP networks. SLIP is relatively old for the computer age (it was developed in 1984), and although it hasn't "timed out" yet, it does lack some of the features that are available in PPP.

Each node in a SLIP connection must have a static IP address; that is, you can't use nifty Windows NT features such as DHCP and WINS. Unlike PPP, SLIP does not support NetBEUI or IPX; you must use TCP/IP with SLIP. Also, SLIP cannot encrypt logon information.

A RAS client running Windows NT can connect to a SLIP host; however, NT 4.0 does not support SLIP services from a RAS server.

PPP

Point-to-Point Protocol (PPP) was originally conceived as a deluxe version of SLIP. Like SLIP, PPP is an industry standard for point-to-point communications. But PPP offers several advantages over SLIP. Most notably, PPP isn't limited to TCP/IP; PPP also supports IPX, NetBEUI, and several other network protocols, such as AppleTalk and DECnet.

Because PPP supports so many protocols, it allows much more flexibility in configuring network communications. Windows NT automatically binds RAS to TCP/IP, NetBEUI, and IPX if those protocols are installed at the same time as RAS.

Another advantage of PPP is that it supports encrypted passwords.

PPTP

Point-to-Point Tunneling Protocol (PPTP) is related to PPP, but it is different enough—and important enough—to deserve its own section. PPTP lets you transmit PPP packets over a TCP/IP network securely. Because the Internet is a TCP/IP network, PPTP enables highly private network links over the otherwise highly public Internet. PPTP connections are encrypted, making them nearly impenetrable to virtual voyeurs.

In fact, PPTP is part of an emerging technology called Virtual Private Networks (VPNs). A VPN provides corporate networks with the same (or close to the same) security over the Internet that they would have over a direct connection.

Another exciting advantage of PPTP (and another reason that it fits nicely into the scheme of the virtual private network) is that PPTP doesn't discriminate among protocols. PPTP is an encapsulation scheme that allows you to transmit packets of any PPP-supported protocol (NetBEUI, IPX, and so on) within a PPTP packet. In this way, you get the effect of transmitting non-TCP/IP protocols over the Internet. A NetBEUI packet is encapsulated and sent over the Internet in a TCP/IP format, and then, at its destination, it is released into the LAN that you are communicating with.

Because PPTP provides intranet privacy over the open Internet, it can significantly reduce costs in some situations. Networks that once would have depended on extravagant direct connections now can hook up via a local Internet service provider.

Table 7.1 summarizes the RAS line protocols and their features.

TABLE 7.1

RAS LINE PROTOCOLS AND FEATURES

Feature	SLIP	PPP	PPTP
Supports NT as server	No	Yes	Yes
Supports NT as client	No	Yes	Yes
Passes TCP/IP	Yes	Yes	Yes
Passes NetBEUI	Yes	Yes	Yes
Passes NWLink	No	Yes	Yes

Feature	*SLIP*	*PPP*	*PPTP*
Supports DHCP over RAS	No	Yes	No
Requires PPP or LAN connection	No	No	Yes
Supports VPNs	No	No	Yes
Supports password encryption	No	Yes	Yes
Supports transmission encryption	No	No	Yes

Routing with RAS

Windows NT RAS can perform some interesting routing functions. These functions are likely to make their way into the Windows NT Server exam, either in the Connectivity section or as part of the protocols objective in the Planning section.

RAS comes with a NetBIOS gateway. A RAS client using the NetBEUI protocol can connect to a RAS server and, using the NetBIOS gateway on the RAS server, can gain access to the remote LAN beyond the gateway regardless of what protocol the LAN is using (see Figure 7.12).

RAS also can act as a TCP/IP or IPX router, and RAS is capable of serving as a Service Advertising Protocol (SAP) agent. (*SAP* is a NetWare protocol that lets servers advertise their services to the network.)

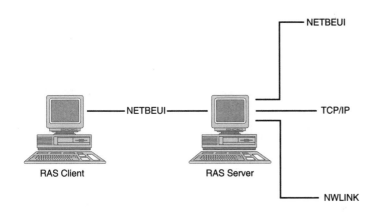

FIGURE 7.12
RAS can act as a NetBIOS gateway, connecting NetBEUI clients with networks using other protocols.

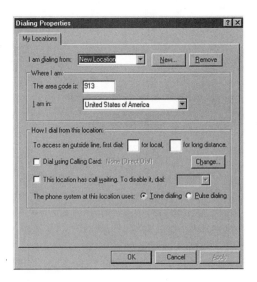

FIGURE 7.13
The Dialing Properties dialog box.

The Telephony API

The Telephony Application Program Interface (TAPI) provides a standard interface with telephony applications. (*Telephony applications* are applications such as a network fax service or an online answering machine that enable a computer to interact with telephone services.) TAPI oversees communication between the computer and the phone system, including initiating, answering, and ending calls. In effect, TAPI is a device driver for the phone system.

Windows NT's basic TAPI settings are set up in the Dialing Properties dialog box shown in Figure 7.13. The Dialing Properties dialog box maintains location and area code settings, as well as calling card settings and a setting for the dialing type (tone or pulse). The first time you run a TAPI-aware application, you have a chance to set up dialing properties. You can also reach the Dialing Properties dialog box directly in several ways, including through the Control Panel's Telephony application and Modems application.

Installing and Configuring RAS

RAS is a network service and, like other network services, is installed and removed via the Services tab of the Control Panel's Network application. In order for a Windows NT machine to act as either a RAS server or a RAS client, the RAS service must be installed (see Step by Step 7.4).

STEP BY STEP

7.4 Installing the RAS Service

1. In the Control Panel, double-click the Network application icon.

2. In the Network dialog box that appears, click the Services tab, and then click Add. The Select Network Service dialog box appears.

3. In the Select Network Service dialog box, choose Remote Access Service from the Network Service list, and then click OK (see Figure 7.14). Windows NT prompts you for

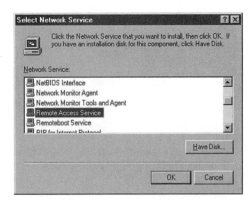

FIGURE 7.14
The Select Network Service dialog box.

the path to the Windows NT installation CD-ROM. Supply that information.

4. Next, Windows NT prompts you for the name of a RAS capable device and an associated communications port (see Figure 7.15). A modem installed on your system typically appears as a default value. If you do not have a modem installed on your system, you will be prompted to install a modem at this time. Click OK to accept the modem, or click the down arrow to choose another RAS capable device on your system.

    You also can install a new modem or an X.25 PAD by using the Install Modem button or the Install X25 Pad button.

5. The Remote Access Setup dialog box appears (see Figure 7.16). Click the Configure button to specify whether to use the port for dial-out connections, dial-in connections, or both. The Port Usage options shown in Figure 7.17 apply only to the port. In other words, you could configure COM1 for Dial Out Only and COM2 for Receive Calls Only.

    In the Remote Access Setup dialog box, you also can add or remove a port entry from the list. The Clone button lets you copy a port configuration.

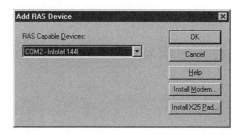

FIGURE 7.15
Selecting a RAS capable device.

FIGURE 7.16
The Remote Access Setup dialog box.

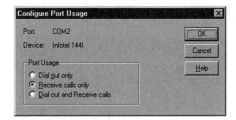

FIGURE 7.17
The Configure Port Usage dialog box.

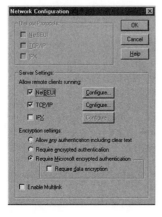

FIGURE 7.18
The Network Configuration dialog box.

6. Click the Network button in the Remote Access Setup dialog box to specify the network protocols for your Remote Access Service to support (see Figure 7.18). The Dial Out Protocols options in the upper portion of the Network Configuration dialog box appear only if you configure the port to dial out. Select one or more server protocols and choose an encryption setting for incoming connections.

You also can enable Multilink protocol. Multilink allows one logical connection to use several physical pathways. However, Multilink will not function if you enable callback security.

7. After you define the RAS settings to your satisfaction, click OK.

8. The Services tab of the Network application appears in the foreground, and you should see Remote Access Service in the list of services. Click the Close button.

9. Windows NT asks whether you want to restart your computer. Choose Yes.

Notice in Figure 7.18 that a Configure button follows each of the Server Settings protocol options. Each Configure button opens a dialog box that lets you specify configuration options for that particular protocol. The following list describes those dialog boxes:

◆ The RAS Server NetBEUI Configuration dialog box lets you specify whether the incoming caller will have access to the entire network or only to the RAS server.

By confining a caller's access to the RAS server, you improve security because the caller can access only one computer, but you reduce functionality because the caller can't access information on other machines.

◆ The RAS Server TCP/IP Configuration dialog box lets you define how the RAS server assigns IP addresses to dial-up clients (see Figure 7.19). You can use DHCP to assign client addresses, or you can configure RAS to assign IP addresses from a static address pool. If you choose to use a static address

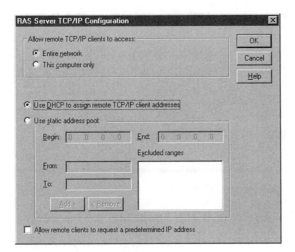

FIGURE 7.19
The RAS Server TCP/IP Configuration dialog box.

pool, enter the beginning and ending addresses in the range. This range must include at least two addresses because one is always given to the server while the other is given to the client dialing in. To exclude a range of addresses within the address pool, enter the beginning and ending addresses in the range you're excluding in the From and To boxes, and then click on the Add button. The excluded range appears in the Excluded Ranges box.

The RAS Server TCP/IP Configuration dialog box also lets you specify whether a client can access the entire network or only the RAS server. By confining a caller's access to the RAS server, you improve security because the caller can access only one computer, but you reduce functionality because the caller can't access information on other machines.

◆ The RAS Server IPX Configuration dialog box lets you specify how the RAS server assigns IPX network numbers (see Figure 7.20).

You also can specify whether a client can access the entire network or only the RAS server. By confining a caller's access to the RAS server, you improve security because the caller can access only one computer, but you reduce functionality because the caller can't access information on other machines.

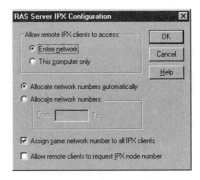

FIGURE 7.20
The RAS Server IPX Configuration dialog box.

Configuring NT Users for RAS

Even when RAS has been configured on your NT Server, by default, users still are not allowed to use Dial-Up Networking. This is because, for security considerations, you must specifically enable Dial-Up Networking for each NT user who is to connect to your server. You set up the necessary configuration by using User Manager on the RAS server (see Step by Step 7.5).

STEP BY STEP

7.5 Enabling Dialin Functions for NT Users

1. Start User Manger or User Manager for Domains.

2. Double-click the user for whom you want to enable dialin capabilities (or select multiple users and choose the File, Properties command).

3. Click the Dialin button to open the Dialin Information dialog box (see Figure 7.21).

4. Select the Grant Dialin Permission to User check box and configure the Call Back options if desired. If you select Set By Caller, the server will prompt a dialin user for a phone number the server will call back; this ensures that the majority of long distance charges are incurred by the server, not by the user. If you select Preset To, you enable security, which ensures that a user can use dialup networking only from a specific number (thus deterring hackers from dialing into your network). A lot of administrative overhead is incurred if the user moves from number to number because this setting will have to be reconfigured frequently.

FIGURE 7.21
Enabling Dialin access for an NT user.

Changing the RAS Configuration

Your RAS configuration might have to be changed as RAS needs change (see Step by Step 7.6).

STEP BY STEP

7.6 Viewing or Changing RAS Configuration

1. Double-click the Network icon in the Control Panel, and then select the Network application's Services tab.

2. Select Remote Access Service from the services list and click on the Properties button.

3. The Remote Access Setup dialog box appears (refer to Figure 7.16). Specify your new RAS configuration as described in steps 5–7 of Step by Step 7.4.

Dial-Up Networking

The Dial-Up Networking application lets you establish remote connections with other computers. The most common uses for Dial-Up Networking include the following:

◆ Accessing an Internet service provider

◆ Accessing a remote Windows NT computer or domain

Step by Step 7.7 goes through the procedure for opening the Dial-Up Networking application.

STEP BY STEP

7.7 Opening the Dial-Up Networking Application

1. Choose Start, Programs, Accessories.

2. Click the Dial-Up Networking icon. Figure 7.22 shows the Dial-Up Networking dialog box.

FIGURE 7.22
The Dial-Up Networking dialog box.

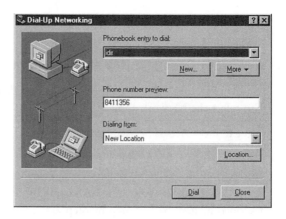

Dial-Up Networking maintains a list of phonebook entries. A *phonebook entry* is a bundle of information that Windows NT needs to establish a specific connection. You can use the Dial-Up Networking application to create a phonebook entry for your access provider, your Windows NT domain, or any other dial-up connection (see Step by Step 7.8). When it's time to connect, select a phonebook entry from the drop-down menu at the top of the screen and click on the Dial button. If you access the phonebook entry often, you can create a desktop shortcut that lets you access the phonebook entry directly.

STEP BY STEP

7.8 Creating a Phonebook Entry

1. Click the New button in the Dial-Up Networking dialog box to open the New Phonebook Entry dialog box (see Figure 7.23).

2. In the New Phonebook Entry dialog box, select the Basic tab, specify a name for the entry, enter an optional comment, and enter the phone number you want Windows NT to dial to make the connection. The Alternates button beside the phone number box lets you specify a prioritized list of alternative phone numbers. You also can specify a different modem or configure a modem from the Basic tab.

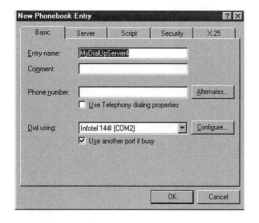

FIGURE 7.23
The Basic tab of the New Phonebook Entry dialog box.

3. Click the Server tab, and then specify the communications protocol for the dial-up server (by choosing from the Dial-Up Server Type drop-down list) and choose the network protocol (see Figure 7.24). If you select the TCP/IP network protocol, click the TCP/IP Settings button to configure TCP/IP settings (see Figure 7.25).

4. Choose the Script tab to view the connection's logon properties (see Figure 7.26). You can tell Windows NT to display a terminal window after dialing or to run a logon script after dialing. (A terminal window enables you to interactively log on to the remote server in terminal mode.)

   The Run This Script option enables you to automate the logon process. For more information on dial-up logon scripts, click on the Edit Script buttonto access a file called SWITCH.INF that provides instructions and sample logon scripts.

   The Before Dialing button lets you specify a terminal window or a logon script to execute before you dial.

5. From the Security tab, you can configure the logon to require encrypted authentication, or you can elect to accept any authentication including clear text (see Figure 7.27). You also can specify data encryption.

6. The X.25 tab shown in Figure 7.28 serves only for X.25 service (described earlier in this chapter). Select an X.25 access provider from the Network combo box, and then enter the requested information.

7. After you make changes to the various tabs of the New Phonebook Entry dialog box, click OK. The new phonebook entry appears in the Dial-Up Networking dialog box.

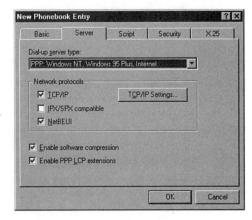

FIGURE 7.24
The Server tab of the New Phonebook Entry dialog box.

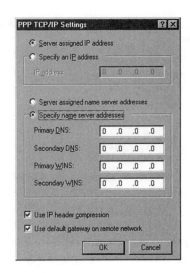

FIGURE 7.25
The PPP TCP/IP Settings dialog box.

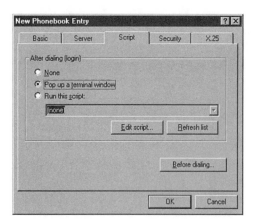

FIGURE 7.26
The Script tab of the New Phonebook Entry dialog box.

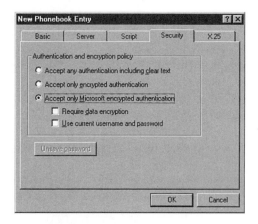

FIGURE 7.27
The New Phonebook Entry Security tab.

FIGURE 7.28
The X.25 tab of the New Phonebook Entry dialog box.

Editing a Phonebook Entry and Other Options

The More button in the Dial-Up Networking dialog box offers several options. Figure 7.29 shows the More menu.

The following list describes the most often used option on the More menu.

♦ *Edit Entry and Modem Properties.* Returns you to the setup tabs you configured in the preceding section (refer to Figures 7.23 through 7.28).

♦ *Create Shortcut to Entry.* Creates a shortcut to the active phonebook entry (specified in the Phonebook Entry to Dial dropdown list, shown in Figure 7.22).

♦ *Monitor Status.* Opens the Control Panel Dial-Up Networking Monitor. This monitor allows you to see the current connection status of a selected device. You can see how long the current connection has been in place, how much data has been transferred in and out, and whether errors have been detected.

♦ *User preferences.* Opens a User Preferences dialog box that presents the following four tabs:

Dialing. Lets you specify dialing options, such as the number of redial attempts and the time between redial attempts. You also can use the Dialing tab to enable or disable Autodial (see the following section). Figure 7.30 shows the Dialing tab.

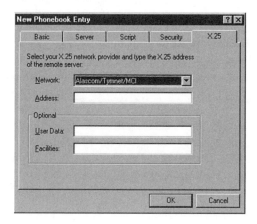

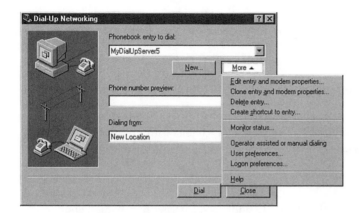

FIGURE 7.29
The Dial-Up Networking More menu.

Callback. Tells Windows NT what to do if the server you connect to offers callback. You can specify a number, you can elect to skip callback, or you can tell NT to prompt at the time callback is offered.

Appearance. Offers some dial-time interface options (see Figure 7.31).

Phonebook. This lets you specify a Dial-Up Networking phonebook. Phonebook entries are stored in a file with the .pbk extension. The default phonebook is the system phonebook. Using the Phonebook tab, you can place an entry in your personal phonebook (a user-specific phonebook), or you can choose a different phonebook.

◆ *Logon Preferences.* Configures Dialing, Callback, Appearance, and Phonebook settings for a remote Windows NT logon. The Logon Preferences options are very similar to the User Preferences options in the previous list. The difference is that the User Preferences options apply to a user who is already logged on to Windows NT and is trying to connect to a remote machine, whereas the Logon Preferences apply to a user who isn't yet logged on to Windows NT but wants to log on directly to a Windows NT domain via a remote connection. The Windows NT Ctrl+Alt+Del Logon dialog box includes the Logon Using Dial-Up Networking check box. If you enable this check box and log on using Dial-Up Networking, the preferences you set in the Logon Preferences dialog box apply.

NOTE

Logon Preferences Not Available to Everyone The Logon Preferences dialog box doesn't appear unless you log on as an administrator.

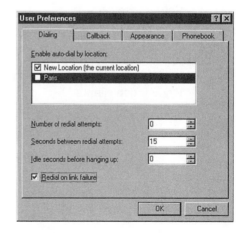

FIGURE 7.30
The User Preferences Dialing tab.

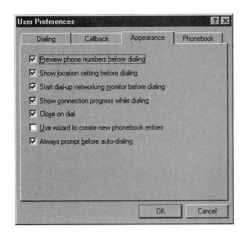

FIGURE 7.31
The User Preferences Appearance tab.

The Location button in the Dial-Up Networking dialog box lets you set a dialing prefix or suffix or specify a Telephony dialing location (refer to Figure 7.22).

Autodial

Windows NT includes a feature called Autodial. Autodial automatically associates network connections with Phonebook entries. This means that if you attempt to access a file or directory that can be accessed only via a dial-up connection, Windows NT attempts to make the dial-up connection automatically.

Autodial supports IP addresses, Internet host names, and NetBIOS names. By default, Autodial is enabled. You can enable or disable Autodial for specific calling locations using the settings on the Dialing tab of the User Preferences dialog box (refer to Figure 7.30).

CASE STUDY: MUGS PHOTOGRAPHIC IMPRINTING

ESSENCE OF THE CASE

The essence of this case is interoperability between NetWare and Windows NT. In point form, the following factors are necessary:

- Access from NetWare clients to NT Server resources

- Access from Windows clients to NetWare resources

- Logon access to NetWare server from NT Workstation clients

SCENARIO

As it does in many companies, networking and a need for a network solution grew one circumstance at a time at Mugs Photographic Imprinting, a research and development company specializing in silk-screening. As a result, they currently have a hodgepodge of technology solutions.

The engineering department currently has a NetWare solution: They have a Novell 3.11 server with Windows 95 clients running the Novell 32-bit client. On it, they keep all their engineering data, as well as financial information relating to the research and development aspects of the company.

On the other hand, MIS and Accounting currently have an NT-based network, with two NT Servers and a mixture of Windows 95 and Windows NT clients.

CASE STUDY: MUGS PHOTOGRAPHIC IMPRINTING

The company's five-year plan is to completely move toward a Microsoft solution. However, Engineering is hesitant to do this in the short term because of the current investment in NetWare training. Instead, what they would like to do is start slowly by replacing some of the Windows 95 clients with NT Workstations, both to increase security on those stations and to get some users familiar with the NT environment.

Despite the resistance to complete change, it is becoming increasingly evident that some sharing of information is necessary between the departments. Therefore, your task is to allow the Novell clients to access resources on the MIS NT servers and to allow occasional access of the NetWare server from the MIS machines.

ANALYSIS

The implementation of a solution follows three tracks. First, you must allow NetWare clients to have access to NT Server resources. This can be accomplished by adding the NWLink protocol to the NT Servers and installing File and Print Services for NetWare. This will then allow access from the NetWare resources (of course, you will also have to enable security access to the accounts accessing the resources).

Second, you must allow Windows clients (95 or NT) to have occasional access to NetWare resources. Therefore, you will want to install Gateway Services for NetWare on one or both of the NT Servers. You can then configure the NetWare sever to allow this gateway to function and then share NetWare resources on the NT Server. This requires no modification to the configuration of the Windows clients who are logging in to the NT domain.

Finally, to enable new NT Workstation clients to log on to the NetWare server and access its resources, you will have to install Client Services for NetWare on the NT Workstation machines. When you do so, NWLink will automatically be installed, too. Then you can configure the NetWare client to log on to the desired server.

A SUMMARY OF THE REQUIREMENTS AND SOLUTIONS IN THIS CASE STUDY

Requirement	Solution Provided By
Access from NetWare clients to NT Server resources	Adding NWLink to servers and installing FPNW on servers
Occasional access to NetWare server from Windows clients	Configuring GSNW on NT Server
Login access to NetWare servers from NT Workstation	Installing CSNW on workstations

CHAPTER SUMMARY

KEY TERMS

Before taking the exam, make sure you are familiar with the definitions of and concepts behind each of the following key terms. You can use the glossary (Appendix A) for quick reference purposes.

- Gateway Services for NetWare (GSNW)

- Client Services for NetWare (CSNW)

- File and Print Services for NetWare (FPNW)

- Directory Service Manager for NetWare (DSMN)

- Migration Tool for NetWare

- Server Message Block (SMB)

- Remote Access Service (RAS)

- Point-to-Point Protocol (PPP)

- Point-to-Point Tunneling Protocol (PPTP)

- Multilink protocol

- Callback

- Serial Line Interface Protocol (SLIP)

- Telephony API

The topics covered in this chapter can be categorized under two headings: NetWare connectivity and RAS.

In the NetWare connectivity section, you learned about the services available to allow interoperability between NT Servers and NetWare servers and clients. This includes services that allow NT clients to access NetWare resources (GSNW and CSNW), as well as services that allow NetWare clients to access file and print resources on NT Servers (FPNW). In addition, you looked at the Directory Service Manager for NetWare (DSMN), an add-on service that allows for the synchronization of NetWare accounts on NT Servers. Finally, you learned about the Migration Tool for NetWare, which makes the process of moving NetWare resources and users onto NT domain controllers manageable.

In the RAS section, you studied the setup and implementation of Remote Access Service on NT Servers. This included examining the protocols supported, the configuration of the service for client access, and the configuration of TAPI settings for clients.

APPLY YOUR LEARNING

Exercises

7.1 Creating a Share with Gateway Services for NetWare

In this exercise, you learn how to create a gateway to a NetWare directory using GSNW.

Estimated Time: 20 minutes

This chapter described how to create a gateway to a NetWare directory using Gateway Services for NetWare. If you have access to both a NetWare network and an NT network, it is helpful to try the process yourself as a learning exercise. If you don't have access to a NetWare network, take a moment to review the following procedure (also described earlier in the chapter) and do as much as you can from the Windows NT end. For example, install the Gateway Services for NetWare service and start the GSNW application in Control Panel. Attempt to become familiar with the features of the Gateway Services for NetWare dialog box and the Configure Gateway dialog box.

1. Open the Control Panel's Network application, select the Services tab, and click Add. Select Gateway (and Client) Services for NetWare from the Network Service list. Then click OK. Windows NT asks for the location of the files (typically, the installation CD-ROM). Windows NT then asks if you want to restart your system. Click Yes to restart your system.

2. Create a group called NTGATEWAY on the NetWare server.

3. Create a user account on the NetWare server for the gateway, and then add the gateway user account to the NTGATEWAY group. You can use NetWare's SYSCON utility to create the

NTGATEWAY group and the gateway's user account.

4. Double-click the GSNW icon in Control Panel. The Gateway Service for NetWare dialog box appears (refer to Figure 7.3). To configure Windows NT to act as a gateway, click the Gateway button.

5. The Configure Gateway dialog box appears (refer to Figure 7.4). Click the Enable Gateway check box. In the Gateway Account text box, enter the name of the account you created on the NetWare server. Below the account name, enter the password for the account, and then retype the password in the Confirm Password text box.

6. To create a new share for the NetWare directory or volume, click the Add button. You are asked to enter a share name and a network path to the NetWare resource. You then can enter a drive letter for the share.

7. From another SMB-compatible computer on the Microsoft network (Windows NT, Windows 95, or Windows for Workgroups), access the gateway computer through Network Neighborhood. Look for the drive letter you entered in step 5 for the NetWare directory. Double-click the drive letter and browse the NetWare files.

7.2 Using Autodial

This exercise shows you how to use Windows NT RAS in a practical situation and lets you try out Windows NT's Autodial feature.

Estimated Time: 20 minutes

1. Log on to a Windows NT domain using Dial-Up Networking. (Check the Logon Using Dial-Up

APPLY YOUR LEARNING

Networking check box below the domain name in the Windows NT Logon dialog box.) If you're already connected directly to the domain, unhook the network cable at the back of your computer so you will truly be remote.

> **NOTE**
>
> **Configure the Phonebook Entry First** When you log on using Dial-Up Networking, Windows NT asks for a Dial-Up Networking phonebook entry. Make sure you already have a phone-book entry for this connection. Also, be sure the RAS service is working on the domain. (This chapter described how to configure RAS and Dial-Up Networking.)

2. Locate a text file or a word processing document on a shared directory somewhere on the domain using Network Neighborhood icon in Explorer. (Use a file type that your computer is configured to recognize automatically; click on the Explorer's View, Options command and choose the File Types tab for a list of registered file types. A .txt file or a Write file should work.)

3. If Explorer can't find the other computers in the domain, pull down the Explorer menu and choose Find, Computer. In the Find: Computer dialog box (see Figure 7.32), enter the name of the computer with the shared directory you want to access. Then click on the Find Now button. The computer will appear as an icon in the Find: Computer dialog box. Double-click on the icon for a list of shared resources.

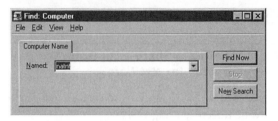

FIGURE 7.32
The Find: Computer dialog box.

4. When you've located a file on the remote share, right-click on the file and choose Create Shortcut from the shortcut menu that appears. Create a shortcut to the file and drag the shortcut to the desktop on your own computer.

5. Double-click the shortcut to make sure it opens the file.

6. Shut down your system.

7. Log on again, but this time, don't use Dial-Up Networking. (Deselect the Logon Using Dial-Up Networking check box.) You may get a message that says Windows NT could find the domain controller and logged you on using cached account information. Click OK.

8. Wait until the logon process is finished. Then double-click the shortcut to the file on the remote domain.

9. If you selected the Always Prompt Before Auto-Dialing check box in the Appearances tab of the Dial-Up Networking User Preferences dialog box, Windows NT will ask if you want to initiate a connection with the remote file. Click Yes. Autodial will automatically dial the remote net-work and attempt to initiate a connection to the file referenced in the shortcut.

APPLY YOUR LEARNING

Review Questions

1. What is required to allow a computer to access NetWare Resources through an NT Server computer configured with Gateway Services for NetWare?

2. What is required for a Windows NT computer to access a client/server application on a NetWare Server?

3. What is required for a Windows NT computer to directly access a printer shared on a NetWare server?

4. How can you configure two modems to work as one for the purposes of RAS connection from a Windows NT client?

5. How can you change the information in a Dial-Up Networking phonebook entry?

Exam Questions

The following questions will test your knowledge of the information in this chapter. For additional questions, see New Riders' exclusive test engine product, Top Score, on the CD-ROM that accompanies this book.

1. The Migration Tool for NetWare is not capable of preserving which of the following?

   A. Accounts

   B. Passwords

   C. Files

   D. Effective rights

2. Which of the following enables a NetWare client machine to access Microsoft SQL Server on a Windows NT Server system?

   A. IPX with NetBIOS

   B. Client Services for NetWare (CSNW)

   C. File and Print Services for NetWare (FPNW)

   D. NWLink

3. After creating a NetWare gateway using GSNW, you can create a share on the gateway machine for NetWare files by using

   A. GSNW.

   B. Explorer or My Computer.

   C. The Control Panel's Server application.

   D. Any of the above.

4. Which of the following services enables your Windows NT Server machine to access file and print resources on a NetWare server?

   A. File and Print Services for NetWare (FPNW)

   B. Client Services for NetWare (CSNW)

   C. Gateway Services for NetWare (GSNW)

   D. Directory Service Manager for NetWare (DSMN)

5. What is the name of the utility that enables remote users to access a network through an NT Workstation or Server?

   A. Remote Control

   B. Remote Access Service

   C. Remote Network Service

   D. The Internet

APPLY YOUR LEARNING

6. **Problem:** Whirling Dervish Tree Planting Inc. has an NT domain with Microsoft Windows NT Workstation and Windows NT Server machines running TCP/IP. On the same LAN, there is also a single NetWare server. They need for people to be able to dial in to the system and get access to resources but have not done any client or server configuration to allow that.

Required Result:

To allow NT clients to be able to dial in to the network and access resources on the Microsoft and NetWare servers.

Optional Results:

To allow all clients who are working on the LAN to be able to access the NetWare server's file resources.

To not have to reconfigure any client except to allow them to dial in to the network.

Proposed Solution:

Install and configure RAS on all remote client machines to allow TCP/IP and NWLink protocols. Install CSNW on all the remote client machines and configure for connection to the NetWare server. Install and configure RAS on an NT Server machine on the LAN and configure it to allow TCP/IP and NWLink to pass to the entire network. Finally, modify the account properties for the Dialin users to allow them to dial in to the network.

Analysis:

Which of the following statements best describes the proposed solution?

A. This solution fulfills the required result as well as both optional results.

B. This solution fulfills the required result and one of the optional results.

C. This solution fulfills the required result but does not fulfill either of the optional results.

D. This solution does not meet the required result.

7. What feature lets RAS use more than one communication channel at a time for the same connection?

A. Multinet

B. Multilink

C. ISDN

D. Multichannel

8. Identify the two serial protocols that a RAS client supports.

A. IEEE 802.2 and X.25

B. Ethernet and token ring

C. SLIP and PPP

D. ESLIP and PPTP

9. Which of the serial protocols supports the NetBEUI, IPX/SPX, and TCP/IP transport protocols over RAS?

A. PPP

B. SLIP

C. PPTPS

D. IEEE 802.2

APPLY YOUR LEARNING

10. You want to let users connect to your local area network using the Internet. However, you're concerned that security might be a problem. Which protocol should you use to ensure a reliable connection and secure transmission of information?

    A. PPP

    B. SLIP

    C. IEEE 802.2

    D. PPTP

11. A user calls you and states that although he's able to connect to his NT Workstation via RAS, he cannot see any resources on the network. What could be causing the problem?

    A. The user is using a userid that isn't configured to have network access via RAS.

    B. He's dialing in with a protocol configured for "This Computer Only" when it needs to be configured for the "Entire Network."

    C. He needs to use a different protocol. NetBEUI isn't routable, so he can't see any other devices on the network if he's using it as his dial-in protocol.

    D. He needs to configure his RAS server to use ISDN because the PSTN can support only a limited amount of bandwidth.

12. A user is trying to dial in to the NT Server-based RAS server. The user is connecting, but he gets disconnected immediately and receives a message that he isn't an authorized dial-in user. What is the first thing you should do?

    A. Restart the NT Server because one of the modems must be disabled.

    B. Change the security configuration options on the RAS server to enable any authentication method, including clear text.

    C. Check to make sure the user has dial-in permissions in User Manager for Domains.

    D. Tell the user to restart his remote system and try again.

13. You have an NT Server configured as a RAS client, and you're trying to copy a file from a NetWare server over your RAS connection. You have installed the NWLink-compatible transport protocol at your remote computer, but you still cannot connect to the NetWare server. What did you forget to do?

    A. You need to install and configure the Gateway Services for NetWare (GSNW) so you can access a NetWare server using file and print services.

    B. You need to install the FPNW (File and Print Services for NetWare) on the RAS server to gain access to the NetWare servers.

    C. You must dial in to the NetWare server directly.

    D. You have to change your protocol to TCP/IP and install TCP/IP on the NetWare server.

14. Several salespeople dial in to your network via RAS. How can you configure the security options in RAS to minimize the users' long distance phone charges?

    A. Configure the user's Dial-Up Networking software to use PPTP, which bypasses the PSTN billing computers and gives the users free long distance service.

B. Configure the RAS service to perform a call-back based on the number specified by the user dialing in to the RAS server. The server authenticates the logon and then disconnects and calls the user back at the specified number.

C. Issue the users long distance calling cards and have their RAS calls billed directly to the company.

D. Make sure the users are calling only from public telephones and are making collect calls to the RAS server. Then configure the RAS server to accept collect calls.

15. Users would like to be able to connect to the Internet from home using the company's T1 connection. You configure RAS to allow your users to dial in. What protocol must they use to dial in to the RAS server?

A. IEEE 802.2

B. Ethernet

C. NetBEUI

D. TCP/IP

16. Your management is concerned that allowing access to the network via RAS may open up security problems. What features does RAS support that help alleviate some of these concerns?

A. RAS supports the U.S. government's DES (Data Encryption Standard) and encrypts all data going across the communication channel.

B. RAS, in fact, can be more secure than a LAN connection because of the callback security, encryption of userid and password information, and PPTP features.

C. RAS is not secure over standard PSTN connections unless data-scrambling equipment is used on both ends of the connection.

D. You can obtain a C2 level version of the RAS product, which meets U.S. government standards for security.

17. Which statement below correctly identifies the differences between connecting to a RAS server running on Windows NT Workstation and connecting to a RAS server running on Windows NT Server?

A. When connecting to NT Workstation, you can access only the shared resources on that machine. When connecting to NT Server, you can access resources on the entire network.

B. When connecting to NT Workstation, you can access shared resources on the entire network, except for resources on NetWare Servers; to connect to NetWare resources, you must connect to an NT Server.

C. Because it supports up to 256 simultaneous connections, you could be connected using RAS to an NT Server while others are also connected using RAS; with NT Workstation, you would be the only RAS user connected.

D. Because it supports up to 256 simultaneous connections, you could be connected using RAS to an NT Workstation while others are also connected using RAS; with NT Server, other processes prevent more than one simultaneous RAS connection, which means you can be the only one connected using RAS.

APPLY YOUR LEARNING

18. You want remote TCP/IP RAS clients to have access to the entire TCP/IP network, but right now they can connect only to the RAS server machine. Which of the following will enable the client to reach the network?

   A. Choose the Entire Network check box in the Server tab of Dial-Up Networking's Edit Phonebook Entry dialog box.

   B. Choose the Entire Network radio button in the Remote Access Permissions dialog box of the Remote Access Admin application.

   C. Choose the Entire Network radio button in the TCP/IP Configuration dialog box accessible via the Network button in the Remote Access Setup dialog box.

   D. A, B, and C are all necessary.

Answers to Review Questions

1. All that is required for a computer to access NetWare resources through an NT Gateway is SMB, Server Message Block. This is available on all Microsoft client computers. For more information, see the section "Gateway Services for NetWare."

2. In order to access a client/server application on a NetWare server, an NT computer must have the NWLink protocol installed. The actual interaction between the client and the server is handled by the application itself and is not a product of the operating system configuration. For more information, see the section "Server and Client/Server Applications."

3. In order for a Windows NT computer to directly access a shared printer on a NetWare server, both the NWLink protocol and Client Services for NetWare (CSNW) must be installed. On an NT Server machine, you must install Gateway Services for NetWare (GSNW) in order to get CSNW. For more information, see the section "Client Services for NetWare (CSNW) and the GSNW Client."

4. In order for two modems to work as one from an NT client, you must do the following:

   a. Physically install two modems and ensure separate telephone connectivity to each (two phone lines).

   b. Install both modems under NT.

   c. Install the RAS service.

   d. In RAS configuration, enable Multilink.

   e. Ensure that the RAS server is also configured for Multilink.

For more information, see the section "Configuring Remote Access Service."

5. To change a phonebook entry, you perform these steps:

   a. Open My Computer and double-click the Dial-Up Networking icon.

   b. From the Phonebook Entry to Dial drop-down list, select the phonebook entry you want to modify.

   c. Click the More button, and then select Edit Entry and Modem Properties to open the Edit Phonebook Entry dialog box.

For more information, see the section "Editing a Phonebook Entry and Other Options."

APPLY YOUR LEARNING

Answers to Exam Questions

1. **B.** Although the Migration Tool for NetWare preserves most NetWare information, it cannot read the encrypted passwords stored on the NetWare server and, therefore, cannot preserve them on the NT side. For more information, see the section "Migration Tool for NetWare."

2. **A.** Although some resource access from NetWare to NT requires FPNW, accessing a SQL server does not. The only requirement is that the NetBIOS interface be available, which you can accomplish by installing IPX/SPX on the NetWare client. For more information, see the section "Server and Client/Server Applications."

3. **A.** Setting up shares is part of the configuration of Gateway Services for NetWare. You cannot configure shares on the NT machine any other way. For more information, see the section "Gateway Services for NetWare (GSNW)."

4. **C.** In order for an NT Server machine to act as a NetWare client, you must install GSNW. This includes both the Gateway service as well as the Client service. For more information, see the section "Client Services for NetWare (CSNW) and the GSNW Client."

5. **B.** Remote Access Service is a service installed on either an NT Server or NT Workstation that allows remote users to connect through that RAS machine and have network connectivity as if they were actually connected to the LAN. On NT Server, RAS allows up to 256 simultaneous connections; on NT Workstation, RAS allows only a single connection. For more information, see the section "Configuring Remote Access Service (RAS)."

6. **C.** This solution fulfills the required result but does not fulfill either of the optional results. Although this solution will allow all dialup clients to access both Microsoft and NetWare resources, it does require reconfiguration of the clients over and above the RAS configuration (installation of CSNW and NWLink), and it does nothing to allow LAN clients to access the NetWare server. A better option might have been to configure a GSNW on an NT Server in addition to the RAS configuration for the clients. For more information, see the sections "Client Services for NetWare (CSMN) and the GSNW Client," "Installing and Configuring RAS," and "Configuring NT Users for RAS."

7. **B.** The Multilink protocol allows for the simultaneous use of multiple communications channels. In the case of two equal channels (56KB modems, for example), the user would get twice the throughput. In order for Multilink to work, both the client and the server must be configured for Multilink, and callback cannot be configured. For more information, see the section "Configuring Remote Access Service (RAS)."

8. **C.** NT-based RAS clients can connect to RAS servers that are configured to use either SLIP or PPP. NT-based servers, however, do not support SLIP. For more information, see the section "RAS Line Protocols."

9. **A.** Only PPP supports all three network protocols over serial lines. For more information, see the section "RAS Line Protocols."

10. **D.** PPTP is an encapsulation protocol that encrypts network packets and sends them over the Internet. This allows for secure transmission of information over the inherently insecure

APPLY YOUR LEARNING

Internet. For more information, see the section "RAS Line Protocols."

11. **B.** For each protocol configured to work with RAS, you can set the properties to allow users to see the whole network or just the RAS server they are dialing into. This RAS server must be configured to not let RAS connections see beyond it. For more information, see the section "Installing and Configuring RAS."

12. **C.** Dialing in to an NT Server is not all there is to RAS. If you want to connect to a RAS server, you must be configured to do so in the user database. From User Manager, open the user's Properties dialog box, click the Dialin button, and grant the user dialin privileges. For more information, see the section "Configuring NT Users for RAS."

13. **A.** Whether you're connecting to a NetWare server using RAS or from a LAN, you must have a client configured that is capable of connecting. Because you are dialing in using an NT Server, you must install GSNW in order to access the file you need. For more information, see the section "Client Services for NetWare (CSNW) and the GSNW Client."

14. **B.** Two options enable callback capabilities to users; however, one requires a fixed number to which the server will call. By configuring dial-up settings in User Manager to require the server to dial a number of the users' choice, you can ensure that the amount of time the users spend on calls they are paying for is minimal. This option also allows for the salespeople to call from any number and have the server call that number

back. For more information, see the section "Installing and Configuring RAS."

15. **D.** The protocol used to connect to the Internet is TCP/IP, regardless of how the connection is established. Whether the user is on a LAN connecting to the Internet or is connecting through a RAS server, TCP/IP must be used. For more information, see the section "Configuring Remote Access Service (RAS)."

16. **B.** A variety of security features make RAS a very secure method of network connection. Callback to a static phone number ensures that you must be at a specific place in order to connect via RAS, and the addition of PPTP ensures that the data that's transmitted is encrypted en-route. For more information, see the section "Configuring Remote Access Service (RAS)."

17. **C.** In terms of access to the network, NT Server and NT Workstation provide identical RAS server features. In addition, access to NetWare resources depends on how the RAS client is configured more than it does on the RAS server (or on whether there is an NT Server running GSNW on the network). It is NT Server that provides 256 simultaneous connections; NT Workstation provides only one. For more information, see the section "Configuring Remote Access Service (RAS)."

18. **C.** To configure a TCP/IP client dialing in through RAS to be able to access the entire network, select the Entire Network radio button in the TCP/IP Configuration dialog box accessible via the Network button in the Remote Access Setup dialog box. For more information, see the section "Installing and Configuring RAS."

Suggested Readings and Resources

1. Microsoft Official Curriculum course 803:
   Administering Microsoft Windows NT 4.0

   • Module 2: Setting Up User Accounts

2. Microsoft Official Curriculum course 922*:
   Supporting Microsoft Windows NT 4.0 Core
   Technologies*

   • Module 12: Remote Access Service

   • Module 14: Interoperating with Novell
     NetWare

3. Networking Supplement Manual - MS
   Windows NT Server 4.0

   • Chapter 5: Understanding Remote Access
     Service

   • Chapter 6: Installing and Configuring
     Remote Access Service Microsoft TCP/IP
     Architecture

   • Chapter 7: RAS Security

   • Chapter 11: Point-to-Point Tunneling
     Protocol (PPTP)

   • Chapter 12: Overview of NetWare
     Compatibility Features

   • Chapter 13: Gateway Service for NetWare

   • Chapter 14: Migration Tool for NetWare

4. MS Windows NT Server 4.0 Resource Kit

   • Chapter 6: Internet Connectivity Using
     the Remote Access Service

5. Microsoft TechNet CD-ROM

   • MS NT Server Technical Notes: Windows
     NT Server 4.0 Deployment Guide –
     NetWare Integration

6. Web sites

   • www.microsoft.com/train.cert

   • www.prometric.com/testingcandidates
     /assessment/_chosetest.html (take online
     assessment tests)

Microsoft provides the following objectives for "Monitoring and Optimization":

Monitor performance of various functions by using Performance Monitor. Functions include processor, memory, disk, and network.

▶ This objective is necessary because someone certified in the use of Windows NT Server technology must understand the fundamentals of server optimization and be able to use the Performance Monitor to view the status of major subsystems under various conditions. This entails understanding the different views of Performance Monitor and the subsystems that are likely to cause performance problems or show problem areas.

Identify performance bottlenecks.

▶ This objective is necessary because someone certified in the use of Windows NT Server technology must know the potential sources of a performance bottleneck, how to identify the source, and how to rectify the problem.

CHAPTER 8

Monitoring and Optimization

STUDY STRATEGIES

▶ Microsoft does not put a great deal of emphasis on performance monitoring in its 70-67 (NT Server) exam; it leaves that to the Enterprise exam. However, it does expect you to know the performance monitoring tools that are available to you and how to use them. When reading this chapter, you need to focus on two particular concepts: the theoretical aspects of performance in general and the practical use of Performance Monitor to view performance characteristics.

▶ The theoretical aspects of performance are just that—theoretical. You can't touch your processor or directly see it work. All you can do is understand that certain tasks use the processor more intensely than others and that, if your server is performing those tasks, you need a fast processor. The bottom line is that you have to study and memorize the subsystems discussed here and know how each is related to performance. This chapter gives you tips on how to improve performance based on what your server does, without even touching the monitoring tools; be aware of those.

▶ Of course, you can't get away with not touching your computer at all for this module. Because Microsoft has provided Performance Monitor as a tool with which you can analyze performance and locate bottlenecks, you need to understand how it is used. You don't need to know all the objects and all the counters associated with it. However, you do need to know about the different views and what you would use each one for. (That is the kind of thing you will be tested on.) In addition, you need to be able to read a Chart view and to use the theory you know and—understanding the relationships between the different objects—interpret the results.

INTRODUCTION

As with any computer solution, the performance of your applications on Windows NT depends on the combination of hardware and software on your system. A good match of the two provides a cost-effective computing solution. A mismatch of the two, however, results in inefficient use of resources or inadequate performance. Fortunately, Windows NT has many self-optimizing characteristics that don't require user intervention. With some careful planning, a typical installation can show some decent performance without the need for tinkering with obscure parameters in the Registry. This chapter looks at some of the steps you can take to make your Windows NT system (and your network) run more efficiently. You will also learn about a useful tool called Performance Monitor that will help you monitor and analyze what is going on within your system.

PERFORMANCE OPTIMIZATION

Optimal performance seems simple enough to define: completing a task in the shortest amount of time. Optimizing the performance of a system is a matter of arranging the resources of the system in such a way that the desired task is finished as quickly as possible. It means getting the best results with the hardware and software you have.

Optimization of a task on your system, then, consists of measuring and analyzing the resource demands of the task to determine what can be done to make it finish in a shorter period of time.

Before you can get truly optimal performance from your system, however, you need to answer some very important questions:

◆ What task or tasks on the system are most important?

◆ Do you want to optimize the utilization of the hardware, or the speed of a particular application or service?

Performance Objectives

The answers to the above questions determine what you should measure and how to decide whether your performance is "optimal." On a file server, for example, the objective could be to service clients' requests for files as quickly as possible. By measuring the number of bytes transferred to all the server's clients across the network in a given period of time, you can tell whether changes you make to the system's configuration make performance better or worse.

On the other hand, what would be "optimal performance" for a primary domain controller (PDC) that's responsible for replicating a large account database to many backup domain controllers (BDCs)? In such a case, the objective would be to achieve synchronization of the account database throughout the WAN in a timely manner, with the minimum amount of network traffic. Therefore, to know whether performance is optimal, you need to measure two things: the amount of time it takes for changes to the account database to be implemented on all domain controllers, and the amount of network traffic the domain synchronization generates.

Optimizing performance of a database server might include this objective: Provide the fastest response time for queries against the customer service database. If your goal is to complete the database task as quickly as possible regardless of how that impacts other processes on the system, optimization could cause non-database tasks to run more slowly than before.

Yet another performance goal could be to make the most efficient use of resources to get the greatest amount of work completed by all processes on the system. To achieve this goal, you need to optimize overall throughput and efficiency, making certain that bottlenecks created by other processes do not block processes.

After you optimize performance of your application (that is, get the best performance from the hardware and software you have), the next question is whether that level of performance meets your business goals. You may have the best performance possible with your existing system, but to get adequate performance, you may need to upgrade one or more components, such as memory, disk, or processor.

The best way to know what you can do to improve performance is to measure it. Gathering data on how your system performs under various circumstances gives you the information you need to make appropriate changes to your system.

Windows NT Tunes Itself

One of Microsoft's design goals for Windows NT was that it should not require a user to make changes to Registry settings to get good performance. One of the problems regarding optimizing performance with any operating system is that what passes for "optimal configuration" changes as the demands on the system fluctuate. For example, how large should the paging file be? At one point in the day, a large paging file might be optimal, while a few hours or minutes later, a smaller paging file might be optimal.

Asking users and administrators to make these kinds of frequent configuration changes is not practical, and yet leaving a static configuration would inevitably lead to inefficiencies. So Microsoft decided to let the operating system itself handle evaluating settings, such as the size of the disk cache and paging file, and adjust them dynamically as resource demands change.

As a result, Windows NT does most of the task of optimizing overall performance of the system without any manual changes to Registry parameters. Windows NT dynamically adjusts the balance between the size of the disk cache and the amount of RAM used for applications, for example, in response to resource demands on the system.

Reasons to Monitor Performance

Although there is little to tune in NT itself, you still have several reasons to monitor system performance, which are covered in the following sections.

Optimizing Specific Tasks

If you want to optimize a particular application on your server, monitoring system performance can tell you whether changing your hardware would enable your application to run faster. It also can uncover contention for resources by multiple applications.

If you are setting up a database server, for example, performance data can tell you whether you have excess capacity to handle additional work, or whether you have a resource shortage affecting performance. If other applications are competing for the same resources as your database application, you can move the other applications to another server that is less busy.

Troubleshooting Performance Problems

One of the most difficult kinds of performance problems to troubleshoot is diagnosing transient network problems. A sudden increase in interrupts generated by a malfunctioning network card can bring server performance to a screeching halt as the processor handles all the interrupts. If you monitor key indicators of network performance (number of errors, number of interrupts processed, and so on), you can be alerted of problems as they occur.

Planning for Future Needs

Another reason to monitor performance is that it enables you to detect changes in the way the server is being used by users. If users are using a file server more frequently to store very large files, for example, the increased demands for file services can be measured and documented.

By anticipating changes in demand for the server's resources, you can take appropriate action before performance suffers.

Configuration Changes That Affect Performance

You can change many things that affect overall system performance. The following strategies have the effect of shifting the demands for resources to achieve higher throughput.

Adding or Upgrading Hardware Components

This section furnishes examples of common hardware upgrades that may improve performance of their respective subsystems. Table 8.1 shows objects and upgrade options for them.

TABLE 8.1

HARDWARE SYSTEMS AND UPGRADE OPTIONS

Object	*Upgrade Options*
Processor	Upgrade the speed of the processor.
	Add another processor (for example, two Pentium processors on an SMP system).
	Upgrade the secondary cache.
Memory	Add more RAM. Having adequate RAM reduces the need for paging memory to and from the hard disk.
	Remove RAM shadowing. Shadowing of the ROM BIOS in RAM does not improve performance under Windows NT. Disabling this feature can, therefore, make more memory available to the system.
Disks	Replace slow disks with faster ones.
	Use NTFS for partitions larger than 400MB.
	Use a defragmentation tool if disks become fragmented.
	Upgrade from IDE to SCSI.
	Use a controller with the highest possible transfer rate and best multitasking functionality.
	Isolate disk I/O-intensive tasks on separate physical disks or disk controllers.
	Create a stripe set to gain the advantage of simultaneous writes to multiple disks (if your hardware will support it).
Network	Get a network card with the widest data bus available on your system. If your system has a PCI bus, for example, use a PCI network adapter instead of an ISA adapter. This consideration is especially important for network servers.
	Divide your network into multiple networks, attaching the server to each network with a different adapter. Allocating the server requests across the two separate interfaces alleviates congestion at the server.
Fault Tolerance	If you're using software-based fault tolerance (such as striping with parity or RAID-5), use a hardware-based solution instead. Using RAID-5 implemented in hardware takes the burden of calculating the parity information off the processor.
	If the goal is the greatest availability of data, you could consider mirroring (via Windows NT fault-tolerant drivers) two hardware-based RAID-5 arrays. In addition, solutions for Windows NT such as Octopus from Octopus Technologies enable mirroring of entire servers.

Removing Unnecessary Software Components

To optimize your system, you can remove any software components that are using precious processor and memory resources. These software components fall into three categories: device drivers, network protocols, and services.

Device Drivers

Any drivers that are loaded into memory but are not used should be removed. For example, if you have a SCSI driver loaded for a non-existent adapter, remove it. If you have an extra network adapter installed that is not currently connected to the network, remove the driver.

Network Protocols

Remove any unnecessary network protocols. If all your systems can communicate using NWLink, for example, remove NetBEUI. Loading protocols that are not necessary increases network traffic and processing overhead without improving performance.

You can remove the bindings for a protocol selectively instead of removing the entire protocol component, by using the Bindings tab of the Control Panel's Network application (see Figure 8.1). With the options on the Bindings tab you can enable and disable network bindings. In the figure, the circular mark beside NetBEUI Protocol indicates that it has been disabled for the Server service. That means this server will no longer service file and print requests that come via NetBEUI.

Services

Any services that this server does not need to provide should be either disabled or configured to start manually. If a server will not be providing print services, for example, you can disable the Spooler service.

You can display the list of installed services, as shown in Figure 8.2, by choosing the Services application in the Control Panel. You can free up wasted processor and memory resources by disabling unneeded services.

> **WARNING**
>
> **Understand What You Remove**   Be extremely careful when removing or disabling components in Windows NT. Removing the wrong components can make your system unstable or prevent it from booting. If you remove one of NT's standard drivers by mistake, you can run the Windows NT Setup program (WINNT32.EXE) to refresh the system files.

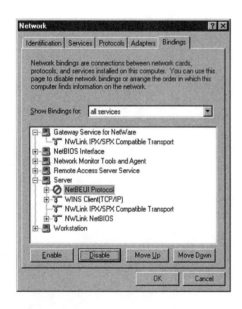

FIGURE 8.1
The Bindings tab in the Network dialog box allows you to see and selectively modify the bindings for adapters, services, and protocols.

Replacing Inefficient Software

If applications or drivers on your system use system resources ineffi-
ciently, you may not be able to make a particular application run
faster. A poorly coded application or device driver can adversely
affect performance of the entire system.

If your performance monitoring uncovers a software component that
makes unacceptably large resource demands, the solution is to
replace the offending software.

Changing Windows NT Performance Parameters

Several relatively easy-to-change settings can make a substantial difference in performance.

Optimizing the Paging File

The Virtual Memory Manager in Windows NT is responsible for
managing all the memory pages on the system, including physical
memory (RAM) and virtual memory (the paging file). Whenever an
application makes a reference to a page of memory that isn't currently
located in physical RAM, a page fault occurs. Excessive paging activity dramatically affects overall system performance. Adding RAM
reduces the need for paging. So when in doubt, add more RAM!

You configure the size of the paging file in the Virtual Memory dialog box (see Figure 8.3). To open the Virtual Memory dialog box,
click on the Change button in the Performance tab of the Control
Panel's System application. When the system starts up, Windows NT
creates a paging file (PAGEFILE.SYS) and sets its size to the minimum value in the Virtual Memory dialog box. The Virtual Memory
Manager then monitors system activity and increases the size of the
paging file up to the maximum value if it determines that paging
would be more efficient.

The following are general recommendations regarding the virtual
memory settings:

◆ Consider spreading the paging file across multiple disks if your
hardware supports writing to those disks at the same time.

◆ Move the paging file to the disk(s) with the lowest amount of
total disk activity (see Figure 8.4).

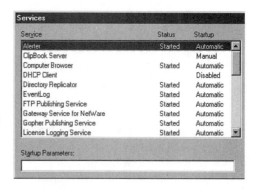

FIGURE 8.2
Disable unneeded services through the
Services dialog box.

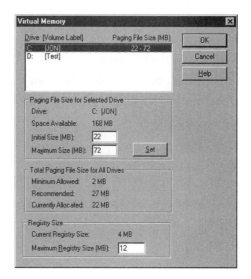

FIGURE 8.3
To increase the size of your paging file, use the
Virtual Memory dialog box, which is accessible
from the System application.

NOTE

Replace 16-Bit Applications with 32-Bit Applications When Possible A 32-bit application will generally run faster than a 16-bit application. Upgrading to a version of software specifically written for a 32-bit platform may increase performance. The one disclaimer here is that many software upgrades include a lot of extra features that may actually slow down the general performance of the software.

NOTE

Starting and Stopping Services from a Command Prompt You can start and stop services from the command prompt. To stop the Spooler service, for example, type the following command:

```
net stop spooler
```

To start the Spooler service, type this command:

```
net start spooler
```

You can combine the NET START command with the AT command to start and stop services as needed, either locally or on another system:

```
at \\myserver 12:00 net start
spooler
```

This technique is useful when you need certain services (such as directory replication) across slow WAN links only at certain times of the day.

FIGURE 8.4
Moving the paging file from the boot partition and spreading it across multiple physical disks can optimize pagefile access.

The following are general recommendations and cautions regarding paging files:

◆ If you plan to use Windows NT's Recovery feature, which writes out debugging information if a stop error occurs to disk, your swap file must be as large as the amount of physical RAM present on the system and must reside on the boot partition.

◆ Monitor the size of the paging file under peak usage, and then set the minimum size to that value. Making the minimum paging file size large enough eliminates the need for Virtual Memory Manager to increase its size (and saves processor cycles).

◆ To determine the amount of RAM you need to add in order to reduce paging activity, use a tool such as Performance Monitor to determine the amount of memory each application needs. Then remove applications (noting their working set sizes) until paging activity falls within acceptable limits. The amount of memory freed up by terminating those applications is the amount of physical RAM the system requires.

Optimizing the Server Service

Another setting that can affect performance is the configuration of the Server service. To access the Server dialog box (see Figure 8.5), choose the Services tab in the Control Panel's Network application, select the Server service, and click on the Properties button.

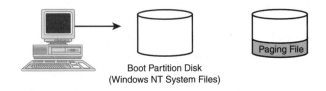

Boot Partition Disk
(Windows NT System Files)

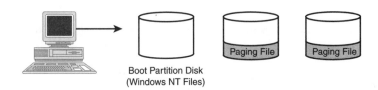

Boot Partition Disk
(Windows NT Files)

By default, Windows NT Server is configured to work best as a file server for 64 or more users. Changing the Server service settings adjusts the amount of RAM and other resources allocated for the Server service to use. Table 8.2 provides a description of each of these settings.

TABLE 8.2

SERVER SERVICE OPTIMIZATION

Setting	Description
Minimize Memory Used	Up to 10 connections
Balance	Up to 64 connections
Maximize Throughput for File Sharing	64 or more connections, large file cache (for file servers)
Maximize Throughput for Network Application	64 or more connections, small file cache (for servers)

NOTE

Put Paging File on Low Activity Disks It's better to put the paging file on the disk(s) with the lowest amount of disk activity. If your system has two disks, consider putting the paging file on the disk that isn't the boot disk. (The boot disk contains Windows NT system files.) If you have multiple disks, try distributing the paging file among all disks except the boot disk.

Optimizing Other Services

For other services on your system, you might have to adjust Registry settings in order to attain optimal performance. Table 8.3 lists some common values for standard Windows NT services that would be a good starting point for evaluation.

If you have installed additional services on your system, research the Registry parameters associated with those services for performance-enhancement opportunities.

TABLE 8.3

SOME COMMON REGISTRY VALUES FOR STANDARD WINDOWS NT SERVICES

Service	Value
Net Logon	Pulse, Pulse Concurrency, Pulse Maximum, Replication Governor
Directory Replication	Interval, Guard Time
Computer Browser	Hidden, IsDomainMaster, MaintainServer-List
Spooler	DefaultSpoolDirectory, PriorityClass

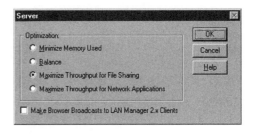

FIGURE 8.5

The Server dialog box, accessible through the Services tab of the Control Panel's Network application, can be used to optimize server performance for specific uses.

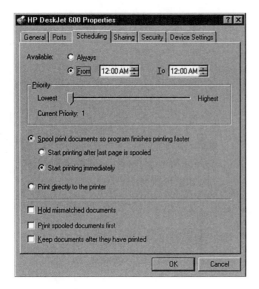

FIGURE 8.6
The Scheduling tab of a printer's Properties dialog box enables you to specify when the printer will be available.

Rescheduling Resource-Intensive Tasks

Demands for resources on a server often fluctuate widely at different times of day. A server running an accounting package meets its greatest demands at the end of an accounting period. A logon server typically experiences a spike in authentication requests at the beginning of the day. Print servers often experience their heaviest demands during late morning and late afternoon. Shifting some of the demand from the peak period to other times can help alleviate the load on the server. In addition, any task that competes for resources with your primary application should be scheduled to non-peak hours. Figure 8.6 shows the scheduling options for a printer.

If you have a batch job that is processor intensive, for example, do not schedule it to run on a domain controller at 8:00 a.m., when most users are logging on and logon authentication demands are at their greatest. Shift demands for resources to times when you have a surplus of the resource available.

Moving Tasks to Another System

If you find that you cannot resolve a resource shortage in an acceptable way on your own system, you may be able to move the demand to another machine that has idle resources. For example, if you have two applications on a server and both are I/O-intensive, you may be able to improve performance of both applications by moving one of them to another less-busy server as illustrated in Figure 8.7.

In a client/server application, you might also be able to spread out the load of your application by running portions of it using the idle processing capacity of other systems on the network.

Before You Change Anything

Before you can make any of these changes, you must first do some detective work. You have to be able to isolate which resource on the system has become the bottleneck; then you have to discover the source of the demand for that resource.

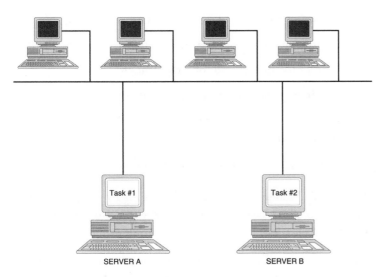

FIGURE 8.7
Spread out the server workload to increase performance.

Suppose you find that while a certain task is being performed, the processor is busy 100 percent of the time. You cannot automatically conclude that you need a faster processor. First you have to determine why the processor was busy. If your system has a memory shortage, for example, the processor could be busy handling the increased need for managing virtual memory. Alternatively, your task could have invoked another process that was ill-behaved and consumed the processor.

This kind of investigative work requires a measurement tool that can tell you what is really going on with your system. That tool is the Performance Monitor.

PERFORMANCE MONITOR

Monitor performance of various functions by using Performance Monitor. Functions include processor, memory, disk, and network.

By far, the most useful tool for measuring performance on NT systems is Performance Monitor. Performance Monitor is installed in the Administrative Tools program group by default. You can use Performance Monitor for the following tasks:

◆ Measuring the demand for resources on your system

◆ Identifying bottlenecks in your system performance

◆ Monitoring the behavior of individual processes

◆ Monitoring the performance of remote systems

◆ Generating alerts to inform you that an exception condition has occurred

◆ Exporting performance data for analysis using other tools

Performance Monitor is essential for monitoring your system. You can use it to gather everything from general indicators of system health to details on individual processes on the system.

You can configure Performance Monitor to record a variety of statistical measurements (called *counters*) for a variety of system hardware and software components (called *objects*). Each object has its own collection of counters. The System object, for example, has counters that measure Processor Queue Length, System Calls/Sec, and so on. The Paging File object has counters that measure %Usage and %Usage Peak.

Windows NT Server exam objectives specify that you should be familiar with how to use Performance Monitor to measure processor, memory, disk, and network functions. Performance Monitor comes with Processor, Memory, and PhysicalDisk objects (all with associated counters) for measuring processor, memory, and disk functions. The Server object and the Network Segment object are two good indicators of network functions.

This section offers some guidelines on detecting bottlenecks and discusses some of the counters you can use to measure processor, memory, disk, and network activity. The exercises at the end of this chapter provide step-by-step instructions on how to use Performance Monitor to create charts, logs, and reports.

Performance Monitor Views

Performance Monitor has four views. Each one is different, and each one fulfills a specific purpose in monitoring your system. The four views are

◆ The *Chart* view plots the counters you select in a continuous chart (refer to Exercise 8.1).

◆ The *Alert* view automatically alerts a network official if a predetermined counter threshold is surpassed.

◆ The *Log* view saves your system performance data to a log file.

◆ The *Report* view displays system performance data in a report format.

Although they are different, the Performance Monitor views do have commonalities. For each, you can ask the Performance Monitor to watch or show information for different objects (like your memory, disk, network), and each object has different counters (which are like statistics for the object). They all have configurable intervals to determine how often statistics should be gathered and either displayed, saved, or reported on.

After you take a look at the different views, you will learn about some of the specific objects and counters that you may want to watch.

Chart View

Chart view is the real-time "watch-as-you-monitor" view (see Figure 8.8). It is designed for you to sit and watch. This allows you to observe performance—both good and bad—as it happens. Chart view can be configured to show either a line graph or a histogram. The difference between the two is that the graph appears to move at the gathering intervals, whereas the histogram has bars that stay fixed and simply grow or shrink in size. You can configure a reporting interval to determine how often new information is displayed.

Although chart view is really designed to be watched, you can export chart data into either a .csv or a .tsv format (csv is comma delimited, and tsv is tab delimited). Then you could analyze the data in a spreadsheet and generate a new graph using that medium.

Configuration of Chart view (see Step by Step 8.1) is basically divided into two segments: the data you want to capture and the form you want to see it in.

FIGURE 8.8
Performance Monitor's Chart view allows you to
see server performance in real-time.

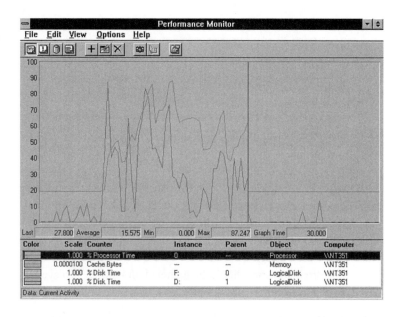

FIGURE 8.8
Performance Monitor's Chart view allows you to
see server performance in real-time.

STEP BY STEP

8.1 Configuring Chart View

1. Start Performance Monitor by choosing Start, Programs, Administrative Tools (Common), Performance Monitor.

2. From the View menu, choose Chart.

3. Choose Menu, Add to Chart to open the Add to Chart dialog box (see Figure 8.9).

4. In the Add to Chart dialog box, add a counter by specifying the server you want to monitor, the object you want to monitor, and the counter you want to see for that object. If the object you want to monitor has more than one instance (multiple physical hard drives or processors, for example), you can choose the specific object to monitor, or you can monitor the total of all objects.

   Configure the look of the line generated from the counter by choosing your preferences from the Color, Scale, Width, and Style boxes.

   Click the Add button to add the counter to the chart (or click Done to exit the Add to Chart dialog box).

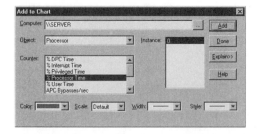

FIGURE 8.9
The Add to Chart dialog box allows you to add
counters and configure their appearance.

5. From the Options menu, choose Chart to see the chart options (see Figure 8.10).

6. In the Chart Options dialog box, configure the general look of the chart, as well as the chart type (Graph or Histogram) and the update frequency (manual if you want the chart updated only when you ask).

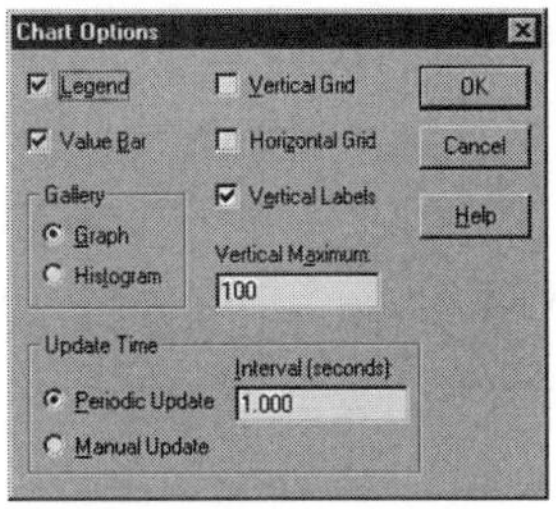

FIGURE 8.10
The Chart Options dialog box allows you to configure the general operation and appearance of the Chart view.

Alert View

The Alert view (shown in Figure 8.11) allows you to set thresholds that the Performance Monitor is to watch for. When a specific counter crosses the threshold you have set for it, an alert is generated. This alert could be an entry made in the NT Event log, or it could be a message sent to a specific computer on the network. By configuring alerts, you can remain aware of system events without having to watch your servers all the time.

Like Chart view, the Alert view can be configured (see Step by Step 8.2). You can specify the interval at which Performance Monitor checks for alert conditions.

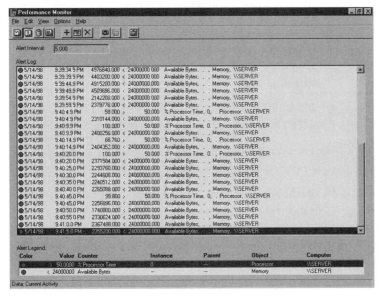

FIGURE 8.11
The Alert view allows you to set thresholds for counters and have Performance Monitor issue alerts when those thresholds are crossed.

FIGURE 8.12
The Add to Alert dialog box allows you to add counters and configure their thresholds.

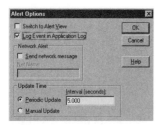

FIGURE 8.13
The Alert Options dialog box allows you to configure the general operation and appearance of the Alert view.

STEP BY STEP

8.2 Configuring Alert View

1. Start Performance Monitor by choosing Start, Programs, Administrative Tools (Common), Performance Monitor.

2. From the View menu, choose Alert.

3. Choose Menu, Add to Alert to open the Add to Alert dialog box (see Figure 8.12).

4. In the Add to Alert dialog box, add a counter by specifying the server you want to monitor, the object you want to monitor, and the counter you want to see for that object. If the object you want to monitor has more than one instance (multiple physical hard drives or processors, for example), you can choose the specific object to monitor, or you can monitor the total of all objects.

   For the selected counter, configure the threshold condition you want to watch for by choosing Over or Under in the Alert If field and then typing a threshold value.

   Choose a color to be identified with the alert in the alert list that will tell you which of the alert conditions have been configured and when they happen.

   If desired, indicate if a program should run when the alert happens and whether it should run each time or just the first time.

   Click the Add button to add the counter to the chart (or click Done to exit the Add to Alert dialog box).

5. From the Options menu, choose Alert to see the alert options (see Figure 8.13).

6. In the Alert Options dialog box, configure the alert interval and the type of notification you desire. You can be alerted in any or all of the following ways: The Alert view comes to the foreground of your server; an event is written to the NT Event log; or a message is sent to a specific computer (specify the computer name, but do not use \\ in front of it).

Log View

The Log view is unlike the other views in that it does not generate information that can be analyzed by it. Based on the parameters you set, the Log view creates a log file that can be exported or analyzed by any of the other view types. The advantage of this view is that it can capture data over a long period of time to be analyzed in a static state.

The Log view cannot be configured to capture specific counters; it simply captures all the counters available for the objects you want to log (see Figure 8.14). Various counters can then be displayed using the view you choose to analyze the log with. Like the other views, you can configure the Log view to capture data at specific intervals (see Step by Step 8.3). However, logs are often configured to capture data with wider intervals because they usually capture data over an extended period of time and are used to determine long-term performance trends.

NOTE

Remember to Start the Messenger Service In order for a message to be sent to another machine when an alert occurs, the Messenger service must be running on both the server and the recipient machine. In addition, the name specified to send to in the Net Name field must be available on the network.

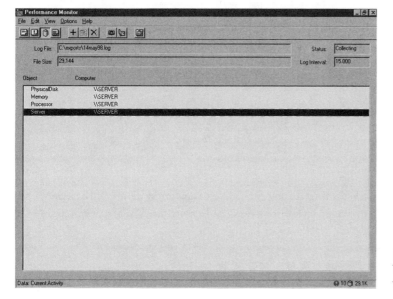

FIGURE 8.14
The Log View allows you to capture data to a file for analysis at a later time.

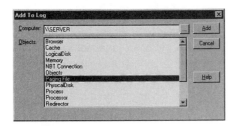

FIGURE 8.15
The Add to Log dialog box allows you to add objects to be logged.

FIGURE 8.16
The Log Options dialog box allows you to configure the log interval and the location of the log file.

STEP BY STEP

8.3 Configuring Log View

1. Start Performance Monitor by choosing Start, Programs, Administrative Tools (Common), Performance Monitor.

2. From the View menu, choose Log.

3. Choose Menu, Add to Log to open the Add to Log dialog box (see Figure 8.15).

4. In the Add to Log dialog box, specify the server you want to monitor and the objects you want to monitor. You can drag over multiple objects or use the Ctrl+*click* method to choose multiple noncontiguous objects.

   Click the Add button to add the object(s) to the log (or click Done to exit the Add to Log dialog box).

5. From the Options menu, choose Log to see the log options (see Figure 8.16).

6. In the Log Options dialog box, configure the log interval and the name and location of the log file. When you're ready to begin logging, click the Start Log button.

7. When the logging period is complete, open the Options menu, choose Log, and click the Stop Log button. Then click the Save button to save the log to disk.

After creating the log file, you can analyze it in any of the other Performance Monitor views, as demonstrated in Step by Step 8.4.

STEP BY STEP

8.4 Analyzing a Log File

1. Start Performance Monitor by choosing Start, Programs, Administrative Tools (Common), Performance Monitor.

2. From the View menu, choose the view you want to use to view the logged information.

3. From the Options menu, choose Data From. The Data From dialog box appears (see Figure 8.17).

4. In the Data From dialog box, choose the Log File option button and enter the path of the log file (or browse for it by using the ellipsis button).

5. If you want to see the log for a certain slice of time only, choose Edit, Time Window. Then in the Input Log File Timeframe dialog box, drag the end points of the gray time window to the positions desired (see Figure 8.18).

6. Add counters to the view and analyze it as though the data were live.

FIGURE 8.17
The Data From dialog box allows you to indicate whether the data for the current view is live (Current Activity) or from a log file.

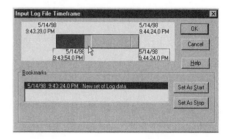

FIGURE 8.18
The Input Log File Timeframe dialog box allows you to focus in on a specific slice of time captured in the log file.

Report View

Like the Chart view, the Report view shows information as it happens. The difference is that there is no graph, and as a result, you can see no historical information as you watch the marker progress across your screen. Instead, the Report view shows you counters categorized by object and shows statistical information for the state of those counters as of the last reporting interval (see Figure 8.19).

Like charts, reports can be exported to .csv or .tsv formats so you can analyze a snapshot of data at a specific point in time. Step by Step 8.5 walks you through the configuration of a Report view.

STEP BY STEP

8.5 Configuring Report View

1. Start Performance Monitor by choosing Start, Programs, Administrative Tools (Common), Performance Monitor.

2. From the View menu, choose Report.

3. Choose Menu, Add to Report to open the Add to Report dialog box (see Figure 8.20).

WARNING

Log File Remains in Effect Until You Change It or Exit Performance Monitor If you choose to analyze a log file but then want to go back to monitoring current activity, you must choose Options, Data From and select Current Activity. Otherwise, you will continue to view data from the log file you last looked at. The log file remains in view until you exit Performance Monitor. When you restart, it reverts back to the default setting of Current Activity.

FIGURE 8.19
The Report view displays a report of system statistics as of the last reporting interval.

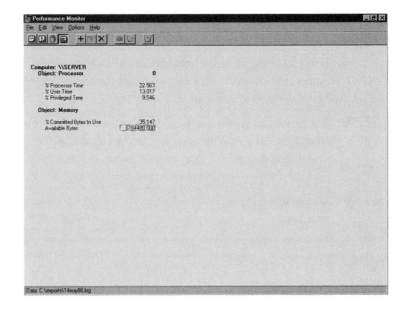

4. In the Add to Report dialog box, specify the server you want to monitor and the objects and counters you want to monitor.

   Click the Add button to add the object to the report (or click Done to exit the Add to Report dialog box).

5. From the Options menu, choose Report to see the report options (see Figure 8.21).

6. In the Report Options dialog box, configure the report interval.

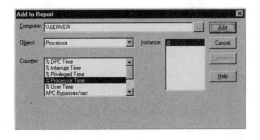

FIGURE 8.20
The Add to Report dialog box allows you to add counters to the report.

FIGURE 8.21
The Report Options dialog box allows you to configure the general operation and appearance of the Report view.

Bottleneck—The Limiting Resource

Identify performance bottlenecks.

When you understand the tools you need for measuring your system's performance, you are ready to dig into the data to determine how to improve performance. This section presents a simple strategy for detecting the part of your system that has become a performance bottleneck.

The bottleneck on your system is the resource that limits the rate at which a task can be completed. If the resource was faster or if you had more of it, the task would finish sooner. If your task uses processor, network, and disk resources but mostly spends time using the disk, for example, the disk is the bottleneck. After you identify the bottleneck, you can resolve it by changing or reallocating your resources (such as adding a faster hard disk).

The simplest way to detect the bottleneck on your system is to examine the amounts of time the various components of your system consume when completing a task. The component that uses the most time to complete its portion of the task is the bottleneck.

Suppose you use Performance Monitor to determine that, when executing your task, Windows NT consumes .5 seconds of processor time, .1 second accessing the network, and .8 seconds accessing the disk. During most of the time the task is running, the processor and network are sitting idle waiting for the disk (see Figure 8.22). After you add a faster hard disk, the disk access drops to .4 seconds, but the processor still takes .5 seconds. Now the processor is the bottleneck.

Overall Performance Indicators

A reasonable place to start in monitoring server performance in Windows NT is to watch a number of general counters in Performance Monitor. These counters can provide a great deal of insight into the performance of the system as a whole. If you are not certain what to monitor, start with these counters, and then gather more detail as you determine which component is the bottleneck.

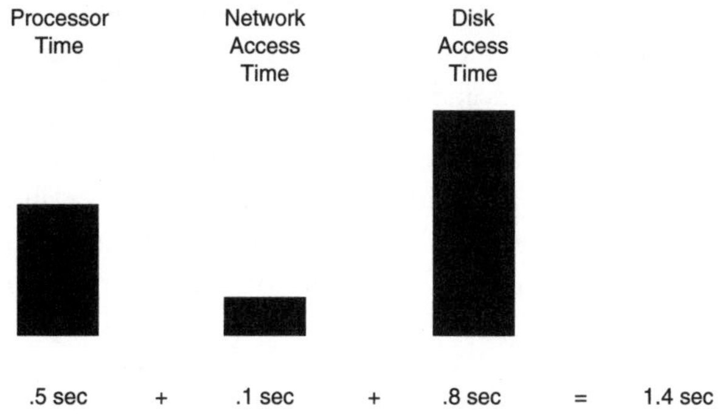

> **NOTE** **Strange But True** Although it sounds backward, it is true: Windows NT boots from the system partition and then loads the system from the boot partition.

FIGURE 8.22
Identifying a bottleneck means taking all factors into account.

N O T E

The Bottleneck Is the Limiting Factor The subtask that consumes the greatest share of execution time is the bottleneck. In Figure 8.22, the disk is the bottleneck.

N O T E

One Performance Monitor for Multiple Servers You can use Performance Monitor to monitor these counters on your system regularly and to log the activity to disk. If you need to monitor multiple servers, you can monitor all of them from one Performance Monitor session by adding counters from each of the systems.

N O T E

High Processor Activity May Indicate Other Problems High levels of processor activity can result from two situations (other than the handling of a processor-intensive task). First, if your system is low on memory, the processor is required to handle a number of memory swaps to deal with the maintenance of virtual memory. Second, if a hardware device is generating a large number of interrupts, the processor is busy handling those messages. In both of those situations, however, replacing the processor with a faster one may be unwarranted because the root cause is not processor specific.

Table 8.4 lists five counters that can give a good indication of overall system health.

TABLE 8.4

COUNTERS THAT INDICATE OVERALL PERFORMANCE

Object	*Counter*
Processor	%Processor Time
Memory	Pages/Sec
Physical Disk	%Disk Time
Server	Bytes Total/Sec
Network Segment	%Network Utilization

The following sections describe the counters listed in Table 8.4, as well as some other important counters you may need to check when measuring the performance of the processor, memory, physical disk, and server. You should be familiar with these counters for the Windows NT Server exam.

The Processor Object

The following are useful counters for the processor object.

◆ *Processor Time.* This counter measures the amount of time the processor spends executing a non-idle thread. In effect, it is the percentage of time the processor was busy. If the average value exceeds 80 percent, the processor could be the bottleneck.

◆ *Interrupts/Sec.* This counter measures the number of interrupts the processor handles per second. An increase in the number of interrupts can indicate hardware failures in I/O devices such as disk controllers and network cards.

◆ *System: Processor Queue Length.* This counter measures the number of threads waiting in the queue for an available processor. Generally, if the number of threads in the queue exceeds two, you have a problem with processor performance.

The Memory Object

In general, the symptoms of a memory shortage on the system are a busy processor (managing the virtual memory) and a high level of disk activity on the disk that contains the page file (accessing the disk to read and write memory pages). The following are counters you will need to monitor to analyze memory performance.

◆ *Pages/Sec.* This counter measures the number of times a memory page had to be paged in to memory or out to the disk. An increase in this value indicates an increase in paging activity.

◆ *Available Bytes.* This counter measures the amount of physical memory available. When this value falls below 1MB, you are getting excessive paging.

The PhysicalDisk and LogicalDisk Objects

Before you can use Performance Monitor to monitor disk activity, you must enable the disk performance counters. Otherwise, all values for the disk counters report zeroes in Performance Monitor.

To turn on the disk performance counters, log on as a user with administrative privileges and type the following:

```
diskperf -y
```

The PhysicalDisk object measures the performance of a physical disk. The LogicalDisk object records parameters pertaining to a logical disk. (A logical disk is a partition or logical drive that is accorded a drive letter, such as C, D, and so on).

> **NOTE**
>
> **Starting Disk Counters on a Remote Computer** To start the disk counters on a remote computer, add the computer name to the `diskperf` command like this:
>
> ```
> diskperf -y \\computername
> ```

DISKPERF ITSELF USES RESOURCES

The disk objects are not enabled by default because they do use some resources to run. On a 486 system, Microsoft claims an increase of 1–2 percent on disk and processor utilization when running DISKPERF. On the other hand, it claims that the impact on a Pentium system is negligible. This low resource utilization, coupled with the fact that enabling DISKPERF requires a server restart, would indicate that starting DISKPERF is a recommended procedure. This ensures that disk performance analysis can be done easily with little impact on the system. Regardless, because most NT Servers are currently Pentium systems, the performance impact will not be noticeable.

You will want to monitor the following counters to analyze disk performance:

◆ *PhysicalDisk: %Disk Time.* This counter reports the percentage of time the physical disk was busy reading or writing.

◆ *PhysicalDisk: Avg. Disk Queue Length.* This counter measures the average number of requests for a given disk (both read and write requests).

◆ *LogicalDisk: %Disk Time.* This counter reports the percentage of time that the logical disk (for example, drive C) was busy. To monitor the total activity of all the partitions on a single disk drive, use the Physical Disk: %Disk Time counter.

◆ *LogicalDisk: Disk Queue Length.* This counter measures the number of read and write requests waiting for the logical disk to become available. If this counter exceeds two, disk performance is suffering.

The Server Object

The Server component is responsible for handling all SMB-based requests for sessions and file and print services. If the Server service becomes the bottleneck, requests from clients are denied, forcing retries and creating slower response times and increased traffic. The following list represents the counters you will want to monitor to gauge server performance.

◆ *Bytes Total/Sec.* This counter measures the number of bytes sent to and received from the network. It provides an overall indication of how much information the Server service is handling. When the combined total of this counter for all your servers nears the maximum throughput for your network medium, you have run out of network capacity and need to subdivide the network.

◆ *Pool Nonpaged Failures and Pool Paged Failures.* This counter measures the number of times a request from the server to allocate memory failed. These failures indicate a memory shortage.

Establishing Baseline Performance Data

Many of the counters that Performance Monitor provides cannot be interpreted without some baseline data to which to compare them. The number of bytes read per second from the disk varies tremendously depending on the type of drive and controller you have. The historical data for these counters, however, can provide a basis for comparison.

It is a good idea to log performance from your servers regularly and at various times of the day. Then if you do encounter a performance problem, you can look at the historical data to see how the demands on the server have changed over time. If you see changes in the percent of free space on the disk or the number of bytes that the Server component is handling, for example, you can make appropriate adjustments in the hardware before a performance problem develops.

With the right combination of hardware and software, Windows NT Server requires minimal to no tuning. Determining the right hardware for your needs, however, is critical to getting the best performance. Knowing how to interpret performance data for your system can help you understand how changes to your hardware will affect performance.

CASE STUDY: SLINGSHOT TRAINING

ESSENCE OF THE CASE

The essence of this case can be summarized in a number of points:

- NT Server has a predictable pattern of heavy use for short periods of time.

- The use of Server and Network resources centers almost exclusively on data transfer.

SCENARIO

Slingshot Training is a major U.S. computer applications training company. Slingshot teaches about 60 different courses, spanning a wide variety of operating system platforms and application manufacturers.

In order to ensure consistency in the classroom and predictability of application performance by its students and instructors, Slingshot Training has implemented a download and installation system to prepare each classroom for the next

continues

CASE STUDY: SLINGSHOT TRAINING

continued

day's course. This system consists of a complete format of the hard drive on each student computer and an installation of both the operating system and an application software suite.

The configuration of each city's branch consists of a single NT Server (used to hold and distribute installation files) and 80–100 client machines that are refreshed every day. This refresh happens between 4:00 and 5:00 p.m. During the rest of the day, the download server is rarely used, and the network remains relatively idle.

As applications have become more complex and larger, download times have increased significantly, and the personnel at the branches have become increasingly frustrated. The server, a 133MHz Pentium, has 32MB of RAM and two 4GB IDE hard drives. The hard drives each have about 50MB of free space on them. The network consists of Category 5 cabling running token ring, and the server has a 16MB ISA adapter. You have been called in to analyze the situation and make recommendations.

ANALYSIS

Although a definitive conclusion cannot be reached given the data presented, a number of factors must be considered for analysis.

The first is a surface analysis of the hardware. It is obvious that the hardware is at least a couple of years old (which you can tell simply by looking at the specifications). Although that does not necessarily mean it will not function in this environment any longer, consideration must be given to the availability of faster and higher-throughput devices. In addition, given the application of the server, you must consider the components and configuration that will give the best results.

The major hardware subsystems that you have to consider are: Processor, Memory, Disks, and Network. And in all of these, speed and quantity are paramount to performance. Right off, you will have to consider the need to add more RAM and replace IDE disks with higher-capacity SCSI drives. This will improve disk access overall. In addition, you may also consider upgrading the network from 16MB token ring to 100MB ethernet for more throughput (the Category 5 cabling is capable of supporting network traffic at those speeds). The processor may or may not be a factor in the reduction of download speeds.

In order to actually test the system for bottlenecks, you will have to run Performance Monitor. You can establish a baseline by running Performance Monitor during the day to determine the typical usage of the system. After you establish that, you can compare your heavy-load figures against the baseline. You will then want to run Performance Monitor on several different days between 4:00 and 5:00 p.m. to get a good log of heavy usage data. You should probably log counters from the four major hardware subsystems and then analyze the results in a static Chart view.

Finally, after you analyze the captured logs, you can compare them against the initial hardware recommendations to see which of your initial insights agree with the monitored data.

Armed with this information, you can make a case for upgrading the system. In addition, after hardware modifications have been made, you may want to recommend periodic analysis to watch for other bottlenecks and progressive system degradation.

CHAPTER SUMMARY

This chapter dealt with optimizing the performance of your NT Server through hardware analysis and upgrades and through performance monitoring and tuning. Many performance problems are caused by inadequate hardware that can be identified by comparing it against recommended specifications and by upgrading to faster components periodically. However, in some cases, bottlenecks are not always easy to spot, and therefore, Performance Monitor becomes an invaluable tool for establishing performance baselines and then comparing performance figures for servers under load to those baselines. This may identify components that need to be upgraded or replaced.

KEY TERMS

Before taking the exam, make sure you are familiar with the definitions of and concepts behind each of the following key terms. Appendix A is a glossary of terms that you can use for quick reference purposes.

- Performance Monitor
- Object
- Counter
- Chart view
- Log view
- Report view
- Alert view
- Reporting interval
- Bottleneck

APPLY YOUR LEARNING

Exercises

8.1   Creating a Chart in Performance Monitor

This exercise will help you do the following: Become familiar with the process of creating and reading a Performance Monitor chart; understand the basic components of the Performance Monitor main window and the Add to Chart dialog box; and learn how to turn on disk performance counters by using the diskperf command.

Estimated Time: 25 minutes

1. Choose Start, Programs, Administrative Tools, and click on Performance Monitor. The Performance Monitor window appears.

2. Choose Edit, Add to Chart (see Figure 8.23). The Add to Chart dialog box appears (see Figure 8.24).

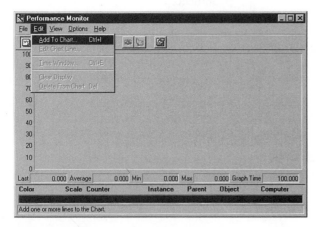

FIGURE 8.23
From the Performance Monitor window, you can add new counters to configure the current view.

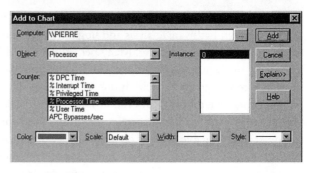

FIGURE 8.24
The Add to Chart dialog box allows you to add counters for specific objects.

You also can open the Add to Chart dialog box by clicking on the plus sign in the toolbar of the Performance Monitor window.

3. The Computer text box at the top of the Add to Chart dialog box will be set to the default (the local system). You can click the ellipsis button to the right of the Computer text box to access a browse list of computers on the network if you want to monitor another computer.

4. The Object combo box tells Performance Monitor which object you want to monitor. Choose the PhysicalDisk object. If you have more than one physical disk on your system, a list of your physical disks appears in the Instances box to the right of the Object box. The Instances box lists all instances of the selected object. If necessary, choose a physical disk instance.

5. In the Counter list box, scroll through the list of counters for the PhysicalDisk object. If you feel like experimenting, select a different object in the Object box. Notice that the different object is accompanied by a different set of counters. Switch back to the PhysicalDisk object and

APPLY YOUR LEARNING

choose the %Disk Time counter. Click on the Explain button. A description of the %Disk Time counter appears at the bottom of the dialog box.

6. Click on the Done button to close the Add to Chart dialog box.

7. In the Performance Monitor main window, you'll see a vertical line sweeping across the chart from left to right. You also might also see a faint-colored line at the bottom of the chart recording a %Disk Time value of 0. If so, you have not enabled the disk performance counters for your system. (If the disk performance counters are enabled on your system, you should see a spiked line that looks like the readout from an electro-cardiogram. Go on to step 8.)

If you need to enable the disk performance counters, click on the Start button and go to the command prompt. Enter the command **diskperf –y**. Reboot your system and repeat steps 1–7. (You do not have to browse through the Object and Counter lists this time.) You should now see a spiked line representing the percentage of time that the physical disk is busy reading or writing.

8. Choose Edit, Add to Chart. Select the PhysicalDisk object and choose the counter Avg. Disk Queue Length. Click on the Add button, and then choose the counter Avg. Disk Bytes/Read. Click on the Add button again. Then click on the Done button.

9. Examine the Performance Monitor main window. All three of the counters you selected should be tracing out spiked lines on the chart (see Figure 8.25). Each line is a different color. A table at the bottom of the window shows which counter goes with which color. The table also

gives the scale of the output, the instance, the object, and the computer.

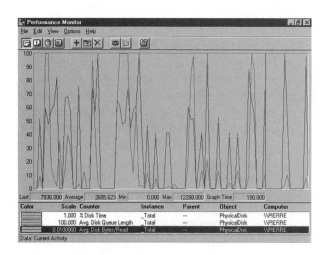

FIGURE 8.25
The Performance Monitor Chart view. By default, it is updated every second with current performance information.

10. Below the chart (but above the table of counters) is a row of statistical parameters labeled Last, Average, Min, Max, and Graph Time. These parameters pertain to the counter selected in the table at the bottom of the window. Select a different counter and some of the values will change. The Last value is the counter value over the last second. Graph Time is the time it will take (in seconds) for the vertical line that draws the chart to sweep across the window.

11. Start Windows NT Explorer. Select a file (a graphics file or a word processing document) and choose Edit, Copy. Then go to another directory and choose Edit, Paste. Minimize Explorer and return to the Performance Monitor main window.

APPLY YOUR LEARNING

The disk activity caused by your Explorer session will be reflected in the spikes of the counter lines.

12. Choose Options, Chart, and the Chart Options dialog box appears (see Figure 8.26), providing a number of options governing the chart display. The Update Time frame enables you to choose an update interval. The update interval tells Performance Monitor how frequently it should update the chart with new values. (If you choose the Manual Update option, the chart is updated only when you press Ctrl+U or choose Options, Update Now.) Experiment with the Chart Options dialog box, or click on the Cancel button.

FIGURE 8.26
The Chart Options dialog box allows you to configure the look of your charts, as well as the update interval and display type (graph versus histogram).

13. Choose File, Exit to exit Performance Monitor. The Save Chart Settings and Save Chart Settings As options in the File menu enable you to save the collection of objects and counters you are using now so you can monitor the same counters later without having to set them up again. The Export Chart option enables you to export the data to a file that you can open with a spreadsheet

or database application. The Save Workspace option saves the settings for your chart as well as any settings for alerts, logs, or reports specified in this session. You will learn more about alerts, logs, and reports in Exercise 8.2.

8.2 Performance Monitor Alerts, Logs, and Reports

In this exercise, you will learn about the alternative views (Alert view, Log view, and Report view) available through the View menu of Performance Monitor, and you will learn how to log performance data to a log file.

Estimated Time: 25 minutes

1. Choose Start, Programs, Administrative Tools, and Performance Monitor. The Performance Monitor main window appears.

2. Choose View, Alert.

3. Click on the plus sign in the toolbar or choose Edit, Add to Alert. The Add to Alert dialog box appears; it is similar to the Add to Chart dialog box, except you will notice two additional items at the bottom (see Figure 8.27).

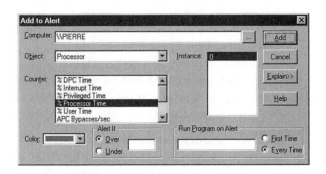

FIGURE 8.27
The Add to Alert dialog box allows you to add a new counter to the Alert view.

APPLY YOUR LEARNING

4. The default object in the Object combo box should be the Processor object. The default counter in the Counter list box should be %Processor Time. In the Alert If area, select the Over radio button and enter the value **5%** in the text box.

In the Run Program on Alert area, type **SOL** in the text box and select the First Time radio button. This configuration tells Performance Monitor to execute Windows NT's Solitaire program when the %Processor Time exceeds five percent.

> **WARNING**
>
> **Use the First Time Radio Button**
> It is important to select the First Time radio button; otherwise, Performance Monitor will execute a new instance of Solitaire every time the %Processor Time exceeds five percent, which happens every time Performance Monitor executes a new instance of Solitaire. In other words, if you try this experiment without selecting the First Time radio button, you'll probably have to close Performance Monitor or reboot your system to stop the incessant shuffling and dealing.

5. Click on the Add button, and then click on the Done button. The Alert Legend at the bottom of the Performance Monitor window describes the active alert parameters. The Alert Log shows every instance of an alert (see Figure 8.28).

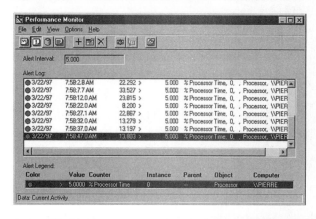

FIGURE 8.28
The Performance Monitor Alert Log identifies the occurrences of the alert conditions you configured.

6. Make some change to your desktop. (Hide or reveal the taskbar or change the size of the Performance Monitor window—anything that will cause a five percent utilization of the processor.) The Solitaire program should miraculously appear on your screen. In a real alert situation, Performance Monitor would execute an alert application instead of starting a card game.

7. Choose Edit, Delete Alert.

8. Choose View, Log. The Log view saves performance data to a log file instead of displaying it onscreen.

9. Choose Edit, Add to Log. Notice that only the objects appear in the Add to Log dialog box. The counters and instances do not appear because Performance Monitor automatically logs all counters and all instances of the object to the log file.

Select the Memory object and click on Add. If you want, you can select another object, such as the Paging File object, and then click on Add again. When you finish adding objects, click on Done.

10. Choose Options, Log. The Log Options dialog box appears (see Figure 8.29). Here you can designate a log file that Performance Monitor will use to log the data.

In the File Name text box, enter the name **exer2**.

You also can specify an update interval. The Manual Update radio button specifies that the file won't be undated unless you press Ctrl+U or choose Options, Update Now.

Click on the Start Log button to start saving data to the log. Wait a few minutes, and then return to the Log Options dialog box and click on the Stop Log button.

FIGURE 8.29
The Log Options dialog box allows you to specify a name and location for your log file and to configure the update interval.

11. Choose View, Chart.

12. Choose Options, Data From. Note that the default source is Current Activity. (That is why the chart you created in Exercise 8.1 took its data from current system activity.)

The alternative to logging current activity is to use data from a log file. Click on the Log File radio button, click on the ellipsis button to the right of Log File, and then select the **exer2** file you created in step 10. Click on OK.

13. Choose Edit, Add to Chart.

Click on the down arrow of the Object combo box. Notice that your only object choices are the Memory object and any other objects you selected in step 9. Select the Memory object. Browse through the counter list and select Pages/Sec. Click on the Add button. Select any other memory counters you want to display, and then click on the Add button. Click on Done.

14. The log file's record of the counters you selected in step 13 appears in the chart in the Performance Monitor main window. Notice that, unlike the chart you created in Exercise 8.1, this chart does not continuously sweep out new data. That is because this chart represents static data from a previous finite monitoring session.

15. Choose Edit, Time Window. A time window enables you to focus on a particular time interval within the log file (see Figure 8.30).

Set the beginning and end points of your time window by adjusting the gray start and stop sliders on the time window slide bar. The Bookmarks frame enables you to specify a log file bookmark to use as a start or stop point. (You can create a bookmark by choosing Options, Bookmark while collecting data to the log file or by clicking on the book in the Performance Monitor toolbar.)

Click on OK to view the data for the time interval.

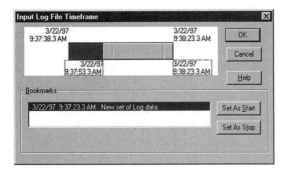

FIGURE 8.30
The Input Log File Timeframe dialog box allows you to specify the specific period within the total captured time for which you want to look at data.

> **NOTE**
> **A Time Window Is Very Useful in a Real-Time Situation** In this example, because you collected data only for a few minutes, using the Time Window option might seem unnecessary. If you collected data for a longer period, however, and you wanted to zero in on a particular event, a time window would be very useful.

16. Choose View, Report. Then choose Options, Data From. In the Data From dialog box, select the radio button labeled Current Activity. Report view displays the performance data in a report instead of in a graphics format.

17. Choose Edit, Add to Report. Select the Processor object and choose the %Processor Time, %Interrupt Time, and Interrupts/Sec counters (hold down the Ctrl key to select all three), and then click on Add.

Select the PhysicalDisk object and choose the %Disk Time, Avg. Disk Queue Length, and Current Disk Queue Length counters. Click on the Add button.

Select the Memory object and choose the Pages/Sec, Page Faults/Sec, and Available Bytes counters. Click on the Add button. Then click on Done.

18. Examine the main report window. Performance Monitor displays a report of the performance data in a hierarchical format, with counters listed under the appropriate objects.

19. Choose File, Exit to exit Performance Monitor.

Review Questions

1. You are attempting to monitor disk performance statistics using Performance Monitor; however, all the statistics show 0. Why?

2. By default, for how many users and for what tasks is the Windows NT Server service configured?

3. What does the Performance Monitor counter Bytes Total/Sec measure?

4. What four views are available in Performance Monitor?

Exam Questions

1. For the most part, how much time should you spend tuning and optimizing Windows NT?

   A. At least an hour a day.

   B. Most of the first week after the initial installation.

   C. None.

   D. Very little. For the most part, NT is self-tuning and requires very little user intervention.

2. Which of the following is the major tool for gathering information and identifying bottlenecks?

   A. Tune—T

   B. Monitor

   C. Performance Monitor

   D. Server Manager

3. Before you can tune a file server for optimum performance, which one of the following questions must you answer?

   A. How much money do you have to spend on new hardware?

   B. What types of tasks is the file server expected to perform?

   C. This question has no answer; simply put, tuning is the process of putting the fastest hardware in your computer.

   D. In what type of business is the company using the file server? (For certain companies, you cannot tune NT because of U.S. government restrictions.)

4. A curious user tells you that while reading a major computer periodical, he came across this statement: "All computer systems have a bottleneck of some type." Why is this so?

   A. A computer system is only as fast as its slowest component. On any system, you may remove one bottleneck, but you always expose another.

   B. The article was incorrect. For example, your file server has absolutely no bottlenecks.

   C. The article was referring to non-Windows NT systems. Microsoft has designed the NT system to continually self-adjust, thus eliminating bottlenecks.

   D. Because you always upgrade components as soon as new ones are available, you eliminate any potential bottlenecks before they become apparent.

5. Which statement is true regarding the type of hardware you should place in a heavily used file server?

   A. The equipment in the server is not important because nobody actually uses the server to run applications.

   B. You should always spend the most money on the server hardware.

   C. When designing a file server, always pick the hardware that exploits the full bus speed if possible (for example, SCSI hard drives, PCI bus network cards, and so on).

   D. You should use the same type of computer hardware as the workstations so the users get good response time; hardware from the same vendor works better together.

6. To optimize the network components in an NT Workstation or Server, which one of the following should you do?

   A. You do not need to do anything. NT automatically optimizes the network components.

   B. You should remove unused adapter cards and protocols.

   C. You should always have TCP/IP, NetBEUI, and NWLink installed, even if your computers are using only one protocol. This leaves more paths open in case one protocol becomes unusable.

   D. You should never use any protocol but TCP/IP.

7. Which of the following automatically swaps data in physical RAM out to disk and back?

   A. The Virtual Memory Manager

   B. The Virtual Device Driver

   C. HIMEM.EXE

   D. EMM386.EXE

8. Which of the following is the paging file that Windows NT creates?

   A. RAMPAGE.SYS

   B. SYS$RAM.SYS

   C. PAGEFILE.SYS

   D. VIRAM.SYS

9. What are some of the things you can do to make the system use virtual memory more efficiently? Select all that apply.

   A. Spread out the paging file across multiple hard drives.

   B. Move the paging file to the drive where the Windows NT system files are located.

   C. Move the paging file away from the drive where the Windows NT system files are located.

   D. Monitor the size of the paging file under peak usage, and then set the minimum size of the paging file to that value. This saves time when the system has to expand the paging file.

10. Which Performance Monitor object and counter measure the amount of time the CPU is busy?

    A. Processor: %Busy Time

    B. Processor: %Processor Time

    C. System: %Processor Time

    D. System: TotalProcessorUsage

11. While monitoring system performance in Performance Monitor, you notice that the number of interrupts per second has doubled. You haven't increased the number of users or added any new applications to the server. What does an increase of this counter mean?

    A. Nothing. It is normal for this counter to increase over time.

    B. It could mean that you have a potential hardware problem and that a piece of hardware is generating many more interrupts than normal.

    C. It indicates that the network card is the bottleneck in the system and should be replaced.

    D. It indicates that the CPU is the bottleneck in the system and should be replaced or upgraded.

APPLY YOUR LEARNING

12. You're trying to explain the System: Processor Queue Length counter in Performance Monitor to a co-worker. Which of the following statements best describes the function of this counter?

    A. It measures the amount of activity on the CPU.

    B. It indicates the number of threads waiting for CPU time.

    C. It indicates the number of users waiting to log on to the domain.

    D. It indicates the total CPU usage across all CPUs in the system. You see a number for this counter only if your computer has more than one CPU.

13. You're trying to get some statistics that measure the total amount of network traffic. Which Performance Monitor counter should you check?

    A. Pool Nonpaged Failures

    B. Total Network Bytes/Sec

    C. Bytes Total/Sec

    D. Network: %Network Bytes

14. You notice an increase in the number of Pool Nonpaged Failures. What does that indicate?

    A. You need to add more RAM to the server.

    B. The hard disk is failing, and the system must continually retry to allocate page file space.

    C. The system is using the RAM installed in the system, and the server is running efficiently.

    D. You need to upgrade the RAM in the system by installing faster EDO memory.

Answers to Review Questions

1. Your statistics are probably showing 0 because you have not turned on the disk counters. Because these counters use some system resources in their operation, they are not turned on by default. However, the performance loss is negligible on most systems, and keeping them running is usually not a problem. You can enable the disk counters with the command diskperf -y. For more information, see the section "The PhysicalDisk and LogicalDisk Objects."

2. The Windows NT Server service is configured for the setting Maximize Throughput for File Sharing. This means that it is optimized for networks with more than 64 users and is set to use the maximum amount of memory for file-sharing. This can be set by double-clicking the Server service in the Services tab of the Network Properties dialog box. For more information, see the section "Optimizing the Server Service."

3. The Bytes Total/Sec counter measures the general health of your Server service. By measuring the total amount of data coming in to and going out of your server, it gives a good indication of the efficiency of that service and the amount of room that's available on the network to handle more data. As the amount of data being handled approaches the total capacity of the network, you need to consider subnetting your network to reduce the total amount of data flowing on each net. For more information, see the section "The Server Object."

4. The Performance Monitor has four views: Chart, Alert, Log, and Report. Each view has a different use and can be configured separately. For more information, see the section "Performance Monitor Views."

Answers to Exam Questions

1. **D.** Because NT is self-tuning, you should have to assess the performance of your servers only periodically. If assessment uncovers serious degradation of performance, you will want to analyze the causes immediately. For more information, see the section "Windows Tunes Itself."

2. **C.** Performance Monitor is used to establish baselines and then to gather information for analysis against those baselines. For more information, see the section "Performance Monitor."

3. **B.** Tuning means optimizing a server for its intended task. It does no good to tune for something that is unnecessary (such as increasing network efficiency and output for a server that runs large scale standalone statistical analysis applications). For more information, see the section "Performance Objectives."

4. **A.** A bottleneck is defined as the limiting resource. No matter how efficient or fast or powerful your system is, one component will always be the slowest or least efficient or weakest link. This may not be easily evident because the system may not ever be pushed to its limit; however, the bottleneck is still present. For more information, see the section "Bottleneck—The Limiting Resource."

5. **C.** In file server applications, speed of throughput is paramount. This means that everything from the disk to the network adapter must be as fast as possible. This means you should make sure you have fast hard drives, fast network adapters, and enough RAM to ensure that caching of data can be as efficient as possible. For more information, see the section "Performance Objectives."

6. **B.** Removing all unnecessary networking hardware and software is very important in optimizing network efficiency. The more protocols and services are installed, the more network traffic is generated with every network command. The more adapters there are, the more points of network communication are present (in some cases this is good, in others this is bad). For more information, see the section "Configuration Changes That Affect Performance."

7. **A.** The Virtual Memory Manager is responsible for handling the interaction between physical RAM, virtual RAM, and the disk subsystem. For more information, see "Configuration Changes That Affect Performance."

8. **C.** The file that the VMM uses for paging is called PAGEFILE.SYS, and it is located on the root of each volume that's configured to have a paging file. For more information, see the section "Configuration Changes That Affect Performance."

9. **A, C, and D.** You can do a number of things to increase the efficiency with which your system uses the paging file. First, by creating more than one paging file, you increase both the amount of virtual memory available and the efficiency of access. Second, by moving the paging file off the boot partition, you can reduce the conflict in disk subsystem usage with other system tasks. Finally, in systems that see heavy use of virtual memory, by configuring the paging file to be as large as it normally expands to, you can save some system overhead that would be used to allocate space to an expanding paging file. For more information, see the section "Configuration Changes That Affect Performance."

APPLY YOUR LEARNING

10. **B.** The object Processor: %Processor Time measures the total amount of time (as a percentage of total time) the processor is being used. For more information, see the section "Overall Performance Indicators."

11. **B.** If the number of interrupts increases suddenly without a change to system configuration or usage patterns that is a sure sign of hardware problems. Some piece of hardware is generating far more interrupts than it previously did. You will have to isolate the hardware problem, and then repair or replace the defective component. For more information, see the section "Reasons to Monitor Performance."

12. **B.** Any queue is a line waiting for some service. The processor queue is a line of threads waiting to be processed. Queue length that consistently measures 2 or greater may indicate a need for an additional processor on your system. For more information, see the section "Overall Performance Indicators."

13. **B.** The total amount of network traffic is measured through the Total Network Bytes/Sec counter. For more information, see the section "Overall Performance Indicators."

14. **A.** This counter indicates the failure of a system request to allocate memory. This is frequently caused by a lack of physical RAM and indicates the need for an increase in RAM. For more information, see the section "Overall Performance Indicators."

Suggested Readings and Resources

1. Microsoft Official Curriculum course 922: *Supporting Microsoft Windows NT 4.0 Core Technologies*
   - Module 18: Troubleshooting Resources

2. Microsoft Official Curriculum course 689: *Supporting Microsoft Windows NT Server 4.0 Enterprise Technologies*
   - Module 2: Microsoft Windows NT Server 4.0 Analysis and Optimization

3. Microsoft TechNet CD-ROM
   - *Concepts and Planning – MS Windows NT Server 4.0*
   - Chapter 8: Monitoring Performance

4. Web sites
   - www.microsoft.com/train.cert
   - www.prometric.com/testingcandidates/ assessment/ chosetest.html (take online assessment tests)

Microsoft provides the following objectives for "Troubleshooting":

Choose the appropriate course of action to take to resolve installation failures.

▶ This objective is necessary because someone certified in the use of Windows NT Server technology must understand the process of installation and be able to troubleshoot and resolve problems that occur in the installation process.

Choose the appropriate course of action to take to resolve boot failures.

▶ This objective is necessary because someone certified in the use of Windows NT Server technology must understand the NT boot process and be able to troubleshoot and resolve problems that occur when booting.

Choose the appropriate course of action to take to resolve configuration errors.

▶ This objective is necessary because someone certified in the use of Windows NT Server technology must understand the proper configuration of NT and be able to troubleshoot and resolve problems relating to general configuration.

Choose the appropriate course of action to take to resolve printer problems.

▶ This objective is necessary because someone certified in the use of Windows NT Server technology must understand the NT print process and architecture and be able to troubleshoot and resolve problems relating to printing.

CHAPTER 9

Troubleshooting

Choose the appropriate course of action to take to resolve RAS problems.

▶ This objective is necessary because someone certified in the use of Windows NT Server technology must understand the configuration and operation of a RAS server and client interaction and be able to troubleshoot and resolve problems that occur when using RAS.

Choose the appropriate course of action to take to resolve connectivity problems.

▶ This objective is necessary because someone certified in the use of Windows NT Server technology must understand the networking and security architecture of NT and be able to troubleshoot and resolve problems with connectivity (or the lack thereof).

Choose the appropriate course of action to take to resolve resource access problems and permission problems.

▶ This objective is necessary because someone certified in the use of Windows NT Server technology must understand the security model of NT and be able to troubleshoot and resolve resource access problems that occur as a result of incorrect permissions or incorrect sharing procedures.

Choose the appropriate course of action to take to resolve fault-tolerance failures. Fault-tolerance methods include: tape backup, mirroring, stripe set with parity, and disk duplexing.

▶ This objective is necessary because someone certified in the use of Windows NT Server technology must understand the software implementation of fault tolerance in NT and be able to troubleshoot and resolve resource access problems that occur as a result of systems failures.

▶ In a poll that Microsoft conducted among troubleshooters to determine what made for successful troubleshooting, more than half of the troubleshooting successes could be related to experience—either with the computer system or with the specific problem. This indicates that the best knowledge to have is knowledge of how the system works and what problems you might face. Just as bank tellers are trained not on how to spot counterfeit money but on how to spot the real stuff, you should focus most of your attention not on what might go wrong and how to fix it but on how a good working NT Server looks. In this way, you will be able to more easily detect a problem and determine its cause.

▶ Troubleshooting questions on the NT Server exam are rarely as straightforward as "You are troubleshooting a problem with RAS...." Instead, a need for troubleshooting is implied in scenario questions, and you will have to put your troubleshooting skills to work to figure out what is the best course of action. Scenario questions on the NT Server exam are often worded so as to confuse you into thinking a particular piece of information is important when it is not. Become familiar with working systems, and when you are familiar, you will instantly know if something is wrong (like the bank teller who handles a piece of counterfeit money after thousands of real bills have passed through her hands). Then your experience and instincts will tell you where to go to solve the problem.

▶ Having said all that, you still must have a good methodology for troubleshooting, and you must know what kinds of problems are likely to crop up both in a production environment and on the exam. Become very familiar with the categories of troubleshooting covered in this chapter and understand the problems that might arise from incorrect configuration or system failure. Also know what solutions make the most sense in a given situation.

INTRODUCTION

The subject of Windows NT troubleshooting is as broad as the subject of Windows NT. Almost any task you perform in Windows NT may someday require troubleshooting. All the material in the preceding chapters is important to your achieving an understanding of troubleshooting. The more you know, the easier time you will have solving problems. The best tool for troubleshooting is an understanding of the underlying processes within NT. When something trips up, try to figure out what it tripped on, and you will be on your way to knowing why. In that vein, you may want to review some of the performance optimization techniques in Chapter 8, "Monitoring and Optimization," as you prepare for the "Troubleshooting" section of the NT Server exam.

GENERAL TROUBLESHOOTING TECHNIQUES

Microsoft presents a basic troubleshooting model that it identifies using the acronym DETECT, which stands for Discover, Explore, Track, Execute, Check, Tie up. The following list outlines the DETECT troubleshooting model.

◆ *Discover the problem.* Talk to users and look at the systems in question to determine what the problem is. Find out what software is running and what versions of operating systems and service packs are being used. Gather as much information as you can to figure out what the real problem is. It may take a lot of work to go from point A when the user says, "My computer won't work" to point B when you discover that the user has been receiving a message indicating the primary domain controller could not be located.

◆ *Explore the boundaries.* Determine the scope of the problem and whether it is reproducible. Does it happen only at specific times of the day? Is other software running when it happens? Is the same problem occurring in other locations on your site? And does TechNet record the problem as common and solvable?

◆ *Track the possible approaches.* Brainstorm—either alone or with others—to determine the possible approaches to solving the problem. Include solutions that have been tried in the past (especially if they have been successful).

◆ *Execute an approach.* Implement the approach that you determine is most likely to succeed. Don't forget to consider possible problems that might occur and take steps to avoid making the problem worse. If it is possible that some working system might be rendered inoperable by your changes, back up the data or disconnect it from the network. Be sure to make copies of all the files you propose to change, especially the Registry.

◆ *Check for success.* Determine if your solution worked, and consider whether the solution is permanent or whether the system is likely to return to the problem state. If it is likely to reoccur, will the same fix work again, and can a user implement it him- or herself?

◆ *Tie up loose ends.* Document your successes and failures as you work through the problem. Then gather the notes you made during the brainstorming and implementation of your solution so that you will have them for similar solutions. If you feel that the solution you used was not the best (even though it resulted in a successful repair), be sure to document that so you can try another solution next time. Also be sure that the user who placed the call (if it was someone other than yourself who discovered the problem) is satisfied that the problem is resolved; this will instill confidence in you and in your systems.

What follows are a number of sections in which specific problems are discussed. Be sure to keep in mind that the information presented really only helps you with the exploration and tracking stages of the troubleshooting model. The rest must be up to you to work out in the situations you find yourself in.

TROUBLESHOOTING INSTALLATION

Choose the appropriate course of action to take to resolve installation failures.

The Windows NT installation process is remarkably easy for the user, but you still may experience occasional problems (see Chapter 2, "Installation and Configuration Part 1: Installation of NT Server"). One of the more common installation failures happens because the hardware simply cannot support NT. This may be because the devices are not supported (are not on the HCL), or it may be the result of insufficient RAM or disk space. However, Microsoft has made it easy to avoid the former problem.

The NT Server CD-ROM contains a useful tool called the NT Hardware Qualifier that you can use to determine if your hardware can support NT. The NTHQ is a floppy disk that you boot your system to. Using the HCL that is present on the CD-ROM, the NTHQ tries to detect your hardware and determine whether it will support NT. This is not a foolproof process, though, because the HCL on the NT Server CD-ROM is now well out-of-date. However, you know that if your computer passes the test of the NTHQ, your hardware will support NT Server for sure. If it fails, you still may be able to run NT on your computer. But before you attempt to do so, you'll have to manually check your components against the most current HCL (found on the Microsoft TechNet CD or on the Microsoft Web site).

The first step toward using the NTHQ is creating the floppy disk (see Step by Step 9.1).

STEP BY STEP

9.1 Creating an NTHQ Floppy Disk

1. Insert the NT Server CD-ROM into your CD-ROM drive.

2. Insert a formatted disk into your floppy disk drive.

3. On the CD-ROM, navigate to the \Support\HqTool folder and run MAKEDISK.BAT. This places the files needed to run NTHQ on the disk.

After creating the NTHQ disk, you can test a machine as described in Step by Step 9.2.

STEP BY STEP

9.2 Testing a Computer Using the NTHQ Disk

1. Place the NTHQ disk into the floppy drive and reboot the computer; the machine should boot to the NTHQ disk.

2. After some initialization (a couple of minutes), you are presented with a dialog box that prompts you to click Yes to continue. Do so.

3. A Detection Method (Comprehensive or Safe) dialog box appears, asking you to choose the detection mode. If you have not tried to detect devices on this machine before, choose Comprehensive Detect. If the NTHQ has already failed once, choose Safe Detect to skip over those components that have already caused the NTHQ to fail.

4. When the detection process is complete, you are presented with a dialog box that summarizes the components detected. At the bottom of this summary are a variety of buttons allowing you to look at specific categories: motherboard, network, video, storage, and so on. Click the Compatibility button to see the report on device failure. Any device that was detected but was not found on the HCL will have "No" listed beside it. Check the most current HCL to see if that device is listed there. If it's not, check to see if an NT 4.0 driver is available for it from the manufacturer. If the device is not on the current HCL and no NT 4.0 driver is available, you will have to upgrade the hardware component before you can install NT on your computer.

In addition to HCL incompatibilities, Microsoft identifies the following common installation problems and solutions:

◆ *Media errors.* If there seems to be a problem with the Windows NT Installation CD-ROM or floppy disks, ask Microsoft Sales to replace the disk. Call 800-426-9400.

◆ *Insufficient disk space.* Delete unnecessary files and folders, compress NTFS partitions, reformat an existing partition or use Setup to create more space, and then create a new partition with more space.

◆ *Non-supported SCSI adapter.* Boot to a different operating system (that can use the SCSI adapter) and run WINNT from the installation CD-ROM. Then try a network installation and replace the unsupported adapter with a supported adapter on the Hardware Compatibility List.

◆ *Failure of dependency service to start.* Verify the protocol and adapter configuration in the Control Panel's Network application and make sure the local computer has a unique name.

◆ *Inability to connect to the domain controller.* Verify account name and password, make sure the domain name is correct, make sure the primary domain controller is functioning properly, and verify protocol and adapter configuration settings by backing up in the installation process and changing your network adapter parameters. If you just finished installing or upgrading, make sure there is a computer account for your machine in the domain accounts database.

◆ *Error in assigning domain name.* Make sure the NT domain name isn't identical to some other NT domain, workgroup, or computer name on the network.

TROUBLESHOOTING BOOT FAILURES

Choose the appropriate course of action to take to resolve boot failures.

You usually know when you have a problem with the boot process—because you can't boot. The boot process is one of the most common sources of problems in Windows NT. The problem may be that one of the essential boot files has been lost or is corrupt. Try booting from the Windows NT boot disk and perform an emergency repair if necessary. (The emergency repair process is described later in this chapter.)

To diagnose a boot problem, you must understand the boot process. This section focuses on booting Windows NT and troubleshooting the boot process. It covers various diagnostic and troubleshooting utilities that are useful to this end. Before you can use any of these Win32 programs, however, you need to be able to boot into Windows NT. If you can't do that, all of Microsoft's tools are useless to you. Therefore, the first type of troubleshooting you should understand is how to deal with problems you might encounter when booting the computer into Windows NT.

Booting Up

The boot process begins when your computer accesses the hard drive's Master Boot Record (MBR) to load Windows NT. If your system fails during the Power On Self Test (POST), the problem isn't NT-related; instead, it is a hardware issue. What happens after the MBR program loads depends on the type of computer you are using.

The Intel Boot Sequence

On Intel x86-based computers, the boot sector of the active partition loads a file called NTLDR. Similar to IO.SYS for MS-DOS or Windows 95, NTLDR is a hidden, system, read-only file in the root of your system partition, and it is responsible for loading the rest of the operating system. NTLDR carries out the following steps:

1. Switches the processor to the 32-bit flat memory model necessary to address 4GB of RAM.

2. Starts the minifile system driver necessary for accessing the system and boot partitions. This minifile system driver contains just enough code to read files at boot time. The full file systems are loaded later.

3. Displays a Boot Loader menu that gives the user a choice of which operating system to load and waits for a response. The options for the Boot Loader menu are stored in a hidden read-only file named BOOT.INI that's stored in the root of your system partition. (This file is discussed in greater depth later in the chapter.)

4. If Windows NT is the selected system, NTLDR invokes the hardware detection routine to determine the hardware required. NTDETECT.COM (the same program that detects the hardware during NTSETUP) performs the hardware detection. NTDETECT.COM builds the hardware list and returns it to NTLDR. NTDETECT.COM is a hidden, system, read-only file in the root of the system partition.

5. Loads the kernel of the operating system. The kernel is called NTOSKRNL.EXE, and you can find it in the <winnt_root>\ SYSTEM32 directory. At this point, the screen clears and displays OS Loader V4.00.

6. Loads the Hardware Abstraction Layer (HAL). The HAL is a single file (HAL.DLL) that contains the code necessary to mask interrupts and exceptions from the kernel.

7. Loads SYSTEM, the HKEY_LOCAL_MACHINE\SYSTEM hive in the Registry. You can find the corresponding file in the <winnt_root>\SYSTEM32\CONFIG directory.

8. Loads the boot-time drivers. Boot-time drivers have a start value of 0. These values are loaded in the order in which they are listed in HKEY_LOCAL_MACHINE\SYSTEM\ CurrentControlSet\ Control\ServiceGroupOrder. Each time a driver loads, a dot is added to the series following the OS Loader V4.00 at the top of the screen. If the /sos switch is used in BOOT.INI, the name of each driver appears on a separate line as each is loaded. The drivers are not initialized yet.

9. Passes control, along with the hardware list collected by NTDETECT.COM, to NTOSKRNL.EXE.

After NTOSKRNL.EXE takes control, the boot phase ends and the load phases begin.

The RISC Boot Sequence

On a RISC-based computer, the boot process is much simpler because the firmware does much of the work that NTLDR and company does on the Intel platform. RISC-based computers maintain hardware configuration in their firmware (also called non-volatile RAM), so they don't need NTDETECT.COM. Their firmware also contains a list of valid operating systems and their locations, so they don't need BOOT.INI either.

RISC-based machines don't look for the Intel-specific NTLDR to boot the operating system; instead, they always look for a file called OSLOADER.EXE. This file is handed the hardware configuration data from the firmware. It then loads NTOSKRNL.EXE, HAL.DLL, and SYSTEM, and the boot process concludes.

Booting to Windows 95, MS-DOS, or OS/2

On Intel-based computers, you can install Windows NT Server with Windows NT Workstation, Windows 95, MS-DOS, or other installations of Windows NT Server. The boot loader screen offers the user a choice of Windows NT Server 4, Windows NT Workstation 4, Microsoft Windows, MS-DOS, or a combination of those four. If the user chooses a non–Windows NT operating system, a file called BOOTSECT.DOS is loaded and executed.

BOOTSECT.DOS is a hidden, system, read-only file in the root of the system partition. It contains the information that was present in the boot sector before Windows NT was installed. If a user chooses Windows 95 from the boot menu, for example, BOOTSECT.DOS loads IO.SYS and passes control to it.

BOOT.INI

Although NTLDR invokes the Boot Loader menu, BOOT.INI, an editable text file, controls it. (It is read-only, so you must remove that attribute before editing it.) BOOT.INI is the only INI file that Windows NT uses—if, indeed, you can actually say that NT uses it. After all, Windows NT is not loaded when this file is called on.

BOOT.INI has only two sections: [boot loader] and [operating systems]. The [boot loader] section defines the operating system that boots by default, and the [operating systems] section defines the other operating systems that can be booted.

The BOOT.INI file contains paths to boot files for the operating systems listed in it. In the case of NT operating systems, this path is defined in ARC format; otherwise, the path is presented as a DOS path. DOS paths, such as C:\MSDOS, are very straightforward and require no explanation. ARC paths, on the other hand, can be very obscure in their contraction and interpretation. It is, therefore, necessary to discuss them at this point.

ARC Paths

ARC paths provide a means of defining the location of a file based on physical location—specifically, based on the controller card, physical disk, and partition on which the directory is stored. Because the drive labeled G: could be physically anywhere, the ARC path convention was adopted as the way to tell the NT boot process where the boot files are located.

An ARC path can take one of two forms:

multi(0)disk(0)rdisk(0)partition(1)\WINNT

or

scsi(0)disk(0)rdisk(0)partition(1)\WINNT

The first parameter (either multi or scsi) identifies the physical number of the controller being referenced, starting from 0 and counting up from there. If multi is used, it indicates either a non-scsi controller or a scsi controller with its BIOS enabled. If scsi is used, it indicates a scsi controller with its BIOS disabled.

The second and third parameters (disk and rdisk) are really a set of alternatives: Only one is used in any circumstance. Both the disk and rdisk parameters indicate the physical disk (associated with the controller indicated in the previous parameter). If the first parameter is multi, the disk parameter is ignored and the rdisk parameter is used. If the first parameter is scsi, the disk parameter is used and the rdisk parameter is ignored. Like the controller parameter, the counter associated with the hard disk parameter begins at 0 and increments from there.

The fourth parameter (partition) indicates the partition on the disk specified in either the second or the third parameter. Unlike the first three parameters, the counter for the partition begins at 1 and increments from there.

The final parameter is the path on the partition described in which the NT boot files are located. This path is frequently (but not always) WINNT.

The ARC path of each NT installation on any given computer is automatically placed into the BOOT.INI file in the system partition. If nothing ever changes on your server, you will never have to manipulate that file. However, if new partitions are created on your hard drives or if new hard drives or disk controllers are installed, the ARC paths might need to be updated.

ARC paths are based on physical configuration of your computer. When the configuration changes, the ARC paths in your BOOT.INI file are not automatically modified. As a result, some changes will render your system unbootable. This will not prevent NT from functioning properly after it is booted; however, it may prevent it from starting properly. In order to understand this, you need to understand how ARC numbers are assigned to partitions.

When you create a new partition using the Disk Administrator, the ARC numbers assigned to the partitions are re-evaluated. The numbers are generated as follows:

1. The first primary partition on each disk gets the number 1.

2. Each additional primary partition is then given a number, incrementing up from 1.

3. Each logical drive is then given a number in the order they appear in the Disk Administrator.

For example, suppose you have a hard drive partitioned like the one shown in Figure 9.1.

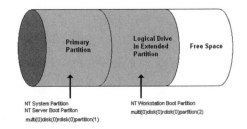

FIGURE 9.1

In the original configuration, the Workstation boot files are stored on partition 2.

As you can see, a primary partition contains the system and boot information for NT server, and the first logical drive contains the boot files for NT Workstation. All is well until you create a new primary partition in the free space on the hard drive (see Figure 9.2).

When you create the new primary partition, that partition gets the number that is one more than the first primary partition; in this case, the new partition is now number 2. This makes the partition with the Workstation files number 3. Unfortunately, because the BOOT.INI file still thinks it is to go to partition 2, when you choose Workstation from the boot list, the boot fails and you see this message:

```
Windows NT could not start because the following file is
missing or corrupt
```

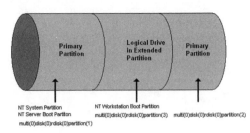

FIGURE 9.2

In the new configuration, the Workstation boot files are stored on partition 3 because the new primary partition is now partition 2.

```
<winntroot>\system32\ntoskrnl.exe
Please reinstall a copy of the above file
```

The solution to this problem can take either of two forms. You can boot to an operating system that will still start (in this case NT Server will still boot) and then change the BOOT.INI file from there. Alternatively, you can boot from a recovery disk that has the correct BOOT.INI file, and then modify the BOOT.INI file from within Workstation. (See "Troubleshooting the Boot Process" for more information on creating a recovery disk.) This method is often used on a system that has only one operating system to boot.

[boot loader]

The [boot loader] section of BOOT.INI defines the operating system that will be loaded if the user doesn't make a selection within a defined period of time. By default, you see something like this:

```
[boot loader]
timeout=30
default=multi(0)disk(0)rdisk(0)partition(1)\WINNT
```

The timeout parameter is the length of time (in seconds) that NTLDR has to wait for the user to make a decision. If timeout is set to 0, the default operating system loads immediately. If it is set to –1, the menu remains onscreen until the user makes a decision.

The default parameter defines the actual path, in ARC-compliant form, to the directory that contains the files for the default operating system—which usually is the last operating system installed, unless someone has changed this entry. The easiest way to change the default operating system and the timeout setting is by using the Control Panel's System application. Select the Startup/Shutdown tab and change the values in the System Startup frame (see Figure 9.3). You can edit BOOT.INI directly, but remember that a mistyped character in NOTEPAD.EXE or EDIT.COM could prevent your system from booting properly.

[operating systems]

The [operating systems] section contains a reference for every operating system available to the user from the Boot Loader menu, as well as any special switches necessary to customize the Windows NT environment. One of these entries must match the default= entry in the [boot loader] section. Otherwise, you end up with two entries onscreen for the same OS, one of which has "(default)" after it. In

> **WARNING**
>
> **Do Not Ignore Messages in Disk Administrator** The NT Disk Administrator will not change your BOOT.INI file. However, if you create a partition in the NT Disk Administrator that necessitates the modification of the BOOT.INI file, a message will inform you of that. Do not ignore those messages because you may leave your NT Server unbootable. Although the solution to this boot problem is relatively simple, if you do not recognize the problem immediately, you might become frustrated and might reinstall NT unnecessarily.

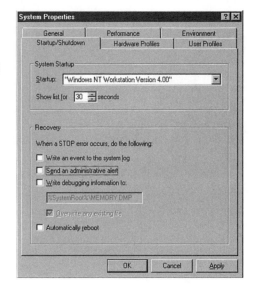

FIGURE 9.3

You can change the default operating system on the Startup/Shutdown tab in the System Properties dialog box.

all likelihood, only one of these will work. Trial-and-error should quickly discern which one.

Note that the paths are in ARC format with a label in quotation marks, which displays as an onscreen selection. Here's an example of an [operating systems] section:

```
multi(0)disk(0)rdisk(0)partition(1)\WINNT="Windows NT
Workstation ~Version 4.00"
multi(0)disk(0)rdisk(0)partition(1)\WINNT="Windows NT
Workstation ~Version 4.00 [VGA mode]" /basevideo /sos
c:\="Windows 95"
```

This example shows two entries for the same Windows NT Workstation installation, but the second one includes two switches (/basevideo and /sos) that customize the Windows NT boot and load process. These and other BOOT.INI switches are covered in the next section.

BOOT.INI Switches

This section describes several useful switches you can include in the [operating systems] section of BOOT.INI. The only way to include a switch is to manually edit the BOOT.INI file. If you decide to do so, be sure to remove the read-only attribute from the file before editing it, and be sure that you save the altered file as a text file if you use a word processor that normally saves in another format.

Here are the available switches:

♦ /basevideo The /basevideo switch tells Windows NT to load the standard VGA driver instead of the optimized driver written for your video card, which is useful, for example, if your monitor breaks and is replaced by one that doesn't support the same resolution or refresh rate that your last one did. If you can't see, it is awfully hard to get into Control Panel to change the video settings. Selecting the VGA mode entry uses the standard VGA 640×480, 16-color driver that works with almost every monitor.

♦ /sos The /sos switch enumerates to the screen each driver as it loads during the kernel load phase. If Windows NT hangs during this phase, you can use the /sos switch to determine which driver caused the problem.

◆ `/noserialmice=[COMx¦COMx,y,z_]`   When Windows NT boots, NTDETECT.COM looks for, among other things, the presence of serial mice. Sometimes this detection routine misfires and identifies modems or other devices as serial mice. Then, when Windows NT loads and initializes, the serial port is unavailable and the device is unusable because Windows NT is expecting a serial mouse. In other instances, the serial mouse detection signal can shut down a UPS connected to the serial port.

By itself, the `/noserialmice` switch tells NTDETECT.COM not to bother looking for serial mice. Used with a specific COM port(s), NTDETECT.COM still looks for serial mice, but not on the port(s) specified.

◆ `/crashdebug`   The `/crashdebug` switch turns on the Automatic Recovery and Restart feature, which you can also configure using the Control Panel's System application. In fact, when you configure this feature through Control Panel, what you are doing is merely adding this switch to the OS path in BOOT.INI.

◆ `/nodebug`   Programmers often use a special version of Windows NT that includes debugging symbols useful for tracking down problems in code. This version of Windows NT runs slowly compared to the retail version, owing to the extra overhead in tracking every piece of executing code. To turn off the monitoring in this version of NT, add the `/nodebug` switch to the OS path in BOOT.INI.

◆ `/maxmem:`*n*   Memory parity errors can be notoriously difficult to isolate. The `/maxmem` switch helps. When followed with a numeric value, this switch limits Windows NT's usable memory to the amount specified in the switch. This switch also is useful for developers using high-level workstations, who want to simulate performance on a lower-level machine.

◆ `/scsiordinal:`*n*   If your system has two identical SCSI controllers, you need a way to distinguish one from the other. The `/scsiordinal` switch is used to assign a value of 0 to the first controller and 1 to the second.

Kernel Initialization Phase

After all the initial drivers are loaded, the screen turns blue, and the text height shrinks; the kernel initialization phase has begun. Now the kernel and all the drivers loaded in the previous phase are initialized. The Registry begins to flesh out. The CurrentControlSet is copied to the CloneControlSet, and the volatile HARDWARE key is created. The system Registry hive is then scanned once more for higher-level drivers configured to start during system initialization. These drivers with a start value of 1 (such as the keyboard and mouse) are then loaded and initialized. Dots appear on the screen; each represents a device driver that's being loaded.

Services Load Phase

Here the Session Manager scans the system hive for a list of programs that must run before Windows NT fully initializes. These programs may include AUTOCHK.EXE, the boot-time version of CHKDSK.EXE that examines and repairs any problems within a file system, or AUTOCONV.EXE, which converts a partition from FAT to NTFS. These boot-time programs are stored in the following key:

HKEY_LOCAL_MACHINE\SYSTEM\CurrentControlSet\ Control\Session Manager\BootExecute

After those programs are run, the page file(s) are created based on the locations specified in this key:

HKEY_LOCAL_MACHINE\SYSTEM\CurrentControlSet\ Control\Session Manager\Memory Management

Next, the SOFTWARE hive loads from <winnt_root>\SYSTEM32\ CONFIG. Session Manager then loads the Client/Server (CSR) subsystem and any other required subsystems from this key:

HKEY_LOCAL_MACHINE\System\CurrentControlSet\Control \Session Manager\SubSystems\Required

Finally, drivers that have a start value of 2 (Automatic) load.

NOTE **Troubleshoot Driver Load Using DRIVERS.EXE** The Windows NT Resource Kit includes a command-line utility called DRIVERS.EXE that reports the name of all successfully loaded drivers. If you have any doubts about a driver's capability to successfully load and initialize, try DRIVERS.EXE.

Windows Start Phase

After the Win32 subsystem starts, the screen switches into GUI mode. In other words, it looks like Windows. The WinLogon process is invoked, which displays the Welcome dialog box. Although users can go ahead and log on at this point, the system might not respond for a few more moments while the Service Controller initializes the Computer Browser, Workstation, Server, Spooler, and other automatic services.

The critical file at this point is SERVICES.EXE, which actually starts Alerter, Computer Browser, EventLog, Messenger, NetLogon, NT LM Security Support Provider, Server, TCP/IP NetBIOS Helper, and Workstation. A missing or corrupt SERVICES.EXE file cripples your Windows NT–based computer.

SERVICES.EXE starts its services by calling the appropriate DLLs, listed here:

Alerter	NT LM Security Support Provider
ALRSVC.DLL	NTLMSSPS.DLL
Computer Browser	Server
BROWSER.DLL	SRVSVC.DLL
EventLog	TCP/IP NetBIOS Helper
EVENTLOG.DLL	LMHSVC.DLL
Messenger	Workstation
MSGSVC.DLL	WKSSVC.DLL
NetLogon	
NETLOGON.DLL	

After a user successfully logs on to the system, the LastKnownGood control set is updated, and the boot is considered good. Until a user logs on for the first time, though, the boot/load process technically remains unfinished. So a problem that Windows NT cannot detect but that a user can see (such as a video problem) can be resolved by falling back on the LastKnownGood configuration.

Control Sets and LastKnownGood

A *control set* is a collection of configuration information used by Windows NT during the boot process. A special control set called LastKnownGood plays a special role in troubleshooting the boot process.

After the system boots and a user logs on successfully, the current configuration settings are copied to the LastKnownGood control set in the Registry. These settings are preserved so that if the system cannot boot successfully the next time a user attempts to log on, the system can fall back on LastKnownGood, which—as the name implies—is the last configuration known to facilitate a "good" boot. LastKnownGood is stored in the Registry under HKEY_LOCAL_MACHINE\SYSTEM\CurrentControlSet.

The key to understanding LastKnownGood lies in recognizing that it is updated the first time (and only the first time) a user logs on to Windows NT after a reboot. If you notice something dicey (if, for example, you changed the settings for a driver that now refuses to load), you can power down and restart the system using the LastKnownGood configuration. If you notice something wrong but still log on to the system, you are telling it that everything is okay—that this is a configuration that facilitates a good boot. The system then overwrites the LastKnownGood control set, and what you essentially end up with is a "LastKnownBad" configuration.

To boot with the LastKnownGood configuration, press the Spacebar when prompted during the boot process. You are presented with the Hardware Profile/Configuration Recovery menu. Select a hardware profile and enter L for the LastKnownGood configuration.

Sometimes Windows NT boots using LastKnownGood of its own volition. However, this occurs only if the normal boot process produces severe or critical errors when loading device drivers.

LastKnownGood does not do you any good if files are corrupt or missing. You must use the emergency repair process in such situations.

Troubleshooting the Boot Process

A variety of things could cause a boot failure. Maybe one of the boot files is missing; maybe the BOOT.INI file is not configured correctly; maybe a driver is corrupt; maybe the Registry is corrupt; or maybe the system or boot partition was on a hard disk that failed. All of these problems can be repaired through one method or another. Those methods are outlined in the sections that follow.

Corrupt or Missing Boot Files

If, when you boot, you get a message that NTLDR, NTDETECT.COM, or BOOTSECT.DOS cannot be found, the file really might be missing or corrupt. However, it may simply be that the boot process is looking in the wrong place. In any event, corruption in the system files (NTLDR, NTDETECT.COM, and BOOT.INI) can be repaired by booting to a recovery disk and then copying good files to overwrite the bad ones.

In NT, using a recovery disk is the closest you'll come to booting to a floppy disk. With a DOS boot disk, the complete bootable operating system can be stored on a single floppy disk. With NT, only a part of the boot process can be performed from disk (that's the part played by the system partition on the hard drive in an NT machine). This partition holds enough information to allow NT to begin the initial stage of bootup, whereupon control transfers to the boot partition (where NTOSKRNL.EXE resides). Fortunately, a recovery disk does contain the NTLDR, NTDETECT.COM, and BOOT.INI files and, therefore, can be used to boot NT as long as the boot partition remains intact on your hard drive. (See Step by Step 9.3 for instructions on how to create a recovery disk.)

STEP BY STEP

9.3 Creating a Recovery Disk for an INTEL-Based System

1. Format a floppy disk from within NT. This first step is important because a disk formatted from any other operating system will not boot NT.

Recovery Disk Files Are All Generic

The files on the recovery disk are hardware specific, but unlike the Registry, none of them are installation specific. This means that, although you should create a recovery disk before a problem occurs, one could be created from any NT computer (Workstation or Server) that has the same processor platform. The only tricky part to using a recovery disk created in that way is replacing NTBOOTDD.SYS should your computer need it.

NTBOOTDD.SYS is the driver for a SCSI drive that does not have its BIOS enabled. You can obtain it by copying NTBOOTDD.SYS from another machine with the same SCSI driver or by copying it from the NT Server or Workstation CD. Be aware, however, that this file is not called NTBOOT-DD.SYS; it is called by the name of the drive type on the CD. Therefore, you will have to locate the proper driver and copy it to your disk, changing its name to NTBOOTDD.SYS in the process. For example, if you had an Adaptec 2940 controller on an Intel-based computer, you would locate the file AIC78XX.SYS in the I386 folder on the NT Server CD-ROM and copy it to your recovery disk, and you would change its name to NTBOOTDD.SYS in the process.

2. *For INTEL-based Servers,* copy the following files onto the disk:

- NTLDR
- NTDETECT.COM
- BOOT.INI
- BOOTSECT.DOS (if you want to be able to boot to DOS)
- NTBOOTDD.SYS (for SCSI disks without SCSI BIOS enabled)

  For RISC-based Servers, copy the following files onto the disk:
- OSLOADER.EXE
- HAL.DLL
- *.PAL from System partition (for ALPHA-based Servers)

3. Modify the BOOT.INI file for the Server you are creating the recovery disk for.

4. Test the disk by inserting it into the floppy drive of the machine in which it is to be used and rebooting. If all is well, the disk should initiate boot, and then NT should load normally.

NTOSKRNL.EXE Missing or Corrupt

As with the boot files mentioned previously, a message saying the NTOSKRNL is missing or corrupt might actually indicate that the file is missing or corrupt. But, again, it may simply indicate that the NT boot process cannot find it. If booting to a recovery disk does not alleviate the problem, you will have to initiate an emergency repair to copy a new version of NTOSKRNL.EXE onto your Server. This process is described in the section "The Emergency Repair Process," later in the chapter.

Faulty Driver Causes Stop Error on Boot

An incorrect or corrupt driver could cause an NT Stop error (blue screen) to occur during boot. If this happens, you will have to replace the faulty driver in order to boot NT again. However, replacing the driver will be a tricky problem if you cannot boot NT far enough to copy the new driver onto your system. Even discovering which driver is giving you the problem may be quite a feat. Unfortunately, the solution to this kind of problem is beyond the scope of this book; fortunately for you, it is also beyond the scope of the NT Server exam.

Registry Configuration Causes Boot to Fail

Because the Registry is the source of most of the configuration of your NT Server system, problems in it could manifest themselves in a variety of ways. One way configuration problems show up is in a system boot failure. This is one of the many reasons it is inadvisable to make modifications to your NT Registry unless you know exactly what the implications of your changes will be (and even then, you should make them only after taking precautions to ensure you can recover from any problems that might arise).

If a Registry setting prevents your NT Server from booting, it may be possible to repair the problem using the emergency repair process. This process is discussed in depth in the section "The Emergency Repair Process," later in the chapter.

DOS or Windows SYS Command Prevents NT from Booting

If, somehow, you or someone else ran the SYS command from DOS or Windows 95 on your NT Server, NT will no longer boot. If this happens, you will have to initiate an emergency repair in order to fix the problem. This process is discussed in depth in the section "The Emergency Repair Process," later in this chapter.

Faulty Drive Media Causes Boot to Fail

Aside from reinstalling NT Server, not much can be done to repair a problem with faulty media. If you have been diligent in making server backups and have kept your emergency repair disk current, after NT is restored, you will be able to restore configuration and all other drive information from the backups and the ERD. If not, you will have learned a valuable lesson about keeping restoration mechanisms handy and up-to-date.

The Emergency Repair Process

As you may recall from Chapter 2, the installation process enables you to create an emergency repair directory and emergency repair disk, both of which are backup copies of Registry information, (which come in handy if you can't boot Windows NT because of missing or corrupt files). It is now time to take a look at ways in which the emergency repair process can aid a troubled Windows NT installation.

Emergency Repair Directory Versus Emergency Repair Disk

Installation always creates the emergency repair directory. You can find it in <winnt_root>\REPAIR. You can create an emergency repair disk as well. Do you need both? Well, no, not really. The directory serves just as well as the disk unless the directory itself becomes corrupt, or the drive itself dies, in which case you're stuck. The disk serves as a backup in case of an extreme emergency.

Both the directory and disk are computer-specific, at least in part. Although you can sometimes borrow an emergency repair disk from another computer, you generally should assume otherwise. Keep a separate emergency repair disk for each computer, and tag it with the serial number of the computer because names and locations change over time. Don't leave these disks in the hands of users. Keep them with an administrator in a secure but accessible location.

Table 9.1 lists and describes the files on the emergency repair disk.

TABLE 9.1

FILES ON THE EMERGENCY REPAIR DISK

Files	Description
SETUP.LOG	A text file that contains the names of all the Windows NT installation files, along with checksum values for each. If any of the files on your hard drive are missing or corrupt, the emergency repair process should detect them with the aid of this hidden, system, and read-only file.
SYSTEM._	A compressed copy of the Registry's SYSTEM hive. This is the Windows NT control set collection.
SAM._	A compressed copy of the Registry's SAM hive. This is the Windows NT user accounts database.
SECURITY.__	A compressed copy of the Registry's SECURITY hive. This is the Windows NT security information, which includes SAM and the security policies.
SOFTWARE._	A compressed copy of the Registry's SOFTWARE hive. This hive contains all Win32 software configuration information.
DEFAULT._	A compressed copy of the system default profile.
CONFIG.NT	The VDM version of the MS-DOS CONFIG.SYS file.
AUTOEXEC.NT	The VDM version of the MS-DOS AUTOEXEC.BAT file.
NTUSER.DA_	A copy of the file NTUSER.DAT (which contains user profile information) from the directory winnt_root\profiles\ Defaultuser.

RDISK.EXE

Both the emergency repair disk and directory are created during installation, but neither is updated automatically at any time thereafter. To update the emergency repair information, use the hidden utility RDISK.EXE. To start RDISK, choose Start, Run and type **RDISK**. Because RDISK.EXE is in the search path (\<winnt_root>\SYSTEM32), you do not have to specify the full path. Some administrators just add the RDISK program to the Administrative Tools group.

RDISK offers two options for administrators: Update Repair Info and Create Repair Disk (see Figure 9.4).

FIGURE 9.4

The Emergency Repair Disk Utility allows you to update the repair information stored in the \Repair folder and allows you to create a new repair disk based on that information.

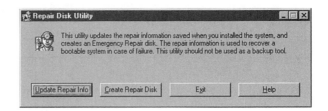

Update Repair Info

The Update Repair Info button updates only the emergency repair directory, although it does prompt for the creation/update of an emergency repair disk immediately following successful completion of the directory update. Always update the directory before creating the disk because the disk will be created using the information in the directory.

Create Repair Disk

If the information in the repair directory is up-to-date, you may choose to create or update an emergency repair disk. You don't have to use a preformatted disk for the repair disk. RDISK formats the disk regardless.

A significant limitation of RDISK that you should definitely know about is that it will not update the DEFAULT._, SECURITY, or SAM files in the repair directory (or disk). In other words, you may update your repair disk week-to-week, but none of your account changes are being backed up. To do a complete emergency repair update, you must run RDISK.EXE using the undocumented /S switch. This takes a while, especially if your account database is quite large. It is better, however, than losing all your accounts if and when disaster strikes.

Starting the Emergency Repair Process

Regarding the emergency repair directory and the emergency repair disk, you need to recognize that you can't boot from either or use either from within Windows NT. To actually invoke the emergency repair process, you must access the original three Windows NT Setup disks. If you don't have the original disks handy, you generate them from the CD by using the WINNT command and either the /O or the /OX switch. Chapter 2 includes more information on the

> **WARNING**
>
> **NT Does Not Support an Emergency Repair That Spans More Than One Disk** A large limitation for an NT implementation of any significant size is that the emergency repair information can become larger than a single disk can handle. Unfortunately, if this happens, NT will not prompt you for a second disk when creating the ERD; instead, it will abort with an error message telling you that the emergency repair disk is full. Although failure of this process is beyond the scope of the NT Server exam, it would be well worth your while to investigate ways to reduce the size of the total repair package that NT tries to copy to your repair disk. If you search Microsoft TechNet using the term "Emergency Repair," you will find many helpful articles.

WINNT.EXE program. Because these disks are generic, any set will do, regardless of which NT Server machine they were created on. In fact, you can create them from any machine that has a functioning CD-ROM drive.

If you think back to installation, you might recall that the Setup process actually gives you the initial choice to either install Windows NT or repair an existing installation. Pressing R on this screen invokes the emergency repair process. Don't be concerned when the Setup process then continues its pace through the rest of the three setup disks. That is normal.

The emergency repair process gives you several options. You can select any or all of the options in the emergency repair menu. (The default is to undertake all repair options.) After you select your repair options, Setup attempts to locate your hard drive. When it finds your hard drive, Setup asks whether you want to use an emergency repair disk or whether you want Setup to search for your repair directory. You then encounter a series of restoration choices based on the repair options you select and the problems Setup uncovers as it analyzes your system. The next few sections discuss the emergency repair options.

Inspect Registry Files

At this point, the process gets computer-specific. If your Registry becomes corrupt, only your own emergency repair disk can save you—no one else's can. You granularly select to repair any combination of the SYSTEM, SOFTWARE, DEFAULT, and SECURITY/SAM hives, and these are copied directly from the repair directory or disk. You don't need the original source CD or disks for this procedure.

Inspect Startup Environment

The files required to boot Windows NT were listed earlier in this chapter. If any of these files is mistakenly deleted or becomes corrupted, choose Inspect Startup Environment to repair them. You can use anyone's emergency repair disk for this option because these files are generic across all Windows NT installations (for the same platform, anyway). You do need to produce the original installation CD, however, before the repair process can replace the files.

**Applied Service Packs May Cause
Verification to Fail** If you have
applied service packs to your NT
Server system, validation will fail
because service packs often modify
NT system files. The validation
process checks the current system
files against the files on the CD-
ROM and flags them as being corrupt if they are not the same.
However, sometimes files are
flagged as being corrupt only
because the repair process recognizes the valid changes that the
Service Packs have made. You can
check this by examining the
FILES.LST file on each Service Pack
to determine which files have been
changed. If you suspect a file is
corrupt, replace it, but be sure to
reapply the Service Pack after your
system has been repaired.

Verify Windows NT System Files

This option often takes time, but it systematically inspects every file
in the Windows NT directory tree and compares each with the
checksum values in SETUP.LOG. If it determines that any files are
missing or corrupt, the repair process attempts to replace them.
Again, you need the original disks or CD when using this option.

Inspect Boot Sector

If you upgrade to a new version of DOS and suddenly find that you
cannot boot to Windows NT anymore, your boot sector probably
has been replaced. The MS-DOS or Windows 95 SYS command is
notorious for trashing the Windows NT boot sector. The emergency
repair disk solves this problem, and you don't even need a computer-
specific ERD. You can borrow anybody's.

TROUBLESHOOTING CONFIGURATION ERRORS

Choose the appropriate course of action to take to resolve configuration errors.

Configuration errors are another common source of hardship for
network professionals. Configuration errors are often introduced by
a user or an administrator installing new software or a new device.

Some common device problems are resource conflicts (such as interrupt conflicts) and SCSI problems. Sometimes these problems manifest themselves at boot time. Sometimes they don't appear until you
try to access the misconfigured device. Device error reports appear in
the Event Log (described later in this chapter). Use Windows NT
Diagnostics to check resource settings. If the error is the result of a
recent configuration change, you can reboot the system and boot to
the LastKnownGood configuration.

If a Windows NT service doesn't start, check Event Viewer. Or,
check the Control Panel's Services application to make sure the service is installed and configured to start.

Windows NT includes some important tools you can use to look for configuration errors:

◆ Event Viewer

◆ Windows NT Diagnostics

◆ System Recovery

In the following sections, you will learn about these tools in detail. You will also learn how to fend off a catastrophic misconfiguration by backing up your Registry.

Event Viewer

If your Windows NT–based computer manages to boot successfully yet still isn't performing correctly, the first thing to check is the system Event Log, where all critical system messages are stored.

Windows NT includes the Event Viewer application for viewing the messages stored in the System, Security, and Application log files (see Figure 9.5). To start Event Viewer, choose Start, Programs, Administrative Tools (Common), Event Viewer.

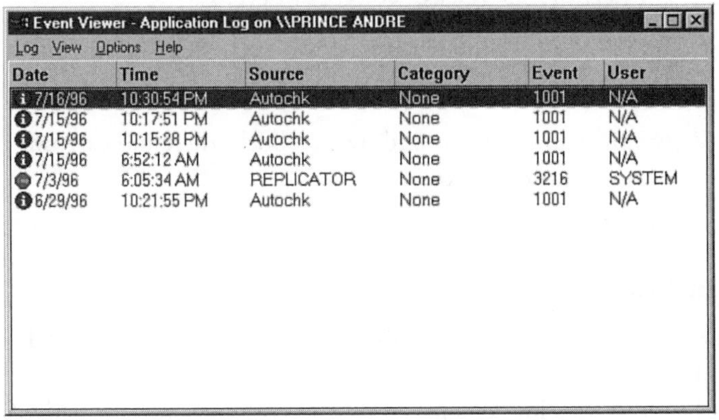

FIGURE 9.5
The Event Viewer enables you to view events written to the three NT log files: System, Security, and Application.

System Log

The System log, the default view in Event Viewer, is maintained by the operating system. It tracks three kinds of events:

◆ *Errors.* Symbolized by Stop signs, these indicate the failure of a Windows NT component or device, or perhaps an inability to start. These errors are common on notebook computers when Windows NT fails to start the network components because PCMCIA network cards are not present.

◆ *Warnings.* Symbolized by exclamation points, these indicate an impending problem. Low disk space on a partition triggers a warning, for example.

◆ *Information events.* Symbolized by the traditional "I" in a blue circle, these indicate an event that is significant but not troublesome. Successful starting of a service or the calling of a browser election causes such an event to be recorded.

Security Log

The Security log remains empty until you enable auditing through User Manager. After you enable auditing, the audited events reside here. The Security log tracks two types of events:

◆ *Success audits.* Symbolized by a key, these indicate successful security access.

◆ *Failure audits.* Symbolized by a padlock, these indicate unsuccessful security access.

Application Log

The Application log collects messages from native Windows NT applications (refer to Figure 9.5). If you aren't using any Win32 applications, this log remains empty. As you move toward native Windows NT programs, check this log occasionally, and certainly check it when you suspect a problem.

Securing Event Logs

Ordinarily, anyone can view the Event Log information. Some administrators, however, might not want guests to have this sort of access. By using the Registry, you can place one restriction on Event Viewer: You can prohibit guests from accessing the System or Application log. To do so, go to the following Registry location, where *<log_name>* is either System or Application:

HKEY_LOCAL_MACHINE\System\CurrentControlSet\Services
\EventLog\~*<log_name>*

You need to add a value called RestrictGuestAccess of type REG_DWORD and set it equal to 1. To re-enable guest access to either log, set the appropriate RestrictGuestAccess value to 0 or just delete the value altogether.

Configuring Event Viewer

By default, log files can reach 512KB, and events are overwritten after seven days. You can change these settings in the Event Log Settings dialog box (see Figure 9.6), which you open by choosing Log Settings from the Log menu in Event Viewer.

The Save As option in the Log menu enables you to save the log either as an Event Log file (with an .EVT extension), which makes it available for examination on another computer at a future time, or as a comma-separated value text file (with a .TXT extension) for importing into a spreadsheet or database. The format you select depends on the spreadsheet or database program you will use for the text file you import. Choose the Log, Select Computer command to view events on another computer (of course, you must have an administrator-level account on the remote Windows NT–based computer to succeed).

Using Event Viewer

At some point, every Windows NT user receives this infamous message:

```
One or more services failed to start. Please see the Event
Viewer for details.
```

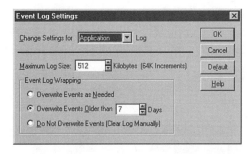

FIGURE 9.6
The Event Log Settings dialog box allows you to configure the size of each log, as well as whether and when log wrapping should occur.

NOTE **The Event Log in a C2 Security Environment** C2 environments require that all log information be retained. No information may be overwritten because overwriting events may allow a security break to escape unnoticed after it is overwritten. This isn't the default setting; however, using it can result in a very large and unwieldy log file.

This message appears when the first user logs on to the system after at least one Windows NT component fails to load successfully. As directed, you should immediately proceed to Event Viewer.

To find the source of the problem, look at the system log under the Event heading. Somewhere toward the top of the column, you should find an Event code of 6005. (By default, the logs list the most recent events at the top of the list, so start scanning at the top of the list to make sure you find the most recent 6005 event.) If you look under the Source heading for this event, it should read EventLog, and it is an informational message. Event 6005 means that the EventLog service was successfully started. Any events that appear chronologically earlier than 6005 are events logged during system boot. Investigate these events, particularly the errors, because they may reveal the source of your problem.

To examine an event message, double-click on an event to open the Event Detail dialog box (see Figure 9.7).

Note the identifying information for the event:

◆ Date of the event

◆ Time of the event

◆ User account that generated the event, if applicable (usually found in the Security log)

◆ Computer on which the event occurred

◆ Event ID (the Windows NT Event code)

◆ Source Windows NT component that generated the event

◆ Type of event (error, warning, and so on)

◆ Category of event (Logon/Logoff audit, for example)

◆ Description of the event

◆ Data in hexadecimal format (useful to a developer or debugger)

Regarding the above items, the event descriptions have come a long way since cryptic MS-DOS error messages. Some Windows NT messages tell you everything you need to know:

```
The D drive is almost full. The files will need to be
backed up and then deleted from the D drive.
```

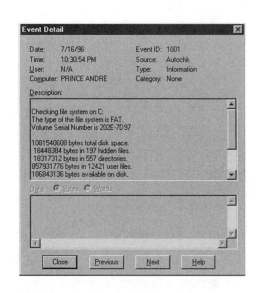

FIGURE 9.7
The Event Detail dialog box shows detailed information for an event in the Event Log.

Perhaps others tell you too much:

```
Could not look up the assoc block for an NBT association.
Check if the message read is corrupted. WINS looks at bit
11-14 of the message to determine if the assoc. is from
another WINS or from an NBT node. It is possible that the
bits are corrupted or that there is a mismatch between
what the two WINS servers expect to see in those bits
(maybe you changed the value to be put in code and not
increment the version number set during assoc. setup).
```

And sometimes progress seems to work in reverse:

```
A DosDevIoctl or DosFsCtl to NETWKSTA.SYS failed. The data
shown is in the format:DWORD approx CS:IP of call to ioctl
or fsctlWORD error code WORD ioctl or fsctl number.
```

Just write down the error message, and then search TechNet for an explanation or call Microsoft's Product Support Services; they know what to do with the information.

You also can filter events so that only certain events are listed onscreen. Note that doing so doesn't delete messages from the Event Log; rather, it controls which of the logged events appear in Event Viewer at any given time. To filter events, choose the View, Filter Events command. You can filter by the following fields:

N O T E **Saving the Hexidecimal Data with the Event Description** If you want to save the hexadecimal data along with the event description, be certain to save the events as .EVT files. The hex data doesn't save with .TXT files.

- ◆ Event date and time
- ◆ Event type (error, warning, and so on)
- ◆ Source (atdisk, browser, and so on)
- ◆ User
- ◆ Computer
- ◆ Event ID

If you attempt to filter an Event Log imported from another computer, you can filter only for components installed on your own machine. In other words, the filters are read from your own Registry, not from the Event Log file itself.

Windows NT Diagnostics

Windows NT Diagnostics provides a tidy interface for much of the information in the HKEY_LOCAL_MACHINE Registry subtree. Like its ancestor, MSD from Windows 3.1, Windows NT

Diagnostics can create incredibly detailed and valuable system configuration reports. One thing you cannot do with Windows NT Diagnostics, though, is edit the system configuration.

Figure 9.8 shows the Windows NT Diagnostics dialog box. To start Windows NT Diagnostics, choose Start, Programs, Administrative Tools (Common), Windows NT Diagnostics.

The Windows NT Diagnostics dialog box includes the following nine tabs:

◆ *Version.* Displays information stored under HKEY_LOCAL_ MACHINE\Software\Microsoft\Windows NT\CurrentVersion, including the build number, registered owner, and Service Pack update information.

◆ *System.* Displays information stored under HKEY_LOCAL_ MACHINE\Hardware, including CPU and other device identification information.

◆ *Display.* Displays information on the video adapter and adapter settings.

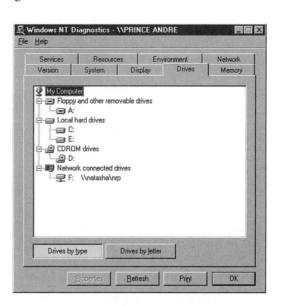

FIGURE 9.8

In the Windows NT Diagnostics dialog box, you can view all the hardware configurations on your NT Server.

◆ *Drives.* Lists all drive letters in use and their types, including drive letters for floppy drives, hard disks, CD-ROM and optical drives, and network connections. Double-click on a drive letter to display a drive Properties dialog box. The General tab of the drive Properties dialog box shows byte and cluster information for the drive (see Figure 9.9). The File System tab of the drive Properties dialog box shows file system information (see Figure 9.10).

◆ *Memory.* Displays current memory load, as well as physical and virtual memory statistics.

◆ *Services.* Displays service information stored under HKEY_LOCAL_MACHINE\System\CurrentControlSet\ Services, including status. Click on the Devices button to display driver information stored under HKEY_LOCAL_MACHINE\ System\CurrentControlSet\Control, including status.

◆ *Resources.* Displays device information listed by interrupt and port, and also by DMA channels and UMB locations in use.

◆ *Environment.* Displays environment variables for command prompt sessions (set under the Control Panel's System application).

◆ *Network.* Displays network component configuration and status.

System Recovery

The Recovery utility is a tool you can use to record debugging information, alert an administrator, or reboot the system in the event of a Stop error. (A Stop error causes Windows NT to stop all processes.) To configure the Recovery utility, start the Control Panel's System application and click on the Startup/Shutdown tab (shown in Figure 9.11).

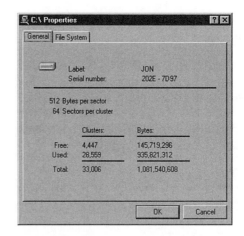

FIGURE 9.9
The General tab of the drive Properties dialog box shows you basic information about the drive including its name, serial number, and space allotments.

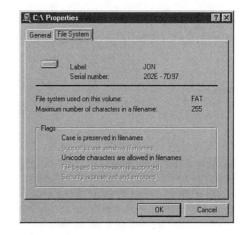

FIGURE 9.10
The File System tab of the drive Properties dialog box shows you information about the file system and the types of features that system supports.

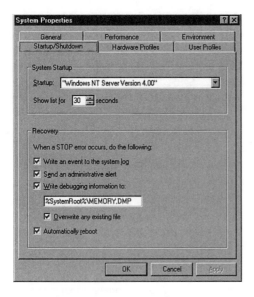

FIGURE 9.11
The Startup/Shutdown tab of the System Properties dialog box has a Recovery section in which you can configure the action to be taken when a stop error occurs.

NOTE **Why "Hives"?** You may be wondering why these files are called *hives*. Reportedly, one of the Windows NT developers thought the Registry resembled a massive beehive with all its tunnels and chambers, and so coined the term.

The bottom frame of the Startup/Shutdown tab is devoted to the following Recovery options:

◆ *Write an Event to the System Log.*

◆ *Send an Administrative Alert.*

◆ *Write Debugging Information to (Specify a Filename).* In the event of a Stop error, the SAVEDUMP.EXE program dumps everything in memory to the pagefile and marks the location of the dump. When you restart your system, Windows NT copies the memory dump from the pagefile to the file specified in the Startup/Shutdown tab. You can then use a program called DUMPEXAM.EXE in the \Support directory of the Windows NT CD-ROM to study the contents of the memory dump and determine what caused the Stop error.

◆ *Automatically Reboot.* You might not want your server to sit idle after a Stop error. This option instructs Windows NT to automatically reboot after a Stop error.

Backing Up the Registry

By now, you're should be aware of the danger of tampering with the Registry. Safety demands that you back up the Registry before making any Registry modification. It is also useful to know which files are involved in a backup of the Registry.

Before you get into a discussion of Registry files, you should be familiar with the term "hive." A *hive* is a binary file that contains all the keys and values within a branch of the Registry. Not every key is a hive. Some keys are contained within hives, and others are never written to disk at all (such as HKEY_LOCAL_MACHINE\ Hardware, which you learned about earlier in the chapter).

Two files are associated with each hive. One file is named after the hive and has no extension, and the other is identically named but has a .LOG extension (with the exception of SYSTEM, which has a SYSTEM.ALT counterpart for reasons to be explained shortly). Both files reside in the \<winnt_root>\SYSTEM32\CONFIG directory. Most of the hives loaded at any given time are residents of

HKEY_LOCAL_MACHINE, and the others belong to
HKEY_USERS.

Here is a list of the Registry hives:

- ◆ HKEY_LOCAL_MACHINE\SAM (SAM, SAM.LOG)

- ◆ HKEY_LOCAL_MACHINE\SECURITY (SECURITY,
  SECURITY.LOG)

- ◆ HKEY_LOCAL_MACHINE\SOFTWARE (SOFTWARE,
  SOFTWARE.LOG)

- ◆ HKEY_LOCAL_MACHINE\SYSTEM (SYSTEM,
  SYSTEM.ALT)

- ◆ HKEY_USERS\.DEFAULT (DEFAULT, DEFAULT.LOG)

- ◆ HKEY_USERS*<user_sid>* (*<user_profile>*,
  <user_profile>.LOG)

The LOG files provide fault tolerance for the Registry. Whenever
configuration data changes, the changes are written to the .LOG file
first. Then the first sector of the actual hive is flagged to indicate that
an update is taking place. The data is transferred from the log to the
hive, and then the update flag on the hive is lowered. If the computer were to crash after the flag is raised but before it is lowered,
some—if not all—of the data will quite possibly become corrupt. If
that happens, when Windows NT restarts, it detects that the flag is
still raised on the hive, and it uses the .LOG file to redo the update.

The SYSTEM file is the only one for which there is no .LOG file.
Because the SYSTEM hive contains critical information that must
be loaded intact to load enough of the operating system to process
the log files, a duplicate of SYSTEM is maintained as SYSTEM.ALT.
This file functions just like a log file, except that the entire file is
mirrored (instead of just the changes). If the computer crashes during an update to the SYSTEM branch of the Registry, the integrity
of the SYSTEM hive is still preserved. If the data had not yet been
fully committed to SYSTEM.ALT, the SYSTEM hive is still preserved in its original configuration. If the data had not yet been fully
committed to SYSTEM, SYSTEM.ALT would be used to redo the
update.

Now that you know which files are connected with the Registry, do you need to back them all up? No. In fact, the .LOG files are so transitory that they would be useless by the time the backup is complete. You may want to back up the user profile information if you are going to alter user-specific information, but usually these settings are potentially harmless. SAM and SECURITY are off-limits for editing, so you can't hurt them at all.

The files of greatest importance are SYSTEM and SOFTWARE, which usually are so small they can fit on a floppy disk. Consequently, just copying the files to a disk is rather tempting. However, do not give in to that temptation.

Registry files usually are in a state of flux and are constantly open for read/write access. The Windows NT Backup program usually skips over these files for that reason. Probably the best way to back up the SYSTEM and SOFTWARE files is to use the Repair Disk application, another hidden application in the \<winnt_root>\SYSTEM32 directory. The section "RDISK.EXE," earlier in this chapter, discussed the Repair Disk utility known as RDISK.EXE.

Backing Up Individual Keys

You can create your own hive files by saving an entire branch of the Registry starting from any key you choose. You do so by choosing Registry, Save Key in Registry Editor. To load the hive into the Registry of another Windows NT computer, choose Registry, Restore Key.

If you want to work with the key only temporarily, you can use the Restore Volatile command instead of the Restore Key command. The key still loads into the Registry at the selected location, but it doesn't reload the next time the system restarts.

TROUBLESHOOTING PRINTER PROBLEMS

Choose the appropriate course of action to take to resolve printer problems.

Printing has always been troublesome, regardless of the operating system. Although Windows NT handles printing better than most systems do, you still should make a concerted effort to avoid certain potential printing pitfalls.

If you can't print to a printer, try a different printer to see whether the problem also appears there. You can also try printing from a different account. Overall, make sure that the printer is plugged in and turned on and that it has paper. Remove and re-create the printer if necessary.

When you try to isolate printing problems, following these guidelines can be helpful:

1. Check the cable connections and the printer port to verify that the printing device is on and the cables are all securely fitted. This precaution may seem rather obvious, but the simplest of things cause some of the most perplexing problems.

2. To verify that the correct printer driver is installed and configured properly, establish the type of printing device (such as PCL, PostScript, and so on) and verify that the correct driver type has been installed. From the printer property page, print a test page to make sure you get a clear printout. If necessary, reinstall the printer driver. If a printer driver needs to be updated, use the Printers folder to install and configure the new printer driver.

3. Verify that the printer is selected, either explicitly in the application or as the default printer. Most Windows NT applications have a Printer Setup menu or toolbar button. When printing by means of OLE or some other indirect means, you need to specify a default printer.

4. Verify that enough hard disk space is available to generate the print job, especially on the partition that has the spooler directory specified, which, by default, is the system partition (that is, the winnt_root partition).

5. Run the simplest application possible (for example, Notepad) to verify that you can print from other applications within Windows NT. If you run into problems printing from the application (other than a Win32-based application), check the appropriate application subsystem (for example, DOS, Win16, POSIX, or OS/2).

6. Print to a file (FILE:) and then copy the output file to a printer port. If this works, the problem is related to the spooler or data transmission. If this doesn't work, the problem is application- or driver-related.

Spooling Problems

By default, spooled print jobs reside in the \<winnt_root>\ SYSTEM32\SPOOL\PRINTERS directory until completely printed. If a Windows NT–based computer is acting as a print server for the network, make sure plenty of free disk space is available on the partition that contains the default spool directory. Spooled print jobs can be quite large and can eat up disk space more quickly than you might think, especially during peak printing periods. Also, keeping this partition defragmented improves printing performance. Because Windows NT doesn't include a defrag utility, you need to use a third-party utility (or boot to MS-DOS if you are using the FAT file system).

If you have more room on another partition, you may change the default spool directory via options on the Advanced tab of the Server Properties dialog box (see Step by Step 9.4).

STEP BY STEP

9.4 Changing the Location of the Spool File

1. From the Start menu, choose Settings, Printers.

2. From the Printers dialog box, choose File, Server Properties.

3. In the Print Server Properties dialog box, click the Advanced tab and fill in the new spooler path (see Figure 9.12).

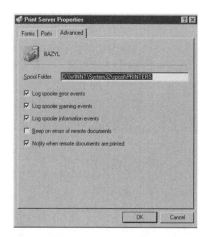

FIGURE 9.12
The Advanced tab of the Print Server Properties dialog box allows you to specify a new path for the spool file.

You can also change the spool directory in the Registry by adding a value called DefaultSpoolDirectory of type REG_SZ to the following key and entering the path to the new spool directory:

HKEY_LOCAL_MACHINE\System\CurrentControlSet\Control
\Print\Printers

You need to restart the spooler service (or the computer itself) for
the change to take effect.

You can also assign a separate spool directory for each individual
printer. To do so, you enter the path to the new spool directory as
the data for the value SpoolDirectory in the following key, where
<Printer> is the name of the printer you want to redirect:

HKEY_LOCAL_MACHINE\System\CurrentControlSet\Control
\Print\~Printers*<Printer>*

Again, you need to restart the Spooler service to put this change into
effect.

Printing from Non–Windows-Based Applications

Non–Windows-based applications (such as MS-DOS–based applications) require their own printer drivers if the application requires any
kind of formatted output other than plain ASCII text. WordPerfect
for MS-DOS, for example, does not even allow the user to print a
document unless there is a WordPerfect-specific and printer-specific
driver installed because non–Windows-based applications are not
written to conform to or take advantage of the Windows APIs. In
addition, you may need to use the NET USE LPT1: *servername*\
printername command to enable the DOS-based application to
print.

Printing and Computer Crashes

When a document prints, two files are created for the print job and
placed in the spool directory (which is, by default, <winnt_root>\
SYSTEM32\SPOOL\PRINTERS). One of the files has an .SPL
extension; it is the actual print job spool file. The other file, which
has an .SHD extension, is a shadow file that contains information
about the job, including its owner and priority. These files remain in

the spool directory until the jobs finish printing, at which point they are deleted.

In the event of a system crash, some spool and shadow files may be left over from jobs that were waiting to be printed. When the Spooler service restarts (along with the rest of the system), the printer should process these files immediately. However, sometimes they become corrupted during the crash and get stuck. Be certain, therefore, to check the spool directory once in a while and delete any spool and shadow files with old date/time stamps. How old is old depends on how long it takes to print a job on your printer. Certainly anything from days, weeks, or months ago should be deleted.

If a print job appears to be stuck in the printer and you cannot delete it, try this solution: Stop the Spooler service via the Control Panel Services application and delete the .SPL and .SHD files for that job from the spool directory. You will need to match the date/time stamp on the files and those in Print Manager to determine which files are causing the problem.

Printing Too Slow or Workstation Too Sluggish

Windows NT Workstation assigns priority 7 to the Spooler service, which puts printing on an equal footing with other background applications. Windows NT Server, which favors printing over background applications, assigns priority 9 to the Spooler service, putting it neck-and-neck with the foreground applications.

If the priority for printing has been changed or if you desire to change its priority, you can do so through the Registry. To change the priority class for the Spooler service, add a value called PriorityClass of type REG_DWORD to HKEY_LOCAL_MACHINE\System\CurrentControlSet\Control\ Print and set it equal to the priority class desired. If this value is set to 0 or is not present, the default is used (7 for Windows NT Workstation, or 9 for Windows NT Server).

TROUBLESHOOTING **RAS**

Choose the appropriate course of action to take to resolve RAS problems.

Most RAS problems result from initial configuration problems. You may have to endure a few trial-and-error failures before things work consistently, but after they work themselves out, the possible ongoing problems will be minimal. However, for users who dial–in to your network, this is their only source of access. Therefore, you will need to ensure that you fully understand the problems that may occur and the solutions to them. You would hate to have the VP of Finance try to dial into your computer from home or a hotel room only to find that RAS is not working properly.

An important thing to note with RAS (and in any function that depends on services) is that some services are configured to start automatically and others are not. When installed, RAS is not configured to start automatically on system boot; instead, it is set to be started manually. That means that if you do not manually start RAS or configure it to start automatically, it will not respond to client requests, even if everything else is configured correctly. This illustrates a basic principle of troubleshooting: Don't assume the problem is serious until you have checked to see if it is trivial. Step by Step 9.5 walks you through the process of checking RAS status and startup configuration.

STEP BY STEP

9.5 Checking and Modifying RAS Start Status

1. Open the Control Panel and double-click the Services icon.

2. Scroll through the Services list until you find Remote Access Server. By default, the Status field will be blank (to indicate that the service is not running), and the Startup field will be set to Manual.

3. Double-click the Remote Access Server entry to display the Service dialog box. Choose Automatic in the Startup

Type field, and then click OK to complete the startup change.

4. In the Services dialog box, click the Start button to start the RAS service. When it has started, click Close to exit back to the Control Panel.

If RAS isn't working, check the Event Viewer. Several RAS events appear in the System log. You might also check the Control Panel's Dial-Up Networking Monitor application. The Status tab of Dial-Up Networking displays statistics on current conditions, including connection statistics and device errors.

If you are having problems with PPP, you can log PPP debugging information to a file called PPP.LOG in the \<winnt_root>\System32\Ras directory. To log PPP debugging information to PPP.LOG, change the Registry value for the following subkey to 1:

\HKEY_LOCAL_MACHINE\System\CurrentControlSet\Services\Rasman\PPP\Logging

Microsoft identifies the following common RAS problems and some possible solutions:

◆ *User permission.* A common but easily remedied cause of RAS failure is insufficient permission given to the user in User Manager. If the user is not enabled for remote login, RAS login will always fail.

◆ *Authentication.* RAS authentication problems often stem from incompatible encryption methods. Try to connect using the Allow Any Authentication Including Clear Text option (described earlier in this chapter). If you can connect using clear text but you can't connect using encryption, you know the client and server encryption methods are incompatible.

◆ *Callback with Multilink.* If a client makes a connection using Multilink over multiple phone lines and he has callback enabled, the server will call back using only a single phone line (in other words, Multilink functionality is lost). RAS can use only one phone number for callback. If the Multilink connection uses two channels over an ISDN line, the server can still use Multilink on the callback.

◆ *Autodial at logon.* At logon, when Explorer is initializing, it might reference a shortcut or some other target that requires an Autodial connection, which causes Autodial to spontaneously dial a remote connection during logon. The only way to prevent this is to either disable Autodial or eliminate the shortcut or other target causing the Autodial to occur.

TROUBLESHOOTING CONNECTIVITY PROBLEMS

Choose the appropriate course of action to take to resolve connectivity problems.

Network problems often are caused by cables, adapters, or IRQ conflicts, or problems with transmission media. Protocol problems also can disrupt the network. Use a diagnostics program to check the network adapter card. Use a cable analyzer to check the cabling. Finally, use Network Monitor (described in the next section) or a network protocol analyzer to check network traffic.

If you are using TCP/IP, you often can isolate the problem by *pinging* other computers on your network. Exercise 1.2 in Chapter 1 described a common diagnostic procedure using the ping command:

1. Ping the 127.0.0.1 (the loopback address).

2. Ping your own IP address.

3. Ping the address of another computer on your subnet.

4. Ping the default gateway.

5. Ping a computer beyond the default gateway.

Check the Control Panel Services application to ensure that the Server and Workstation services (and any other vital services that might affect connectivity) are running properly. If the Server service on your NT Server is not running, no one will be able to access the server. If the Workstation service is not running, your server will not

---

EXAM TIP

Some Situations Dictate Pinging the Gateway First   Although theoretically you should follow the steps on this page to ensure that TCP/IP is working properly, if you ping the default gateway first, you can be sure that steps 1–3 would also produce successful results. Watch for questions that imply problems with TCP/IP connectivity, and try to determine whether a single ping will dismiss some avenues of problem. For example, suppose you're trying to access a computer by name but cannot hit it. To uncover the problem, you should ping the default gateway first to establish TCP/IP configuration, then ping the computer by name, and then ping it by address. If you can successfully ping by address but not by name, you probably have a TCP/IP address resolution problem and not a TCP/IP configuration problem. In that case, you would want to check the WINS or DNS configuration next.

be able to access any other machine. Check the Bindings tab in the Control Panel's Network application to ensure that the services are bound to applications and adapters.

Network Monitor

Windows NT Server 4 includes a tool called Network Monitor. Network Monitor captures and filters packets and analyzes network activity. The Network Monitor included with Windows NT Server can monitor incoming and outgoing network traffic only on the system on which it is installed. Another version of Network Monitor, found in Microsoft's Systems Management Server package, can operate in promiscuous mode, which means it can monitor all network traffic anywhere on the network.

To install Windows NT Server's Network Monitor, start the Network application in Control Panel and click on the Services tab. Click on the Add button, and then select Network Monitor from the Network Services list. After Network Monitor is installed, it appears in the Administrative Tools program group. Figure 9.13 shows the Network Monitor main screen.

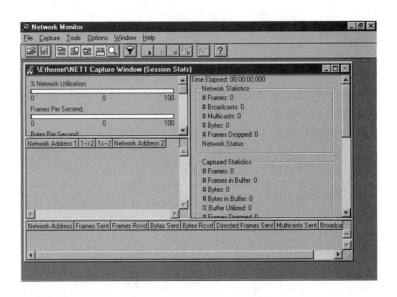

FIGURE 9.13

From the Network Monitor main screen you can configure the operation of Network Monitor and observe it as it captures network data.

The Network Monitor window is divided into four sections or *panes*. This section describes each of the four Network Monitor panes and the various parameters and statistics you can monitor with Network Monitor.

The Graph pane (in the upper-left corner) shows the current network activity in a series of five bar charts. Note the scroll bar to the right of the Graph pane. To view the bar charts (not shown in Figure 9.13), scroll down or drag the lower border down until the hidden charts are exposed.

The Graph pane contains the following five bar graphs:

◆ %Network Utilization

◆ Frames Per Second

◆ Bytes Per Second

◆ Broadcasts Per Second

◆ Multicasts Per Second

Below the Graph pane is the Session Stats pane. The Session Stats pane indicates the exchange of information from two nodes on the network, the amount of data, and the direction of travel. This data is limited to a per-session basis.

The Session Stats pane reports only on the first 128 sessions it finds. However, you can specify a particular session by creating a capture filter.

The Session Stats pane collects information on the following four areas:

◆ *Network Address 1.* The first node included in a network session.

◆ *1->2.* The number of packets sent from the first address to the second.

◆ *1<-2.* The number of packets sent from the second address to the first.

◆ *Network Address 2.* The second node included in the network session.

On the right side of the display window is the Total Stats pane, which reveals information relevant to all activity on the entire network. Whether statistics are supported depends on the network adapter. If a given network adapter isn't supported, Unsupported replaces the label.

The Total Stats information is divided into five categories:

◆ *Network Statistics,* which lists statistics for Total Frames, Total Broadcasts, Total Multicasts, Total Bytes, Total Frames Dropped, and Network Status.

◆ *Captured Statistics,* which lists statistics for Captured Frames, Captured Frames in Buffer, Captured Bytes, Captured Bytes in Buffer, Percentage of Allotted Buffer Space in Use, and Captured Packets Dropped.

◆ *Per Second Statistics,* which lists statistics for Frames, Bytes/Second, Broadcasts/Second, Multicasts/Second, and %Network Utilization.

◆ *Network Card (MAC) Statistics,* which lists statistics for Total Frames, Total Broadcasts, Total Multicasts, and Total Bytes.

◆ *Network Card (MAC) Error Statistics,* which lists statistics for Total Cyclical Redundancy Check (CRC) Errors, Total Dropped Frames Due to Inadequate Buffer Space, and Total Dropped Packets Due to Hardware Failure(s).

At the bottom of the display window is the Station Stats pane, which displays information specific to a workstation's activity on the network. The Station pane reports on only the first 128 sessions it finds. However, you can specify a particular session using a capture filter.

In this pane, you can sort data based on any category by right-clicking on the column label. The following eight categories constitute the Station pane:

◆ *Network Address.* The network address for which the statistics shown have been compiled (there will be one entry for every network address that interacted with the machine running Network Monitor).

NOTE

The Network Status Value The Network Status value is always normal if you use an ethernet network. If you use token ring, the Network Status value indicates the status of the ring.

◆ *Frames Sent.* The total number of frames sent from the network address to the machine running Network Monitor since the capture began.

◆ *Frames Rcvd.* The total number of frames received by the machine running Network Monitor from the network address since the capture began.

◆ *Bytes Sent.* The total number of bytes of data sent from the network address to the machine running Network Monitor since the capture began.

◆ *Bytes Rcvd.* The total number of bytes of data received by the machine running Network Monitor from the network address since the capture began.

◆ *Directed Frames Sent.* The total number of frames sent by the network address that were directed to a specific address.

◆ *Multicasts Sent.* The total number of frames sent by the network address that were directed at a multicast address.

◆ *Broadcasts Sent.* The total number of frames sent by the network address that were broadcast instead of being directed.

TROUBLESHOOTING ACCESS AND PERMISSION PROBLEMS

Choose the appropriate course of action to take to resolve resource access problems and permission problems.

If you can't log on, first make sure you are using the correct username and password. Also, make sure that the correct domain or workgroup (or the local machine) is selected in the Domain drop-down list of the Logon dialog box. If you still can't log on, try logging on using another account. If other accounts are working normally, check the settings for your account in User Manager for Domains. If you can't log on from any account, repair the accounts database by using the emergency repair process.

One of the worst culprits for logon problems is the Caps Lock key. If you (or another user) cannot log on, make sure you are not typing the password in all caps.

If a user can't access a file, a share, a printer, or some other resource, check the resource permissions. Try connecting using a different account. Try accessing a similar resource to see whether the problem also appears there. Make sure the user has spelled the name of the resource correctly.

Check the Control Panel Services application to ensure that the NetLogon service, the Server service, and the Workstation service are running properly, and then check the Bindings tab in the Control Panel's Network application to ensure that the services are bound to applications and adapters. The NetLogon service must be started on both the NT computer that you are logging in from and the domain controller that will validate your logon. This service is the mechanism that transmits and receives account name and password information and ensures that domain security can validate it.

You can also check User Manager for Domains to verify that the user's group memberships haven't changed or that a change to a group rights setting hasn't inadvertently denied the user access to the resource.

Check System Policy Editor for restrictions on the user's access to computers or other resources.

RECOVERING FROM FAULT-TOLERANCE FAILURES

Choose the appropriate course of action to take to resolve fault-tolerance failures. Fault-tolerance methods include tape backup, mirroring, stripe set with parity, and disk duplexing.

Fault tolerance is the ability to recover from failure in a quick and easy way. Despite the presence of fault-tolerance systems, problems will have to be resolved. Disk striping with parity, for example, allows your system to continue to function when a hard drive fails, but your system will be crippled until the failed drive can be replaced. This section talks about recovery techniques that can be used to allow fault-tolerance systems to recover from hardware failure.

NT Backup

The most important fault-tolerance system you can put into place on your server is a good backup schedule. Not even the most sophisticated RAID software or hardware implementation can prevent the need to recover data from a backup at some time. Disk-striping with parity, for example, cannot tolerate multiple hard drives failing at once. Moreover, no fault-tolerance system can tolerate the physical destruction from fire, flood, earthquake, and other natural disasters. Finally, it must also be noted that no system will allow you to recover from certain user errors. If someone who has authority makes incorrect changes, no fault-tolerance system can prevent that from happening. Therefore, having backups is essential if your system is to survive physical disaster or catastrophic user error.

The NT Backup utility is built into the NT operating system and is available on both NT Server and NT Workstation. In addition to the software being built in, some administrative structures have also been automatically created to allow for ease of use. This includes the presence of the local Backup Operators group on every NT machine and the presence of special user permissions to allow the backing up and restoring files and directories.

Backups can be initiated by anyone with the user right to "Back Up Files and Directories." By default, the local groups Administrators, Backup Operators, and Server Operators have this right. However, any user or group can be granted the right to perform this operation.

To start the NT Backup utility, choose Start, Programs, Administrative Tools (Common), Backup.

NT Backup is configured to detect and back up to an installed tape drive. If you do not have a tape drive in your NT Server, you cannot perform backups using NT Backup. When Backup starts, if you have no tape unit, an error message appears (see Figure 9.14).

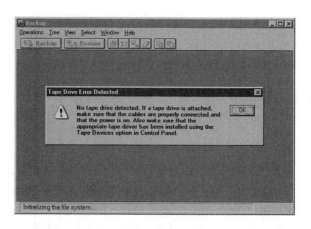

FIGURE 9.14
This message warns you that Backup will not work without a tape drive.

Backup Does Not Back Up to the Sector Level The NT Backup program does not back up to the sector level. This means that you cannot restore your NT system onto a bare hard drive using this utility. Instead you must reinstall NT onto the system to be recovered and then restore the data and Registry from there.

Backing Up Files and Directories

The NT Backup program supports five backup types, allowing you to create a backup routine designed for practicality, efficiency, and ease of recovery. The types differ based on which files they back up (all files or only those that have not been marked as backed up) and whether they mark files as backed up. Table 9.2 outlines the backup types, which files they back up, and whether they mark files as backed up.

TABLE 9.2

BACKUP TYPES AVAILABLE IN NT BACKUP

Type	Backs Up	Marks?
Normal	All selected files and folders	Yes
Copy	All selected files and folders	No
Incremental	Selected files and folders not marked as backed up	Yes
Differential	Selected files and folders not marked as backed up	No
Daily Copy	Selected files and folders changed that day	No

The marker that is set on a file is called the *archive attribute*. When a file changes, the archive attribute is cleared. That enables the Backup program to determine which files need to be backed up and which ones were backed up on another tape.

The Normal backup (sometimes referred to as a Full backup) backs up all the files you select and sets the archive attribute.

Running a Copy backup is basically the same as using the XCOPY command to copy to a tape: It makes a copy of selected files and folders but does not modify the archive attribute. This ensures that you can archive information to a tape without interfering with the backup process.

The Incremental backup backs up only those selected files and folders that have been changed since the last backup. In other words, if a Normal backup is done on Monday night, the Incremental done on Tuesday night would back up only those files changed since the Normal backup. In addition, the archive attributes are set on all files that are backed up so that an Incremental backup on Wednesday backs up only those files that have changed since the Incremental on Tuesday.

Like the Incremental backup, the Differential backup backs up only those files that have changed since the last backup. The difference is that this backup type does not set the archive attribute. In other words, if you ran a Normal backup on Monday night and you do a Differential backup on Tuesday, it will back up only those files changed since Monday night. However, because the archive attributes are not set, a Differential backup on Wednesday again backs up everything that has changed since the Monday backup.

The Daily Copy backup is used to back up those files changed on a specific day (which Backup detects by looking at the Change date in the file properties). This backup type does not set the archive attribute, so it does not affect the backup process.

Backup Strategies

Most backup strategies involve some combination of Normal backups with either Differential or Incremental backups. It does not make sense from a practical perspective to do Normal backups daily because you end up backing up your whole system day after day. Instead, a Normal backup is generally done at the start or end of the week, and then a smaller backup is done daily to ensure that daily changes are captured. This combination of a weekly Normal backup and some sort of daily backup ensures that, at most, one day of information could be lost in the event of a disk failure.

As for what kind of daily backup to do, well, that depends on how long you want to spend running daily backups versus how long you might want to spend performing a recovery. If you do Incremental backups on a daily basis, your daily backups will be relatively small because you are backing up only a single day's information. On the other hand, if you do a differential backup daily, the amount of information stored per tape increases as the week wears on because the archive attributes are not being marked. Therefore, if you run a Normal backup on Monday night and an Incremental backup on Thursday, the Thursday Incremental contains only Thursday's data (whereas a Thursday Differential would contain Tuesday, Wednesday, and Thursday's data).

On the other hand, when it comes time to restore information, one method will definitely take more time and effort on your part. If you need to restore back to Thursday in a Normal/Incremental environment, you will have to apply the Normal backup from Monday, followed by Tuesday's incremental, Wednesday's incremental, and Thursday's incremental. In a Normal/Differential environment, you will have to apply only the Normal and then Thursday's Differential, which contains everything from Monday to Thursday.

Performing a Backup

Performing a backup involves two basic steps: indicating the scope of the backup and setting the backup properties. Indicating the scope simply means telling the backup program which folders and/or files are to be backed up (and on which machines). Setting the backup properties involves configuring the backup type, setting the device to back up to, naming the backup set, and configuring logging if necessary. Step by Step 9.6 describes the procedure for performing a backup.

STEP BY STEP

9.6 Performing a Backup

1. Establish drive mappings to remote computers that you want to back up on the tape you are currently using. This is necessary because NT Backup will back up only from local drives; but of course, a mapped drive is treated as a local drive.

---

2. Start the NT Backup program by choosing Start, Programs, Administrative Tools (Common), Backup. The main Backup window appears (see Figure 9.15).

3. For each drive on which you want to back up information, double-click the drive to display an Explorer window (see Figure 9.16). Beside each drive, folder, and file is a check box. By clicking the check box, you indicate that you want to include that element in the backup. If you select a drive, its entire contents will be backed up; if you select a folder, its entire contents will be backed up; if you select a file, only that single file will be backed up.

4. To set the backup properties, select Operations, Backup. Then fill in the appropriate fields in the Backup Information dialog box (see Figure 9.17). The properties available include the name of the backup set (in the Tape Name field), verification options, Registry backup, access restriction, backup type, and log file location and type.

5. Click the OK button to initiate the backup process.

EXAM TIP

Be Aware of How to Back Up the Registry On the exam, you may be asked how to back up the Registry. Be aware that there is a check box labeled Backup Local Registry in the Backup Information dialog box. That check box allows you to specify Registry backup. Also note that you cannot back up the Registry of a local machine using this method; you may be tested on that as well.

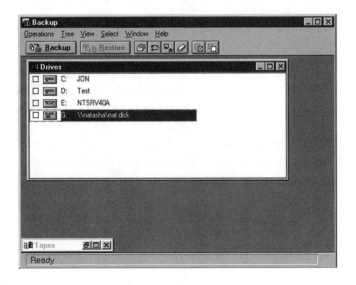

FIGURE 9.15
From the Backup window, you can intiate backups or restore files.

FIGURE 9.16
Select drives, folders, and files to include in the backup's scope by clicking the check box to the left of each element's name in the Explorer window.

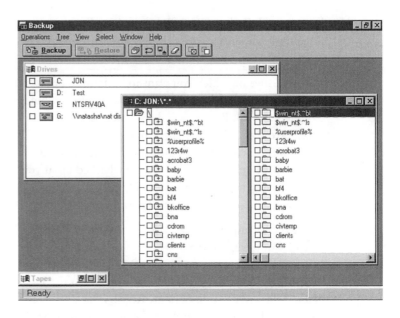

Restoring Files and Directories

Restoring backed up information is necessary in a variety of situations: when disk failure occurs, when a user requests the restoration of data that was deleted or changed and cannot be manually recovered, or simply to exercise your tapes.

The last option, exercising your tapes, is less of a fault recovery process and more for backup insurance. Like all media, tapes are subject to environmental influence. As a result, the quality of a backup degrades over time, even in an environmentally controlled vault. There is nothing worse than trying to restore information and finding that the tape contains errors. Periodically restoring information to a test system ensures that critical data is available in case it should ever need to be restored from a tape.

The restoration of data from a backup set requires the user right "Restore Files and Folders," which can be given to any user but is granted by default to the local groups Administrators, Backup Operators, and Server Operators.

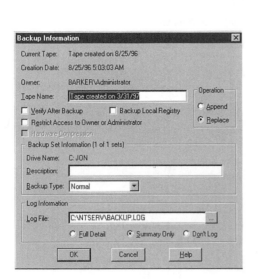

FIGURE 9.17
Configure the backup type and options in the Backup Information dialog box.

When you do restore data, the default method is to restore it to the same location it came from. You can, if you desire, restore it to another location. If you restore it to the same location it came from, you will want to make sure it is restored with the same NTFS permissions it had before so that all users who had access to the data originally still have access after the restore. If you are restoring to another computer (one that does not have the same user directory the original computer did), you will want to restore without NTFS permissions. The restored data is then accessible on the new system, and it will inherit the permissions of the folder into which it is restored.

The procedure for restoring from a backup follows in Step by Step 9.7.

STEP BY STEP

9.7 Restoring a File or Directory Using Backup

1. Start the NT Backup program by choosing Start, Programs, Administrative Tools (Common), Backup.

2. Insert the tape from which you want to recover into the tape drive.

3. From the Window menu, choose Tapes, and a list of tapes appears in the Backup window (see Figure 9.18).

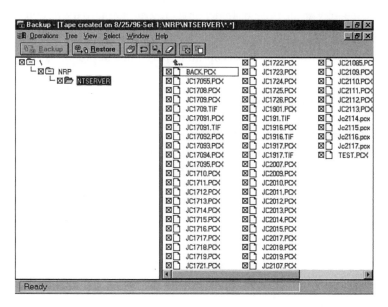

FIGURE 9.18

From the list of tapes in the right pane, you can select the files to restore.

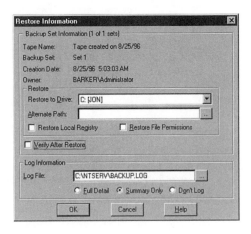

FIGURE 9.19
In the Restore Information dialog, you can configure the characteristics of your restore procedure.

4. In the right pane, select the files and folders you want to restore by selecting the check box to the left of each element.

5. From the Operations menu, choose Restore. The Restore Information dialog box appears (see Figure 9.19).

6. In the Restore Information dialog box, indicate the restore characteristics. You can indicate where you want the data restored (both drive and path name), whether you want to restore the Registry and file permissions, and the location and detail level of the log file that will be produced.

7. Click the OK button to initiate the restore.

Running Backup from a Command Prompt

You also can execute the NT Backup utility from a command prompt, with switches to indicate the properties of the backup. You can even do this from within a batch file for your convenience.

Running Backup from a command prompt is essentially the same as running it from the GUI interface except that you can indicate the scope only at the drive or folder level. You do not have the option of backing up certain individual files.

The syntax for running Backup from the command prompt is as follows:

```
ntbackup operation path
```

where *operation* is the name of the operation (backup, restore, and so on), and *path* is the path to the directory you're backing up. Table 9.3 shows some of the available switches and their functions.

TABLE 9.3

NTBACKUP SWITCHES

a	Causes the backup set to be appended after the last backup set. (If you don't specify, /a will overwrite existing backup sets on the tape.)

Switch	Function
/d "*text*"	Enables you to add a description of the data in the backup set.
/l	Specifies the filename for a backup log.
/r	Restricts access to the backup to the owner or an administrator. The /r parameter is ignored if /a is also specified.
/t {*option*}	Enables you to specify the backup type (Normal, Incremental, Daily, Differential, Copy).
/v	Verifies tape content when the backup completes.

To illustrate the use of Backup from the command line, suppose you wanted to perform a backup with the following parameters:

◆ Perform a normal backup of drives C, D, and E.

◆ Restrict access to the owner or administrator.

◆ Apply the description "Full backup of drives C, D, and E" to all three backup sets.

◆ Perform a verification pass upon completion of the backup.

◆ Record the results of the session in a log file named C:\LOG\LOG.TXT.

To meet all those requirements, you would type the following at the command line:

```
NTBackup Backup C: D: E: /t Normal /v /r /d "Full Backup
of drives C, D, and E" /l "C:\LOG\LOG.TXT"
```

For a complete description of options for the NTBACKUP command, see Windows NT Online Help.

Recovering from a Failed Mirror Set

When a mirror set fails, the remaining drive becomes an orphan. To maintain service until the mirror is repaired, the fault-tolerant device directs all I/O requests to the healthy partition. This can carry on indefinitely until you reboot the server, at which point the restart may fail.

If the boot and/or system partitions are on the mirror set, you may find that a reboot is impossible because the BOOT.INI file (if it can be located during the boot process) may be pointing to the physical drive that failed. As a result, you will have to use a recovery disk to restart your system and then repair the mirror set (see Step by Step 9.8).

STEP BY STEP

9.8 Repairing a Broken Mirror Set

1. Shut down your NT server and physically replace the failed drive.

2. If required, boot NT using a recovery disk.

3. Start the Disk Administrator by choosing Start, Programs, Administrative Tools (Common), Disk Administrator.

4. Select the mirror set by clicking on it.

5. From the Fault Tolerance menu, choose Break Mirror. This exposes the remaining partition as a volume separate from the failed one.

6. Reestablish the mirror set if desired by selecting the partition you desire to mirror and a portion of free space equal in size and then choosing the Fault Tolerance, Establish Mirror command.

Recovering from a Failed Element of a Stripe Set with Parity

As in the failure of a mirror set, the partition that fails in a stripe set with parity becomes an orphan. In addition, the fault-tolerant device redirects I/O requests to the remaining partitions in the set to enable reconstruction. So that this can be done, the data is stored in RAM by using the parity bits (which slows system performance dramatically).

In order to restore a stripe set with parity, you will have to replace the disk that failed and then regenerate the stripe set using the Disk Administrator (see Step by Step 9.9). It is recommended that you perform a backup on the data in the stripe set before you attempt the repair to ensure that if the set proves unrecoverable, you will be able to restore the data from backup.

STEP BY STEP

9.9 Regenerating a Stripe Set with Parity

1. Shut down your NT Server and physically replace the failed drive.

2. Start the Disk Administrator by choosing Start, Programs, Administrative Tools (Common), Disk Administrator.

3. Select the stripe set with parity by clicking on it.

4. Select an area of free space as large as or larger than the portion of the stripe set that was lost when the disk failed.

5. Choose Fault Tolerance, Regenerate.

You must close the Disk Administrator and restart the system before the process can begin. After the system restarts, the information from the existing partitions in the stripe set are read into memory and re-created on the new member. This process is completed in the background, so the stripe set with parity isn't active in the Disk Administrator until it finishes.

Troubleshooting Partitions and Disks

When you install Windows NT, your initial disk configuration is saved on the emergency repair disk and in the directory \<winnt_root>\Repair. The RDISK utility does update the disk configuration information stored on the repair disk and in the repair directory. You can also save or restore the disk configuration by using Disk Administrator (see the section "Saving and Restoring Configuration Information," earlier in this chapter).

You should periodically update emergency configuration information in case you ever need to use the emergency repair process or you ever want to upgrade to a newer version of Windows NT. Otherwise, NT restores the original configuration that was saved when you first installed Windows NT.

CASE STUDY: NT SERVER FREQUENTLY EXPERIENCES STOP

ESSENCE OF THE CASE

Here are the essential elements of this case:

- The server in question is experiencing a high number of Stop errors.

- The problem cannot be repaired using the setup disks and the ERD the user has.

- The problem manifests itself during local user interaction with the Server.

- The problems have increased in recent weeks.

- This server is essential, and unless it's absolutely necessary, the user does not want to reinstall NT on it.

SCENARIO

A client calls you in to repair a production server. This machine has been running for approximately a month and has a considerable number of user accounts, data, and applications on it. The symptoms of the problem are that the machine blue-screens at almost every command or action performed locally. When it's started and left alone, the machine functions perfectly. Users can connect to it, it validates logon, and it functions well as a print server. However, if someone tries to log on locally after the machine boots, about 50 percent of the time the server experiences a Stop error before the desktop appears. The rest of the time, if someone tries to access the system properties to examine the Stop error recovery properties, the system experiences a Stop error.

The client has tried performing an emergency repair, but when the NT Setup process initiates, a Stop error is generated and the setup fails.

All instances of the Stop error generate the same error code referencing the NTOSKRNL.

When queried, the user cannot think of a time when Stop errors did not occur, but he is convinced that they have increased in the last couple of weeks, when more configuration of the Server has been required.

ANALYSIS

The errors that are manifesting themselves point to a fundamental problem with the NT configuration on this server. If this were a test machine that could be broken down easily, that would be the simplest solution. However, in this case, that

CASE STUDY: NT SERVER FREQUENTLY EXPERIENCES STOP

is not an option (at least not until all other avenues of repair have been tried). Using the DETECT model, you note the following:

1. *Discover the problem.* The server experiences Stop errors on a frequent basis.

2. *Explore the boundaries.* The problem is reproducible; sooner or later, local user interaction with the Server results in a Stop error. It does not, however, occur when users connect over the network.

3. *Track the possible approaches.* In brainstorming sessions, you come up with the following suggestions

   - Repair with ERD

   - Remove services and adapters

   - Create new user accounts

   - Remove protocols

   - Reinstall NT

In addition you consult with other NT professionals regarding their experience with this sort of problem, but you come up with no solutions.

Finally, you record the Stop screen error message from the upper left-hand corner of the screen, and armed with that reference, you do a search in TechNet. It yields a result telling you that you have a corrupt file and should attempt an emergency repair.

4. *Execute an approach.* You decide to revisit the possibility of an emergency repair. You know that one has already been attempted, and when you try, you also get a Stop error when booting from the Setup disks. Probing a little more, you discover that both the NT installation and the Setup disks were created from a network share. You begin to suspect that there is a problem with the files in that share. Creating a new set of Setup disks from the NT Server CD-ROM, you again attempt a setup; this one is successful. You are able to use the ERD to discover that the NTOSKRNL is corrupt and replace it.

5. *Check for success.* Upon rebooting the server you find that, in all the situations where Stop errors occurred, they no longer do. Documenting what you have discovered to this point, you ask the user who called you to continue to work with the system and to document all Stop errors that occur. One month later, he has recorded no more error conditions.

6. *Tie up loose ends.* After the server has been running for a few months without problems, you are convinced that the problem is resolved. You document the solution so that if you encounter it again, you will be armed with a solution to try right away.

CHAPTER SUMMARY

KEY TERMS

Before taking the exam, make sure you are familiar with the definitions of and concepts behind each of the following key terms. Use Appendix A, Glossary, for quick reference purposes.

- DETECT model
- NTHQ
- HCL
- MBR
- NTLDR
- NTDETECT.COM
- NTOSKRNL.EXE
- BOOT.INI
- ARC-path
- /SOS
- LastKnownGood
- BOOTSECT.DOS
- NTBOOTDD.SYS
- OSLOADER.EXE
- recovery disk
- emergency repair disk
- RDISK.EXE
- Event Viewer
- Security log
- System log

Beginning with a suggested approach to troubleshooting (the DETECT model), this chapter covered a number of areas you might need to troubleshoot. The areas included installation, boot, configuration, printing, RAS, connectivity, access and permissions, and fault tolerance.

The point of this chapter was to give you a framework for understanding the kinds of issues that may arise in troubleshooting NT Server problems, both in a production environment and on the exam.

- Application log
- hive
- Network Monitor
- Normal backup
- Incremental backup
- Differential backup
- regenerate

APPLY YOUR LEARNING

Exercises

The following exercises will help to reinforce the concepts you learned in this chapter. Although they are not all-inclusive, they do give you an overview of some of the tools and procedures discussed.

9.1   Booting with /SOS

In this exercise, you learn how to initiate a Windows NT boot by using the /sos switch, which enumerates each driver as the drivers load during the kernel load phase.

Estimated Time: 20 minutes

1. Start the Notepad accessory application and open the BOOT.INI file in the root directory of the system partition. In the Notepad Open dialog box, don't forget to select All Files in the Files of Type box. The extension may not appear in the browse list. (The file name may appear as *boot*, without the extension. If you aren't sure you have the right file, right-click on the file and select Properties. Examine the MS-DOS name setting in the file Properties dialog box.)

2. Figure 9.20 shows the BOOT.INI file in Notepad. Find the line with the text string "Windows NT Server Version 4.00 [VGA]." Make sure the string is followed by the switches /basevideo and /sos. If you're confident your system uses a VGA video driver, skip to step 6; otherwise, continue with step 4.

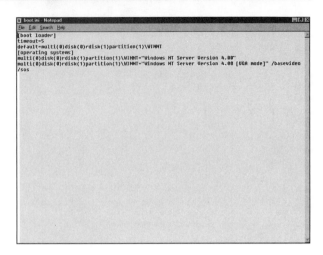

FIGURE 9.20
This is the BOOT.INI file of an NT server that boots only to NT.

3. Save the BOOT.INI file to a different file name (such as BOOT.TMP) by using the File, Save As command.

4. Delete the /basevideo switch in the line with the text string "Windows NT Server Version 4.00 [VGA]." The /sos switch should remain. Change the text in the square brackets from "VGA" to "sos."

5. Save the file as BOOT.INI.

   You may have to use the Save As command to save BOOT.INI. Verify the filename in the File Name box. Step 3 may have changed the default file name.

6. Close Notepad and shut down your system.

7. Reboot Windows NT. When the boot menu appears, choose the "sos" option (or the VGA option if you skipped steps 3–5).

APPLY YOUR LEARNING

8. Watch the names of the drivers display onscreen as they load. (Watch carefully because they will disappear quickly from the screen.) The drivers, like the BOOT.INI entries, will appear in ARC format. If you experience a boot failure, you can use this technique to determine which driver crashed or hung the system.

9. Log on to Windows NT. Restore the BOOT.INI file to its original state, either by inserting "VGA" and "/basevideo" using Notepad or by copying the BOOT.TMP file back to BOOT.INI. When you're finished, open BOOT.INI and make sure it is back to normal.

> **NOTE**
> **Be Sure to Reset the BOOT.INI File**
> Step 9 is very important. You may not use the VGA boot option again for months or even years, and when you do, you may not remember that you tried this exercise.

9.2 Creating a Recovery Disk

In this exercise, you create and test a recovery disk.

Estimated Time: 10 minutes

1. Insert a disk into your floppy drive.

2. Format the disk from within Windows NT using My Computer or Windows Explorer.

3. Open an Explorer window and copy whichever of the following files are on your system partition to the floppy disk (the files present will vary depending on your processor and hard drive

type): NTLDR, NTDETECT.COM, NTBOOTDD.SYS, BOOT.INI, OSLOADER.EXE, HAL.DLL, and *.PAL.

4. Restart your NT Server with the disk in the drive. You should see the floppy run throughout the initial boot phase until the boot partition is located.

9.3 Updating Emergency Repair Information and Creating an Emergency Repair Disk

In this exercise, you will update the repair information in the /REPAIR folder on your hard drive and you will create an emergency repair disk.

Estimated Time: 10 minutes

1. Choose Start, Run and type **RDISK** in the Run dialog box.

2. In the Repair Disk Utility dialog box, click the Update Repair Info button.

3. When prompted, click Yes to initiate repair information update.

4. After the configuration is saved, you will be prompted to create a new emergency repair disk. Click the Yes button to initiate the ERD creation process.

5. When prompted, insert a floppy disk in the floppy drive and click the Yes button.

6. When the ERD has been created, a message appears telling you that you should secure this disk against unauthorized access. Click OK to continue.

7. Click Exit to close the repair disk utility.

APPLY YOUR LEARNING

> **NOTE**
>
> **If You Get a Message About the ERD Being Full**   If you get a message about the emergency repair disk being full, don't worry; your ERD is complete enough to finish the next exercise. However, if this were a production situation, you would want to consult TechNet white papers about reducing the size of your /REPAIR data so that it all fits on a single floppy disk.

9.4   Examining System Files Using the Emergency Repair Process

In this exercise, you will use the ERD you created in the last exercise to verify the system files on your NT Server. It is assumed that you have the three Setup disks required to initiate setup on an NT Server. If you do not, create them before you begin this exercise.

Estimated Time: 20 minutes

1. Insert the disk labeled Windows NT Server Setup Boot Disk into the floppy drive of your NT Server and restart your machine.

2. When prompted, insert the disk labeled Windows NT Server Setup Disk #2 and press Enter to continue.

3. When the Windows NT Server Setup screen appears, press R to initiate the repair process.

4. When the repair screen appears, using the up arrow on your keyboard, move the highlight bar up to the Inspect Registry Files line and press

Enter to deselect it. Repeat this for all lines except Verify Windows NT System Files.

5. Move the highlight bar to the line that reads Continue (Perform Selected Tasks) and press Enter to continue.

6. When asked to detect mass storage devices, press Enter to continue.

7. When prompted, insert the disk labeled Windows NT Server Setup Disk #3 and press Enter to continue.

8. When the list of recognized mass storage devices is presented, press Enter to continue.

9. When asked if you have an ERD for this server, press Enter to continue.

10. When prompted, insert the Windows NT emergency repair disk and press Enter to continue.

11. When told that your hard disk will be examined for corruption, press Enter to continue.

12. When prompted, insert the Windows NT Server CD-ROM in the CD-ROM drive and press Enter.

13. If you are prompted to repair files that are deemed corrupt, press ESC each time. Because your system is not really in need of repair, we can assume that each of the files found has been modified by a legitimate process—probably by the application of a service pack. Continue to press ESC when additional files are identified.

14. When prompted, remove the ERD from your floppy drive and press Enter to restart your server.

APPLY YOUR LEARNING

Review Questions

1. What is the LastKnownGood configuration and what do you need to do in order to boot with it?

2. What files are required on a recovery disk on an Intel-based Server with IDE hard drives?

3. What priority does Windows NT Server assign to the print Spooler service?

4. What would cause an NT computer to begin dialing a phone number at the end of the logon process?

5. Which local groups are, by default, given rights to perform backups and restore data using the NT Backup program?

6. What is an ARC path and what is the significance of ARC paths in the NT boot process?

7. A user calls to tell you that when dialing into your recently configured RAS server she keeps getting messages indicating that the server is not responding to RAS requests. What do you check first?

8. What is the general procedure for recovering from the failure of a disk in a stripe set with parity?

Exam Questions

1. A user calls and says that he can't log on to the system. He is getting a message that says NT cannot log you on. Check your userid and password information and try again (or something to that effect). What would you check?

A. Make sure that the user types in the correct password and userid combination. Also check that the user has entered the password in the correct case and is specifying the correct domain name.

B. Nothing. It's a normal message that the user would get when the server is down for maintenance.

C. Log on as administrator and restart the domain controller to clear out any unused connections. When the server comes back up, the user should be able to log on.

D. Using IPCONFIG, check the TCP/IP address of the client to ensure that it is using the same subnet mask as the server.

2. You received a message during the boot process that a dependency service failed to start. Where should you check for more information?

A. The file server error log.

B. In Event Viewer, under the Security log.

C. In Event Viewer, under the System log.

D. In Server Manager, under the System log.

3. You have turned on auditing, but you cannot remember where the system puts the audit information. Where do you need to look?

A. In Event Viewer, under the Security log.

B. In Event Viewer, under the System log.

C. In Auditcon, under the Security section.

D. At the command prompt, type **NET Show Audit**.

APPLY YOUR LEARNING

4. You're looking for a particular message in the Event Viewer System log, but there are so many messages you can't find the one you're looking for. How can you display messages of a certain type?

   A. You cannot. Event Viewer shows all the messages in the System log.

   B. You must set up Event Viewer to store only messages of the type you're looking for and then restart the system.

   C. You can filter the log by choosing View, Filter Events.

   D. You must first export the data to an ASCII file and then use the Edit program to find the specific data you seek.

5. Your manager informs you that you need to inventory all company computers running NT Workstation and NT Server. Which NT utility can you use to safely determine the amount of RAM, type of CPU, and other information about the computers in question?

   A. You must purchase the 32-bit version of PC Tools. This program gives you the required information.

   B. No tools will run under NT because they would have to access the hardware directly, which isn't allowed under NT.

   C. You must manually edit the Registry and search for the information you need.

   D. Use the Windows NT Diagnostics utility.

6. A user calls you and says that while he was running Windows NT Diagnostics, he attempted to change the type of CPU that was reported but could not. Why couldn't he?

   A. NT Diagnostics only shows information. You cannot make any modifications using this tool.

   B. The type of CPU cannot be changed with NT Diagnostics. The user must use Registry Editor to make such a change manually.

   C. The user must make the CPU change in CMOS setup, not in NT Diagnostics.

   D. No CPU information is available in NT Diagnostics.

7. You're on a telephone call with Microsoft, and the support engineer asks you which version of the operating system you're running. How can you find this out? Choose all that apply.

   A. You cannot. You must contact your network administrator for the information.

   B. The support engineer should be able to look up your product registration information.

   C. Run Windows NT Diagnostics and choose Version.

   D. Check the Registry under the key HKEY_LOCAL_MACHINE\Software\Microsoft\Windows NT\CurrentVersion.

8. You're having problems with Stop errors on a computer running Windows NT Server. How can you set the recovery options that tell the system what action to perform in the event of a Stop error?

   A. You can set these options under Control Panel, System.

   B. You cannot. The system automatically places an event in the System log and then restarts the computer.

APPLY YOUR LEARNING

C. You must configure a process to start whenever a Stop error is encountered by using the command line utility AT.

D. Use the Control Panel, Network option to configure the action to be taken when a Stop error is encountered.

9. Which set of files is required to boot Windows NT on an Intel-x86 based computer?

A. NTLDR, BOOT.INI, NTDETECT.COM, NTOSKRNL.EXE, NTBOOTDD.SYS

B. NTLDR, BOOT.MNU, NTDETECT.EXE, OSLOADER, NTBOOTDD.SYS

C. OSLOADER, NTOSKRNL.EXE, NTDETECT.COM, NTBOOTDD.SYS

D. NTLDR, BOOT.INI, NTDETECT.COM, NTOSKRNL.EXE

10. Which file is used on an Intel-x86 based computer for computers that have SCSI hard drive controllers with the BIOS disabled?

A. OSLOADER.EXE

B. BOOTSCSI.SYS

C. NTBOOTDD.SYS

D. NTBOOTSCSI.SYS

11. What is the best explanation of the function of the NTDETECT.COM program?

A. It reads the hardware configuration data from a RISC-based computer and passes it on to the OSLOADER program.

B. It reads the hardware configuration information from a computer with a Plug and Play BIOS and updates the Registry.

C. It scans the hardware in the computer and reports the list back to NTLDR for later inclusion in the Registry.

D. It initializes the hardware on a computer with a Plug and Play BIOS.

12. You receive a phone call from a user who asks if she can somehow reduce the amount of time her computer takes to boot. She also would like to change the default operating system from MS-DOS to NT Workstation. Which utility would you advise her to use to accomplish this?

A. Control Panel, Boot.

B. Control Panel, System.

C. Server Manager.

D. None of the above. These things are configured on a user-by-user basis in the users' profiles.

13. You receive a telephone call from a user who accidentally changed the SCSI controller card driver and now the computer won't boot NT. It stops at the blue screen and gives him a system error. What would you suggest?

A. Tell the user to boot into DOS and rerun the Windows NT Setup program.

B. Suggest that the user go out and purchase and install the SCSI device that he selected.

C. Tell the user that he now needs to reinstall NT.

D. Suggest that the user select the LastKnowGood configuration during NT booting. Then have the user remove the incorrect driver.

14. You're trying to understand the ARC-naming conventions in your BOOT.INI file. Which is a valid ARC path for a computer with an IDE drive as the boot device?

    A. scsi(0)disk(1)rdisk(0)partition(1)

    B. scsi(1)disk(1)rdisk(0)partition(1)

    C. multi(1)disk(0)rdisk(1)partition(1)

    D. multi(1)disk(1)rdisk(0)partition(2)

15. What does the /basevideo switch in the BOOT.INI file specify?

    A. To load NT, but not to use any upper memory blocks.

    B. To load NT using the resolution specified by your last driver configuration for the display.

    C. To load NT, but to select the standard VGA mode 640×480.

    D. To load NT, but not in graphics mode. Load only the command-line version of NT.

16. You're having a problem loading NT on your workstation. It appears that a driver may not be loading correctly, but you can't tell which drivers are loading and which ones aren't. What command-line switch can you add to the BOOT.INI file to see a list of the drivers loading during the boot process?

    A. /sos

    B. /basevideo

    C. /crashdebug

    D. /listdrivers

17. Which utility enables you to create an emergency repair disk?

    A. Disk Administrator

    B. ERD.EXE

    C. BOOTNT.COM

    D. RDISK.EXE

18. If you receive the message I/O Error accessing boot sector file multi(0)disk(0)rdisk(0) partition(1):\bootsect.dos, which one of the critical boot files is missing?

    A. NTLDR

    B. NTDETECT.COM

    C. BOOTSECT.DOS

    D. MSDOS.SYS

19. What is the BOOTSECT.DOS file?

    A. A copy of the information that was originally on the boot sector of the drive before NT was installed. You use it to boot an operating system other than NT.

    B. A copy of the information needed to boot a RISC-based computer.

    C. The file that detects the hardware installed on a PC with a Plug and Play BIOS.

    D. The file that contains the boot menu selections.

20. If your BOOTSECT.DOS file becomes corrupted, can you copy this file from another NT-based computer?

    A. Yes.

    B. No.

C. Yes, if the computer is configured exactly like yours.

D. No, but you can create it from DOS using the RDISK.EXE utility.

21. **Scenario:** An NT Server that you administrate has a five partition RAID 5 implementation. One partition of the set fails, leaving the system sluggish but still functional.

Required Result:

To restore the system to pre-failure working order with the least amount of time spent.

Optional Desired Results:

To increase the total number of partitions from 5 to 10.

To eliminate the need for backups in the future.

Proposed Solution:

Shut down the NT Server and replace the hard drive that failed. Restart the system and start the Disk Administrator. Delete the stripe set with parity using the Fault Tolerance menu, and then re-create it, including the replaced disk and five others to increase the total number of partitions to 10.

Analysis:

Which of the following statements best describes the proposed solution?

A. The proposed solution produces the required result and both of the optional desired results.

B. The proposed solution produces the required result and one of the optional desired results.

C. The proposed solution produces the required result but does not produce either of the optional desired results.

D. The proposed solution does not produce the required result.

22. **Scenario:** An NT Server that you administrate has a five partition RAID 5 implementation. One partition of the set fails, leaving the system sluggish but still functional.

Required Result:

To restore the system to pre-failure working order with the least amount of time spent.

Optional Desired Result:

To increase the total number of partitions from 5 to 10.

To eliminate the need for backups in the future.

Proposed Solution:

Shut down the NT Server and replace the hard drive that failed. Restart the system and start the Disk Administrator. Select the stripe set with parity and a section of free space on the newly replaced drive. From the Fault Tolerance menu, choose Regenerate. Reboot the NT Server.

Analysis:

Which of the following statements best describes the proposed solution?

A. The proposed solution produces the required result and both of the optional desired results.

B. The proposed solution produces the required result and one of the optional desired results.

APPLY YOUR LEARNING

C. The proposed solution produces the required result but does not produce either of the optional desired results.

D. The proposed solution does not produce the required result.

23. You're concerned that your boot partition is filling up with print jobs and the disk may soon run out of disk space. What can you do?

A. Change the location of the spool file using the Advanced tab of the Server Properties dialog box to point to a hard disk partition that has more free disk space.

B. Nothing. You cannot change where NT puts the spooled print jobs.

C. Install a larger hard disk in the system.

D. Install another hard disk in the system and span the boot partition over the newly installed disk.

24. After you change a computer's disk partitioning scheme with the Disk Administrator program, what utility should you use to update the emergency repair disk?

A. Disk Administrator

B. BOOTUP.EXE

C. FDISK

D. RDISK

Answers to Review Questions

1. The LastKnownGood configuration is a set of Registry settings defining the hardware configuration settings as of the last successful login. It is useful because it can be used to back out of what would otherwise be a permanent settings modification. You can invoke LastKnownGood by rebooting your computer and, when prompted, pressing the Spacebar followed by the letter "L." For more information on LastKnownGood, see the section "Booting Up."

2. The files required on a recovery disk for an Intel-based server with an IDE hard drive are: BOOT.INI, NTLDR, NTDETECT.COM, and NTOSKRNL.EXE. For more information, see the section "Troubleshooting the Boot Process."

3. The Spooler service is assigned the priority of 9 by NT Server. This can be adjusted through Registry settings to give the spooler more or less priority. For more information, see the section "Printing Too Slow or Workstation Too Sluggish."

4. At logon, when Explorer is initializing, it might reference a shortcut or some other target that requires an Autodial connection, causing Autodial to spontaneously dial a remote connection during logon. The only way to prevent this is to disable Autodial or to eliminate the shortcut or other target causing the Autodial to occur. For more information, see the section "Troubleshooting RAS."

APPLY YOUR LEARNING

5. The local groups that, by default, are given the right to perform backups and restore data are Administrators, Backup Operators, and Server Operators. For more information, see the section "NT Backup."

6. An ARC path is an industry standard shorthand for defining the position of a folder on a disk based on the physical configuration of hardware instead of the logical configuration of drive letters. ARC paths are used in the BOOT.INI file to identify the physical position of the boot files for NT boot (frequently found in the WINNT folder). For more information, see the section "Arc Paths."

7. If this RAS server has just been configured, the first thing to check before redoing the entire configuration is whether the RAS service is started. By default, the RAS service is configured to start manually, not automatically. Therefore, if you did not start it, and if you did not configure it to start automatically, it is likely that the service is not started and cannot respond. For more information, see the section "Troubleshooting RAS."

8. This is the general procedure for recovering from a failed disk in a stripe set with parity: Shut down your NT Server and physically replace the failed drive; start the Disk Administrator by choosing Start, Programs, Administrative Tools (Common), Disk Administrator; select the stripe set with parity by clicking on it; select an area of free space as large as or larger than the portion of the stripe set that was lost when the disk failed; choose Fault Tolerance, Regenerate. For more information, see the section "Recovering from a Failed Element of a Stripe Set with Parity."

Answers to Exam Questions

1. **A.** This message appears when a user can locate a machine to validate logon but that validation is failing. This is frequently caused by an incorrect password or username. For more information, see the section "Troubleshooting Access and Permission Problems."

2. **C.** Messages about system events failing (like dependencies) are found in the Event Viewer's System log. For more information, see the section "Event Viewer."

3. **A.** Auditing is a security issue. Therefore, to see audited events, go to the Event Viewer and look at the Security log. For more information, see the section "Event Viewer."

4. **C.** In any log, you can pare down the list of displayed events by using a filter. With the correct log displayed, choose View, Filter Events and specify the filter criteria. For more information, see the section "Event Viewer."

5. **D.** The Windows NT Diagnostics utility allows you to see all the computer's hardware configuration, including RAM and CPU. For more information, see the section "Windows NT Diagnostics."

6. **A.** NT Diagnostics is a reporting tool, not a configuration tool. You cannot change the information reported on in the Diagnostics tool from within the tool itself. By replacing hardware and reconfiguring it in the Control Panel, you can change what is displayed in NT Diagnostics. For more information, see the section "Windows NT Diagnostics."

7. **C, D.** Both NT Diagnostics and the Registry key HKEY_LOCAL_MACHINE\Software\Microsoft\Windows NT\CurrentVersion will tell you what version of NT you are running. For more information, see the section "Windows NT Diagnostics."

8. **A.** From the Startup/Shutdown tab of the System program (accessible from the Control Panel), you can configure the recovery settings for determining what the system should do if a Stop error occurs. For more information, see the section "System Recovery."

9. **A.** The minimum files required to boot Windows NT on an Intel platform are BOOT.INI, NTLDR, NTDETECT.COM, and NTOSKRNL.EXE. In some cases, you might need NTBOOTDD.SYS if you have a SCSI drive with the BIOS disabled, but that will not happen very often. For more information, see the section "Booting Up."

10. **C.** NTBOOTDD.SYS is the generic name given to the driver for a SCSI hard drive controller without the BIOS enabled. This file is found on the system partition and must be present on a recovery disk. For more information, see the section "Booting Up."

11. **C.** NTDETECT.COM is a program that, on an Intel-based computer, scans the hardware and reports to the NTLDR. Eventually, the information discovered by NTDETECT.COM is included in the Registry. For more information, see the section "Booting Up."

12. **B.** The amount of time a computer takes to boot is, in some part, controlled by the initial boot screen presented by BOOT.INI. You can modify this and the default operating system that's booted by using the Startup/Shutdown tab of the Control Panel's System application. For more information, see the section "Booting Up."

13. **D.** If a configuration problem is detected before the next successful login, the LastKnownGood configuration can be used to revert to previous settings. The user should invoke LastKnownGood and then ensure that the proper driver is being used. For more information, see the section "Booting Up."

14. **C.** The only choice that could be a valid ARC path for a computer with an IDE drive as the boot device is multi(1)disk(0)rdisk(1)partition(1). The scsi(x) setting is used only for SCSI drives with BIOS disabled, and the disk(x) setting is always used with scsi(x). For more information, see the section "Booting Up."

15. **C.** /basevideo is equivalent to the Windows 95 Safe mode, which tells NT to use a generic VGA video driver in 640×480 mode. This allows you to recover from video configuration errors. For more information, see the section "Booting Up."

16. **A.** The command line switch /sos lists drivers as they are loaded during boot. For more information, see the section "Booting Up."

17. **D.** An emergency repair disk can be created using the RDISK.EXE program, invoked at a command line. For more information, see the section "The Emergency Repair Process."

18. **C.** This message indicates that you have chosen to boot to a non-NT operating system and that BOOTSECT.DOS is missing. For more information, see the section "Booting Up."

APPLY YOUR LEARNING

19. **A.** BOOTSECT.DOS is a file that contains the boot information that was present on the primary partition when NT was installed. It is necessary to boot any non-NT operating system. For more information, see the section "Booting Up."

20. **A.** Yes. This file is generic, and copying it will allow you to boot to DOS. For more information, see the section "Booting Up."

21. **D.** This solution does not produce the desired result because, by deleting the stripe set with parity, you lose all the data that was contained in it. Instead, you should have regenerated it. Without backing up and restoring the data, there is no way to increase the number of partitions the stripe set uses, and there is no way to completely eliminate the need for backups. For more information, see the section "Recovering from a Failed Element in a Stripe Set with Parity."

22. **C.** This solution produces the desired result but does not produce either of the optional results. Without backing up and restoring the data, there is no way to increase the number of partitions the stripe set uses, and there is no way to completely eliminate the need for backups. For more information, see the section "Recovering from a Failed Element in a Stripe Set with Parity."

23. **A.** Using the Advanced tab of the Server Properties dialog box (accessible from the Printers window), you can change the location of the spool file. For more information, see the section "Spooling Problems."

24. **D.** The utility used in all cases to update the emergency repair disk is RDISK.EXE. For more information, see the section "The Emergency Repair Process."

Suggested Readings and Resources

The following are some recommended readings in the area of Troubleshooting:

1. Microsoft Official Curriculum course 803: *Administering Microsoft Windows NT 4.0*

   • Module 8: Administering Network Printers

   • Module 9: Auditing Resources and Events

   • Module 11: Backing Up and Restoring Data

2. Microsoft Official Curriculum course 922: *Supporting Microsoft Windows NT 4.0 Core Technologies*

   • Module 2: Installing Windows NT

   • Module 3: Configuring the Windows NT Environment

   • Module 7: Managing Fault Tolerance

   • Module 12: Remote Access Service

   • Module 17: The Windows NT Boot Process

   • Module 18: Troubleshooting Resources

3. Microsoft Official Curriculum Course 689: *Supporting Microsoft Windows NT 4.0 Enterprise Technologies*

   • Unit 3: Microsoft Windows NT Server 4.0 Network Analysis and Optimization

   • Unit 4: Troubleshooting Microsoft Windows NT Server 4.0 in an Enterprise Environment

4. *MS Windows NT Server 4.0 Networking Guide* (Microsoft Press; Also available in the Windows NT Server Resource Kit)

   • Chapter 2: Network Security and Domain Planning

   • Chapter 12: Troubleshooting Tools and Strategies

5. *MS Windows NT Server 4.0 Resource Guide* (Microsoft Press; Also available in the Windows NT Server Resource Kit)

   • Chapter 2: Printing

   • Chapter 3: Disk Management Basics

   • Chapter 4: Planning a Reliable Configuration

   • Chapter 5: Preparing for and Performing a Recovery

   • Chapter 6: Troubleshooting Startup and Disk Problems

   • Chapter 7: Disk, File System, and Backup Utilities

   • Chapter 8: General Troubleshooting

6. Microsoft TechNet CD-ROM

   • *Concepts and Planning: MS Windows NT Server 4.0*

   • Chapter 6: Backing Up and Restoring Network Files

   • Chapter 7: Protecting Data

Suggested Readings and Resources

- Chapter 9: Monitoring Events

- Chapter 10: Monitoring Your Network

7. Web sites

  - www.microsoft.com/ntserver (check out the online seminars)

- www.microsoft.com/train_cert

- www.prometric.com/testingcandidates/ assessment/chosetest.html (take online assessment tests)

FINAL REVIEW

Fast Facts: Windows NT Server 4 Exam

Fast Facts: Windows NT Server 4 Enterprise Exam

Fast Facts: Windows NT Workstation 4 Exam

Fast Facts: Networking Essentials Exam

Study and Exam Prep Tips

Practice Exam

Now that you have thoroughly read through this book, worked through the exercises and got as much hands on exposure to NT Server as you could, you've now booked your exam. This chapter is designed as a last minute cram for you as you walk out the door on your way to the exam. You can't re-read the whole book in an hour, but you will be able to read this chapter in that time.

This chapter is organized by objective category, giving you not just a summary, but a rehash of the most important point form facts that you need to know. Remember that this is meant to be a review of concepts and a trigger for you to remember wider definitions. In addition to what is in this chapter, make sure you know what is in the glossary because this chapter does not define terms. If you know what is in here and the concepts that stand behind it, chances are the exam will be a snap.

PLANNING

Remember: Here are the elements that Microsoft says they test on for the "Planning" section of the exam.

◆ Plan the disk drive configuration for various requirements. Requirements include: choosing a file system and fault tolerance method

◆ Choose a protocol for various situations. Protocols include: TCP/IP, NWLink IPX/SPX Compatible Transport, and NetBEUI

Minimum requirement for installing NT Server on an Intel machine is 468DX/33, 16MB of RAM, and 130MB of free disk space.

The login process on an NT Domain is as follows:

1. WinLogon sends the user name and password to the Local Security Authority (LSA).

Fast Facts: Windows NT Server 4 Exam

2. The LSA passes the request to the local NetLogon service.

3. The local NetLogon service sends the logon information to the NetLogon service on the domain controller.

4. The NetLogon service on the domain controller passes the information to the domain controller's Security Accounts Manager (SAM).

5. The SAM asks the domain directory database for approval of the user name and password.

6. The SAM passes the result of the approval request to the domain controller's NetLogon service.

7. The domain controller's NetLogon service passes the result of the approval request to the client's NetLogon service.

8. The client's NetLogon service passes the result of the approval request to the LSA.

9. If the logon is approved, the LSA creates an access token and passes it to the WinLogon process.

10. WinLogon completes the logon, thus creating a new process for the user and attaching the access token to the new process.

The system partition is where your computer boots and it must be on an active partition.

The boot partition is where the WINNT folder is found and it contains the NT program files. It can be on any partition (not on a volume set, though).

NT supports two forms of software-based fault tolerance: Disk Mirroring (RAID 1) and Stripe Sets with Paritiy (RAID 5).

Disk Mirroring uses 2 hard drives and provides 50% disk space utilization.

Stripe sets with Parity use between 3 and 32 hard drives and provides a (n-1)/n*100% utilization (n = number of disks in the set).

Disk duplexing provides better tolerance than mirroring because it does mirroring with separate controllers on each disk.

NT Supports 3 file systems: NTFS, FAT, and CDFS (it no longer supports HPFS, the OS/2 file system nor does it support FAT32, a file system used by Windows 95).

The following table is a comparison of NTFS and FAT features:

Table 1.1 shows a quick summary of the differences between file systems:

SUMMARY TABLE 1
FAT VERSUS NTFS COMPARISON

Feature	FAT	NTFS
File name length	255	255
8.3 file name compatibility	Yes	Yes
File size	4 GB	16 EB
Partition size	4 GB	16 EB
Directory structure	Linked list	B-tree
Local security	No	Yes
Transaction tracking	No	Yes
Hot fixing	No	Yes
Overhead	1 MB	>4 MB
Required on system partition for RISC-based computers	Yes	No
Accessible from MS-DOS/ Windows 95	Yes	No
Accessible from OS/2	Yes	No
Case-sensitive	No	POSIX only
Case preserving	Yes	Yes

Feature	FAT	NTFS
Compression	No	Yes
Efficiency	200 MB	400 MB
Windows NT formattable	Yes	Yes
Fragmentation level	High	Low
Floppy disk formattable	Yes	No

The following is a table to summarize the protocols commonly used by NT for network communication:

SUMMARY TABLE 2
PRIMARY PROTOCOL USES

Protocol	Primary Use
TCP/IP	Internet and WAN connectivity
NWLink	Interoperability with NetWare
NetBEUI	Interoperability with old Lan Man networks

The main points regarding TCP/IP are as follows:

◆ Requires IP Address, and Subnet Mask to function (default Gateway if being routed)

◆ Can be configured manually or automatically using DHCP server running on NT

◆ Common address resolution methods are WINS and DNS

INSTALLATION AND CONFIGURATION

Remember: Here are the elements that Microsoft says they test on for the "Installation and Configuration" section of the exam.

◆ Install Windows NT Server on Intel-based platforms.

◆ Install Windows NT Server to perform various server roles. Server roles include: Primary domain controller, Backup domain controller, and Member server.

◆ Install Windows NT Server by using various methods. Installation methods include: CD-ROM, Over-the-network, Network Client Administrator, and Express versus custom.

◆ Configure protocols and protocol bindings. Protocols include: TCP/IP, NWLink IPX/SPX Compatible Transport, and NetBEUI.

◆ Configure network adapters. Considerations include: changing IRQ, IObase, and memory addresses and configuring multiple adapters.

◆ Configure Windows NT server core services. Services include: Directory Replicator, License Manager, and Other services.

◆ Configure peripherals and devices. Peripherals and devices include: communication devices, SCSI devices, tape devices drivers, UPS devices and UPS service, mouse drivers, display drivers, and keyboard drivers.

◆ Configure hard disks to meet various requirements. Requirements include: allocating disk space capacity, providing redundancy, improving security, and formatting.

◆ Configure printers. Tasks include: adding and configuring a printer, implementing a printer pool, and setting print priorities.

◆ Configure a Windows NT Server computer for various types of client computers. Client computer types include: Windows NT Workstation, Microsoft Windows 95, and Microsoft MS-DOS-based.

The Hardware Compatibility list is used to ensure that NT supports all computer components.

NT can be installed in 3 different configurations in a domain: Primary Domain Controller, Backup Domain Controller, and Member Server.

Two sources can be used for installation files: CD-ROM or network share (which is the hardware specific files from the CD copied onto a server and shared).

Three Setup diskettes are required for all installations when a CD-ROM is not supported by the operating system present on the computer at installation time (or if no operating system exists and the computer will not boot from the CD-ROM.)

WINNT and WINNT32 are used for network installation; WINNT32 for installations when NT is currently present on the machine you are installing to and WINNT when it is not.

The following table is a summary of the WINNT and WINNT32 switches:

SUMMARY TABLE 3
WINNT AND WINNT32 SWITCH FUNCTIONS

Switch	Function
/B	Prevents creation of the three setup disks during the installation process
/S	Indicates the location of the source files for NT installation (e.g., /S:D:\NTFiles)
/U	Indicates the script file to use for an unattended installation (e.g., /U:C:\Answer.txt)
/UDF	Indicates the location of the uniqueness database file which defines unique configuration for each NT machine being installed (e.g., /UDF:D:\Answer.UDF)
/T	Indicates the place to put the temporary installation files
/OX	Initiates only the creation of the three setup disks

Switch	Function
/F	Indicates not to verify the files copied to the setup diskettes
/C	Indicates not to check for free space on the setup diskettes before creating them

To remove NT from a computer you must do the following:

1. Remove all the NTFS partitions from within Windows NT and reformat them with FAT (this ensures that these disk areas will be accessible by non-NT operating systems).

2. Boot to another operating system, such as Windows 95 or MS-DOS.

3. Delete the Windows NT installation directory tree (usually WINNT).

4. Delete pagefile.sys.

5. Turn off the hidden, system, and read-only attributes for NTBOOTDD.SYS, BOOT.INI, NTLDR, and NTDETECT.COM and then delete them. You might not have all of these on your computer, but if so, you can find them all in the root directory of your drive C.

6. Make the hard drive bootable by placing another operating system on it (or SYS it with DOS or Windows 95 to allow the operating system with does exist to boot).

The Client Administrator allows you to do the following:

◆ Make Network Installation Startup disk: shares files and creates bootable diskette for initiating client installation.

◆ Make Installation Disk Set: copies installation files to diskette for installing simple clients like MS-DOS network client 3.0.

◆ Copy Client-Based Network Administration Tools: creates a folder which can be attached to from Windows NT Workstation and Windows 95 clients to install tools for administering an NT Server from a workstation.

MANAGING RESOURCES

Remember: Here are the elements that Microsoft says they test on for the "Managing Resources" section of the exam.

◆ Manage user and group accounts. Considerations include: managing Windows NT groups, managing Windows NT user rights, administering account policies, and auditing changes to the user account database.

◆ Create and manage policies and profiles for various situations. Policies and profiles include: local user profiles, roaming user profiles, and system policies.

◆ Administer remote servers from various types of client computers. Client computer types include: Windows 95 and Windows NT Workstation.

◆ Manage disk resources. Tasks include: copying and moving files between file systems, creating and sharing resources, implementing permissions and security, and establishing file auditing.

Network properties dialog box lets you install and configure the following:

◆ Computer and Domain names

◆ Services

◆ Protocols

◆ Adapters

◆ Bindings

When configuring NWLink ensure that if more than one frame type exists on your network that you don't use AutoDetect or only the first frame type encountered will be detected from then on.

The following table shows you three TCP/IP command-line diagnostic tools and what they do:

SUMMARY TABLE 4
TCP/IP COMMAND LINE DIAGNOSTIC TOOLS

Tool	Function
IPConfig	Displays the basic TCP/IP configuration of each adapter card on a computer (with/all displays detailed configuration information)
Ping	Determines connectivity with another TCP/IP host by sending a message that is echoed by the recipient if received
Tracert	Traces each hop on the way to a TCP/IP host and indicates points of failure if they exist

Network adapter card configuration of IRQ and I/O port address may or may not be configurable from the Network Properties dialog box; it depends on the card.

To allow NT computers to participate in a domain, a computer account must be created for each one.

Windows 95 clients need special profiles and policies created on a Windows 95 machine and then copied onto an NT Server to participate in domain profile and policy configuration.

Windows 95 clients need printer drivers installed on an NT Server acting as a print controller to print to an NT controller printer.

Typical services tested for NT Server are listed and described in the following table:

SUMMARY TABLE 5
NT SERVER SERVICES AND THEIR FUNCTIONS

Service	Function
DNS	Provides TCP/IP address resolution using a static table and can be use for non-Microsoft hosts
WINS	Provides TP/IP address resolution using a dynamic table and can be used for Microsoft hosts
DHCP	Provides automatic configuration of TCP/IP clients for Microsoft clients
Browser	Provides a list of domain resources to Network Neighborhood and Server Manager
Replicator	Provides import and export services for automated file distribution between NT computers (Servers can be export and import, Workstations can only be import)

REGEDT32.EXE and REGEDIT are used to view and modify registry settings in NT

The five registry subtrees are:

- **HKEY_LOCAL_MACHINE.** Stores all the computer-specific configuration data.

- **HKEY_USERS.** Stores all the user-specific configuration data.

- **HKEY_CURRENT_USER**. Stores all configuration data for the currently logged on user.

- **HKEY_CLASSES_ROOT.** Stores all OLE and file association information.

- **HKEY_CURRENT_CONFIG.** Stores information about the hardware profile specified at start-up.

REGEDT32.EXE allows you to see and set security on the registry and allows you to open the registry in read-only mode, but does not allow you to search by key value.

NT checking for serial mice at boot may disable a UPS. To disable that check, place the /noserialmice in the boot line in the BOOT.INI file.

The SCSI adapters icon in the Control Panel lets you add and configure SCSI devices as well as CD-ROM drives.

Many changes made in the disk administrator require that you choose the menu Partition, Commit Changes for them to take effect.

Although you can set drive letters manually, the following is how NT assigns letters to partitions and volumes:

1. Beginning from the letter C:, assign consecutive letters to the first primary partition on each physical disk.

2. Assign consecutive letters to each logical drive, completing all on one physical disk before moving on to the next.

3. Assign consecutive letters to the additional primary partitions, completing all on one physical disk before moving on to the next.

Disk Administrator allows for the creation of two kinds of partitions (primary and extended) and four kinds of volumes (volume set, stripe set, mirror set, and stripe set with parity). The following table is a summary of their characteristics:

SUMMARY TABLE 6
PARTITION CHARACTERISTICS

Object	Characteristics
Primary partition	Non-divisible disk unit which can be marked active and can be made bootable.
	Can have up to four on a physical drive.
	NT system partition must be on a primary.
Extended partition	Divisible disk unit which must be divided into logical disks (or have free space used in a volume) in order to function as space storage tool.
	Can have only one on a physical drive.
	Logical drive within can be the NT boot partition.
Volume Set	Made up of 2-32 portions of free space which do not have to be the same size and which can be spread out over between 1 and 32 disks of many types (IDE, SCSI, etc.).
	Can be added to if formatted NTFS.
	Cannot contain NT boot or system partition.
	Removing one portion of the set destroys the volume and the data is lost.
	Is not fault tolerant.
Stripe Set	Made up of 2-32 portions of free space which have to be the same size and which can be spread out over between 2 and 32 disks of many types (IDE, SCSI, etc.).
	Cannot be added to and removing one portion of the set destroys the volume and the data is lost.
	Is not fault tolerant.
Mirror Set	Made up of 2 portions of free space which have to be the same size and which must be on 2 physical disks.
	Identical data is written to both mirror partitions and they are treated as one disk.
	If one disk stops functioning the other will continue to operate.
	The NT Boot and System partitions can be held on a mirror set.
	Has a 50% disk utilization rate.
	Is fault tolerant.
Stripe Set with Parity	Made up of 3-32 portions of free space which have to be the same size and must be spread out over the same number of physical disks.
	Maintains fault tolerance by creating parity information across a stripe.
	If one disk fails, the stripe set will continue to function, albeit with a loss of performance.
	The NT Boot and System partitions cannot be held on a Stripe Set with Parity.
	Is fault tolerant.

Disk Administrator can be used to format partitions and volumes either FAT or NTFS.

If you have any clients who access a shared printer that are not using NT or are not using the same hardware platform as your printer server then you must install those drivers when you share the printer.

By assigning different priorities for printers associated with the same print device you can create a hierarchy among users' print jobs, thus ensuring that the print jobs of some users print sooner than others.

By adjusting the printer schedule you can ensure that jobs sent to particular printers are only printed at certain hours of the day.

A printer has permissions assigned to it. The following is a list of the permissions for printers.

◆ **No Access.** Completely restricts access to the printer.

◆ **Print.** Allows a user or group to submit a print job, and to control the settings and print status for that job.

◆ **Manage Documents.** Allows a user or group to submit a print job, and to control the settings and print status for all print jobs.

◆ **Full Control.** Allows a user to submit a print job, and to control the settings and print status for all documents as well as for the printer itself. In addition, the user or group may share, stop sharing, change permissions for, and even delete the printer.

Printer pools consist of one or more print devices that can use the same print driver controlled by a single printer.

MS-DOS users must have print drivers installed locally on their computers.

The assignment of permissions to resources should use the following procedure:

1. Create user accounts.

2. Create global groups for the domain and populate the groups with user accounts.

3. Create local groups and assign them rights and permissions to resources and programs in the domain.

4. Place global groups into the local groups you have created, thereby giving the users who are members of the global groups access to the system and its resources.

The built-in local groups in a Windows NT Domain are as follows:

◆ Administrators

◆ Users

◆ Guests

◆ Backup Operators

◆ Replicator

◆ Print Operators

◆ Server Operators

◆ Account Operators

The built-in global groups in an NT Domain are as follows:

◆ Domain Admins

◆ Domain Users

◆ Domain Guests

The system groups on an NT server are as follows:

◆ Everyone

◆ Creator Owner

◆ Network

◆ Interactive

The built-in users on an NT server are as follows:

◆ Administrator

◆ Guest

The following table describes the buttons on the User Properties dialog box and their functions:

SUMMARY TABLE 7
BUTTONS ON THE USER PROPERTIES DIALOG BOX

Button	Function
Groups	Enables you to add and remove group memberships for the account. The easiest way to grant rights to a user account is to add it to a group that possesses those rights.
Profile	Enables you to add a user profile path, a logon script name, and a home directory path to the user's environment profile. You learn more about the Profile button in the following section.
Hours	Enables you to define specific times when the users can access the account. (The default is always.)
Logon To	Enables you to specify up to 8 workstations from which the user can log on. (The default is all workstations.)
Account	Enables you to provide an expiration date for the account. (The default is never.) You also can specify the account as global (for regular users in this domain) or domain local.

The following table is a summary of the account policy fields:

SUMMARY TABLE 8
ACCOUNT POLICY FIELDS

Button	Function
Maximum Password Age	The maximum number of days a password can be in effect until it must be changed.
Minimum Password Age	The minimum number of days a password must stay in effect before it can be changed.
Minimum Password Length	The minimum number of characters a password must include.
Password Uniqueness	The number of passwords that NT remembers for a user; these passwords cannot be reused until they are no longer remembered.
Account Lockout	The number of incorrect passwords that can be input by a user before the account becomes locked. Reset will automatically set the count back to 0 after a specified length of time. In addition the duration of lock-out is either a number of minutes or forever (until an administrator unlocks it).
Forcibly disconnect remote users from server when logon hours expire	In conjunction with logon hours, this checkbox enables forcible disconnection of a user when authorized hours come to a close.
Users must log on in order to change password	Ensures that a user whose password has expired cannot change his or her password but has to have it reset by an administrator.

Account SIDs are unique; therefore, if an account is deleted, the permissions cannot be restored by recreating an account with the same name.

Local profiles are only available from the machine on which they were created, whereas roaming profiles can be accessed from any machine on the network.

A mandatory profile is a roaming profile that users cannot change. They have the extension .MAN.

Hardware profiles can be used with machines that have more than one hardware configuration (such as laptops).

The System Policy editor (POLEDIT) has two modes, Policy File mode and Registry Mode.

The application of system policies is as follows:

1. When you log in, the NT Config.pol is checked. If there is an entry for the specific user, then any registry settings indicated will be merged with, and overwrite if necessary, the users registry.

2. If there is no specific user entry, any settings for groups that the user is a member of will be applied to the user.

3. If the user is not present in any groups and not listed explicitly then the Default settings will be applied.

4. If the computer that the user is logging in on has an entry, then the computer settings are applied.

5. If there is not a computer entry for the user then the default computer policy is applied.

Windows 95 policies are not compatible with NT and therefore Windows 95 users must access a Windows 95 policy created on an Windows 95 machine and copied to an NT machine and named Config.Pol.

The Net Use command line can be used to map a drive letter to a network share; using the /persistent switch ensures that it is reconnected at next logon.

FAT long file names under NT have 8.3 aliases created to ensure backward compatibility. The following is an example of how aliases are generated from 5 files that all have the same initial characters:

Team meeting Report #3.doc	TEAMME~1.DOC
Team meeting Report #4.doc	TEAMME~2.DOC
Team meeting Report #5.doc	TEAMME~3.DOC
Team meeting Report #6.doc	TEAMME~4.DOC
Team meeting Report #7.doc	TE12B4~1.DOC

A long file name on a FAT partition uses one file name for the 8.3 alias and then one more FAT entry for every 13 characters in the name.

A FAT partition can be converted to NTFS without loss of data through the command line

CONVERT <drive>: /FS:NTFS

NTFS supports compression as a file attribute that can be set in the file properties.

Compression can be applied to a folder or a drive and the effect is that the files within are compressed and any file copied into it will also become compressed.

Compression can be applied through the use of the COMPACT.EXE program through the syntax

COMPACT <file or directory path> [/switch]

The available switches for COMPACT are as follows:

SUMMARY TABLE 9
COMPACT Switches

Switch	Function
/C	Compress
/U	Uncompress
/S	Compress an entire directory tree
/A	Compress hidden and system files
/I	Ignore errors and continue compressing
/F	Force compression even if the objects are already compressed
/Q	Display only summary information

Share-level permissions apply only when users access a resource over the network, not locally. The share-level permissions are:

- **No Access**. Users with No Access to a share can still connect to the share, but nothing appears in File Manager except the message You do not have permission to access this directory.

- **Read.** Allows you to display folder and file names, display file content and attributes, run programs, open folders inside the shared folder.

- **Change.** Allows you to create folders and files, change file content, change file attributes, delete files and folders, do everything READ permission allows.

- **Full Control.** Allows you to change file permissions and do everything change allows for.

Share-level permissions apply to the folder that is shared and apply equally to all the contents of that share.

Share-level permissions apply to any shared folder, whether on FAT or NTFS.

NTFS permissions can only be applied to any file or folder on an NTFS partition.

The actions that can be performed against an NTFS object are as follows:

- Read (R)
- Write (W)
- Execute (X)
- Delete (D)
- Change Permissions (P)
- Take Ownership (O)

The NTFS permissions available for folders are summarized in the following table:

SUMMARY TABLE 10
NTFS Folder Permissions

Permission	Action permitted
No Access	none
List	RX
Read	RX
Add	WX
Add & Read	RXWD
Change	RXWD
Full Control	RXWDPO

The NTFS permissions available for files are summarized in the following table:

SUMMARY TABLE 11
NTFS FILE PERMISSIONS

Permission	Action permitted
No Access	none
Read	RX
Add & Read	RX
Change	RXWD
Full Control	RXWDPO

If a user is given permission to a resource and a group or groups that the user is a member is also given access then the effective permission the user has is the cumulation of all of the user permissions. This applies unless any of the permissions are set to No Access in which case the user has no access to the resource.

If a user is given permission to a shared resource and is also given permission to that resource through NTFS permissions then the effective permission is the most restrictive permission.

The File Child Delete scenario manifests itself when someone has full control to a folder but is granted a permission which does not enable deletion (Read or No Access, for example). The effect is that a user will be able to delete files inside the folder even though sufficient access does not appear to be present.

To close the File Child Delete loophole, do not grant a user Full Control access to a folder but instead, use special Directory permissions to assign RXWDPO access, this eliminates the File Child Delete permission.

Access Tokens do not refresh and a user needs to log off and log back on if changed permissions are to take effect.

MONITORING AND OPTIMIZATION

Remember: Here are the elements that Microsoft says they test on for the "Monitoring and Optimization" section of the exam.

◆ Monitor performance of various functions by using Performance Monitor. Functions include: processor, memory, disk, and network.

◆ Identify performance bottlenecks.

Performance monitor has 4 views: chart, alert, log, and report.

The subsystems that are routinely monitored are: Memory, Disk, Network, and Processor.

Disk counters can be enabled through the command line:

   Diskperf –y

Or

   Diskperf –ye (for RAID disks and volumes)

TROUBLESHOOTING

Remember: Here are the elements that Microsoft says they test on for the "Troubleshooting" section of the exam.

◆ Choose the appropriate course of action to take to resolve installation failures.

◆ Choose the appropriate course of action to take to resolve boot failures.

◆ Choose the appropriate course of action to take to resolve configuration errors.

◆ Choose the appropriate course of action to take to resolve printer problems.

◆ Choose the appropriate course of action to take to resolve RAS problems.

◆ Choose the appropriate course of action to take to resolve connectivity problems.

◆ Choose the appropriate course of action to take to resolve fault tolerance problems. Fault-tolerance methods include: tape backup, mirroring, stripe set with parity, and disk duplexing.

The acronym DETECT can be used to define the troubleshooting process and stands for:

◆ Discover the problem.

◆ Explore the boundaries.

◆ Track the possible approaches.

◆ Execute an Approach.

◆ Check for success.

◆ Tie up loose ends.

An NTHQ diskette can test a computer to ensure that NT will successfully install on it.

The following list identifies possible sources of installation problems:

◆ Media errors

◆ Insufficient disk space

◆ Non-supported SCSI adapter

◆ Failure of dependancy service to start

◆ Inability to connect to the domain controller

◆ Error in assigning domain name

The files involved in the boot process are identified in the following table for both Intel and RISC machines:

SUMMARY TABLE 12
FILES INVOLVED IN THE BOOT PROCESS

Intel	*RISC*
NTLDR	OSLOADER.EXE
BOOT.INI	NTOSKRNL.EXE
NTDETECT.COM	
NTOSKRNL.EXE	

In the NT boot process (in BOOT.INI) ARC paths define the physical position of the NT operating system files and come in two forms:

Scsi(0)disk(0)rdisk(0)partition(1)\WINNT

Multi(0)disk(0)rdisk(0)partition(1)\WINNT

SCSI arc paths define hard drives which are SCSI and which have their bios disabled. The relevant parameters are:

◆ SCSI: the SCSI controller starting from 0

◆ DISK: the physical disk starting from 0

◆ PARTITION: the partition on the disk stating from 1

◆ \folder: the folder in which the NT files are located

MULTI arc paths define hard drives which are non-SCSI or SCSI with their bios enabled. The relevant parameters are:

◆ MULTI: the controller starting from 0

◆ RDISK: the physical disk starting from 0

◆ PARTITION: the partition on the disk stating from 1

◆ \folder: the folder in which the NT files are located

Partitions are numbered as follows:

1. The first primary partition on each disk gets the number 0.

2. Each additional primary partition then is given a number, incrementing up from 0.

3. Each logical drive is then given a number in the order they appear in the Disk Administrator.

Switches on boot lines in the boot.ini file define additional boot parameters. The following table lists the switches you need to know about and their function:

SUMMARY TABLE 13
Boot.ini File Switches

Switch	Function
/basevideo	Loads standard VGA video driver (640x480, 16 color)
/sos	Displays each driver as it is loaded
/noserialmice	Prevents autodetection of serial mice on COM ports which may disable a UPS connected to the port

A recovery disk can be used to bypass problems with system partition. Such a disk contains the following files (broken down by hardware platform):

SUMMARY TABLE 14
Files on a Fault-tolerant Boot Diskette

Intel	RISC
NTLDR	OSLOADER.EXE
NTDETECT.COM	HAL.DLL

Intel	RISC
BOOT.INI	*.PAL (for Alpha machines)
BOOTSECT.DOS (allows you to boot to DOS)	
NTBOOTDD.SYS (the SCSI driver for a hard drive with SCSI bios not enabled)	

An Emergency repair disk can be used to recover an NT system if the registry becomes corrupted and must be used in conjunction with the three setup diskettes used to install NT.

The RDISK programs allows you to update the \REPAIR folder which in turn is used to update your repair diskette.

The Event Viewer allows you to see three log files: System Log, Security Log, and Application Log.

The Windows NT Diagnostics program allows you to see (but not modify) configuration settings for much of your hardware and environment.

The course of action to take when a stop error occurs (blue screen) can be configured from the System Properties dialog box (in the Control Panel) on the Startup/Shutdown tab.

To move the spool file from one partition to another, use the Advanced Tab on the Server Properties dialog box; this can be located from the File, Server Properties menu in the printers dialog box.

Common RAS problems include the following:

◆ User Permission: user not enabled to use RAS in User Manager for Domains.

◆ Authentication: often caused by incompatible encryption methods (client using different encryption than server is configured to receive).

◆ Callback with Multilink: Client configured for callback but is using multilink; server will only call back to a single number, thereby removing multilink functionality.

◆ Autodial at Logon: Shortcuts on desktop referencing server-based applications or files causes autodial to kick in when logon is complete.

User can't login may be caused by a number of factors including:

◆ Incorrect user name or password

◆ Incorrect domain name

◆ Incorrect user rights (inability to log on locally to an NT machine, for example)

◆ Netlogon service on server is stopped or paused

◆ Domain controllers are down

◆ User is restricted in system policies from logging on at a specific computer

The right to create backups and restore from backups using NT Backup is granted to the groups Administrators, Backup Operators, and Server Operators by default.

NT Backup will only backup files to tape, no other media is supported.

The following table summarizes the backup types available in NT backup:

SUMMARY TABLE 15
BACKUP TYPES AVAILABLE IN NTBACKUP

Type	Backs Up	Marks?
Normal	All selected files and folders	Yes
Copy	All selected files and folders	No
Incremental	Selected files and folders not marked as backed up	Yes
Differential	Selected files and folders not marked as backed up	No

Type	Backs Up	Marks?
Daily Copy	Selected files and folders changed that day	No

The local registry of a computer can be backed up by selecting the Backup Local Registry checkbox in the Backup Information dialog box.

Data from tape can be restored to the original location or to an alternate location and NTFS permissions can be restored or not, however, you cannot change the names of the objects being restored until the restore is complete.

Backup can be run from a command line using the NTBACKUP command in the syntax:

Ntbackup backup path [switches]

Some command line backup switches are shown in the following table:

SUMMARY TABLE 16
NTBACKUP COMMAND LINE SWITCHES

Switch	Function
/a	Append the current backup to the backup already on the tape
/v	verify the backed up files when complete
/d "text"	Add an identifying description to the backup tape
/t option	specify the backup type. Valid options are: normal, copy, incremental, differential, and daily

To recover from a failed mirror set you must do the following:

1. Shut down your NT server and physically replace the failed drive.

2. If required, boot NT using a recovery disk.

3. Start the Disk Administrator using the menu Start, Programs, Administrative Tools (Common), Disk Administrator.

4. Select the mirror set by clicking on it.

5 From the Fault Tolerance menu choose Break Mirror. This action exposes the remaining partition as a volume separate from the failed one.

6. Reestablish the mirror set if desired by selecting the partition you desire to mirror and a portion of free space equal in size and choosing the menu Fault Tolerance, Establish Mirror.

To regenerate a stripe set with parity do the following:

1. Shut down your NT server and physically replace the failed drive.

2. Start the Disk Administrator using the menu Start, Programs, Administrative Tools (Common), Disk Administrator.

3. Select the stripe set with parity by clicking on it.

4. Select an area of free space as large or larger than the portion of the stripe set that was lost when the disk failed.

5. Choose Fault Tolerance, Regenerate.

Hopefully, this has been a helpful tool in your final review before the exam. You might find after reading this that there are some places in the book you need to revisit. Just remember to stay focused and answer all the questions. You can always go back and check the answers for the questions you are unsure of. Good luck!

The fast facts listed in this section are designed as a refresher of key points and topics that are required to succeed on the Windows NT server 4.0 in the Enterprise exam. By using these summaries of key points, you can spend an hour prior to your exam to refresh key topics, and ensure that you have a solid understanding of the objectives and information required for you to succeed in each major area of the exam.

The following are the main categories Microsoft uses to arrange the objectives:

◆ Planning

◆ Installation and configuration

◆ Managing resources

◆ Connectivity

◆ Monitoring and optimization

◆ Troubleshooting

For each of these main sections, or categories, the assigned objectives are reviewed, and following each objective, review material is offered.

WINDOWS NT SERVER 4 ENTERPRISE EXAM

PLANNING

Plan the implementation of a directory services architecture. Considerations include the following:

◆ Selecting the appropriate domain model

◆ Supporting a single logon account

◆ Enabling users to access resources in different domains

The main goals of directory services are the following:

◆ One user, one account

◆ Universal resource access

◆ Centralized administration

◆ Directory synchronization

To ensure that you are selecting the best plan for your network, always address each of the goals of directory services.

The requirements for setting up a trust are as follows:

◆ The trust relationship can be established only between Windows NT Server domains.

◆ The domains must be able to make an RPC connection. To establish an RPC connection, you must ensure that a network connection exists between the domain controllers of all participating domains.

◆ The trust relationship must be set up by a user with administrator access.

◆ You should determine the number and type of trusts prior to the implementation.

◆ You must decide where to place the user accounts, as that is the trusted domain.

Trust relationships enable communication between domains. The trusts must be organized, however, to achieve the original goal of directory services. Windows NT domains can be organized into one of four different domain models:

◆ The single-domain model

◆ The single-master domain model

◆ The multiple-master domain model

◆ The complete-trust model

Table 1 summarizes the advantages and disadvantages of the domain models.

TABLE 1
PROFILING THE DOMAIN MODELS

Domain Model	Advantages	Disadvantages
Single-domain model	Centralized administration.	Limited to 40,000 user accounts. No trust relationships. No distribution of resources.
Single-master domain model	Centralized administration. Distributed resources.	Limited to 40,000 user accounts.
Multiple-master domain model	Unlimited number of user accounts; each master domain can host 40,000 user accounts. Distributed resources. Complex trust relationships.	No centralized administration of user accounts.
Complete-trust model	Unlimited number of user accounts; each domain can host 40,000 user accounts. Complex trust relationships.	No centralized administration of user accounts.

Plan the disk drive configuration for various requirements. Requirements include choosing a fault-tolerance method.

Windows NT Server 4 supports the following fault-tolerant solutions:

◆ RAID Level 0 (disk striping)

◆ RAID Level 1 (disk mirroring)

◆ RAID Level 5 (disk striping with parity)

A comparison of the three fault-tolerance options might help to summarize the information and to ensure that you have a strong understanding of the options available in Windows NT Server 4 (see Table 2).

Choose a protocol for various situations. The protocols include the following:

◆ TCP/IP

◆ TCP/IP with DHCP and WINS

◆ NWLink IPX/SPX Compatible Transport Protocol

◆ Data Link Control (DLC)

◆ AppleTalk

Windows NT Server 4 comes bundled with several protocols that can be used for interconnectivity with other systems and for use within a Windows NT environment. You examine the various protocols, then try to define when each protocol best fits your network needs. The protocols discussed to prepare you for the enterprise exam are the following:

◆ **NetBEUI.** The NetBEUI protocol is the easiest to implement and has wide support across platforms. The protocol uses NetBIOS broadcasts to locate other computers on the network. This process of locating other computers requires additional network traffic and can slow down your entire network. Because NetBEUI uses broadcasts to locate computers, it is not routable; in other words, you cannot access computers that are not on your physical network. Most Microsoft and IBM OS/2 clients support this protocol. NetBEUI is best suited to small networks with no

TABLE 2
SUMMARY OF FAULT-TOLERANCE OPTIONS IN WINDOWS NT SERVER 4

Disk Striping	Disk Mirroring/ Disk Duplexing	Disk Striping with Parity
No fault tolerance.	Complete disk duplication.	Data regeneration from stored parity information.
Minimum of two physical disks, maximum of 32 disks.	Two physical disks	Minimum of three physical disks, maximum of 32 disks.
100 percent available disk utilization.	50 percent available disk utilization.	Dedicates the equivalent of one disk's space in the set for parity information. The more disks, the higher the utilization.
Cannot include a system/boot partition.	Includes all partition types.	Cannot include a system/boot partition.
Excellent read/write performance.	Moderate read/write performance.	Excellent read and moderate write performance.

requirements for routing the information to remote networks or to the Internet.

◆ **TCP/IP.** Transmission Control Protocol/Internet Protocol, or TCP/IP, is the most common protocol—more specifically, it is the most common suite of protocols. TCP/IP is an industry-standard protocol that is supported by most network operating systems. Because of this acceptance throughout the industry, TCP/IP enables your Windows NT system to connect to other systems with a common communication protocol.

The following are advantages of using TCP/IP in a Windows NT environment:

- The capability to connect dissimilar systems

- The capability to use numerous standard connectivity utilities, including File Transfer Protocol (FTP), Telnet, and PING

- Access to the Internet

If your Windows NT system is using TCP/IP as a connection protocol, it can communicate with many non-Microsoft systems. Some of the systems it can communicate with are the following:

- Any Internet-connected system

- UNIX systems

- IBM mainframe systems

- DEC Pathworks

- TCP/IP-supported printers directly connected to the network

◆ **NWLink IPX/SPX Compatible.** The IPX protocol has been used within the NetWare environment for years. By developing an IPX-compatible protocol, Microsoft enables Windows NT systems to communicate with NetWare systems.

NWLink is best suited to networks requiring communication with existing NetWare servers and for existing NetWare clients.

Other utilities must be installed, however, to enable the Windows NT Server system to gain access into the NetWare security. Gateway Services for NetWare/Client Services for NetWare (GSNW/CSNW) must be installed on the Windows NT server to enable the computer to be logged on to a NetWare system. GSNW functions as a NetWare client, but it also can share the connection to the Novell box with users from the Windows NT system. This capability enables a controlled NetWare connection for file and print sharing on the NetWare box, without requiring the configuration of each NT client with a duplicate network redirector or client.

◆ **DataLink Control.** The DLC protocol was originally used for connectivity in an IBM mainframe environment, and maintains support for existing legacy systems and mainframes. The DLC protocol is also used for connections to some network printers.

◆ **AppleTalk.** Windows NT Server can configure the AppleTalk protocol to enable connectivity with Apple Macintosh systems. This protocol is installed with the Services for the Macintosh included with your Windows NT Server CD-ROM. The AppleTalk protocol enables Macintosh computers on your network to access files and printers set up on the Windows NT server. It also enables your Windows NT clients to print to Apple Macintosh printers.

The AppleTalk protocol is best suited to connectivity with the Apple Macintosh.

INSTALLATION AND CONFIGURATION

Install Windows NT Server to perform various server roles. Server roles include the following:

◆ Primary domain controller

◆ Backup domain controller

◆ Member server

The following are different server roles into which Windows NT Server can be installed:

◆ **Primary Domain Controller.** The Primary Domain Controller (PDC) is the first domain controller installed into a domain. As the first computer in the domain, the PDC creates the domain. This fact is important to understand because it establishes the rationale for needing a PDC in the environment. Each domain can contain only one PDC. All other domain controllers in the domain are installed as Backup Domain Controllers. The PDC handles user requests and logon validation, and it offers all the standard Windows NT Server functionality. The PDC contains the original copy of the Security Accounts Manager (SAM), which contains all user accounts and security permissions for your domain.

◆ **Backup Domain Controller.** The Backup Domain Controller (BDC) is an additional domain controller used to handle logon requests by users in the network. To handle the logon requests, the BDC must have a complete copy of the domain database, or SAM. The BDC also runs the Netlogon service; however, the Netlogon service in a BDC functions a little differently than in a PDC. In the PDC, the Netlogon

service handles synchronization of the SAM database to all the BDCs.

◆ **Member server.** In both of the domain controllers, PDC or BDC, the computer has an additional function: The domain controllers handle logon requests and ensure that the SAM is synchronized throughout the domain. These functions add overhead to the system. A computer that handles the server functionality you require without the overhead of handling logon validation is called a *member server*. A member server is a part of the domain, but it does not need a copy of the SAM database and does not handle logon requests. The main function of a member server is to share resources.

After you have installed your computer into a specific server role, you might decide to change the role of the server. This can be a relatively easy task if you are changing a PDC to a BDC or vice versa. If you want to change a domain controller to a member server or member server to a domain controller, however, you must reinstall into the required server role. A member server has a local database that does not participate in domain synchronization. In changing roles, a member server must be reinstalled to ensure that the account database and the appropriate services are installed.

Configure protocols and protocol bindings. Protocols include the following:

◆ TCP/IP

◆ TCP/IP with DHCP and WINS

◆ NWLink IPX/SPX Compatible Transport Protocol

◆ DLC

◆ AppleTalk

You install a new protocol in Windows NT Server through the Network Properties dialog box.

> N O T E
> **NetBEUI Not Discussed**   This list does not include the NetBEUI protocol, as there are no configuration options available for this protocol.

Following are the protocols, and the configuration options available with each:

◆ **TCP/IP.** The following tabs are available for configuration in the Microsoft TCP/IP Properties dialog box:

   • **IP Address.** The IP Address tab enables you to configure the IP address, the subnet mask, and the default gateway. You also can enable the system to allocate IP address information automatically through the use of the DHCP server.

   An IP address is a 32-bit address that is broken into four octets and used to identify your network adapter card as a TCP/IP host. Each IP address must be a unique address. If you have any IP address conflicts on your computer, you cannot use the TCP/IP protocol.

   Your IP address is then grouped into a subnet. The process you use to subnet your network is to assign a subnet mask. A *subnet mask* is used to identify the computers local to your network. Any address outside your subnet is accessed through the default gateway, also called the *router*. The default gateway is the address of the router that handles all routing of your TCP/IP information to computers, or hosts, outside your subnet.

• **DNS.** The DNS tab shows you the options available for configuring your TCP/IP protocol to use a DNS server. The Domain Name System (DNS) server translates TCP/IP host names of remote computers into IP addresses. Remember that an IP address is a unique address for each computer. The DNS server contains a database of all the computers you can access by host name. This database is used when you access a Web page on the Internet. Working with the naming scheme is easier than using the IP address of the computer.

• **WINS Address.** The WINS Address tab enables you to configure your primary and secondary Windows Internet Names Services (WINS) server addresses. WINS is used to reduce the number of NetBIOS broadcast messages sent across the network to locate a computer. By using a WINS server, you keep the names of computers on your network in a WINS database. The WINS database is dynamic.

   In configuring your WINS servers, you can enter your primary WINS server and a secondary WINS server. Your system searches the primary WINS server database first, then the secondary database if no match was found in the primary one.

• **DHCP Relay.** The DHCP relay agent is used to find your DHCP servers across routers. DHCP addresses are handed out by the DHCP servers. The client request, however, is made with a broadcast message. Broadcast messages do not cross routers; therefore, this protocol might place some restrictions on your systems. The solution is to use a DHCP relay agent to assist the clients in finding the DHCP server across a router.

In configuring your DHCP relay agent, you can specify the seconds threshold and the maximum number of hops to use in searching for the DHCP servers. At the bottom of the tab, you can enter the IP addresses of the DHCP servers you want to use.

- **Routing.** In an environment in which multiple subnets are used, you can configure your Windows NT Server as a multihomed system. In other words, you can install multiple network adapters, each connecting to a different subnet. If you enable the Enable IP Forwarding option, your computer acts as a router, forwarding the packets through the network cards in the multihomed system to the other subnet.

◆ **NWLINK IPX/SPX Compatible.** The configuration of the NWLink protocol is simple in comparison to the TCP/IP protocol. It is this simplicity that makes it a popular protocol to use.

The NWLink IPX/SPX Properties dialog box has two tabs:

- **General.** On the General tab, you have the option to assign an internal network number. This eight-digit hexadecimal number format is used by some programs with services that can be accessed by NetWare clients.

  You also have the option to select a frame type for your NWLink protocol. The frame type you select must match the frame type of the remote computer with which you need to communicate. By default, Windows NT Server uses the Auto Frame Type Detection setting, which scans the network and loads the first frame type it encounters.

- **Routing.** The Routing tab of the NWLink IPX/SPX Properties dialog box is used to enable or disable the Routing Information Protocol (RIP). If you enable RIP routing over IPX, your Windows NT Server can act as an IPX router.

◆ **DLC.** The configuration of DLC is done through Registry parameters. The DLC protocol is configured based on three timers:

- **T1.** The response timer
- **T2.** The acknowledgment delay timer
- **Ti.** The inactivity timer

The Registry contains the entries that can be modified to configure DLC. You can find the entries at

HKEY_LOCAL_MACHINE\SYSTEM\Current ControlSet\Services\DLC\Parameters\ELNKIII *adapter name*

◆ **AppleTalk.** To install the AppleTalk protocol, you install Services for Macintosh.

Table 3 reviews the protocols that you can configure for your NT enterprise (including the subcomponents—tabs—of each protocol).

TABLE 3
PROTOCOLS TO CONFIGURE

Protocol	Subcomponent (Tab)
TCP/IP	IP Address
	DNS
	WINS Address
	DHCP Relay
	Routing
NWLink IPX/SPX Compatible	General
	Routing
AppleTalk	General
	Routing

The binding order is the sequence your computer uses to select which protocol to use for network communications. Each protocol is listed for each network-based service, protocol, and adapter available.

The Bindings tab contains an option, Show Bindings for, that can be used to select the service, adapter, or protocol you want to modify in the binding order. By clicking the appropriate button, you can enable or disable each binding, or move up or down in the binding order.

Configure Windows NT Server core services. Services include the following:

◆ Directory Replicator

◆ Computer Browser

In this objective, you look at configuring some of the core services in the Windows NT Server. These services are the following:

◆ **Server service.** The Server service answers network requests. By configuring Server service, you can change the way your server responds and, in a sense, the role it plays in your network environment. To configure Server service, you must open the Network dialog box. To do this, double-click the Network icon in the Control Panel. Select the Services tab. In the Server dialog box, you have four optimization settings. Each of these settings modifies memory management based on the role the server is playing. These options are the following:

• **Minimize Memory Used.** The Minimize Memory Used setting is used when your Windows NT Server system is accessed by less than 10 users.

This setting allocates memory so a maximum of 10 network connections can be properly maintained. By restricting the memory for

network connections, you make more memory available at the local or desktop level.

• **Balance.** The Balance setting can be used for a maximum of 64 network connections. This setting is the default when using NetBEUI software. Like the Minimize setting, Balance is best used for a relatively low number of users connecting to a server that also can be used as a desktop computer.

• **Maximize Throughput for File Sharing.** The Maximize Throughput for File Sharing setting allocates the maximum amount of memory available for network connections. This setting is excellent for large networks in which the server is being accessed for file and print sharing.

• **Maximize Throughput for Network Applications.** If you are running distributed applications, such as SQL Server or Exchange Server, the network applications do their own memory caching. Therefore, you want your system to enable the applications to manage the memory. You accomplish this by using the Maximize Throughput for Network Applications setting. This setting also is used for very large networks.

◆ **Computer Browser service.** The Computer Browser service is responsible for maintaining the list of computers on the network. The browse list contains all the computers located on the physical network. As a Windows NT Server, your system plays a big role in the browsing of a network. The Windows NT Server acts as a master browser or backup browser.

The selection of browsers is through an election. The election is called by any client computer or when a preferred master browser computer starts up. The election is based on broadcast messages.

Every computer has the opportunity to nominate itself, and the computer with the highest settings wins the election.

The election criteria are based on three things:

- The operating system (Windows NT Server, Windows NT Workstation, Windows 95, Windows for Workgroups)

- The version of the operating system (NT 4.0, NT 3.51, NT 3.5)

- The current role of the computer (master browser, backup browser, potential browser)

◆ **Directory Replicator service.** You can configure the Directory Replicator service to synchronize an entire directory structure across multiple servers.

In configuring the directory service, you must select the export server and all the import servers. The export server is the computer that holds the original copy of the directory structure and files. Each import server receives a complete copy of the export server's directory structure. The Directory Replicator service monitors the directory structure on the export server. If the contents of the directory change, the changes are copied to all the import servers. The file copying and directory monitoring is completed by a special service account you create. You must configure the Directory Replicator service to use this service account. The following access is required for your Directory Replicator service account:

- The account should be a member of the Backup Operators and Replicators groups.

- There should be no time or logon restrictions for the account.

- The Password Never Expires option should be selected.

- The User Must Change Password At Next Logon option should be turned off.

When configuring the export server, you have the option to specify the export directory. The default export directory is C:\WINNT\system32\repl\export\.

In the Import Directories section of the Directory Replication dialog box, you can select the import directory. The default import directory is C:\WINNT\system32\repl\import.

Remember that the default directory for executing logon scripts in a Windows NT system is C:\WINNT\system32\repl\import\scripts.

Configure hard disks to meet various requirements. Requirements include the following:

◆ Providing duplication

◆ Improving performance

All hard disk configuration can be done using the Disk Administrator tool. The different disk configurations you need to understand for the enterprise exam are the following:

◆ **Stripe set.** A stripe set gives you improved disk read and write performance; however, it supplies no fault tolerance. A minimum of two disks is required, and the configuration can stripe up to 32 physical disks. A stripe set cannot include the system partition.

◆ **Volume set.** A volume set enables you to extend partitions beyond one physical disk; however, it supplies no fault tolerance. To extend a volume set, you must use the NTFS file system.

◆ **Disk mirroring.** A mirror set uses two physical disks and provides full data duplication. Often referred to as RAID level 1, disk mirroring is a useful solution to assigning duplication to the system partition, as well as any other disks that might be in the system.

◆ **Stripe set with parity.** A stripe set with parity enables fault tolerance in your system. A minimum of three physical disks is required, and a maximum of 32 physical disks can be included in a stripe set with parity. A stripe set with parity cannot include the system partition of your Windows NT system.

The solution that supplies the best duplication and optimization mix is the stripe set with parity.

Configure printers. Tasks include the following:

◆ Adding and configuring a printer

◆ Implementing a printer pool

◆ Setting print priorities

The installation of a printer is a fairly simplistic procedure and is not tested heavily on the exam; however, the printer pool is a key point. The items to remember about printer pools are as follows:

◆ All printers in a printer pool must be able to function using the same printer driver.

◆ A printer pool can have a maximum of eight printers in the pool.

Configure a Windows NT Server computer for various types of client computers. Client computer types include the following:

◆ Windows NT Workstation

◆ Windows 95

◆ Macintosh

The Network Client Administrator is found in the Administrative Tools group. You can use the Network Client Administrator program to do the following:

◆ **Make a Network Installation Startup Disk.** This option creates an MS-DOS boot disk that contains commands required to connect to a network server and that automatically installs Windows NT Workstation, Windows 95, or the DOS network clients.

◆ **Make an Installation Disk Set.** This option enables the creation of installation disks for the DOS network client, LAN Manager 2.2c for DOS, or LAN Manager 2.2c for OS/2.

◆ **Copy Client-Based Network Administration Tools.** This option enables you to share the network administration tools with client computers. The client computers that can use the network administration tools are Windows NT Workstation and Windows 95 computers.

◆ **View Remoteboot Client Information.** This option enables you to view the remoteboot client information. To install remoteboot, go to the Services tab of the Network dialog box.

When installing a client computer, you must ensure that your Windows NT system is prepared for and configured for the client. The Windows clients can connect to the Windows NT server without any configuration required on the server; however, some configuration is required on the client computers. For the Apple Macintosh client, the NT server must install the services for the Macintosh, which includes the AppleTalk protocol. This protocol enables the seamless connection between the Windows NT system and the Apple clients.

MANAGING RESOURCES

Manage user and group accounts. Considerations include the following:

◆ Managing Windows NT user accounts

◆ Managing Windows NT user rights

◆ Managing Windows NT groups

◆ Administering account policies

◆ Auditing changes to the user account database

AGLP stands for Accounts/Global Groups/Local Groups/Permissions. When you want to assign permissions to any resource, you should follow a few simple rules. All user accounts are placed into global groups, and global groups get assigned into local groups. The local groups have the resources and permissions assigned to them.

When you are working with groups across trust relationships, the following guidelines are useful:

◆ Always gather users into global groups. Remember that global groups can contain only user accounts from the same domain. You might have to create the same named global group in multiple domains.

◆ If you have multiple account domains, use the same name for a global group that has the same types of members. Remember that when multiple domains are involved, the group name is referred to as DOMAIN\GROUP.

◆ Before the global groups are created, determine whether an existing local group meets your needs. There is no sense in creating duplicate local groups.

◆ Remember that the local group must be created where the resource is located. If the resource is on

a Domain Controller, create the local group in the Domain Account Database. If the resource is on a Windows NT Workstation or Windows NT Member Server, you must create the group in that system's local account database.

◆ Be sure to set the permissions for a resource before you make the global groups a member of the local group assigned to the resource. That way, you set the security for the resource.

Create and manage policies and profiles for various situations. Policies and profiles include the following:

◆ Local user profiles

◆ Roaming user profiles

◆ System policies

You can configure system policies to do the following:

◆ Implement defaults for hardware configuration— for all computers using the profile or for a specific machine.

◆ Restrict the changing of specific parameters that affect the hardware configuration of the participating system.

◆ Set defaults for all users in the areas of their personal settings that the users can configure.

◆ Restrict users from changing specific areas of their configuration to prevent tampering with the system. An example is disabling all Registry editing tools for a specific user.

◆ Apply all defaults and restrictions on a group level rather than just a user level.

Some common implementations of user profiles are the following:

◆ Locking down display properties to prevent users from changing the resolution of their monitor. Display properties can be locked down as a whole or on each individual property page of display properties. You adjust this setting by clicking the Control Panel, Display, Restrict Display option of the Default User Properties dialog box.

◆ Setting a default color scheme or wallpaper. You can do this by clicking the Desktop option of the Default User Properties dialog box.

◆ If you want to restrict access to portions of the Start menu or desktop, you can do this by clicking the Shell, Restrictions option of the Default User Properties dialog box.

◆ If you need to limit the applications that the user can run at a workstation, you can do so by clicking the System, Restrictions option of the Default User Properties dialog box. You can also use this option to prevent the user from modifying the Registry.

◆ You can prevent users from mapping or disconnecting network drives by clicking the Windows NT Shell, Restrictions option of the Default User Properties dialog box.

Profiles and policies can be very powerful tools to assist in the administrative tasks in your environment. The following list reviews each of the main topics covered in this objective:

◆ **Roaming profiles.** The user portion of the Registry is downloaded from a central location, allowing the user settings to follow the user anywhere within the network environment.

◆ **Local profiles.** The user settings are stored at each workstation and are not copied to other computers. Each workstation that you use will have different desktop and user settings.

◆ **System policies.** System policies enable the administrator to restrict user configuration changes on systems. This enables the administrator to maintain the settings of the desktop of systems without the fear that a user can modify them.

◆ **Computer policies.** Computer policies allow the lockdown of common machine settings that affect all users of that computer.

Administer remote servers from various types of client computers. Client computer types include the following:

◆ Windows 95

◆ Windows NT Workstation

This objective focuses on the remote administration tools available for your Windows NT Server. The following list summarizes the key tools:

◆ **Remote Administration Tools for Windows 95.** Allows User Manager, Server Manager, Event Viewer, and NTFS file permissions to be executed from the Windows 95 computer.

◆ **Remote Administration for Windows NT.** Allows User Manager, Server Manager, DHCP Manager, System Policy Editor, Remote Access Admin, Remote Boot Manager, WINS Manager, and NTFS file permissions to be executed from a Windows NT machine.

◆ **Web Based Administration.** Allows for common tasks to be completed through an Internet connection into the Windows NT Server.

Manage disk resources. Tasks include the following:

◆ Creating and sharing resources

◆ Implementing permissions and security

◆ Establishing file auditing

Windows NT has two levels of security for protecting your disk resources:

- ◆ Share permissions

- ◆ NTFS permissions

NTFS permissions enable you to assign more comprehensive security to your computer system. NTFS permissions can protect you at the file level. Share permissions, on the other hand, can be applied only to the folder level. NTFS permissions can affect users logged on locally or across the network to the system where the NTFS permissions are applied. Share permissions are in effect only when the user connects to the resource through the network.

The combination of Windows NT share permissions and NTFS permissions determines the ultimate access a user has to a resource on the server's disk. When share permissions and NTFS permissions are combined, no preference is given to one or the other. The key factor is which of the two effective permissions is the most restrictive.

For the exam, remember the following tips relating to managing resources:

- ◆ Users can be assigned only to global groups in the same domain.

- ◆ Only global groups from trusted domains can become members of local groups in trusting domains.

- ◆ NTFS permissions are assigned only to local groups in all correct test answers.

- ◆ Only NTFS permissions give you file-level security.

CONNECTIVITY

Configure Windows NT Server for interoperability with NetWare servers by using various tools. The tools include the following:

- ◆ Gateway Service for NetWare

- ◆ Migration Tool for NetWare

Gateway Service for NetWare (GSNW) performs the following functions:

- ◆ GSNW enables Windows NT Servers to access NetWare file and print resources.

- ◆ GSNW enables the Windows NT Servers to act as a gateway to the NetWare file and print resources. The Windows NT Server enables users to borrow the connection to the NetWare server by setting it up as a shared connection.

The Migration Tool for NetWare (NWCONV) transfers file and folder information and user and group account information from a NetWare server to a Windows NT domain controller. The Migration Tool can preserve the folder and file permissions if it is being transferred to an NTFS partition.

Connectivity between Windows NT and a NetWare server requires the use of GSNW. If the user and file information from NetWare is to be transferred to a Windows NT Server, the NetWare Conversion utility, NWCONV, is used for this task. The following list summarizes the main points in this section on NetWare connectivity:

- ◆ GSNW can be used as a gateway between Windows NT clients and a NetWare server.

- ◆ GSNW acts as a NetWare client to the Windows NT Server, allowing the NT server to have a connection to the NetWare server.

◆ GSNW is a service in Windows NT, and is installed using the Control Panel.

◆ For GSNW to be used as a gateway into a NetWare server, a gateway user account must be created and placed in a NetWare group called NTGATEWAY.

◆ In configuring the GSNW as a gateway, you can assign permissions to the gateway share by accessing the GSNW icon in the Control Panel.

◆ For GSNW to be functional, the NWLINK IPX/SPX protocol must be installed and configured.

◆ To convert user and file information from a NetWare server to a Windows NT server, you can use the NWCONV.EXE utility.

◆ NWCONV requires that GSNW be installed prior to any conversion being carried out.

◆ To maintain the NetWare folder- and file-level permissions in the NWCONV utility, you must convert to an NTFS partition on the Windows NT system.

Install and configure multiprotocol routing to serve various functions. Functions include the following:

◆ Internet router

◆ BOOTP/DHCP Relay Agent

◆ IPX router

Multiprotocol routing gives you flexibility in the connection method used by your clients, and in maintaining security. Check out the following:

◆ **Internet router.** Setting up Windows NT as an Internet router is as simple as installing two network adapters in the system, then enabling IP routing in the TCP/IP protocol configuration. This option enables Windows NT to act as a

static router. Note that Windows NT cannot exchange Routing Information Protocol (RIP) routing packets with other IP RIP routers unless the RIP routing software is installed.

◆ **IPX router.** You enable the IPX router by installing the IPX RIP router software by choosing Control Panel, Networks, Services.

After installing the IPX RIP router, Windows NT can route IPX packets over the network adapters installed. Windows NT uses the RIP to exchange its routing table information with other RIP routers.

The inclusion of the industry-standard protocols, and tools to simplify the configuration and extension of your NT network into other environments, makes this operating system a very powerful piece of your heterogenous environment. The following are the main factors to focus on for this objective:

◆ A strong understanding of the functionality of each of the Windows NT protocols—with a strong slant toward TCP/IP and the configuration options available. Understanding and configuration of the DHCP server are also tested on this exam.

◆ The services used to resolve the IP addresses and names of hosts in a TCP/IP environment. DNS service, WINS Service, the Hosts file, and the LMHosts files are among the services tested.

◆ The routing mechanisms available in Windows NT. These mechanisms are powerful, and largely unknown to the vast majority of NT administrators. Ensure that you review the configuration and functionality of Internet or IP routing, as well as the IPX routing tools available.

Install and configure Internet Information Server, and install and configure Internet services. Services include the following:

- The World Wide Web

- DNS

- Intranets

Internet Information Server (IIS) uses Hypertext Transfer Protocol (HTTP), File Transfer Protocol (FTP), and the Gopher service to provide Internet publishing services to your Windows NT Server computer.

IIS provides a graphical administration tool called the Internet Service Manager. With this tool, you can centrally manage, control, and monitor the Internet services in your Windows NT network. The Internet Service Manager uses the built-in Windows NT security model, so it offers a secure method of remotely administering your Web sites and other Internet services.

IIS is an integrated component in Windows NT Server 4.0. The IIS services are installed using the Control Panel, Networks icon or during the installation phase. The following list summarizes the key points in installing and configuring IIS:

- The three Internet services included in IIS are HTTP, FTP, and Gopher.

- HTTP is used to host Web pages from your Windows NT server system.

- FTP is a protocol used for transferring files across the Internet using the TCP/IP protocol.

- Gopher is used to create a set of hierarchical links to other computers or to annotate files or folders.

- The Internet Service Manager is the utility used to manage and configure your Internet services in IIS.

- The Internet Service Manager has three views that you can use to view your services. The three views are Report View, Servers View, and Services View.

Install and configure Remote Access Service (RAS). Configuration options include the following:

- Configuring RAS communications

- Configuring RAS protocols

- Configuring RAS security

RAS supports the Serial Line Internet Protocol (SLIP) and Point-to-Point Protocol (PPP) line protocols, and the NetBEUI, TCP/IP, and IPX network protocols.

RAS can connect to a remote computer using any of the following media:

- **Public Switched Telephone Network (PSTN).** (PSTN is also known simply as the phone company.) RAS can connect using a modem through an ordinary phone line.

- **X.25.** A packet-switched network. Computers access the network through a Packet Assembler Disassembler (PAD) device. X.25 supports dial-up or direct connections.

- **Null modem cable.** A cable that connects two computers directly. The computers then communicate using their modems (rather than network adapter cards).

- **ISDN.** A digital line that provides faster communication and more bandwidth than a normal phone line. (It also costs more, which is why not everybody has it.) A computer must have a special ISDN card to access an ISDN line.

RAS is designed for security. The following are some of RAS's security features:

- **Auditing.** RAS can leave an audit trail, enabling you to see who logged on when and what authentication they provided.

◆ **Callback security.** You can enable the RAS server to use callback (hang up all incoming calls and call the caller back), and you can limit callback numbers to prearranged sites that you know are safe.

◆ **Encryption.** RAS can encrypt logon information, or it can encrypt all data crossing the connection.

◆ **Security hosts.** In case Windows NT is not safe enough, you can add an extra dose of security by using a third-party intermediary security host—a computer that stands between the RAS client and the RAS server and requires an extra round of authentication.

◆ **PPTP filtering.** You can tell Windows NT to filter out all packets except ultra safe Point-to-Point Tunneling Protocol (PPTP) packets.

RAS can be a very powerful and useful tool in enabling you to extend the reaches of your network to remote and traveling users. The following list summarizes main points for RAS in preparation for the exam:

◆ RAS supports SLIP and PPP line protocols.

◆ With PPP, RAS can support NetBEUI, NWLINK, and TCP/IP across the communication line.

◆ RAS uses the following media to communicate with remote systems: PSTN, X.25, Null Modem cable, and ISDN.

◆ The RAS security features available are auditing, callback security, encryption, and PPTP filtering.

◆ To install RAS, click the Network icon in the Control Panel.

MONITORING AND OPTIMIZATION

Establish a baseline for measuring system performance. Tasks include creating a database of measurement data.

You can use numerous database utilities to analyze the data collected. The following are some of the databases that Microsoft provides:

◆ Performance Monitor

◆ Microsoft Excel

◆ Microsoft Access

◆ Microsoft FoxPro

◆ Microsoft SQL Server

The following list summarizes the key items to focus on when you are analyzing your computer and network:

◆ Establish a baseline measurement of your system when functioning at its normal level. Later, you can use the baseline in comparative analysis.

◆ Establish a database to maintain the baseline results and any subsequent analysis results on the system, to compare trends and identify potential pitfalls in your system.

◆ The main resources to monitor are memory, the processor, the disks, and the network.

The following list summarizes the tools used to monitor your NT server that are available and are built into Windows NT Server 4.0:

◆ Server Manager

◆ Windows NT Diagnostics

◆ Response Probe

◆ Performance Monitor

◆ Network Monitor

Monitor performance of various functions by using Performance Monitor. Functions include the following:

◆ Processor

◆ Memory

◆ Disk

◆ Network

To summarize the main views used within Performance Monitor, review the following list:

◆ **Chart view.** This view is very useful for viewing the objects and counters in a real-time mode. This mode enables you to view the data in a graphical format. You can also use the chart view to view the contents of a log file.

◆ **Log view.** This view enables you to set all the options required for creating a log of your system resources or objects. After this log is created, you can view it by using the chart view.

◆ **Alert view.** Use the alert view to configure warnings or alerts of your system resources or objects. In this view, you can configure threshold levels for counters and can then launch an action based on the threshold values being exceeded.

◆ **Report view.** The report view enables you to view the object and counters as an averaged value. This view is useful for comparing the values of multiple systems that are configured similarly.

When monitoring the disk, remember to activate the disk counters using the command diskperf –y. If you do not enter this command, you can select counter but will not see any activity displayed. In the case of a software RAID system, start diskperf with the -ye option.

When you want to monitor TCP/IP counters, make sure that SNMP is installed. Without the SNMP service installed, the TCP/IP counters are not available.

Performance Monitor is a graphical utility that you can use for monitoring and analyzing your system resources within Windows NT. You can enable objects and counters within Performance Monitor; it is these elements that enable the logging and viewing of system data.

In preparing you for this objective, this section introduces numerous objects and counters that you use with Performance Monitor. To prepare for the exam, you need to understand the following key topics:

◆ The four views available in Performance Monitor are the report view, the log view, the chart view, and the alert view.

◆ The main resources to monitor in any system are the disk, the memory, the network, and the processor.

◆ Each of the main resources is grouped as a separate object, and within each object are counters. A counter is the type of data available from a type of resource or object. Each counter might also have multiple instances. An instance is available if multiple components in a counter are listed.

◆ To enable the disk counters to be active, you must run the DISKPERF utility.

Monitor network traffic by using Network Monitor. Tasks include the following:

◆ Collecting data

◆ Presenting data

◆ Filtering data

Network Monitor is a network packet analyzer that comes with Windows NT Server 4. Actually, two versions of Network Monitor are available from Microsoft.

The first version comes with Windows NT Server 4 (simple version). This version can monitor the packets (frames) sent or received by a Windows NT Server 4 computer. The second version comes with Microsoft Systems Management Server (full version). This version can monitor all traffic on the network.

By fully understanding the various components found while analyzing traffic, you will be more successful in locating potential network bottlenecks and offering relevant optimization recommendations. The main components that need to be monitored with your network traffic analysis are the following:

◆ Locate and classify each service. Analyze the amount of traffic generated from each individual service, the frequency of the traffic, and the overall effect the traffic has on the network segment.

◆ Understand the three different types of frames: broadcast, multicast, and directed.

◆ Review the contents of a frame and ensure that you can find the destination address, source address, and data located in each frame.

The following points summarize the key items to understand in building a strong level of knowledge in using Network Monitor as a monitoring tool:

◆ Two versions of Network Monitor are available: the scaled-down version that is built into the Windows NT Server operating system, and the full version that is a component of Microsoft Systems Management Server.

◆ The Network Monitor windows consist of four sections: Graph, Session Statistics, Station Statistics, and Total Statistics.

◆ After Network Monitor captures some data, you use the display window of Network Monitor to view the frames. The three sections of the display window are the Summary pane, the Detail pane, and the Hexadecimal pane.

Identify performance bottlenecks and optimize performance for various results. Results include the following:

◆ Controlling network traffic

◆ Controlling the server load

To optimize the logon traffic in your Windows NT network, you should consider four main points:

◆ Determine the hardware required to increase performance.

◆ Configure the domain controllers to increase the number of logon validations.

◆ Determine the number of domain controllers needed.

◆ Determine the best location for each of the domain controllers.

The following are a few good points to follow in optimizing file-session traffic:

◆ Remove any excess protocols that are loaded.

◆ Reduce the number of wide area network (WAN) links required for file transfer.

The following are three points to consider when attempting to optimize server browser traffic:

◆ Reduce the number of protocols.

◆ Reduce the number of entries in the browse list.

◆ Increase the amount of time between browser updates.

Trust relationships generate a large amount of network traffic. In optimizing your system, attempt to keep the number of trusts very low.

TROUBLESHOOTING

Choose the appropriate course of action to take to resolve installation failures.

Troubleshooting a Windows NT system requires that you have a strong understanding of the processes and tools available to you. To be an effective troubleshooter, first and foremost you must have experience. The following is a list of some common installation problems:

◆ Hard disk problems

◆ Unsupported CD-ROMs

◆ Network adapter problems and conflicts

◆ Naming problems (each computer must be uniquely named, following the NetBIOS naming conventions)

Always use the hardware compatibility list to ensure that your components are supported by Windows NT.

Choose the appropriate course of action to take to resolve boot failures.

For startup errors, try the following:

◆ Check for missing files that are involved in the boot process, including NTLDR, NTDE-TECT.COM, BOOT.INI, NTOSKRNL.EXE, and OSLOADER (RISC).

◆ Modify BOOT.INI for options.

◆ Create an NT boot disk for bypassing the boot process from the hard disk.

◆ Use the Last Known Good option to roll back to the last working set of your Registry settings.

Choose the appropriate course of action to take to resolve configuration errors. Tasks include the following:

◆ Backing up and restoring the Registry

◆ Editing the Registry

You can resolve many problems that you encounter within Windows NT by configuring the Registry. However, before you make any Registry configurations, you must have a strong understanding of the keys within the Registry and always back up the Registry prior to making any modifications to ensure a smooth rollback if additional problems occur. The following are the main tools used to modify the Registry:

◆ REGEDT32

◆ REGEDIT

For configuration problems, remember the following:

◆ Using the Registry for configuration and troubleshooting can cause additional problems if you do not maintain a full understanding of the Registry.

◆ Always back up the Registry prior to editing the contents.

◆ You can back up and restore the local Registry by using REGEDT32.

Choose the appropriate course of action to take to resolve printer problems.

For troubleshooting printers, you should do the following:

◆ Understand and review the overview of the printing process.

◆ Understand the files involved in the printing process.

◆ As a first step in troubleshooting a printer, always verify that the printer is turned on and online.

◆ Note that the most common errors associated with a printer are an invalid printer driver or incorrect resource permissions set for a user.

Choose the appropriate course of action to take to resolve RAS problems.

The following is a list of some of the problems that you might encounter with RAS:

◆ You must ensure that the protocol you are requesting from the RAS client is available on the RAS server. There must be at least one common protocol or the connection will fail.

◆ If you are using NetBEUI, ensure that the name you are using on the RAS client is not in use on the network to which you are attempting to connect.

◆ If you are attempting to connect using TCP/IP, you must configure the RAS server to provide you with an address.

You can use the Remote Access Admin tool to monitor the ports as well as the active connections of your RAS server.

Numerous RAS settings can cause some problems with your RAS connections. Ensure that you understand the installation process, as well as any configuration settings required to enable your RAS server. You can avoid some of the common problems that can occur by doing the following:

◆ Ensuring that the modem and communication medium are configured and functional prior to installing RAS. It can be very difficult to modify settings after the installation, so it is recommended to have all hardware tested and working first.

◆ Verifying that dial-in permissions have been enabled for the required users. This small task is commonly forgotten in your RAS configuration.

Choose the appropriate course of action to take to resolve connectivity problems.

To test and verify your TCP/IP settings, you can use the following utilities:

◆ IPCONFIG

◆ PING

The most effective method for troubleshooting connectivity is to understand thoroughly the installation and configuration options of each of the network protocols. If you understand the options available, you can narrow down the possible problem areas very quickly. Also ensure that you use utilities such as IPCONFIG and PING to test your connections.

Choose the appropriate course of action to take to resolve resource access and permission problems.

You should keep in mind two main issues about permissions:

◆ The default permissions for both share and NTFS give the Windows NT group Everyone full control over the files and folders. Whenever you format a drive as NTFS or first share a folder, you should remove these permissions. The Everyone group contains everyone, including guests and any other user who, for one reason or another, can connect to your system.

◆ The NTFS folder permission delete takes precedence over any file permissions. In all other cases, the file permissions take precedence over the folder permissions.

Choose the appropriate course of action to take to resolve fault-tolerance failures. Fault-tolerance methods include the following:

◆ Tape backup

◆ Mirroring

◆ Stripe set with parity

In using the NTBACKUP tool, the primary thing that you need to do is to determine the frequency and type of backup that you will do. There are three main types of backups that you might want to perform:

◆ **Full.** This backs up all the files that you mark, and marks the files as having been backed up. This is the longest of the backups because it transfers the most data.

◆ **Differential.** This backs up all the files that have changed since the last backup. A differential backup does not mark the files as being backed up. As time passes since the last full backup, the differentials become increasingly larger. However, you need only reload the full backup and the differential to return to the position of the last backup.

◆ **Incremental.** This backs up any files that have changed since the last backup, and then marks them as having been backed up. If your system crashes, you need to start by loading a full backup and then each incremental backup since that full backup.

If you are mirroring the system partition, the disks and partitions should be absolutely identical. Otherwise, the MBR/DBR (master boot record/disk boot record) that contains the driver information will not be correct.

Although ARC naming looks complicated, it is really rather simple. The name is in four parts, of which you use three. The syntax is as follows:

```
multi/scsi(#)disk(#)rdisk(#)partition(#)
```

The following list outlines the parts of the name:

◆ **multi/scsi.** You use either multi or scsi, not both. Use multi in all cases except when using a scsi controller that cannot handle int13 (hard disk access) BIOS routines. Such cases are uncommon. The number is the logical number of the controller with the first controller being 0, the second being 1, and so forth.

◆ **disk.** When you use a scsi disk, you use the disk parameter to indicate which of the drives on the controller is the drive you are talking about. Again, the numbers start at 0 for the first drive and then increase for each subsequent drive.

◆ **rdisk.** Use this parameter for the other controllers in the same way as you use the disk parameter for scsi.

◆ **partition.** This is the partition on the disk that you are pointing at. The first partition is 1, the second is 2, and so forth. Remember that you can have up to four primary partitions, or three primary and one extended. The extended partition is always the last one, and the first logical drive in the partition will have the partition's number. Other drives in the extended partition each continue to add one.

Breaking a mirror set. The boot floppy will get the operating system up and running. You should immediately back up the mirrored copy of the mirror set. To back up the drive, you must break your mirror set. To do this, perform the tasks outlined in Step by Step FF.1.

STEP BY STEP

FF.1 Breaking the Mirror Set

1. Run the Disk Administrator.

2. From the Disk Administrator, click the remaining fragment of the mirrored set.

3. Choose Fault Tolerance, Break Mirror set from the menu.

   At the end of these three steps, you should notice that the mirror set has been broken, and you can now back up the drive.

Regenerating a stripe set with parity. Fixing a stripe set with parity is simple. Perform the tasks outlined in Step by Step FF.2 to regenerate your stripe set with parity.

STEP BY STEP

FF.2 Regenerating the Stripe Set

1. Physically replace the faulty disk drive.

2. Start the Disk Administrator.

3. Select the stripe set with parity that you need to repair and then Ctrl+click the free space of the drive you added to fix the stripe set.

4. Choose Fault Tolerant, Regenerate. Note that this process can take some time, although the process takes less time than restoring from tape.

   The drives regenerate all the required data from the parity bits and the data bits, and upon completion your stripe set with parity is completely functional.

◆ **Share permissions.** A common problem when troubleshooting share resources is in the share permissions. Ensure that the minimum functional permissions have been assigned. Always remove the Everyone group from having full control of a share.

◆ **Combining NTFS and share permissions.** When combining these permissions, remember that NT uses the most restrictive of the permissions when combining. As a rule, use the NTFS permissions as the highest level of permissions, and use the share permissions mainly for access to the folder or share.

◆ **Tape backups.** In any system that you are using, ensure that you have a good backup strategy. Any component in your system can be faulty, and it is your responsibility to have a recovery plan in case of emergencies.

◆ **Disk mirroring.** If you are implementing disk mirroring in your system, ensure that you have created a fault-tolerant boot disk that you can use in case of drive failure. By having this disk pre-configured and handy, you can break the mirror set and replace the drive with very little down-time for your server.

◆ **Stripe set with parity.** This system automatically regenerates data if a drive is faulty. Although your system performance will dramatically decline, it is still a functional box and you risk no possibility of losing any data. If you find that a drive in your stripe set is faulty, replace the drive and use the regenerate command from the Disk Administrator.

Perform advanced problem resolution. Tasks include the following:

◆ Diagnosing and interpreting a blue screen

◆ Configuring a memory dump

◆ Using the event log service

Three utilities come with Windows NT that enable you to work with the memory dump files that are created. You can find all of these utilities on the Windows NT Server CD-ROM. Each utility can be a very helpful tool. The following list briefly describes these utilities:

◆ **DUMPCHK.** This utility checks that the dump file is in order by verifying all the addresses and listing the errors and system information.

◆ **DUMPEXAM.** This creates a text file that can provide the same information that was on the blue screen at the time the stop error occurred.

You need the symbol files and the kernel debugger extensions as well as IMAGEHLP.DLL to run DUMPEXAM.

◆ **DUMPFLOP.** This utility backs up the dump file to a series of floppies so that you can send them to Microsoft.

The following list summarizes the key points required for this objective:

◆ The Event Viewer is a very powerful troubleshooting tool. The three logs that can be viewed through the Event Viewer are the system log, the application log, and the security log.

◆ Cross-reference the events in the Event Viewer with knowledge base articles found on Microsoft TechNet for troubleshooting help.

◆ Interpreting blue screens can be very difficult. Use memory dump files and the following utilities to view your memory dumps to help you isolate the problem:

  • DUMPCHK

  • DUMPEXAM

  • DUMPFLOP

◆ If the problem persists, you might have to use the kernel debugger that is included on the NT Server CD-ROM in the \Support\debug folder.

◆ You can use the kernel debugger to monitor a remote machine through a null modem, or by using the RAS service into a machine that is connected to the problematic computer through a null modem.

WINDOWS NT WORKSTATION 4 EXAM

Now that you have thoroughly read through this book, worked through the exercises, and picked up as much hands-on exposure to NT Workstation as possible, you're ready to take your exam. This chapter is designed to be a last-minute cram for you as you walk out the door on your way to the exam. You can't re-read the whole book in an hour, but you will be able to read this chapter in that time. This chapter is organized by objective category and summarizes the basic facts you need to know regarding each objective. If you know what is in here, chances are the exam will be a snap.

PLANNING

Remember: Here are the elements that Microsoft says they test on in the "Planning" section of the exam.

◆ Create unattended installation files.

◆ Plan strategies for sharing and securing resources.

◆ Choose the appropriate file system to use in a given situation. File systems and situations include: NTFS, FAT, HPFS, security, and dual-boot systems.

The files used for unattended installation are

◆ An unattended answer file (UNATTEND.TXT)

◆ A uniqueness database file (a .UDF file)

◆ SYSDIFF.EXE

◆ WINDIFF.EXE

Some switches available for WINNT32.EXE are useful for unattended installations:

◆ /u:*answerfile* (where *answerfile* might be UNATTEND.TXT, for example)

◆ /s:*sourcepath* (where *sourcepath* might be e:\i386, for example)

◆ /udf:*userid*,x:\udf.txt

The content of the OEM directory is copied to the destination machine before NT is installed to allow for additional file or application installation after NT has been installed.

SYSDIFF.EXE can be used to create a snapshot file, a difference file, and/or an .INF file.

.INF files are preferred over difference files because .INF files contain instructions on how to install the software, whereas the difference file contains the whole software package in one large file.

WINDIFF.EXE is used to compare one NT system to another.

The built-in groups in NT Workstation are

◆ Users

◆ Power Users

◆ Administrators

◆ Guests

◆ Backup Operators

◆ Replicator

Table 1 lists the default rights assigned to users or groups on an NT Workstation.

Table 2 lists the built-in capabilities of the built-in groups.

TABLE 1
ASSIGNMENT OF DEFAULT USER RIGHTS

Right	Administrators	Power Users	Users	Guests	Everyone	Backup Operators
Access This Computer from the Network	X	X				X
Back Up Files and Directories	X					X
Change the System Time	X	X				
Force Shutdown from a Remote System	X	X				
Load and Unload Device Drivers	X					
Log On Locally	X	X	X	X	X	X
Manage Auditing and Security Log	X					
Restore Files and Directories	X					X
Shut Down the System	X	X	X		X	X
Take Ownership of Files or Other Objects	X					

TABLE 2
BUILT-IN USER CAPABILITIES

Built-In Capability	Administrators	Power Users	Users	Guests	Everyone	Backup Operators
Create and Manage User Accounts	X	X				
Create and Manage Local Groups	X	X				
Lock the Workstation	X	X	X	X	X	X
Override the Lock of the Workstation	X					
Format the Hard Disk	X					
Create Common Groups	X	X				
Share and Stop Sharing Directories	X	X				
Share and Stop Sharing Printers	X	X				

The following special groups are maintained by NT:

◆ Network

◆ Interactive

◆ Everyone

◆ Creator Owner

Table 3 shows the advantages and disadvantages of storing home directories on a server and on a local computer.

Table 4 shows the advantages and disadvantages of running applications from a server and from a local machine.

TABLE 3
HOME DIRECTORIES ON THE SERVER VERSUS HOME DIRECTORIES ON THE LOCAL COMPUTER

Server-Based Home Directories	*Local Home Directories*
Centrally located so that users can access them from any location on the network.	Available only on the local machine. For roaming users (who log in from more than one computer on the network), the directory is not accessible from other systems.
During a regular backup of the server, information in users' home directories is also backed up.	Often users' local workstations are not backed up regularly as part of a scheduled backup process. If a user's machine fails, the user cannot recover the lost data.
Windows NT does not provide a way to limit the size of a user's directory. Thus, if a lot of information is being stored in home directories, the directories use up a lot of server disk space.	If a user stores a lot of information in his home directory, the space is taken up on his local hard drive instead of the server.
If the server is down, the user won't have access to her files.	The user has access to his files even when the network is down because the files are stored locally.
Some network bandwidth is consumed due to the over-the-network access of data or files.	No network traffic is generated by a user accessing his or her files.

TABLE 4
SHARED NETWORK APPLICATIONS VERSUS LOCALLY INSTALLED APPLICATIONS

Shared Network Applications	*Locally Installed Applications*
Take up less disk space on the local workstation.	Use more local disk space.
Easier to upgrade/control.	Upgrades must "touch" every machine locally.
Use network bandwidth.	Use no network bandwidth for running applications.
Slower response time because applications are accessed from the server.	Faster, more responsive.
If the server is down, users can't run applications.	Users can run applications regardless of server status.

NT Workstation supports the following file formats:

 ◆ FAT16 (a universal standard format)

 ◆ NTFS (an NT proprietary format)

 ◆ CDFS (CD-ROM format)

NT Workstation does not support these file formats:

 ◆ FAT32 (supported by Windows 95 OSR2 and Windows 98)

 ◆ HPFS (supported by OS/2)

Table 5 provides a comparison between FAT and NTFS.

TABLE 5
COMPARISON OF NTFS AND FAT FILE SYSTEMS USING WINDOWS NT WORKSTATION

Feature	FAT	NTFS
Support for long filenames (up to 255 characters)	Yes	Yes
Compression	No	Yes
Security	No	Yes
Dual-boot capabilities with non–Windows NT systems	Yes	No
Maximum file/partition size	4GB	16EB
Recommended partition size	0–400MB	400MB–16EB
Capability to format a floppy	Yes	No
Recoverability (transaction logging)	No	Yes

INSTALLATION AND CONFIGURATION

Remember: Here are the elements that Microsoft says they test on in the "Installation and Configuration" section of the exam.

◆ Install Windows NT Workstation on an Intel platform in a given situation.

◆ Set up a dual-boot system in a given situation.

◆ Remove Windows NT Workstation in a given situation.

◆ Install, configure, and remove hardware components for a given situation. Hardware components include: network adapter drivers, SCSI device drivers, tape device drivers, UPSs, multimedia devices, display drivers, keyboard drives, and mouse drivers.

◆ Use Control Panel applications to configure a Windows NT Workstation computer in a given situation.

◆ Upgrade to Windows NT Workstation 4.0 in a given situation.

◆ Configure server-based installation for wide-scale deployment in a given situation.

NTHQ.EXE (available on the Workstation CD-ROM) can be used to evaluate a computer for NT installation. It is used to verify hardware and produce a report indicating which components are and are not on the HCL.

Table 6 lists the minimum hardware requirements for NT Workstation installation.

NT Workstation supports four installation types. Table 7 lists the components installed with each of the four installation types.

TABLE 6
WINDOWS NT WORKSTATION 4.0 MINIMUM INSTALLATION REQUIREMENTS

Component	Minimum Requirement
CPU	32-bit Intel x86-based (80486/33 or higher) microprocessor or compatible (the 80386 microprocessor is no longer supported)
	Intel Pentium, Pentium Pro, or Pentium II microprocessor
	Digital Alpha AXP-based RISC microprocessor
	MIPS Rx400-based RISC microprocessor
	PowerPC-based RISC microprocessor
Memory	Intel x86-based computers: 12MB RAM
	RISC-based computers: 16MB RAM
Hard disk	Intel x86-based computers: 110MB
	RISC-based computers: 148MB
Display	VGA or better resolution
Other drives	Intel x86-based computers require a high-density 3 $\frac{1}{2}$" floppy drive and a CD-ROM drive (unless you are planning to install Windows NT over a network)
Optional	Network adapter card
	Mouse or other pointing device, such as a trackball

TABLE 7
VARYING COMPONENTS IN FOUR SETUP OPTIONS

Component	Typical	Portable	Compact	Custom
Accessibility options	X	X	None	All options
Accessories	X	X	None	All options
Communications programs	X	X	None	All options
Games			None	All options
Windows Messaging			None	All options
Multimedia	X	X	None	All options

Windows NT Workstation can be installed using a variety of procedures given different circumstances:

◆ Locally, by using the three Setup floppy disks and a CD-ROM

◆ Locally, by using the CD-ROM and creating and using the three Setup floppy disks

◆ Locally, using the CD without Setup floppy disks, but by booting instead to an operating system that recognizes the CD-ROM

◆ Locally, by booting to the CD-ROM from a computer that recognizes the CD-ROM as a boot device

◆ Over the network, by creating and using the three Setup floppy disks

◆ Over the network, but without the Setup floppies

When you're installing NT on a computer with an existing operating system present, if the computer recognizes either the CD-ROM or a supported network adapter and connection to a network share on which the installation files are present, you can use one of two programs to install NT:

◆ **WINNT.EXE.** For installation from existing non-NT operating systems

◆ **WINNT32.EXE.** For installation or upgrade from existing NT installations

Table 8 describes the switches available for use with WINNT.EXE and WINNT32.EXE.

Dual booting is a method of installing two operating systems on a single machine and letting the user choose which will boot at startup time (only one can be booted at any time).

TABLE 8
SWITCHES FOR MODIFYING THE **WINNT.EXE** AND **WINNT32.EXE** INSTALLATION PROCESSES

Switch	Effect
/b	Prevents creation of the three Setup boot disks. Create a temporary folder named WIN_NT.˜BT and copy to it the boot files that would normally be copied to the three floppies. The contents of the temporary folder are used instead of the Setup boot disks to boot the machine when the user is prompted to restart.
/c	Skips the step of checking for available free space. (This switch cannot be used with WINNT32.EXE.)
/I:*inf_file*	Specifies the name of the Setup information file. The default filename is DOSNET.INF.
/f	Prevents verification of files as they are copied. (This switch cannot be used with WINNT32.EXE.)
/l	Creates a log file called $WINNT.LOG, which lists all errors that occur as files are being copied to the temporary directory. (This switch cannot be used with WINNT32.EXE.)
/ox	Creates the three Setup boot disks and then stops.
/s:*server_path*	Specifies the location of the installation source files.
/u	Allows all or part of an installation to proceed unattended (as detailed in Chapter 1, "Planning"). The /b option for floppyless installation is automatically invoked, and the /s option for location of the source files must be used. The /u option can be followed with the name of an answer file to fully automate installation.
/udf	During an unattended installation, specifies settings unique to a specific computer, which are contained in a uniqueness database file (see Chapter 1).
/w	This *undocumented* flag enables the WINNT.EXE program to execute in Windows (normally, it must be executed from an MS-DOS command prompt).
/x	Prevents creation of the three Setup boot disks. You must already have the three boot disks.

NT Workstation can dual boot with any of the following operating systems:

- ◆ MS-DOS
- ◆ Microsoft Windows (3.1, 3.11, 95, 98)
- ◆ OS/2
- ◆ Microsoft Windows NT (Server or Workstation, any version)

Dual booting with an operating system other than NT (Server or Workstation) requires that at least the primary partition be formatted FAT.

If you remove NT Workstation from a machine, you must SYS (for the OS that remains) on the primary partition to remove the following:

- ◆ All paging files (C:\PAGEFILE.SYS)
- ◆ C:\BOOT.INI, C:\BOOTSECT.DOS, C:\NTDETECT.COM, C:\NTLDR (these are hidden, system, read only files)
- ◆ *.PAL (on Alpha computers)
- ◆ NTBOOTDD.SYS (on computers with SCSI drives with the BIOS disabled)
- ◆ The *winnt_root* folder
- ◆ The C:\Program files\Windows Windows NT folder

Most device drivers not written for NT 4.0 will not work with NT 4.0 (that includes network adapter drivers for NT 3.51 and Windows 95).

All mass storage device installation and settings (including those for tape drives and IDE hard drives) are configured from the SCSI icon in the Control Panel.

During boot, NT's automatic hardware detection process can cause a UPS to shut off because of a pulse that's sent through the COM port to detect a serial mouse. This can be prevented by including the /noserialmice switch in the boot line of the BOOT.INI file.

MANAGING RESOURCES

Remember: Here are the elements that Microsoft says they test on in the "Managing Resources" section of the exam.

- ◆ Create and manage local user accounts and local group accounts to meet given requirements.
- ◆ Set up and modify user profiles.
- ◆ Set up shared folders and permissions.
- ◆ Set permissions on NTFS partitions, folders, and files.
- ◆ Install and configure printers in a given environment.

Using local groups to assign rights and permissions on an NT Workstation can reduce administrative overhead.

The following account policies can be set from the User Manager:

- ◆ **Maximum Password Age.** This option enables you to specify how long a user's password is valid. The default is that passwords expire in 42 days.

- ◆ **Minimum Password Age.** This specifies how long a user must keep a particular password before she can change it again. If you force a user to change her password, and you leave this set to Allow Changes Immediately, after the user has changed her password once, she can change it right back to the old one. If you are requiring password changes for security reasons, this breaks down your security. For that reason, you may want to set a minimum password age.

- ◆ **Minimum Password Length.** The default on Windows NT is to allow blank passwords. Once again, for security reasons, you may not want to allow this. You can set a minimum password length of up to 14 characters, which is the maximum password length allowed under Windows NT.

◆ **Password Uniqueness.** If you want to force users to use a different password each time they change their passwords, you can set a value for password uniqueness. If you set the password uniqueness value to remember two passwords, when a user is prompted to change her password, she cannot use the same password again until she changes her password for the third time. The maximum password uniqueness value is 24.

◆ **Lockout After Bad Logon Attempts.** Setting a value for this option prevents the account from being used after this number is reached, even if the right password is finally entered. If you set this value to five, which is the default when Account Lockout is enabled, on the sixth attempt, a person cannot log on to Windows NT—even if the user (or hacker) types in the correct username and password.

◆ **Reset Counter After.** This value specifies when to refresh the counter for bad logon attempts. The default value is 30 minutes. That means if Account Lockout is set to five and a user tries to log on unsuccessfully four times, he can stop, wait 45 minutes, and then try again. The counter will have been reset by then, and he can try to log on five more times before the account will be locked out.

◆ **Lockout Duration.** This value specifies how long the account should remain locked if the lockout counter is exceeded. It is generally more secure to set Lockout Duration to forever so that the administrator must unlock the account. That way, the administrator is warned of the activity on that account.

◆ **Users Must Log On to Change Password.** This setting requires a user to log on successfully before changing his password. If a user's password expires, the user cannot log on until the administrator changes the password for the user.

Home directories can be created so that each user who logs on has a specific location on the local machine or the network where he or she can store personal information.

In order to use RAS, a user must be granted dial-in permission in the User Manager.

You create new accounts through User Manager. Two accounts are created automatically when NT is installed: Administrator and Guest.

The following password options can be configured for a user when the account is created:

◆ **User Must Change Password at Next Logon.** When this is selected (which is the default when creating new users), the user is prompted to change his password when he logs on to Windows NT. This setting is not compatible with the account policy that forces a user to log on to change his password. If both are selected, the user must contact the administrator to change the password.

◆ **User Cannot Change Password.** Setting this option prevents a user from changing her password. If both this setting and User Must Change Password are selected, you get an error message stating that you cannot check both options for the same user when you attempt to add the account.

◆ **Password Never Expires.** You can use this option to override the setting for password expiration in the Account Policy. This option tends to be used for accounts that will be assigned to services, but it can be granted to user accounts as well. If you have both this option and User Must Change Password at Next Logon selected, a warning tells you that the user will not be required to change her password.

◆ **Account Disabled.** Instead of deleting a user's account when he or she leaves the company, it is a good idea to disable the account. If the user will be replaced, it is likely that the new individual who's hired will need the same rights and permissions the previous user had. By disabling the account, you prevent the previous employee from accessing your Windows NT Workstation or domain. When the new individual is hired, however, you can rename the old account to the new name and have the user change the password.

◆ **Account Locked Out.** This option is visible only if you have Account Lockout enabled in the Account Policy. You, as an administrator, can never check this box; it will be grayed out. The only time this box is available is when a user's account has been locked out because it has exceeded the specified number of bad logon attempts. If the Lockout Duration is set to forever, the administrator must go into that user's account and uncheck the Account Locked Out check box.

Table 9 lists the buttons available from a user's Properties dialog box in User Manager.

TABLE 9
USER PROPERTY BUTTONS IN USER MANAGER

Button	Enables You to Modify...
Groups	The groups the user is a member of
Profile	The user's profile path, login script path, and home directory location
Account	The user's account expiration date and account type
Hours	The hours a user can log in to the computer
Dialin	Whether the user can dial in using RAS and what callback features (if any) are enabled

You can create account templates to reduce the amount of administration that's required to create groups of similar accounts. Accounts created from a template inherit the template's configuration for the following features:

◆ Account Description option

◆ User Must Change Password at Next Logon option

◆ User Cannot Change Password option

◆ Password Never Expires option

◆ Group memberships

◆ All user-environment profile properties

◆ All dial-in properties

In account configuration, the %UserName% variable can represent individual users' login names whenever they're needed to access or create a folder. (For example, you might use it when creating home folders called by the users' login names.)

When a user leaves the company, it is always better to disable his account than to delete it for the following reasons:

◆ A disabled account cannot be used to log in (rendering it unuseable).

◆ Deleting an account also deletes the SID associated with it, thus removing the permissions for that user from all locations on the network.

◆ A user whose account is deleted will have to have her permissions restored everywhere if she should return.

◆ Renaming an account grants the permissions of the former user to the new user.

Local groups can be created to grant access to Workstation resources and to assign users' rights on the system. The following local groups are created when NT Workstation is installed:

◆ **Administrators.** The Administrators group has full control over the Windows NT Workstation. This account has the most control on the computer. However, members of the Administrators group do not automatically have control over all files on the system. By using an NTFS partition, a user can configure a file's permissions to restrict access from the administrator. If the administrator needs to access the file, she can take ownership of the file and then access it. Administrative privilege is one of three levels of privilege you can assign to a user in Windows NT. It is the highest level of privilege that can be assigned.

◆ **Guests.** The Guests group is used to give someone limited access to the resources on the Windows NT Workstation. The Guest account is automatically added to this group. The Guests group is one of the three levels of privilege you can assign to a Windows NT user account.

◆ **Users.** The Users group provides a user with the necessary rights to use the computer. By default, all accounts created on Windows NT Workstation are put into the Users group, except for the built-in Administrator and Guest accounts. User privilege is one of the three levels of privilege you can assign in Windows NT.

◆ **Power Users.** The Power Users group gives members the ability to perform certain system tasks without giving them complete administrative control over the machine. One of the tasks a power user can perform is the sharing of directories. An ordinary user on Windows NT Workstation cannot share directories.

◆ **Backup Operators.** The Backup Operators group gives its members the ability to bypass the security placed on any file when using the NT Backup utility. This allows them complete resource access, but only for the specialized job of backing up files, not for general access.

◆ **Replicator.** The Replicator group is used only to enable directory replication. This process allows file transfer to take place between an export computer (which must be an NT Server) and an import computer (which can be NT Workstation or NT Server). You will not see questions regarding this group and its service on the NT Workstation exam; but if you want more information, you can consult the NT Server book in this MCSE series.

Group accounts cannot be renamed.

User profiles fall into two categories: local and roaming. In addition, roaming user profiles fall into two categories: mandatory and personal. A local profile is located on a specific machine and takes effect only when a user logs onto that machine. A roaming profile is available over the network and can be accessed from any machine that has network connectivity to the machine holding the profile. Mandatory profiles (which have the extension .MAN) are read only and, therefore, cannot be changed by a user.

Shared folders allow users to access Workstation resources from the network (by default, no resources are made generally accessible to users over the network).

The following permissions are available on shared folders:

◆ **No Access.** If a user or group is given the No Access permission to a shared folder, that user or group cannot open the shared folder even though he will see the shared folder on the network. The

No Access permission overrides all other permissions a user or group might have to the folder.

◆ **Read.** The Read permission allows a user or group to display files and subfolders within the shared folder. It also allows the user or group to execute programs that might be located within the shared folder.

◆ **Change.** The Change permission allows a user or group to add files or subfolders to the shared folder and to append or delete information from existing files and subfolders. The Change permission also encompasses everything included within the Read permission.

◆ **Full Control.** If a user or group is given the Full Control permission, that user or group has the ability to change the file permissions and to perform all tasks allowed by the Change permission.

In order to share a folder on an NT Workstation, you must have that right. It is given by default to the built-in Administrators and Power Users groups.

You can share a folder remotely by using the Server Manager. Shares can be created, modified, or removed from a folder through the folder share permissions (accessible by right-clicking the folder and choosing Sharing).

If a user is given individual permission to access a folder and is also a member of one or more groups which are given access, the user's effective permission is the combination of the permissions (the highest level). This is true unless one of the permissions is No Access, in which case the No Access permission prevails over all others.

The permission granted to a share is also the permission granted to the tree structure inside that share. Sharing one folder within another shared folder gives two points of access and, potentially, two levels of access to the same resource.

Shared permissions apply only to network access; NTFS permissions apply both over the network and locally.

Table 10 describes the access permissions available on NTFS.

TABLE 10
STANDARD NTFS PERMISSIONS

Permission	Folder	File
Read (R)	Enables the user to display the folder and subfolders, attributes, and permissions	Enables the user to display the file, its attributes, and its permissions
Write (W)	Enables the user to add files or folders, change attributes for the folder, and display permissions	Enables the user to change file attributes and add or append data to the file
Execute (X)	Enables the user to make changes to subfolders, display permissions, and display attributes	Enables the user to run a file if it is an executable and display attributes and permissions
Delete (D)	Enables the user to remove the folder	Enables the user to remove the file
Change Permission (P)	Enables the user to modify folder permissions	Enables the user to modify file permissions
Take Ownership (O)	Enables the user to take ownership of the folder	Enables the user to take ownership of a file

Table 11 lists the standard NTFS file permissions and the granular permissions that comprise them.

TABLE 11
STANDARD NTFS FILE PERMISSIONS

Standard File Permission	Individual NTFS Permissions
No Access	(None)
Read	(RX)
Change	(RWXD)
Full Control	(All Permissions)

Table 12 lists the standard NTFS folder permissions and the default file permissions for files within those folders.

You (or any user) can take ownership of an NTFS resource provided that you meet one or more of the following criteria:

◆ **You must be the owner of the file or folder.** You must be the user who created it.

◆ **You must have been granted Full Control.** This includes the ability to Change Permissions (P).

◆ **You must have been given special access to Change Permissions (P).** A user can be given just this one permission to a file or folder.

◆ **You must have been given special access to Take Ownership (O).** With the ability to Take Ownership, a user can give himself the right to Change Permissions (P).

◆ **You must be a member of the Administrators group.**

If a user is granted individual NTFS permissions to a resource and is also a member of one or more groups that have been granted access, the effective permission for the user is the cumulative permission from all the access levels. This is the case unless any level is No Access, in which case the No Access level prevails over all others.

When shared permissions are combined with NTFS permissions for accessing a resource over the network, the lowest permission (share or NTFS) prevails. If the user is accessing locally, however, only NTFS permission applies.

TABLE 12
STANDARD NTFS FOLDER PERMISSIONS

Standard Folder Permissions	Individual NTFS Folder Permissions	Individual NTFS File Permissions
No Access	(None)	(None)
Read	(RX)	(RX)
Change	(RWXD)	(RWXD)
Add	(WX)	(Not Applicable)
Add & Read	(RWX)	(RX)
List	(RX)	(Not Applicable)
Full Control	(All)	(All)

When you copy a file from one folder to another, the permissions of the destination folder are applied to the new copy of the file. When you move a file from one folder to another and the folders are on different partitions, the permissions on the destination folder apply to the moved file. When you move a file from one folder to another on the same partition, the file retains its original permissions.

It's important that you remember the definitions of the following printing terms:

◆ **Printer**. The software component for printing. Also referred to as a *logical printer*, it is the software interface between the application and the print device.

◆ **Print device.** The actual hardware the paper comes out of. This is what you would traditionally think of as a printer. In Windows NT terminology, however, it is called a print device.

◆ **Print job.** The information that is sent to the print device. It contains both the data and the commands for print processing.

◆ **Print spooler.** A collection of DLLs (Dynamic Link Libraries) that accept, process, schedule, and distribute print jobs.

◆ **Creating a printer.** The process of defining a printer from your Windows NT Workstation. When you create a printer, you specify that the machine on which you are creating it will be the print server for that print device. You must create a printer if no other Windows NT system has created it yet, or if the print device is on a non–Windows NT operating system such as Windows 95.

◆ **Connecting to a printer.** A process that is necessary when the print device has already been defined by another Windows NT system and a printer has been created on that Windows NT system. If that is the case, in order to use the printer, you just need to connect to the printer from your Windows NT Workstation.

◆ **Print server.** The computer that created the printer and on which the printer is defined. Typically this is a Windows NT Server. However, a Windows NT Workstation or even a Windows 95 system can act as a print server.

◆ **Print queue.** The list of print jobs on the print server that are waiting to print.

◆ **Printer driver.** The software that enables applications to communicate properly with the print device.

◆ **Spooling.** The process of storing documents on the hard disk and then sending them to the printer. After the document has been stored on the hard disk, the user regains control of the application.

You can configure a printer pool by assigning two or more printer ports to the same printer and enabling printer pooling.

To allow other users to access a printer over the network, you must share the printer. Printer permissions can be set to control access to a printer. Table 13 lists those permissions.

TABLE 13
CAPABILITIES GRANTED WITH PRINTER PERMISSIONS

Capability	Full Control	Manage Documents	Print	No Access
Print documents	X	X	X	
Pause, resume, restart, and cancel the user's own documents	X	X	X	
Connect to a printer	X	X	X	
Control job settings for all documents	X	X		
Pause, restart, and delete all documents	X	X		
Share a printer	X			
Change printer properties	X			
Delete a printer	X			
Change printer permissions		X		

In a printer's properties dialog box, you can set the availability of the printer to allow it to hold documents until a certain time of the day.

Spool settings include the following options:

◆ **Spool Print Documents So Program Finishes Printing Faster.** If you choose this option, the documents will spool. This option has two choices within it:

  • *Start Printing After Last Page Is Spooled.* This prevents documents from printing until they are completely spooled. The application that is printing is not available during the spooling. To use this option, you must have enough space on the partition of the spool directory to hold the entire print job.

  • *Start Printing Immediately.* This enables a document to start printing before it has spooled completely, which speeds up printing.

◆ **Print Directly to the Printer.** This prevents the document from spooling. Although it speeds up printing, this is not an option for a shared printer, which would must support multiple incoming documents simultaneously.

◆ **Hold Mismatched Documents.** This prevents incorrect documents from printing. Incorrect documents are those that do not match the configuration of the printer.

◆ **Print Spooled Documents First.** Spooled documents will print ahead of partially spooled documents, even if they have a lower priority. This speeds up printing.

◆ **Keep Documents After They Have Printed.** Documents remain in the spooler after they have been printed.

If the print queue becomes jammed, you can clear corrupted print items by stopping and restarting the Spooler service from the Services icon in the Control Panel. The spool directory is, by default, located in Systemroot\system32\spool\printers, but that location can be changed via the File menu in the printer properties dialog box.

CONNECTIVITY

Remember: Here are the elements that Microsoft says they test on in the "Connectivity" section of the exam.

- ◆ Add and configure the network components of Windows NT Workstation.

- ◆ Use various methods to access network resources.

- ◆ Implement Windows NT Workstation as a client in a NetWare environment.

- ◆ Use various configurations to install Windows NT Workstation as a TCP/IP client.

- ◆ Configure and install Dial-Up Networking in a given situation.

- ◆ Configure Microsoft Peer Web Services in a given situation.

NDIS 4.0 enables the following on an NT Workstation computer:

- ◆ An unlimited number of network adapter cards.

- ◆ An unlimited number of network protocols can be bound to a single network adapter card.

- ◆ Independence between protocols and adapter card drivers.

- ◆ Communication links between adapter cards and their drivers.

The major characteristics of TCP/IP include the following:

- ◆ Routing support

- ◆ Connectivity with the Internet

- ◆ Interoperability with most possible operating systems and computer types

- ◆ Support as a client for Dynamic Host Configuration Protocol (DHCP)

- ◆ Support as a client for Windows Internet Name Service (WINS)

- ◆ Support as a client for Domain Name System (DNS)

- ◆ Support for Simple Network Management Protocol (SNMP)

The following are the major characteristics of NWLink:

- ◆ Connectivity with NetWare resources

- ◆ Routing support

- ◆ Supported by a wide variety of other operating systems

- ◆ Large installation base

The main characteristics of NetBEUI include

- ◆ No routing support.

- ◆ Transmissions are broadcast-based and, therefore, generate a lot of traffic.

- ◆ Fast performance on small LANs.

- ◆ Small memory overhead.

- ◆ No tuning options.

DLC protocol is primarily used for connecting NT Workstations to printers directly attached to the network through network interface cards.

Two network programming interfaces are available to allow programmers to access the network:

◆ **NetBIOS (Network Basic Input/Output System).** The original network API supported by Microsoft. IBM originally developed NetBIOS.

◆ **Windows Sockets (also called WinSock).** A newer network API originally developed by the UNIX community. Now Microsoft also supports it.

Table 14 describes the IPC mechanisms available in NT Workstation.

The Network applet in the Control Panel allows you to change names, services, protocols, adapters, and bindings for network configuration.

In order to be part of an NT domain, an NT computer must have an account that was created by someone with the right to add computer accounts in the domain (by default, an administrator).

If NWLink is installed and NT is left to autoconfigure the frame type, NT will expect 802.2 frames unless others are detected, in which case it will configure to the frame type it sees first. To use multiple NWLink frame types, you must make a Registry setting change.

Client Services for NetWare gives an NT Workstation the capability to access files and printers from a NetWare server, provided that NWLink is also installed on the Workstation. When installed on an NT Workstation, NWLink allows the workstation to connect to an application running on a NetWare server.

TABLE 14
TYPES OF INTERPROCESS COMMUNICATIONS

IPC Mechanism	*Typical Uses*
Named pipes	Named pipes establish a guaranteed bidirectional communications channel between two computers. After the pipe is established, either computer can read data from or write data to the pipe.
Mailslots	Mailslots establish a unidirectional communications channel between two computers. Receipt of the message is not guaranteed, and no acknowledgment is sent if the data is received.
Windows Sockets (WinSock)	WinSock is an API that enables applications to access transport protocols such as TCP/IP and NWLink.
RPCs	RPCs enable the various components of distributed applications to communicate with one another via the network.
Network Dynamic Data Exchange (NetDDE)	NetDDE is an older version of an RPC that is based on NetBIOS.
Distributed ActiveX Component Object Model (DCOM)	DCOM is an RPC based on Microsoft technology; it enables the components of a distributed application to be located on multiple computers across a network simultaneously.

TCP/IP is the default protocol installed on NT Workstation and requires at least a TCP/IP address and subnet mask to function properly. You can configure an NT Workstation to automatically receive TCP/IP configuration information from a DHCP server by selecting the Obtain Address from DHCP Server option button in the TCP/IP Properties dialog box. Two tools, IPCONFIG and PING, can be used to test the configuration and function of TCP/IP on your NT Workstation.

NT Workstation can act as a RAS client or a RAS server with one concurrent incoming connection. As a client, it can connect to servers using the SLIP, PPP, and PPTP protocols; as a client, it supports incoming connections using PPP or PPTP. Whether acting as a RAS client or a RAS server, an NT Workstation must have the RAS service installed. Table 15 lists the features of the three line protocols mentioned here.

PPTP connections require a PPP or LAN connection to a server with a Virtual Private Network (VPN) configured on it and provide for secure and encrypted communication.

In order for a user to log on to an NT Workstation using RAS, the user account must be configured in User Manager to allow dialin.

Peer Web Services allows for FTP, WWW, and Gopher connections from Internet or intranet clients.

TABLE 15
RAS LINE PROTOCOLS AND FEATURES

Feature	SLIP	PPP	PPTP
Supports NT as server	No	Yes	Yes
Supports NT as client	Yes	Yes	Yes
Passes TCP/IP	Yes	Yes	Yes
Passes NetBEUI	No	Yes	Yes
Passes NWLink	No	Yes	Yes
Supports DHCP over RAS	No	Yes	No
Requires PPP or LAN connection	No	No	Yes
Supports VPNs	No	No	Yes
Supports password encryption	No	Yes	Yes
Supports transmission encryption	No	No	Yes

RUNNING APPLICATIONS

Remember: Here are the elements that Microsoft says they test on in the "Running Applications" section of the exam.

- Start applications on Intel and RISC platforms in various operating system environments.

- Start applications with various priorities.

NT Workstation supports (to a greater or lesser extent) applications written for the following operating systems:

- Windows NT and Windows 95

- MS-DOS

- Windows 3.x

- OS/2

- POSIX

MS-DOS applications invoke an NT Virtual DOS machine, which emulates a DOS environment. Windows 16-bit applications invoke an NT Virtual DOS machine (unless one is already running) and then run a Win16 emulator called WOW.EXE.

By default, Win16 applications all run in the same NTVDM. However, if desired, you can configure them to run in separate NTVDMs. The following list summarizes the advantages and disadvantages of running Win16 applications in separate NTVDMs.

Advantages:

- Win16 applications will now use preemptive multitasking. An ill-behaved Win16 application will no longer prevent other Win16 applications from executing normally because each Win16 application will have its own memory space and thread of execution.

- Win16 applications will now be more reliable because they will not be affected by the problems of other Win16 applications.

- Win16 applications can now take advantage of multiprocessor computers. When Win16 applications are run in a common NTVDM, they must share a single thread of execution. The generation of individual NTVDMs also creates individual threads of execution, and each thread can potentially be executed on a different processor. The operating system could now schedule each NTVDM's thread of execution to run on whichever processor is available. In a system with multiple processors, this can lead to multiprocessing. If the Win16 applications were running in a common NTVDM, their single thread of execution would be able to run only on a single processor, no matter how many processors existed on the computer.

- Windows NT will enable Win16 applications running in separate memory spaces to continue to participate in OLE and dynamic data exchange (DDE).

Disadvantages:

- There is additional overhead in running separate NTVDMs.

- Some older Win16 applications did not use the standards of OLE and DDE. These applications would not function properly if they were run in separate memory spaces. These applications must be run in a common memory space to function correctly. Lotus for Windows 1.0 is an example of this type of application.

NT offers four methods for running Win16 applications in separate NTVDMs:

◆ Anytime you start a Win16 application from the Start menu using the Run option, you can select the Run in Separate Memory Space option. This technique must be applied every time an application is run from the Run dialog box.

◆ At a command prompt, you can start a Win16 application using the command syntax start /separate *application*. For example, to start Word 6.0 you could type the following:

```
start /separate c:\office16\word\winword.exe
```

This technique must be applied every time the application is run from a command prompt.

◆ Shortcuts that point to Win16 applications can be configured to always run in a separate memory space. To do that, use the appropriate option on the Shortcut tab of the properties dialog box for the shortcut. Although this causes an application to run in a separate memory space every time the shortcut is used, it applies only to the particular shortcut that's modified, and not to any other shortcuts that have been created to that application.

◆ You can configure all files with a particular extension to always run in a separate memory space when the data document is double-clicked on in the Windows NT Explorer. To do this, you edit the File Types tab of the View, Options properties.

The OS/2 subsystem allows you to run OS/2 1.x character-based applications on Intel machines. On RISC machines, you must run OS/2 applications in NTVDMs by using the /FORCEDOS switch when running the applications from a command prompt or shortcut. You configure OS/2 applications by editing a CONFIG.SYS file using an OS/2 text editor. This creates a temporary file that is then converted to Registry settings (no CONFIG.SYS file is actually stored on the hard drive).

NT provides POSIX.1 support in its POSIX subsystem. This subsystem supports the following features for POSIX applications:

◆ **Case-sensitive file naming.** NTFS preserves case for both directory and filenames.

◆ **Hard links.** POSIX applications can store the same data in two differently named files.

◆ **An additional time stamp on files.** This tracks the last time the file was accessed. The default on FAT volumes is to track only the last time the file was modified.

Application support differs across different hardware platforms. Table 16 lists the kinds of support that applications have. *Binary* means that the same application will run across all hardware platforms; *source* means that a different compile is required for each hardware platform.

TABLE 16
APPLICATION COMPATIBILITY ACROSS WINDOWS NT PLATFORMS

Platform	MS-DOS	Win16	Win32	OS/2	POSIX
Intel	Binary	Binary	Source	Binary	Source
Alpha	Binary	Binary	Source*	Binary**	Source
Mips	Binary	Binary	Source	Binary**	Source
PowerPC	Binary	Binary	Source	Binary**	Source

* Third-party utilities such as Digital FX!32 enable Win32-based Intel programs to execute on Digital Alpha AXP microprocessors. Although these utilities are interpreting the code on-the-fly, they end up performing faster on the Alpha as a result of the increased processor speed.
** Only bound applications can be run on the three RISC hardware platforms. They will run in a Windows NTVDM because the OS/2 subsystem is not provided in RISC-based versions of Windows NT.

All applications run at a default priority set by the application itself (between 0 and 31). This priority determines its relative access to the CPU and, as a result, how quickly it responds to user interaction.

You can assign priority levels to applications through the use of command prompt switches. Table 17 lists the priority levels, their base priorities, and the commands you use to assign them.

NT boosts the priority of the application in the foreground by anywhere from 0 to 2 points (this ensures that foreground applications are more responsive than background applications). The "boost from" base is set on the Performance tab of the Control Panel's System application.

TABLE 17
BASE PRIORITY LEVELS UNDER WINDOWS NT

Priority Level	Base Priority	Command Line
Low	4	start /low executable.exe
Normal	8	start /normal executable.exe
High	13	start /high executable.exe
Realtime	24	start /realtime executable.exe

MONITORING AND OPTIMIZATION

Remember: Here are the elements that Microsoft says they test on in the "Monitoring and Optimization" section of the exam.

◆ Monitor system performance by using various tools.

◆ Identify and resolve a given performance problem.

◆ Optimize system performance in various areas.

Task Manager (accessible by right-clicking the taskbar and choosing Task Manager) allows you to see and end applications and processes on your system.

Performance Monitor allows you to monitor counters for specific computer and application objects and to tune the performance of your computer based on what you find.

In order to monitor disk counters, you must first enable them through the use of the command DISKPERF -y (or DISKPERF -YE for volume sets and RAID disks).

Table 18 describes the objects you will find in the Performance Monitor (others may be present depending on the services or applications you have installed).

Four views are available in the Performance Monitor:

◆ **Chart view.** Real-time line graphs of counters.

◆ **Log view.** Stored statistics useable by other views at a later time.

◆ **Alert view.** Monitored thresholds that generate events if the thresholds are crossed.

◆ **Report view.** Real-time text-displayed statistics on counters.

Performance Monitor can be used to monitor a local machine or an NT Server or Workstation to which the user has Administrative rights.

TABLE 18
COMMON OBJECTS ALWAYS AVAILABLE IN THE PERFORMANCE MONITOR

Object	Description
Cache	The file system cache is an area of physical memory that holds recently used data.
Logical Disk	Disk partitions and other logical views of disk space.
Memory	Random access memory used to store code and data.
Objects	Certain system software objects.
Paging File	File used to support virtual memory allocated by the system.
Physical Disk	Hardware disk unit.
Process	Software object that represents a running program.
Processor	Hardware unit that executes program instructions.
Redirector	File system that diverts file requests to network servers.
System	Counters that apply to all system hardware and software.
Thread	The part of a process that uses the processor.

The Server Manager allows you to see who is currently logged on to a computer and what resources they are using, to see available shares on your Workstation, to start or stop sharing resources, and to see what type of access is being made to all in-use resources.

WINMSD allows you to view configuration information about your computer.

You may want to monitor and tune the following components:

- ◆ Memory
- ◆ Processor
- ◆ Disks
- ◆ Network

The Event Viewer allows you to view information logged to any of three logs:

- ◆ **System log.** A log of events detected by NT that have to do with system functioning (the starting and stopping of services or their failure).
- ◆ **Security log.** A log of audited events that have to do with resource access (success or failure).
- ◆ **Application log.** A log of events recorded by applications running on NT that are configured to create such events.

You can archive any of these logs for viewing at a later time or for event archive.

An emergency repair disk enables you to recover Registry and system settings should they become corrupt. By performing the following two steps, you can be sure your ERD remains up-to-date:

1. Using the RDISK.EXE utility, update the Repair directory to save the repair information on your hard drive.

2. Using the RDISK.EXE utility, write the Repair information to a floppy disk.

You can perform a repair by booting to and using the three installation disks required to install NT from a CD-ROM and by specifying that you want to repair your system when asked.

The LastKnownGood configuration is a set of Registry settings that record the state of the NT configuration at the time of the last successful login. If you encounter problems with your system resulting from a change you've made in the current session, reboot and choose to restore LastKnownGood. Every time you log in, the LastKnownGood configuration is overwritten with the current configuration of your hardware (whether it functions properly or not).

TROUBLESHOOTING

Remember: Here are the elements that Microsoft says they test on in the "Troubleshooting" section of the exam.

- ◆ Choose the appropriate course of action to take when the boot process fails.
- ◆ Choose the appropriate course of action to take when a print job fails.
- ◆ Choose the appropriate course of action to take when the installation process fails.
- ◆ Choose the appropriate course of action to take when an application fails.
- ◆ Choose the appropriate course of action to take when a user cannot access a resource.
- ◆ Modify the Registry using the appropriate tool in a given situation.
- ◆ Implement advanced techniques to resolve various problems.

The acronym DETECT can be used to define the troubleshooting process:

D	Discover the problem
E	Explore the boundaries
T	Track the possible approaches
E	Execute an approach
C	Check for success
T	Tie up loose ends

Table 19 identifies the files involved in the boot process for both Intel and RISC machines.

TABLE 19
BOOT PROCESS FILES

Intel	*RISC*
NTLDR	OSLOADER.EXE
BOOT.INI	NTOSKRNL.EXE
NTDETECT.COM	
NTOSKRNL.EXE	
NTBOOTDD.SYS (for SCSI drives with BIOS disabled)	

In the NT boot process (in BOOT.INI), ARC paths define the physical position of the NT operating system files. ARC paths follow one of two formats:

scsi(0)disk(0)rdisk(0)partition(1)*folder*

multi(0)disk(0)rdisk(0)partition(1)*folder*

The first type, scsi ARC paths, define hard drives that are SCSI but have the BIOS disabled. The relevant parameters are

◆ **scsi.** The SCSI controller, starting from 0.

◆ **disk.** The physical disk, starting from 0.

◆ **partition.** The partition on the disk, starting from 1.

◆ ***folder*.** The folder in which the NT files are located.

The second type, multi ARC paths, define hard drives that are non-SCSI or are SCSI with the BIOS enabled. The relevant parameters are

◆ **multi.** The controller, starting from 0.

◆ **rdisk.** The physical disk, starting from 0.

◆ **partition.** The partition on the disk, starting from 1.

◆ ***folder*.** The folder in which the NT files are located.

Partitions are numbered according to the following pattern:

1. The first primary partition on each disk gets the number 1.

2. Each additional primary partition is then given a number, incrementing up from 1.

3. Each logical drive is then given a number in the order they appear in the Disk Administrator.

Switches on boot lines in the BOOT.INI file define additional boot parameters. Table 20 lists the switches you need to know and their functions.

TABLE 20
BOOT.INI SWITCHES

Switch	Function
/basevideo	Loads standard VGA video driver (640×480, 16-color)
/sos	Displays each driver as it is loaded
/noserialmice	Prevents autodetection of serial mice on COM ports, which can disable a UPS connected to the port

A recovery disk can be used to bypass problems with a system partition. This disk must be formatted in NT and will contain the files listed in Table 21 (broken down by hardware platform).

TABLE 21
FILES ON THE RECOVERY DISK

Intel	RISC
NTLDR	OSLOADER.EXE
NTDETECT.COM	HAL.DLL
BOOT.INI	*.PAL (for Alpha machines)
BOOTSECT.DOS (allows you to boot to DOS)	
NTBOOTDD.SYS (the SCSI driver for a hard drive with SCSI BIOS not enabled)	

An emergency repair disk can be used to repair an NT system if the Registry becomes corrupted. The repair disk must be used in conjunction with the three setup disks used to install NT.

The RDISK program allows you to update the \REPAIR folder, which in turn is used to update your repair disk.

The following list identifies possible sources of installation problems:

◆ Media errors

◆ Insufficient disk space

◆ Non-supported SCSI adapters

◆ Failure of dependency service to start

◆ Inability to connect to the domain controller

◆ Error in assigning domain names

Application failures generally result from incorrect application configuration, not from incorrect NT configuration.

If applications do not run, check the following:

◆ An MS-DOS application may be trying to access hardware directly.

◆ Two Win16 applications running in the same NTVDM may be conflicting.

◆ Win32 applications may be compiled for a different processor.

Services are interrelated: If one service fails, it may affect others as well. Therefore, you need to make sure that you get to the root of a service failure, and you're not just treating the symptoms.

Two programs are available for viewing and modifying the Registry:

◆ REGEDIT.EXE

◆ REGEDT32.EXE

The Network Monitor tool can be used to analyze network traffic in and out of the adapter on an NT Workstation computer.

Twelve chapters of this book have looked at objectives and components of the Microsoft Networking Essentials exam. After reading all of that, what is it that you must really know? What should you read as you sit and wait in the parking lot of the testing center—right up until the hour before going in to gamble your $100 and pride?

The following material covers the salient points of the 12 previous chapters and the points that make excellent test fodder. Although there is no substitute for real-world, hands-on experience, knowing what to expect on the exam can be equally meaningful. The information that follows is the networking equivalent of *Cliffs Notes*, providing the information you must know in each of the four sections to pass the exam. Don't just memorize the concepts given; attempt to understand the reason why they are so, and you will have no difficulties passing the exam.

Fast Facts

NETWORKING ESSENTIALS EXAM

STANDARDS AND TERMINOLOGY

The Standards and Terminology section is designed to test your understanding and knowledge of terms used in networking, as well as some of the more common standards that have been implemented in the industry.

Define Common Networking Terms for LANs and WANs

The Networking Essentials exam does not really test on definitions of terms. You are asked questions though, and, based on these questions, you need to understand the definitions of the terms used in order to successfully answer the questions.

The best mechanism to study for this area would be to be able to review the key terms found in every chapter and provide the correct definition for each term. Below is a list of some of the more general networking terms you should be aware of.

◆ **peer-to-peer networking**. A networking model where both the services and the client are performed by the same computer.

◆ **client/server networking**. A networking model where a specific role of providing services or acting as a client (not both) is performed by a computer.

◆ **centralized computing**. A form of computing where all the processing is done by one central computer.

◆ **distributed computing**. A form of computing where all the processing is shared by many different computers.

◆ **file services**. Services allowing for the storage and access of files.

◆ **print services**. Services that allow the sharing of a printer.

◆ **file and print server**. A server that provides file and print services.

◆ **application server**. A server that provides some high-end application used by many different computers.

◆ **token-ring network**. A network that follows a logical topology of a ring, but a physical topology of a star. The computers are connected to a concentrator known as an MSAU or MAU. Computers rely on the possession of a token before the transmission of data on the network. This type of network is known as a deterministic network.

◆ **ethernet network**. This type of a network is run as a logical bus, but can take on the physical topology of a bus or a star. The concentrator used by these computers, when in a star topology, is called a hub. This type of network is known as a contention-based network because each device contends with every other device for network access.

◆ **LAN**. Also known as a Local Area Network. Often characterized by fast transmission speeds and short distances between devices, and by the fact that the company running the network has control over all devices and transmission media.

◆ **WAN**. Also known as a Wide Area Network. When compared to a LAN, a WAN is often characterized by lower data transmission rates and the coverage of long distances, and by the fact that a third party is involved with the supply and maintenance of the transmission media.

Compare a File and Print Server with an Application Server

A file server is a service that is involved with giving access to files and directories on the network. The purpose of the file server is to give large numbers of users access to a centrally stored set of files and directories.

A print server is a computer or device that gives large number of users access to a centrally maintained printing device. A computer that is a file server often acts as print server, too. These types of computers are known as file and print servers.

An application server is responsible for running applications such as Exchange Server or SQL Server on the network. Application servers perform services that often require a more advanced level of processing than a user's personal computer is able to provide.

Compare User-Level Security with Access Permission Assigned to a Shared Directory on a Server

User-level security is a security model in which access to resources is given on a user-by-user basis, a group-by-group basis, or both. This type of access restriction allows an administrator to grant access to resources and affords users seemless access to those resources. User-level security is offered by Windows NT in both the workgroup and domain models.

The permissions to a shared directory are:

◆ **Read**. The user is allowed to read files within a share. He can also see all files and subdirectories.

◆ **Change**. The user can modify existing files and directories and create new files and directories within the share.

◆ **Full Control.** The user can see, modify, delete, and take ownership of all files and directories within the share.

◆ **No Access**. The user cannot access any files or directories within the share.

Share-level permissions apply to anyone accessing the share over the network and do not apply to users who are interactive on the computer where the share resides. Share-level permissions can be set on both FAT and NTFS partitions.

Compare a Client/Server Network with a Peer-to-Peer Network

A client/server network is one in which a computer has a specific role. A server is a computer, often with more RAM, more hard drive space, and a faster CPU than the other machines. A server services requests from clients. These requests could be for the use of files and printers, application services, communication services, and database services.

Clients are the computers on which users work. These computers typically are not as powerful as servers. Client computers are designed to submit requests to the server.

Peer-to-peer networks are made up of several computers that play the roles of both a client and a server; thus there is no dedicated computer running file and printer services, application services, communication services, or database services.

Compare the Implications of Using Connection-Oriented Communications with Connectionless Communications

In general, connection-oriented communication differs from connectionless communication as follows:

◆ **Connection-oriented mode**. Error correction and flow control are provided at internal nodes along the message path.

◆ **Connectionless mode**. Internal nodes along the message path do not participate in error correction and flow control.

In connection-oriented mode, the chain of links between the source and destination nodes forms a kind of logical pathway connection. The nodes forwarding the data packet can track which packet is part of which connection. This enables the internal nodes to provide flow control as the data moves along the path. For example, if an internal node determines that a link is malfunctioning, the node can send a notification message backward through the path to the source computer. Furthermore, because the internal node distinguishes among individual, concurrent connections in which it participates, this node can transmit (or forward) a "stop sending" message for one of its connections without stopping all communications through the node. Another feature of connection-oriented communication is that internal nodes provide error correction at each link in the chain. Therefore, if a node detects an error, it asks the preceding node to retransmit.

SPX and TCP are two major examples of connection-oriented protocols.

Connectionless mode does not provide these elaborate internal control mechanisms; instead, connectionless mode relegates all error-correcting and retransmitting processes to the source and destination nodes. The end nodes acknowledge the receipt of packets and retransmit if necessary, but internal nodes do not participate in flow control and error correction (other than simply forwarding messages between the end nodes).

IPX and UDP are two major examples of connection-oriented protocols.

The advantage of connectionless mode is that connectionless communications can be processed more quickly and more simply because the internal nodes only forward data and thus don't have to track connections or provide retransmission or flow control.

Distinguish Whether SLIP or PPP Is Used as the Communications Protocol for Various Situations

Two other standards vital to network communication are Serial Line Internet Protocol (SLIP) and Point-to-Point Protocol (PPP). SLIP and PPP were designed to support dial-up access to networks based on the Internet transport protocols. SLIP is a simple protocol that functions at the Physical layer, whereas PPP is a considerably enhanced protocol that provides Physical layer and Data Link layer functionality.

Windows NT supports both SLIP and PPP from the client end using the Dial-Up Networking application. On the server end, Windows NT RAS (Remote Access Service) supports PPP but doesn't support SLIP. In other words, Windows NT can act as a PPP server but not as a SLIP server.

PPP

PPP was defined by the Internet Engineering Task Force (IETF) to improve on SLIP by providing the following features:

◆ Security using password logon

◆ Simultaneous support for multiple protocols on the same link

◆ Dynamic IP addressing

◆ Improved error control

Different PPP implementations might offer different levels of service and negotiate service levels when connections are made. Because of its versatility, interoperability, and additional features, PPP has surpassed SLIP as the most popular serial-line protocol.

SLIP

Developed to provide dial-up TCP/IP connections, SLIP is an extremely rudimentary protocol that suffers from a lack of rigid standardization in the industry, which sometimes hinders different vendor implementations of SLIP from operating with each other.

SLIP is most commonly used on older systems or for dial-up connections to the Internet via SLIP-server Internet hosts.

Certain dial-up configurations cannot use SLIP for the following reasons:

◆ SLIP supports the TCP/IP transport protocol only. PPP, however, supports TCP/IP, as well as a number of other transport protocols, such as NetBEUI, IPX, AppleTalk, and DECnet. In addition, PPP can support multiple protocols over the same link.

◆ SLIP requires static IP addresses. Because SLIP requires static, or preconfigured, IP addresses, SLIP servers do not support the Dynamic Host Configuration Protocol (DHCP), which assigns IP addresses dynamically or when requested. (DHCP enables clients to share IP addresses so that a relatively small number of IP addresses can serve a larger user base.) If the dial-up server uses DHCP to assign an IP address to the client, the dial-up connection won't use SLIP.

◆ SLIP does not support dynamic addressing through DHCP so SLIP connections cannot dynamically assign a WINS or DNS server.

Define the Communication Devices that Communicate at Each Level of the OSI Model

◆ **Repeater**. Operates at the Physical layer of the OSI model. The purpose of a repeater is to regenerate a signal, allowing a signal to travel beyond the maximum distance specified by the transmission media.

◆ **Hub**. Operates at the Physical layer. A hub is a concentrator that connects 10BASE-T cabling together on an Ethernet network. Some hubs also have the capability to act as a repeater.

◆ **MSAU**. Operates at the Physical layer. An MSAU performs the same purpose of a hub, but is used on token-ring networks.

◆ **Network Interface Card (NIC)**. Operates at the Data Link layer. A NIC is responsible for converting information in a computer to a signal that will be sent on the transmission media.

◆ **Bridge**. Operates at the Data Link layer of the OSI mode. A bridge is responsible for isolating network traffic on a cable segment. It performs this task by building address tables that contain the MAC address or hardware addresses of devices on ether side of it.

◆ **Router**. Operates at the Network layer of the OSI model. It is responsible for connecting different segments that have dissimilar logical network addresses.

◆ **Gateway**. Can appear at any level of the OSI model but is primarily seen at the Network layer and higher. The purpose of a gateway is to convert one network protocol to another.

Describe the Characteristics and Purpose of the Media Used in IEEE 802.3 and IEEE 802.5 Standards

The various media types used by the IEEE 802.3 and 802.5 are discussed below.

IEEE 802.3

This standard defines characteristics related to the MAC sublayer of the Data Link layer and the OSI Physical layer. Except for one minor distinction—frame type—IEEE 802.3 Ethernet functions identically to DIX Ethernet v.2.

The MAC sublayer uses a type of contention access called *Carrier Sense Multiple Access with Collision Detection (CSMA/CD)*. This technique reduces the incidence of collision by having each device listen to the network to determine whether it's quiet ("carrier sensing"); a device attempts to transmit only when the network is quiescent. This reduces but does not eliminate collisions because signals take some time to propagate through the network. As devices transmit, they continue to listen so they can detect a collision should it occur. When a collision occurs, all devices cease transmitting and send a "jamming" signal that notifies all stations of the collision. Each device then waits a random amount of time before attempting to transmit again. This combination of safeguards significantly reduces collisions on all but the busiest networks.

The IEEE 802.3 Physical layer definition describes signaling methods (both baseband and broadband), data rates, media, and topologies. Several Physical layer variants also have been defined. Each variant is named following a convention that states the signaling rate (1 or 10) in Mbps, baseband (BASE) or broadband (BROAD) mode, and a designation of the media characteristics.

The following list details the IEEE 802.3 variants of transmission media:

- **1BASE5**. This 1-Mbps network utilizes UTP cable with a signal range up to 500 meters (250 meters per segment). A star physical topology is used.

- **10BASE5**. Typically called Thick Ethernet, or Thicknet, this variant uses a large diameter (10 mm) "thick" coaxial cable with a 50-ohm impedance. A data rate of 10 Mbps is supported with a signaling range of 500 meters per cable segment on a physical bus topology.

- **10BASE2**. Similar to Thicknet, this variant uses a thinner coaxial cable that can support cable runs of 185 meters. (In this case, the "2" only indicates an approximate cable range.) The transmission rate remains at 10 Mbps, and the physical topology is a bus. This variant typically is called Thin Ethernet, or Thinnet.

- **10BASE-F**. This variant uses fiber-optic cables to support 10-Mbps signaling with a range of four kilometers. Three subcategories include *10BASE-FL* (fiber link), *10BASE-FB* (fiber backbone), and *10BASE-FP* (fiber passive).

- **10BROAD36**. This broadband standard supports channel signal rates of 10 Mbps. A 75-ohm coaxial cable supports cable runs of 1,800 meters (up to 3,600 meters in a dual-cable configuration) using a physical bus topology.

- **10BASE-T**. This variant uses UTP cable in a star physical topology. The signaling rate remains at 10 Mbps, and devices can be up to 100 meters from a wiring hub.

- **100BASE-X**. This proposed standard is similar to 10BASE-T but supports 100 Mbps data rates.

IEEE 802.5

The IEEE 802.5 standard was derived from IBM's Token Ring network, which employs a ring logical topology and token-based media-access control. Data rates of 1, 4, and 16 Mbps have been defined for this standard.

Explain the Purpose of NDIS and Novell ODI Network Standards

The *Network Driver Interface Specification (NDIS)*, a standard developed by Microsoft and the 3Com Corporation, describes the interface between the network transport protocol and the Data Link layer network adapter driver. The following list details the goals of NDIS:

- To provide a vendor-neutral boundary between the transport protocol and the network adapter card driver so that an NDIS-compliant protocol stack can operate with an NDIS-compliant adapter driver.

◆ To define a method for binding multiple protocols to a single driver so that the adapter can simultaneously support communications under multiple protocols. In addition, the method enables you to bind one protocol to more than one adapter.

The *Open Data-Link Interface (ODI)*, developed by Apple and Novell, serves the same function as NDIS. Originally, ODI was written for NetWare and Macintosh environments. Like NDIS, ODI provides rules that establish a vendor-neutral interface between the protocol stack and the adapter driver. This interface also enables one or more network drivers to support one or more protocol stacks.

PLANNING

The planning section on the exam tests your ability to apply networking components and standards when designing a network.

Select the Appropriate Media for Various Situations

Media choices include:

◆ Twisted-pair cable

◆ Coaxial cable

◆ Fiber-optic cable

◆ Wireless

Situational elements include:

◆ Cost

◆ Distance limitations

◆ Number of nodes

Summary Table 1 outlines the characteristics of the cable types discussed in this section.

Summary Table 2 compares the different types of wireless communication media in terms of cost, ease of installation, distance, and other issues.

SUMMARY TABLE 1
COMPARISON OF CABLE MEDIA

Cable Type	Cost	Installation	Capacity	Range	EMI
Coaxial Thinnet	Less than STP	Inexpensive/easy	10 Mbps typical	185 m	Less sensitive than UTP
Coaxial Thicknet	Greater than STP Less than Fiber	Easy	10 Mbps typical	500 m	Less sensitive than UTP
Shielded Twisted-Pair (STP)	Greater than UTP Less than Thicknet	Fairly easy	16 Mbps typical up to 500 Mbps	100 m typical	Less sensitive than UTP
Unshielded twisted-pair (UTP)	Lowest	Inexpensive/easy	10 Mbps typical up to 100 Mbps	100 m typical	Most sensitive
Fiber-optic	Highest	Expensive/ Difficult	100 Mbps typical	Tens of Kilometers	Insensitive

SUMMARY TABLE 2
COMPARISON OF WIRELESS MEDIA

Cable Type	Cost	Installation	Distance	Other Issues
Infrared	Cheapest of all the wireless	Fairly easy; may require line of sight	Under a kilometer	Can attenuate due to fog and rain
Laser	Similar to infrared	Requires line of site	Can span several kilometers	Can attenuate due to fog and rain
Narrow band radio	More expensive than infrared and laser; may need FCC license	Requires trained technicians and can involve tall radio towers	Can span hundreds of kilometers	Low power devices can attenuate; can be eavesdropped upon; can also attenuate due to fog, rain, and solar flares
Spread spectrum radio	More advanced technology than narrow band radio, thus more expensive	Requires trained technicians and can involve tall radio towers	Can span hundreds of kilometers	Low power devices can attenuate; can also attenuate due to fog, rain, and solar flares
Microwave	Very expensive as it requires link to satellites often	Requires trained technicians and can involve satellite dishes	Can span thousands of kilometers	Can be eavesdropped upon; can also attenuate due to fog, rain, and solar flares

Select the Appropriate Topology for Various Token-Ring and Ethernet Networks

The following four topologies are implemented by Ethernet and token-ring networks:

◆ **Ring**. Ring topologies are wired in a circle. Each node is connected to its neighbors on either side, and data passes around the ring in one direction only. Each device incorporates a receiver and a transmitter and serves as a repeater that passes the signal to the next device in the ring. Because the signal is regenerated at each device, signal degeneration is low. Most ring topologies are logical, and implemented as physical stars. Token-ring networks follow a ring topology.

◆ **Bus**. Star topologies require that all devices connect to a central hub. The hub receives signals from other network devices and routes the signals

to the proper destinations. Star hubs can be interconnected to form tree or hierarchical network topologies. A star physical topology is often used to physically implement a bus or ring logical topology that is used by both Ethernet and token-ring networks.

◆ **Star**. Star topologies require that all devices connect to a central hub. The hub receives signals from other network devices and routes the signals to the proper destinations. Star hubs can be interconnected to form tree or hierarchical network topologies. A star physical topology is often used to physically implement a bus or ring logical topology that is used by both Ethernet and token-ring networks.

◆ **Mesh**. A mesh topology is really a hybrid model representing a physical topology because a mesh topology can incorporate all of the previous topologies. The difference is that in a mesh topology every device is connected to every other device on the network. When a new device is added, a connection to all existing devices must be made. Mesh topologies can be used by both Ethernet and token-ring networks.

Select the Appropriate Network and Transport Protocol or Protocols for Various Token-Ring and Ethernet Networks

Protocol choices include:

◆ DLC

◆ AppleTalk

◆ IPX

◆ TCP/IP

◆ NFS

◆ SMB

Data Link Control (DLC)

The Data Link Control (DLC) protocol does not provide a fully functioning protocol stack. In Windows NT systems, DLC is used primarily to access to Hewlett-Packard JetDirect network-interface printers. DLC also provides some connectivity with IBM mainframes. It is not a protocol that can be used to connect Windows NT or 95 computers together.

AppleTalk

AppleTalk is the computing architecture developed by Apple Computer for the Macintosh family of personal computers. Although AppleTalk originally supported only Apple's proprietary LocalTalk cabling system, the suite has been expanded to incorporate both Ethernet and token-ring Physical layers. Within Microsoft operating systems, AppleTalk is only supported by Windows NT Server. Windows NT Workstation and Windows 95 do not support AppleTalk. AppleTalk cannot be used for Microsoft to Microsoft operating system communication, only by NT servers supporting Apple clients.

The LocalTalk, EtherTalk, and TokenTalk Link Access Protocols (LLAP, ELAP, and TLAP) integrate AppleTalk upper-layer protocols with the LocalTalk, Ethernet, and token-ring environments.

Apple's *Datagram Deliver Protocol (DDP)* is a Network layer protocol that provides connectionless service between two sockets. The AppleTalk Transaction Protocol (ATP) is a connectionless Transport layer protocol. Reliable service is provided through a system of acknowledgments and retransmissions. The *AppleTalk File Protocol (AFP)* provides file services and is responsible for translating local file service requests into formats required for network file services. AFP directly translates command syntax and enables applications to perform file format translations. AFP is responsible for file system security and verifies and encrypts logon names and passwords during connection setup.

IPX

The *Internetwork Packet Exchange Protocol (IPX)* is a Network layer protocol that provides connectionless (datagram) service. (IPX was developed from the XNS protocol originated by Xerox.) As a Network layer protocol, IPX is responsible for internetwork routing and maintaining network logical addresses. Routing uses the RIP protocol (described later in this section) to make route selections. IPX provides similar functionality as UDP does in the TCP/IP protocol suite.

IPX relies on hardware physical addresses found at lower layers to provide network device addressing. IPX also uses sockets, or upper-layer service addresses, to deliver packets to their ultimate destinations. On the client, IPX support is provided as a component of the older DOS shell and the current DOS NetWare requester.

TCP/IP

TCP/IP is a broad protocol that covers many different areas. This summary presents some of the most important protocols within the TCP/IP protocol suite.

Internet Protocol (IP)

The *Internet Protocol (IP)* is a connectionless protocol that provides datagram service, and IP packets are most commonly referred to as IP datagrams. IP is a packet-switching protocol that performs the addressing and route selection.

IP performs packet disassembly and reassembly as required by packet size limitations defined for the Data Link and Physical layers being implemented. IP also performs error checking on the header data using a checksum, although data from upper layers is not error-checked.

Transmission Control Protocol (TCP)

The *Transmission Control Protocol (TCP)* is an internetwork connection-oriented protocol that corresponds to the OSI Transport layer. TCP provides full-duplex, end-to-end connections. When the overhead of end-to-end communication acknowledgment isn't required, the User Datagram Protocol (UDP) can be substituted for TCP at the Transport (host-to-host) level. TCP and UDP operate at the same layer.

TCP corresponds to SPX in the NetWare environment (see the NetWare IPX/SPX section). TCP maintains a logical connection between the sending and receiving computer systems. In this way, the integrity of the transmission is maintained. TCP detects any problems in the transmission quickly and takes action to correct them. The tradeoff is that TCP isn't as fast as UDP, due to the number of acknowledgments received by the sending host.

TCP also provides message fragmentation and reassembly and can accept messages of any length from upper-layer protocols. TCP fragments message streams into segments that can be handled by IP. When used with IP, TCP adds connection-oriented service and performs segment synchronization, adding sequence numbers at the byte level.

Windows Internet Naming Services (WINS)

Windows Internet Naming Service (WINS) provides a function similar to that of DNS, with the exception that it provides a NetBIOS name to IP address resolution. This is important because all of Microsoft's networking requires the capability to reference NetBIOS names. Normally NetBIOS names are obtained with the issuance of broadcasts, but because routers normally do not forward broadcasts, a WINS server is one alternative that can be used to issue IP addresses to NetBIOS name requests. WINS servers replace the need for LMHOSTS files on a computer.

Domain Name System (DNS)

The Domain Name System (DNS) protocol provides host name and IP address resolution as a service to client applications. DNS servers enable humans to use logical node names, utilizing a fully qualified domain name structure to access network resources. Host names can be up to 260 characters long. DNS servers replace the need for HOSTS files on a computer.

Network File System (NFS)

Network File System (NFS), developed by Sun Microsystems, is a family of file-access protocols that are a considerable advancement over FTP and Telnet. Since Sun made the NFS specifications available for public use, NFS has achieved a high level of popularity.

Server Messaging Blocks (SMB)

One protocol that is slightly independent is Microsoft's Server Messaging Blocks (SMB). SMBs are Microsoft's equivalent to NCP packets. Like NCP packets, SMBs operate at the Application layer of the OSI model.

SMBs allow machines on a Microsoft network to communicate with one another. Through the use of SMBs, file and print services can be shared. SMBs can use TCP/IP, NWLink (IPX/SPX), and NetBEUI because SMBs utilize a NetBIOS interface when communicating. For more information on NetBIOS names, see the following section.

Select the Appropriate Connectivity Devices for Various Token-Ring and Ethernet Networks

Connectivity devices include:

◆ **Repeaters**. Repeaters regenerate a signal and are used to expand LANs beyond cabling limits.

◆ **Bridges**. Bridges know the side of the bridge on which a node is located. A bridge passes only packets addressed to computers across the bridge, so a bridge can thus filter traffic, reducing the load on the transmission medium.

◆ **Routers**. Routers forward packets based on a logical (as opposed to a physical) address. Some routers can determine the best path for a packet based on routing algorithms.

◆ **Brouters**. A brouter is a device that is a combination of a bridge and a router, providing both types of services.

◆ **Gateways**. Gateways function under a process similar to routers except that gateways can connect dissimilar network environments. A gateway replaces the necessary protocol layers of a packet so that the packet can circulate in the destination environment.

List the Characteristics, Requirements, and Appropriate Situations for WAN Connection Services

WAN connection services include:

◆ X.25

◆ ISDN

◆ Frame relay

◆ ATM

X.25

X.25 is a packet-switching network standard developed by the International Telegraph and Telephone Consultative Committee (CCITT), which has been renamed the International Telecommunications Union (ITU). The standard, referred to as *Recommendation X.25*, was introduced in 1974 and is now implemented most commonly in WANs.

At the time X.25 was developed, this flow control and error checking was essential because X.25 was developed around relatively unreliable telephone line communications. The drawback is that error checking and flow control slow down X.25. Generally, X.25 networks are implemented with line speeds up to 64 Kbps, although actual throughput seems slower due to the error correction controls in place. These speeds are suitable for the file transfer and terminal activity that comprised the bulk of network traffic when X.25 was defined, most of this traffic being terminal connections to mainframes. Such speeds, however, are inadequate to provide LAN-speed services, which typically require speeds of 1 Mbps or better. X.25 networks, therefore, are poor choices for providing LAN application services in a WAN environment. One advantage of X.25, however, is that it is an established standard that is used internationally. This, as well as lack of other services throughout the world, means that X.25 is more of a connection service to Africa, South America, and Asia, where a lack of other services prevails.

ISDN

The original idea behind ISDN was to enable existing phone lines to carry digital communications, and it was at one time touted as a replacement to traditional analog lines. Thus, ISDN is more like traditional telephone service than some of the other WAN services. ISDN is intended as a dial-up service and not as a permanent 24-hour connection.

ISDN separates the bandwidth into channels. Based upon how these channels are used, ISDN can be separated into two classes of service:

◆ **Basic Rate (BRI)**. Basic Rate ISDN uses three channels. Two channels (called B channels) carry the digital data at 64 Kbps. A third channel (called the D channel) provides link and signaling information at 16 Kbps. Basic Rate ISDN thus is referred to as 2B+D. A single PC transmitting

through ISDN can use both B channels simultaneously, providing a maximum data rate of 128 Kbps (or higher with compression).

◆ **Primary Rate (PRI)**. Primary Rate supports 23 64 Kbps B channels and one 64 Kbps D channel. The D channel is used for signaling and management, whereas the B channels provide the data throughput.

In a BRI line, if the line was currently being used for voice, this would only allow one of the B channels to be available for data. This effectively reduces the throughput of the BRI to 64 Kbps.

Frame Relay

Frame Relay was designed to support the *Broadband Integrated Services Digital Network (B-ISDN)*, which was discussed in the previous section. The specifications for Frame Relay address some of the limitations of X.25. As with X.25, Frame Relay is a packet-switching network service, but Frame Relay was designed around newer, faster fiber-optic networks.

Unlike X.25, Frame Relay assumes a more reliable network. This enables Frame Relay to eliminate much of the X.25 overhead required to provide reliable service on less reliable networks. Frame Relay relies on higher-level protocol layers to provide flow and error control.

Frame Relay typically is implemented as a public data network and, therefore, is regarded as a WAN protocol. The scope of Frame Relay, with respect to the OSI model, is limited to the Physical and Data Link layers.

Frame Relay provides permanent virtual circuits that supply permanent virtual pathways for WAN connections. Frame Relay services typically are implemented at line speeds from 56 Kbps up to 1.544 Mbps (T1).

Customers typically purchase access to a specific amount of bandwidth on a frame-relay service. This bandwidth is called the *committed information rate (CIR)*, a data rate for which the customer is guaranteed access. Customers might be permitted to access higher data rates on a pay-per-use temporary basis. This arrangement enables customers to tailor their network access costs based on their bandwidth requirements.

To use Frame Relay, you must have special Frame Relay-compatible connectivity devices (such as frame-relay-compatible routers and bridges).

Asynchronous Transfer Mode (ATM)

Asynchronous Transfer Mode (ATM) is a high-bandwidth switching technology developed by the ITU Telecommunications Standards Sector (ITU-TSS). An organization called the ATM Forum is responsible for defining ATM implementation characteristics. ATM can be layered on other Physical layer technologies, such as Fiber Distributed Data Interface (FDDI) and SONET.

Several characteristics distinguish ATM from other switching technologies. ATM is based on fixed-length 53-byte cells, whereas other technologies employ frames that vary in length to accommodate different amounts of data. Because ATM cells are uniform in length, switching mechanisms can operate with a high level of efficiency. This high efficiency results in high data transfer rates. Some ATM systems can operate at an incredible rate of 622 Mbps; a typical working speed for an ATM is around 155 Mbps.

The unit of transmission for ATM is called a cell. All cells are 53 bytes long and consist of a 5-byte header and 48 bytes of data. The 48-byte data size was selected by the standards committee as a compromise to suit both audio- and data-transmission needs. Audio information, for instance, must be delivered with little latency (delay) to maintain a smooth flow of sound. Audio engineers therefore preferred a small cell so that cells

would be more readily available when needed. For data, however, large cells reduce the overhead required to deliver a byte of information.

Asynchronous delivery is another distinguishing feature of ATM. "Asynchronous" refers to the characteristic of ATM in which transmission time slots don't occur periodically but are granted at irregular intervals. ATM uses a technique called *label multiplexing*, which allocates time slots on demand. Traffic that is time-critical, such as voice or video, can be given priority over data traffic that can be delayed slightly with no ill effect. Channels are identified by cell labels, not by specific time slots. A high-priority transmission need not be held until its next time slot allocation. Instead, it might be required to wait only until the current 53-byte cell has been transmitted.

IMPLEMENTATION

The Implementation section of the exam tests your knowledge of how to implement, test, and manage an installed network.

Choosing an Administrative Plan to Meet Specified Needs, Including Performance Management, Account Management, and Security

Administrative plans can be broken down into three areas: performance management, account management, and security.

Performance Management

Performance management is best done through the establishment of a baseline of the network performance and a baseline of a computer's performance. Based upon the information in a baseline, the administrators of the network can establish when network or computer performance is abnormal.

Account Management

Account management within Windows NT is done through the use of groups. In a workgroup model, there exist local groups, or groups that are local to the computer. These groups are not seen on other machines in the network. Users are placed into these local groups and assigned permissions to resources, such as printers, shares, or files and directories.

Windows 95 computers do not have built-in groups. There also is no account database on a Windows 95 computer to provide user accounts.

Windows NT domain models do make use of user accounts and groups. Like the workgroup model, the domain model has user accounts and local groups. A domain model also has global groups. Global groups reside on a domain controller and can be referenced as a resource user by any Windows NT computer within the domain sharing resources.

Security

Windows 95 computers have the capability to provide share-level security, which involves password protecting resources.

Windows NT computers can provide user-level security, in which users are granted access to resources on a user or local group basis (workgroups and domains support this) and a global group basis (only domains support this).

Choosing a Disaster Recovery Plan for Various Situations

Disaster recovery applies to many different components on the network. The following sections describe the most common issues and solutions used in a disaster recovery program.

Uninterruptible Power Supply (UPS)

An uninterruptible power supply (UPS) is a special battery (or sometimes a generator) that supplies power to an electronic device in the event of a power failure. UPSs commonly are used with network servers to prevent a disorderly shutdown by warning users to log out. After a predetermined waiting period, the UPS software performs an orderly shutdown of the server. Many UPS units also regulate power distribution and serve as protection against power surges. Remember that in most cases, a UPS generally does not provide for continued network functionality for longer than a few minutes. A UPS is not intended to keep the server running through a long power outage, but rather to give the server time to do what it needs before shutting down. This can prevent the data loss and system corruption that sometimes result from sudden shutdown.

Tape Backup

Tape backups are done to store data offline in the event that the hard drive containing the data fails. There are three types of tape backups:

◆ **Full backup**. Backs up all specified files.

◆ **Incremental backup**. Backs up only those files that have changed since the last backup.

◆ **Differential backup**. Backs up the specified files if the files have changed since the last backup. This type doesn't mark the files as having been backed up, however. (A differential backup is somewhat like a copy command. Because the file is not marked as having been backed up, a later differential or incremental backup will back up the file again.)

RAID 1

In level 1, drives are paired or mirrored with each byte of information being written to each identical drive. You can duplex these devices by adding a separate drive controller for each drive. Disk mirroring is defined as two hard drives (one primary, one secondary) that use the same disk channel or controller cards and cable. Disk mirroring is most commonly configured by using disk drives contained in the server. Duplexing is a form of mirroring that involves the use of a second controller and that enables you to configure a more robust hardware environment.

RAID 5

RAID 5 uses striping with parity information written across multiple drives to enable fault-tolerance with a minimum of wasted disk space. This level also offers the advantage of enabling relatively efficient performance on writes to the drives, as well as excellent read performance.

Striping with parity is based on the principle that all data is written to the hard drive in binary code (ones and zeros). RAID 5 requires at least three drives because this version writes data across two of them and then creates the parity block on the third. If the first byte is 00111000 and the second is 10101001, the system computes the third by adding the digits together using this system:

1+1=0, 0+0=0, 0+1=1, 1+0=1

The sum of 00111000 and 10101001 is 10010001, which would be written to the third disk. If any of the

disks fail, the process can be reversed and any disk can be reconstructed from the data on the other two. Recovery includes replacing the bad disk and then regenerating its data through the Disk Administrator. A maximum of 32 disks can be connected in a RAID 5 array under Windows NT.

Given the Manufacturer's Documentation for the Network Adapter, Install, Configure, and Resolve Hardware Conflicts for Multiple Network Adapters in a Token-Ring or Ethernet Network

The following resources are configurable on network adapter cards:

- ◆ IRQ
- ◆ Base I/O port address
- ◆ Base memory address
- ◆ DMA channel
- ◆ Boot PROM
- ◆ MAC address
- ◆ Ring speed (token-ring cards)
- ◆ Connector type

Not all network adapter cards have all of these resources available for configuration. These resource settings on the network adapter card must be different than the settings found on other components used within the computer.

Some network adapter cards use jumper settings to configure these settings, others use software, and others can have this done through the operating system software, such as Windows 95 and Windows NT. The method of configuration is dependent upon the manufacturer.

Implementing a NetBIOS Naming Scheme for All Computers on a Given Network

NetBIOS is an interface that provides NetBIOS-based applications with access to network resources. Every computer on a Windows NT network must have a unique name for it to be accessible through the NetBIOS interface. This unique name is called a computer name or a NetBIOS name.

On a NetBIOS network, every computer must have a unique name. The computer name can be up to 15 characters long. A NetBIOS name can include alphanumeric characters and any of the following special characters:

! @ # $ % ^ & ( ) - _ ' { } . ~

Note that you cannot use a space or an asterisk in a NetBIOS name. Also, NetBIOS names are not case sensitive.

Selecting the Appropriate Hardware and Software Tools to Monitor Trends in the Network

The hardware and software tools described in the next five sections are used to monitor trends in a network.

Protocol Analyzer

This can be a hardware or software tool to analyze the traffic in a network. Protocol analyzers capture packets on a network and display their contents. The software version of this tool supplied by Microsoft is Network Monitor. Network Monitor ships with Windows NT as a scaled-down version that can only capture data between the host computer and those to which the host talks.

Event Viewer

This software tool is found on Windows NT. It reports one of three event types:

◆ **System Events**. Those generated by the operating system.

◆ **Application Events**. Those generated by any application that is programmed to make event calls to the Event Viewer.

◆ **Auditing**. Any auditing being performed on NTFS partitions or by users interacting with the network.

Performance Monitor

Windows NT's Performance Monitor tool lets you monitor important system parameters for the computers on your network in real time. Performance Monitor can keep an eye on a large number of system parameters, providing a graphical or tabular profile of system and network trends. Performance Monitor also can save performance data in a log for later reference. You can use Performance Monitor to track statistical measurements (called *counters*) for any of several hardware or software components (called *objects*).

System Monitor

Windows 95 includes a program called System Monitor that also allows information to be collected on the Windows 95 machine in real time. System Monitor collects information on different categories of items on the system. System Monitor is not as detailed as Windows NT's Performance Monitor.

Simple Network Management Protocol (SNMP)

SNMP is a TCP/IP protocol used to perform management operations on a TCP/IP network. SNMP-enabled devices allow for information to be sent to a management utility (this is called a *trap*). SNMP devices also allow for the setting and extraction of information (this is done by the issuance of a set or get command) found in their Management Information Base (MIB).

TROUBLESHOOTING

The Troubleshooting section of the exam covers many of the topics covered in previous sections. Emphasis of this section is to test your understanding of what can cause problems, and how to fix them.

Identifying Common Errors Associated with Components Required for Communications

The utilities described in the next four sections can be used to diagnose errors associated with components required for communications.

Protocol Analyzers

Protocol analyzers are either hardware or software products used to monitor network traffic, track network performance, and analyze packets. Protocol analyzers can identify bottlenecks, protocol problems, and malfunctioning network components.

Digital Volt Meter (DVM)

Digital volt meters are handheld electronic measuring tools that enable you to check the voltage of network cables. They also can be used to check the resistance of terminators. You can use a DVM to help you find a break or a short in a network cable.

DVMs are usually inexpensive battery-operated devices that have either a digital or needle readout and two metal prongs attached to the DVM by some wires a foot or more in length. By sending a small current through the wires and out through the metal prongs, resistance and voltages of terminators and wires can be measured.

Time-Domain Reflectometers (TDR)

Time-domain reflectometers send sound waves along a cable and look for imperfections that might be caused by a break or a short in the line. A good TDR can detect faults on a cable to within a few feet.

Oscilloscope

An oscilloscope measures fluctuations in signal voltage and can help find faulty or damaged cabling. Oscilloscopes are often more expensive electronic devices that show the signal fluctuations on a monitor.

Several diagnostic software tools provide information on virtually any type of network hardware, as well. A considerable number of diagnostic software packages are available for a variety of prices.

A common software tool distributed with most network cards is a Send/Receive package. This software tool allows two computers with network cards and cables to connect to each other. This tool does not rely on a networked operating system, nor can it be used to send data. It simply sends packets from one computer to the other, establishing that the network cards and underlying transmission media are connected and configured properly.

Diagnosing and Resolving Common Connectivity Problems with Cards, Cables, and Related Hardware

Most network problems occur on the transmission media or with the components that attach devices to the transmission media. All of these components operate at the Physical, DataLink, or Network levels of the OSI model. The components that connect PCs and enable them to communicate are susceptible to many kinds of problems.

Troubleshooting Cables and Connectors

Most network problems occur at the OSI Physical layer, and cabling is one of the most common causes. A cable might have a short or a break, or it might be attached to a faulty connector. Tools such as DVMs and TDRs help search out cabling problems.

Cabling problems can cause three major problems: An individual computer cannot access the network, a group of computers cannot access the network, or none of the computers can access the network.

On networks that are configured in a star topology, an individual cable break between the computer and hub or MSAU causes a failure in communication between

that individual computer and the rest of the network. This type of cable break does not cause problems between all of the other computers on the network.

A cable break in cables connecting multiple hubs causes a break in communications between the computers on one side of the cable break and the computers on the other side of the cable break. In most cases, the communications between computers within the broken segment can continue.

In the case of MSAU, the breakage of a cable connecting MSAUs often causes all computers on the ring to fail because the ring is not complete. A break in the cable on a bus topology also causes all computers on the network segment to be unable to communicate with any other computers on the network.

Try the following checks when troubleshooting network cabling problems:

◆ With 10BASE-T, make sure the cable used has the correct number of twists to meet the data-grade specifications.

◆ Look for electrical interference, which can be caused by tying the network cable together with monitor and power cords. Fluorescent lights, electric motors, and other electrical devices can cause interference if they are located too close to cables. These problems often can be alleviated by placing the cable away from devices that generate electromagnetic interference or by upgrading the cable to one that has better shielding.

◆ Make sure that connectors are pinned properly and crimped tightly.

◆ If excess shielding on coaxial cable is exposed, make sure it doesn't ground out the connector.

◆ Ensure that coaxial cables are not coiled tightly together. This can generate a magnetic field around the cable, causing electromagnetic interference.

◆ On coaxial Ethernet LANs, look for missing terminators or terminators with improper resistance ratings.

◆ Watch out for malfunctioning transceivers, concentrators, or T-connectors. All of these components can be checked by replacing the suspect devices.

◆ Test the continuity of the cable by using the various physical testing devices discussed in the previous section or by using a software-based cable testing utility.

◆ Make sure that all the component cables in a segment are connected. A user who moves his client and removes the T-connector incorrectly can cause a broken segment.

◆ Examine cable connectors for bent or broken pins.

◆ On token-ring networks, inspect the attachment of patch cables and adapter cables. Remember, patch cables connect MSAUs, and adapter cables connect the network adapter to the MSAU.

One advantage of a token-ring network is its built-in capability to monitor itself. token-ring networks provide electronic troubleshooting and, when possible, actually make repairs. When the token-ring network can't make its own repairs, a process called *beaconing* narrows down the portion of the ring in which the problem is most likely to exist.

Troubleshooting Network Adapter Cards

Network problems often result from malfunctioning network adapter cards. The process of troubleshooting the network adapter works like any other kind of troubleshooting process: Start with the simple. The following list details some aspects you can check if you think your network adapter card might be malfunctioning:

◆ Make sure the cable is properly connected to the card.

◆ Confirm that you have the correct network adapter card driver and that the driver is installed properly. Be sure the card is properly bound to the appropriate transport protocol.

◆ Make sure the network adapter card and the network adapter card driver are compatible with your operating system. If you use Windows NT, consult the Windows NT hardware compatibility list. If you use Windows 95 or another operating system, rely on the adapter card vendor specifications.

◆ Test for resource conflicts. Make sure another device isn't attempting to use the same resources. If you think a resource conflict might be the problem, but you can't pinpoint the conflict using Windows NT Diagnostics, Windows 95's Device Manager, or some other diagnostic program, try removing all the cards except the network adapter and then replacing the cards one by one. Check the network with each addition to determine which device is causing the conflict.

◆ Run the network adapter card's diagnostic software. This will often indicate which resource on the network card is failing.

◆ Examine the jumper and DIP switch settings on the card. Make sure the resource settings are consistent with the settings configured through the operating system.

◆ Make sure the card is inserted properly in the slot. Reseat if necessary.

◆ If necessary, remove the card and clean the connector fingers (don't use an eraser because it leaves grit on the card).

◆ Replace the card with one that you know works. If the connection works with a different card, you know the card is the problem.

Token-ring network adapters with failure rates that exceed a preset tolerance level might actually remove themselves from the network. Try replacing the card. Some token-ring networks also can experience problems if a token-ring card set at a ring speed of 16 Mbps is inserted into a ring using a 4 Mbps ring speed, and vice versa.

Troubleshooting Hubs and MSAUs

If you experience problems with a hub-based LAN, such as a 10BASE-T network, you often can isolate the problem by disconnecting the attached workstations one at a time. If removing one of the workstations eliminates the problem, the trouble may be caused by that workstation or its associated cable length. If removing each of the workstations doesn't solve the problem, the fault may lie with the hub. Check the easy components first, such as ports, switches, and connectors, and then use a different hub (if you have it) to see if the problem persists. If your hub doesn't work properly, call the manufacturer.

If you're troubleshooting a token-ring network, make sure the cables are connected properly to the MSAUs, with ring-out ports connecting to the ring-in ports throughout the ring. If you suspect the MSAU, isolate it by changing the ring-in and ring-out cables to bypass the MSAU. If the ring is now functional again, consider replacing the MSAU. In addition, you might find that if your network has MSAUs from more than one manufacturer, they are not wholly compatible. Impedance and other electrical characteristics can show slight differences between manufacturers, causing intermittent network problems. Some MSAUs (other than the 8228) are active and require a power supply. These MSAUs fail if they have a blown fuse or a bad power source. Your problem also might result from a misconfigured MSAU port. MSAU ports using the hermaphrodite connector need to be reinitialized with the setup tool. Removing drop cables and reinitializing each

MSAU port is a quick fix that is useful on relatively small token-ring networks.

Isolating problems with patch cables, adapter cables, and MSAUs is easier to do if you have a current log of your network's physical design. After you narrow down the problem, you can isolate potential problem areas from the rest of the network and then use a cable tester to find the actual problem.

Troubleshooting Modems

A modem presents all the potential problems you find with any other device. You must make sure that the modem is properly installed, that the driver is properly installed, and that the resource settings do not conflict with other devices. Modems also pose some unique problems because they must connect directly to the phone system, they operate using analog communications, and they must make a point-to-point connection with a remote machine.

The online help files for both Windows NT and Windows 95 include a topic called the Modem Troubleshooter. The Modem Troubleshooter leads you to possible solutions for a modem problem by asking questions about the symptoms. As you answer the questions (by clicking the gray box beside your answer), the Modem Troubleshooter zeroes in on more specific questions until (ideally) it leads you to a solution.

Some common modem problems are as follows:

◆ **Dialing problems**. The dialing feature is improperly configured. For instance, the modem isn't dialing 9 to bypass your office switchboard, or it is dialing 9 when you're away from your office. The computer also could be dialing an area code or an international code when it shouldn't. Check the dialing properties for the connection.

◆ **Connection problems**. You cannot connect to another modem. Your modem and the other modem might be operating at different speeds.

Verify that the maximum speed setting for your modem is the highest speed that both your modem and the other modem can use. Also make sure the Data Bits, Parity, and Stop Bits settings are consistent with the remote computer.

◆ **Digital phone systems**. You cannot plug a modem into a telephone line designed for use with digital phone systems. These digital phone systems are commonplace in most office environments.

◆ **Protocol problems**. The communicating devices are using incompatible line protocols. Verify that the devices are configured for the same or compatible protocols. If one computer initiates a connection using PPP, the other computer must be capable of using PPP.

Repeaters, Bridges, and Routers

Issues dealing with repeaters, bridges, and routers are often more technically advanced than those covered in a book such as Networking Essentials. Companies such as Cisco, Bay Networks, and 3Com have their own dedicated books and courses on dealing with the installation, configuration, and troubleshooting of repeaters, bridges, and routers. In general, there are some basic troubleshooting steps you can do when working with these three devices.

Repeaters are responsible for regenerating a signal sent down the transmission media. The typical problem with repeaters is that they do not work—that is, the signal is not being regenerated. If this is the case, the signal being sent to devices on the other side of the repeater from the sending device will not receive the signal.

Problems with bridges are almost identical to that of a repeater. The signal being sent to devices on the other side of the bridge from the sending device will be received. Other issues with bridges are that the table of

which devices are on which interface of the bridge can get corrupt. This can lead from one to all machines not receiving packets on the network. Diagnostic utilities provided by the bridge's manufacturer can resolve this type of problem.

Problems with routers can be complex, and troubleshooting them often involves a high level of understanding of the different protocols in use on the network, as well as the software and commands used to program a router. There are generally two types of router problems.

The first router problem that is commonly found is that packets are just not being passed through because the router is 'dead' or simply not functioning. The second common problem with routers is that the routing tables within the routers are corrupted or incorrectly programmed. This problem either leads to computers on different networks being unable to communicate with each other or to the fact that certain protocols simply do not work.

Resolve Broadcast Storms

A *broadcast storm* is a sudden flood of broadcast messages that clogs the transmission medium, approaching 100 percent of the bandwidth. Broadcast storms cause performance to decline and, in the worst case, computers cannot even access the network. The cause of a broadcast storm is often a malfunctioning network adapter, but a broadcast storm also can be caused when a device on the network attempts to contact another device that either doesn't exist or for some reason doesn't respond to the broadcast.

If the broadcast messages are viable, a network-monitoring or protocol-analysis tool often can determine the source of the storm. If the broadcast storm is caused by a malfunctioning adapter throwing illegible packets onto the line, and a protocol analyzer can't find the source, try to isolate the offending PC by removing computers from the network one at a time until the line returns to normal.

Identify and Resolve Network Performance Problems

If your network runs slower than it used to run (or slower than it ought to run), the problem might be that the present network traffic exceeds the level at which the network can operate efficiently. Some possible causes for increased traffic are new hardware (such as a new workstation) or new software (such as a network computer game or some other network application). A generator or another mechanical device operating near the network could cause a degradation of network performance. In addition, a malfunctioning network device could act as a bottleneck. Ask yourself what has changed since the last time the network operated efficiently, and begin there with your troubleshooting efforts.

A performance monitoring tool, such as Windows NT's Performance Monitor or Network Monitor, can help you look for bottlenecks that are adversely affecting your network. For instance, the increased traffic could be the result of increased usage. If usage exceeds the capacity of the network, you might want to consider expanding or redesigning your network. You also might want to divide the network into smaller segments by using a router or a bridge to reduce network traffic. A protocol analyzer can help you measure and monitor the traffic at various points on your network.

Study and Exam Prep Tips

This chapter provides you with some general guidelines for preparing for the exam. It is organized into three sections. The first section addresses your pre-exam preparation activities, covering general study tips. This is followed by an extended look at the Microsoft Certification exams, including a number of specific tips that apply to the Microsoft exam formats. Finally, it addresses changes in Microsoft's testing policies and how they might affect you.

To better understand the nature of preparation for the test, it is important to understand learning as a process. You probably are aware of how you best learn new material. Maybe outlining works best for you, or maybe you are a visual learner who needs to "see" things. Whatever your learning style, test preparation takes time. While it is obvious that you can't start studying for these exams the night before you take them, it is very important to understand that learning is a developmental process. Understanding the process helps you focus on what you know and what you have yet to learn.

Thinking about how you learn should help you recognize that learning takes place when we are able to match new information to old. You have some previous experience with computers and networking, and now you are preparing for this certification exam. Using this book, software, and supplementary materials will not just add incrementally to what you know. As you study, you actually change the organization of your knowledge to integrate this new information into your existing knowledge base. This will lead you to a more comprehensive understanding of the tasks and concepts outlined in the objectives and related to computing in general. Again, this happens as an iterative process rather than a singular event. Keep this model of learning in mind as you prepare for the exam, and you will make better decisions on what to study and how much to study.

STUDY TIPS

There are many ways to approach studying, just as there are many different types of material to study. However, the tips that follow should work well for the type of material covered on the certification exams.

Study Strategies

Although individuals vary in the ways they learn information, some basic principles of learning apply to everyone. You should adopt some study strategies that take advantage of these principles. One of these principles is that learning can be broken into various depths. *Recognition* (of terms, for example) exemplifies a surface level of learning: You rely on a prompt of some sort to elicit recall. *Comprehension or understanding* (of the concepts behind the terms, for instance) represents a deeper level of learning. The ability to analyze a concept and apply your understanding of it in a new way or to address a unique setting represents further depth of learning.

Your learning strategy should enable you to know the material a level or two deeper than mere recognition. This will help you to do well on the exam(s). You will know the material so thoroughly that you can easily handle the recognition-level types of questions used in multiple-choice testing. You will also be able to apply your knowledge to solve novel problems.

Macro and Micro Study Strategies

One strategy that can lead to this deeper learning includes preparing an outline that covers all the objectives and subobjectives for the particular exam you are working on. You should then delve a bit further into the material and include a level or two of detail beyond the stated objectives and subobjectives for the exam. Finally, flesh out the outline by coming up with a statement of definition or a summary for each point in the outline.

This outline provides two approaches to studying. First, you can study the outline by focusing on the organization of the material. Work your way through the points and subpoints of your outline with the goal of learning how they relate to one another. For example, be sure you understand how each of the main objective areas is similar to and different from one another. Then do the same thing with the subobjectives. Also, be sure you know which subobjectives pertain to each objective area and how they relate to one another.

Next, you can work through the outline and focus on learning the details. Memorize and understand terms and their definitions, facts, rules and strategies, advantages and disadvantages, and so on. In this pass through the outline, attempt to learn detail as opposed to the big picture (the organizational information that you worked on in the first pass through the outline).

Research shows that attempting to assimilate both types of information at the same time seems to interfere with the overall learning process. Separate your studying into these two approaches, and you will perform better on the exam than if you attempt to study the material in a more conventional manner.

Active Study Strategies

In addition, the process of writing down and defining the objectives, subobjectives, terms, facts, and definitions promotes a more active learning strategy than merely reading the material does. In human information processing terms, writing forces you to engage in more active encoding of the information. Simply reading over it constitutes passive processing.

Next, determine whether you can apply the information you have learned by attempting to create examples and scenarios of your own. Think about how or where you could apply the concepts you are learning. Again, write down this information to process the facts and concepts in a more active fashion.

The hands-on nature of the Step by Step tutorials and the exercises at the end of the chapters provide further active learning opportunities that will reinforce concepts.

Common Sense Strategies

Finally, you should also follow common sense practices in studying: Study when you are alert, reduce or eliminate distractions, take breaks when you become fatigued, and so on.

Pre-Testing Yourself

Pre-testing allows you to assess how well you are learning. One of the most important aspects of learning is what has been called "meta-learning." Meta-learning has to do with realizing when you know something well or when you need to study some more. In other words, you recognize how well or how poorly you have learned the material you are studying. For most people, this can be difficult to assess objectively on their own. Therefore, practice tests are useful because they reveal more objectively what you have and have not learned. You should use this information to guide review and further studying. Developmental learning takes place as you cycle through studying, assessing how well you have learned, reviewing, and assessing again, until you feel you are ready to take the exam.

You may have noticed the practice exam included in this book. Use it as part of this process. In addition to the Practice Exam, the Top Score software on the CD-ROM also provides a variety of ways to test yourself before you take the actual exam. By using the Top Score Practice Exams, you can take an entire practice test. By using the Top Score Study Cards, you can take an entire practice exam or you can focus on a particular objective area, such as Planning, Troubleshooting, or Monitoring and Optimization. By using the Top Score Flash Cards, you can test your knowledge at a level beyond that of recognition; you must come up with the answers in your own words. The Flash Cards also enable you to test your knowledge of particular objective areas.

You should set a goal for your pre-testing. A reasonable goal would be to score consistently in the 90-percent range (or better). See Appendix D, "Using the Top Score Software," for more detailed explanation of the test engine.

Exam Prep Tips

Having mastered the subject matter, the final preparatory step is to understand how the exam will be presented. Make no mistake about it, a Microsoft Certified Professional (MCP) exam will challenge both your knowledge and your test-taking skills! This section starts with the basics of exam design, reviews a new type of exam format, and concludes with hints that are targeted to each of the exam formats.

The MCP Exam

Every MCP exam is released in one of two basic formats. What's being called *exam format* here is really little more than a combination of the overall exam structure and the presentation method for exam questions.

Each exam format utilizes the same types of questions. These types or styles of questions include multiple-rating (or scenario-based) questions, traditional multiple-choice questions, and simulation-based questions. It's important to understand the types of questions you will be asked and the actions required to properly answer them.

Understanding the exam formats is essential to good preparation because the format determines the number of questions presented, the difficulty of those questions, and the amount of time allowed to complete the exam.

Exam Format

There are two basic formats for the MCP exams: the traditional fixed-form exam and the adaptive form. As its name implies, the fixed-form exam presents a fixed set of questions during the exam session. The adaptive format, however, uses only a subset of questions drawn from a larger pool during any given exam session.

Fixed-Form

A fixed-form, computerized exam is based on a fixed set of exam questions. The individual questions are presented in random order during a test session. If you take the same exam more than once, you won't necessarily see the exact same questions. This is because two or three final forms are typically assembled for every fixed-form exam Microsoft releases. These are usually labeled Forms A, B, and C.

The final forms of a fixed-form exam are identical in terms of content coverage, number of questions, and allotted time, but the questions themselves are different. You may have noticed, however, that some of the same questions appear on, or rather are shared across, different final forms. When questions are shared across multiple final forms of an exam, the percentage of sharing is generally small. Many final forms share no questions, but some older exams may have ten to fifteen percent duplication of exam questions on the final exam forms.

Fixed-form exams also have a fixed time limit in which you must complete the exam. The Top Score software on the CD-ROM that accompanies this book provides fixed-form exams.

Finally, the score you achieve on a fixed-form exam (which is always reported for MCP exams on a scale of 0 to 1,000) is based on the number of questions you answer correctly. The exam passing score is the same for all final forms of a given fixed-form exam.

The typical format for the fixed-form exam is this:

◆ 50–60 questions

◆ 75–90 minute testing time

◆ Question review is allowed, including the opportunity to change your answers

Adaptive Form

An adaptive form exam has the same appearance as a fixed-form exam, but it differs in both how questions are selected for presentation and how many questions actually are presented. Although the statistics of adaptive testing are fairly complex, the process is concerned with determining your level of skill or ability with the exam subject matter. This ability assessment begins with the presentation of questions of varying levels of difficulty and ascertains at what difficulty level you can reliably answer them. Finally, the ability assessment determines if that ability level is above or below the level required to pass that exam.

Examinees at different levels of ability will then see quite different sets of questions. Examinees who demonstrate little expertise with the subject matter will continue to be presented with relatively easy questions. Examinees who demonstrate a high level of expertise will be presented progressively more-difficult questions. Both individuals may answer the same number of questions correctly, but because the higher-expertise examinee can correctly answer more-difficult questions, he or she will receive a higher score and is more likely to pass the exam.

The typical design for the adaptive form exam is this:

◆ 20–25 questions

◆ 90 minute testing time (although this is likely to be reduced to 45–60 minutes in the near future)

◆ Question review is not allowed, providing no opportunity to change your answers

The Adaptive Exam Process

Your first adaptive exam will be unlike any other testing experience you have had. In fact, many examinees have difficulty accepting the adaptive testing process because they feel they were not provided the opportunity to adequately demonstrate their full expertise.

You can take consolation in the fact that adaptive exams are painstakingly put together after months of data gathering and analysis and are just as valid as a fixed-form exam. The rigor introduced through the adaptive testing methodology means that there is nothing arbitrary about what you'll see! It is also a more efficient means of testing that requires less time to conduct and complete.

As you can see from Figure 1, a number of statistical measures drive the adaptive examination process. The one that's most immediately relevant to you is the ability estimate. Accompanying this test statistic are the standard error of measurement, the item characteristic curve, and the test information curve.

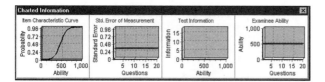

FIGURE 1
Microsoft's adaptive testing demonstration program.

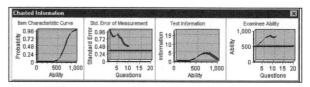

FIGURE 2
The changing statistics in an adaptive exam.

The standard error, which is the key factor in determining when an adaptive exam will terminate, reflects the degree of error in the exam ability estimate. The item characteristic curve reflects the probability of a correct response relative to examinee ability. Finally, the test information statistic provides a measure of the information contained in the set of questions the examinee has answered, again relative to the ability level of the individual examinee.

When you begin an adaptive exam, the standard error has already been assigned a target value below which it must drop for the exam to conclude. This target value reflects a particular level of statistical confidence in the process. The examinee ability is initially set to the mean possible exam score, which is 500 for MCP exams.

As the adaptive exam progresses, questions of varying difficulty are presented. Based on your pattern of responses to those questions, the ability estimate is recalculated. Simultaneously, the standard error estimate is refined from its first estimated value of one toward the target value. When the standard error reaches its target value, the exam terminates. Thus, the more consistently you answer questions of the same degree of difficulty, the more quickly the standard error estimate drops and the fewer questions you will end up seeing during the exam session. This situation is depicted in Figure 2.

As you might suspect, one good piece of advice for taking an adaptive exam is to treat every exam question as if it is the most important. The adaptive scoring algorithm is attempting to discover a pattern of responses

that reflects some level of proficiency with the subject matter. Incorrect responses almost guarantee that additional questions must be answered (unless, of course, you get every question wrong). This is because the scoring algorithm must adjust to information that is not consistent with the emerging pattern.

New Question Types

A variety of question types can appear on MCP exams. Examples of multiple-choice questions and scenario-based questions appear throughout this book and the Top Score software. Simulation-based questions are new to the MCP exam series.

Simulation Questions

Simulation-based questions reproduce the look and feel of key Microsoft product features for the purpose of testing. The simulation software used in MCP exams has been designed to look and act, as much as possible, just like the actual product. Consequently, answering simulation questions in an MCP exam entails completing one or more tasks just as if you were using the product itself.

The format of a typical Microsoft simulation question is straightforward. It presents a brief scenario or problem statement along with one or more tasks that must be completed to solve the problem. The next section provides an example of a simulation question for MCP exams.

A Typical Simulation Question

It sounds obvious, but the first step when you encounter a simulation is to carefully read the question (see Figure 3). Do not go straight to the simulation application! Assess the problem being presented and identify the conditions that make up the problem scenario. Note the tasks that must be performed or outcomes that must be achieved to answer the question, and then review any instructions on how to proceed.

The next step is to launch the simulator by using the button provided. After clicking the Show Simulation button, you will see a feature of the product, like the dialog box shown in Figure 4. The simulation application will partially cover the question text on many test center machines. Feel free to reposition the simulation or to move between the question text screen and the simulation using hot-keys and point-and-click navigation or even by clicking the simulation launch button again.

It is important to understand that your answer to the simulation question is not recorded until you move on to the next exam question. This gives you the added capability to close and reopen the simulation application (using the launch button) on the same question without losing any partial answer you may have made.

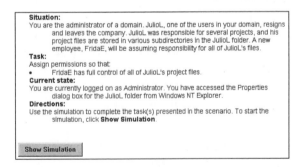

Situation:
You are the administrator of a domain. JulioL, one of the users in your domain, resigns and leaves the company. JulioL was responsible for several projects, and his project files are stored in various subdirectories in the JulioL folder. A new employee, FridaE, will be assuming responsibility for all of JulioL's files.
Task:
Assign permissions so that:
• FridaE has full control of all of JulioL's project files.
Current state:
You are currently logged on as Administrator. You have accessed the Properties dialog box for the JulioL folder from Windows NT Explorer.
Directions:
Use the simulation to complete the task(s) presented in the scenario. To start the simulation, click **Show Simulation**.

FIGURE 3
Typical MCP exam simulation question with directions.

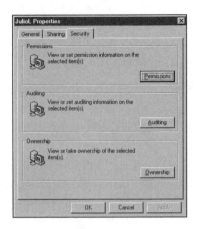

FIGURE 4
Launching the simulation application.

The third step is to use the simulator as you would the actual product to solve the problem or perform the defined tasks. Again, the simulation software is designed to function, within reason, just as the product does. But don't expect the simulation to reproduce product behavior perfectly. Most importantly, do not allow yourself to become flustered if the simulation does not look or act exactly like the product. Figure 5 shows the solution to the sample simulation problem.

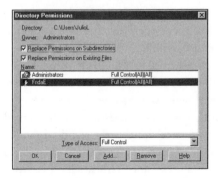

FIGURE 5
The solution to the simulation example.

There are two final points that will help you tackle simulation questions. First, respond only to what is being asked in the question. Do not solve problems that you are not asked to solve. Second, accept what is being asked of you. You may not entirely agree with conditions in the problem statement, the quality of the desired solution, or sufficiency of defined tasks to adequately solve the problem. Always remember that you are being tested on your ability to solve the problem as it has been presented.

The solution to the simulation problem shown in Figure 5 perfectly illustrates both of these points. As you'll recall from the question scenario (refer to Figure 3), you were asked to assign appropriate permissions to a new user called FridaE. You were not instructed to make any other changes in permissions. Thus, if you had modified or removed Administrator permissions, this item would have been scored wrong on an MCP exam.

Putting It All Together

Given all these different pieces of information, the task is now to assemble a set of tips that will help you successfully tackle the different types of MCP exams.

More Pre-Exam Preparation Tips

Generic exam preparation advice is always useful. Follow these general guidelines:

◆ Become familiar with the product. Hands-on experience is one of the keys to success on any MCP exam. Review the exercises and the Step by Step tutorials in the book.

◆ Review the current exam preparation guide on the Microsoft MCP Web site. The documentation Microsoft makes publicly available over the Web identifies the skills every exam is intended to test.

◆ Memorize foundational technical detail as appropriate. But remember, MCP exams are generally heavy on problem solving and application of knowledge more than they are on questions that require only rote memorization.

◆ Take any of the available practice tests. We recommend the one included in this book and those you can create using the Top Score software on the CD-ROM. While these are fixed-format exams, they provide preparation that is also valuable for taking an adaptive exam. Because of the nature of adaptive testing, it is not possible for these practice exams to be offered in the adaptive format. However, fixed-format exams provide the same types of questions as adaptive exams and are the most effective way to prepare for either type of exam. As a supplement to the material included with this book, try the free practice tests available on the Microsoft MCP Web site.

◆ Look on the Microsoft MCP Web site for samples and demonstration items. These tend to be particularly valuable for one significant reason: They allow you to become familiar with any new testing technologies before you encounter them on an MCP exam.

During the Exam Session

Similarly, the generic exam-taking advice you've heard for years applies when taking an MCP exam:

◆ Take a deep breath and try to relax when you first sit down for your exam. It is very important to control the pressure you may (naturally) feel when taking exams.

◆ You will be provided scratch paper. Take a moment to write down any factual information and technical detail that you committed to short-term memory.

◆ Carefully read all information and instruction screens. These displays have been put together to give you information relevant to the exam you are taking.

◆ Accept the Non-Disclosure Agreement and pre-liminary survey as part of the examination process. Complete them accurately and quickly move on.

◆ Read the exam questions carefully. Reread each question to identify all relevant detail.

◆ Tackle the questions in the order they are presented. Skipping around won't build your confidence; the clock is always counting down.

◆ Don't rush, but at the same time, don't linger on difficult questions. The questions vary in degree of difficulty. Don't let yourself be flustered by a particularly difficult or verbose question.

Fixed-Form Exams

Building from this basic preparation and test-taking advice, you also need to consider the challenges presented by the different exam designs. Because a fixed-form exam is composed of a fixed, finite set of questions, add these tips to your strategy for taking a fixed-form exam:

◆ Note the time allotted and the number of questions appearing on the exam you are taking. Make a rough calculation of how many minutes you can spend on each question, and use that number to pace yourself through the exam.

◆ Take advantage of the fact that you can return to and review skipped or previously answered questions. Mark the questions you can't answer confidently, noting the relative difficulty of each question on the scratch paper provided. When you reach the end of the exam, return to the more difficult questions.

◆ If there is session time remaining when you have completed all questions (and you aren't too fatigued!), review your answers. Pay particular attention to questions that seem to have a lot of detail or that required graphics.

◆ As for changing your answers, the rule of thumb here is *don't*! If you read the question carefully and completely and you felt like you knew the right answer, you probably did. Don't second-guess yourself. If, as you check your answers, one stands out as clearly incorrect, however, of course you should change it. But if you are at all unsure, go with your first impression.

Adaptive Exams

If you are planning to take an adaptive exam, keep these additional tips in mind:

◆ Read and answer every question with great care. When reading a question, identify every relevant detail, requirement, or task that must be performed and double-check your answer to be sure you have addressed every one of them.

◆ If you cannot answer a question, use the process of elimination to reduce the set of potential answers, and then take your best guess. Stupid mistakes invariably mean additional questions will be presented.

◆ Forget about reviewing questions and changing your answers. Once you leave a question, whether you've answered it or not, you cannot return to it. Do not skip any questions either. If you do, that question is counted as incorrect!

Simulation Questions

You may encounter simulation questions on either the fixed-form or adaptive form exam. If you do, keep these tips in mind:

◆ Avoid changing any simulation settings that don't pertain directly to the problem solution. Solve the problem you are being asked to solve and nothing more.

◆ Assume default settings when related information has not been provided. If something has not been mentioned or defined, it is a non-critical detail that does not factor in to the correct solution.

◆ Be sure your entries are syntactically correct, paying particular attention to your spelling. Enter relevant information just as the product would require it.

◆ Close all simulation application windows after you complete the simulation tasks. The testing system software is designed to trap errors that could result when using the simulation application, but trust yourself over the testing software.

◆ If simulations are part of a fixed-form exam, you can return to skipped or previously answered questions and change your answer. However, if you choose to change your answer to a simulation question, or if you even attempt to review the settings you've made in the simulation application, your previous response to that simulation question will be deleted. If simulations are part of an adaptive exam, you cannot return to previous questions.

FINAL CONSIDERATIONS

Finally, a number of changes in the MCP program will impact how frequently you can repeat an exam and what you will see when you do.

◆ Microsoft has instituted a new exam retake policy. This new rule is "two and two, then one and

two." That is, you can attempt any exam twice with no restrictions on the time between attempts. But after the second attempt, you must wait two weeks before you can attempt that exam again. After that, you will be required to wait two weeks between subsequent attempts. Plan to pass the exam in two attempts; if that's not possible, increase your time horizon for receiving an MCP credential.

◆ New questions are being seeded into the MCP exams. After performance data has been gathered on new questions, they will replace older questions on all exam forms. This means that the questions appearing on exams will change regularly.

◆ Many of the current MCP exams will be republished in adaptive format in the coming months. Prepare yourself for this significant change in testing format, as it is entirely likely that this will become the new preferred MCP exam format.

These changes mean that the brute-force strategies for passing MCP exams may soon completely lose their viability. So if you don't pass an exam on the first or second attempt, it is entirely possible that the exam will change significantly in form. It could be updated from fixed-form to adaptive form, or it might have a different set of questions or question types.

The intention of Microsoft is clearly not to make the exams more difficult by introducing unwanted change. Their intent is to create and maintain valid measures of the technical skills and knowledge associated with the different MCP credentials. Preparing for an MCP exam has always involved not only studying the subject matter, but also planning for the testing experience itself. With these changes, this is now more true than ever.

Practice Exam

This element consists of 55 questions that are representative of what you should expect on the actual exam. You will find that the questions here are all multiple choice, however, and not simulations, because of the limitations of paper testing. Still, this exam should help you determine how prepared you are for the real exam, and provide a good base for what you will still need to review.

As you take this exam, treat it as you would the real exam: time yourself (about 90 minutes), and answer each question carefully, marking the ones you wish to go back and double check. You will find the answers and their explanations at the end of the exam.

Once you have taken this exam, remember to load the CD-ROM, and check out New Riders' exclusive Top Score test engine, which is one of the best on the market. (See appendixes C and D for more information).

1. Under which platform can Windows NT server be installed? Select all that apply.

   a. Intel

   b. MIPS RISC

   c. Apple Macintosh

   d. Power PC

   e. UNIX

2. Windows NT server can support many types of applications. Which applications are supported with a basic installation of NT server 4.0? Select all that apply.

   a. MS-DOS applications that access the hardware directly

   b. UNIX POSIX-compliant software

   c. 16-bit and 32-bit applications

   d. OS/2 Warp with Presentation Manager

   e. NT specifically compiled software

3. NT can be installed in several LAN topologies. Which of the following will be acceptable under NT?

   a. Ethernet

   b. Coax

   c. FDDI

   d. RAS

   e. TokenRing

4. You are installing a new network and wish to use 100 Mbps fast Ethernet. Which of the following cable types can be used? Select all that apply.

   a. UTP category 3

   b. Coax

   c. TCP category 5

   d. STP category 5

   e. Fiber

5. What file type must be used to install NT on a RISC-based computer? Select the best answer.

   a. NTFS for everything

   b. FAT for everything

   c. FAT for the System partition and NTFS for the boot partition

d. NTFS for the system partition and FAT for the boot partition

e. Either FAT or NTFS for the system partition and the boot partition.

6. Which of the following files are part of the system partition for NT 4.0? Select all that apply.

a. NTdetect.com

b. NTstart.com

c. Boot.ini

d. NToskrnl

e. NTLDR

7. When a new partition is added to the system, which files should be verified before the system is restarted?

a. NTDETECT.com

b. Boot.ini

c. Autoexec.bat

d. Config.sys

e. NTLDR

8. What needs to be considered when a second network card is added to a computer? Select all that apply.

a. Each card must have its own protocol.

b. Each card must have its own drivers.

c. Each card must have its own resources.

d. Both cards must be installed at the same time.

e. Both cards must be setup in the network application of the control panel.

9. On a busy network, what can you do to increase overall performance? Select the best and most practical answer.

a. Remove all the network cards.

b. Disable any bindings that are not needed.

c. Remove services that are not needed.

d. Shut down any computer that is not in use.

e. Configure the routers to not propagate broadcasts.

10. Which of the following computers can be a member of a domain? Select all that apply.

a. An NT server acting as a BDC

b. An NT server acting as a Stand-alone server

c. An NT workstation

d. Windows 95 computer

e. An MS-DOS system

11. What type of system is responsible for directory synchronization?

a. A BDC

b. An NT server running the directory synchronization service

c. A PDC

d. A BDC setup to handle replication

e. A NT server

12. Which of the following statements best describes the proper way of assigning rights and permissions to users?

a. Users are assigned rights directly, but they get their permissions from Local groups.

b. Users are assigned permissions directly but they get their user rights from Local groups.

c. Users are placed in Local groups which are given user rights and permissions.

d. Users are placed in Global groups which are placed into local groups that are given rights and permissions.

e. Users are placed into local groups which are placed into global groups which are given rights and permissions.

13. An NT member server cannot change Domains. True or False?

a. True

b. False

14. How can an NT workstation join a domain? Select all that apply.

a. The administrator can add the computer name of the workstation to the domain using the User Manager for Domains.

b. The administrator can add the computer name of the workstation to the domain using the Server Manager.

c. The administrator can change the domain name of the Domain on the Identification tab of the Network application and can provide an administrative account name and password instead.

d. The user can change the name of the Domain on the Identification tab of the Network application and can provide his own account name and password.

e. The administrator can change the domain name during login.

15. What is the purpose of placing a user's home directory in a network share if the user logs on at a Windows 95 and NT Workstation? Select all that apply.

a. Central backup.

b. A common file system -Windows 95 can read files on NTFS if they are on the network, but not locally.

c. Windows 95 clients store their roaming profiles in the home directory.

d. NT clients store their roaming profiles in the home directory.

e. NT clients must have their home directories on the server.

16. An administrator needs to control passwords. Several users have been changing their passwords back to the originals each time they are forced to change. You configure NT to remember a history of five passwords but they simply change the password five times in a row then back to the original. What can you do to force them to have a different password for at least six months?

a. Do not allow the users to change their passwords.

b. Set a minimum password length set of 6 months.

c. Set the minimum password history to 6 months.

d. Set the minimum password age to 6 months.

e. Set the minimum password age to 1 month.

17. Each user, group and NT computer object has a unique SID. When an object is deleted, what happens to the object's rights and permissions?

    a. The rights and permissions are removed and cannot be reactivated.

    b. The ACL of objects will show an unknown object under the deleted object's permissions.

    c. The ACL of rights will be cleaned up automatically.

    d. The rights and permissions are reinstated when the original object is re-created.

    e. The rights and permissions are displayed as deleted in the ACLs.

18. NT provides a series of user rights assigned to built-in groups, and those rights cannot be modified. True or False?

    a. True

    b. False

19. What is the difference between the Winnt and Winnt32 programs?

    a. Winnt is for an upgrade only; Winnt32 is for a full installation.

    b. Winnt is an 8-bit application that runs on all systems; Winnt32 can be used only on NT.

    c. Winnt is a 16-bit application that runs on MS-DOS and NT systems; Winnt32 is used to upgrade from Windows 95.

    d. Winnt is for MS-DOS and Windows95 upgrades; Winnt32 is for a full installation.

    e. Winnt is for MS-DOS and Windows95; Winnt32 is for NT upgrades.

20. What is the difference between the system partition and the boot partition? Select all that apply.

    a. There is no difference when NT is installed on drive C:.

    b. The boot partition contains the boot.ini file and the system partition contains the system and system32 folders.

    c. The boot partition contains the system and system32 folders, and the system partition contains the boot.ini file.

    d. The terms "system" and "boot partitions" are interchangeable in all cases.

    e. The system partition contains all the files needed to start up NT, and the boot partition is a hidden partition that presents the user with a list of operating systems on the computer.

21. A DOS client can connect to an NT share. Which of the following commands will successfully connect the client? Select all that apply.

    a. `Net Connect k: \\cal_down\download`.

    b. `Net Use k: //cal_down\download`.

    c. `Net Use k: \\cal_down\download`.

    d. `Net Connect k: //cal_down\download`.

    e. `Net Use k: \\cal_down\downloading`.

22. Which of the following cannot be assigned as a permission on a share under NT 4.0? Select all that apply.

    a. Read.

    b. Write.

    c. No Access.

    d. Change.

    e. Take Ownership.

23. Which of the following statements about share permissions and NTFS permissions is true?

   a. Share permissions always override NTFS permissions.

   b. NTFS permissions always override Share permissions.

   c. Share permissions and NTFS permissions are cumulative.

   d. The combined effective permissions are the most restrictive between Share and NTFS.

   e. Share permissions exist on Servers whereas NTFS local permissions exist only on workstations.

24. A user tries to share a folder on her NT workstation but fails. What could be the problem?

   a. The user must turn on File and Print sharing.

   b. The user must be a member of Domain Admins in order to share a folder.

   c. The user must be a member of the Server Operators on her workstation.

   d. The share user right must be given to the user account in order for her to access the share menus.

   e. The user must be a member of the local administrators or power user group.

25. If a directory or file has a No Access permission for a group, only users in that group who are administrators have access. True or False?

   a. True

   b. False

26. What component(s) of an Access Token does a user obtain during logon? Select all that apply.

   a. The user's name and SID

   b. The user's password (encrypted for safety)

   c. The group SID to which the user belongs

   d. The user's rights

   e. A list of resources the user can access.

27. What is the difference between a printer and a print device?

   a. The printer is the physical hardware; the printing device is the software component.

   b. The printing device is the physical hardware and the printer is the software components.

   c. Nothing; the two are interchangeable.

28. Which network protocol is used to connect directly to an HP jet direct network printer? Select all that apply.

   a. TCP/IP

   b. HP direct

   c. DLC

   d. NetBeui

   e. NWLink

29. Several users in your network connect to three different shared printers. Users complain they never know which printer is free. How can you alleviate this?

   a. Install the printer monitor tool on all users' systems so they can monitor all printers and select the printer they want to use.

   b. Set up the printers on three separate systems and then assign one third of the users permissions to user on each one.

c. Set up the printers in a printer pool and distribute the print devices all over the network.

d. Set up the printers in a printer pool and locate the print devices in close proximity to each other.

e. Have each user open the print queue for each printer before he prints so he can monitor the queue and select a printer accordingly.

30. Which NT tool is used to create a Client installation boot disk?

a. Client Manager

b. Client Administrator

c. Network Client Administrator

d. Network Client Manager

e. Client installation Manager

31. What is the difference between a user profile and a user policy?

a. A user profile contains all the restrictions the administrator wants to implement; the user policy contains the user's preferences.

b. A user profile defines the user on the network (including her full name and department, and phone numbers); the user policy affects which functions can the user perform.

c. A user profile contains the user's preferences; the user policy defines the rights the administrator wants to implement on the user.

d. A user profile defines the user on the network; the user policy contains the password guidelines.

e. The user profile contains the user's preferences; the user policy contains the password guidelines.

32. Which type of profile will regenerate a common environment each time the user logs on even if he has made changes? Select two answers.

a. A policy entry

b. A common profile

c. A shared profile

d. A mandatory profile

e. A common shared policy

33. What is the difference between a stripe set and a volume set? Select all that apply.

a. A stripe set stores data on the first hard drive and then moves the subsequent drives; a volume set saves data across all drives equally.

b. A stripe set stores data across all drives equally; a volume set fills up the first drive initially.

c. A stripe set offers fault tolerance; a volume set does not.

d. A stripe allows the use of multiple drives (up to 32); a volume set can use only two drives.

e. A stripe set requires partitions of equal size over multiple drives; a volume set can make use of different size partitions.

34. A stripe set can use drives of different types (such as IDE and SCSI) in the same set. True or False?

a. True

b. False

35. What is the difference between how a stripe set with parity and a mirror set respond when a drive crashes?

    a. The mirror set fails completely, whereas the stripe set with parity continues to work as if nothing happened.

    b. The mirror set continues to work off the mirror partition, whereas the stripe set with parity requires the administrator's intervention.

    c. There is no difference. Both systems recover automatically. However, the administrator will eventually need to replace the damaged drive.

    d. The mirror set requires the administrator's intervention before the system can continue, whereas the stripe set with parity can rebuild the missing information from the parity data store on the other drives without administrative intervention. The access time will be a little lower as the information is reconstructed, however.

36. Which of the following can be used to automate backups under Windows NT?

    a. Scheduler

    b. AT

    c. Backup Admin

    d. WinAT

    e. Backup utility

37. What backup utility can be used from the Resource Kit to back up the Registry while the system is operational?

    a. Regedit

    b. Regedt32

    c. Rdisk

    d. Regback

    e. Regrest

38. How can you monitor invalid login attempts? Select all that apply.

    a. Use the Login administrator.

    b. Use the auditing tools in the User Manager.

    c. Use the auditing tools in the Server Manager.

    d. You cannot audit invalid logins, but you can track accounts that are locked out.

    e. Use the event viewer.

39. Which of the following must be used to configure the pagefile under Windows NT 4.0? Select all that apply.

    a. The device manager

    b. The System icon in the control panel

    c. Windows NT diagnostics

    d. The server manager

    e. The server icon in the control panel

40. The logs in the event viewer can be viewed with a basic text editor. True or False?

    a. True

    b. False

41. A Windows NT 4.0 upgrade has failed. The system was running Windows 95 and the new installation path was set to c:\windows (the same directory as Windows95). The administrator believed they would be able to keep all the properties and applications. What can be done to recover the Windows 95 system?

a. Run the uninstall command that is stored on the Emergency Recovery Disk. Everything will return to Windows 95 settings.

b. Reboot the system, and Windows 95 will recover. NT does not modify the previous OS until the installation is successful.

c. Nothing can be done. The Windows 95 settings are lost. Reformat the drive and reinstall Windows 95.

d. Reboot the system and Windows NT will recover and continue the installation. When the installation is complete, you can perform the uninstall.

e. Reboot the system and select Windows from the startup menu. NT always saves the old OS and places an entry in the Boot.ini file.

42. An administrator would like to upgrade from NT 3.51 to NT 4.0 but maintain the settings of NT 3.51. The administrator decides to use Winnt32 and select a new directory for Windows NT 4.0 just in case the installation fails. Has the administrator fulfilled the original requirements? Why or why not?

a. Yes. Winnt32 is used for upgrades from NT 3.51.

b. Yes. Winnt32 is used for upgrades, and a new directory will keep the configuration safe in case of a failed upgrade. As long as the administrator points to the original NT 3.51 directory during the installation, NT 4.0 will copy the registry settings it needs.

c. No. Winnt32 will override all the NT 3.51 settings. NT 3.51 and NT 4.0 are not compatible and cannot be upgraded.

d. No. This scenario will create a dual boot, not an upgrade. NT 4.0 should have been placed in the same directory as NT 3.51.

e. No. Winnt32 is used only for a full new installation of NT 4.0. Winnt should have been used.

43. An NT server is currently partitioned with a 50 Mb FAT partition as drive C: and a 750 MB Extended partition with logical drive D:. The administrator decided to add another primary partition on the same drive. The administrator rebooted the system as prompted but was unable to start up NT. The error message Unable to find NTOSKRNL appeared when the administrator choose the option to load NT. How can the administrator get the system back online?

a. The NT server is damaged beyond repair. The administrator must reinstall the software in the same directory, and all settings will be maintained.

b. Use an NT boot disk to sys the drive; this will rebuild the partition numbering order.

c. Run the Emergency Repair process and rebuild the boot sector of the drive.

d. Remove the additional partition using Fdisk, and then restart the system. NT will recover.

e. Using an NT boot disk modify the boot.ini to locate the new partition number that contains the boot files.

44. An NT server fails to start up after changes were made in the Registry. What tools can be used to try to recover? Select all that apply.

a. Use the Last Known Good configuration.

b. Reboot using the Emergency Repair Disk.

c. Reboot using an NT boot disk and restore the registry using REGRest.

d. Use the emergency repair process including the three startup disks and the ERD.

e. Reboot using an NT boot disk and run Regedit to reverse the changes made previously.

45. A user calls the help desk to complain that when she changed the desktop resolution to super VGA the screen became all messed up and she cannot change it back. What do you suggest?

    a. Use the CTRL+ALT+DEL keys to reboot the computer. NT will recover automatically with its VGA fallback mode.

    b. Use the ALT+F4 keys to shut down the system or hit the off switch if you cannot tell where you are. Once NT restarts, the VGA fallback mode will kick in automatically and restore the settings to VGA.

    c. Shut down the server and restart using the VGA item in the Boot.ini menu. Then when you're in NT change the settings back to VGA.

    d. Retrace your steps backward in NT until you have undone the changes.

    e. Reboot and run an Emergency Repair. Have NT repair the VGA mode.

46. Your office shared a UNIX printer with UNIX and NT users. While the UNIX users have no problems accessing the printer, the NT users do not seem to be able to connect. What must be done to help the NT users to connect? Select all that apply.

    a. Install TCP/IP.

    b. Install TCP/IP printing.

c. Share the UNIX printer with NT users using the gateway services.

d. Install the Printer on an NT system and share it with gateway services.

e. Install the DLC protocol.

47. Three new laser printers were purchased for a particular department, and now everyone is arguing how best to put them to use. What would you suggest? Select the best answer.

    a. Install the printers on three different systems and share to everyone.

    b. Install the printers on the MS-exchange server and share to everyone.

    c. Install the printers on a single dedicated system as a printer pool and share to everyone.

    d. Install the printers on a single workstation and share to groups based on need, assigning the managers the highest priority.

    e. Install each printer with a different priority and share accordingly.

48. A user connects with two modems and has Multilink. The administrator has set up several modems on the RAS server and enabled callback. The user connects and gets authenticated, but when the server calls back, only one modem is in use. What can be done to get both modems to connect?

    a. The call back will only work on one modem. Once the call has been reconnected simply re-dial the second modem and a second call back will take place.

    b. The call back needs to have two phone numbers to dial back.

    c. Enable the RAS server to use two lines for dial-out.

d. The call back feature needs to have Multilink enabled.

e. Call back will simply not support Multilink.

49. What does Microsoft's encryption software MS-CHAP stand for?

a. Certified Handshake Authorization Protocol

b. Challenge Handshake Authentication Protocol

c. Certified Handshake Authentication Protocol

d. Challenge Handshake Authorization Protocol

50. In a mixed environment several Microsoft clients need access to a Novell server. As the administrator you do not want to install the Novell client on all systems, so you install Gateway services for Novell on an NT server. However, users are complaining that they cannot save files to some folders on the Novell Server. What can be done to resolve the problem? Select all that apply.

a. Make sure the users have write access to the Novell share.

b. Make sure the Gateway account has write access to the Novell share.

c. Gateway services need to give write permissions to the Gateway account for the NT share.

d. Gateway services need to give write permissions to the user accounts for the NT share.

e. Make sure the Gateway services account is also a member of the Novell group GATEWAY.

51. To connect to a client/server program on a Novell server, what is the minimum configuration on an NT server? Select all that apply.

a. A common protocol such as TCP/IP or NWLink

b. A Novell client such as Gateway services or Novell's client 32

c. The client software portion of the client/server application

d. Must have an ODI compatible network card driver

e. A common frame type

52. Sara was given full control for the Report share on the server. The Sales group (of which Sara is a member) has read-only access to the share. Under Local NTFS permission the group everyone has change permission to the shared folder. What permission does Sara have to the files in the shared folder on the server?

a. Sara has the most restrictive permission, which is read-only.

b. Sara has cumulative permission, which is full control.

c. Sara has the permission of the group, which is read-only.

d. Sara has the most restrictive between full control (cumulative for the share—read and full control) and the NTFS local permission, which is change.

e. The permission on the files is not affected by the share permissions because files cannot be shared. Sara will have no access to the files because they are not explicitly listed.

53. Mike calls and tell you that of the 15 co-workers on the NT network, only some can access the permissions that he has created. You verify the share permissions and find that in this group everyone has read access. What could be causing the problems with some users? Select all that apply.

    a. Only some users belong to the group everyone.

    b. Only some of the users have the client for Microsoft installed.

    c. Mike has restricted the number of concurrent connections.

    d. Mike does not have 10 valid user licenses.

    e. Mike needs to identify by name all the men who will need access to the folder.

54. What is the difference between a differential backup and an incremental backup?

    a. The differential backup will back up only files that have been modified; the incremental will back up all the files.

    b. Incremental backup will back up only the files that have been modified; the differential will back up all the files.

    c. Both types will back up only the files that have been modified but incremental will change the archive bit, and differential will not.

    d. Both types will back up only the files that have been modified but differential will change the archive bit, and incremental will not.

    e. Both types will change the archive bit but differential will use a new tape whereas incremental can add to an existing tape.

55. By default, where are the logon scripts and policy files stored on a Domain Controller?

    a. c:\winnt\system\drivers\etc

    b. c:\winnt\system32\drivers\etc

    c. c:\winnt\system\repl\import\scripts

    d. c:\winnt\system32\repl\import\scripts

    e. c:\winnt\system32\scripts

ANSWERS AND EXPLANATIONS

1. **A - B - D.** Intel , Apple Power PC, DEC alpha and MIPS RISC chip are all supported. On the Server CD, look for the different subdirectories with the names of the platforms. For more information, see "Chapter 2 Installation and Configuration, Part 1."

2. **B - C.** MS-DOS applications that do not access the hardware directly will be supported. That includes 16- and 32-bit applications with Microsoft's NT compatible icon. OS/2 from a basic install can support only 1.x character-based software.

3. **A - C - D - E.** Coax is a type of cable. NT can support a network through Ethernet, token ring and FDDI on a LAN or WAN. RAS is used over a WAN to connect back to a network.

4. **B - D - E.** UTP category 3 might work, but it is not certified at the high speed. TCP is not a cable type.

5. **C.** A minimum of 2 MB must be in place as a bootable partition to create the system partition. The System partition can be either FAT or NTFS. For more information, see "Chapter 2, Installation and Configuration, Part 1."

6. **A - C - E.** The NTLDR is read first to setup the system with the appropriate resources to read the Boot.ini, which will offer a list of operating systems or the location of NTOSKRNL (usually in the Winnt subdirectory). NTdetect is used to confirm hardware settings on the system. For more information, see Chapter 9, "Troubleshooting."

7. **B.** When a new partition is created, it might modify the numbering scheme that the boot.ini is relying on. Always count the primary partition first on each physical disk, followed by extended partitions. If the system reboots and the boot.ini file does not find the NTOSKRNL, the user will be faced with an error message. For more information, see Chapter 1, "Planning."

8. **C - E.** Each card must be using a unique non-conflicting IRQ and other resources as needed. Both cards are set up in the same network tool via the control panel. The cards can be configured to use the same or different protocols and be bound to the same or different services. For more information, see Chapter 3, "Installation and Configuration, Part 2."

9. **B.** Bindings are used to establish a connection between services, protocols, and adapters on the network. Disabling a binding is easy and can be reversed. Any service not required on a network protocol or card can be disabled to free up network traffic. For more information, see Chapter 3, "Installation and Configuration, Part 2."

10. **A - B - C.** A BDC must be a member of a domain. A stand-alone server and a workstation can join a domain if a computer name has been registered in the domain. Windows 95 and MS-DOS systems can log in to a domain but they are not a member of the domain. For more information, see Chapter 3, "Installation and Configuration, Part 2."

11. **C.** A PDC is responsible for all account database synchronization. A BDC will accept any changes passed to it by the PDC, but it will not initiate any changes.

12. **D.** Users should be placed into Global groups in the domain. Each resource is assigned permissions to local groups, which contain Global groups. Other combinations will work but require more administration in the long run as users are added and removed. For more information, see Chapter 5, "Managing Resources, Part 1."

13. **B.** False. As long as the computer name of the member server is registered in the domain, it can join. A member server cannot be a member of more than one domain at a time. For more information, see Chapter 3, "Installation and Configuration, Part 2."

14. **B - C.** The administrator must add the computer name of the system that will join the domain in one of two ways: through the server manager tool on a domain controller or at the workstation itself through a remote administration command that is performed by providing the domain to join as well as an administrative account and password. For more information, see Chapter 3, "Installation and Configuration, Part 2."

15. **A - B - C.** Having files on the server will help with central backup procedure, allow users to be more mobile, and enable Windows 95 clients to keep their files in a secure file system like NTFS. Another plus would be that Windows 95 clients can have their profiles roam around the network with them. For more information, see Chapter 5, "Managing Resources, Part 1."

16. **E.** The password history setting will force the user to change their password five times before they can change back to the original. If each password must be kept for a one month, the original

password can only be used once in six months. For more information, see Chapter 5, "Managing Resources, Part 1."

17. **B.** Every object has an Access Control List that contains all users and groups as well as the rights or permissions assigned. When a user or group object is deleted, an unknown user is listed until the system can update its entries. For more information see Chapter 5, "Managing Resources, Part 1."

18. **B.** Default rights assigned to built-in groups are for convenience only. They establish a safe environment to start working in. All entries can be modified as needed. For more information, see Chapter 5, "Managing Resources, Part 1."

19. **E.** Winnt is a 16 bit application that is used for a full installation of NT starting from MS-DOS or Windows 95. Winnt32 can be run only from a true 32-bit operating system like NT. NT cannot be upgraded from MS-DOS or Windows 95 even though it can be installed from them. For more information, see Chapter 1, "Planning."

20. **A - C.** The system partition is used to start up the computer and present the user with options listed in the boot.ini file. The boot partition is used to start up the NT operating system. When NT is installed on drive C: the boot and system partitions become one and the same. For more information, see Chapter 1, "Planning."

21. **C - E.** Net Use can connect a drive by using a UNC of up to 12 characters. The // symbols are used for Internet FQDN, whereas the \\ symbols are used for UNC names.

22. **B - E.** Write is part of the change permission. In a share permission, there are only four options: Read, Change, Full Control, and No Access. Take Ownership and write are NTFS local permissions. For more information, see Chapter 6, "Managing Resources, Part 2."

23. **D.** When share and NFTS permissions are combined the most restrictive combination will be enforced when a user tries to access a resource over the network. If the user is accessing the resource locally, however, Share permissions have no impact. For more information, see Chapter 6, "Managing Resources, Part 2."

24. **B - E.** On an NT server or workstation, the local administrator and Power users groups have the rights to share folders. On a Domain Controller the administrators, domain admins, and Server Operators groups have the rights to share. The server operator group does not exist on a workstation. Making a person a member of the Domain Admins group will make him a local administrator on all NT workstations that are part of the domain. This last option would work, but it gives the user account far more power than is needed. For more information, see Chapter 6, "Managing Resources, Part 2."

25. **B.** False. All users including administrators will have the No Access permission assigned to them. The only way an administrator can override this permission is if he takes local ownership of the object. This would not go unnoticed, though, because the original owner would lose ownership. For more information, see Chapter 6, "Managing Resources, Part 2."

26. **A - C - D.** The user's password is only used to generate the access token at logon. The password is not included in the access token. The SID for the account, the groups the user belongs to, and the user rights they have are the only elements included in the access token. The access token is presented to each object the user tries to access in order to determine appropriate rights and permissions. For more information, see Chapter 6, "Managing Resources, Part 2."

27. **B.** Microsoft uses the term print device to represent the actual hardware that outputs to printed papers. The printer is the print driver and configuration settings on the server that send information to the print device. For more information, see Chapter 4, "Installation and Configuration, Part 3."

28. **A - C.** TCP/IP and DLC are used to connect directly to printers. Other protocols are used to connect to other servers that might have a printer attached. For more information, see Chapter 4, "Installation and Configuration, Part 3."

29. **D.** The printer or shared resources contain a setting called Print Pool that allows the administrator to select multiple printer ports. All users are assigned the same printer, but the first available printer will be used to de-spool the print job. Because the user is not sure which printer is going to receive the print job, it is best to locate the printers close together. For more information, see Chapter 4, "Installation and Configuration, Part 3."

30. **C.** The Network Client Administrator is used to create a DOS boot disk that will log on and connect to a client share containing client software and launch the installation. For more information, see Chapter 3, "Installation and Configuration, Part 2."

31. **C.** The user profile contains desktop and start menu preferences. If a user has a roaming profile these preferences will follow the user around the network. A policy or policy file implements configuration settings or restrictions on a user, group, or computer on the network. A policy will be merged into the local system's registry. For more information, see Chapter 5, "Managing Resources, Part 1."

32. **A - D.** A policy will be read into the registry at each logon. All environment settings can be

reestablished at this time, overriding any changes the user may have made. A mandatory profile will not save any changes when the user logs out. For more information, see Chapter 5, "Managing Resources, Part 1."

33. **B - E.** A Stripe set saves data in 64 K blocks across all drives in the set. For this reason a stripe set requires partitions of equal size. A volume set fills up the first drive in the set before moving to subsequent drives. For a volume set partitions or drives do not need to be the same size. Neither provides fault tolerance. For more information, see Chapter 4, "Installation and Configuration, Part 3."

34. **A.** True. A stripe set can make use of any drive that is active on the NT system. For more information, see Chapter 4, "Installation and Configuration, Part 3."

35. **D.** The mirror set will not be able to switch over automatically. The administrator must break the mirror and rename the valid copy. A stripe set with parity stores parity (duplicate) information across all the drives. When one drive fails, the system is able to re-create the information from the parity sectors on the remaining drives. When a new drive is inserted to replace the defective one, the administrator must run a Regenerate command from the Disk Administrator to rebuild the drive. For more information, see Chapter 4, "Installation and Configuration, Part 3."

36. **B - D.** AT is a command line utility used to automated activities. The backup utility can be started using the AT command. WinAT is simply the windows graphical version of AT.

37. **D.** Regback is found in the resource kit and can be used to backup the registry files while NT is fully functional. Regedit and Regedt32 are used to export part of the registry tree and Rdisk can

be used to back up part of the configuration files used to rebuild a system. Regrest is used to restore the registry. For more information, see Chapter 4, "Installation and Configuration, Part 3."

38. **B - E.** The auditing logins must be enabled in User Manager for Domains. The invalid attempts will all be listed in the event viewer under the security log. For more information, see Chapter 5, "Managing Resources, Part 1."

39. **B.** The system application contains a tab for configuring the Pagefile; while NT diagnostic can display only the current settings of the pagefile. For more information, see Chapter 4, "Installation and Configuration, Part 3."

40. **B.** False. The logs can be viewed only from the event viewer. However, they can be saved as another file type if necessary. For more information, see Chapter 8, "Monitoring and Optimization."

41. **C.** Windows 95 and NT cannot be in the same directory because they use the same file names. NT cannot upgrade a 95 system because the registries are not compatible. In this case the installation of 95 is lost as soon as the NT installation started. Reformatting the hard drive will clean up the system so a fresh install can take place. For more information, see Chapter 1, "Planning."

42. **D.** No. This scenario will create a dual boot, not an upgrade. NT 4.0 should have been placed in the same directory as NT 3.51. NT 4.0 will read the registry from NT 3.51 if it is installed in the same directory only. For more information, see Chapter 1, "Planning."

43. **E.** The Boot.ini file contains a numbering scheme that is not changed when new partitions are created. NT will count all primary partitions first, and then move on to the extended partitions. In this case the extended partition D was

number 2 on the drive initially. When the new primary partition was created, it became number 2 and the D: drive became number 3. This change must be reflected in the boot.ini. A boot.ini file can be created or copied from any other NT server. Changing the entry to number 3 allows NT to boot and then allow the administrator to modify the original boot.ini file. For more information, see Chapter 9, "Troubleshooting."

44. **A - C - D.** The last known good configuration may contain the values that were present before the changes took place. However, it may not fix all the problems or may not even be presented if NT is severely damaged. Using the ERD requires use of the three NT OS disks that will prompt repair. If the registry was backed up using REGBack from the resource kit, use the REGRest to restore the settings. For more information, see Chapter 9, "Troubleshooting."

45. **C.** The VGA menu on boot.ini appears before NT is started. Once you're in NT, the display should be clear under VGA. Change the settings back to a resolution the monitor can handle and always test the configuration before accepting it. Then reboot NT normally. For more information, see Chapter 9, "Troubleshooting."

46. **A - B - E.** The printer will connect by using TCP/IP and the printing utilities. NT will be able to access the Unix printer using the LPR utility. DLC may also be used to connect to a unix printer. For more information, see Chapter 4, "Installation and Configuration, Part 3."

47. **C.** A printer pool ensures that a printing device is almost always available. A user does not need to monitor or choose a printing device because the first available printer will be used. For more information, see Chapter 4, "Installation and Configuration, Part 3."

48. **E.** At this point Multilink does not work with Call back. If the user wants to use Multilink he cannot use call back. For more information, see Chapter 9, "Troubleshooting."

49. **B.** Challenge Handshake Authentication Protocol. For more information, see Chapter 7, "Connectivity."

50. **B - D.** The Gateway services accounts need to access the Novell share, whereas the Microsoft users need to have write permission to the NT share. In most cases, the Gateway account or the NTGateway group it must belong to has full access to the Novell server, and share permissions are controlled on the NT server. For gateway services to function at all, the service account used by Gateway services must already be a member of the NTGateway group on the Novell server. For more information, see Chapter 7, "Connectivity."

51. **A - C - E.** A file and print sharing client is not required. NT can run TCP/IP or Nwlink. A common frame type is needed if Nwlink is in place. For more information, see Chapter 4, "Installation and Configuration, Part 3."

52. **D.** The most restrictive permissions between full control (share permission) and change (NTFS permission) is change for Sara. For more information, see Chapter 6, "Managing Resources, Part 2."

53. **C.** The maximum number of concurrent connections will restrict users trying to access a share. By default on an NT workstation, that number is 10. On a server, the default is unlimited. For more information, see Chapter 6, "Managing Resources, Part 2."

54. **C.** Only files that have been modified since the last backup will be included in an incremental or differential backup. The archive bit is reset on an incremental backup. This means the files can be selected for backup every night but will be included only if they have been modified since the previous backup. A differential backup will not reset the archive bit and will include all selected files every night in the backup.

55. **D.** The folder Winnt\system32\repl\import\ scripts is shared as NETLOGON on all Domain Controllers. The repl stands for directory replication. If the logon scripts and policies need to be copied automatically to all Domain Controllers, this is the default export directory for directory replication.

APPENDIXES

A Glossary

B Overview of the Certification Process

C What's On the CD-ROM

D Using the Top Score Software

Glossary

A

access token   A Windows NT object describing a user account and group memberships. This object is provided by the Local Security Authority when logon and validation are successful, and it is attached to all user processes.

account lockout   A Windows NT Server security feature that locks a user account if a certain number of failed logon attempts occur within a specified amount of time (based on account policy lockout settings). Locked accounts cannot log on.

account policy   Controls the way passwords must be used by all user accounts of a domain or of an individual computer. Specific settings include minimum password length, how often a user must change his or her password, and how often users can reuse old passwords. Account policy can be set for all user accounts in a domain when administering a domain and for all user accounts of a single workstation or member server when administering a computer.

active partition   The disk partition that has been designated as being bootable. Although up to four partitions on an NT system can be capable of booting, only one can be active at any one time.

administrative share   A network share that is created and maintained by the Windows NT operating systems. Administrative shares are hidden and are accessible only by users in the local Administrators account.

All disk partitions have administrative shares associated with them (such as C$ for drive C).

Alert View   A Performance Monitor view in which thresholds for counters are set and then actions are taken when those thresholds are crossed.

application log   A Server log that's accessible from the Event Viewer. This log records messages, warnings, and errors generated by applications running on your NT Server or Workstation.

ARC-path   The Advanced RISC Computing path is an industry standard method for identifying the physical location of a partition on a hard drive. ARC-paths are used in the BOOT.INI file to identify the location of NT boot files.

B

backup browser   A computer chosen by an election process to maintain a list of resources on a network. A master browser directs clients' requests for resources on a network to the backup browser.

backup domain controller (BDC)   In a Windows NT Server domain, this is a computer running Windows NT Server that receives a copy of the domain's directory database, which contains all account and security policy information for the domain. The copy is synchronized periodically and automatically with the master copy on the primary domain controller (PDC). BDCs also authenticate user logons and can be promoted to function as PDCs as needed. Multiple BDCs can exist on a domain. *See also* member server; primary domain controller (PDC).

binding   A process that establishes the communication channel between a protocol driver (such as TCP/IP) and a network card.

boot partition   The volume, formatted for either an NTFS or FAT file system, that contains the Windows NT operating system and its support files. The boot partition can be (but does not have to be) the same as the system partition. *See also* partition; FAT; NTFS.

BOOT.INI   A file located on the system partition of an NT Server or Workstation that is responsible for pointing the boot process to the correct boot files for the operating system chosen in the boot menu.

BOOTSECT.DOS   A file located on the system partition that contains information required to boot an NT System to MS-DOS if a user requests it.

bottleneck   The system resource that is the limiting factor in speed of processing. All systems have a bottleneck of some sort; the question is whether the bottleneck is significant in the context in which a Server finds it.

browser   Called the Computer Browser service, the browser maintains an up-to-date list of computers and provides that list to applications when requested. This list is kept up-to-date through consultation with a master browser or backup browser on the network. It provides the computer lists displayed in the Network Neighborhood, Select Computer, and Select Domain dialog boxes and (for Windows NT Server only) in the Server Manager window.

C

call back   A security feature enabled in the configuration of a RAS server, which requires that a RAS server call a client at a specific phone number (system- or user-configured) after a client initiates a RAS connection to the server. This feature is used either to transfer the bulk of long distance charges to the server instead of the user or to ensure that a user is authentic by confirming that he is at a specific location (and thus verifying that he's not a hacker trying to gain unauthorized access to a network via RAS).

Chart View   A view in the Performance Monitor in which a dynamically updated line graph or histogram displays data for the counters selected in the view configuration.

Client Access License   A license that's required by all users connecting to an NT server, which provides legal access to NT Server resources.

Client Administration Tools   A set of applications that allow for the administration of an NT Domain Controller from a Windows 95 or Windows NT Workstation, or Windows NT Server computer. The Client Administration Tools provide the most commonly used administration tools but do not provide complete administrative functionality.

Client Services for NetWare (CSNW)   Included with Windows NT Workstation, enabling workstations to make direct connections to file and printer resources at NetWare servers running NetWare 2.x or later.

COMPACT.EXE   A command-line utility used to compress files on NTFS volumes. To see command line options, type compact /? at the command prompt. You can also access this utility by right-clicking any file or directory on an NTFS volume in Windows NT Explorer, clicking Properties, and changing the compression attribute for the files.

Control Panel   A folder containing a number of applets (applications) with which you configure and monitor your system running Windows NT. This includes configuring hardware, software, network configurations, service startup parameters, and system properties.

CONVERT.EXE   A command-line utility used to convert an NT volume from FAT to NTFS. The command syntax is CONVERT `<drive letter>`: /fs:NTFS (for example, CONVERT C: /fs:NTFS to convert drive C).

counter   A specific component of a Performance Monitor object that has a displayable value. For example, for the Memory object, one counter is Available Bytes.

D

default gateway   In TCP/IP, the intermediate network device on the local network that has knowledge of the network IDs of the other networks in the Internet so it can forward packets to other gateways until the packet is eventually delivered to a gateway connected to the specified destination.

DETECT   A troubleshooting acronym indicating a recommended method for approaching NT problems. DETECT stands for Discover, Explore, Track, Execute, Check, Tie Up.

differential backup   A backup method that backs up all files whose archive attributes are not set but does not set the archive attribute of the files it backs up.

directory replication   The process of copying a master set of directories from a server (called an export computer) to specified servers or workstations (called import computers) in the same or other domains. Replication simplifies the task of maintaining identical sets of directories and files on multiple computers

because only a single master copy of the data must be maintained. Files are first replicated when they are added to an exported directory and then every time a change is saved to the file.

Directory Service Manager for NetWare (DSMN) An NT add-on that provides directory synchronization between an NT Network and a NetWare network.

Disk Administrator   An administration program that allows an NT administrator to create, format, and maintain hard drive partitions, volumes, and fault-tolerant mechanisms.

disk duplexing   A mirror set created with two hard drives controlled by separate disk controller cards. Disk duplexing provides more fault tolerance than standard mirror sets do because it ensures that a controller card failure will not bring down the mirror set.

disk mirroring   A fault-tolerance method that provides a fully redundant, or shadow, copy of data (a mirror set). Mirror sets provide a twin for a selected disk; all data written to the primary disk is also written to the shadow or mirror disk. This enables you to have instant access to another disk with a redundant copy of the information on a failed disk.

disk striping with parity   A method of data protection in which data is striped in large blocks across all the disks in an array. Data redundancy is provided by the parity information.

domain   In Windows NT, a collection of computers defined by the administrator of a Windows NT Server network that share a common directory database. A domain provides access to the centralized user accounts and group accounts maintained by the domain administrator. Each domain has a unique name.

domain master browser   A kind of network name server that keeps a browse list of all the servers and domains on the network. The domain master browser for a domain is always the primary domain controller.

Domain Name System (DNS)   DNS offers a static hierarchical name service for TCP/IP hosts. The network administrator configures the DNS with a list of hostnames and IP addresses, allowing users of workstations configured to query the DNS to specify remote systems by hostname instead of by IP address. For example, a workstation configured to use DNS name resolution could use the command ping *remotehost* instead of ping 1.2.3.4 if the mapping for the system named *remotehost* was contained in the DNS database.

Dynamic Host Configuration Protocol (DHCP)   A protocol that offers dynamic configuration of IP addresses and related information through the DHCP Server service running on an NT Server. DHCP provides safe, reliable, and simple TCP/IP network configuration, prevents address conflicts, and helps conserve the use of IP addresses through centralized management of address allocation.

E

Emergency Repair Disk   A floppy disk containing configuration information for a specific NT Server or Workstation. This disk is created and updated using the RDISK utility and can be used in conjunction with the three NT setup disks to recover from many NT system failures resulting from file Registry corruption.

Event Viewer   An administrative utility used to look at event logs. The event viewer provides three logs: system, security, and application.

export computer   In directory replication, a server from which a master set of directories is exported to specified servers or workstations (called import computers) in the same or other domains.

extended partition   Created from free space on a hard disk, an extended partition can be subpartitioned into zero or more logical drives. Only one of the four partitions allowed per physical disk can be an extended partition, and no primary partition needs to be present to create an extended partition.

F

FAT (File Allocation Table)   A table or list maintained by some operating systems to keep track of the status of various segments of disk space used for file storage. Also referred to as the FAT file system, this method is used to format hard drives in DOS, Windows 95, and OS/2, and it can be used in Windows NT.

FAT32   A variation of FAT that provides for more efficient file storage. This FAT variation is available only on Windows 95 and Windows 98 and is not readable by Windows NT.

fault tolerance   System of ensuring data integrity when hardware failures occur. In Windows NT, the FTDISK.SYS driver provides fault tolerance. In Disk Administrator, fault tolerance is implemented through the use of mirror sets, stripe sets with parity, and volume sets.

File and Print Services for NetWare (FPNW)   A service installed on an NT server that provides NetWare clients the ability to access an NT server for the purposes of reading files and printing to NT-controlled printers. In order for this to work, the NT Server must have NWLink installed on it.

filename alias   An 8.3 compatible short filename given to a long filename that's created on an NT computer so that MS-DOS and Windows 3.x clients can read the file.

frame type   The type of network package generated on a network. In NT configuration, this refers to the type of network packages sent by a NetWare server that an NT client is configured to accept.

G

Gateway Services for NetWare (GSNW)   Included with Windows NT Server, this service enables a computer running Windows NT Server to connect to NetWare servers. Creating a gateway enables computers running only Microsoft client software to access NetWare resources through the gateway.

global group   For Windows NT Server, a group that can be used in its own domain, member servers and workstations of its domain, and trusting domains. In all those places, it can be granted rights and permissions and can become a member of local groups. However, it can contain user accounts only from its own domain. Global groups offer a means of grouping users from inside the domain to give them rights both in and out of the domain.

Global groups cannot be created or maintained on computers running Windows NT Workstation. However, for Windows NT Workstation computers that participate in a domain, domain global groups can be granted rights and permissions at those workstations, and they can become members of local groups at those workstations.

group account   A collection of user accounts. Giving a user account membership in a group gives that user all the rights and permissions granted to the group.

H

Hardware Compatibility List (HCL)   The Windows NT Hardware Compatibility List lists all devices supported by Windows NT. The latest version of the HCL can be downloaded from the Microsoft Web Page (microsoft.com) on the Internet.

hidden share   A network share that is configured not to show up in browse lists but that a user can connect to explicitly if he knows the share name. You create a hidden share by appending a dollar sign ($) to the end of a share name, as in SECRET$. All administrative shares are hidden shares.

hive   A section of the Registry that appears as a file on your hard disk. The Registry subtree is divided into hives (named for their resemblance to the cellular structure of a beehive). A hive is a discrete body of keys, subkeys, and values that is rooted at the top of the Registry hierarchy. A hive is backed by a single file and a .log file, which are in either the %SystemRoot%\system32\config folder or the %SystemRoot%\profiles\username folder. By default, most hive files (Default, SAM, Security, and System) are stored in the %SystemRoot%\system32\config folder. The %SystemRoot%\ profiles folder contains the user profile for each user of the computer. Because a hive is a file, it can be moved from one system to another, but it can only be edited using Registry Editor.

HKEY_LOCAL_MACHINE   A Registry subtree that maintains all the configuration information for the local machine, including hardware settings and settings for installed software.

I - J - K

import computer   In directory replication, the server or workstation that receives copies of the master set of directories from an export server.

incremental backup   A backup method that backs up all files whose archive attributes are not set and that sets the archive attribute of the files it backs up.

installation disk set   A set of floppy disks that contain a minimal configuration of NT used to initiate NT installation and repair.

IP address   Used to identify a node on a network and to specify routing information. Each node on the network must be assigned a unique IP address (usually the network ID) plus a unique host ID assigned by the network administrator. This address is typically represented in dotted-decimal notation, with the decimal values of the octets separated by periods (for example, 138.57.7.27).

In Windows NT, the IP address can be configured statically on the client or configured dynamically through DHCP.

IPCONFIG   A command-line utility that is used to determine the current TCP/IP configuration of a local computer. It is also used to request a new TCP/IP address from a DHCP server through the use of the /RELEASE and /RENEW switches. The /ALL switch shows a complete list of TCP/IP configurations.

IPX/SPX   Transport protocols used in Novell NetWare networks. Windows NT implements IPX through NWLink.

L

LastKnownGood configuration   A set of Registry settings that records the hardware configuration of an NT computer during each successful login. LastKnownGood can be used to recover from an incorrect hardware setup as long as logon does not occur between the time the configuration was changed and the time the LastKnownGood was invoked.

License Manager   An administrative utility that allows you to track the purchase of client access licenses for an NT Server and/or Domain.

licensing mode   An indicator of what kind of licensing is being used on an NT Server. The choices are Per Server and Per Seat.

local group   For Windows NT Workstation, a group that can be granted permissions and rights only for its own workstation. However, it can contain user accounts from its own computer and (if the workstation participates in a domain) user accounts and global groups both from its own domain and from trusted domains.

For Windows NT Server, a group that can be granted permissions and rights only for the domain controllers of its own domain. However, it can contain user accounts and global groups both from its own domain and from trusted domains.

Local groups provide a means of grouping users from both inside and outside the domain to be used only at domain controllers of the domain.

local profile   A profile stored on a local machine, and which is accessible only to users who log onto the NT computer locally.

Local Security Authority (LSA)   The NT process responsible for directing logon requests to the local Security Accounts Manager (SAM) or to the SAM of a domain controller via the NetLogon service. The LSA is responsible for generating an access token when a user logon is validated.

Log View   A Performance Monitor view in which the configuration of a log is determined. Logs have no dynamic information; however, the resulting file can be analyzed using any of the other Performance Monitor views.

logical drive   A subpartition of an extended partition on a hard disk.

M

mandatory profile   A profile that is downloaded to the user's desktop each time he or she logs on. A mandatory user profile is created by an administrator and assigned to one or more users to create consistent or job-specific user profiles. They cannot be changed by the user and remain the same from one logon session to the next.

Master Boot Record (MBR)   The place on the disk that the initial computer startup is directed to go to initiate operating system boot. The MBR is located on the primary partition.

master browser   A kind of network name server that keeps a browse list of all the servers and domains on the network. Also referred to as a browse master.

member server   A computer that runs Windows NT Server but is not a primary domain controller (PDC) or backup domain controller (BDC) of a Windows NT domain. Member servers do not receive copies of the directory database.

Migration Tool for NetWare   A tool included with Windows NT, enabling you to easily transfer user and group accounts, volumes, folders, and files from a NetWare server to a computer running Windows NT Server.

multi-boot   A computer that runs two or more operating systems. For example, Windows 95, MS-DOS, and Windows NT operating systems can be installed on the same computer. When the computer is started, any one of the operating systems can be selected. Also known as dual boot.

multilink protocol   Multilink combines multiple physical links into a logical "bundle." This aggregate link increases your bandwidth.

N

NetBEUI   A network protocol usually used in small department-sized local area networks of 1 to 200 clients. It is non-routable and is, therefore, not a preferred WAN protocol.

NetLogon   For Windows NT Server, this process performs authentication of domain logons and keeps the domain's directory database synchronized between the primary domain controller and the other backup domain controllers of the domain.

network adapter   An expansion card or other device used to connect a computer to a local area network (LAN). Also called a network card, network adapter card, adapter card, or network interface card (NIC).

network monitor   An administrative utility installed on an NT computer when the Network Monitor Tools and Agent service is installed. The network monitor provided with NT allows you to capture and analyze network traffic coming into and going out of the local network card. The SMS version of network monitor runs in promiscuous mode, which allows monitoring of traffic on the local network.

network protocols   Communication "languages" that allow networked computer and devices to communicate with one another. Common network protocols are TCP/IP, NetBEUI, NWLink, and DLC (used for communicating with networked printers such as HP DirectJet).

network service   A process that performs a specific network system function and often provides an application programming interface (API) for other processes to call. Windows NT services are RPC-enabled, meaning that their API routines can be called from remote computers.

non-browser   A computer that is configured to never participate in browser elections and that, therefore, can never become a master browser or backup browser.

normal backup   Sometimes referred to as a full backup, this method backs up all files and then sets the archive attribute of those files it backs up.

NTBOOTDD.SYS   The driver for a SCSI boot device that does not have its BIOS enabled. NTBOOTDD.SYS is found on an NT system partition and is required for creation of a fault-tolerant boot disk.

NTCONFIG.POL   A file that defines an NT system policy.

NTDETECT.COM   The program in the NT boot process that's responsible for generating a list of hardware devices. This list is later used to populate part of the HKEY_LOCAL_MACHINE subtree in the Registry.

NTFS   An advanced file system designed for use specifically within the Windows NT operating system. It supports file system recovery, extremely large storage media, long filenames, and various features for compatibility with the POSIX subsystem. It also supports object-oriented applications by treating all files as objects with user-defined and system-defined attributes.

NTFS compression   A compression type supported only on an NTFS volume. This supports file-level compression and is dynamic.

NTFS permissions   Local permissions on NTFS volumes, which allow for the restriction of both local and network access to files and folders.

NTHQ   A program that executes from a floppy disk and that allows you to automatically check the hardware on a computer against the HCL for NT compatibility.

NTLDR   The program responsible for booting an NT system. It is invoked when an NT computer is started, and it is responsible for displaying the boot menu (from the BOOT.INI file) and starting the NTDETECT.COM program.

NTOSKRNL.EXE   The program responsible for maintaining the core of the NT operating system. When NTLDR completes the boot process, control of NT is handed over to the NTOSKRNL.

NWLink   A standard network protocol that supports routing and can support NetWare client-server applications, where NetWare-aware Sockets-based applications communicate with IPX\SPX Sockets-based applications.

O - P - Q

object   A specific system category for which counters can be observed in Performance Monitor. Objects whose counters are frequently monitored are Memory, Processor, Network, and PhysicalDisk.

OSLOADER.EXE   The program on a RISC-based machine that's responsible for the function of the NTLDR on an INTEL-based machine.

partition   A portion of a physical disk that functions as though it were a physically separate unit.

per-client licensing mode   An NT licensing mode that allocates server access on a per-person basis (not on a per-connection basis). Using a per-client license, a user can connect to many NT servers simultaneously.

Performance Monitor   An administrative application used to monitor object counters on an NT computer in order to determine bottlenecks in the system and to increase overall efficiency.

per-server licensing mode   An NT licensing mode that allocates server access on a per-connection basis. This licensing mode allocates a certain number of simultaneous connections to a server, and when that number of connections is reached, no more users are allowed to access the server.

persistent connection   A network connection from a client to a server, which is automatically reestablished when disconnected.

ping   A command used to verify connections to one or more remote hosts. The PING utility uses the ICMP echo request and echo reply packets to determine whether a particular IP system on a network is functional. The PING utility is useful for diagnosing IP network or router failures.

Point to Point Protocol (PPP)   A set of industry-standard framing and authentication protocols that is part of Windows NT RAS and ensures interoperability with third-party remote access software. PPP negotiates configuration parameters for multiple layers of the OSI model.

Point to Point Tunneling Protocol (PPTP)   PPTP is a new networking technology that supports multiprotocol virtual private networks (VPNs), enabling remote users to access corporate networks securely across the Internet by dialing into an Internet service provider (ISP) or by connecting to the Internet directly.

potential browser   A computer that is not currently functioning as a browser on a network but which could become one if necessary.

primary domain controller (PDC)   In a Windows NT Server domain, the computer running Windows NT Server that authenticates domain logons and maintains the directory database for a domain. The PDC tracks changes made to accounts of all computers on a domain. It is the only computer to receive these changes directly. A domain has only one PDC.

primary partition   A partition is a portion of a physical disk that can be marked for use by an operating system. There can be up to four primary partitions (or up to three if there is an extended partition) per physical disk. A primary partition cannot be subpartitioned.

print device   Refers to the actual hardware device that produces printed output.

printer   Refers to the software interface between the operating system and the print device. The printer defines where the document will go before it reaches the print device (to a local port, to a file, or to a remote print share, for example), when it will go, and various other aspects of the printing process.

printer driver   A program that converts graphics commands into a specific printer language, such as PostScript or PCL.

printer pool   A group of two or more identical print devices associated with one printer.

protocol   *See* network protocols.

R

RDISK.EXE   A program used to create and update Emergency Repair Disks and the /REPAIR folder on an NT system.

recovery disk   A floppy disk that contains the files required by NT to begin the boot process and to point to the boot partition. The files required for an INTEL system are: BOOT.INI, NTDETECT.COM, NTLDR, and NTBOOTDD.SYS (if the hard drive is SCSI with BIOS disabled).

REGEDIT.EXE   One of two Registry editors available in NT. This one has the same interface as the Registry Editor available in Windows 95 and provides key value searching.

REGEDT32.EXE   One of two Registry editors available in NT. This one has a cascaded subtree interface and allows you to set Registry security.

regenerate The process of rebuilding a replaced hard drive in a stripe set with parity after hard drive failure. This process can be initiated from the Disk Administrator.

Registry The Windows NT Registry is a database repository for information about a computer's configuration. It is organized in a hierarchical structure and is comprised of subtrees and their keys, hives, and value entries.

Registry key A specific Registry entry that has a configurable value.

Registry tree A collection of similar Registry keys. HKEY_LOCAL_MACHINE is an example of a Registry tree.

Remote Access Service (RAS) A service that provides remote networking for telecommuters, mobile workers, and system administrators who monitor and manage servers at multiple branch offices. Users with RAS on a Windows NT computer can dial in to remotely access their networks for services such as file and printer sharing, electronic mail, scheduling, and SQL database access.

Report View A view in the Performance Monitor that displays data in a single-page format of current counter values.

reporting interval In Performance Monitor, the interval at which a new set of statistical information is processed and delivered to the view or views currently operating.

roaming profile The profile that is enabled when an administrator enters a user profile path into the user account. The first time the user logs off, the local user profile is copied to that location. Thereafter, the server copy of the user profile is downloaded each time the user logs on if it is more current than the local copy, and it is updated each time the user logs off.

S

SCSI adapter SCSI is an acronym for small computer system interface, a standard high-speed parallel interface defined by the American National Standards Institute (ANSI). A SCSI adapter is used to connect microcomputers to peripheral devices, such as hard disks and printers, and to other computers and local area networks.

Security Accounts Manager (SAM) The NT process that's responsible for querying the directory database to locate a specific username and password combination when a user attempts to logon.

security log Records security events and can be viewed through the Event Viewer. This helps track changes to the security system and identify any possible breaches of security. For example, depending on the Audit settings in User Manager or User Manager for Domains, any attempts to log on the local computer may be recorded in the security log. The security log contains both valid and invalid logon attempts, as well as events related to resource use (such as creating, opening, and deleting files).

Serial Line Interface Protocol (SLIP) An older industry standard that is part of Windows NT RAS and that ensures interoperability with third-party remote access software. Windows NT supports SLIP as a client but not as a server; in other words, an NT machine can connect to a SLIP server but cannot itself be a SLIP server.

Server Message Block (SMB) A file-sharing protocol designed to allow systems to transparently access files that reside on remote systems.

service A process that performs a specific system function and often provides an application programming interface (API) for other processes to call. Windows NT services are RPC-enabled, meaning that their API routines can be called from remote computers.

share permissions   A set of permissions controlling access to a network share when users attempt to access the share from over the network. Share permissions do not apply to local users of a system and can be applied only at the folder level.

sharing   The process of making a resource available on the network. This resource could be a drive, a folder, or a printer.

/SOS   A BOOT.INI switch indicating that during boot of NT Server or Workstation, the list of loading drivers should be displayed. This switch is used for troubleshooting and is normally configured as part of the [VGA] boot option.

spooler   Software that accepts documents sent by a user to be printed and then stores those documents and sends them, one-by-one, to available printer(s).

standalone server   An NT server that participates as part of a workgroup and not as a part of a domain.

stripe set   A method for saving data across identical partitions on different drives. A stripe set does not provide fault tolerance.

subnet mask   A 32-bit value that allows the recipient of IP packets to distinguish the network ID portion of the IP address from the host ID.

system groups   One or more groups maintained by NT for special purposes. The Everyone group is an example of a system group; it cannot be changed because its membership is defined and maintained by NT.

system log   The system log contains events logged by the Windows NT components and can be looked at through Event Viewer. For example, the failure of a driver or other system component to load during startup is recorded in the system log.

system partition   The volume that contains the hardware-specific files needed to load Windows NT.

system policy   Settings created with the System Policy Editor to control user work environments and actions and to enforce system configuration for Windows NT clients. System policies can be implemented for specific users, groups, or computers or for all users. A system policy for users overwrites settings in the current user area of the Registry, and a system policy for computers overwrites the current local machine area of the Registry. If you have clients who are using Windows 95, separate system policies need to be created for them on a Windows 95 system because NT system policies are not compatible with 95.

T

TCP/IP   An acronym for Transmission Control Protocol/Internet Protocol, TCP/IP is a set of networking protocols that enable communication across interconnected networks made up of computers with diverse hardware architectures and various operating systems. TCP/IP includes standards for how computers communicate and conventions for connecting networks and routing traffic.

Take Ownership   The user right that enables the ownership of a resource to be transferred from one user to another. By default, Administrators have the ability to take ownership of any NT resource.

Telephony API (TAPI)   A system used by certain programs to make data, fax, and voice calls. Those programs include the Windows NT applets HyperTerminal, Dial-Up Networking, Phone Dialer, and other Win32 communications applications written for Windows NT.

TRACERT   A TCP/IP troubleshooting utility that traces the route from one host to another. This utility can locate the source of transmission breakdown between TCP/IP hosts.

U

UNC (Universal Naming Convention) name   A full Windows NT name of a resource on a network. It conforms to the format *servername**sharename*, where *servername* is the name of the server and *sharename* is the name of the shared resource. UNC names of directories or files can also include the directory path under the share name, in which case they adhere to the following syntax:

   *servername**sharename**directory**filename*

UPS   A battery-operated power supply connected to a computer to keep the system running during a power failure.

user account   An account that contains all the information that defines a user to Windows NT. This includes such things as the username and password required for the user to log on, the groups in which the user account has membership, and the rights and permissions the user has for using the system and accessing its resources. For Windows NT Workstation, user accounts are managed with User Manager. For Windows NT Server, user accounts are managed with User Manager for Domains.

User Manager for Domains   A Windows NT Server tool used to manage security for a domain or an individual computer. This tool enables an administrator to maintain user accounts, groups, and security policies.

user profile   Configuration information that is retained on a user-by-user basis is saved in a user profile. This information includes all the user-specific settings of the Windows NT environment, such as the desktop arrangement, personal program groups and the program items in those groups, screen colors, screen savers, network connections, printer connections, mouse settings, window size and position, and more.

When a user logs on, the user's profile is loaded, and the user's Windows NT environment is configured according to that profile.

V - W - X - Y - Z

volume set   A combination of partitions on a physical disk that appear as one logical drive.

Windows Internet Name Service (WINS)   A name resolution service that resolves Windows NT networking computer names to IP addresses in a routed environment. A WINS server handles name registrations, queries, and releases.

WinLogon   The NT process that initiates login by presenting the logon dialog box to the user.

WINNT.EXE   The program used to install Windows NT from a non-NT platform.

WINNT32.EXE   The program used to install or upgrade Windows NT from an NT platform.

workgroup   For Windows NT, a workgroup is a collection of computers that are grouped for viewing purposes. Each workgroup is identified by a unique name.

Overview of the Certification Process

You must pass rigorous certification exams to become a Microsoft Certified Professional. These certification exams provide a valid and reliable measure of your technical proficiency and expertise. The closed-book exams are developed in consultation with computer industry professionals who have on-the-job experience with Microsoft products in the workplace. These exams are conducted by an independent organization—Sylvan Prometric—at more than 1,200 Authorized Prometric Testing Centers around the world.

Currently Microsoft offers six types of certification, based on specific areas of expertise:

◆ **Microsoft Certified Professional (MCP).** Persons who attain this certification are qualified to provide installation, configuration, and support for users of at least one Microsoft desktop operating system, such as Windows NT Workstation. In addition, candidates can take elective exams to develop areas of specialization. MCP is the initial or first level of expertise.

◆ **Microsoft Certified Professional + Internet (MCP+Internet).** Persons who attain this certification are qualified to plan security, install and configure server products, manage server resources, extend service to run CGI scripts or ISAPI scripts, monitor and analyze performance, and troubleshoot problems. The expertise required is similar to that of an MCP with a focus on the Internet.

◆ **Microsoft Certified Systems Engineer (MCSE).** Persons who attain this certification are qualified to effectively plan, implement, maintain, and support information systems with Microsoft Windows NT and other Microsoft advanced systems and workgroup products, such as Microsoft Office and Microsoft BackOffice. MCSE is a second level of expertise.

◆ **Microsoft Certified Systems Engineer + Internet (MCSE+Internet).** Persons who attain this certification are qualified in the core MCSE areas and are qualified to enhance, deploy, and manage sophisticated intranet and Internet solutions that include a browser, proxy server, host servers, database, and messaging and commerce components. In addition, an MCSE+Internet–certified professional will be able to manage and analyze Web sites.

◆ **Microsoft Certified Solution Developer (MCSD).** Persons who attain this certification are qualified to design and develop custom business solutions by using Microsoft development tools, technologies, and platforms, including Microsoft Office and Microsoft BackOffice. MCSD is a second level of expertise with a focus on software development.

◆ **Microsoft Certified Trainer (MCT).** Persons who attain this certification are instructionally and technically qualified by Microsoft to deliver

Microsoft Education Courses at Microsoft-authorized sites. An MCT must be employed by a Microsoft Solution Provider Authorized Technical Education Center or a Microsoft Authorized Academic Training site.

NOTE

Stay in Touch For up-to-date information about each type of certification, visit the Microsoft Training and Certification World Wide Web site at http://www.microsoft.com/train_cert. You must have an Internet account and a WWW browser to access this information. You also can call the following sources:

· Microsoft Certified Professional Program:
800-636-7544

· Sylvan Prometric Testing Centers:
800-755-EXAM

· Microsoft Online Institute (MOLI):
800-449-9333

How to Become a Microsoft Certified Professional (MCP)

To become an MCP, you must pass one operating system exam. The following list contains the names and exam numbers of all the operating system exams that will qualify you for your MCP certification (a * denotes an exam that is scheduled to be retired):

◆ Implementing and Supporting Microsoft Windows 95, #70-064 (formerly #70-063)

◆ Implementing and Supporting Microsoft Windows NT Workstation 4.02, #70-073

◆ Implementing and Supporting Microsoft Windows NT Workstation 3.51, #70-042*

◆ Implementing and Supporting Microsoft Windows NT Server 4.0, #70-067

◆ Implementing and Supporting Microsoft Windows NT Server 3.51, #70-043*

◆ Microsoft Windows for Workgroups 3.11–Desktop, #70-048*

◆ Microsoft Windows 3.1, #70-030*

◆ Microsoft Windows Architecture I, #70-160

◆ Microsoft Windows Architecture II, #70-161

How to Become a Microsoft Certified Professional + Internet (MCP+Internet)

To become an MCP with a specialty in Internet technology, you must pass the following three exams:

◆ Internetworking Microsoft TCP/IP on Microsoft Windows NT 4.0, #70-059

◆ Implementing and Supporting Microsoft Windows NT Server 4.0, #70-067

◆ Implementing and Supporting Microsoft Internet Information Server 3.0 and Microsoft Index Server 1.1, #70-077

OR Implementing and Supporting Microsoft Internet Information Server 4.0, #70-087

How to Become a Microsoft Certified Systems Engineer (MCSE)

MCSE candidates must pass four operating system exams and two elective exams. The MCSE certification path is divided into two tracks: the Windows NT 3.51 track and the Windows NT 4.0 track.

The following lists show the core requirements (four operating system exams) for the Windows NT 3.51 track, the core requirements for the Windows NT 4.0 track, and the elective courses (two exams) you can choose from for either track.

The four Windows NT 3.51 track core requirements for MCSE certification are:

◆ Implementing and Supporting Microsoft Windows NT Server 3.51, #70-043*

◆ Implementing and Supporting Microsoft Windows NT Workstation 3.51, #70-042*

◆ Microsoft Windows 3.1, #70-030*

  OR Microsoft Windows for Workgroups 3.11, #70-048*

  OR Implementing and Supporting Microsoft Windows 95, #70-064

  OR Implementing and Supporting Microsoft Windows 98, #70-098

◆ Networking Essentials, #70-058

The four Windows NT 4.0 track core requirements for MCSE certification are:

◆ Implementing and Supporting Microsoft Windows NT Server 4.0, #70-067

◆ Implementing and Supporting Microsoft Windows NT Server 4.0 in the Enterprise, #70-068

◆ Microsoft Windows 3.1, #70-030*

  OR Microsoft Windows for Workgroups 3.11, #70-048*

  OR Implementing and Supporting Microsoft Windows 95, #70-064

  OR Implementing and Supporting Microsoft Windows NT Workstation 4.0, #70-073

  OR Implementing and Supporting Microsoft Windows 98, #70-098

◆ Networking Essentials, #70-058

For both the Windows NT 3.51 and the Windows NT 4.0 track, you must pass two of the following elective exams for MCSE certification:

◆ Implementing and Supporting Microsoft SNA Server 3.0, #70-013

  OR Implementing and Supporting Microsoft SNA Server 4.0, #70-085

◆ Implementing and Supporting Microsoft Systems Management Server 1.0, #70-014*

  OR Implementing and Supporting Microsoft Systems Management Server 1.2, #70-018

  OR Implementing and Supporting Microsoft Systems Management Server 2.0, #70-086

◆ Microsoft SQL Server 4.2 Database Implementation, #70-021

  OR Implementing a Database Design on Microsoft SQL Server 6.5, #70-027

  OR Implementing a Database Design on Microsoft SQL Server 7.0, #70-029

◆ Microsoft SQL Server 4.2 Database Administration for Microsoft Windows NT, #70-022

OR System Administration for Microsoft SQL
Server 6.5 (or 6.0), #70-026

OR System Administration for Microsoft SQL
Server 7.0, #70-028

◆ Microsoft Mail for PC Networks 3.2-Enterprise,
#70-037

◆ Internetworking with Microsoft TCP/IP on
Microsoft Windows NT (3.5–3.51), #70-053

OR Internetworking with Microsoft TCP/IP on
Microsoft Windows NT 4.0, #70-059

◆ Implementing and Supporting Microsoft
Exchange Server 4.0, #70-075*

OR Implementing and Supporting Microsoft
Exchange Server 5.0, #70-076

OR Implementing and Supporting Microsoft
Exchange Server 5.5, #70-081

◆ Implementing and Supporting Microsoft Internet
Information Server 3.0 and Microsoft Index
Server 1.1, #70-077

OR Implementing and Supporting Microsoft
Internet Information Server 4.0, #70-087

◆ Implementing and Supporting Microsoft Proxy
Server 1.0, #70-078

OR Implementing and Supporting Microsoft
Proxy Server 2.0, #70-088

◆ Implementing and Supporting Microsoft Internet
Explorer 4.0 by Using the Internet Explorer
Resource Kit, #70-079

How to Become a Microsoft Certified Systems Engineer + Internet (MCSE+Internet)

MCSE+Internet candidates must pass seven operating
system exams and two elective exams. The following
lists show the core requirements and the elective courses (of which you need to pass two exams).

The seven MCSE+Internet core exams required for certification are:

◆ Networking Essentials, #70-058

◆ Internetworking with Microsoft TCP/IP on
Microsoft Windows NT 4.0, #70-059

◆ Implementing and Supporting Microsoft
Windows 95, #70-064

OR Implementing and Supporting Microsoft
Windows NT Workstation 4.0, #70-073

OR Implementing and Supporting Microsoft
Windows 98, #70-098

◆ Implementing and Supporting Microsoft
Windows NT Server 4.0, #70-067

◆ Implementing and Supporting Microsoft
Windows NT Server 4.0 in the Enterprise,
#70-068

◆ Implementing and Supporting Microsoft Internet
Information Server 3.0 and Microsoft Index
Server 1.1, #70-077

OR Implementing and Supporting Microsoft
Internet Information Server 4.0, #70-087

◆ Implementing and Supporting Microsoft Internet
Explorer 4.0 by Using the Internet Explorer
Resource Kit, #70-079

You must also pass two of the following elective exams:

- ◆ System Administration for Microsoft SQL Server 6.5, #70-026

- ◆ Implementing a Database Design on Microsoft SQL Server 6.5, #70-027

- ◆ Implementing and Supporting Web Sites Using Microsoft Site Server 3.0, #70-056

- ◆ Implementing and Supporting Microsoft Exchange Server 5.0, #70-076

   OR Implementing and Supporting Microsoft Exchange Server 5.5, #70-081

- ◆ Implementing and Supporting Microsoft Proxy Server 1.0, #70-078

   OR Implementing and Supporting Microsoft Proxy Server 2.0, #70-088

- ◆ Implementing and Supporting Microsoft SNA Server 4.0, #70-085

How to Become a Microsoft Certified Solution Developer (MCSD)

MCSD candidates must pass two core technology exams and two elective exams. The following lists show the required technology exams, plus the elective exams that apply toward obtaining the MCSD.

You must pass the following two core technology exams to qualify for MCSD certification:

- ◆ Microsoft Windows Architecture I, #70-160

- ◆ Microsoft Windows Architecture II, #70-161

You must also pass two of the following elective exams to become an MSCD:

- ◆ Microsoft SQL Server 4.2 Database Implementation, #70-021

   OR Implementing a Database Design on Microsoft SQL Server 6.5, #70-027

   OR Implementing a Database Design on Microsoft SQL Server 7.0, #70-029

- ◆ Developing Applications with C++ Using the Microsoft Foundation Class Library, #70-024

- ◆ Implementing OLE in Microsoft Foundation Class Applications, #70-025

- ◆ Programming with Microsoft Visual Basic 4.0, #70-065

   OR Developing Applications with Microsoft Visual Basic 5.0, #70-165

- ◆ Microsoft Access 2.0 for Windows-Application Development, #70-051

   OR Microsoft Access for Windows 95 and the Microsoft Access Development Toolkit, #70-069

- ◆ Developing Applications with Microsoft Excel 5.0 Using Visual Basic for Applications, #70-052

- ◆ Programming in Microsoft Visual FoxPro 3.0 for Windows, #70-054

Becoming a Microsoft Certified Trainer (MCT)

To understand the requirements and process for becoming a Microsoft Certified Trainer (MCT), you need to obtain the Microsoft Certified Trainer Guide document from the following WWW site:

```
http://www.microsoft.com/train_cert/mct/
```

From this page, you can read the document as Web pages, or you can display or download it as a Word file.

The MCT Guide explains the four-step process of becoming an MCT. The general steps for the MCT certification are described here:

1. Complete and mail a Microsoft Certified Trainer application to Microsoft. You must include proof of your skills for presenting instructional material. The options for doing so are described in the MCT Guide.

2. Obtain and study the Microsoft Trainer Kit for the Microsoft Official Curricula (MOC) course(s) for which you want to be certified. You can order Microsoft Trainer Kits by calling 800-688-0496 in North America. Other regions should review the MCT Guide for information on how to order a Trainer Kit.

3. Pass the Microsoft certification exam for the product for which you want to be certified to teach.

4. Attend the Microsoft Official Curriculum (MOC) course for which you want to be certified. You do this so that you can understand how the course is structured, how labs are completed, and how the course flows.

> **WARNING**
>
> **Be Sure to Get the MCT Guide!**
> You should consider the preceding steps to be a general overview of the MCT certification process. The precise steps that you need to take are described in detail on the WWW site mentioned earlier. Do not mistakenly believe the preceding steps make up the actual process you need to take.

If you are interested in becoming an MCT, you can receive more information by visiting the Microsoft Certified Training (MCT) WWW site at http://www.microsoft.com/train_cert/mct/ or call 800-688-0496.

What's on the CD-ROM

This appendix offers a brief rundown of what you'll find on the CD-ROM that comes with this book. For a more detailed description of the newly developed Top Score test engine, exclusive to Macmillan Computer Publishing, see Appendix D, "Using the Top Score Software."

TOP SCORE

Top Score is a test engine developed exclusively for Macmillan Computer Publishing. It is, we believe, the best test engine available because it closely emulates the format of the standard Microsoft exams. In addition to providing a means of evaluating your knowledge of the exam material, Top Score features several innovations that help you to improve your mastery of the subject matter. For example, the practice tests allow you to check your score by exam area or category, which helps you determine which topics you need to study further. Other modes allow you to obtain immediate feedback on your response to a question, explanation of the correct answer, and even hyperlinks to the chapter in an electronic version of the book where the topic of the question is covered. Again, for a complete description of the benefits of Top Score, see Appendix D.

Before you attempt to run the Top Score software, make sure that autorun is enabled. If you prefer not to use autorun, you can run the application from the CD by double-clicking the START.EXE file from within Explorer.

EXCLUSIVE ELECTRONIC VERSION OF TEXT

As alluded to above, the CD-ROM also contains the electronic version of this book in Portable Document Format (PDF). In addition to the links to the book that are built into the Top Score engine, you can use that version of the book to help you search for terms you need to study or other book elements. The electronic version comes complete with all figures as they appear in the book.

COPYRIGHT INFORMATION AND DISCLAIMER

Macmillan Computer Publishing's Top Score test engine: Copyright 1998 New Riders Publishing. All rights reserved. Made in U.S.A.

Using the Top Score Software

GETTING STARTED

The installation procedure is very simple and typical of Windows 95 or Window NT 4 installations.

1. Put the CD into the CD-ROM drive. The autorun function starts, and after a moment, you see a CD-ROM Setup dialog box asking you if you are ready to proceed.

2. Click OK, and you are prompted for the location of the directory in which the program can install a small log file. Choose the default (C:\Program Files\), or type the name of another drive and directory, or select the drive and directory where you want it placed. Then click OK.

3. The next prompt asks you to select a start menu name. If you like the default name, click OK. If not, enter the name you would like to use. The Setup process runs its course.

When setup is complete, icons are displayed in the MCSE Top Score Software Explorer window that is open. For an overview of the CD's contents, double-click the CD-ROM Contents icon.

If you reach this point, you have successfully installed the exam(s). If you have another CD, repeat this process to install additional exams.

INSTRUCTIONS ON USING THE TOP SCORE SOFTWARE

Top Score software consists of the following three applications:

◆ Practice Exams

◆ Study Cards

◆ Flash Cards

The Practice Exams application provides exams that simulate the Microsoft certification exams. The Study Cards serve as a study aid organized around specific exam objectives. Both are in multiple-choice format. Flash Cards are another study aid that require responses to open-ended questions, which test your knowledge of the material at a level deeper than that of recognition memory.

To start the Study Cards, Practice Exams, or Flash Cards applications, follow these steps:

1. Begin from the overview of the CD contents (double-click the CD-ROM Contents icon). The left window provides you with options for obtaining further information on any of the Top Score applications as well as a way to launch them.

2. Click a "book" icon, and a listing of related topics appears below it in Explorer fashion.

3. Click an application name. This displays more detailed information for that application in the right window.

4. To start an application, click its book icon. Then click on the Starting the Program option. Do this for Practice Exams, for example. Information appears in the right window. Click on the button for the exam, and the opening screens of the application appear.

Further details on using each of the applications follow.

Using Top Score Practice Exams

The Practice Exams interface is simple and straightforward. Its design simulates the look and feel of the Microsoft certification exams. To begin a practice exam, click the button for the exam name. After a moment, you see an opening screen similar to the one shown in Figure D.1.

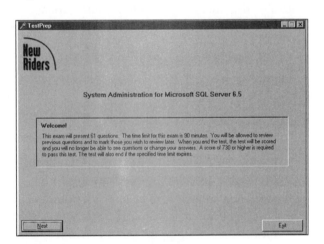

FIGURE D.1
Top Score Practice Exams opening screen.

Click on the Next button to see a disclaimer and copyright screen. Read the information, and then click Top Score's Start button. A notice appears, indicating that the program is randomly selecting questions for the practice exam from the exam database (see Figure D.2). Each practice exam contains the same number of items as the official Microsoft exam. The items are selected from a larger set of 150–900 questions. The random selection of questions from the database takes some time to retrieve. Don't reboot; your machine is not hung!

N O T E   **Some Exams Follow a New Format**
The number of questions will be the same for traditional exams. However, this will not be the case for exams that incorporate the new "adaptive testing" format. In that format, there is no set number of questions. See the chapter entitled "Study and Exam Prep Tips" in the Final Review section of the book for more details on this new format.

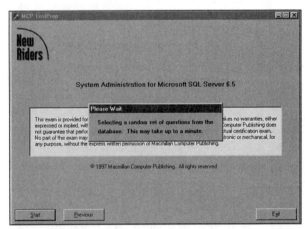

FIGURE D.2
Top Score's Please Wait notice.

After the questions have been selected, the first test item appears. See Figure D.3 for an example of a test item screen.

Notice several important features of this window. The question number and the total number of retrieved questions appears in the top-left corner of the window in the control bar. Immediately below that is a check box labeled Mark, which enables you to mark any exam item you would like to return to later. Across the screen from the Mark check box, you see the total time remaining for the exam.

The test question is located in a colored section (it's gray in the figure). Directly below the test question, in the white area, are response choices. Be sure to note that immediately below the responses are instructions about how to respond, including the number of responses required. You will notice that question items requiring a single response, such as that shown in Figure D.3, have radio buttons. Items requiring multiple responses have check boxes (see Figure D.4).

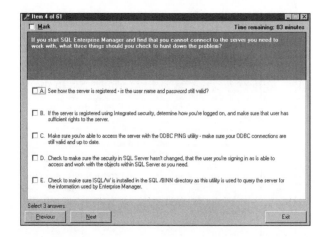

FIGURE D.4
A Top Score test item requiring multiple responses.

Some questions and some responses do not appear on the screen in their entirety. You will recognize such items because a scroll bar appears to the right of the question item or response. Use the scroll bar to reveal the rest of the question or response item.

The buttons at the bottom of the window enable you to move back to a previous test item, proceed to the next test item, or exit Top Score Practice Exams.

Some items require you to examine additional information referred to as *exhibits*. These screens typically include graphs, diagrams, or other types of visual information that you will need in order to respond to the test question. You can access Exhibits by clicking the Exhibit button, also located at the bottom of the window.

After you complete the practice test by moving through all of the test questions for your exam, you arrive at a summary screen titled Item Review (see Figure D.5).

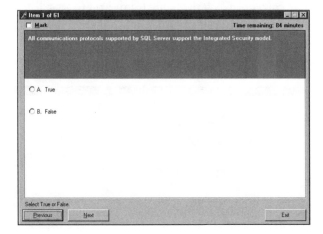

FIGURE D.3
A Top Score test item requiring a single response.

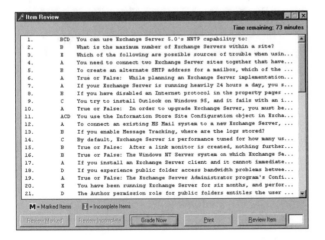

FIGURE D.5
The Top Score Item Review window.

This window enables you to see all the question numbers, your response(s) to each item, any questions you have marked, and any you've left incomplete. The buttons at the bottom of the screen enable you to review all the marked items and incomplete items in numeric order.

If you want to review a specific marked or incomplete item, simply type the desired item number in the box in the lower-right corner of the window and click the Review Item button. This takes you to that particular item. After you review the item, you can respond to the question. Notice that this window also offers the Next and Previous options. You can also select the Item Review button to return to the Item Review window.

> **NOTE** **Your Time Is Limited** If you exceed the time allotted for the test, you do not have the opportunity to review any marked or incomplete items. The program will move on to the next screen.

After you complete your review of the practice test questions, click the Grade Now button to find out how you did. An Examination Score Report is generated for your practice test (see Figure D.6). This report provides you with the required score for this particular certification exam, your score on the practice test, and a grade. The report also breaks down your performance on the practice test by the specific objectives for the exam. Click the Print button to print out the results of your performance.

You also have the option of reviewing those items that you answered incorrectly. Click the Show Me What I Missed button to view a summary of those items. You can print out that information if you need further practice or review; such printouts can be used to guide your use of Study Cards and Flash Cards.

Using Top Score Study Cards

To start the software, begin from the overview of the CD contents. Click the Study Cards icon to see a listing of topics. Clicking Study Cards brings up more detailed information for this application in the right window.

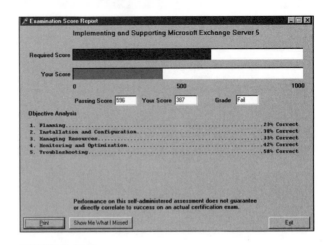

FIGURE D.6
The Top Score Examination Score Report window.

To launch Study Cards, click on Starting the Program. In the right window, click on the button for the exam in which you are interested. After a moment, an initial screen similar to that of the Practice Exams appears.

Click on the Next button to see the first Study Cards screen (see Figure D.7).

The interface for Study Cards is very similar to that of Practice Exams. However, several important options enable you to prepare for an exam. The Study Cards material is organized according to the specific objectives for each exam. You can opt to receive questions on all the objectives, or you can use the check boxes to request questions on a limited set of objectives. For example, if you have already completed a Practice Exam and your score report indicates that you need work on Planning, you can choose to cover only the Planning objectives for your Study Cards session.

You can also determine the number of questions presented by typing the number of questions you want into the option box at the right of the screen. You can control the amount of time you will be allowed for a review by typing the number of minutes into the Time Limit option box immediately below the one for the number of questions.

When you're ready, click the Start Test button, and Study Cards randomly selects the indicated number of questions from the question database. A dialog box appears, informing you that this process could take some time. After the questions are selected, the first item appears, in a format similar to that in Figure D.8.

Respond to the questions in the same manner you did for the Practice Exam questions. Radio buttons signify that a single answer is required, while check boxes indicate that multiple answers are expected.

Notice the menu options at the top of the window. You can pull down the File menu to exit from the program. The Edit menu contains commands for the copy function and even allows you to copy questions to the Windows clipboard.

Should you feel the urge to take some notes on a particular question, you can do so via the Options menu. When you pull it down, choose Open Notes, and Notepad opens. Type any notes you want to save for later reference. The Options menu also allows you to start over with another exam.

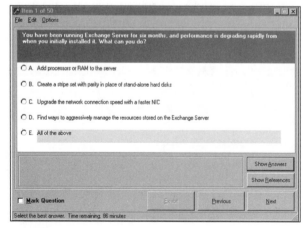

FIGURE D.8
A Study Cards item.

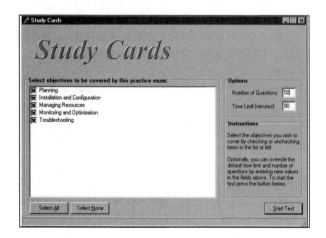

FIGURE D.7
The first Study Cards screen.

The Study Cards application provides you with immediate feedback of whether you answered the question correctly. Click the Show Answers button to see the correct answer, and it appears highlighted on the screen as shown in Figure D.9.

Study Cards also includes Item Review, Score Report, and Show Me What I Missed features that function the same as those in the Practice Exams application.

Using Top Score Flash Cards

Flash Cards offer a third way to use the exam question database. The Flash Cards items do not offer you multiple-choice answers to choose from; instead, they require you to respond in a short answer/essay format. Flash Cards are intended to help you learn the material well enough to respond with the correct answers in your own words, rather than just by recognizing the correct answer. If you have the depth of knowledge to answer questions without prompting, you will certainly be prepared to pass a multiple-choice exam.

You start the Flash Cards application in the same way you did Practice Exams and Study Cards. Click the Flash Cards icon, and then click Start the Program.

Click the button for the exam you are interested in, and the opening screen appears. It looks similar to the example shown in Figure D.10.

You can choose Flash Cards according to the various objectives, as you did Study Cards. Simply select the objectives you want to cover, enter the number of questions you want, and enter the amount of time you want to limit yourself to. Click the Start Test button to start the Flash Cards session, and you see a dialog box notifying you that questions are being selected.

The Flash Cards items appear in an interface similar to that of Practice Exams and Study Cards (see Figure D.11).

Notice, however, that although a question is presented, no possible answers appear. You type your answer in the white space below the question (see Figure D.12).

Compare your answer to the correct answer by clicking the Show Answers button (see Figure D.13).

You can also use the Show Reference button in the same manner as described earlier in the Study Cards sections.

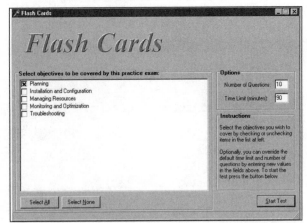

FIGURE D.10
The Flash Cards opening screen.

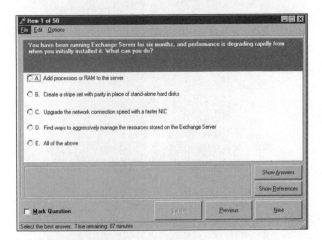

FIGURE D.9
The correct answer is highlighted.

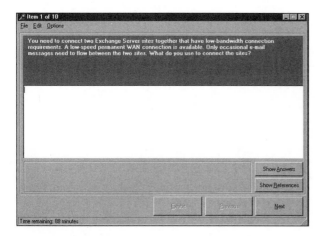

FIGURE D.11
A Flash Cards item.

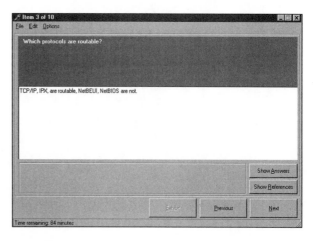

FIGURE D.12
A typed answer in Flash Cards.

The pull-down menus provide nearly the same functionality as those in Study Cards, with the exception of a Paste command on the Edit menu instead of the Copy Question command.

Flash Cards provide simple feedback; they do not include an Item Review or Score Report. They are intended to provide you with an alternative way of assessing your level of knowledge that will encourage you to learn the information more thoroughly than other methods do.

SUMMARY

The Top Score software's suite of applications provides you with several approaches to exam preparation. Use Practice Exams to do just that—practice taking exams, not only to assess your learning, but also to prepare yourself for the test-taking situation. Use Study Cards and Flash Cards as tools for more focused assessment and review and to reinforce the knowledge you are gaining. You will find that these three applications are the perfect way to finish off your exam preparation.

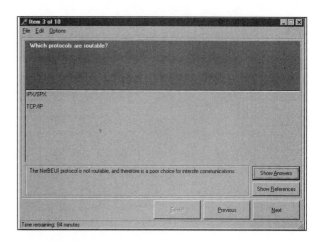

FIGURE D.13
The correct answer is shown.

Index

SYMBOLS

/sos switch (BOOT.INI file), 463, 468
540MB limit (addressing IDE hard disks), 62

A

Access Control Entries, *see* ACEs
access tokens, 21, 357
Account Operators domain controllers local group, 262
accounts
    administrator-level
      (member server group accounts), 258
    disabling versus deleting, 584
ACEs (Access Control Entries), 343
    accessing resources, 355-356
      handles, 357
    groups or users, 346
      adding/deleting, 348
active partitions, 28, 200-201
adapter cards (Windows NT Server 4.0 installation), 76
Adapters tab, Network (Control Panel), 104, 117-118
Add & Read directory-level permission, 345
Add directory-level permission, 345
Add Printer Wizard
    local computers, 216-219
    network print servers, 219
administrative shares, 334-335
Administrative Tools (Network Client Administrator), 82-83
Administrator accounts
    passwords, 74, 260
    user accounts, 265-266
Administrators group
    domain controllers local group, 260-261
    member server local group, 263
    printer permissions, 229
Advanced tab, print server properties, 222

Alert view, Performance Monitor, 429-430
aliases (Windows 95 and Windows NT comparisons), 323-325
AppleTalk, 609
applets, Control Panel, 174-175
    Devices, 181-182
    Display, 191-192
    Keyboard, 189-190
    Modems, 187, 190
    Mouse, 191
    Multimedia, 183
    PC Card, 187
    Ports, 183
    SCSI Adapters, 185-186
    System, 175-180
    Tape Devices, 186-187
    UPS (Uninterruptible Power Supply), 184-185
applications
    Dial-Up Networking, 395-396
      options, 398, 400
      phonebook entries, 396-397
    FPNW (File and Print Services for NetWare), 380
    priority levels, 595
    RAS (Remote Access Service), 390
    Running Applications exam section, 593-595
    shared versus local, 578
    Win16 (running in NTVDMs), 593-594
Application log (Event Viewer), 482
ARC paths (booting), 598
    BOOT.INI file, 465-467
archive attributes, 504, 506
assigning drive letters (partitions), 196, 198
Asynchronous Transfer Mode (ATM), 613
audio, Multimedia Control Panel applet, 183
auditing
    events (account-related), 280
    NTFS resources, 342-343
    RAS (Remote Access Service) security, 386
AUTOCHK.EXE utility, 470
AUTOCONV.EXE utility, 326, 470
Autodial feature, 400

F

M

X - Z

TRAINING GUIDES
THE NEXT GENERATION

MCSE Training Guide:
Networking Essentials,
Second Edition

1-56205-919-X,
$49.99, 9/98

MCSE Training Guide:
TCP/IP, Second
Edition

1-56205-920-3,
$49.99, 10/98

MCSD Training
Guide: Microsoft
Visual Basic 6,
Exam 70-176

0-7357-0031-1,
$49.99, Q1/99

MCSE Training Guide:
Windows NT Server 4,
Second Edition

1-56205-916-5,
$49.99, 9/98

MCSE Training Guide:
SQL Server 7
Administration

0-7357-0003-6,
$49.99, Q1/99

TRAINING GUIDES
FIRST EDITIONS

Your Quality Elective Solution

MCSE Training Guide: Systems Management
Server 1.2, 1-56205-748-0

MCSE Training Guide: SQL Server 6.5
Administration, 1-56205-726-X

MCSE Training Guide: SQL Server 6.5
Design and Implementation, 1-56205-830-4

MCSE Training Guide: Windows 95, 70-064
Exam, 1-56205-880-0

MCSE Training Guide: Exchange Server 5,
1-56205-824-X

MCSE Training Guide: Internet Explorer 4,
1-56205-889-4

MCSE Training Guide: Microsoft Exchange
Server 5.5, 1-56205-899-1

MCSE Training Guide: IIS 4, 1-56205-823-1

MCSD Training Guide: Visual Basic 5,
1-56205-850-9

MCSD Training Guide: Microsoft Access,
1-56205-771-5

MCSE Training Guide:
Windows NT Server 4
Enterprise, Second
Edition

1-56205-917-3,
$49.99, 9/98

MCSE Training Guide:
SQL Server 7 Design
and Implementation

0-7357-0004-4,
$49.99, Q1/99

MCSE Training Guide:
Windows NT
Workstation 4,
Second Edition

1-56205-918-1,
$49.99, 9/98

MCSD Training Guide:
Solution Architectures

0-7357-0026-5,
$49.99, Q1/99

MCSE Training Guide:
Windows 98

1-56205-890-8,
$49.99, Q4/98

MCSD Training Guide:
Visual Basic 6, Exam
70-175

0-7357-0002-8,
$49.99, Q1/99

FAST TRACK SERIES

The Accelerated Path to Certification Success

Fast Tracks provide an easy way to review the key elements of each certification technology without being bogged down with elementary-level information.

These guides are perfect for when you already have real-world, hands-on experience. They're the ideal enhancement to training courses, test simulators, and comprehensive training guides. *No fluff, simply what you really need to pass the exam!*

LEARN IT FAST

Part I contains only the essential information you need to pass the test. With over 200 pages of information, it is a concise review for the more experienced MCSE candidate.

REVIEW IT EVEN FASTER

Part II averages 50–75 pages, and takes you through the test and into the real-world use of the technology, with chapters on:

1) Fast Facts Review Section
2) Hotlists of Exam-Critical Concepts
3) Sample Test Questions
4) The Insider's Spin (on taking the exam)
5) Did You Know? (real-world applications for the technology covered in the exam)

 MCSE Fast Track: Networking Essentials

1-56205-939-4, $19.99, 9/98

 MCSE Fast Track: Windows 98

0-7357-0016-8, $19.99, Q4/98

 MCSE Fast Track: Windows NT Server 4

1-56205-935-1, $19.99, 9/98

 MCSE Fast Track: Windows NT Server 4 Enterprise

1-56205-940-8, $19.99, 9/98

 MCSE Fast Track: Windows NT Workstation 4

1-56205-938-6, $19.99, 9/98

 MCSE Fast Track: TCP/IP

1-56205-937-8, $19.99, 9/98

 MCSE Fast Track: Internet Information Server 4

1-56205-936-X, $19.99, 9/98

 MCSD Fast Track: Solution Architectures

0-7357-0029-X, $19.99, Q1/99

 MCSD Fast Track: Visual Basic 6, Exam 70-175

0-7357-0018-4, $19.99, Q4/98

 MCSD Fast Track: Visual Basic 6, Exam 70-176

0-7357-0019-2, $19.99, Q4/98

TESTPREP SERIES

Practice and cram with the new, revised Second Edition TestPreps

Questions. Questions. And more questions. That's what you'll find in our New Riders *TestPreps*. They're great practice books when you reach the final stage of studying for the exam. We recommend them as supplements to our *Training Guides*.

What makes these study tools unique is that the questions are the primary focus of each book. All the text in these books support and explain the answers to the questions.

✓ **Scenario-based questions** challenge your experience.

✓ **Multiple-choice questions** prep you for the exam.

✓ **Fact-based questions** test your product knowledge.

✓ **Exam strategies** assist you in test preparation.

✓ **Complete yet concise explanations of answers** make for better retention.

✓ **Two practice exams** prepare you for the real thing.

✓ **Fast Facts** offer you everything you need to review in the testing center parking lot.

Practice, practice, practice, pass with New Riders TestPreps*!*

MCSE TestPrep: Networking Essentials, Second Edition

0-7357-0010-9, $19.99, 11/98

MCSE TestPrep: Windows 95, Second Edition

0-7357-0011-7, $19.99, 11/98

MCSE TestPrep: Windows NT Server 4, Second Edition

0-7357-0012-5, $19.99, 12/98

MCSE TestPrep: Windows NT Server 4 Enterprise, Second Edition

0-7357-0009-5, $19.99, 11/98

MCSE TestPrep: Windows NT Workstation 4, Second Edition

0-7357-0008-7, $19.99, 11/98

MCSE TestPrep: TCP/IP, Second Edition

0-7357-0025-7, $19.99, 12/98

MCSE TestPrep: Windows 98

1-56205-922-X, $19.99, Q4/98

FIRST EDITIONS

MCSE TestPrep: SQL Server 6.5 Administration, 0-7897-1597-X

MCSE TestPrep: SQL Server 6.5 Design and Implementation, 1-56205-915-7

MCSE TestPrep: Windows 95 70-64 Exam, 0-7897-1609-7

MCSE TestPrep: Internet Explorer 4, 0-7897-1654-2

MCSE TestPrep: Exchange Server 5.5, 0-7897-1611-9

MCSE TestPrep: IIS 4.0, 0-7897-1610-0

HOW TO CONTACT US

IF YOU NEED THE LATEST UPDATES ON A TITLE THAT YOU'VE PURCHASED:

1) Visit our Web site at www.newriders.com.

2) Click on the DOWNLOADS link, and enter your book's ISBN number, which is located on the back cover in the bottom right-hand corner.

3) In the DOWNLOADS section, you'll find available updates that are linked to the book page.

IF YOU ARE HAVING TECHNICAL PROBLEMS WITH THE BOOK OR THE CD THAT IS INCLUDED:

1) Check the book's information page on our Web site according to the instructions listed above, or

2) Email us at support@mcp.com, or

3) Fax us at (317) 817-7488 attn: Tech Support.

IF YOU HAVE COMMENTS ABOUT ANY OF OUR CERTIFICATION PRODUCTS THAT ARE NON-SUPPORT RELATED:

1) Email us at certification@mcp.com, or

2) Write to us at New Riders, 201 W. 103rd St., Indianapolis, IN 46290-1097, or

3) Fax us at (317) 581-4663.

IF YOU ARE OUTSIDE THE UNITED STATES AND NEED TO FIND A DISTRIBUTOR IN YOUR AREA:

Please contact our international department at international@mcp.com.

IF YOU WISH TO PREVIEW ANY OF OUR CERTIFICATION BOOKS FOR CLASSROOM USE:

Email us at pr@mcp.com. Your message should include your name, title, training company or school, department, address, phone number, office days/hours, text in use, and enrollment. Send these details along with your request for desk/examination copies and/or additional information.

WE WANT TO KNOW WHAT YOU THINK

To better serve you, we would like your opinion on the content and quality of this book. Please complete this card and mail it to us or fax it to 317-581-4663.

Name _____

Address _____

City _____ State _____ Zip _____

Phone _____ Email Address _____

Occupation _____

Which certification exams have you already passed? _____
_____
_____
_____

Which certification exams do you plan to take? _____
_____
_____
_____

What influenced your purchase of this book?
❏ Recommendation   ❏ Cover Design
❏ Table of Contents   ❏ Index
❏ Magazine Review   ❏ Advertisement
❏ Reputation of New Riders ❏ Author Name

How would you rate the contents of this book?
❏ Excellent   ❏ Very Good
❏ Good   ❏ Fair
❏ Below Average   ❏ Poor

What other types of certification products will you buy/have you bought to help you prepare for the exam?
❏ Quick reference books   ❏ Testing software
❏ Study guides   ❏ Other

What do you like most about this book? Check all that apply.
❏ Content   ❏ Writing Style
❏ Accuracy   ❏ Examples
❏ Listings   ❏ Design
❏ Index   ❏ Page Count
❏ Price   ❏ Illustrations

What do you like least about this book? Check all that apply.
❏ Content   ❏ Writing Style
❏ Accuracy   ❏ Examples
❏ Listings   ❏ Design
❏ Index   ❏ Page Count
❏ Price   ❏ Illustrations

What would be a useful follow-up book to this one for you?_____
Where did you purchase this book? _____
Can you name a similar book that you like better than this one, or one that is as good? Why?_____
_____
_____

How many New Riders books do you own? _____
What are your favorite certification or general computer book titles? _____
_____

What other titles would you like to see us develop?_____
_____

Any comments for us? _____
_____
_____
_____

Fold here and Scotch tape to mail

Place
Stamp
Here

New Riders
201 W. 103rd St.
Indianapolis, IN 46290